Lecture Notes in Computer Science 2750

Edited by G. Goos, J. Hartmanis, and J. van Leeuwen

Springer
Berlin
Heidelberg
New York
Hong Kong
London
Milan
Paris
Tokyo

Thanasis Hadzilacos   Yannis Manolopoulos
John F. Roddick   Yannis Theodoridis (Eds.)

Advances in Spatial and Temporal Databases

8th International Symposium, SSTD 2003
Santorini Island, Greece, July 24-27, 2003
Proceedings

Springer

Series Editors

Gerhard Goos, Karlsruhe University, Germany
Juris Hartmanis, Cornell University, NY, USA
Jan van Leeuwen, Utrecht University, The Netherlands

Volume Editors

Thanasis Hadzilacos
Yannis Theodoridis
Computer Technology Institute
11 Akteou and Poulopoulou St., 11851 Athens, Greece
E-mail: thh@cti.gr, ytheod@unipi.gr

Yannis Manolopoulos
Aristotle University, 56124 Thessaloniki, Greece
E-mail: manolopo@csd.auth.gr

John F. Roddick
Flinders University, P.O. Box 2100
Adelaide, 5001, Australia
E-mail: roddick@infoeng.flinders.edu.au

Cataloging-in-Publication Data applied for

A catalog record for this book is available from the Library of Congress

Bibliographic information published by Die Deutsche Bibliothek
Die Deutsche Bibliothek lists this publication in the Deutsche Nationalbibliographie;
detailed bibliographic data is available in the Internet at <http://dnb.ddb.de>.

CR Subject Classification (1998): H.2, H.3, H.4, I.2.4

ISSN 0302-9743
ISBN 3-540-40535-6 Springer-Verlag Berlin Heidelberg New York

Springer-Verlag Berlin Heidelberg New York
a member of BertelsmannSpringer Science+Business Media GmbH

http://www.springer.de

© Springer-Verlag Berlin Heidelberg 2003
Printed in Germany

Typesetting: Camera-ready by author, data conversion by DA-TeX Gerd Blumenstein
Printed on acid-free paper   SPIN: 10929315   06/3142   5 4 3 2 1 0

Preface

On behalf of the Program Committee, it was our pleasure to welcome the participants to the beautiful Greek island of Santorini and, in particular, to the Eighth International Symposium on Spatial and Temporal Databases, SSTD 2003. The SSTD series represents some of the most exciting research in the field of spatial and temporal databases and this volume contains 30 excellent papers, 28 accepted through peer review to the conference and two invited keynote papers.

Interest in the field of spatio-temporal databases continues to grow. Significantly, of the papers submitted, many have ceased to deal with just one or other of spatial and temporal databases, choosing instead to focus on the rich confluence of these areas to deal with spatio-temporal semantics and systems. This was a trend foreshadowed in the renaming of the conference in 1999 and is to be welcomed.

Following an international call for papers, 105 papers were submitted and reviewed thoroughly by an international panel of experts in the field. The number of papers submitted represents a record number for the conference and shows a vibrant and growing interest in the theory and applications of the area. Of the submitted papers, 28 were accepted (giving an acceptance rate of 27%) and the final papers, modified in the light of the comments from the referees, appear in this volume.

Two invited papers were also presented: the first from Prof. Christian Jensen of Aalborg University in Denmark and the second from Dr. John Herring of Oracle Corporation. Two tutorials were also held with the conference, one on Location Management and Moving Objects Databases by Ouri Wolfson and another on Spatio-Temporal Data Mining by Sanjay Chawla.

We would like to thank the Program Committee for giving of their time and expertise so freely. Following the refereeing itself, as is often the case, there was substantial discussion on various aspects of some papers to ensure that the papers presented were the best available. This takes time and effort and we appreciate the efforts of those involved.

The organizing team at the Computer Technology Institute deserve much credit for their essential contribution. Vasilis Delis and Dieter Pfoser arranged technical and publicity issues, Lena Gourdoupi and Aggeliki Stamatopoulou managed the registration process. Furthermore we would like to thank Antonis Sidiropoulos at the University of Thessaloniki for managing the Web-based paper reviewing system and the local teams at Magma-Heliotopos Conferences and the Nomikos Conference Center in Santorini for their excellent services in preparing and hosting the event.

The symposium was sponsored by Microsoft Hellas and Marathon Data Systems, and it was held in cooperation with the Computer Technology Institute and the University of Piraeus. We thank these organizations for their support.

July 2003

Yannis Manolopoulos
John F. Roddick
Program Chairs
Thanasis Hadzilacos
Yannis Theodoridis
General Chairs

Program Committee

Program Chairs

Yannis Manolopoulos, Aristotle University of Thessaloniki, Greece
John Roddick, Flinders University, Australia

Program Committee Members

Dave Abel, CSIRO, Australia
Walid Aref, Purdue University, USA
Lars Arge, Duke University, USA
Elisa Bertino, University of Milan, Italy
Michael Böhlen, Aalborg University, Denmark
Thomas Brinkhoff, Fachhochschule Oldenburg, Germany
Edward Chan, University of Waterloo, Canada
Jan Chomicki, University of Buffalo, USA
Curtis Dyreson, Washington State University, USA
Fabio Grandi, University of Bologna, Italy
Jim Gray, Microsoft, USA
Ralf Hartmut Güting, Fernuniversität Hagen, Germany
Erik Hoel, ESRI, USA
Kathleen Hornsby, University of Maine, USA
Christian S. Jensen, Aalborg University, Denmark
Christopher Jones, Cardiff University, UK
George Kollios, Boston University, USA
Ravi-Kanth Kothuri, Oracle, USA
Dik Lun Lee, Hong Kong UST, China SAR
Scott Leutenegger, Denver University, USA
Nikos Lorentzos, Agricultural University of Athens, Greece
Mario Nascimento, University of Alberta, Canada
Raymond Ng, University of British Columbia, Canada
Dimitris Papadias, Hong Kong UST, China SAR
Michel Scholl, INRIA, France
Bernhard Seeger, University of Marburg, Germany
Richard Snodgrass, University of Arizona, USA
Ioana Stanoi, IBM, USA
Jianwen Su, University of California at Santa Barbara, USA
Nectaria Tryfona, CTI, Greece
Vassilis Tsotras, University of California, Riverside, USA
Jeff Vitter, Duke University, USA
Agnès Voisard, Free University, Berlin, Germany
Kyu-Young Whang, KAIST, South Korea

Peter Widmayer, ETH Zurich, Switzerland
Jef Wijsen, University of Mons-Hainaut, Belgium
Ouri Wolfson, University of Illinois, Chicago, USA

Additional Referees

Ning An
Luzius Anderegg
Alessandro Artale
Michael Cammert
Jorge Campos
Hu Cao
Reynold Cheng
Jörg Derungs
Cedric Du Mouza
Matt Duckham
Jeff Erickson
James Farrugia
Enrico Franconi
Anders Friis-Christensen
Xiang Fu
Thanaa Ghanem
David Gross-Amblard
Marios Hadjieleftheriou
M. Hammad
Christoph Heinz
Fabian Hennecke
Haibo Hu
Piotr Indyk
Dimitrios Katsaros
Jürgen Krämer
Lars Kulik
Christian Lang
Bin Lin
Bin Liu
Nikos Mamoulis

Federica Mandreoli
Artūras Mažeika
George Mihaila
Mohamed Mokbel
Hoda Mokhtar
Apostolos N. Papadopoulos
Kjetil Nørvåg
Alexandros Nanopoulos
Marc Nunkesser
Dieter Pfoser
Conrad Pomm
Octavian Procopiuc
Siva Ravada
Maria Rita Scalas
Simonas Šaltenis
Martin Schneider
Qiongmao Shen
Chengyu Sun
Gabor Szabo
Yangui Tao
Yufei Tao
Shiby Thomas
Goce Trajcevski
Jan Vahrenhold
Yujun Wang
Min Wang
Bo Xu
Huabei Yin
Jun Zhang
Baihua Zheng

Organizing Committee

Co-chairs

Thanasis Hadzilacos, Greek Open University and CTI
Yannis Theodoridis, University of Piraeus and CTI

Members

Vasilis Delis, CTI - Technical Coordination and Tutorials
Lena Gourdoupi, CTI - Registration and Local Arrangements
Dieter Pfoser, CTI - Publicity
Antonis Sidiropoulos, Aristotle University of Thessaloniki

Sponsors and Supporting Organizations

Major Sponsor

Sponsor

Supporting Organizations

University of Piraeus

Table of Contents

Data Mining and Warehousing

Distance-Based Queries

Mobility and Moving Points Management

Modeling and Languages

Similarity Processing

Systems and Implementation Issues

Data Modeling for Mobile Services
in the Real World

Christian S. Jensen, Torben Bach Pedersen, Laurynas Speičys, and Igor Timko

Department of Computer Science, Aalborg University, Denmark

Abstract. Research contributions on data modeling, data structures, query processing, and indexing for mobile services may have an impact in the longer term, but each contribution typically offers an isolated solution to one small part of the practical problem of delivering mobile services in the real world. In contrast, this paper describes holistic concepts and techniques for mobile data modeling that are readily applicable in practice. Focus is on services to be delivered to mobile users, such as route guidance, point-of-interest search, road pricing, parking payment, traffic monitoring, etc. While geo-referencing of content is important, it is even more important to relate content to the transportation infrastructure. In addition, several sophisticated, integrated representations of the infrastructure are needed.

1 Introduction

The integration of location-based content and the reuse of content across multiple services will be central to the cost-effective delivery of competitive mobile services as well as to the rapid development of new mobile services. Appropriate data modeling is therefore essential to the delivery of quality mobile services.

Knowledge of the user's location is central to many mobile services. Knowledge of the transportation infrastructure in which the user is moving is often also essential to a mobile service. A general-purpose foundation for the delivery of location-based services requires that multiple, integrated representations of the infrastructure are available. In addition, content (also termed business data) must be geo-referenced and must be positioned with respect to the infrastructure.

The paper offers the reader insight into the real-world challenges to data modeling for mobile services, and it describes an approach to data modeling that meets the challenges. The approach is being used by the Danish road directorate and Danish company Euman [2]. It is our hope that this paper will shed light on the application domain of mobile services, will demonstrate some of the complexity of the inherent data management problem, and will inform future research.

Much related research in the area of computer science makes simple assumptions about the problem setting. The transportation infrastructure is often not taken into account. As a result, the notions of proximity used are inappropriate

T. Hadzilacos et al. (Eds.): SSTD 2003, LNCS 2750, pp. 1–9, 2003.

to many services. Further, only a limited range of services can be supported. Other research reduces a transportation infrastructure to a graph, but does not consider other aspects of the infrastructure. The present paper takes steps towards integrating these contributions, thus taking first steps towards making the advances from the scientific domain relevant in practice. In the industrial domain, linear referencing [4, 6] has been used quite widely for the capture of content located along linear elements (e.g., routes) in transportation infrastructures. In addition, a generic data model, or ER diagram, has been recommended for the capture of different aspects of entire transportation infrastructures and related content [5], and a number of variants of this model have been reported in the literature (see [3] for further references). The data model presented in this paper employs linear referencing, and it improves on other data models in several respects. Most notably, it is the only model known to us that integrates different representations of a transportation infrastructure via a purely internal model of the infrastructure. In a sense, this approach is a "geographical generalization" of the use of surrogate keys for the management of business data.

The paper is structured as follows. The case study in the next section describes key data modeling challenges. Sect. 3 describes the data modeling approach that meets the challenges. Finally, Sect. 4 summarizes the paper.

2   Case Study

We proceed to illustrate data modeling challenges posed by mobile services.

2.1   Requirements

The kinds of queries to be supported induce requirements. A simple type of query computes the distance from a user's current position to a point of interest, such as an art gallery or a nature park. Another type of query concerns route planning, where, e.g., the user wants to retrieve the "shortest" route to a certain point of interest while passing one or more points of interest enroute. Yet another type of query retrieves the "nearest" point of interest such as a particular type of store or gas station. The terms "shortest" and "nearest" may be given several meanings. For example, they may be based on Euclidean distance or the anticipated travel time along the road network.

Queries such as these depend on two types of data: the transportation infrastructure and the "remaining" data. The remaining data is sometimes termed business data or content. Examples include the points of interest mentioned above.

To position a service user wrt. the infrastructure, it is necessary to georeference the infrastructure. To perform route planning, a graph-like representation of the transportation infrastructure is helpful. To position some content, e.g., information about accidents, wrt. the infrastructure, a so-called knownmaker representation of the infrastructure is required. Next, in order to support queries such as those listed above, the business data must be geo-referenced as well as positioned wrt. all the different representations of the infrastructure. The implication is that the infrastructure representations must be interrelated, meaning that it must be possible to translate from one representation to another.

2.2   Content

Content generally falls into one of two categories. First, *point data* concerns entities that are located at a specific geographic location and have no relevant spatial extent. This type of data is attached to specific points in the transportation infrastructure. Second, *interval data* concern data that are considered to relate to a *part* of a road and are thus attached to intervals of given roads. Interval data can be categorized as being (1) *overlapping versus non-overlapping* and (2) *covering versus non-covering*.

Non-overlapping, covering content includes speed limits and road surface type. Non-overlapping, non-covering content includes u-turn restrictions and road constructions, as well as more temporary phenomena such as traffic congestion and jams. Examples of overlapping, non-covering content includes tourist sights. A scenic mountain top and a castle may be visible from overlapping stretches of the same road. Other part of roads have no sights. Another example is warning signs. Overlapping, covering content include service availabilities, e.g., a car repair service may be available from some service provider anywhere, and several repair service providers may be available in areas.

2.3   Transportation Infrastructure

We proceed to describe the actual infrastructure that is to be modeled. To be specific, we consider two consecutive "intersections" along a single road. Aerial photos are given in Fig. 1. The road we consider first stretches from West to East (a), then bends and goes from South-West to North-East (b). We describe each intersection in turn.

While our road is generally a bidirectional highway with one lane in each direction and no median strip dividing the traffic, the first intersection introduces a median and includes two bidirectional exit and entry roads. Major concerns underlying this design are those of safety and ease of traffic flow. Vehicles traveling East, i.e., using the lower lane of the highway, must use the first road to the right for exiting. A short deceleration lane is available. The second road connected to the right side of the highway is used by vehicles originating from the crossing road that wish to travel East on the highway. A short acceleration lane is available. A similar arrangement applies to the highway's upper lane.

At the second intersection, in Fig. 1(b), the highway has two lanes in each direction, a median, and four unidirectional exit/entry lanes. A vehicle traveling North-East, i.e., using the right lane of the highway, can decelerate in the long exit lane, while North-East bound vehicles must enter and can accelerate via the long right entry lane.

It should be clear that a transportation infrastructure is not just a mathematical graph. While some aspects may be described as a directed, non-planar

(a) First Intersection   (b) Second Intersection

Fig. 1. Aerial Photos of Road Intersections

graph, many other aspects are left unaccounted for by such a simple representation.

3   Data Modeling

The data model provides three external, user-accessible, representations of the transportation infrastructure, namely the *kilometer post*, *link-node*, and *geographic* representations, which are connected by an internal *segment* representation. The core of the data model is given in Fig. 2. When referring to this figure, we use capital letters and italics, e.g., ROAD and *r_id*, to denote table names and attributes, respectively.

3.1   Kilometer-Post Representation

The kilometer-post representation (the most commonly used type of known-marker representation) is used for road administration. It is convenient for relating a physical location to a location stored in a database and vice versa. Location is expressed in terms of the road, the distance marker on the road

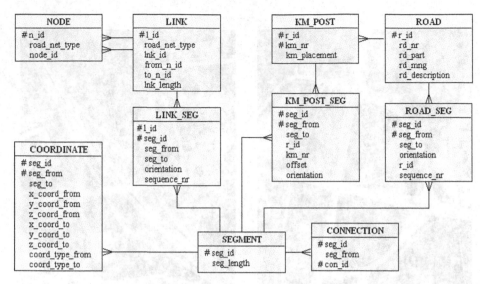

Fig. 2. Core Data Model

(e.g., kilometer post), and the offset from the distance marker. The representation is used by administrative authorities for collecting and utilizing data on field conditions, i.e., for entering content into the system. Primitive technological means, such as a simple measuring device and map and a ruler, suffice for identifying a position on a road, rendering the use of the representation cost effective and thus practical.

Table ROAD captures the administrative identification of roads, using the following attributes: the internal surrogate road id r_id, the external road number rd_nr, the road part rd_part (physically separate lanes, etc.), the road management authority rd_mng, and the external name of the road $rd\_description$. Table KM_POST captures information on road distance markers, namely the full kilometer distance km_nr from the start of road r_id, possibly with an offset $km\_placement$ from the physical marker (used, e.g., when the logical marker is in the middle of an intersection). The kilometer-post representation of the case study is seen in Fig. 3. Imaginary markers (with residual meter offsets from the full kilometer in parentheses) are used to mark beginnings of road parts.

3.2   Link-Node Representation

The link-node representation is based on the concepts of weighted undirected and directed mathematical graphs. A node is a road location with a significant change of traffic properties, e.g., an intersection. A link is a route that connects two nodes. Such a representation abstracts away geographical detail, but preserves the topology of the transportation infrastructure. For this reason, node-link representations are suitable for tasks such as traffic and route planning. The former task refers to (re)designing road networks taking traffic flows

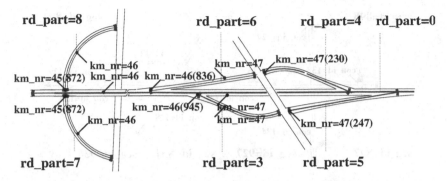

Fig. 3. Kilometer Post Infrastructure Representation

into consideration. In this case, undirected graphs are sufficient. The latter task refers to finding traversable routes in road networks that satisfy certain criteria. Directed graphs that capture traffic directions are appropriate for this task. The representation allows several *road network types*, e.g., a coarse-grained one for traffic planning and a fine-grained one for route planning.

Table NODE captures nodes, i.e., the internal surrogate id *n_id*, the road network type *road_net_type*, and a generic *node_id* that spans all road network types. Table LINK captures a link from start node *from_n_id* to end node *to_n_id* of length *lnk_length*. Links also have identifier attributes analogous to those of nodes, i.e., the *road_net_type*, the generic *lnk_id*, and the unique *l_id*.

3.3   Geographical Representation

The geographical representation captures the geographical coordinates of the transportation infrastructure. The coordinate representation enables users to directly reference location rather than measure distances along roads from certain locations, such as kilometer posts. Additionally, the representation is used by geography-related applications, such as cartographic systems or certain GISs, that operate on coordinate data.

Table COORDINATE captures a three-dimensional point given by (*x_coord_from*, *y_coord_from*, *z_coord_from*) on the center-line of a road. Several levels of detail are possible; these are captured by attribute *coord_type_from*. Attributes *x_coord_to*, *y_coord_to*, *z_coord_to*, and *coord_type_to* indicate the next 3D point on the segment. They are redundant and used to enhance the efficiency of query processing. Attributes *seg_id*, *seg_from*, and *seg_to*, map the two points of the tuple to the segment representation, described next.

3.4   Segment Representation

The internal segment representation models an infrastructure as a collection of segments that intersect at connections (locations where there is an exchange of

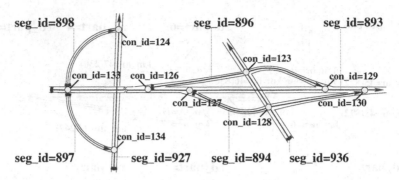

Fig. 4. Segment-Based Infrastructure Representation

traffic). This representation preserves the network topology and captures the complete set of roadways.

The positions of any content (e.g., speed limits, accident reports) are given by references to segments. In addition, the external representations of the infrastructure are mapped to the segment representation in a way that establishes one-to-one mappings between all the representations, i.e., the segment representation is the *integrator* of the different representations. For this reason, the segment representation is used by content integrators for efficient content position maintenance and translation between the external representations. The segment representation is purely internal to the system.

Table SEGMENT captures segments with unique id *seg_id* and length *seg_length*. A row in table CONNECTION describes that segment *seg_id* intersects with a connection point identified by *con_id*. The intersection of the segment with the connection point occurs at *seg_from* units from the start of the segment. The segment representation of the case study is illustrated in Fig. 4.

3.5 Interrelating the Representations

As pointed out earlier, we need the ability to translate among the different external infrastructure representations. This is achieved by connecting the kilometer-post representation and the node-link representation to the segment representation, which is already integrated with the geographical representation.

In our model, these connections are recorded by the tables KM_POST_SEG and ROAD_SEG for the kilometer-post representation and by table LINK_SEG for the link-node representation. We consider the latter two tables only.

As for the kilometer-post representation, a row in table ROAD_SEG relates (a section of) a road part *r_id* to a part of a segment *seg_id*. The (section of the) road part positioned by a row corresponds to the section of the related segment with end points at *seg_from* and *seg_to* units from the start of the segment. The attribute *orientation* indicates whether or not the directions of linear referencing along the segment and along the road part coincide. Attributes *rd_id* and *seg_id* are foreign keys that reference the tables ROAD and SEGMENT, respectively.

Further, since road parts do not overlap, the pair (*seg_id*, *seg_from*) is the primary key of the table. Finally, *sequence_nr* is an ordinal number of the road part section. It is used for distinguishing among different sections of the same road part and to "reconstruct" road parts from a collection of segment sections.

Note that table KM_POST_SEG alone fully defines the relation between the kilometer-post and other representations. Table ROAD_SEG is merely included for query efficiency—it contains redundant information.

As regards the link-node representation, a record in table LINK_SEG positions (a section of) a link *Lid* within a segment *seg_id*. The attribute *orientation* indicates whether the directions of linear referencing along the segment and of the link coincide. The other attributes have the same semantics as do their counterparts in table ROAD_SEG. Attributes *Lid* and *seg_id* are the foreign keys that point to the primary keys in tables LINK and SEGMENT, respectively.

3.6   Integration of Content

In our model, each type of content is allocated a separate descriptive table. For example, tables ACCIDENT and SERVICE describe instances of road accidents and car repair service providers, respectively. Further, each type of content is associated with a table that positions the content with respect to the infrastructure in the segment representation, e.g, a table ACCIDENT_SEG captures accident position and SERVICE_SEG captures service availability ranges.

The principles of positioning interval data with respect to segments are described above. In particular, the tables for interval content have schemas similar to those of tables ROAD_SEG and LINK_SEG. The positioning of point data is analogous to the positioning of connections (see above).

The same content must be accessible via different infrastructure representations. Given a type of content, a (possibly materialized) view can be created for each necessary external representation to allow easy and fast access.

4   Summary

Mobile, location-based information services, such as traffic, weather, tourist, and safety-related services, are seen as a very important new type of application. Such services depend on the availability of geo-related content, on multiple representations of the geographical infrastructure in which the users are traveling, and on the integration of the content with the infrastructure. This paper presents a case study with requirements, and it covers data modeling in response to the requirements, concentrating on infrastructure representations: the kilometer post, node-link, geographical, and segment representations, and on the integration of these with each other and the related content.

We hope this paper will expose to the data management research community some of the challenges faced when building a system capable of delivering high-quality mobile services in practice.

Danish company Euman is building a content integration and delivery system that uses an approach to data modeling that is quite similar to the one described in this paper.

Acknowledgments

We thank Christian Hage at Euman A/S for many discussions on the paper's topics. This work was supported in part by two grants from the Danish Centre for IT Research. The photos in Fig. 1 were made available by COWI, who hold the rights to the photos.

References

[1] P. Djernæs, O. Knudsen, E. Sørensen, and S. Schrøder. VIS-brugerhåndbog: Vejledning i opmåling og inddatering. 58 pages, 2002. (In Danish)

[2] Euman. http://www.euman.com 1

[3] C.S. Jensen, T.B. Pedersen, L. Speicys, and I. Timko. Integrated Data Management for Mobile Services in the Real World. *VLDB Conf.*, 2003 (to appear) 2

[4] C. Murray. Oracle Spatial User Guide and Reference, Release 9.2. *Oracle Corporation*, 486 pp., 2002 2

[5] NCHRP. A Generic Data Model for Linear Referencing Systems. *Transportation Research Board, Washington, DC*, 28 pp., 1997 2

[6] P. Scarponcini. Generalized Model for Linear Referencing in Transportation. *GeoInformatica* 6(1):35–55, 2002 2

Performance Evaluation
of Main-Memory R-tree Variants

Sangyong Hwang[1], Keunjoo Kwon[1], Sang K. Cha[1], and Byung S. Lee[2]

[1] Seoul National University
{syhwang,icdi,chask}@kdb.snu.ac.kr
[2] University of Vermont
bslee@cs.uvm.edu

Abstract. There have been several techniques proposed for improving the performance of main-memory spatial indexes, but there has not been a comparative study of their performance. In this paper we compare the performance of six main-memory R-tree variants: R-tree, R*-tree, Hilbert R-tree, CR-tree, CR*-tree, and Hilbert CR-tree. CR*-trees and Hilbert CR-trees are respectively a natural extension of R*-trees and Hilbert R-trees by incorporating CR-trees' quantized relative minimum bounding rectangle (QRMBR) technique. Additionally, we apply the optimistic, latch-free index traversal (OLFIT) concurrency control mechanism for B-trees to the R-tree variants while using the GiST-link technique. We perform extensive experiments in the two categories of sequential accesses and concurrent accesses, and pick the following best trees. In sequential accesses, CR*-trees are the best for search, Hilbert R-trees for update, and Hilbert CR-trees for a mixture of them. In concurrent accesses, Hilbert CR-trees for search if data is uniformly distributed, CR*-trees for search if data is skewed, Hilbert R-trees for update, and Hilbert CR-trees for a mixture of them. We also provide detailed observations of the experimental results, and rationalize them based on the characteristics of the individual trees. As far as we know, our work is the first comprehensive performance study of main-memory R-tree variants. The results of our study provide a useful guideline in selecting the most suitable index structure in various cases.

1   Introduction

With the emergence of ubiquitous computing devices (e.g., PDAs and mobile phones) and the enabling technologies for locating such devices, the problem of managing and querying numerous spatial objects poses a new scalability challenges [JJ+01]. Since such environment involves a huge number of spatial updates and search operations, existing disk-resident DBMS may not scale up enough to meet the high performance requirement. In this regard, main-memory DBMS (MMDBMS) promises a solution to the scalability problem as the price of memory continues to drop.

T. Hadzilacos et al. (Eds.): SSTD 2003, LNCS 2750, pp. 10-27, 2003.
© Springer-Verlag Berlin Heidelberg 2003

MMDBMS aims at achieving high transaction performance by keeping the database in main memory and limiting the disk access only to the sequential log writing and occasional checkpointing. Recent research finds that MMDBMS accomplishes up to two orders-of-magnitude performance improvements over disk-resident DBMS by using MMDB-specific optimization techniques. For example, the differential logging scheme improves the update and recovery performance of MMDBMS significantly by enabling fully parallel accesses to multiple logs and backup partition disks [LKC01]. Furthermore, with the primary database resident in memory without the complex mapping to disk, MMDBMS can focus on maximizing the CPU utilization. Techniques have been proposed to improve the search performance of B+-trees by utilizing the L2 cache better [RR00, CGM01, BMR01].

For multidimensional databases, our previous work on the cache-conscious R-tree (CR-tree) focuses on an inexpensive compression of minimum bounding rectangles (MBRs) to reduce L2 cache misses during a main-memory R-tree search [KCK01]. Specifically, the CR-tree uses a *quantized relative representation of MBR* (QRMBR) as the key. This compression effectively makes the R-tree wider for a given index node size, thus improving the search performance with reduced L2 cache misses. To handle dimensionality curse for the high-dimensional disk-resident R-tree, a similar technique called A-tree has been proposed independently [SY+02].

To handle concurrent index updates in real-world database applications while leveraging off-the-shelf multiprocessor systems, we have previously proposed the *optimistic latch-free index traversal* (OLFIT) as a cache-conscious index concurrency control technique that incurs minimal cache miss overhead [CH+01]. A conventional index concurrency control like lock coupling ([BS77]) pessimistically latches index nodes on every access, and incurs many coherence cache misses on shared-memory multiprocessor systems. OLFIT, based on a pair of node read and update primitives, completely eliminates latch operations during the index traversal. It has been empirically shown that OLFIT combined with the link technique ([LY81]) scales the search and update performance of B+-tree almost linearly on the shared-memory multiprocessor system.

To provide a useful guidance on selecting the most appropriate main memory spatial index structure in different cases, this paper investigates the search and update performance of main-memory R-tree variants experimentally in the sequential and concurrent access environments. To ensure a fair comparison, some of the existing R-tree variants need to be upgraded. For this purpose, we first apply the QRMBR technique to R*-tree and Hilbert R-tree and call the resulting trees the CR*-tree and the Hilbert CR-tree, respectively. Thus, the main-memory R-tree variants consist of R-tree, R*-tree, Hilbert R-tree, CR-tree, CR*-tree, and Hilbert CR-tree. Additionally, we apply the OLFIT to these R-tree variants, and for this we use the GiST-link technique instead of the B-link technique [KMH97].

In the sequential access experiments, the CR*-tree shows the best search performance and the Hilbert R-tree shows the update performance. Others (i.e., R-tree, R*-tree, CR-tree) are significantly below the two. The concurrent access experiments confirm the efficacy of the OLFIT in the scalability of search and update performance. The result shows that the Hilbert CR-tree is the best in the search performance if the data is uniformly distributed whereas CR*-tree is the best if the data is skewed, and the Hilbert R-tree is the best in the update performance. In both experiments, we judge that the Hilbert CR-tree is the best overall considering *both* the search and the update.

This paper is organized as follows. Section 2 briefly introduces the QRMBR and the OLFIT. Section 3 describes how we implement main-memory R-tree variants with the QRMBR technique. Section 4 elaborates on the concurrency control of main-memory R-trees. Section 5 presents the experimental result of index search and update performance for sequential and concurrent accesses. Section 6 summarizes the paper and outlines further work.

2   Background

2.1   Quantized Relative Representation of an MBR for the CR-tree

The quantized relative representation of an MBR (QRMBR) is a compressed representation of an MBR, which allows packing more entries in an R-tree node [KCK01]. This leads to a wider index tree, better utilization of cache memory, and consequently faster search performance. The QRMBR is done in two steps: representing the coordinates of an MBR relative to the coordinates of the "reference MBR" and quantizing the resulting relative coordinates with a fixed number of bits. The reference MBR of a node encloses all MBRs of its children. Relative coordinates require a smaller number of significant bits than absolute coordinates and, therefore, allow a higher compression in the quantization step.

The high performance of the QRMBR technique comes from the following two points. First, the compression is computationally simple and doable only with the data already cached, that is, the reference MBR and the MBR to be compressed. Second, the overlap-check between a QRMBR and a query rectangle can be done by computing the QRMBR of the query rectangle and comparing it with the given QRMBR. This property allows the overlap-check to be done by compressing the query rectangle once instead of decompressing the QRMBR of every node encountered during the search.

2.2   OLFIT Concurrency Control of Main-Memory B+-trees

Concurrency control of main-memory indexes typically uses latches placed inside an index node. A latch operation involves a memory-write, whether the operation is for acquiring or releasing a latch and whether the latch is in a shared-mode or an exclusive-mode. In the case of a conventional index concurrency control, a cache block containing a latch is invalidated even if the index is not updated. The optimistic, latch-free index traversal (OLFIT) concurrency control reduces this kind of cache misses by using two primitives for node accesses: UpdateNode and ReadNode [CH+01]. These primitives use a version as well as a latch in each node as shown in the following algorithms.

Algorithm UpdateNode
U1. Acquire the latch.
U2. Update the content of the node.
U3. Increment the version.
U4. Release the latch.

Algorithm ReadNode
R1. Copy the value of the version into a register.
R2. Read the content of the node.
R3. If the latch is locked, go to Step R1.
R4. If the current value of the version is different from the copied value in the register, go to Step R1.

Step R3 and Step R4 of ReadNode guarantee that transactions read a consistent version of a node without holding any latch. Specifically, Step R3 checks if the node is being updated by another transaction, and Step R4 checks if the node has been updated by another transaction while the current transaction is reading the content in Step R2. Consequently, if the read operation in Step R2 is interfered by any other concurrent update, the transaction cannot pass either Step R3 or Step R4 since the condition of either one becomes true.

Provided with the two primitive operations, Cha et al. combines the B-link technique with the primitives to support the concurrency control of B+-trees. The B-link technique places a high key and a link pointer in each node. A high key is the upper bound of all key values in a node, and a link pointer is a pointer to the right neighbor of the node [LY81]. The purpose of a link pointer is to provide an additional method for reaching a node, and the purpose of a high key is to determine whether to traverse through the link pointer or not. All splits are done from left to right, and a new node splitting from a node becomes its right neighbor. These link pointers make all nodes that split from a node reachable from the original node and make the correct child node reachable without lock coupling in the case of concurrent splits of nodes.

3   Main-Memory R-tree Variants

3.1   Overview

The *R-tree* is a height-balanced tree for indexing multi-dimensional keys [Gut84]. Other variants considered in this section are founded on this structure. Each node is associated with an MBR that encompasses the MBRs of all descendents of the node. The search operation traverses the tree to find all leaf nodes of which the MBRs overlap the query rectangle. On insertion of a new entry, the R-tree finds the leaf node that needs the least area enlargement of its MBR in order to contain the MBR of the new node.

The *R*-tree* is a variant of the R-tree that uses a different insertion policy and overflow treatment policy for better search performance [BK+90]. While traversing the tree for inserting a new entry, it chooses the internal node that needs the least *area* enlargement of its MBR and the leaf node that needs the least *overlap* enlargement of its MBR. However, this policy degrades the update performance because the CPU cost of finding such a leaf node is quadratic with the number of entries [BK+90]. Therefore, using the least overlap enlargement is left as an optional policy. If a node overflows then, before splitting it, the R*-tree first tries to reinsert part of the entries that are the farthest from the center of the node's MBR. This reinsertion improves the search performance by dynamically reorganizing the tree structure. However, it makes the concurrency control difficult without latching the whole tree. Compared with the split algorithm of the R-tree that considers only the area, that of the R*-tree considers the area, the margin, and the overlap, and achieves better clustering.

The *Hilbert R-tree* uses the Hilbert curve to impose a total order on the entries in an index tree [KF94]. Since all entries are totally ordered by their Hilbert values, the insertion and deletion algorithms are the same as those of the B+-tree except adjusting the MBRs of nodes to cover all descendent MBRs. The Hilbert R-tree was originally proposed to improve the *search* performance of *disk*-resident R-trees. However, here we use the Hilbert value-based ordering to improve the *update* performance of *main-memory* R-trees. Specifically, in the insertion algorithm, the R-tree or the R*-tree examines the MBRs of all nodes encountered to find the node with the least area or overlap enlargement, but the Hilbert R-tree uses a binary search on the total ordering and, therefore, performs only simple value comparisons. In the case of a node overflow, the R-tree or the R*-tree examines all entries in the node and separates them into two groups, but the Hilbert R-tree simply moves half the ordered entries to a new node. In the deletion algorithm, the R-tree or the R*-tree first searches the tree given the MBR of the entry to delete and this search may visit multiple paths. However, the Hilbert R-tree removes an entry with its Hilbert value and does not visit multiple paths. The total ordering in the Hilbert R-tree has another advantage. While the R-tree and R*-tree are non-deterministic in allocating the entries to a node and thus different sequences of insertions result in different tree structures, the Hilbert R-tree does not suffer from such non-determinism.

By applying the QRMBR technique of the CR-tree to R*-tree and Hilbert R-tree, we obtain the cache-conscious R-tree variants *CR*-tree* and *Hilbert CR-tree*, respectively. Their search and update algorithms are the same as those of their non-cache-conscious counterparts except that they use QRMBRs instead of MBRs for search and adjust QRMBRs instead MBRs for update. The QRMBR technique improves the search performance significantly in return for a slight degradation of the update performance caused by the overhead of adjusting QRMBRs.

3.2   Node Structures

Fig. 1 shows the node structures of the R-tree variants. C denotes the control information comprising the number of entries in the node and the level of the node in the tree. R denotes the reference MBR used in the QRMBR technique. Each node of the CR-tree, CR*-tree, and Hilbert CR-tree contains uncompressed MBRs corresponding to the QRMBRs to improve the concurrency and update performance. The reason for this is that the QRMBR technique requires re-computing all the QRMBRs in a node when the reference MBR of the node changes. Since the QRMBR technique is a lossy compression scheme, without uncompressed MBRs the recomputation of the QRMBRs requires visiting all children.

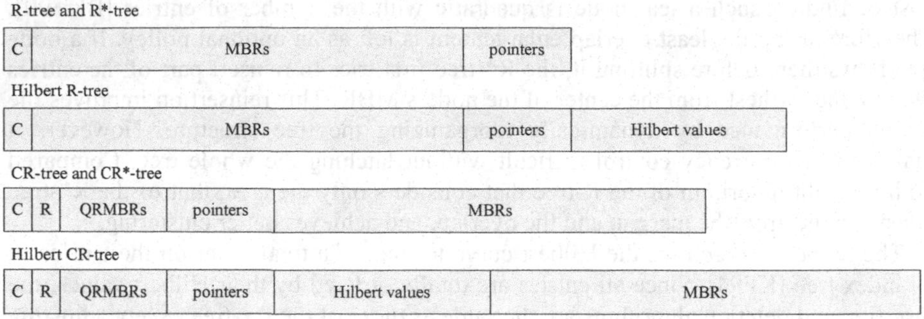

R-tree and R*-tree

C	MBRs	pointers

Hilbert R-tree

C	MBRs	pointers	Hilbert values

CR-tree and CR*-tree

C	R	QRMBRs	pointers	MBRs

Hilbert CR-tree

C	R	QRMBRs	pointers	Hilbert values	MBRs

Fig. 1. Node structures of the R-tree variants (C: control information, R: reference MBR)

The QRMBRs and the Hilbert values make the node size bigger and, therefore, increase the memory consumption. This overhead, however, is not significant. For example, we will see in Table 1 at section 5.1.2 that the largest gap is only 3.2 times between Hilbert CR-trees and R/R*-trees when the node size is 128 bytes. Moreover, increasing the node size does not entail increasing the memory access cost as much. For example, the Hilbert CR-tree, whose node size is the biggest by containing both the QRMBRs and the Hilbert values, reads only the control information, reference MBR, QRMBRs, and pointers for a search operation. Likewise, an update operation reads only the control information, pointers, and Hilbert values before it reaches a leaf node.

4   Concurrency Control of Main-Memory R-trees

4.1   Link Technique for R-trees

The OLFIT for main-memory B+-trees improves the performance of concurrent accesses by reducing the coherence cache misses, combined with The B-link technique [CH+01]. For R-trees, We use OLFIT with the GiST-link technique [KMH97]. Like the B-link technique, the GiST-link technique requires all the nodes at each level to be chained together through link pointers. The GiST-link technique uses a node sequence number (NSN) to determine if the right neighbor needs to be examined. The NSN is taken from a counter called the global NSN, which is global in the entire tree and increases monotonically. During a node split, this counter is incremented and the new value is assigned to the original node. The new sibling node inherits the original node's old NSN. A traversal can now determine whether to follow a link or not by memorizing the global NSN value when reading the parent and comparing it with the NSN of the current node. If the latter is higher, the node must have been split and, therefore, the operation follows the links until it encounters a node whose NSN is less than or equal to the one originally memorized.

```
// Note that QRMBR is used instead of MBR for CR, CR*, and Hilbert CR-trees.
procedure search(query_rectangle)
1.  gnsn:= global_nsn;
2.  push(stack, [root, gnsn]);
3.  while(stack is not empty) {
4.    [node, nsn]= pop(stack);
5.  RETRY:
6.    stack_savepoint = get_savepoint(stack);
7.    result_savepoint:= get_savepoint(result);
8.    saved_version:= node.version;
9.    if (nsn < node.nsn) push(stack, [node.link, nsn]);
10.   if (node is internal) {
11.     gnsn:= global_nsn;
12.     for (each entry [MBR, pointer] in node) {
13.       if (overlaps(query_rectangle, MBR)) push(stack, [pointer, gnsn]);
14.     }
15.   }
16.   else {   // node is a leaf
17.     for (each entry [MBR, pointer] in node) {
18.       if (overlaps(query_rectangle, MBR)) add(result, pointer);
19.     }
20.   }
21.   if (node.latch is locked or node.version ≠ saved_version) {
22.     rollback(stack, stack_savepoint);
23.     rollback (result, result_savepoint);
24.     goto RETRY;
25.   }
26. }
```

Fig. 2. Traversal with the OLFIT for search

In the case of the Hilbert R-tree and the Hilbert CR-tree, we use the GiST-link technique only for the search. We use the B-link technique for the insertion and the deletion because the index entries are totally ordered by their Hilbert values. Link pointers are for dual use as either B-links or GiST-links. In this paper, we consider only the 1-to-2 split for the Hilbert R-tree and the Hilbert CR-tree because the GiST-link technique does not allow redistribution of entries between nodes.

4.2   Search Algorithm of R-tree Variants Using OLFIT

Fig. 2 shows the algorithm for performing R-tree search while using the GiST-link based OLFIT. First, in Lines 1 and 2, it pushes the pointer to the root node and the global NSN into the stack. Then, in Line 4 it pops the pointer to a node and the associated global NSN from the stack and reads the corresponding node. If the popped node is an internal node, then in Lines 11~14 it pushes into the stack all pointers to the child nodes whose MBRs (or QRMBRs) overlap the query rectangle. If the node is a leaf node, then in Lines 17~19 it adds all pointers to the data objects whose MBRs (or QRMBRs) overlap the query rectangle to the search result. This procedure is repeated until the stack is empty.

Each time it iterates, the pointer to a node is pushed with the value of the global NSN When the pointer to a node in the stack is used to visit a node, in Line 9 the global NSN pushed together is compared with the NSN of the node. If the latter is higher, the node must have been split and, therefore, the link pointer of the node is pushed into the stack together with the original global NSN. This guarantees that the right siblings that split off the original node will also be examined later on.

Lines 5~8 and Lines 21~25 are specific to the OLFIT. Line 8, which saves the version of the node, corresponds to Step R1 of the ReadNode primitive in Section 2.2. Line 21, which checks the state of the latch and the version of the node, corresponds to Steps R3 and R4. That is, while reading the node, if the search operation is interfered by other concurrent updates on the node, the condition in Line 21 becomes true and the search operation retries to read the node. (Refer to Line 24 and Line 5). Before the retry, in Lines 22~23 the stack and the result are rolled back to the state recorded in Lines 6~7 before reading the node. The repeatable-read transaction isolation level is achieved by locking all pointers to data objects in the result buffer.

4.3   Update Algorithm of R-tree Variants OLFTI

For performing R-tree updates while using the OLFIT concurrency control, the Hilbert R-tree and the Hilbert CR-tree use the B-link technique and the other variants use the GiST-link technique. The insertion operation first looks for the leaf node to hold the new entry, and the deletion operation first looks for the leaf node holding the entry to delete. As in the search, the ReadNode primitive presented in Section 2.2 is used in the process. After finding the target leaf, the operations update the leaf node and propagate the update upward using the UpdateNode primitive presented in Section 2.2. We omit the detailed algorithm due to space limit. Interested readers are referred to [TR02].

5   Experimental Evaluation

In this section, we compare the index access performance of the main memory R-tree variants with respect to such attributes as data size, data distribution, query selectivity, index node size, the number of parallel threads, and update ratio (= the number of updates / the total number of searches and updates combined). We run our experiments on a Sun Enterprise 5500 server with 8 CPUs (UltraSPARC II, 400MHz) running Solaris 7. Each CPU has 8Mbyte L2 cache whose cache line size is 64 bytes.

5.1   Setup

5.1.1   Data and Queries

We use three data sets containing hundred thousand (100K), one million (1M), and ten million (10M) data rectangles each. All rectangles have the same size 4m × 4m, and their centers are either uniformly distributed or skewed within a 40km × 40km region. Skewed data are simulated with the Gaussian distribution of mean 20,000m and standard deviation 200m.

We use two region queries, where the regions are specified with square windows whose centers are distributed uniformly within the 40km × 40km region. The window sizes are 126m × 126m and 400m × 400m and the resulting selectivity values are 0.001% and 0.01%, respectively.

Table 1. Node fanout, Index height and Index size for different node sizes (data size=1M, uniform dist.)

Node size (bytes)	Fanout						Height						Index size (Mbytes)					
	R	R*	HR	CR	CR*	HCR	R	R*	HR	CR	CR*	HCR	R	R*	HR	CR	CR*	HCR
128	5	5	3	4	4	3	11	11	34	13	13	34	50	50	149	65	65	159
256	11	11	8	9	9	7	7	7	8	8	8	9	39	39	54	50	50	65
384	18	18	13	15	15	11	6	6	7	6	6	7	35	34	49	42	41	57
512	24	24	17	20	20	15	5	5	6	6	6	6	34	33	47	41	40	54
1024	50	50	35	41	41	31	4	4	5	5	5	5	32	31	44	39	38	50
2048	101	101	72	84	84	63	4	4	4	4	4	4	31	30	42	37	36	48
3072	152	152	109	127	127	95	3	3	4	4	4	4	31	30	42	37	36	47

Updates are performed as a sequence of random moves. Each move deletes an entry at the coordinates $<x, y>$ and inserts it into a new position at $<x\pm30r_1, y\pm30r_2>$ where r_1 and r_2, $0\le r_1, r_2\le1$, are random numbers. This random move is one of the cases that can be generated using the GSTD software [TN00] and is typical of moving objects. Assuming cars are moving at 100km/hour (= 30m/second), we choose 30m for the variation. The variation does not affect the update performance significantly because the update operation consists of independent two operations, delete and insert.

5.1.2 Indexes

We implement the R-tree and its five variants R*-tree, Hilbert R-tree, CR-tree, CR*-tree, and Hilbert CR-tree. (In this section, we label them as R, R*, HR, CR, CR*, and HCR) We allow duplicate key values in these indexes and initialize them by inserting data rectangles and the associated pointers. We set the pointer size to 4bytes as we run our experiment in the 32-bit addressing mode. Additionally, we use 4-byte QRMBRs in the CR, CR*, and Hilbert CR-trees. In the R*-tree and the CR*-tree, we do not use the reinsertion because it makes the concurrency control difficult without latching the whole tree, nor we use the least overlap enlargement policy because it improves the search performance only slightly at the expense of significant update performance.

Table 1 shows the node fanout, index height, and index size of the main-memory R-tree variants created on the data of size 1M. The numbers are based on the index entry size 20 bytes for the R and R*-tree, 24 bytes for the CR and CR*-tree, 28 bytes for the Hilbert R-tree, and 32 bytes for the Hilbert CR-tree.

5.1.3   Experimental Outline

We perform two kinds of experiments: the sequential access experiment and the concurrent access experiment. In each experiment, we measure the throughput of a sequence of search (i.e., range query) and update (i.e., random move) operations. Operation/sec refers to the number of executed operations divided by the total execution time.

In the sequential access experiment, we initialize indexes by inserting data objects in sequence and perform searches using a sequence of region queries mentioned above. In the concurrent access experiment, we initialize indexes inserting data objects concurrently in eight threads and then compare the concurrent search and update performance between the OLFIT and the conventional latched-based link technique [LY81, KMH97]. The performed searches and updates are the same as those in the sequential access experiment and are divided evenly to each thread. We also compare the performance among OLFIT techniques for a mixture of searches and updates mixed at different ratios.

We omit such a mixture of operations in the sequential experiment because the resulting performance is a linear interpolation between the results from searches only and updates only and, thus, is calculated without running the actual experiment. In the concurrent case, the performance from the mixture is not an interpolation because search and update may interfere with each other.

The way QRMBR and OLFIT techniques improve the throughput is by reducing the number of L2 cache misses. There are, however, other factors contributing to improving the throughput as well, like the number of instructions in the code. Since main memory performance is particularly sensitive to code implementations, serious attention should be paid to removing code-specific biases among the R-tree variants. In this regard, we demonstrate the consistency between the performance measured as the throughput and the performance measured as the number of cache misses (using the *Perfmon* tool [Enb99]).

There is no R-tree variant winning consistently in all possible cases. Therefore, it could be misleading to rank the variants by their search or update performance without considering the complexity of the comparisons. In this regard, we have performed a benchmark of 288 test cases generated as a combination of the attributes mentioned above and selected the winners by their rates of winning the cases. The results obtained are consistent with those obtained in the experiments presented in this section. We omit the results due to space limit. Interested readers are referred to [TR02].

5.2   Sequential Access Performance

Fig. 3 shows the sequential access performance for different node sizes when one million data rectangles (1M) are uniformly distributed, and Fig. 4 shows the same information when the data rectangles have the Gaussian distribution. From Fig. 3(a)-(b) and Fig. 4(a)-(b), we make the following observations about the search performance for both data distributions alike. First, they confirm that the QRMBR technique improves the search performance significantly. That is, a cache-conscious version (i.e., CR, CR*, HCR) is better than its non-cache-conscious counterpart (i.e., R, R*, HR). Second, CR*-trees show the best search performance, which is attributed to not only the QRMBR technique but also the well-clustered nodes generated with the R*-tree split algorithm. Third, the search performance fluctuates as the index node size increases. This reflects the dual effect of increasing the fanout – it increases the cost of reading a node but decrease the overall search cost by reducing the tree height.

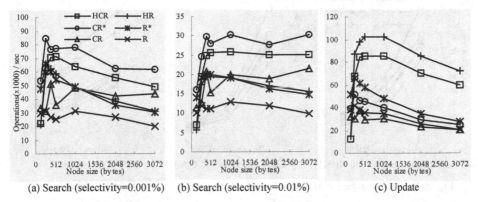

(a) Search (selectivity=0.001%)   (b) Search (selectivity=0.01%)   (c) Update

Fig. 3. Sequential access performance w.r.to node size (data size = 1M, uniform dist.)

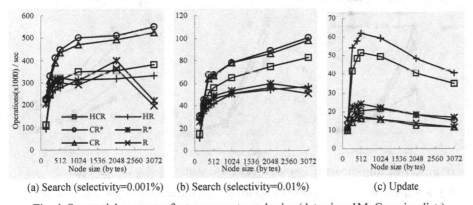

(a) Search (selectivity=0.001%)   (b) Search (selectivity=0.01%)   (c) Update

Fig. 4. Sequential access performance w.r.to node size (data size=1M, Gaussian dist.)

From the same figures, we see that Hilbert CR-trees perform better than CR-trees in uniformly distributed data but worse in skewed data. That is, skewed data gives a disadvantage to Hilbert CR-trees. This result contradicts Kamel and Faloutsos's conjecture [KF94] that skewness of data gives a favor to Hilbert R-trees. The cause is the difference in the experimental settings. For instance, their experiment uses 2-to-3 split in Hilbert R-trees and reinsertion in R*-trees whereas ours does not.

From Fig. 3(c) and Fig. 4(c), we make the following observations about the update performance for both data distributions. First, they confirm that the Hilbert value-based ordering improves the update performance significantly. That is, Hilbert R-trees are better than R-trees and R*-trees, and Hilbert CR-trees are better than CR-trees and CR*-trees. Second, the update performance of Hilbert R-trees is better than that of Hilbert CR-trees. This is due to the Hilbert CR-tree's overhead of maintaining the QRMBRs. Third, CR*-trees show poor update performance, unlike their excellent search performance. This is due to the computational overhead of R*-tree insertion for finding the leaf node with the minimum overlap enlargement and splitting a node.

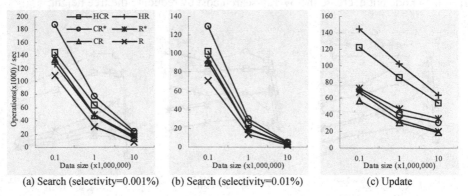

(a) Search (selectivity=0.001%)   (b) Search (selectivity=0.01%)   (c) Update

Fig. 5. Sequential access performance w.r.to data size (node size=1024B, uniform dist.)

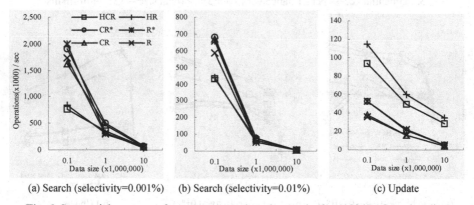

(a) Search (selectivity=0.001%)   (b) Search (selectivity=0.01%)   (c) Update

Fig. 6. Sequential access performance w.r.to data size (node size=1024B, Gaussian dist.)

Fig. 5 and Fig. 6 show the search and update performance with respect to the size of data with each of the two distributions. First, it appears that the performance gap among the R-tree variants decreases as the data size increases. This is true for the absolute performance, but it is the opposite for the relative performance. The reason for this increase is that the increase of data size causes more cache misses and consequentially highlights the performance gain of the QRMBR.

Second, with uniformly distributed data, the performance rank among the R-tree variants is the same for all data sizes whereas, with the skewed data, the cache-conscious versions lose advantage in the search performance as the data size decreases. This happens partly due to the computation overhead of the QRMBR method for reducing the number of cache misses. In addition, three factors reduce the effectiveness of the QRMBR. First, if the data is small enough to fit in the cache, a cache miss hardly occurs and, therefore, there is little gain from the QRMBR. Second, data skew reduces the gap between the size of a parent node's MBR and the size of its child node's MBR, and this diminishes the effectiveness of the relative representation of an MBR and, as a result, increases the quantization errors. Third, these quantization errors are higher for lower query selectivity. The aforementioned instance in Fig. 6(a) is the worst case caused by the accumulation of these three factors.

From all these observations about sequential access performance, we judge that Hilbert CR-trees are the best considering both the search performance and the update performance. These trees are not the first choice in any category, but are consistently the second or the third choice by a small margin in most cases. In summary, we conclude that CR*-trees are the best choice for the search performance only, Hilbert R-trees are the best choice for the update performance only, and Hilbert CR-trees are the best choice when considering both.

5.3   Concurrent Access Performance

Fig. 7 shows the search and update performance for different numbers of threads, contrasted between the conventional latch-based and the OLFIT-based concurrency control, given the data with size 1M and the uniform distribution. (We omit the results obtained with the Gaussian distribution data due to space limit. Most observations are same as in the uniform distribution case.) We set the node size to 512 bytes, which is the median of the seven different node sizes used. Besides, we consider only the CR*-tree, Hilbert R-tree, and Hilbert CR-tree because the other three variants are poorer in both the search and update performance.

From this figure, we make the following observations. First, they confirm the advantage of the OLFIT in the concurrent search and update performance. That is, as the number of threads increases, CR*-trees, Hilbert R-trees, and Hilbert CR-trees become significantly better with the OLFIT than with the Latch. Second, the relative search performance among the R-tree variants differs between the two data distributions. Specifically, the best search performer is Hilbert CR-trees for the uniform distribution and CR*-trees for the Gaussian distribution. The reason is that data skew is not favorable to Hilbert R-trees, as discussed in the sequential access case. Third, the update performance shows the same relative performance as in the sequential access experiment.

Fig. 8 shows the concurrent search and update performance with respect to the data size for the uniform distribution given the number of threads 4. (We omit the results from the Gaussian distribution and other number of threads for the same reason as above.) We make the following observations. First, like the case of sequential access performance, the absolute performance gap decreases among the R-tree variants while the relative performance gap increases as the data size increases. Second, the performance advantage of the OLFIT over the Latch becomes more noticeable for smaller data and queries with lower selectivity. We draw the following reasons for this. First, smaller data size increases the coherence cache miss rate because evidently it increases the possibility of cached data being invalidated by another processor. Second, in the case of higher query selectivity, queries access nodes near the leaves in addition to those near the root. This causes other types of cache misses (e.g., capacity cache miss) to occur as well and, as a result, reduces the relative adverse effect of the coherence cache misses.

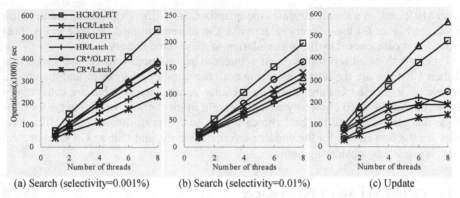

Fig. 7. Concurrent access performance w.r.to the number of threads (data size=1M, uniform)

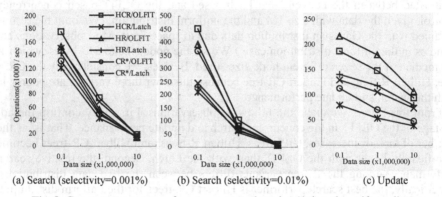

Fig. 8. Concurrent access performance w.r.to data size (4 threads, uniform dist.)

Fig. 9 and Fig. 10 show the concurrent access performance for different update ratios for each of the two data distributions. The OLFIT is used for the concurrency control and the number of threads is fixed to eight. We make the following observations from these figures. First, the winners change places as the update ratio changes. The pattern is slightly different between the two data distributions. In the case of the uniform distribution, Hilbert CR-trees are the best in the low to middle range of the update ratio and Hilbert R-trees are the best in the high range. Hilbert CR-trees fall below Hilbert R-trees as the cost of managing QRMBR increases. In the case of the Gaussian distribution, CR*-trees are the best or comparable to Hilbert CR-trees in the low range, Hilbert CR-trees are the best in the middle range, and Hilbert R-trees are the best in the high range. The initial lead of CR*-trees is due to the relatively poor search performance of Hilbert R-trees and Hilbert CR-trees against skewed data. CR*-trees fall below the other two as the number of updates increases due to the increasing computational overhead. Second, related to the first observation, Hilbert CR-trees have an advantage over the other two trees at the higher query selectivity.

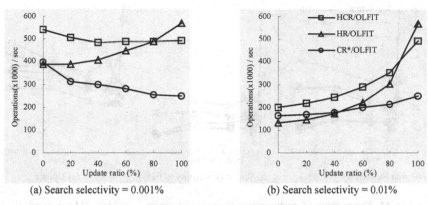

(a) Search selectivity = 0.001%   (b) Search selectivity = 0.01%

Fig. 9. Concurrent access performance w.r.to update ratios (8 threads, data size=1M, uniform)

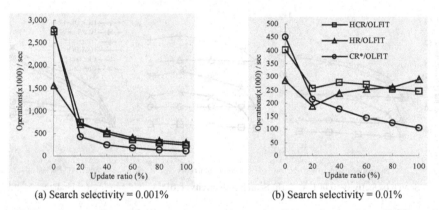

(a) Search selectivity = 0.001%   (b) Search selectivity = 0.01%

Fig. 10. Concurrent access performance w.r.to update ratios (8 threads, data size=1M,Gaussian)

From all these observations about concurrent access performance, we make the same judgment as in the sequential access performance. Hilbert CR-trees are the best choice for the search performance if the data is distributed uniformly whereas CR*-trees are the best if the data is skewed, Hilbert R-trees are the best choice for the concurrent update performance, and Hilbert CR-trees are the best choice when considering both.

5.4   Consistency with the Number of Cache Misses

Fig. 11 shows the number of cache misses in sequential accesses for different node sizes when one million data rectangles are uniformly distributed, and Fig. 12 shows the number in concurrent accesses for different numbers of threads. We do not show the case of skewed data because the observed results are the same.

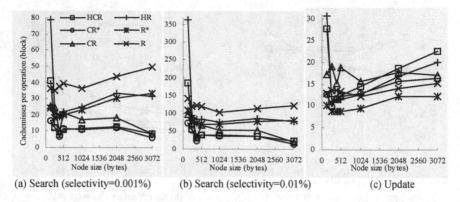

Fig. 11. The number of cache misses (Sequential access, data size=1M, uniform)

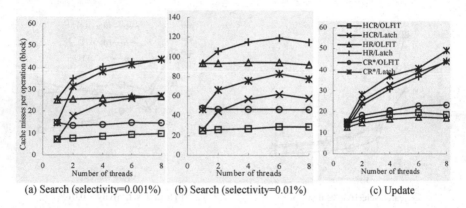

Fig. 12. The number of cache misses (Concurrent access, data size=1M, uniform)

The numbers of cache misses of the R-tree variants in Fig. 11(a)-(b) are ranked exactly in the reverse order of the throughputs in Fig. 3(a)-(b), and the numbers in Fig. 11(c) are almost in the reverse order of those in Fig. 3(c). In Fig. 11(c), the HCR-tree and the HR-tree incur more cache misses than the other R-tree variants despite showing the best update performance in Fig. 3(c). This is because an insertion in HCR-trees and HR-trees needs far less computation than the other R-tree variants for choosing the appropriate leaf node. Fig. 12 shows that the number of cache misses of the variants are ranked in the reverse order of the throughputs in Fig. 7(a)-(c), including the update case. We see that the numbers hardly increase with the number of threads if OLFIT is used, whereas they do increase if Latch is used. This confirms the advantage of OLFIT over Latch in concurrency control.

6   Summary and Further Work

In this paper, we compared the sequential and concurrent access (search and update) performance of the main-memory R-tree and its five variants – R*-tree, Hilbert R-tree, CR-tree, CR*-tree, and Hilbert CR-tree – while applying the QRMBR technique for faster search performance and the OLFIT technique for better concurrency control. We used the GiST-link technique to apply the OLFIT technique to the R-tree variants. Naturally, the QRMBR improved the index search performance and the OLFIT improved the concurrency.

We conducted experiments for evaluating the performance in terms of the throughput. As a result, we found the following trees performing the best in each category: in sequential accesses, CR*-trees for search, Hilbert R-trees for update, and Hilbert CR-trees when considering both and, in concurrent accesses, Hilbert CR-trees for searching uniformly distributed data, CR*-trees for searching skewed data, Hilbert R-trees for update, and Hilbert CR-tree for a mixture of search and update except an update-intensive case. We also demonstrated that the throughput results were not biased by the code implementations by showing the consistency between the observations based on the number of cache misses and those based on the throughput.

We also demonstrated that the throughput results were not biased by the code implementation by showing the consistency between the observations based on the number of cache misses and those based on the throughput.

All queries considered in this paper are range search queries. We plan to pursue further experiments using the nearest neighbor queries. Like range search queries, these queries involve traversing R-trees while pushing nodes into and popping nodes from a stack. Therefore, they are amenable to tree structures clustered so that more index entries can be examined with the same block cached. Compared with range queries, however, nearest neighbor queries incur higher computation cost and, therefore, clustering is more important than compression to search performance.

Currently our R-tree search algorithm does not prevent the phantom phenomenon. To our knowledge, there does not exist any algorithm addressing this problem for main-memory indexes. We are currently working on it.

Other further works include using real (dynamic) geographical data sets instead of synthetic ones and using different process architecture like MPP instead of SMP. As MPP incurs higher communication cost among processors than SMP, we expect the advantage of the OLFIT over the latch-based concurrency control should become eminent. We also plan to incorporate the R-tree variants into a main memory spatial data management system and perform a benchmark comparison instead of simulation.

References

[BMR01] Philip Bohannon, Peter McIlroy, and Rajeev Rastogi, "Improving Main-Memory Index Performance with Partial Key Information", In *Proc. of ACM SIGMOD Conf.*, 2001, pages 163-174.

[BS77]   Rudolf Bayer and Mario Schkolnick, "Concurrency of Operations on B-Trees", *Acta Informatica 9*, 1977, pages 1-21.

[BK+90] Norbert Beckmann, Hans-Peter Kriegel, Ralf Schneider, and Bernhard Seeger, "The R*-tree: An Efficient and Robust Access Method for Points and Rectangles", In *Proc. of ACM SIGMOD Conf.*, 1990, pages 322-331.

[CGM01] Shimin Chen, Philip B. Gibbons, and Todd C. Mowry, "Improving Index Performance through Prefetching", In *Proc. of ACM SIGMOD Conf.*, 2001, pages 235-246.

[CH+01] Sang K. Cha, Sangyong Hwang, Kihong Kim, and Keunjoo Kwon, "Cache-Conscious Concurrency Control of Main-Memory Indexes on Shared-Memory Multiprocessor Systems", In *Proc. of VLDB Conf.*, 2001

[Enb99] R. Enbody, Perfmon Performance Monitoring Tool, 1999, available from http://www.cps.msu.edu/~enbody/perfmon.html.

[Gut84] Antonin Guttman, "R-trees: A Dynamic Index Structure for Spatial Searching", In *Proc. of ACM SIGMOD Conf.*, 1984, pages 125-135.

[JJ+01] Ravi Jain, Christian S. Jensen, Ralf-Hartmut Güting, Andreas Reuter, Evaggelia Pitoura, Ouri Wolfson, George Samaras, and Rainer Malaka, "Managing location information for billions of gizmos on the move— what's in it for the database folks?", *IEEE ICDE 2001 Panel*.

[KCK01] Kihong Kim, Sang K. Cha, and Keunjoo Kwon, "Optimizing Multidimensional Index Trees for Main Memory Access", In *Proc. of ACM SIGMOD Conf.*, 2001, pages 139-150.

[KF94] Ibrahim Kamel and Christos Faloutsos, "Hilbert R-tree: An Improved R-tree using Fractals", In *Proc. of VLDB Conf.*, 1994, pages 500-509.

[KMH97] Marcel Kornacker, C. Mohan, and Joseph M. Hellerstein, "Concurrency and Recovery in Generalized Search Trees", In *Proc. of ACM SIGMOD Conf.*, 1997, pages 62-72.

[LKC01] Juchang Lee, Kihong Kim, and Sang K. Cha, "Differential Logging: A Commutative and Associative Logging Scheme for Highly Parallel Main Memory Database", In *Proc. of IEEE ICDE Conf.*, 2001, pages 173-182.

[LY81] Philip L. Lehman and S. Bing Yao, "Efficient Locking for Concurrent Operations on B-Trees", *ACM TODS*, Vol. 6, No. 4, 1981, pages 650-670.

[RR00] Jun Rao and Kenneth Ross, "Making B+-trees Cache Conscious in Main Memory", In *Proc. of ACM SIGMOD Conf.*, 2000, pages 475-486.

[SY+02] Yasushi Sakurai, Masatoshi Yoshikawa, Shunsuke Uemura, Haruhiko Kojima, "Spatial Index of High-dimensional Data Based on Relative Approximation", *VLDB Journal* 11(2), 2002, pages 93-108

[TN00] Y. Theodoridis and M.A. Nascimento, "Generating Spatio temporal Datasets on the WWW", *ACM SIGMOD Record*, September 2000.

[TR02] Sangyong Hwang, Keunjoo Kwon, Sang K. Cha, Byung S. Lee, "Performance Evaluation of Main-Memory R-tree Variants", *Technical Report*, 2002, available at http://kdb.snu.ac.kr/papers/SSTD03_TR.pdf

The BTR-Tree: Path-Defined Version-Range Splitting in a Branched and Temporal Structure

Linan Jiang[1], Betty Salzberg[2], David Lomet[3], and Manuel Barrena[4]

[1] Oracle Corp.
400 Oracle Parkway, Redwood Shores, CA 94065
linan.jiang@oracle.com
[2] College of Computer Science
Northeastern Univerity
Boston, MA 02115
salzberg@ccs.neu.edu
[3] Microsoft Research
One Microsoft Way, Building 9, Redmond, WA 98052
lomet@microsoft.com
[4] Universidad de Extremadura
Cáceres, Spain
barrena@unex.es

Abstract. There are applications which require the support of temporal data with *branched* time evolution, called *branched-and-temporal* data. In a branched-and-temporal database, both historic versions and current versions are allowed to be updated. We present an access method, the *BTR-Tree*, for branched-and-temporal databases with reasonable space and access time tradeoff. It is an index structure based on the BT-Tree [5]. The BT-Tree always splits at a current version whenever a data page or an index page is full. The BTR-Tree is able to split at a previous version while still keeping the posting property that only one parent page needs to be updated. The splitting policy of the BTR-Tree is designed to reduce data redundancy in the structure introduced by branching. Performance results show that the BTR-Tree has better space efficiency and similar query efficiency than the BT-Tree, with no overhead in search and posting algorithm complexity.

1 Introduction

There are applications which require the support of temporal data with *branched* time evolution, called *branched-and-temporal* data. In a branched-and-temporal database, both historic versions and current versions are allowed to be updated. We present an access method, the *BTR-Tree*, for branched-and-temporal databases with reasonable space and access time tradeoff.

A branched-and-temporal index method not only needs to support *version queries*, such as "show me all the data for branch B at time T", but also needs to support historical queries [6], such as "show me all the previous versions of this record." The BT-tree [5] is the only paginated access method explicitly proposed

T. Hadzilacos et al. (Eds.): SSTD 2003, LNCS 2750, pp. 28–45, 2003.

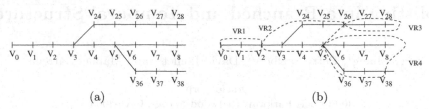

Fig. 1. (a)A version tree. (b) Version ranges of various kinds: $VR1=(v_0,\{v_2\})$, $VR2 = (v_2,\{v_{26}, v_5\})$, $VR3 = (v_{26}, \emptyset)$, and $VR4 = (v_5,\{v_{38}\})$

for branched-and-temporal data in the literature, although many access methods (for example, [3], [1], [8], [10] and [9]) have been proposed for temporal data (no branching), and Lanka and Mays proposed (based on ideas from [2]) the "fully persistent B+-tree" [7], a branch-only access method where no time dimension is considered.

The contribution of this paper is to introduce a new branched and temporal access method, the BTR-tree, based on the BT-tree. New splitting options which diminish version branching in pages and hence improve performance while maintaining the simple posting and searching algorithms of the BT-tree are proposed. In particular, in spite of not splitting at current versions, posting of the information about a split need only be made to one parent of the splitting page.

In Section 2 we review the BT-tree and describe the motivation of the BTR-Tree. Section 3 presents our new splitting algorithms used in the BTR-Tree. Performance results are presented in Section 4. We will conclude in Section 5.

2   BT-Tree Overview and Our Motivation

In this section, we first introduce some preliminary definitions. We will then review the BT-Tree and describe the motivation of the BTR-Tree.

2.1   Preliminaries

Time in a branched-and-temporal database is assumed to be discrete, described by a succession of nonnegative integers. Each branch is assigned a unique branch id, represented by a positive integer. A combination of a branch identifier B and a time stamp T is called a *version*. Sometimes we also denote a version (B, T) to be a version v. V is used to represent the version universe.

The whole version space V can be captured by a rooted *version tree*, whose nodes are the versions, with version v_i being the parent of version v_j if v_j is derived directly from v_i. Version v_0 is the root of the version tree. An example is given in Figure 1 (a).

Given two versions $(B1, T1)$ and $(B2, T2)$, if $(B2, T2)$ is derived from $(B1, T1)$, we denote that $(B1, T1) < (B2, T2)$. $(B2, T2)$ is also called a *descendant* of $(B1, T1)$. A version $(B1, T1)$ is defined to be a descendant of itself. Therefore the set of versions v satisfying $(B1, T1) <= v$ is noted as $des((B1, T1))$. For example, in Figure 1 (a), $v_{25} \in des(v_2)$. If $(B2, T2)$ is a descendant of $(B1, T1)$, we say $(B1, T1)$ is an *ancestor* of $(B2, T2)$.

Branched-and-temporal data is represented by record variants. A *record variant* is characterized by four entries: a branch id, a time stamp, a time-invariant part called a *key*, and a data field. For example, $(3, 80, a, d)$ is a record variant with branch id = 3, time stamp = 80, key = a, and d representing the data value of this record variant. The notation of record variant can also be used to describe the discontinuation of data with a certain key in a specific branch. A *null record variant* $(b, t, k, null)$ indicates that at time t, the record variant with key k in branch b is deleted.

2.2   The BT-Tree Review

The BT-Tree is in fact a DAG. When restricted to one version, it is a tree. Similarly, other versioned structures such as the WOBT tree [3] and the TSB tree [8] are also DAGs, but they are traditionally called trees.

The BT-Tree has many properties in common with the ordinary B-tree. The nodes are disk pages. When page A contains the address of page B, A is a *parent* of B, B is called a *child* of A and there is a directed edge in the DAG from A to B. There is a distinguished page called the *root* which is an entry point for search. Leaf pages are at the same distance from the root page.

Also in common with B-trees, leaf pages contain data and are called *data pages*. Non-leaf pages direct search and contain only search information, not data. These pages are called *index pages*. The BT-Tree stores record variants in data pages. Exact match search (for example, "for a version (B, T) and key value k, what is the data value?") follows a unique path from the root to exactly one leaf, visiting only one page at each level. (Pages are at the same *level* if they are the same distance from the leaves.) The number of index pages is much smaller than the number of data pages. This is because each index page has numerous children.

As in the B-tree, when a new item is to be inserted, search directs the inserter to exactly one leaf. If that leaf page is full, a new leaf page must be allocated and some of the data from the old leaf page must be placed in the new leaf page. This is called a *split*. When a split is made, information is *posted* about the split to a parent node to direct search to the newly allocated node when appropriate.

Unlike the B-tree, which deals only with one-dimensional data, the BT-tree must cope with branching versions. To get an idea how BT-Tree copes with branching versions to achieve both space and query efficiency, we need a few more definitions about branching and versions.

- *Current Version*: A version is *current* if there is no descendent version in the same branch. For example, in Figure 1 (a) versions v_{28}, v_8, and v_{38} (each of them represents a branch and time pair) are all current versions.
- *Start Time and Share Time of a Branch*: If version $(B2, T2)$ is created from version $(B1, T1)$ where $B2 \neq B1$, then branch $B2$ is created from branch

$B1$ with *start time* $T2$ and *share time* $T1$. Version $(B2, T2)$ is also called the *start version* of a branch.

Version Ranges. A *version range* vr is a set of versions represented by the pair $(start(vr), end(vr))$, where *start(vr)* is a version and *end(vr)* is a set of versions satisfying the following condition: if $ev \in end(vr)$, then $start(vr) < ev$ and $\forall ev' \in end(vr)$ and $ev' \neq ev, \neg(ev < ev')$. This condition implies that end versions must be (strict) descendants of the start version and distinct end versions must lie on different branches. For example, in Figure 1 (b), $(v_0, \{v_2\})$ is a version range marked as $VR1$, while $VR = (v_0, \{v_1, v_2\})$ is not a version range because $v_2 \in end(VR)$ and $v_1 \in end(VR)$ and $v_1 < v_2$, in other words, these two end versions v_1 and v_2 lie on same branch.

Since version ranges are sets, we use set notation to describe the relationship among versions and version ranges. Thus, $v \in vr$ if $start(vr) <= v$ and $\forall ev \in end(vr), \neg(ev <= v)$. For example, in Figure 1 (b) $v_{37} \in VR4 = (v_5, \{v_{38}\})$ because $v_5 < v_{37}$ and $\neg(v_{38} <= v_{37})$, while $v_{38} \notin VR4$ because $v_{38} \in end(VR4)$. Similarly $vr1 \subseteq vr2$ if $v \in vr_1$ implies $v \in vr_2$. We freely use set notation and terminology where appropriate.

Note that inside a version range not all branches leading from the start version need be explicitly terminated. Thus, we can have open-ended version ranges. For example, $(v, \emptyset)$ is a version range consisting of version v and every $v' \in des(v)$. Thus $(v_0, \emptyset) = V$, the *version-universe*. Another example of an open-ended version range is shown in Figure 1 (b) where $(v_{26}, \emptyset)$ is the version range marked by $VR3$. The branch in $VR4$ containing v_6, v_7 and v_8 is an open-ended branch. Hence there is no end version for $VR4$ on that branch. Of course, at any given instant, V has some precise number of versions, and even an open-ended range is finite. But additional versions can be added on non-terminated paths, so the number of versions in a range can always increase. For example, in Figure 1 (b), if a new version v_{29} is derived directly from version v_{28}, the new version v_{29} is added to range $VR3$.

Indeed, all version ranges are open-ended in that, with branched versions, it is always possible to add versions to an existing range by producing a new branch from an existing version, even when all current paths to descendants are terminated. For example, for $VR2 = (v_2, \{v_{26}, v_5\})$ in Figure 1 (b), if we create a new version v_{44} from version v_{25}, then the new version v_{44} is added to the version range $VR2$.

There are two important reasons that we define the concept of version ranges. First of all, branched-and-temporal data can be clustered according to version ranges to efficiently support typical version queries. Secondly, to save space, the BT-Tree exploits maximum data sharing among versions in version ranges. For example, in Figure 1 (b), if versions in $VR2$ share the same data value for key k, only one record variant (the one with the earliest time stamp) is needed to represent all the data corresponding to every version in $VR2$ and key k. When record variant (v_2, k, d) (v_2 represents a branch and time pair) is used to

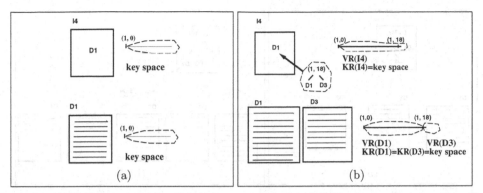

Fig. 2. (a) This is how the BT-Tree gets started. (b) Version-split page $D1$ at $(1, 18)$. We use $VR(I)$ to represent the version range corresponding to page I and $KR(D)$ to represent the key range corresponding to page D

represent all the data corresponding to versions in $VR2$ and key k, we say the record variant (v_2, k, d) is *valid* at versions in $VR2$.

BT-Tree Splits. Each page in the BT-Tree corresponds to a key range and version range and only contains information related to the key range and version range. As shown in Figure 2 (a), when the BT-Tree gets started, there is only one index page and one data page with both pages corresponding to the key space and the entire version space. New record variants are directed to the sole data page $D1$ in the BT-Tree. (Data is represented by horizontal line segments in the figure.)

When an insertion of a new record variant (B, T, k, d) finds insufficient space in a data page, we will split the data page at version (B, T) ((B, T) is always *current* since (B, T, k, d) is a new record variant.) This is called a *version-split*. The BT-Tree only performs version splits at current versions, not previous versions. For example, in Figure 2 (b) at time 18, in order to insert a new record variant we have to version-split data page $D1$ at current version $(1, 18)$. A new page $D3$ corresponding to a new version range $((1, 18), \emptyset)$ and the same key range as the old page $D1$ is created. The old page $D1$ corresponds to the version range $((1, 0), \{(1, 18)\})$. The version tree to the right of the figure shows the corresponding version range and key range of each page.

Any record variants of $D1$ which are still valid at version $(1, 18)$ are *copied* to $D3$. *In general, when an overflowing data page is split at a current version, only the record variant that caused the overflow is moved to the new page, although many existing record variants in the original page are copied to the new page. Therefore the original overflowing page is still full.*

Posting is implemented by replacing the original reference to the old page with a *split history* tree (A similar mechanism has been exploited in previous index structures, such as [4].) The split history tree or *sh-tree* is used within each index page. The sh-tree is a small binary tree containing three types of

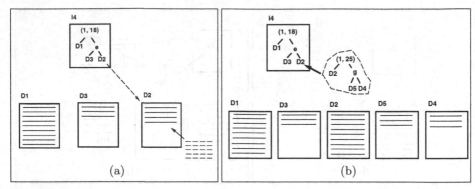

Fig. 3. (a) Version-and-key split data page $D1$ at $(1, 18)$ and e. (b) Version-and-key split data page $D2$. When we try to post to the root page $I4$, we found inefficient space

nodes: *vsh* nodes, *ksh* nodes and *leaf* nodes. A vsh node contains a branch id and a time stamp (indicating a *version*), a ksh node contains a key value while a leaf node contains a disk page address of a child page in the next lower level of the BT-Tree. In Figure 2 (b), the sh-tree that is going to be posted to index page $I4$ (to replace the pointer to page $D1$) contains only one vsh node and two leaf nodes.

We will be using the following information about BT-Trees in designing the new splitting algorithm. *A vsh node (B, T) in an index page divides the lower level BT-Tree rooted at (B, T) into two parts. The right subtree of the vsh node refers to lower level pages whose version range contains descendants of (B, T), while the left subtree of the vsh node refers to pages whose version range contains versions which are not descendants of (B, T).* For example, after we post the sh-tree to page $I4$ in Figure 2 (b), page $D3$ contains all information whose versions are descendant of version $(1, 18)$, and page $D1$ contains all information whose versions are not descendant of version $(1, 18)$.

When version-splitting a data page results in a new data page with the number of record variants exceeding some threshold, a *version-and-key-split* occurs. Specifically, in the BT-Tree, a version-and-key-split is a current version-split followed by a key split. No pure key split (a key split without an immediate preceding current version split) is allowed in BT-Tree. In our running example, since the resulting new page $D3$ after the version-split has too many record variants in it, as shown in Figure 2 (b), we do a version-and-key-split instead, creating two new data pages $D3$ and $D2$, as shown in Figure 3 (a). The sh-tree posted after the version-and-key-split contains an additional ksh node e. A ksh node e divides the lower level BT-Tree rooted at e into two parts. The right subtree of the ksh node refers to lower level pages whose key range contains key values greater than or equal to e while the left subtree of the ksh node contains key values less than e.

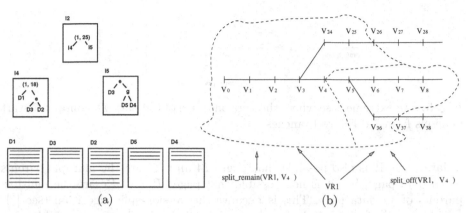

Fig. 4. (a) Version-split the current root page $I4$, creating a new index page $I5$ and a new root $I2$. (b) An example of version range splitting

Now that we've introduced vsh nodes and ksh nodes, the simple *searching algorithm* of the BT-Tree can be easily understood. *Suppose we are searching for a record with version v and key k. When we meet a vsh node (B,T), if v is a descendant of version (B,T), we go right, otherwise we go left. When we meet a ksh node $k1$, if k is greater than or equal to $k1$, we go right, otherwise we go left.*

Notice that in both Figure 2 (b) (version-split page $D1$) and Figure 3 (a) (version-and-key-split page $D1$), the original overflowing page $D1$ remains full after the split. In Figure 3 (a) we also show a lot of new record variants being inserted into data page $D2$ after the version-and-key-split. In Figure 3 (b) we can see that at time 25 we have to version-and-key split page $D2$ creating new data pages $D5$ and $D4$. But when we try to post to the root page $I4$, we find insufficient space. Therefore we version-split the current root page $I4$, creating a new index page $I5$ and a new root $I2$. This is shown in Figure 4 (a). Generally speaking, if a page in the lower level is split at version v and posting to an upper level index page P causes P to overflow, we will split P at version v too. Therefore *both index pages and data pages split at current versions only.* When version-splitting an index page, we will extract an sh-tree which only has ksh nodes. When the size of the resulting sh-tree exceeds a threshold, we do a version-and-key-split as well.

Although we do not intend to repeat the index page split algorithm from [5]) here, we do want to emphasize that version-splitting an index page sometimes creates multiple parents for lower level pages. For example, in Figure 4 (a), after version-splitting index page $I4$, generating page $I5$, data page $D3$ has two parents $I4$ and $I5$. In case of version-and-key splitting an index page (version split the index page first, followed by a key split on the new page created), only the version split, not the key split, might create multiple parents for lower level pages. For example, if $I4$ was version-and-key-split creating two new pages $I5$ and $I5'$, it is possible that both pages $I4$ and $I5$ are the multiple parents of

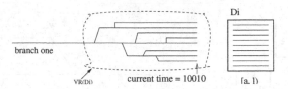

Fig. 5. An extreme case where the version range of the page D_i contains 7 start versions from 7 different branches

a data page. It is also possible that pages $I4$ and $I5'$ are the multiple parents of an data page, but it is not possible that pages $I5$ and $I5'$ are the multiple parents of an data page. This is because the version-split algorithm (see [5]) copies some leaf nodes (a leaf node contains the disk address of a child page) from the old page to the newly created page, hence creating multiple parents for the child page. The key-split followed by the version-split only divides the leaf nodes into two non-intersecting sets with one set of leaf nodes in one page (stored as a tree separated by some keys) and the other set in the other page. The property that *only version-splits not the key splits made after version splits could generate multiple parents* is important in creating our new splitting method for the BTR-Tree.

2.3   Motivation for the BTR-Tree

The performance of the BT-Tree is sensitive to the way branches are created. This is mainly because the BT-Tree always splits at a current version, no matter how branches are created.

Branch creation affects the performance of the BT-Tree through those pages whose version range contains the start version of a branch. An extreme case is shown in Figure 5 where the version range of the page D_i (also denoted as $VR(D_i)$) contains branch one and 7 other different branches whose start versions are in the version range of the page D_i. Assume the key range of page D_i is $[a, l)$. For each of these eight different branches having a new insertion or update involving a record variant with a key within the key range $[a, l)$, the page D_i is going to be accessed. Now suppose that the page D_i is full.

When inserting or updating a full page, we need to split the page no matter which branch the new record variant comes from. After splitting at current version (B, T), later record variants coming from the same branch B will be directed to the newly created page, not the old overflowing page. However, record variants coming from other branches will still be directed to the original overflowing page. But the overflowing page D_i remains full after splitting D_i at a current version. Therefore, any new insertion or update to page D_i will immediately cause another split of page D_i.

Assuming no new branches are created in the version range, the maximum number of times D_i may be split is eight (7 different branches with the start version in $VR(D_i)$ plus branch one whose start version is not in $VR(D_i)$.) Since

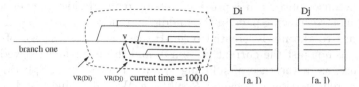

Fig. 6. An example of R-splitting for page D_i

many of the shared record variants may be copied to the new page when splitting a data page, shared record variants could have maximally eight copies in eight different pages, leading to expensive space cost.

Our method of decreasing the number of copies of shared records in cases such as we have shown in Figure 5 (hence ultimately increasing the space efficiency of the indexing structure) is to split the page at a previous version v (not a current version v_c) to decrease the number of branches contained in a page. To describe it more clearly, we define the split operation on the version range.

Definition 2.1 *Let v be a version and vr be a version range with $v \in vr$. Split(vr, v) generates two version ranges:*
split-off(vr, v): The part of the version range that is "split-off" is defined by

- *start(split-off (vr, v)) $= v$,*
- *end(split-off (vr, v)) $= \{v'|v' \in end(vr) \text{ and } v' \in dec(v)\}$.*

Split-off is the subset of vr whose members are descendants of v.
split-remain(vr, v): The part of the version range that "remains" is defined by

- *start(split-remain (vr, v)) $=$ start(vr),*
- *end(split-remain (vr, v)) $= (end(vr) \cup \{start(split-off (vr, v))\} - end(split-off (vr, v))$.*

Split-remain is the subset of vr whose members are not descendants of v.

For example, let's consider the version range $VR1$ in Figure 4 (b). $VR1 = (v_0, \{v_{26}, v_{37}\})$. *Split* $(VR1, v_4)$ generates two version ranges: *split-remain*$(VR1, v_4) = (v_0, \{v_{26}, v_4\})$ and *split-off*$(VR1, v_4) = (v_4, \{v_{37}\})$.

With the definition of *split_off* and *split_remain*, we can illustrate the effect of splitting a page at previous version more clearly. Let's use the page D_i in Figure 5 as an example. After splitting at a previous version v, the version range of the new page created will be *split_off*$(VR(D_i), v)$, while the version range of the old page after the split will be *split_remain*$(VR(D_i), v)$. The number of branches in the original page D_i will be decreased if the split-off contains some of the branch start versions.

Splitting a page at a previous version is different from splitting a page at a current version in that some of the records in the original overflowing page will be *moved* (not just *copied*) to the version range of the newly created page. This is mainly because splitting at a previous version really divides the version range of the original overflowing page in the middle and moves many existing versions (non-current) to the newly created page. Hence the version range of the new page contains not just the current version v_c and those versions derived from v_c in the future, as in the case of splitting at current version v_c. Splitting a page at a non-current version v is called *R-splitting*. We will refine the definition of R-splitting in the next section.

Figure 6 shows R-splitting data page D_i from Figure 5 at version v. The new page will corresponds to the version range enclosed in the bold dotted boundary, which is also the split-off. The starting versions of some branches are included in the split-off. By doing so, all records created in those branches are removed from the original page and some records that are created in ancestor branches of those branches but are inherited by those branches are copied, leaving empty space in both page Di and the newly created page D_j, allowing further insertions and updates to both pages without further page splitting. By including start versions of some branches in the split-off, the number of branches in the version range of the original page D_i is decreased, hence the situation we described in Figure 5 where a full page contains information from many different branches and the page has to be split many times is mitigated.

3 Splitting Using Path-Defined Version Ranges

We call a BT-Tree which is extended to allow R-splitting a *BTR-Tree*. Since a page in a BT-Tree might have multiple parents, R-splitting needs to guarantee that one only needs to post to the parent page that leads the search to the splitting page. This is called *local* splitting.

In order to guarantee a local R-splitting, we explore paths and version ranges associated with paths in the following subsections. We will define a *path* and a *path to a page*. We will give a refined definition of R-splitting. The data page and index page splitting strategy follows. To illustrate these concepts, we use the BT-tree in Figure 7 and the corresponding version tree in Figure 8.

3.1 Definition of Path

Definition 3.1 Path: *A path r is a sequence of the vsh nodes and ksh nodes that channel the search from the root of the BTR-Tree to a data page along with the directions (left or right) to move after encountering these vsh nodes and ksh nodes.*

Given the version tree shown in Figure 8 and a corresponding example shown in Figure 7, the *path r6* is "$(3, 80)L(1, 25)R(1, 50)ReRgR$". This means we met vsh node $(3, 80)$ first, then turn left, then we met vsh node $(1, 25)$ and turn right, after that we met vsh node $(1, 50)$ and turn right, then we met ksh node e and turn right, finally we met ksh node g and turn right. Several other paths are also indicated in Figure 7. These paths all lead to data pages. But paths may also lead to index pages. We make the following definition.

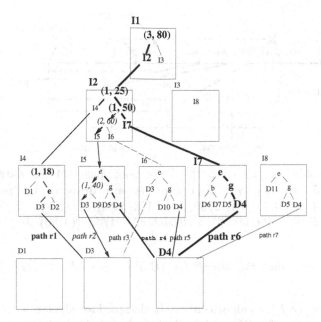

Fig. 7. Examples of A BT-Tree and paths

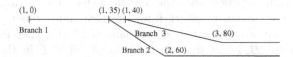

Fig. 8. The version tree of the running example

Definition 3.2 Path to a Page: *If path r goes through an index page or data page P, path(r, P) is defined to be the sequence of the vsh nodes and ksh nodes that channel the search from the root of the BT-Tree to the page P along with the directions (left or right) to move.*

For the same example shown in Figure 7, the *path*(r6, I7) is "(3, 80)L (1, 25)R (1, 50)R".

3.2 The Version Range Associated with a Path

Paths are associated with version ranges. In this section we define the version range of a path and design an algorithm to calculate it.

Definition 3.3 Path Defined Version Range: *For each path r and page P (P could be an index page or a data page) that path r went through, path(r, P) identifies a version range vr, denoted as VR(path(r, P)). VR(path(r, P)) is defined as follows: a version (B, T) is in VR(path(r, P)) if and only if there ex-*

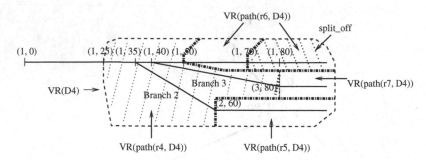

Fig. 9. Version ranges of paths from root page $I1$ to data page $D4$ (path $r4$, $r5$, $r6$ and $r7$ in Figure 7) are disjoint. $VR(path(r4, D4))$ = $((1, 25), \{(1, 50), (3, 80), (2, 60)\})$. $VR(path(r5, D4))$ = $((2, 60), \emptyset)$. $VR(path(r6, D4)) = ((1, 50), \emptyset)$. $VR(path(r7, D4)) = ((3, 80), \emptyset)$

ists a key k such that the search for (B, T, k) through the BTR-Tree follows $path(r, P)$.

Given a $path(r, P)$, an algorithm can be designed to calculate $VR(path(r, P))$. The intuition of the algorithm is based on the fact that a path is actually a search path and $VR(path(r, P))$ is in fact the search space defined by $path(r, P)$. From the search algorithm, we know that the searching space for version v starts with the whole version space as we start from the root index page. A $(B, T)R$ in the path means that version v is a descendant of (B, T), therefore the search space changes with (B, T) as its start version. A $(B, T)L$ in the path means that version v is not a descendant of (B, T), therefore the search space further shrinks with (B, T) as one of its end versions. The detailed algorithm returning the *Start_version* and *End_set* which define $VR(path(r, P))$ is as follows.

1. Initialization
   Start_version $= (B_{start}, T_{start}) = (1, 0)$ $(B_{start}{=}1, T_{start}{=}0)$
   End_set $= \emptyset$.
2. Read the vsh nodes in $path(r, P)$ in order. If the current vsh node is (B', T'), do the following:
   – If (B', T')R:
     • If $T'{>}T_{start}$, then set Start_version $= (B', T')$, and remove from the End_set all versions that are not descendants of Start_version.
     • Otherwise do nothing.
   – If (B', T')L:
     • If (B', T') is not a descendant of the current Start_version (B_{start}, T_{start}), ignore (B', T'), else
     • If $\exists\,(B_i, T_i) \in$ End_set such that (B_i, T_i) is an ancestor of (B', T'), ignore (B', T'), else
     • If $\exists\,(B_i, T_i) \in$ End_set such that (B', T') is an ancestor of (B_i, T_i), then remove from the End_set all versions that are descendants of (B', T') and add (B', T') to End_set.

- Otherwise, add (B', T') to End_set.

In the example shown in Figure 7, $path(r6, I7) =$ "(3, 80) L (1, 25) R (1, 50) R". According to the previous algorithm, $VR(path(r6, I7))$ is (Start_version=(1, 50), End_set $= \emptyset$).

We make two observations here. First, in the process of computing $VR(path(r, P))$, the version range $VR(path(r, P))$ is initialized as the whole version space and it gets smaller and smaller as we go through the algorithm. Hence if page I is a parent of page D and path r goes through both page I and page D, then $VR(path(r, I)) \supseteq VR(path(r, D))$.

Secondly, since $(B, T)L$ in the path leads to non-descendants of (B, T) and $(B, T)R$ in the path leads to descendants of (B, T), the intersection of $VR(path\ r)$ and $VR(path\ s)$ is empty if path r contains $(B, T)L$ and path s contains $(B, T)R$.

3.3   Properties of Paths

In order to develop our new splitting strategy, we are concerned only when paths to a page P visit two different parents of P. If P has only one parent, splitting can occur anywhere without causing posting to more than one parent page. Thus, we will only be interested in paths which diverge at a vsh node. (Paths which diverge at a ksh node will end in different data pages since key splits of index pages split the children into disjoint key ranges.)

Definition 3.4 *path r* **v-diverges** *path s*

Path r v-diverges path s if $\exists$ (B, T) such that path r contains (B, T)L and path s contains (B, T)R.

For example, path $r5$ in Figure 7 v-diverges with path $r6$ because we have $(1, 50)L$ in path $r5$ and $(1, 50)R$ in path $r6$. Our goal in developing a method based on paths will be to assure that, even when a page P has multiple parents, only one of the parents, corresponding to one of the paths to P, will be involved when information about a split of P must be posted.

Consider how a page (such as page $D3$ in Figure 4 (a)) starts to get multiple parent pages. Originally page $D3$ has only one parent (page $I4$ in Figure 3 (a)). Version-splitting page $I4$ at version $(1, 25)$ generates the second parent page (page $I5$) of $D3$. When the version-split creates multiple parents, the two paths to the same page (in our case, the two paths are (see Figure 4 (a)) : one path from root page $I2$ to page $D3$ going through page $I4$, the other path from root page $I2$ to page $D3$ going through page $I5$) are separated by the vsh node that is posted after the version-split (in our case, the vsh node is $(1, 25)$ in the root page $I2$). Since different paths to a same page v-diverge, (again, if the paths diverge at a ksh node, they do not end at the same page) using the induction method, we can show that $VR(path(r, P)) \cap VR(path(s, P)) = \emptyset$ if r and s are different paths to the same page P. An example is shown in Figure 9 where the version range of the four different paths to the same page $D4$ from Figure 7 are disjoint.

If we split page $D4$ in such a way that the split-off (the version range that the new page is responsible for) is contained completely in $VR(path(r6, D4))$, as shown in Figure 9, it is not necessary to post to the other three index pages that the other paths to the same page $D4$ (path $r4$, path $r5$ and path $r7$) are lying in. The intuition is that posting will split one path into two paths and also split the original version range of the path into two disjoint version ranges. Neither of these two disjoint version ranges intersects any version range corresponding to other paths. Now let's refine the definition of R-splitting as follows.

Definition 3.5 *R-splitting: Consider an index page or a data page P and a path(r, P). Let vr satisfy $vr \subseteq VR(path(r, P))$ and the end set of vr is empty. We call splitting page P in such a way that the split off is vr R-splitting. After the split, page P corresponds to version range $(VR(BEFORE(P)) - vr)$ where $BEFORE(P)$ represents the page P before splitting. The new page created out of the split corresponds to the version range vr.*

We will explain later in Section 3.4 why the end set is required to be empty in the definition of R-splitting. Many version ranges vr may satisfy the definition for R-splitting. The next section considers which split-off version range to choose for an R-split.

3.4   The Splitting Strategy

Our motivation in choosing a split-off among several possiblities is to decrease the branching in index and data pages.

We first define the *owning branch of a page*. When the BTR-Tree is initialized, we have one index page and one data page. They contain information about the first branch in the branched-and-temporal database, branch one. The owning branch of the index page and the data page is branch one. New data pages and index pages are created from page splitting. If a new data page or a new index page is created by splitting an existing page at version (B, T) ((B, T) is the start version of the split-off when the page is R-splitting), the owning branch of the data page or the index page is B.

The Data Page Splitting Strategy. When we try to insert a new record variant (B, T, k, d), the search algorithm directs us following *path* r to a data page D. We need to split the data page D if there is not enough space in the data page D for the new record variant. Since (B, T, k, d) is a new record variant, we know that (B, T) is current. We denote the start version of a branch B as $(B, Start$-$time (B))$. The following algorithm is followed when splitting the data page D.

- If B is the owning branch of the data page D, we version-split at the current version (B, T).
- Otherwise, we look at $VR(path(r, D))$. We consider the two cases where the start version of B is in and not in $VR(path(r, D))$.

- If $(B,\ Start\text{-}time\ (B)) \in VR(path(r, D))$, we compute $VR\_splitting = split\_off\,(VR\,(path\,(r, D)), (B,\ Start\text{-}time(B)))$ and look at the End_set S of $VR\_splitting$:
  * $S = \emptyset$: R-split with the split-off to be $VR\_splitting$.
  * $S \neq \emptyset$: split at the current version (B, T).
- Otherwise, we look at the End_set S of $VR(path\,(r, D))$:
  * $S = \emptyset$: R-split with the split-off to be $VR(path(r, D))$.
  * $S \neq \emptyset$: split at the current version (B, T).

The reason that we check the End_set of $VR\_splitting$ before deciding whether to R-split or not is to guarantee that the version space of the data page D after splitting is still a version range (not a union of disjoint version ranges). This enables us to retain the simple searching scheme of the BT-Tree.

The Index Page Splitting Strategy. Assume that the path r is followed to get to a data page D while trying to insert a new record variant. Subsequently, the data page D is split. The parent page of the data page D lying in the path r needs to be updated to reflect the split. As in the BT-Tree, this is achived by posting. If the page D is split at the current version (B, T), we post (B, T). If the page D is R-split, we post (B_{start}, T_{start}), the start version of the split-off. When the posting make the index page (say, I) full, we split the index page I by looking at how the data page D was split:

- If the data page D is split at the current version (B, T), we split the index page I at the current version (B, T), and post (B, T).
- If the data page D is R-split with the split-off to be $VR\_splitting$, we compute a new split-off $VR\_splitting\_I = split\_off\ (VR(path(r, I)), (B_{start},\ T_{start}))$, with (B_{start}, T_{start}) the start version of $VR\_splitting$, and R-Split the index page I with the new split-off $VR\_splitting\_I$. We then post (B_{start}, T_{start}).

For index page R-splitting, we no longer need to check whether the End_set of the split-off $VR\_splitting\_I$ is empty, like we did for the data page splitting case. This is because we can deduce the fact that the End_set of $VR\_splitting\_I$ must be empty from the property of $VR(path(r, I)) \supseteq VR(path(r, D))$ and the fact that the End_set of the split-off for the data page D $VR\_splitting$ is empty.

4   Performance Results

We present some results of our performance comparison between the BTR-Tree and the BT-tree.

We assume all record variants, including *null* record variants, have the same size. A transaction is either an insertion of a record variant with a new key, an update of an existing record variant or a delete of an old record variant.

The database system starts up with only one branch. Other branches are created gradually after a number of transactions occurred in the first branch.

Table 1. The total number of data pages

Update Rate (%)	BT-Tree (A)	BTR-Tree (B)	Improvement ((A-B)/B)
0	7679	6438	19.3%
5	7329	6190	18.4%
10	7025	6052	16.1%
30	6010	5454	10.2%
50	5228	4902	6.7%
70	4161	4007	3.8%

Table 2. The total number of index pages

Update Rate (%)	BT-Tree (A)	BTR-Tree (B)	Improvement ((A-B)/B)
0	474	420	12.9%
5	480	439	9.3%
10	469	416	12.7%
30	378	366	3.3%
50	332	293	6.7%
70	280	273	2.6%

Transactions are randomly assigned to existing branches. We use the intuitive measurement of data page and index page numbers to measure the space cost and the query efficiency.

The number of branches is fixed to be 100. All branches other than the first are randomly created between the 3,000th and 30,000th transaction with a randomly selected ancestor version (other branch creation profiles were also implemented, but since their results were similar, they are not presented here.) The key range of the first branch is [0, 800,000). All other branches are allowed to modify versioned records in key range [0, 600,000). We vary the fraction of updates versus insertions. No deletes are allowed. In these experiments, the height of the BTR-tree never rose above 3. (Consolidation algorithms (see [5]) have been designed to guarantee good version query performance in case of deletes. Experiments show that the effect of consolidation on the BTR-Tree is as same as the BT-Tree.)

We first comment on the space utilization. Table 1 (Table 2) shows that comparison of total number of data pages (index pages) in each index structure. With the new split method, the number of data pages and index pages needed is smaller This is anticipated. The number of times that record variants in a page are going to be copied is less, making the total space cost less.

When the update rate increases, the differences on the space cost get smaller. The reason is as follows. The number of distinctive key values in a page is smaller when the update rate is higher. When a full page is split at a current version, the number of record variants that gets copied to the new page is smaller, making the saving on the number of times that record variants in the page are copied

Table 3. The number of data pages that need to be accessed for the current version query in branch one

Update Rate	BT-Tree	BTR-Tree
0	222	216
5	213	210
10	202	200
30	153	152
50	111	112
70	64	65

in case of R-splitting over the number of times that record variants in the page are copied in case of splitting at a current version less.

Now we comment on the version query efficiency. With 100 branches, the version query efficiency may vary from one branch to another. We compare the version query efficiency of the BT-Tree and the BTR-Tree for branch one. Branch one is considered as a respresentative because it has the maximum number of record variants among the 100 branches. As time proceeds, all other branches may reach a state having as many record variants as branch one now. (The analysis for other branches are similar). We consider the current version query efficiency measured by the number of data pages containing record variants valid at current version. Table 3 shows the number of data pages that needs to be accessed for both the BT-Tree and the BTR-Tree for the current version query in branch one. With low update rate, the query efficiency of the BTR-Tree is slightly better than the BT-Tree. With high update rate, it is almost the same.

5   Conclusion

Based on the BT-tree [5], we have proposed a new splitting algorithm, namely R-splitting, thus creating a new branched-and-temporal index structure, the BTR-tree. Information gathered from the search path enables expanded splitting choices without requiring posting to more than one parent. We have proposed a detailed splitting strategy for the BTR-tree. This strategy aims to decrease the amount of branching in pages while maintaining simple posting and searching algorithms. The performance results show that the BTR-Tree improves the space performance significantly when the space requirement is the most (relatively low update rate). The new splitting strategy improves query performance slightly for the same low update case.

References

[1] Bruno Becker, Stephan Gschwind, Thomas Ohler, Bernhard Seeger, and Peter Widmayer. On optimal multiversion access structures. In *Porc. Symp. on Large Spatial Databases, in Lecture Notes in Computer Science, Vol. 692*, pages 123–141, Singapore, 1993.   29

[2] James R. Driscoll, Neil Sarnak, Daniel D. Sleator, and Robert E. Tarjan. Making
     data structures persistent. *Journal of Computer and System Sciences, 38*, pages
     86–124, 1989. 29

[3] M. C. Easton. Key-sequence data sets on indelible storage. *IBM J. Res. Devel-
     opment*, 30(3):230–241, 1986. 29, 30

[4] G. Evangelidis, David Lomet, and B. Salzberg. The hB-$^{\Pi}$-tree: A Multiattribute
     Index Supporting Concurrency, Recovery and Node Consolidation. *VLDB Jour-
     nal*, 6(1), January 1997. 32

[5] Linan Jiang, Betty Salzberg, David Lomet, and Manuel Barrena. The BT-tree:
     A branched and temporal access method. In *International Conference on Very
     Large Data Bases*, pages 451–460, Cairo, Egypt, September 2000. 28, 34, 35, 43,
     44

[6] Gad M. Landau, Jeanette P. Schmidt, and Vassilis J. Tsotras. Historical queries
     along multiple lines of time evolution. *VLDB Journal, 4*, pages 703–726, 1995.
     28

[7] Sitaram Lanka and Eric Mays. Fully persistent B+-trees. In *Proceedings of the
     ACM SIGMOD conference on Management of Data*, Denver, CO, 1991. 29

[8] David Lomet and Betty Salzberg. The performance of a multiversion access
     method. In *Proceedings of the ACM SIGMOD conference on Management of
     Data*, pages 354–363, 1990. 29, 30

[9] Peter Muth, Patrick O'neil, Achim Pick, and Gerhard Weikum. Design, imple-
     mentation, and performance on the LHAM log-structured history data access
     method. In *Proceedings of the 24th VLDB Conference*, pages 452–463, New York,
     1998. 29

[10] Vassilis J. Tsotras and Nickolas Kangelaris. The snapshot index: An I/O-optimal
     access method for timeslice queries. *Information Systems 20(3)*, pages 237–260,
     1995. 29

Bkd-Tree: A Dynamic Scalable kd-Tree

Octavian Procopiuc[1] *, Pankaj K. Agarwal[1] **,
Lars Arge[1] ***, and Jeffrey Scott Vitter[2] †

[1] Department of Computer Science, Duke University
Durham, NC 27708, USA
{tavi,pankaj,large}@cs.duke.edu
[2] Department of Computer Science, Purdue University
West Lafayette, IN 47907 USA
jsv@purdue.edu

Abstract. In this paper we propose a new index structure, called the Bkd-tree, for indexing large multi-dimensional point data sets. The Bkd-tree is an I/O-efficient dynamic data structure based on the kd-tree. We present the results of an extensive experimental study showing that unlike previous attempts on making external versions of the kd-tree dynamic, the Bkd-tree maintains its high space utilization and excellent query and update performance regardless of the number of updates performed on it.

1 Introduction

The problem of indexing multi-dimensional point data sets arises in many applications and has been extensively studied. Numerous structures have been developed, highlighting the difficulty of optimizing multiple interrelated requirements that such multi-dimensional indexes must satisfy. More precisely, an efficient index must have high space utilization and be able to process queries fast, and these two properties should be maintained under a significant load of updates. At the same time, updates must also be processed quickly, which means that

---

* Supported by the National Science Foundation through research grant EIA–9870734 and by the Army Research Office through MURI grant DAAH04–96–1–0013. Part of this work was done while visiting BRICS, University of Aarhus, Denmark.

** Supported by Army Research Office MURI grant DAAH04–96–1–0013, by a Sloan fellowship, by NSF grants ITR–333–1050, EIA–9870724 and CCR–9732787 and by a grant from the U.S.-Israeli Binational Science Foundation.

*** Supported in part by the National Science Foundation through ESS grant EIA–9870734, RI grant EIA–9972879 and CAREER grant CCR–9984099. Part of this work was done while visiting BRICS, University of Aarhus, Denmark.

† Supported in part by the National Science Foundation through research grants CCR–9877133 and EIA–9870734 and by the Army Research Office through MURI grant DAAH04–96–1–0013. Part of this work was done while visiting BRICS, University of Aarhus, Denmark. Part of this work was done while at Duke University.

the structure should change as little as possible during insertions and deletions. This makes it hard to maintain good space utilization and query performance over time. Consequently, the quality of most indexing structures deteriorates as a large number of updates are performed on them, and the problem of handling massive update loads while maintaining high space utilization and low query response time has been recognized as an important research problem [9].

In this paper we propose a new data structure, called the Bkd-tree, that maintains its high space utilization and excellent query and update performance regardless of the number of updates performed on it. The Bkd-tree is based on a well-known extensions of the kd-tree, called the K-D-B-tree [22], and on the so-called logarithmic method for making a static structure dynamic. As we show through extensive experimental studies, the Bkd-tree is able to achieve the almost 100% space utilization and the fast query processing of a static K-D-B-tree. However, unlike the K-D-B-tree, these properties are maintained over massive updates.

Previous Results. One of the most fundamental queries in spatial databases is the orthogonal *range query* or *window query*. In two dimensions a window query is an axis-aligned rectangle and the objective is to find all points in the database inside the rectangle. Numerous practically efficient multi-dimensional point indexing structures supporting window queries have been proposed, most of which can also answer a host of other query types. They include K-D-B-trees [22], hB-trees [18, 10], and R-trees [13, 6]. If N is the total number of points and B is the number of points that fit in a disk block, $\Omega(\sqrt{N/B} + K/B)$ is the theoretical lower bound on the number of I/Os needed by a linear space index to answer a window query [15]. Here K is the number of points in the query rectangle. In practice, the above indexing structures often answer queries in much fewer I/Os. However, their query performance can seriously deteriorate after a large number of updates. Recently, a number of linear space structures with guaranteed worst-case efficient query and update performance have been developed (see e.g. [5, 15, 12]). The so-called cross-trees [12] and O-trees [15] answer window queries in the optimal number of I/Os and can be updated, theoretically, in $O(\log_B N)$ I/Os, but they are of limited practical interest because a theoretical analysis shows that their average query performance is close to the worst-case performance. See e.g. [11, 3] for more complete surveys of multi-dimensional indexing structures. While some of the above indexing structures are specifically designed for external memory, many of them are adaptations of structures designed for main memory. In this paper we only focus on external memory adaptations of the original main memory kd-tree proposed by Bentley [7] (see also [23]).

External-Memory Dynamic kd-Trees. While static versions of the kd-tree have been shown to have excellent query performance in many practical situations, an efficient dynamic version has proven hard to develop. In the following, we give a brief overview of the internal memory kd-tree structure and then discuss the two most important previous approaches for obtaining external memory dynamic kd-trees. In two dimensions, the kd-tree consists of a height $\lceil \log_2 N \rceil$ binary tree representing a recursive decomposition of the plane by means of axis-orthogonal lines partitioning the point set into two equal subsets.[1] On even levels the line is orthogonal to the x-axis, while on odd levels it is orthogonal to the y-axis. The data points themselves are stored in the leaves, which form a partition of the plane into disjoint rectangular regions containing one point each. In the worst case a window query on a kd-tree requires $O(\sqrt{N} + K)$ time [16], but average case analysis [24] and experiments have shown that in practice it often performs much better. One way of performing an insertion on a kd-tree is to first search down the tree for the leaf corresponding to the rectangle containing the point, and then split this leaf into two in order to accommodate the new point. While this insertion procedure runs efficiently in $O(\log_2 N)$ time, the kd-tree can grow increasingly unbalanced when many insertions are performed, resulting in deteriorating query performance. In fact, the resulting tree is no longer a kd-tree, since the lines in the internal nodes no longer partition the points into equal sized sets. Unfortunately, while many other tree structures can be rebalanced efficiently in time proportional to the root-to-leaf path, it can be shown that in order to rebalance a kd-tree after an insertion, we may need to reorganize large parts of the tree [23]. Thus it seems hard to efficiently support insertions while at the same time maintaining good query performance. These considerations show that the kd-tree is mainly a static data structure with very good window query performance.

One main issue in adapting the kd-tree to external memory is how to assign nodes to disk blocks in order to obtain good space utilization (use close to N/B disk blocks) and good I/O query performance. In the first external memory adaptation of the kd-tree, called the K-D-B-tree [22], the kd-tree is organized as a B$^+$-tree. More precisely, a K-D-B-tree is a multi-way tree with all leaves on the same level. Each internal node v corresponds to a rectangular region and the children of v define a disjoint partition of that region obtained using a kd-tree partitioning scheme. The points are stored in the leaves of the tree, and each leaf and internal node is stored in one disk block. Like a kd-tree, a K-D-B tree can be bulk loaded such that it exhibits excellent space utilization (uses close to N/B blocks) and answers queries I/O-efficiently (worst case optimally in $O(\sqrt{N/B} + K/B)$ but often much better in practice). Unfortunately, it also exhibits the kd-tree insertion characteristics. To insert a point into a K-D-B-tree, a root-to-leaf path is followed in $\lceil \log_B(N/B) \rceil$ I/Os and after inserting the point in a leaf, the leaf and possibly other nodes on the path are split just like in a B$^+$-tree. However, unlike the B$^+$-tree but similar to the kd-tree, the split of an internal node v may result in the need for splits of several of the subtrees rooted at v's children—refer to Figure 1. As a result, updates can be very inefficient and, maybe more importantly, the space utilization can decrease dramatically since the split process may generate many near empty leaves [22].

Following the K-D-B-tree, several other adaptations of the kd-tree to external memory have been proposed. An important breakthrough came with the result

---

[1] For simplicity we only consider two-dimensional kd-trees in this paper. However, all our results work in d dimensions.

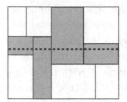

Fig. 1. Splitting a K-D-B-tree node. The outer rectangle corresponds to a node v being split. The darker regions correspond to children that need to be split recursively when v splits

of Lomet and Salzberg [18]. Their structure, called the hB-tree (holey brick tree), significantly improved the update performance over the K-D-B-tree. The better performance was obtained by only splitting nodes on one root-to-leaf path after an insertion. However, to be able to do so, the definition of internal nodes had to be changed so that they no longer corresponded to simple rectangles, but instead to rectangles from which smaller rectangles have been removed (holey bricks). The hB-tree update algorithm is theoretically efficient, although quite complicated. As we show in our experimental results, the hB-tree can still suffer from degenerating space utilization, although to a smaller extent than the K-D-B-tree (see also [10]). All other attempts at externalizing the kd-tree suffer from similar inefficiencies.

Our Results. In this paper, we present the first theoretically and practically efficient *dynamic* adaptation of the kd-tree to external memory. Our structure, which we call the Bkd-tree, maintains the high storage utilization and query efficiency of a static K-D-B-tree, while also supporting updates I/O-efficiently. We have conducted extensive experiments that show that the Bkd-tree outperforms previous approaches in terms of storage utilization and update time, while maintaining similar query performance.

The main ingredients used in the design of the Bkd-tree are an I/O-efficient K-D-B-tree bulk loading algorithm and the so-called logarithmic method for making a static data structure dynamic [8, 21]. Instead of maintaining one tree and dynamically rebalance it after an insertion, we maintain a set of $\log_2(N/M)$ static K-D-B-trees and perform updates by rebuilding a carefully chosen set of the structures at regular intervals (M is the capacity of the memory buffer, in number of points). This way we maintain the close to 100% space utilization of the static K-D-B-tree. The idea of maintaining multiple trees in order to speed up insertion time has also been used by O'Neill et al. [20] and Jagadish et al. [14]. Their structures are used for indexing points on a single attribute and their techniques cannot be extended to efficiently handle multi-dimensional points.

To answer a window query using the Bkd-tree, we have to query all the $\log_2(N/M)$ structures instead of just one, but theoretically we actually maintain the worst case optimal $O(\sqrt{N/B} + K/B)$ query bound. Using an optimal $O(\frac{N}{B} \log_{M/B} \frac{N}{B})$ I/O bulk loading algorithm, an insertion is performed in

$O(\frac{1}{B}(\log_{M/B} \frac{N}{B})(\log_2 \frac{N}{M}))$ I/Os amortized. This bound is much smaller than the familiar $O(\log_B N)$ B$^+$-tree update bound for all practical purposes. One disadvantage of the periodical rebuilding is of course that the update bound varies from update to update (thus the amortized result). However, queries can still be answered while an update (rebuilding) is being performed, and (at least theoretically) the update bound can be made worst case using additional storage [21].

While our Bkd-tree has nice theoretical properties, the main contribution of this paper is a proof of its practical viability. We present the result of an extensive experimental study of the performance of the Bkd-tree compared to the K-D-B-tree using both real-life (TIGER) and artificially generated (uniform) data. In addition, we used a carefully chosen family of data sets to show that both the K-D-B-tree and the hB$^{\Pi}$-tree (an improved version of the hB-tree, see [10]) can have poor space utilization (as low as 28% for the K-D-B-tree and 36% for the hB$^{\Pi}$-tree), while the space utilization of the Bkd-tree is always above 99%. At the same time, an insertion in a Bkd-tree can be up to 100 times faster than an insertion on the K-D-B-tree, in the amortized sense. The main practical question is of course how the use of $\log_2(N/M)$ structures affects the query performance. Even though the theoretical worst case efficiency is maintained, the querying of several structures instead of just one results in an increased number of random I/Os compared to the more localized I/Os in a single structure. Our experiments show that this makes no or relatively little difference, and thus that the dynamic Bkd-tree maintains the excellent query performance of the static K-D-B-tree.

Finally, we regard the demonstration of the practical efficiency of the logarithmic method as an important general contribution of this paper; while the main focus of the paper is on making the kd-tree dynamic, the logarithmic method is applicable to any index structure for which an efficient bulk loading algorithm is known. Thus our results suggest that in general we might be able to make practically efficient static index structures dynamically efficient using the method.

The rest of this paper is organized in three sections. The details of the Bkd-tree are given in Section 2. Then, in Section 3, we describe the hardware, software, and data sets used in our experimental study. The results of the experiments are reported and analyzed in Section 4.

2 Description of the Bkd-Tree

As mentioned, the Bkd-tree consists of a set of balanced kd-trees. Each kd-tree is laid out (or *blocked*) on disk similarly to the way the K-D-B-tree is laid out. To store a given kd-tree on disk, we first modify the leaves to hold B points, instead of just one. In this way, points are packed in N/B blocks. To pack the internal nodes of the kd-tree, we execute the following algorithm. Let B_i be the number of nodes that fit in one block. Suppose first that N/B is an exact power of B_i, i.e., $N/B = B_i^p$, for some p, and that B_i is an exact power of 2. In this case the internal nodes can easily be stored in $O(N/(BB_i))$ blocks in a natural way. Starting from the kd-tree root v, we store together the nodes obtained by performing a breadth-first search traversal starting from v, until B_i nodes have been traversed. The rest of the tree is then blocked recursively. Using this procedure the number of blocks needed for all the internal nodes is $O(N/(BB_i))$, and the number of blocks touched by a root-leaf path—the path traversed during a point query—is $log_{B_i}(N/B)+1 = \Theta(\log_B(N/B))$. If N/B is not a power of B_i, we fill the block containing the kd-tree root with less than B_i nodes in order to be able to block the rest of the tree as above. If N/B is not a power of 2 the kd-tree is unbalanced and the above blocking algorithm can end up under-utilizing disk blocks. To alleviate this problem we modify the kd-tree splitting method and split at rank power of 2 elements, instead of at the median elements. More precisely, when constructing the two children of a node v from a set of p points, we assign $2^{\lfloor \log_2 p \rfloor}$ points to the left child, and the rest to the right child. This way, only the blocks containing the rightmost path—at most $\lceil \log_{B_i}(N/B) \rceil$—can be under-full.

From now on, when referring to a kd-tree, we will mean a tree stored on disk as described above.

2.1   Bulk Loading kd-Trees

Classically, a kd-tree is built top-down, as outlined in Figure 2 (left column). The first step is to sort the input on both coordinates. Then (in Step 2) we construct the nodes in a recursive manner, starting with the root. For a node v, we determine the splitting position by reading the median from one of the two sorted sets associated with v (when splitting orthogonal to the x-axis we use the file sorted on x, and when splitting orthogonal to the y-axis we use the file sorted on y). Finally we scan these sorted sets and distribute each of them into two sets and recursively build the children of v. Since the kd-tree on N points has height $\log_2(N/B)$ and each input point is read twice and written twice on every level, the algorithm performs $O((N/B)\log_2(N/B))$ I/Os, plus the cost of sorting, which is $O((N/B)\log_{M/B}(N/B))$ I/Os [2], for a total of $O((N/B)\log_2(N/B))$ I/Os.

An improved bulk loading method was proposed in [1]. Instead of constructing one level at a time, this algorithm constructs an entire $\Theta(\log_2(M/B))$-height subtree of the kd-tree at a time. The major steps of the algorithm are outlined in Figure 2 (right column). As before, the first step is to sort the input on both coordinates. Then (in Step 2) we build the upper $\log_2 t$ levels of the kd-tree using just three passes over the input file, where $t = \Theta(\min\{M/B, \sqrt{M}\})$. We achieve this by first determining a $t \times t$ grid on the input points: t horizontal (vertical) grid lines are chosen (in Step 2a) so that each horizontal (vertical) strip contains N/t points—refer to Figure 3(a). Then (in Step 2b) the number of points in each grid cell is computed by simply scanning the input file. These counts are stored in a $t \times t$ grid matrix A, kept in internal memory (the size of the matrix, t^2, is at most M). The upper subtree of height $\log_2 t$ is now computed (in step 2c) using a top-down approach. Assume the root node partitions the points using a vertical line. This split line can be determined by first computing (using the cell counts in matrix A) the vertical strip X_k containing the line. After that we can

Algorithm Bulk Load (binary)	Algorithm Bulk Load (grid)
(1) Create two sorted lists;	(1) Create two sorted lists;
(2) Build kd-tree top-down:	(2) Build $\log_2 t$ levels of the kd-tree:
Starting with the root node, do the following steps for each node, in a depth-first-search manner:	(a) Compute t grid lines orthogonal to the x axis and t grid lines orthogonal to the y axis;
(a) Find the partitioning line;	(b) Create the grid matrix A containing the grid cell counts;
(b) Distribute input into two sets, based on partitioning line;	(c) Create a subtree of height $\log_2 t$, using the counts in the grid matrix;
	(d) Distribute input into t sets, corresponding to the t leaves;
	(3) Build the bottom levels either in main memory or by recursing step (2).

Fig. 2. Two algorithms for bulk loading a kd-tree

easily compute which block to read from the list sorted by x-coordinate in order to determine the point defining the split. Next the grid matrix A is split into two new matrices, $A^<$ and $A^>$, storing the grid cell counts from the left and from the right of the split line, respectively. This can be done by scanning the contents of the vertical strip X_k. Figure 3(b) shows how a cell $C_{j,k}$ from the original grid is split into two cells, $C_{j,k}^<$ and $C_{j,k}^>$. The number of points in $C_{j,k}^<$ is stored in $A_{j,k}^<$, and the number of points in $C_{j,k}^>$ is stored in $A_{j,1}^>$, for each j, $1 \leq j \leq t$. Using matrices $A^<$ and $A^>$, the split corresponding to two children of v can be computed recursively. For each node we produce, the size of the matrix A in internal memory grows by t cells. Since $t \leq O(\sqrt{M})$, it still fits in memory after producing $\log_2 t$ levels, that is $2^{\log_2 t} = t$ nodes, of the tree. After producing this number of levels, the resulting subtree determines a partition of the space into t

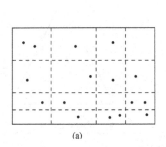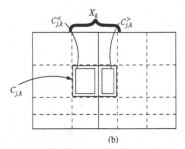

(a)   (b)

Fig. 3. Finding the median using grid cells. (a) Each strip contains N/t points. (b) Cells $C_{j,k}^<$ and $C_{j,k}^>$ are computed by splitting cell $C_{j,k}$

rectangles. At this point we distribute the input points into these rectangles by scanning the input and, for each point p, using the constructed subtree to find the rectangle containing p (Step 2d). If the main memory can hold $t+1$ blocks—one for each rectangle in the partition, plus one for the input—the distribution can be done in $2N/B$ I/Os. This explains the choice of $t = \Theta(\min(M/B, \sqrt{M}))$. Finally, the bottom levels of the tree are constructed (in Step 3) by recursing Step 2 or, if the point set fits in internal memory, by loading it in memory and applying the binary bulk load algorithm to it.

Since Step 2 scans the input points two times, it follows that $\Theta(\log_2(M/B))$ levels of the kd-tree can be built using $O(N/B)$ I/Os. Thus the entire kd-tree is built in $O((N/B)\log_{M/B}(N/B))$ I/Os. This is a factor of $\Theta(\log_2(M/B))$ better than the binary bulk load algorithm. For most practical purposes, the logarithmic factor is at most 3, so the bulk loading complexity is effectively linear.

The algorithm presented in this section uses only the characteristics of the internal memory kd-tree, and not the specific disk layout. Consequently, other I/O-efficient data structures based on the kd-tree can be bulk loaded using this algorithm. In particular, the algorithm can be readily used to bulk load an $\text{hB}^{\varPi}$-tree, which was mentioned as an open problem in [10].

2.2 Dynamic Updates

A Bkd-tree on N points in the plane consists of $\log_2(N/M)$ kd-trees. The ith kd-tree, T_i, is either empty or contains exactly $2^i M$ points. Thus, T_0 stores at most M points. In addition, a structure T_0^M containing at most M points is kept in internal memory. Figure 4 depicts the organization of the Bkd-tree. This organization is similar to the one used by the logarithmic method [8, 21].

The algorithms for inserting and deleting a point are outlined in Figure 5. The simplest of the two is the deletion algorithm. We simply query each of the trees to find the tree T_i containing the point and delete it from T_i. Since there are at most $\log_2(N/M)$ trees, the number of I/Os performed by a deletion is $O(\log_B(N/B)\log_2(N/M))$.

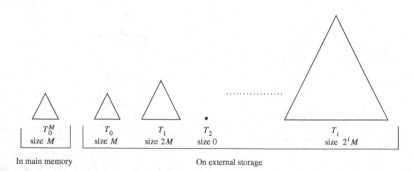

Fig. 4. The forest of trees that makes up the data structure. In this instance, T_2 is empty

Algorithm **Insert**(p)	Algorithm **Delete**(p)
(1) Insert p into in-memory buffer T_0^M;	(1) Query T_0^M with p; if found, delete it
(2) If T_0^M is not full, return; otherwise, find the first empty tree T_k and extract all points from T_0^M and T_i, $0 \le i < k$ into a file F;	and return;
	(2) Query each non-empty tree in the forest (starting with T_0) with p; if found, delete it and return;
(3) Bulk load T_k from the items in F;	
(4) Empty T_0^M and T_i, $0 \le i < k$.	

Fig. 5. The **Insert** and **Delete** algorithms for the Bkd-tree

The insertion algorithm is fundamentally different. Most insertions ($M-1$ out of M consecutive ones) are performed directly on the in-memory structure T_0^M. Whenever T_0^M becomes full, we find the smallest k such that T_k is an empty kd-tree. Then we extract all points from T_0^M and T_i, $0 \le i < k$, and bulk load the tree T_k from these points. Note that the number of points now stored in T_k is indeed $2^k M$ since T_0^M stores M points and each T_i, $1 \le i < k$, stores exactly $2^i M$ points (T_k was the first empty kd-tree). Finally, we empty T_0^M and T_i, $0 \le i < k$. In other words, points are inserted in the in-memory structure and gradually "pushed" towards larger kd-trees by periodic reorganizations of small kd-trees into one large kd-tree. The larger the kd-tree, the less frequently it needs to be reorganized.

To compute the amortized number of I/Os performed by one insertion, consider N consecutive insertions in an initially empty Bkd-tree. Whenever a new kd-tree T_k is constructed, it replaces all kd-trees T_j, $1 \le j < k$, and the in-memory structure T_0^M. This operation takes $O((2^k M/B) \log_{M/B}(2^k M/B))$ I/Os (bulk loading T_k) and moves exactly $2^k M$ points into the larger kd-tree T_k. If we divide the construction of T_k between these points, each of them has to pay $O((1/B) \log_{M/B}(2^k M/B)) = O((1/B) \log_{M/B}(N/B))$ I/Os. Since points are only moving into larger kd-trees, and there are at most $\log_2(N/M)$ kd-trees, a point can be charged at most $\log_2(N/M)$ times. Thus the final amortized cost of an insertion is $O\left(\frac{\log_{M/B}(N/B) \log_2(N/M)}{B}\right)$ I/Os.

2.3   Queries

To answer a window query on the Bkd-tree we simply have to query all $\log_2(N/M)$ kd-trees. The worst-case performance of a window query on one kd-tree storing N points is an optimal $O(\sqrt{N/B} + K/B)$ I/Os, where K is the number of points in the query window. Since the kd-trees that form the Bkd-tree are geometrically increasing in size, the worst-case performance of the Bkd-tree is also $O(\sqrt{N/B} + K/B)$ I/Os. However, since the average window query performance of a kd-tree is often much better than this worst-case performance [24], it is important to investigate how the use of several kd-trees influences the practical performance of the Bkd-tree compared to the kd-tree.

3   Experimental Platform

In this section we describe the setup for our experimental studies, providing detailed information on the software, hardware, and data sets that were used.

Software Platform. We implemented the Bkd-tree in C++ using TPIE. TPIE [4] is a templated library that provides support for implementing I/O-efficient algorithms and data structures. In our implementation we used a block size of 16KB for internal nodes (following the suggestions of Lomet [17] for the B-tree), resulting in a maximum fanout of 512. The leaves of a kd-tree, stored in 16KB blocks as well, contain a maximum of 1364 (key, pointer) elements. We implemented the Bkd-tree using the grid bulk loading algorithm during insertions and a linear array as the internal memory structure T_0^M (more sophisticated data structures can be implemented for better CPU performance). For comparison purposes, we also implemented the K-D-B-tree, following closely the details provided in the original paper [22] regarding the insertion algorithm. As mentioned in the Introduction, the K-D-B-tree is the point of departure for the hB-tree [18] and the hB^{Π}-tree [10]. The latter is the state-of-the-art in indexing data structures for multi-dimensional points. We used the authors' implementation of the hB^{Π}-tree for the space utilization experiments. The provided implementation is in-memory, but it simulates I/Os by counting accesses to data blocks. For the rest of the experiments, we chose not to use this implementation of the hB^{Π}-tree, since we wanted to emphasize the running times of the Bkd-tree for data sets much larger than main memory.

Data Sets. We chose three different types of point sets for our experiments: real points from the TIGER/Line data [25], uniformly distributed points, and points along a diagonal of a square. The real data consists of six sets of points generated from the road features in the TIGER/Line files. *TIGER Set i, $1 \leq i \leq 6$,* consists of all points on CD-ROMs 1 through i. Note that the largest set, TIGER set 6, contains all the points in the road features of the entire United States and its size is 885MB. Table 1 contains the sizes of all 6 data sets. Figure 6(a) depicts TIGER set 1, representing 15 eastern US states. It can be seen that points are somewhat clustered, with clusters corresponding to urban areas. The uniform data consists of six sets, each containing uniformly distributed points in a square region. The smallest set contains 20 million points, while the largest contains 120 million points. Table 2 contains the sizes of all 6 sets. The final group of sets contains points arranged on a diagonal of a square, as shown in Figure 6(b). We used these sets only for space utilization experiments. In all sets, a point consists

Table 1. The sizes of the TIGER sets.

Set	1	2	3	4	5	6
Number of points	15483533	29703113	39523372	54337289	66562237	77383213
Size (MB)	177.25	340.00	452.38	621.94	761.82	885.69

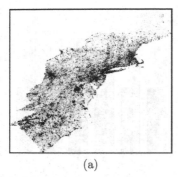
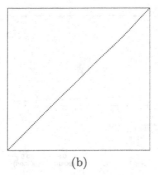

(a)   (b)

Fig. 6. (a) An image of TIGER set 1 (all the points in the road features from 15 eastern US states). The white area contains no points. The darkest regions have the highest density of points. (b) A diagonal data set

of three integer values: the x-coordinate, the y-coordinate, and an ID, for a total of 12 bytes per point. Thus, the largest data set we tested on, containing 120 million points, uses 1.34GB of storage.

Hardware Platform. We used a dedicated Dell PowerEdge 2400 workstation with one Pentium III/500MHz processor, running FreeBSD 4.3. A 36GB SCSI disk (IBM Ultrastar 36LZX) was used to store all necessary files: the input points, the data structure, and the temporary files. The machine had 128MB of memory, but we restricted the amount of memory that TPIE could use to 64MB. The rest was used by operating system daemons. We deliberately used a small memory, to obtain a large data size to memory size ratio.

4 Experimental Results

4.1 Space Utilization

As mentioned previously, the Bkd-tree has close to 100% space utilization. To contrast this to the space utilization of the K-D-B-tree and the hB$^{\Pi}$-tree, we inserted the points from each of the diagonal data sets, sorted by x-coordinate, in all three data structures, and measured the final space utilization. The results are depicted in Figure 7(a). As expected, the Bkd-tree space utilization is almost 100% (between 99.3% and 99.4%). For the K-D-B-tree, the space utilization is as low as 28%, while for the hB$^{\Pi}$-tree it is as low as 38%. In the case of the

Table 2. The sizes of the uniform data sets

Set	1	2	3	4	5	6
Number of points (millions)	20	40	60	80	100	120
Size (MB)	228.88	457.76	686.65	915.53	1144.41	1373.29

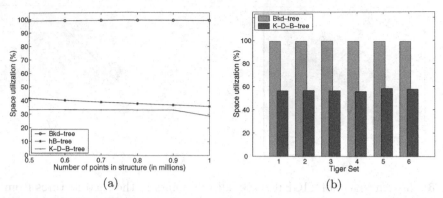

Fig. 7. (a) Space utilization for the diagonal sets. (b) Space utilization for the TIGER sets

K-D-B-tree, the diagonal pattern causes most leaves of the tree to be inside long and skinny rectangles, with points concentrated on one end of the rectangle. When an internal node is split, some of these leaves are cut, resulting in empty leaves. As data sets get larger, the effect is compounded (empty leaves are split as well), resulting in increasingly lower space utilization. In the case of the hB$^{\Pi}$-tree, node splits are not propagated down to leaves. Indeed, the space utilization of the leaves remains at 50% or better, as reported in [10]. However, node splits cause redundancy: Some kd-tree nodes are stored in multiple hB-tree nodes. Consequently, the size of the index grows dramatically, resulting in low fanout, large tree height, and poor overall space utilization. In our experiments, the K-D-B-tree had lower tree height than the corresponding hB$^{\Pi}$-tree.

These results underscore the sensitivity of the K-D-B-tree and the hB$^{\Pi}$-tree to data distribution and insertion order. Indeed, much better space utilization is obtained when the points in a diagonal data set are inserted in random order, rather than sorted on the x coordinate.

To investigate the space utilization for more practically realistic data sets, we repeated the experiment using the TIGER data. The structures were built by repeated insertions, and the order of insertion is given by the order in which the points were stored in the original TIGER/Line data. Unfortunately, we were not able to run the hB$^{\Pi}$-tree experiments in a reasonable amount of time. Experiments on smaller TIGER data sets show the space utilization of the hB$^{\Pi}$-tree to be around 62% (consistent with the results reported in [10] for similar geographic data). Although not as extreme as the diagonal sets, the real life data sets result in relatively poor space utilization—refer to Figure 7(b). For these sets, the space utilization of the K-D-B-tree is around 56%, still far from the 99.4% utilization of the Bkd-tree.

4.2   Bulk Loading Performance

To compare the two kd-tree bulk loading algorithms presented in Section 2.1, we tested them on both the uniform and the real data sets. Figure 8 shows the performance for the uniform data sets and Figure 9 shows the performance for the TIGER data sets. The figures reflect only the building time, leaving out the time needed to sort the data set on each coordinate, which is common for the two methods.

The experiments on uniformly distributed data (Figure 8(a)) show that, in terms of running time, the grid method is at least twice as fast as the binary method and, as predicted by the theoretical analysis, the speedup increases with increased set size. When comparing the number of I/Os (Figure 8(b)), the difference is even larger. To better understand the difference in the number of I/Os performed by the two methods, we can do a "back-of-the-envelope" computation: for the largest size tested, the binary method reads the input file 14 times and writes it 13 times (two reads and two writes for each of the upper levels, and two reads and one write for the lower levels, which are computed in memory), while the grid method reads the input file 5 times and writes it 3 times (one read to compute the grid matrix, two reads and two writes for all the upper levels, and two reads and one write for the lower levels, which are computed in memory). This means that the grid method saves 9 reads of the entire file and, more importantly, 10 writes of the entire input file. To put it differently, the grid method performs less than a third fewer I/Os than the binary method. This corresponds perfectly with the results from Figure 8(b). The difference between the running time speedup (approximately 2) and the I/O speedup (approximately 3) reflects the fact that the grid method is more CPU-intensive.

The experiments on the TIGER data (Figure 9) show a similar pattern. Note that the kd-tree bulk loading performance is independent of the data distribu-

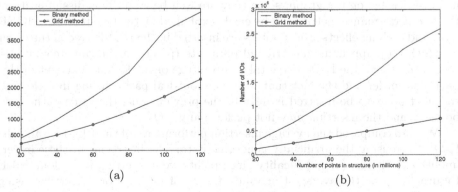

(a)   (b)

Fig. 8. Bulk loading performance on uniform data: (a) Time (in seconds), (b) Number of I/Os

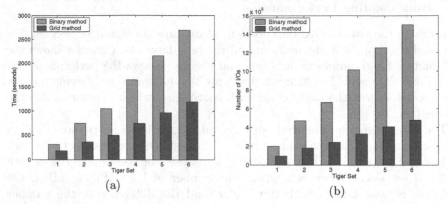

Fig. 9. Bulk loading performance on TIGER data: (a) Time (in seconds), (b) Number of I/Os

tion, which means that the bulk loading performance can be predicted very accurately only from the number of points to be indexed. To illustrate this, consider the uniformly distributed set containing 40 million points, and TIGER set 3, containing 39.5 million points. Comparing the bulk loading times for the two sets, we find virtually identical values.

4.3   Insertion Performance

To compare the average insertion performance of the Bkd-tree with that of the K-D-B-tree, we inserted all the points of each TIGER set into an initially empty structure, and we divided the overall results by the number of points inserted. Figure 10 shows the average time and the average number of I/Os for one insertion. In terms of elapsed time, a Bkd-tree insertion is only twice as fast as a K-D-B-tree insertion. When I/Os are counted, however, the Bkd-tree values are not even visible on the graph, since they are well below 1. This dissimilarity in the two performance metrics can be easily explained by the layout of the TIGER data and caching effects. Since points are inserted in the K-D-B-tree in the order in which they appear in the original data sets (points in the same county are stored together), the K-D-B-tree takes advantage of the locality existent in this particular order and the fact that we cache root-leaf paths during insertions. If the next point to be inserted is next to the previous one, the same path could be used, and the insertion may not perform any I/Os.

We also compared the average insertion performance of the Bkd-tree and the K-D-B-tree using the artificially generated data. The insertions in these experiments exhibit less (or no) locality since points were inserted in random order. Figure 11 shows the average time and number of I/Os for one insertion, using the uniform data sets. For the Bkd-tree, the values were obtained by inserting all points one by one in an initially empty structure and averaging. For the K-D-B-tree, however, we have not been able to perform the same experiment.

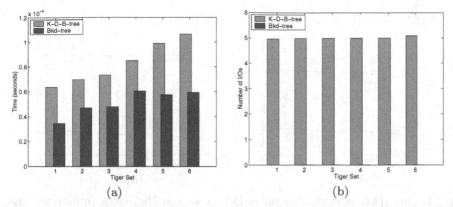

Fig. 10. Insertion performance on K-D-B-trees and Bkd-trees (TIGER data):
(a) Time (in seconds), (b) Number of I/Os

Even for the smallest set, containing 20 million points, inserting them one by
one takes more than 2 days! This is due to the lack of locality in the insertion
pattern; even if all internal nodes are cached, each insertion still makes at least
two I/Os (to read and to write the corresponding leaf) because chances are that
the relevant leaf is not in the cache. This results in 40 million random I/Os for
the 20 million point set.

Since we could not build the K-D-B-tree by repeated insertions, we designed
a different experiment to measure the K-D-B-tree insertion performance. We
bulk loaded a K-D-B-tree using the input points (filling each leaf and node up to
70% of capacity) and then we inserted 1000 random points into that structure.
As predicted by the theoretical analysis, a Bkd-tree insertion is several orders of
magnitude faster than a K-D-B-tree insertion, both in terms of elapsed time and
number of I/Os; in terms of elapsed time, the Bkd-tree insertion is more then 100
times faster than the K-D-B-tree insertion, for all data sizes. In terms of number
of I/Os, the Bkd-tree is up to 230 times faster. The discrepancy between the
two numbers comes, again, from the fact that we cache nodes and leaves. Since
the Bkd-tree implicitly uses the entire main memory as cache, we allowed the
K-D-B-tree to do the same. However, due to the randomness of the data, very
few leaves were found in the cache.

4.4   Query Performance

Although the worst case asymptotic bounds for a window query on a Bkd-tree
and a K-D-B-tree are identical, we expect the Bkd-tree to perform more I/Os,
due to the multiple trees that need to be searched. To investigate this, we queried
a Bkd-tree and a K-D-B-tree with the same window. Figure 12 shows the running
times and number of I/Os of a square-shaped window query that covers 1% of the
points in each of the uniform data sets. These values are obtained by averaging
over 10 queries of the same size, whose position is randomly chosen in the area

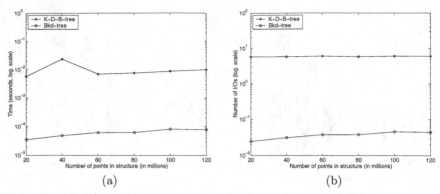

Fig. 11. Insertion performance on K-D-B-trees and Bkd-trees (uniformly distributed data): (a) Time (in seconds), (b) Number of I/Os

covered by the points. It can be seen that the Bkd-tree performs roughly the same number of I/Os as the K-D-B-tree. This somewhat unexpected result is the consequence of a number of factors. First, the average number of kd-trees forming the Bkd-tree is less than $\lceil \log_2(N/M) \rceil$ (the maximum possible). Table 3 shows the number of non-empty kd-trees and the number of maximum kd-trees for each of the 6 uniform data sets. It can easily be shown that in the course of $2^p M$ insertions into an initially empty Bkd-tree, the average number of non-empty kd-trees is $p/2$. As a result, the number of kd-trees that need to be searched during a window query is smaller than the maximum. Second, the individual kd-trees in the Bkd-tree have smaller heights than the K-D-B-tree built on the same data set. This is due to the geometrically decreasing sizes of the kd-trees and to the fact that, as noted in Section 3, the fanout of the Bkd-tree is larger than the fanout of the K-D-B-tree. As a result, the number of internal nodes read during a window query is small. Third, the kd-tree query performance is very efficient for these data sets. Table 4 shows, for the uniform data sets, the number of points returned by the query as a percentage of the total number of points retrieved. As a result, both data structures read roughly the same number of leaf-level blocks, which is close to optimal.

In terms of running time, the K-D-B-tree is faster than the Bkd-tree. This can be explained by the fact that the queries are performed on a bulk loaded K-D-B-tree. The trees constructed by the bulk loading algorithms described in

Table 3. The number of non-empty kd-trees and the maximum number of kd-trees, for each Bkd-tree built on the uniform data sets

Number of points (in millions)	20	40	60	80	100	120
Non-empty kd-trees	3	3	3	4	4	4
Max kd-trees ($\lceil \log_2(N/M) \rceil$)	4	5	6	6	7	7

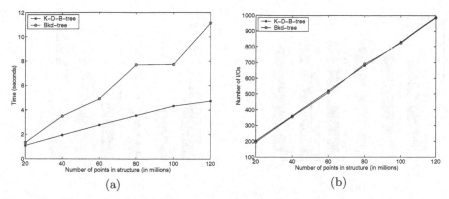

(a)   (b)

Fig. 12. Range query performance on the uniform data (the range area is 1% of entire area): (a) Time (in seconds), (b) Number of I/Os

Section 2.1 exhibit a high level of locality, in the sense that points that are nearby on disk are likely to be spatially close. Queries performed on the K-D-B-tree are able to take advantage of this locality, resulting in a more sequential access pattern. On the other hand, the Bkd-tree has less locality, since multiple trees have to be queried to obtain the final result. In a real-world spatial database the K-D-B-tree is often obtained by repeated insertions. This typically results in a structure with low space utilization and poor locality. This behavior can be observed in the experiments performed on the TIGER sets. As explained in Section 4.3, the K-D-B-tree for the TIGER sets was obtained by repeated insertions. As a result, it exhibits much less locality. Figure 13 shows that the two structures perform similarly in terms of time, attesting to the fact that both structures have to perform some random I/O (the Bkd-tree because it queries multiple kd-trees, and the K-D-B-tree because it exhibits less locality). In terms of I/O, the Bkd-tree is performing half as many I/Os as the K-D-B-tree. This is due to the poor space utilization of the K-D-B-tree, which was shown to be around 56% for the TIGER data sets (see Section 4.1).

In order to measure the effect of the window size on the query performance, we ran a set of experiments with various window sizes. Figure 14 shows the results of these experiments. Both the K-D-B-tree and the Bkd-tree are built on the largest data set, containing 120 million uniformly distributed points.

Table 4. The number of points returned by a window query as a percentage of the total number of points retrieved. For each set, the window covers 1% of the total number of points

Number of points (in millions)	20	40	60	80	100	120
Bkd-tree	78.4	84.7	88.1	86.5	90.4	90.6
K-D-B-tree	74.8	83.6	86.2	87.9	90.2	90.6

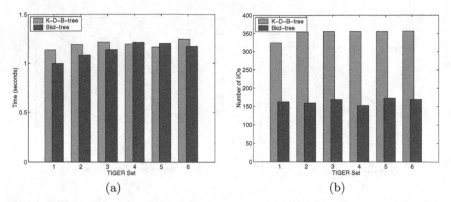

Fig. 13. Range query performance on the TIGER data: (a) Time (in seconds), (b) Number of I/Os

On the graph showing elapsed time, we see again the effects of a freshly bulk loaded K-D-B-tree, resulting in a more sequential I/O pattern than the Bkd-tree. But the I/O performance of the two structures is virtually identical for the entire range of query sizes, confirming the results obtained on the 1% query, namely that the Bkd-tree's window query performance is on par with that of existing data structures. Thus, without sacrificing window query performance, the Bkd-tree makes significant improvements in insertion performance and space utilization: insertions are up to 100 times faster than K-D-B-tree insertions, and space utilization is close to a perfect 100%, even under massive insertions.

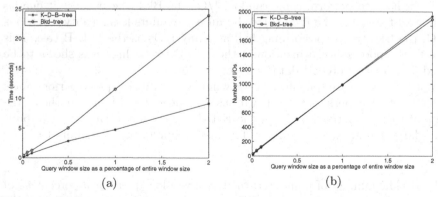

Fig. 14. Performance of range queries of increasing size (the data set consists of 120 million points uniformly distributed in a square): (a) Time (in seconds), (b) Number of I/Os

64   Octavian Procopiuc et al.

Acknowledgments

We would like to thank Georgios Evangelidis for providing us the hB$^{\Pi}$-tree code.

References

[1] P. K. Agarwal, L. Arge, O. Procopiuc, and J. S. Vitter. A framework for index bulk loading and dynamization. In *Proc. Intl. Colloq. Automata, Languages and Programming*, pages 115–127, 2001. 51

[2] A. Aggarwal and J. S. Vitter. The Input/Output complexity of sorting and related problems. *Commun. ACM*, 31:1116–1127, 1988. 51

[3] L. Arge. External memory data structures. In J. Abello, P. M. Pardalos, and M. G. C. Resende, editors, *Handbook of Massive Data Sets*, pages 313–358. Kluwer, 2002. 47

[4] L. Arge, O. Procopiuc, and J. S. Vitter. Implementing I/O-efficient data structures using TPIE. In *Proc. European Symp. on Algorithms*, pages 88–100, 2002. 55

[5] L. Arge, V. Samoladas, and J. S. Vitter. On two-dimensional indexability and optimal range search indexing. In *Proc. ACM Symp. Principles of Database Systems*, pages 346–357, 1999. 47

[6] N. Beckmann, H.-P. Kriegel, R. Schneider, and B. Seeger. The R*-tree: An efficient and robust access method for points and rectangles. In *Proc. SIGMOD Intl. Conf. on Management of Data*, pages 322–331, 1990. 47

[7] J. L. Bentley. Multidimensional binary search trees used for associative searching. *Commun. ACM*, 18(9):509–517, Sept. 1975. 47

[8] J. L. Bentley. Decomposable searching problems. *Inform. Process. Lett.*, 8:244–251, 1979. 49, 53

[9] S. Berchtold, C. Böhm, and H.-P. Kriegel. Improving the query performance of high-dimensional index structures by bulk load operations. In *Proc. Intl. Conf. on Extending Database Technology*, volume 1377 of *Lecture Notes Comput. Sci.*, pages 216–230, 1998. 47

[10] G. Evangelidis, D. Lomet, and B. Salzberg. The hB$^{\Pi}$-tree: A multi-attribute index supporting concurrency, recovery and node consolidation. *The VLDB Journal*, 6:1–25, 1997. 47, 49, 50, 53, 55, 57

[11] V. Gaede and O. Günther. Multidimensional access methods. *ACM Computing Surveys*, 30(2):170–231, 1998. 47

[12] R. Grossi and G. F. Italiano. Efficient cross-tree for external memory. In J. Abello and J. S. Vitter, editors, *External Memory Algorithms and Visualization*, pages 87–106. American Mathematical Society, 1999. Revised version available at ftp://ftp.di.unipi.it/pub/techreports/TR-00-16.ps.Z. 47

[13] A. Guttman. R-trees: A dynamic index structure for spatial searching. In *Proc. SIGMOD Intl. Conf. on Management of Data*, pages 47–57, 1984. 47

[14] H. V. Jagadish, P. P. S. Narayan, S. Seshadri, S. Sudarshan, and R. Kanneganti. Incremental organization for data recording and warehousing. In *Proc. Intl. Conf. on Very Large Data Bases*, pages 16–25, 1997. 49

[15] K. V. R. Kanth and A. K. Singh. Optimal dynamic range searching in non-replicating index structures. In *Proc. Intl. Conf. on Database Theory*, volume 1540 of *Lecture Notes Comput. Sci.*, pages 257–276, 1999. 47

[16] D. T. Lee and C. K. Wong. Worst-case analysis for region and partial region searches in multidimensional binary search trees and balanced quad trees. *Acta Informatica*, 9:23–29, 1977. 48

[17] D. Lomet. B-tree page size when caching is considered. *SIGMOD Record*, 27(3):28–32, 1998. 55

[18] D. B. Lomet and B. Salzberg. The hB-Tree: A multiattribute indexing method with good guaranteed performance. *ACM Trans. on Database Systems*, 15(4):625–658, Dec. 1990. 47, 49, 55

[19] J. Nievergelt, H. Hinterberger, and K. C. Sevcik. The grid file: An adaptable, symmetric multikey file structure. *ACM Trans. on Database Systems*, 9(1):38–71, Mar. 1984.

[20] P. E. O'Neil, E. Cheng, D. Gawlick, and E. J. O'Neil. The log-structured merge-tree (LSM-tree). *Acta Informatica*, 33(4):351–385, 1996. 49

[21] M. H. Overmars. *The Design of Dynamic Data Structures*, volume 156 of *Lecture Notes Comput. Sci.* Springer-Verlag, 1983. 49, 50, 53

[22] J. T. Robinson. The K-D-B-tree: A search structure for large multidimensional dynamic indexes. In *Proc. SIGMOD Intl. Conf. on Management of Data*, pages 10–18, 1981. 47, 48, 55

[23] H. Samet. *The design and analysis of spatial data structures*. Addison-Wesley, 1990. 47, 48

[24] Y. V. Silva Filho. Average case analysis of region search in balanced *k*-d trees. *Inform. Process. Lett.*, 8:219–223, 1979. 48, 54

[25] *TIGER/Line Files, 1997 Technical Documentation*. U.S. Census Bureau, 1998. http://www.census.gov/geo/tiger/TIGER97D.pdf. 55

Efficient Object-Relational Interval Management and Beyond*

Lars Arge and Andrew Chatham

Department of Computer Science
Duke University, Durham,
NC 27708, USA
{large,achatham}@cs.duke.edu

Abstract. Recently, the *object-relational access method paradigm*—the idea of designing index structures that can be built on top of the SQL layer of any relational database server—was proposed as a way to design easy to implement indexes while obtaining strong robustness, performance, and integration into transaction management for free.

In this paper, we describe an object-relational index for the 3-sided range indexing problem. Previously an object-relational index was only known for the interval management problem, which is a special case of the 3-sided range indexing problem. Our new index is efficient in the worst-case, and it can be used to answer all general interval relationship queries efficiently. The previously known index were only able to answer 7 out of 13 possible relationship queries efficiently. We also describe a (limited) experimental study of a simplified version of our structure.

1   Introduction

In order to be successful, any data model in a large database requires efficient index support for its language features. In their pioneering work, Kanellakis et al. [10] showed that the problem of indexing in new data models (such as constraint, temporal, and object models), can be reduced to special cases of two-dimensional indexing—refer to Figure 1. In particular they identified the 3-sided indexing problem to be of major importance. In this problem an index needs to be maintained for a set of points in the plane such that for a query $q = (a, b, c)$ all points (x, y) with $a \leq x \leq b$ and $y \geq c$ can be found efficiently (Figure 1(c)). One major reason for the importance of the 3-sided problem is that the simpler 2-sided problem (Figure 1(b)), or rather the so-called diagonal corner query problem (Figure 1(a)), is equivalent to the interval management problem, that is, the problem of maintaining an index on a set of intervals such that all intervals containing a query point can be found efficiently. Interval management is important in an increasing number of applications [13].

---

* This work was supported in part by the National Science Foundation through ESS grant EIA–9870734, RI grant EIA–9972879, CAREER grant CCR–9984099, and ITR grant EIA–0112849.

T. Hadzilacos et al. (Eds.): SSTD 2003, LNCS 2750, pp. 66–82, 2003.

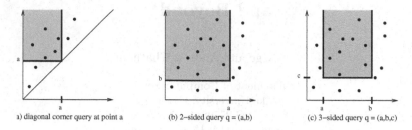

a) diagonal corner query at point a   (b) 2–sided query q = (a,b)   (c) 3–sided query q = (a,b,c)

Fig. 1. Special cases of two-dimensional range queries

While many two-dimensional indexing schemes have been developed in recent years [3, 9] (many even provably optimal), very few of them have made it into commercial database systems [13]. One reason for this is that many of them are quite sophisticated and thus not straightforward to implement. Another main reason is that in order to be of commercial strength, an index needs to be integrated into transaction management, that is, recovery and concurrency control issues need to be addressed. Very recently, the *object-relational access method paradigm* was proposed as a way to overcome this problem [13]. The idea in this paradigm is to design index structures that can be built on top of the pure SQL layer of any relational database server and thus inherit the robustness and transaction management for free. Efficiency is obtained by utilizing the I/O-efficient index for one-dimensional range queries, typically a B^+-tree, underlying virtually any relational system. The relational interval tree (RI-tree) solving the interval management problem was the first structure developed using the object-relational (or simply *relational*) paradigm [13]. Subsequently, the RI-tree has been used in relational index structures for managing general spatial data [14] and for answering general interval relationships queries [15].

In this paper we present several results related to relational index structures. We illustrate that in certain cases the performance of the RI-tree can degenerate significantly, and propose a new relational index that is efficient in the worst case. Our index actually efficiently solves the more general 3-sided range indexing problem, and we also show how it can be used to answer all interval relationship queries efficiently. The previously known index were only able to answer 7 out of 13 possible relationship queries efficiently. Finally, we describe a simplified version of our structure, as well as a (limited) experimental study illustrating that this structure has similar or better query performance than the RI-tree while at the same time requiring significantly less space.

1.1 Memory Model and Previous Results

As mentioned, many efficient two-dimensional indexing structures have been developed in recent years. Refer to recent surveys for a complete overview of these structures [3, 9]. Many of the developed structures are not worst-case efficient, but are relatively simple to implement and perform well in most practical situations. Worst case optimal index structures have been developed for general two-dimensional range searching [4, 11], as well as for the special cases of 3-sided queries [4] and interval management (diagonal corner queries) [5]. The latter two structures are modified versions of the priority search tree of McCreight [16] and interval tree of Edelsbrunner [8]. They both use $O(N/B)$ space, answers queries in $O(\log_B N + T/B)$ I/Os, and can be updated in $O(\log_B N)$ I/Os. In these bounds N is the number of intervals/points in the index, B the number of intervals/points that fits in a disk block, and T the number of intervals/points reported by a query; one block can be transferred between disk and main memory in one I/O operation [1, 12].

While many interval management index structures have been developed (see e.g. [13] for an overview), the RI-tree was the first efficient index to be developed using the object-relational paradigm [13]. Like the index developed in [5], the RI-tree is based on the interval tree [8]. It uses $O(N/B)$ space, can be updated in $O(\log_B N)$ I/Os, and answers a query in $O(h \cdot \log_B N + T/B)$ I/Os. Here h is a parameter reflecting the expansion and granularity of the data space (the height of the so-called *virtual backbone* corresponding to the binary base tree of an interval tree). In [13] it was conjectured that the RI-tree is optimal. The only assumptions made about the underlying relational database management system used in these bounds are that a (one-dimensional) range query on a size N relation can be performed in $O(\log_B N + T/B)$ I/Os, that the relation can be updated in $O(\log_B N)$ I/Os, and that all data element in the relation can be scanned in $O(N/B)$ I/Os. These bounds are obtained by the ubiquitous B^+-tree [6, 7, 12]. In [13] it was also shown that the RI-tree is easy to implement on top of SQL and that it performs well in practice.

As mentioned, the RI-tree has been used in relational index structures for managing general spatial data [14] and for answering general interval relationships queries [15]. While a query in the interval management problem asks for all intervals in the database containing a query point a, a query in an interval relationship query is an interval I and can for example ask for all intervals in the database *containing* I, starting *before* I, or *overlapping* I. In general, there are 13 different interval relationship queries [2]. The RI-tree can be used to answer 7 of these queries in $O(h \cdot \log_B N + T/B)$ I/Os, while the remaining 6 queues may require $O(N/B)$ I/Os [15].

1.2   Our Results

In this paper we present several results related to relational index structures. In Section 2, we review the RI-tree and illustrate that $h = \Omega(\log_2 N)$ for a simple set of intervals, resulting in a query requiring $\Omega(\log_2 N \cdot \log_B N + T/B)$ I/Os. For another set of intervals, we can even have $h = \Omega(N)$, resulting in an $\Omega(N \cdot \log_B N + T/B)$ query bound. In Section 3, we then develop a new relational version of a priority search tree (called the RPS-tree) that can answer 3-sided queries in $O(\log_B^2 N + T/B)$ I/Os. The RPS-tree uses linear space and an update requires $O(\log_B^2 N)$ I/Os. The RPS-tree uses a substructure for storing and querying $O(B^2 \log_B N)$ points, which we describe in Section 4. In Section 5 we show how the RPS-tree can be used to answer *all* 13 interval relationship queries in $O(\log_B^2 N + T/B)$ I/Os.

The RPS-tree is somewhat more complicated than the RI-tree (partly because of this papers focus on worst-case efficiency). In Section 6, we discuss how the RPS-tree can be considerably simplified using ideas similar to the ones used in the RI-tree. The cost of the simplification is that a query now is answered in $O(h \log_B N + T/B)$ I/Os, where h (like in the RI-tree) is a parameter reflecting the expansion and granularity of the data space. Finally, in Section 7, we present a (limited) experimental study illustrating that in practice the SRPS-tree has similar or better query performance than the RI-tree, while at the same time requiring significantly less space.

2 Relational Interval Tree

In this section we review the RI-tree developed by Kriegel et al. [13]. The RI-tree is a relational version of a standard internal memory interval tree [8] and therefore we first review this structure. Note that an interval tree can normally be used to find not only the intervals containing a query point, but more generally all intervals intersecting a query interval. For simplicity we only consider point queries in this section. As mentioned, we consider general interval relationship queries in Section 5. Throughout the rest of the paper, for simplicity, we also assume that all interval endpoint (and point) coordinates are distinct.

2.1 Interval Tree

An interval tree consists of a *base* (or *backbone*) balanced binary tree on the endpoints of the interval in the tree. An interval e is assigned to the highest node v where $e = (x_1, x_2)$ contains the value x_v stored in v. The set of intervals I_v assigned to a node v is stored in two *secondary* structures L_v and R_v. L_v and R_v are search trees on the intervals in I_v sorted according to left and right endpoint, respectively. An interval tree uses linear space since each interval is only stored in two secondary structures.

In order to answer a query with query point a we search down a path of the base tree until we find a or reach a leaf. In each node v on the path we need to find all intervals in I_v containing a: If the search for a continues to the left subtree, the intervals are found by traversing the intervals in L_v from left to right, until a interval not containing a is encountered. All intervals in L_v after this interval (in the sorted order) cannot contain a. Note that this corresponds to performing a range query $(-\infty, a)$ on L_v. Similarly, R_v is used if the search for a continues to the right subtree. To see that the procedure correctly finds all intervals containing a, consider the root r of the base tree and assume without loss of generality that the search for a continues to the left child. Since this means that a is to the left of the point x_r in r, no interval in the subtree rooted in the right child can contain a. The correctness follows, since we find all intervals in I_r containing a and recursively find all intervals in the left subtree containing a.

Since the query procedure visits $O(\log N)$ nodes and uses $O(T_v)$ time to report the relevant T_v intervals in node v, the total time spent on answering a query is the optimal $O(\log N + \sum T_v) = O(\log N + T)$.

To insert a new interval $e = (x_1, x_2)$, we simply search down the tree for the highest node v where e contains x_v. Then we insert e in L_v and R_v using $O(\log N)$ time. We also need to insert the endpoints x_1 and x_2 of e in the base tree. This involves rebalancing the base tree and may result in the need for rearrangement of intervals in the secondary structures of many nodes. This can also be handled in $O(\log N)$ time using a weight-balanced BB[α]-tree [8, 17]. Deletes can be handled in $O(\log N)$ time in a similar way.

2.2   Relational Interval Tree (RI-Tree)

Essentially, the RI-tree is an interval tree where the intervals in the L_v structures of all nodes are stored in a relation L and the intervals in the R_v structures are stored in a relation R. An interval $e = (x_1, x_2)$ in I_v is stored as the tuple (v, x_1, x_2) in L and R, which are indexed on (v, x_1) and (v, x_2), respectively. Using the assumption that a range query can be answered in $O(\log_B N + T/B)$ I/Os, a range query (q_1, q_2) on L_v can be performed in $O(\log_B N + T_v/B)$ I/Os by performing the query $((v, q_1), (v, q_2))$ on L. Thus if we know the, say, h nodes on a path to a query point a, the query can be answered in $O(h \cdot \log_B N + T/B)$ I/Os by issuing h queries on L and R.

The base tree of the RI-tree is not defined as a tree on the endpoints of the intervals in the interval tree. Instead, if the endpoints are in the range $[1, 2^h - 1]$, the elements in the tree can be any number in this range. More precisely, the element in the root of the tree is 2^{h-1} and the other elements in the tree are obtained using simple bisection; the left and right children of the root contain elements $2^{h-1} - 2^{h-1}/2 = 2^{h-2}$ and $2^{h-1} + 2^{h-1}/2 = \frac{3}{2}2^{h-1}$, respectively, and in general $2^{l-1}/2$ is added to and subtracted from the value of the element in a node on level l of the tree to obtain the values of the elements in its children. Refer to Figure 2. The advantage of this is that the base tree does not need to be materialized at all; relations L and R are all that is needed to store the intervals. When performing a query with point a, the "traversal" of the base tree can be performed using simple integer arithmetic without performing any I/O. After this the relevant $O(h)$ range queries can be answered in $O(h \cdot \log_B N + T/B)$ I/Os. The insertion of an interval $e = (x_1, x_2)$ with endpoints in the range $[1, 2^h - 1]$ can be performed in $O(\log_B N)$ I/Os by simply "traversing" the base tree to compute the relevant node v, and then inserting (v, x_1, x_2) in L and R. Inserting an interval with endpoints outside the range $[1, 2^h - 1]$, say $e = (x_1, 2^k - 1)$ with $k > h$, is equally simple to handle; a new root of the virtual base tree containing element 2^{k-1} is constructed and e is inserted as before. Deletes are handled in $O(\log_B N)$ I/Os in a similar way. In [13] methods for handling negative endpoint values and for keeping the tree height adjusted to the actual data distribution (e.g. if the endpoints are clustered close to the upper end of the range $[1, 2^h - 1]$) are also discussed.

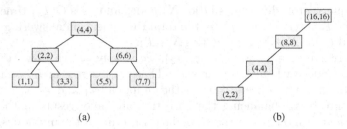

(a)   (b)

Fig. 2. RI-trees. (a) Intervals $(0,0), (1,1) \ldots (7,7)$ result in tree of height at least 3 $(\Omega(\log_2 N))$. (b) Intervals $(2,2), (4,4), (8,8), (16,16)$ results in tree of height 4 $(\Omega(N))$

2.3   Height h of the RI-Tree

In [13] it is claimed that the height h of an RI-tree depends only on the range and size of the intervals stored in the structure. It is certainly true that the presented methods allow the tree structure to adapt to the intervals stored in it. However, there are still simple datasets where h is highly dependent on the number N of intervals in the tree and in these cases the performance of the structure can degenerate. For example, a dataset consisting of unique degenerate intervals (points) results in a tall base tree as a function of N: In this case the (virtual) base tree will contain N nodes, since each interval (point) must be stored in a unique node. Since the tree is binary this means that $h = \Omega(\log_2 N)$ and thus a query will take $\Omega(\log_2 N \cdot \log_B N + T/B)$ I/Os—Refer to Figure 2(a). For the set of intervals $(1,1), (2,2), (4,4) \ldots (2^N, 2^N)$ the height is $\Omega(N)$, resulting in an $\Omega(N \cdot \log_B N + T/B)$ query bound—Refer to Figure 2(b).[1]

3   Relational Priority Search Tree (RPS-Tree)

As discussed in the introduction, the interval management problem solved by the RI-tree is a special case of the 3-sided range searching problem, that is, the problem of maintaining a set of points in the plane such that for a query $q = (a, b, c)$ all points (x, y) with $a \leq x \leq b$ and $y \geq c$ can be found efficiently (Figure 1(c)). To see this, imagine interpreting the interval $[x_1, x_2]$ as the point (x_1, x_2) above the diagonal $y = x$. Since an interval $[x_1, x_2]$ contains a point a if and only if $x_1 \leq a$ and $x_2 \geq a$, finding all intervals containing a corresponds to performing a 2-sided query (with corner point (a, a) on the diagonal line) on the points corresponding to the intervals (Figure 1(a))—a (very) special case of a 3-sided query.

In this section we develop a relational index for answering 3-sided queries. Our so-called RPS-tree is a relational version of the external priority search

---

[1] Note that h can actually be unbounded in the size of N, since we can get a height h tree with just two intervals $(1,1)$ and $(2^h, 2^h)$.

tree [4], modified in a number of nontrivial ways. The structure has improved (worst-case) query and update bounds compared to the RI-tree.

3.1   Structure

The RPS-tree consists of a fanout $\Theta(B)$ balanced base tree on the x-coordinates of the N points stored in the structure, with each leaf containing $\Theta(B \log_B^2 N)$ co-ordinates. The tree has height $O(\log_B N)$ and, like a B^+-tree, each internal node contains $\Theta(B)$ values (x-coordinates) used to guide a search through the tree. A range X_v can naturally be associated with each node v, consisting of all values (x-coordinates) below v. This range is divided into $\Theta(B)$ subranges by the ranges of the children of v (that is, by the values stored in v). We call these subranges *slabs*. A secondary structure U_v for answering 3-sided queries on $O(B^2 \log_B N)$ points is (conceptually) associated with node v. It stores $O(B \log_B N)$ points for each of the $\Theta(B)$ slabs, namely the $B \log_B N$ points (if existing) with the highest y-coordinates among the points that have not been stored in ancestors of v—Refer to Figure 3(a).

In order to make the RPS-tree relational the base tree is not actually manifested. Instead the individual nodes are stored in a relation P indexed by a unique id. One node v contains information about the $O(B)$ values (x-coordinates) associated with it, along with the id's of the corresponding children. Is also contains a constant amount of information about the secondary structure U_n (such as its size). This way a given node v can be obtained in $O(\log_B N)$ I/Os by querying P, which in turn means that a root-leaf path can be traversed in $O(\log_B^2 N)$ I/Os. The secondary structures of all nodes are stored in a linear space relational structure U, such that a 3-sided query on a particular structure U_v can be answered in $O(\log_B N + T_v/B)$ I/Os and such that a point can be inserted and deleted in $O(\log_B N)$ I/Os. We describe this structure in Section 4. Since P uses linear space, and since each point is stored in one secondary structure, the RPS-tree uses linear space.

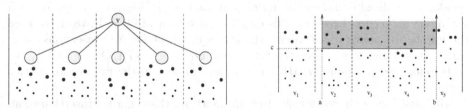

Fig. 3.   (a) An internal node v of the base tree. The $B \log_B N$ highest points in each slab (marked bold) are stored in the secondary structure U_v. (b) Internal node v with children $v_1, v_2, \ldots, v_5$. The points in bold are stored in U_v. To answer a 3-sided query, we report the relevant points in U_v and answer the query recursively in v_2, v_3, and v_5. The query is not extended to v_4 because not all points in U_v from v_4 satisfy the query

3.2 Operations

To answer a 3-sided query (a, b, c) on the RPS-tree, we start at the root of the tree and proceed recursively to the appropriate subtrees; when visiting a node v, we first query the secondary structure U_v (or rather U) and report the relevant points. We then advanced the search to child v_i if it is either along the search path to a or b, or if the entire set of points in U_v from the slab corresponding to v_i were reported—refer to Figure 3(b).

Our query procedure correctly reports all points in the query range: If we do not visit child v_i corresponding to a slab completely spanned by the interval $[a, b]$, it means that at least one point in U_v corresponding to v_i does not satisfy the query. This in turn means that none of the points in the subtree rooted at v_i can satisfy the query.

That we use $O(\log_B^2 N + T/B)$ I/Os to answer a query can be seen as follows. We spend $O(\log_B N + T_v/B)$ I/Os in each node v visited by the query procedure; $O(\log_B N)$ to load v from P and $O(\log_B N + T_v/B)$ to query U. We visit $O(\log_B N)$ nodes on the search paths to the leaf containing a and the leaf containing b. Thus the number of I/Os used in these nodes adds up to $O(\log_B^2 N + T/B)$. Each remaining visited node v is visited because $\Theta(B \log_B N)$ points corresponding to it were reported in its parent. Thus the cost of visiting these nodes adds up to $O(T/B)$.

Disregarding rebalancing of the base tree for now, we insert a point $p = (x, y)$ by searching down the base tree and insert p in U_v of the relevant node v. As previously, we use $O(\log_B N)$ I/Os to load each node on the path. We can also decide in $O(\log_B N)$ I/Os if p needs to be inserted in a given node v: We simply extract the $O(B \log_B N)$ points in U_v from the slab corresponding to the relevant child v_i using a (degenerate) 3-sided query and compare their y-coordinates to y. Insertion of p may result in U_v containing too many points ($> B \log_B N$) from the slab corresponding to v_i. In this case we remove the lowest point in U_v corresponding to v_i and recursively insert it in the subtree rooted in v_i. This way we use $O(\log_B N)$ I/Os in each of $O(\log_B N)$ nodes, for a total of $O(\log_B^2 N)$ I/Os. Note that since an insertion changes N, strictly speaking we should change the number of points ($B^2 \log_B N$) stored in each secondary structure. However, this could require a lot of I/Os. Instead, we keep the number of points in secondary structures constant for $N/2$ insertions, after which we rebuild the entire structure using $O(N \log_B^2 N)$ I/Os, or $O(\log_B^2 N)$ I/Os amortized per point. Further details will appear in the full version of this paper.

Rebalancing of the base tree after an insertion, that is, after insertion of an x-coordinate in the leaves, can also be handled in $O(\log_B^2 N)$ I/Os. Here we only sketch how this is done. The rebalancing is basically done as in a normal B-tree by splitting nodes. When a node v splits into v' and v'', the secondary structure U_v also needs to be split into $V_{v'}$ and $V_{v''}$. We can easily do so in $O(B \log_B N)$ I/Os (Section 4). When v splits, a slab in the parent w of v also splits into two slabs. While the secondary structure U_w contained $B \log_B N$ points corresponding to v, it now needs to contain $2 \cdot B \log_B N$ points corresponding to v' and v''. Thus we need to promote (move) $B \log_B N$ points from secondary structures $U_{v'}$ and $U_{v''}$ to U_w. Promoting one point from, say, $U_{v'}$ to U_w—deleting the topmost point from $U_{v'}$ and inserting it in U_w—can be performed in $O(\log_B N)$ I/Os. Since such a promotion means that $U_{v'}$ now contains too few points from one of the slabs of v', we recursively need to promote a point to $U_{v'}$. We call this process of recursively promoting one point a *bubble-up*; it can be performed in $O(\log_B^2 N)$ I/Os similar to the way we performed a "bubble-down" during an insertion. Since we need to bubble-up $B \log_B N$ points, the split of v costs $O(B \log_B^3 N)$ I/Os in total. Since an insertion can result in $O(\log_B N)$ splits, the total rebalancing cost can be $O(B \log_B^4 N)$. However, rebalancing is only needed when a leaf splits, and since a leaf can only split once per $\Theta(B \log_B^2 N)$ insertions into it (because it contains $\Theta(B \log_B^2 N)$ x-coordinates), the amortized rebalancing cost is $O(\log_B^2 N)$ I/Os. Using ideas from [4] we can even make this bound worst case. Deletions can be handled in $O(\log_B^2 N)$ I/Os in a similar way. Details will appear in the full paper.

Theorem 1. *A set of N points in the plane can be maintained in a RPS-tree of size $O(N/B)$, such that a 3-sided query can be answered in $O(\log_B^2 N + T/B)$ I/Os and such that an update can be performed in $O(\log_B^2 N)$ I/Os.*

4   Structure Containing $O(B^2 \log_B N)$ Points

In this section we describe the linear space relational structure U used for the secondary structure U_v for all nodes v of the RPS-tree, such that a 3-sided query on the $O(B^2 \log_B N)$ points in a particular structure U_v can be answered in $O(\log_B N + T/B)$ I/Os.

4.1   Structure

The structure U_v consists of $O(B)$ *bins* containing $B \log_B N$ points each. Conceptually, we construct these bins as follows. Initially we create $O(B)$ bins $b_1, b_2, \ldots, b_B$ by partitioning the $O(B^2 \log_B N)$ points by their x order (for each $i < j$, if $(x_1, y_1) \in b_i$ and $(x_2, y_2) \in b_j$, then $x_1 \leq x_2$). We associate an *x-range* with each bin in a natural way and order them linearly according to these ranges. Next we mark all bins as *active* and consider sweeping a horizontal line over the bins starting at $y = -\infty$. During the sweep, as soon as two active consecutive bins both contain less than $\frac{1}{2} B \log_B N$ points above the sweep line, we mark the two bins as inactive and create a new active bin containing the (at most) $B \log_B N$ points in the two bins above the sweep-line. The x-range of the new active bin consists of the x-ranges of the two bins it replaces, and the new bin replaces the two inactive bins in the linear order. We associate an *active y-range* with each bin, delimited by the y-coordinates of the point that caused the bin to be created and the point that caused the bin to become inactive. We continue the sweep until only one active bin remains. Since we start with $O(B)$ bins and eliminate two bins every time a new bin is created, we in total create $O(B)$ bins. Since they contain $O(B \log_B N)$ points each, we use $O((B^2/B) \log_B N) = O(B \log_B N)$ space.

A bin of U_v is uniquely defined by its x-range and active y-range, which in turn is defined by four points in the bin. Since U_v contains $O(B)$ bins, the x-range and active y-range of all the bins can be stored in a constant number of *catalog* blocks. When working on U_v we assume that these blocks are in memory. (In the RPS-tree the blocks could for example be stored in the tuple in P encoding v). In order to store U_v in the U relation, we assign each bin of U_v a unique id; a bin with id i containing points $p_1, p_2 \ldots, p_{B \log_B N}$ sorted by x-coordinates is stored as the tuple $(v, i, p_1, p_2, \ldots, p_{B \log_B N})$ in U. The relation U is indexed by (v, i) such that all the points in a given bin of a given U_v can be inserted or extracted in $O(\log_B N + (B \log_B N)/B) = O(\log_B N)$ I/Os.

Given $O(B^2 \log_B N)$ points sorted by x-coordinates we can construct U_v on these points in $O(B \log_B N)$ I/Os: To identify the $O(B \log_B N)$ points in each of the $O(B)$ bins of U_v in $O(B \log_B N)$ I/Os, we implement the sweep as follows. When we create a bin (make it active), we determine the y-coordinate at which fewer than $\frac{1}{2} B \log_B N$ of its points will be above the sweep line. We insert that y-value into a priority queue (implemented using a B-tree). We use the priority queue to find the next possible y-value where bins may need to be coalesced. The total number of calls to the priority queue is $O(B)$, for a total of $O(B \log_B N)$ I/Os. Thus only $O(B \log_B N)$ I/Os are required to construct U_v. Details will appear in the full version of this paper. Finally, after constructing the $O(B)$ bins we can insert them (the points) in U in $O(B \log_B N)$ I/Os.

4.2 Operations

To answer a 3-sided query $q = (a, b, c)$ on U_v, we consider bins whose active y-interval include c, that is, the bins that were active when the sweep line was at $y = c$. These bins contain all the relevant points. To answer the query, we identify the subset of these bins with x-ranges intersecting the interval $[a, b]$. These, say k, bins are consecutive in the linear ordering, and their id's can be identified using the catalog blocks without performing any I/Os. We answer the query by extracting the k bins from U using $O(k \cdot \log_B N)$ I/Os and reporting the relevant points. Note that we can easily report the points in sorted x-order. Two of the loaded bins, the ones containing a and b, may not contain any points at all that satisfy the query. However, since all the bins were active when the sweep-line was at $y = c$, at least half of the remaining bins must contain $\frac{1}{2} B \log_B N$ points that satisfy the query. Thus we have $T > (\lfloor (k-2)/2 \rfloor) \cdot (\frac{1}{2} B \log_B N)$ and therefore a query is answered in $O(k \cdot \log_B N) = O(\log_B N + T/B)$ I/Os.

A point can easily be inserted into or deleted from U_v in $O(\log_B N)$ I/Os amortized using global rebuilding [18]; we simply maintain an extra update bin corresponding to U_v. To perform an update we insert the point to be inserted or deleted in this bin in $O(\log_B N)$ I/Os. Once the bin contains $B \log_B N$ points we construct a new version of U_v out of the points in the old U_v, updated with the points in the update bin. To do so we use $O(B \log_B N)$ I/Os, or $O(1)$ I/Os per update, as discussed above. Note that the $O(B \log_B N)$ construction algorithm requires the points to be given in sorted order by x-coordinates. Such a sorted sequence can easily be obtained in $O(B \log_B N)$ I/Os if we keep the update bin sorted by x-coordinates; the sequence can then be obtained simply by "merging" the points in the update bin with the sorted sequence of point in the old structure, obtained by loading the $O(B)$ bins that were active when the sweep-line was at $-\infty$. When performing a query we of course also need to perform the relevant updates on the output of a query on U_v before reporting the points. Since both the query output and the update bin are sorted, we can easily do so in $O(\log_B N + T/B)$ I/Os. Details will appear in the full paper, where we also discuss how standard techniques can be used to make the update bound worst case.

Lemma 1. *A set of $K \leq B^2 \log_B N$ points can be maintained in a relational structure of size $O(K/B)$, such that a 3-sided range query can be answered in $O(\log_B N + T/B)$ I/Os and such that an update can be performed in $O(\log_B N)$ I/Os.*

5   Interval Relationship Queries

As mentioned, the RI-tree can be used to find not only all intervals containing a query point but all intervals intersecting a query interval. Often we are interested in asking more detailed interval queries, like for example finding all intervals completely containing a query interval. Allen [2] discussed how there in general are 13 interval relationships from which more complicated relationships can be derived. Kriegel et al. [15] showed how the RI-tree can be used to answer 6 of these queries—*meets, finishedBy, starts, startedBy, finishes,* and *metBy*—efficiently in $O(h \log_B N + T/B)$ I/Os, and one other query—*equals*—optimally in $O(\log_B N + T/B)$ I/Os. They also discussed how four of the remaining 6 queries—*overlaps, overlappedBy, contains,* and *containedBy*—can be answered in $O(h \log_B N + T/B + F/B)$ I/O, where F is the number of intervals stored at a particular node in the RI-tree (the so-called *fork node* where the query paths to the two endpoints of the query interval split). Unfortunately, F can be as large as N. They were only able to answer the remaining two queries—*before* and *after*—in $O(N/B)$ I/O in the worst case. Therefore heuristics for improving their average-case behavior are also discussed in [15].

Using our RPS-tree we are able to answer all 13 relationship queries efficiently in $O(\log_B^2 N + T/B)$ I/Os (or $O(h \log_B N + T/B)$ if using the simplified version of the structure described in the next section): One query—*equals*—can easily be answered efficiently using a B-tree, and the remaining 12 queries can be transformed into 3-sided range queries. As an example, consider the *Contains* query asking for all intervals completely containing the query interval. Since a *Contains* query (x, y) ask for all intervals $[x', y']$ such that $x' < x$ and $y' > y$, we can answer the query simply by transforming an interval $[x', y']$ into the point (x', y') above the line $y = x$ and answer the 3-sided query $(-\infty, x, y)$. The remaining queries can be answered in a similar easy way; refer to Figure 4 for the complete set of transformations.

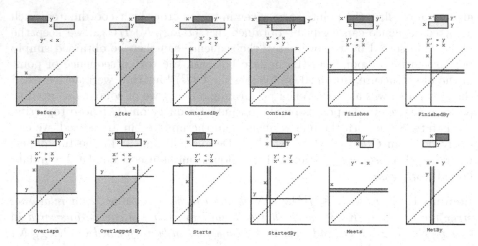

Fig. 4. Transforming interval relationship queries into 3-sided (2-sided) range queries. An interval $[x', y']$ is represented as the point (x', y') above the diagonal line, and the gray regions represent the regions containing the reported points/intervals

6   Simplified Relational Priority Search Tree (SRPS-Tree)

In this section we discuss how the RPS-tree can be considerably simplified using two ideas also utilized in the RI-tree; decreasing the fanout from B to 2, which eliminates the need for secondary structures containing $O(B^2 \log_B N)$ points, and avoiding materializing the base tree, which eliminates the need for base tree rebalancing.

6.1   Structure

As the RPS-tree, the SRPS-tree conceptually consists of a binary base tree on the x-coordinates of the N points, with the actual points stored in secondary structures associated with the internal nodes. Like the RI-tree, the base tree is not materialized. Recall that if the interval endpoints are in the range $[1, 2^h - 1]$, the root of an RI-tree contains the x-coordinate 2^{h-1} and the other nodes in the tree are obtained by bisection. A new root is created if an interval with an endpoint larger than 2^{h-1} is inserted. In our SRPS-tree, a similar addition of a new root would result in the need for a complicated rearrangement of secondary structures. We therefore modify this scheme slightly so that the tree grows at a leaf instead of at the root: If the x-coordinates of the points are in the range $[1, 2^h]$, the root contains $2^0 = 1$ and the l'th node on the rightmost path contains 2^l. Thus the rightmost leaf contains 2^h and the insertion of an x-coordinate larger than 2^h is handled by insertions of new nodes below this leaf. The left child of a node on the rightmost path containing 2^l now contains $2^l - 2^{l-2} = \frac{3}{4}2^l$, and the rest of the nodes in this subtree are obtained by bisection (such that the subtree contains nodes in the range $[2^{l-1}, 2^l]$). In other words, the rightmost paths contains powers of two and the rest of the tree is obtained precisely as in the RI-tree. As previously, a length h path in the tree can be "traversed" without performing I/Os at all.

The secondary structure associated with a node v in the SRPS-tree contains $2B \log_B N$ points: Like in the RPS-tree, the children of v define 2 (vs. B in the RPS-tree) slabs and the secondary structure contains the $B \log_B N$ points (that have not been stored in ancestors of v) with the highest y-coordinates from each of these slabs. However, unlike the RPS-tree, the secondary structure is just a list of points, making the structure extremely simple; the whole structure is stored in *one* relation R—a point (x, y) stored in the secondary structure of node v is stored as the tuple (v, x, y) in R and indexed similarly.

6.2   Operations

Conceptually, we answer a 3-sided query (a, b, c) on the SRPS-tree exactly like we did on the RPS-tree. We start at the root and proceed recursively to the appropriate subtrees. When visiting node v we simply query R to find all points stored in v, report the points satisfying the query, and advance the search to a child w if either a or b is stored below w or if all $B \log_B N$ points corresponding to w were reported. The correctness of this procedure follows exactly as in the RPS-tree case.

Since a query to find all points in R corresponding to v takes $O(\log_B N + (B \log_B N)/B) = O(\log_B N)$ I/Os, we can find all points in v satisfying the 3-sided query using a single query in $O(\log_B N)$ I/Os. As in the RPS-tree case, we can argue that we spend $O(\log_B N)$ I/Os in each node on the two length h paths to a and b, and that the $O(\log_B N)$ costs of each other visited node add up to $O(T/B)$ I/Os in total. Thus a query is answered in $O(h \cdot \log_B N + T/B)$ I/Os.

An insertion or deletion of a point can easily be performed in $O(h \cdot \log_B N)$ I/Os. To insert a point p we proceed down the tree, loading all points in each node using $O(\log_B N)$ I/Os, until we find the node v where p needs to be inserted. As previously, we may need to remove a point after this and insert it recursively below v (what we called a *bubble-down*). A deletion can be performed similarly using a *bubble up*. Note that compared to the RPS-tree, the update procedures are extremely simple since we do not have to worry about rebalancing the base tree.

7   Experimental Evaluation

While theoretical worst-case efficiency is the main focus of the work presented in this paper, we have also performed a limited experimental evaluation of the efficiency of the SRPS-tree. The SRPS-tree was implemented using PL/SQL stored procedures in Oracle 9i and compared with a PL/SQL implementation of the RI-tree (provided by Seidl). We used a 933 MHz Pentium III Xeon platform with 1GB of RAM and an Ultra-SCSI hard drive (running Microsoft Windows 2000). The block size and block cache was set at 2KB and 4MB, respectively, and the number of points associated with each internal node of the SRPS-tree was 100. Below we briefly describe the result of our experiments with both "real life" data and with data designed to illustrating some of the problems with the RI-tree.

7.1 Real-Life Data

To investigate the performance of the SRPS- and RI-trees on relatively uniformly distributed "real life" data, we experimented with a set of 5,745,866 intervals obtained from the x-projection of the two-dimensional road segments for the state of California (from the TIGER/Line data set from the US Bureau of the Census [19]). The intervals were normalized to have endpoints in the range $[0, 10272919]$ and their lengths were in the range $[0, 97671]$ (with average length 660 and standard deviation 34). We built an SRPS-tree and an RI-tree on this set using repeated insertion, where the intervals were inserted in the order they appeared in the TIGER data file. The height of the two trees was 21 and 23, respectively, and they contained 83507 and 477049 nodes, respectively. The first important thing to note is that the RI-tree used more than twice the amount of space of the SRPS-tree (847.1MB versus 312MB). This is an important advantage of the SRPS-tree over the RI-tree, and a result of each interval being represented twice in the RI-tree and only ones in the SRPS-tree. (The size of the RI-tree is not exactly twice the size of the SRPS-tree due to some—otherwise unimportant—implementation details).

We first performed stabbing queries with randomly selected points in the range $[0, 10272919]$; recall that both indexes answer such queries in $O(h \log_B N + T/B)$ I/Os (possibly for different values of h). In the first experiment (with 15 points) we manually flushed the block cache between each query, while in the second experiment (with 5000 points) the structures were allowed to take advantage of the 4MB cache. The average number of physical reads (I/Os) per query for these two experiments are reported in the first part of Table 1. While the RI-tree performance is relatively unaffected by the cache, caching significantly improves the performance of the SRPS-tree. Without caching a stabbing query on the SRPS-tree requires approximately twice as many I/Os as on the RI-tree, while the SRPS-tree requires fewer I/Os than the RI-tree when caching is used. The reason for the improved performance of the SRPS-tree can be explained by the way a query is performed. Recall that a stabbing query with a is equivalent to the 3-sided query $(0, a, a)$, and that when answering such a query the paths from the root to both 0 and a in the SRPS-tree are always traversed. In comparison, only the path to a is traversed in the RI-tree. When caching is utilized during a sequence of stabbing queries on a SRPS-tree, the path to 0 is always cached and the number of I/Os is thus significantly reduced.

Next we performed experiments with *Contains* interval queries. Recall that while such queries can be expressed as 3-sided queries and thus answered in $O(h \log_B N + T/B)$ I/Os by the SRPS-tree, heuristic algorithms are used on the

Table 1. The average number of physical reads per *stabbing* and *Contains* query

	Stabbing		*Contains*	
	RI-tree	SRPS-tree	RI-tree	SRPS-tree
With Cache Flushing	59.4	100.3	61	105.3
Without Cache Flushing	46.5	38.3	40.7	37.9

RI-tree in order to answer them in $O(h \log_B N + T/B + F/B)$ I/Os (here F is the number of interval stored in a certain node of the tree). We randomly selected intervals from the dataset itself and used them as query intervals in two sets of experiments—with and without block cache flushing. The average number of I/Os per query for these two experiments are reported in the second part of Table 1. The results are very similar to the stabbing query results; like stabbing queries, a *Contains* query corresponds to a 3-sided query with one of the x-endpoints being 0. Therefore the SRPS-tree benefits from caching. At the same time, the good RI-tree query performance is maintained since F was relatively small in most queries (and the heuristics performed well). This is a result of the data intervals being relatively small and uniformly distributed.

7.2   Worst-Case Data

To illustrate the RI-trees vulnerability to worst-case datasets (as well as the robustness of the SRPS-tree), we also experimented with a set of 2^{21} random intervals with midpoints and lengths uniformly distributed over the range $[2^{20}, 2^{21}]$. As in the previous experiment, we performed *Contains* queries with randomly selected intervals and repeated the experiment with and without flushing of the block cache. For the RI-tree all intervals were stored in only two nodes, leading to a large value of F in the query I/O-bound and thus a relatively inefficient query performance. For the SRPS-tree on the other hand, the efficient query performance was maintained. Since the size of the query result (query selectivity) influences both the RI-tree and SRPS-tree performance (the T/B-term in their query bound), the query I/O-cost is shown as a function of query selectivity in Figure 5. Note the efficient and predictable performance of the SRPS-tree, while the performance of the RI-tree is highly unpredictable. Note also that (as expected) caching is less important for the SRPS-tree for higher selectivities (since a large number of nodes other than the ones on the paths to 0 and a are visited during a high selectivity query).

7.3   Summary

The main conclusion from our limited experimental study is that with block caching the performance of our SRPS-tree is similar to or better than that of the RI-tree, while at the same time requiring only half the space. Only a small block cache is needed, since it only needs to hold one path of the tree. Furthermore,

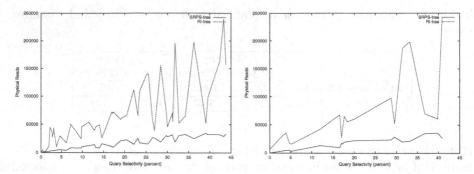

Fig. 5. Physical reads required to answer all *Contains* queries on randomly generated intervals without (left) and with (right) cache flushing (50 queries without flushing and 20 with flushing)

the performance of the SRPS-tree is predictable and good in the worst case, while the RI-tree performance can degenerate on data that are not "nicely" distributed. Note also that the SRPS-tree is relatively easy to implement, and that (unlike the RI-tree) all interval relationship queries can be handled with the same query procedure (a 3-sided queries).

Acknowledgment

We thank Thomas Seidl for helpful discussions and for providing the RI-tree code.

References

[1] A. Aggarwal and J. S. Vitter. The Input/Output complexity of sorting and related problems. *Communications of the ACM*, 31(9):1116–1127, 1988. 68

[2] J. Allen. Maintaining knowledge about temporal intervals. *Communications of the ACM*, 26(11):832–843, 1983. 68, 76

[3] L. Arge. External memory data structures. In J. Abello, P. M. Pardalos, and M. G. C. Resende, editors, *Handbook of Massive Data Sets*, pages 313–358. Kluwer Academic Publishers, 2002. 67

[4] L. Arge, V. Samoladas, and J. S. Vitter. On two-dimensional indexability and optimal range search indexing. In *Proc. ACM Symposium on Principles of Database Systems*, pages 346–357, 1999. 68, 72, 74

[5] L. Arge and J. S. Vitter. Optimal dynamic interval management in external memory. In *Proc. IEEE Symposium on Foundations of Computer Science*, pages 560–569, 1996. 68

[6] R. Bayer and E. McCreight. Organization and maintenance of large ordered indexes. *Acta Informatica*, 1:173–189, 1972. 68

[7] D. Comer. The ubiquitous B-tree. *ACM Computing Surveys*, 11(2):121–137, 1979. 68

[8] H. Edelsbrunner. A new approach to rectangle intersections, part I. *Int. J. Computer Mathematics*, 13:209–219, 1983. 68, 69, 70

[9] V. Gaede and O. Günther. Multidimensional access methods. *ACM Computing Surveys*, 30(2):170–231, 1998. 67

[10] P. C. Kanellakis, S. Ramaswamy, D. E. Vengroff, and J. S. Vitter. Indexing for data models with constraints and classes. *Journal of Computer and System Sciences*, 52(3):589–612, 1996. 66

[11] K. V. R. Kanth and A. K. Singh. Optimal dynamic range searching in non-replicating index structures. In *Proc. International Conference on Database Theory, LNCS 1540*, pages 257–276, 1999. 68

[12] D. E. Knuth. *Sorting and Searching*, volume 3 of *The Art of Computer Programming*. Addison-Wesley, Reading MA, second edition, 1998. 68

[13] H.-P. Kriegel, M. Pötke, and T. Seidl. Managing intervals efficiently in object-relational databases. In *Proc. International Conference on Very Large Databases*, pages 407–418, 2000. 66, 67, 68, 69, 70, 71

[14] H.-P. Kriegel, M. Pötke, and T. Seidl. Interval sequences: An object-relational approach to manage spatial data. In *Proc. International Symposium on Spatial and Temporal Databases*, pages 481–501, 2001. 67, 68

[15] H.-P. Kriegel, M. Pötke, and T. Seidl. Object-relational indexing for general interval relationships. In *Proc. International Symposium on Spatial and Temporal Databases*, pages 522–542, 2001. 67, 68, 76

[16] E. McCreight. Priority search trees. *SIAM Journal on Computing*, 14(2):257–276, 1985. 68

[17] J. Nievergelt and E. M. Reingold. Binary search tree of bounded balance. *SIAM Journal on Computing*, 2(1):33–43, 1973. 70

[18] M. H. Overmars. *The Design of Dynamic Data Structures*. Springer-Verlag, LNCS 156, 1983. 75

[19] *TIGER/Line*^{TM} *Files, 1997 Technical Documentation*. Washington, DC, September 1998. http://www.census.gov/geo/tiger/TIGER97D.pdf. 79

Efficient k-NN Search on Streaming Data Series

Xiaoyan Liu and Hakan Ferhatosmanoğlu

Ohio State University
Department of Computer and Information Science
{liuxia,hakan}@cis.ohio-state.edu

Abstract. Data streams are common in many recent applications, e.g. stock quotes, e-commerce data, system logs, network traffic management, etc. Compared with traditional databases, streaming databases pose new challenges for query processing due to the streaming nature of data which constantly changes over time. Index structures have been effectively employed in traditional databases to improve the query performance. Index building time is not of particular interest in static databases because it can easily be amortized with the performance gains in the query time. However, because of the dynamic nature, index building time in streaming databases should be negligibly small in order to be successfully used in continuous query processing. In this paper, we propose efficient index structures and algorithms for various models of k nearest neighbor (k-NN) queries on multiple data streams. We find scalar quantization as a natural choice for data streams and propose index structures, called VA-Stream and VA$^+$-Stream, which are built by dynamically quantizing the incoming dimensions. VA$^+$-Stream (and VA-Stream) can be used both as a dynamic summary of the database and as an index structure to facilitate efficient similarity query processing. The proposed techniques are update-efficient and dynamic adaptations of VA-file and VA$^+$-file, and are shown to achieve the same structures as their static versions. They can be generalized to handle aged queries, which are often used in trend-related analysis. A performance evaluation on VA-Stream and VA$^+$-Stream shows that the index building time is negligibly small while query time is significantly improved.

1   Introduction

Data streaming has recently attracted the attentions of several researchers [1, 6, 2, 8, 12, 4, 7]. Many emerging applications involve periodically querying a database of multiple data streams. Such kind of applications include online stock analysis, air traffic control, network traffic management, intrusion detection, earthquake prediction, etc. In many of these applications, data streams from various sources arrive at a central system. The central system should be able to discover some useful patterns based on the specifications provided by the user. Due to the streaming nature of the involved data, a query is continuously evaluated to find the most similar pattern whenever new data are coming. Immediate responses are desirable since these applications are usually time-critical and important decisions need to be made upon the query results. The dimensionality

T. Hadzilacos et al. (Eds.): SSTD 2003, LNCS 2750, pp. 83–101, 2003.
© Springer-Verlag Berlin Heidelberg 2003

of the data sets in these applications is dynamically changing over time when new dimensions are periodically appended.

There are many types of scenarios occurring in data stream applications. These scenarios can have either streaming or static queries, and the database either is fixed or consists of data streams. In prior related work [6, 8, 7], only the scenario with streaming queries and fixed time series database is discussed. However, in many important applications, the database itself is formed by streaming data too. For example, in stock market analysis, a database is usually formed by incrementally storing multiple data streams of stock prices. The users are often concerned with finding the nearest neighbors of a specific stock or all pairs of similar stocks. In this scenario, the streaming database is usually sized by a pre-defined window on the most recent dimensions, e.g. the last 30 days, or the last 24 hours, etc. The user-specified stock can be either taken from the streaming database or a fixed stock pattern. In order to be able to respond to the volatility of the stock market, the user requests need to be analyzed continuously whenever new stock prices arrive. In this paper, the scenarios with streaming database instead of fixed database will be studied in order to address these emerging needs. The queries are either fixed or streaming. Several techniques will be proposed respectively to increase the overall query response time for each scenario.

Data stream applications may involve predefined queries as well as ad hoc and online queries. Prior information on the predefined queries can be used to improve the performance. However, for efficient support of ad hoc and online queries it is necessary to build highly dynamic index structures on the data streams. Hence, we are motivated to propose techniques for both cases, i.e., predefined and online queries, in this paper. Since the dimensionality is changing for stream data, it will be beneficial to dynamically index such data to enable the support for efficient query processing. Although index structures in the literature are designed to handle inserting and deleting of new data objects, we are not aware of any mechanisms that handle dynamic dimensionality.

R-tree based index structures have shown to be useful in indexing multi-dimensional data sets [11, 3], but they are not suitable for indexing data streams since they are designed for the cases where the dimensionality is fixed. Based on this observation, we propose an index structure which can accommodate the changing dimensionality of data objects. Since scalar quantization is performed on each dimension independently, the access structure based on such an idea is a better choice for handling dynamic dimensionality. In this paper, we propose effective scalar quantization based indexing techniques for efficient similarity searching on multiple data streams. The proposed technique can be used both as an index and as a summary for the database, which can produce accurate answers to queries in an incremental way.

Our contributions are as follows: we first study the model for processing data streams, formulate several important data streaming scenarios. Both sliding window and infinite window cases are considered for the completeness. We then present an index structure to support efficient similarity search for multiple data streams. The proposed technique is dynamic, update-efficient, and scalable for high dimensions, which are crucial properties for an index to be useful for stream data. To the best of our knowledge, there has been no techniques for indexing data with dynamic dimensionality such as streams. Our method can also be generalized to support the aged query in trend-related analysis of streaming database. In the context of aged query, the users are more interested in the current data than in the past data, and bigger weights will be assigned to more recent dimensions of the data.

This paper consists of five sections. Section 2 describes a stream processing model and then gives a detailed formulation of three different but equally significant data streaming scenarios. In Section 3, a brief review of scalar quantization techniques VA-file and VA$^+$-file is given. We then motivate the need for an adapted version of VA-file and VA$^+$-file, which is specifically used to tackle the problem imposed by dynamic streaming data. At last, the proposed techniques, called VA-Stream and VA$^+$-Stream, are presented in this section. In Section 4, an extensive performance evaluation of proposed techniques is given which shows that significant improvements are achieved by the proposed technique. Finally, Section 5 concludes the paper with a discussion.

2   Streams and Queries

In this section, we start with introducing a general stream processing model, and then discuss several important scenarios in streaming database followed by precise definitions of their related queries.

2.1   Stream Processing Model

Figure 1 shows our general architecture for processing continuous queries over streaming database. The Real Time Stream Manager is responsible for updating the synopsis in real time and archiving the stream data. Whenever there are new data streaming in, the synopsis is changed correspondingly. When a query arrives at Query Processor, the processor will first look at the synopsis in main memory

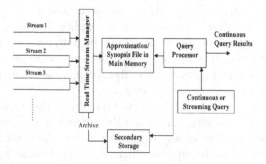

Fig. 1. Stream Processing Model

and eliminate as many disqualified candidates as possible from the whole pool
of data streams. The details regarding how the elimination procedure works will
be discussed in Section 3. After the elimination process, the possible candidates
have been narrowed down to a much smaller set. This set can be used to obtain approximate answers to the queries. For exact answers to the queries, the
processor can read each candidate from the archived data in the secondary storage. The key element in our processing model is Real Time Stream Manager.
It should be able to generate a synopsis which can be used to prune the data
efficiently, so that the secondary storage access time will be greatly minimized
if accurate answers are desired. Moreover, Real Time Stream Manager should
be able to sketch the incoming data streams in a prompt way. The proposed
indexing techniques in this paper will be shown to be capable of processing the
incoming data streams and generate the synopsis in an efficient way. Hence it
can support the implementation of Real Time Stream Manager.

We also look at continuous or streaming queries with either a sliding window
or an infinite window. For queries with a fixed-size sliding window, the size of the
synopsis stays the same, and the accuracy of this synopsis does not suffer from
the evolving dimensionality. However, for queries with an infinite window, though
it can be solved in a way similar to those with fixed-size window, the accuracy
will get sacrificed if the size of synopsis stays the same. Hence, another approach
for queries with an infinite window would be based on an reasonable assumption
that the data streams are aging. That's actually what usually happens in real
world, where people put more emphasis on more recent activities. A discussion
of aged queries can be found in Section 3.4.

2.2   Queries

We define streaming database as a collection of multiple data streams, each of
which arrives sequentially and describes an underlying signal. For example, the
data feeds from a sensor network form a streaming database. Hence, theoretically
the amount of data stored, if stored at all, in a streaming database tends to be
infinite. In this paper, we are considering several important scenarios occurring
in streaming database. See Table 1 for notations and Table 2 for a classification
of these scenarios.

The first scenario occurs when streaming queries are issued to a streaming
database. For example, we have a streaming database containing stock quotes of
companies, which is updated daily, hourly, or even more frequently to include the
new quotes. In this case a query may be posed to find the most similar company
to a given company in terms of the stock price in last 2 months. We formally
define this scenario as QUERY 1, which is shown below.

QUERY 1: Given a streaming database D, let q be the streaming query object
at time position t, the nearest neighbor of q for the last T time period would be
r if $dis(q[t-T,t], r[t-T,t]) \leq dis(q[t-T,t], s[t-T,t])$, $\forall s$ in D.

The second scenario is similar to the first scenario, except in a more general
sense. In the first scenario, we are only interested in the past data sets which are

Table 1. Frequently used notations

Notation	Meaning
x, y	streaming data objects in database
$x[i, j]$	slices of x between time position i and j
$x[., i]$	slices of x up to time position i
q	query object
$len(q)$	the number of dimensions in the query, i.e. the length of q
$dis(x, y)$	the distance function between x and y
D	the streaming database
b	the total number of available bits
b_i	the number of bits assigned to dimension i
σ_i^2	the variance of the data
g_i	the weight of dimension i in an aged query

collected over a certain amount of time period. However, in the second scenario, we are interested in all of the data sets collected up to now. For example, we want to find the company most similar to a given one after considering all the history records of their stock prices. This scenario often occurs when a long-term plan or strategy is concerned, and it is formulated as QUERY 2.

QUERY 2: Given a streaming database D, let q be the streaming query at time position t, the nearest neighbor query of q would be r if $dis(q[., t], r[., t]) \leq dis(q[., t], s[., t])$, $\forall s\ in\ D$.

In the above two scenarios, the streaming query objects usually come from the streaming database. The third scenario occurs when queries are predefined over streaming databases. For example, we have an existing stock bull pattern, and a regular check against the streaming database would find us those companies whose stock price fluctuations match this pattern most. This is an interesting scenario, and we formally define it as QUERY 3.

QUERY 3: Given a streaming database D, let q be the predefined query object at time position t with a fixed length len(q), the nearest neighbor of q would be r if $dis(q, r[t - len(q), t]) \leq dis(q, s[t - len(q), t])$, $\forall s\ in\ D$.

QUERY 1 and QUERY 3 are sized by a sliding window, and QUERY 2 has an infinite window. Their definitions can be easily generalized for k nearest neighbor queries. All these discussed queries are usually characteristics of their continuity, which means the same query will be asked continuously against the database over a period of time and will be evaluated over and over again during that time period. For example, Traderbot [1, 17], a web-site which performs various queries on streaming stock price series, offers a variety of queries similar to the models discussed here.

In order to support these queries, efficient index structures are needed to accommodate the uniqueness of streaming databases, which have (1) high dimensionality (2) dynamically growing/changing dimensions (3) large amount of

Table 2. Summary of Queries in Streaming Database

Query Type	Query	Database
QUERY 1	Streaming data objects	Streaming database with a sliding window
QUERY 2	Streaming data objects	Streaming database with an infinite window
QUERY 3	Predefined data objects	Streaming database with a sliding window

data. In this paper, we propose scalar quantization based indexing technique as a natural choice for handling dimensionality changes. Since the scalar quantization is performed independently on each dimension, when a new dimension is added it can be quantized separately without making major changes to the overall structure. Quantization of data can also serve as the summary to answer queries approximately. Depending on the time and space constraints, scalar quantization-based summary of data can be effectively used as an approximation as well as an index for the actual data. The efficient scalar quantization-based solutions to QUERY 1 and QUERY 2 will be discussed in Section 3.3. For QUERY 3, it can be treated as a special case of QUERY 1 with queries fixed, hence no separate discussions will be made on it.

3   Scalar Quantization Technique

Scalar quantization technique is a way to quantize each dimension independently so that a summary of the database is efficiently captured. It also serves as an index structure for efficient point, range, and k nearest neighbor queries. By observing that there is no cross-interference among dimensions when applying scalar quantization techniques to the traditional databases, we are motivated to apply it to support the similarity search in streaming databases.

3.1   Indexing Based on Vector Approximation

We will first briefly review a scalar quantization technique used in traditional database, Vector-Approximation file (VA-file) [18].

Since conventional partitioning index methods, e.g. R-trees and their variants, suffer from dimensionality curse, VA-file was proposed as an approach to support efficient similarity search in high-dimensional spaces. The VA-file is actually a filter approach based on synopsis files. It divides the data space into 2^b rectangular cells where b is the total number of bits specified by the user [18]. Each dimension is allocated a number of bits, which are used to divide it into equally populated intervals on that dimension. Each cell has a bit representation of length b which approximates the data points that fall into this cell. The VA-file itself is simply an array of these bit vector approximations based on the quantization of the original feature vectors. Figure 2 shows an example of one VA-file for a two-dimensional space when $b = 3$. Nearest neighbor searching in a VA-file has two major phases [18]. In the first phase, the set of all vector approximations is

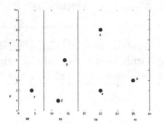

	Vector Data	Vector Approximation
1	(4,2)	00 0
2	(12,1)	01 0
3	(14,5)	01 1
4	(25,2)	10 0
5	(25,8)	10 1
6	(35,3)	11 1

Fig. 2. A two-dimensional example for VA-file

scanned sequentially and lower and upper bounds on the distance of each vector to the query vector are computed. The real distance can not be smaller than the distance between the query vector and the closest point on the corresponding cell. Therefore, the real distance can be lower-bounded by this smallest possible distance. Similarly, the distance of the furthest point in the cell with the query point determines the upper bound of the real distance. In this phase, if an approximation is encountered such that its lower bound exceeds the smallest upper bound found so far, the corresponding objects can be eliminated since at least one better candidate exists. At the end of the first phase, the vectors with the smallest bounds are found to be the *candidates* for the nearest neighbor of the query. In the second phase, the algorithm traverses the real feature vectors that correspond to the candidate set remaining after filtering. The feature vectors are visited in the order of their lower bounds and then exact distances to the query point are computed. One of the advantages of traversing the feature vectors in the order of their lower bounds to the query is that the algorithm can stop at a certain point and does not check the rest of the candidates. If a lower bound is reached that is greater than the k-th actual nearest neighbor distance seen so far, then the algorithm stops retrieving the rest of the candidates.

3.2   VA⁺-File Based Indexing for Non-uniform Data Sets

In the VA-file approach, although there is an option of non-uniform bit allocation among dimensions, no specific algorithm for that option was proposed in [18]. Moreover, each dimension i is divided into 2^{b_i} cells of either equal size, or equal population, which are the two simplest partitionings that only suits a uniformly distributed data set. VA⁺-file [5] is proposed to target non-uniform data sets, and can lead to more efficient searching.

A scalar quantizer [9] is a VA-file together with representative values assigned to each cell. The target is to achieve the least reproduction error, i.e., the least average Euclidean distance between data points and their representatives. The partitioning performed by the VA-file approach can be viewed as a scalar quantization, except that the approach does not care about the representative values for the cells. It is shown in [5] that a scalar quantization designed by directly aiming for the least possible reproduction error would result in much tighter lower and upper bounds for the distances between the query point and the data points. Since tighter lower bounds mean less number of vectors visited in the second phase of the VA-file algorithm, and tighter upper bounds mean better filtering of data in the first phase, VA$^+$-file uses the reproduction error as its minimization objective in order to increase its pruning ability. An approach for designing a scalar quantizer follows these steps:

1. The total available bits specified by the quota is allocated among the dimensions non-uniformly, based on one bit allocation algorithm, shown below as ALGORITHM 1.
2. An optimal scalar quantizer is then designed for each dimension independently, with the allocated number of bits. The Lloyd's algorithm [15, 13], is used here to quantize each dimension optimally. No assumption about data uniformity is needed for this algorithm and data statistics is used instead.

The goal in VA$^+$-file is to approximate a given data set with a minimum number of bits but maximum accuracy. Therefore, it is crucial in VA$^+$-file to analyze each dimension, rather than using the simple uniform bit allocation, so that the resulting accuracy obtained from the approximation can be maximized. Non-uniform bit allocation is an effective way to increase the accuracy of the approximations for any data set.

Let the variance of dimension i be σ_i^2, and the number of bits allocated to dimension i be b_i. Assume the quota is b bits, i.e, $b = \sum_i b_i$ always holds. In quantization theory, a well-known rule is: if for any two dimensions i and j, $\exists\ k \geq 0$, st. $\sigma_i^2 \geq 4^k \sigma_j^2$, then $b_i \geq b_j + k$ [9] and it is shown to be a good heuristic for allocating bits based on the significance of each dimension [5]. The significance of each dimension is decided by its variance.

ALGORITHM 1 Bit Allocation Algorithm for VA$^+$-file:

1. Begin with $d_i = \sigma_i^2$, $b_i = 0$ for all i, and $k = 0$.
2. Let $j = argmax_i d_i$. Then increment b_j and $d_j \leftarrow d_j/4$.
3. Increment k. If $k < b$, go to 2, else stop.

Once the number of bits assigned to each dimension is known, an actual scalar quantizer is designed based on Lloyd's algorithm. This algorithm produces a set of partition points or intervals along each dimension by minimizing the total representation error. It is actually a special case of a popular clustering algorithm, the so-called K-means algorithm in the clustering literature [16].

3.3   VA-Stream Technique for Indexing Streaming Database

Both VA-file and VA$^+$-file are targeted towards traditional database with fixed dimensionality. In order to handle dynamic streaming databases, the approaches should be customized for streaming databases. We call the customized approaches as VA-Stream and VA$^+$-Stream in this paper. Just as VA-file or VA$^+$-file can be viewed as a way to generate the synopsis or summarization of traditional databases, VA-Stream or VA$^+$-Stream is a way to generate dynamic synopsis or summarization for streaming databases with dynamic updates. The proposed approach is an incremental way to update the VA-file or VA$^+$-file to reflect the changes in the databases, and it can eliminate the need to rebuild the whole index structure from scratch. Hence it enables faster query response time.

With the use of scalar quantization techniques, if the data is indexed with a sliding window on recent dimensions, the previously quantized first dimension will be replaced by the quantized new dimension. This is the case for QUERY 1. It is a plain idea but it might get complicated with a need for bit reallocation and optimal quantization. The complexity of the bit reallocation algorithms for different query types depends on whether it is based on VA-file or VA$^+$-file. The bit allocation strategy in regular VA-file approach is quite simple, with the same number of bits equally assigned to each dimension. Hence, in this case the steps to restructure a new vector approximation file are relatively simpler too. The algorithm used to build a new VA-file in order to capture the up-to-date state of the streaming databases is called VA-Stream, and shown as ALGORITHM 2a.

ALGORITHM 2a VA-Stream:

1. Assume the window size for the database is k. Begin with the initial data set of k dimensions, build the original VA-file for this k-dimensional data set, where the total number of available bits b is equally assigned to each dimension. Hence, $b_i = \lfloor \frac{b}{k} \rfloor + 1$, $\forall i$ in $[1, mod(b, k)]$; and $b_i = \lfloor \frac{b}{k} \rfloor$, $\forall i$ in $(mod(b, k), k]$. When new dimension data is coming, let it be j and $j = k + 1$.
2. Let $b_j = b_{(j-k)}$ and $b_{(j-k)} = 0$. Compute the vector approximation for j^{th} dimension, and replace the data for $(j - k)^{th}$ dimension in the VA-file with the newly computed approximation.
3. If there is still new dimension coming, increment j and go to 2, else wait.

The above algorithm can be used to handle QUERY 1 which has a fixed-size sliding window for the data sets. VA-file is used as the index structure. The idea is simple by always keeping the same number of dimensions in VA-file with the new dimension replacing the oldest dimension. However, the power of VA-Stream is limited since it is suitable for data sets with uniform-like distribution. Hence, a more general scheme is needed in order to handle non-uniform data sets. For this purpose, VA$^+$-file can be used as the basis index structure. More complicated bit reallocation algorithm is needed due to the following facts: (1) VA$^+$-file allocates different number of bits to different dimensions in order to deal with the non-uniformity of the data set, and (2) VA$^+$-file quantizes each dimension independently with its assigned bits to achieve the least reproduction error.

For non-uniform data sets, when a new dimension comes, we first evaluate its significance. Thereafter, a *bit reallocation* scheme should be applied in order to justify the significance of each dimension. The number of bits allocated to each dimension is decided by its variance. The same quantization principle applies here : if $\sigma_i^2 \geq 4^k \sigma_j^2$, then $b_i \geq b_j + k$ [9]. The following ALGORITHM 2b illustrates the steps to build an up-to-date VA$^+$-file for streaming databases, and we call it VA$^+$-Stream. This algorithm assigns those extra bits contributed by the oldest dimension based on comparing the variance of new dimension with all other remaining dimensions. When no extra bit is left, this algorithm will continue to check if the new dimension deserves more bits. The detailed algorithm is shown below.

ALGORITHM 2b VA$^+$-Stream:

1. Assume the window size for the database is k. Begin with the initial data set of k dimensions, build the original VA$^+$-file for this k-dimensional data set, where the total number of available bits b is unevenly assigned to k dimensions based on the data distribution. When new dimension data is coming, let the new dimension be $j = k + 1$ and let $b_j = 0$ initially.

2. Let $t = j - k$ be the oldest dimension which we need to take out from VA$^+$-file. Now we have b_t bits available for reallocation. Let $\sigma_i'^2 = \frac{\sigma_i^2}{4^{b_i}}, \forall i$ in $[t, j]$, and it represents the current significance of dimension i after being assigned b_i bits. Let $s = \max_{n=t+1}^{n=j}(\sigma_n'^2)$, then $b_s = b_s + 1$, $\sigma_s'^2 = \frac{\sigma_s'^2}{4}$, and $b_t = b_t - 1$. Repeat this procedure, until $b_t = 0$.

3. When $b_t = 0$, if $\sigma_j'^2 > 4\min_{n=t+1}^{n=j-1}\sigma_n'^2$, more bits need to be extracted from other dimensions for use by dimension j. Let $b_j = b_j + 1$, and $b_s = b_s - 1$, where $s = \min^{-1}{}_{n=t+1}^{n=j-1}\sigma_n'^2$ (min^{-1} returns the index of the minimum). Also $\sigma_j'^2 = \frac{\sigma_j'^2}{4}$, and $\sigma_s'^2 = 4\sigma_s'^2$. Repeat this procedure, until $\sigma_j'^2 \leq 4\min_{n=t+1}^{n=j-1}\sigma_n'^2$. When $\sigma_j'^2 \leq 4\min_{n=t+1}^{n=j-1}\sigma_n'^2$, go to step 4 directly.

4. If $b_j > 0$, quantize the jth dimension based on the number of bits assigned to it, b_j, using Lloyd's algorithm.

5. Check if there are any other dimensions whose bits assignments have been changed during the step 2 and step 3. Re-quantize each of those affected dimensions independently using Lloyd's algorithm.

6. If there is still new dimension coming, increment j and go back to step 2, else wait.

ALGORITHM 2c is a different way to implement the idea of VA$^|$-Stream. It starts with a different perspective by comparing the variance of the oldest dimension with the newest dimension. It is based on the observation that if the variance of the newest dimension is larger than the oldest dimension, it will at least deserve the same number of bits as the oldest dimension. For the details, please refer to [14].

Lemma 1 For any two dimensions s and t represented in VA$^+$-stream or VA$^+$-file, $4\sigma_s'^2 > \sigma_t'^2$.

Proof. By contradiction. If there exists s and t, s.t. $\sigma_s'^2 < \sigma_t'^2$ and also $4\sigma_s'^2 < \sigma_t'^2$, this implies that s should not get its last bit in its last assignment. That will make t deserve that bit. This is contradictory to the current bit assignment. $\square$

Lemma 2 The VA$^+$-file built by ALGORITHM 2b incrementally to reflect the impact of new dimension is the same as the VA$^+$-file built from the scratch for streaming database with new dimensions coming.

Proof. Assume at the beginning, we have a data set of n dimensions, and a VA$^+$-file is built for this n-dimensional data set. Then according to the algorithm for building VA$^+$-file, there must exist a sequence $(1,2,...,n)$, s.t. $b_1 \geq b_2 \geq ... \geq b_n$ and $\sigma_1^2 \geq \sigma_2^2 ... \geq \sigma_n^2$. Here b_i is the number of bits assigned to dimension with sequence index i, σ_i^2 is the variance of each dimensional data. Let $d_i = \frac{\sigma_i{}^2}{4^{b_i}}$. Let s_i denote the index of the ith dimension in the sequence.

Now assume the $(n+1)^{th}$ new dimension comes. Let its variance be σ_{n+1}^2. If we rebuild the whole VA$^+$-file from scratch, then will get a new sequence $(2,3,...,n+1)$, s.t. $b_2 \geq b_3 \geq ... \geq b_{n+1}$, s.t. $\sigma_2^2 \geq \sigma_3^2 ... \geq \sigma_{n+1}^2$. Since the variance of each of dimension is a constant once the data is fixed, the order for the dimensions from dimension 2 to dimension n should stay unchanged though the assigned number of bit might have been changed. Hence, for the new dimension $n+1$, it should only be inserted into a proper place, denoted by s_{n+1}, at the ordered sequence of the last $n-1$ dimensions. Let j be the sequence index of $(n+1)^{th}$ dimension. Hence $b_{s_{n+1}}$ should satisfy the following conditions $\sigma_{j-1} > \sigma_{s_{n+1}} > \sigma_{j+1}$.

If we use VA$^+$-Stream approach, the same sequence will be produced since it compares the variance of new dimension $n+1$ against those of other remaining dimensions until we find a proper bit assignment, say $b_{s_{n+1}}$, s.t. $b_2 \geq b_3 \geq .. \geq b_{j-1} \geq b_{s(n+1)} \geq b_{j+1} ... \geq b_{n+1}$ and $\sigma_1^2 \geq \sigma_2^2 ... \geq \sigma_{j-1}^2 \geq \sigma_{s_{n+1}}^2 \geq \sigma_{j+1}^2 ... \geq \sigma_n^2$.

Now we need to show the number of bits assigned to each dimension from both will be same. Since we already show there is one and only one order for all dimensions based on the variance of each dimension, $\sigma_1^2 \geq \sigma_2^2 ... \geq \sigma_n^2$, the number of assigned bits to each dimension b_i should make a sequence with the same order, $b_1 \geq b_2 \geq ... \geq b_n$. Now a unique order of all dimensions can be obtained based on the variance. Moreover, Lemma 1 shows that the current variance d_i between any two dimensions can not differ by a factor of more than four. Since $d_i = \frac{\sigma_i{}^2}{4^{b_i}}$, we will always assign the same number of bits to the dimension for a total of b bit quota for allocation. $\qquad\qquad\square$

ALGORITHM 2a, 2b and 2c are all used to deal with the streaming data sets with fixed-size sliding window, and suitable for QUERY 1 and QUERY 3. If there is an infinite window, i.e., all available dimensions are involved in queries, and the index size is kept the same, then some bits need to be extracted from those old dimensions for the new dimension. This is the case for QUERY 2. In this case a restructuring on all involved dimensions is needed. An efficient and effective bit reallocation algorithm should be investigated so that the restructuring work can be kept as least as possible while maximizing the accuracy. The following ALGORITHM 3 is the VA$^+$-Stream approach customized for dynamically building VA$^+$-file for processing QUERY 2.

ALGORITHM 3 VA$^+$-Stream:

1. Begin with the initial data set of k dimensions, build the original VA$^+$-file for this k-dimensional data set, where $b_i (1 \leq i \leq k)$ still represents the number of bits already assigned to the ith dimension, When new dimension data is coming, let it be $j = k+1$ and $b_j = 0$.
2. The following rules will apply.
   Case 1: ${\sigma_j'}^2 > 4\min_{n=1}^{n=j-1} {\sigma_n'}^2$

   Let $b_j = b_j + 1$, and $b_s = b_s - 1$ where $s = \min^{-1} {}_{n=1}^{n=j-1} {\sigma_n'}^2$. Also let ${\sigma_j'}^2 = \frac{{\sigma_j'}^2}{4}$, and ${\sigma_s'}^2 = 4{\sigma_s'}^2$. Go back to step 2.
   Case 2: ${\sigma_j'}^2 \leq 4\min_{n=1}^{n=j-1} {\sigma_n'}^2$
   In this case, it means the new jth dimension doesn't matter too much in answering the query while all dimensions are concerned. Let $b_j = 0$. Go to step 3.

3. If $b_j > 0$, quantize the jth dimension based on the number of bits assigned to it, b_j, using Lloyd's algorithm.
4. Check if there are any other dimensions whose bits assignments have been changed during the step 2. Re-quantize each of those affected dimensions independently using Lloyd's algorithm.
5. If there is still new dimension coming, increment j and go to step 2, else wait.

All of the algorithms shown in this section have the flexibility to accommodate new dimensions without the need to rebuild either the VA-file or the VA$^+$-file from scratch. By dynamically changing the VA-file or VA$^+$-file with only modifying a small portion of the index file, it can deliver much faster response to similarity queries.

3.4 Aging Data Stream

Another interesting query in streaming databases is the aged query [10]. For example, in the context of network traffic monitoring, a trend-related analysis is made over data streams to identify some kind of access pattern, more emphasis is usually put on the most recent traffic. It is quite reasonable to think the traffic in this week should be more important than the traffic in the last week since a trend analysis usually focus more on the current events. Let $..., d_{-3}, d_{-2}, d_{-1}, d_0$ be a stream of network traffic data, where d_0 means today's data, d_{-1} means yesterday's data, and so on. A λ-aging data stream will take the following form:

$$... + \lambda(1-\lambda)^3 d_{-3} + \lambda(1-\lambda)^2 d_{-2} + \lambda(1-\lambda)d_{-1} + \lambda d_0.$$

Hence in λ-aging data stream, the weight of the data is decreasing exponentially with time. There are also other types of aging streams, for example, linear aging stream, where the recent data contributes to the data stream with linearly more weight than the older data. In order for the proposed VA$^+$Stream to be able to work for the aging stream database, we need to make the following modifications regarding the heuristic rule for allocating bits. If a weight g_i is specified for dimension i, the following heuristic rule should be used: if for any two dimensions i and $j, \exists k \geq 0$, st. $\sigma_i^2 g_i \geq 4^k \sigma_j^2 g_j$, then $b_i \geq b_j + k$ [9]. The rest of the algorithms remain the same.

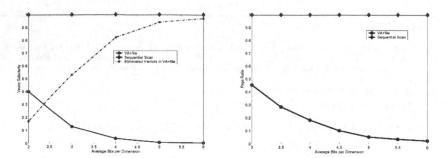

Fig. 3. Vector Selectivity (left) and Page Ratio (right) versus Number of Available Bits in *Stockdata*

4   Performance Evaluation

In this section, we evaluate the performance of the proposed techniques and compare them with other possible approaches. The design of our experiments aims to show the advantage of the proposed approaches in terms of both query response time and index building time.

4.1   Data Sets

For the purpose of performance evaluation, we used several real-life and semi-synthetic data sets from different application domains. We chose our real-life data sets to have high dimensions and streaming nature. The first data set, *Stock Time-series (Stockdata)*, is a time-series data set which contains 360-day stock price movements of 6,500 companies, i.e., 6,500 data points with dimensionality 360. The second data set *Highly Variant Stockdata (HighVariant)* is a semi-synthetic data set based on *Stockdata*, and is of size 6,500 with 360-dimensional vectors too. The generation of the second data set aims at obtaining a data set with high variance across dimensions. The third data set is *Satellite Image Data Set*, which has 270,000 60-dimensional vectors representing texture feature vectors of satellite images. In the context of streaming database, we adapt all the above data sets for our purpose by having the data pretend to come into database one dimension after another dimension. For example, in the case of *Stockdata*, each dimension corresponds to daily stock prices of all companies.

When not stated otherwise, VA+Stream in the following experimental study refers to the implementation version of ALGORITHM 2b and an average of 3 bits per dimension is used to generate the vector approximation file. When not stated otherwise, k is set to be 10 for k-NN queries through our whole experimental study.

4.2   Experiments on Query Performance

As Lemma 2 states that the vector approximation file built by ALGORITHM 2b is the same as the one built from scratch using VA$^+$-file approach, the first thing we want to show is that the generated vector approximation file can support efficient continuous queries in streaming database. We will show the advantage of our approach over sequential scan. The reason we chose the sequential scan as the yardstick here is because of the infeasibility of well-known techniques for stream data besides the well-known dimensionality curse, which make other choices like R-tree and its variants out of the question for efficient k nearest neighbor search.

A group of experiments was first set up to evaluate the performance of the vector approximation file generated by our approach for k-NN queries. Two metrics were used: *vector selectivity* and *page ratio*. Vector selectivity was used to measure how many vectors have been actually visited in order to find the k nearest neighbors of the query. Since vectors actually share pages, the vector selectivity does not exactly reflect the paging activity and query response time during the similarity search. Hence, page ratio was adopted to measure the number of pages visited as a percentage of the number of pages necessary for sequential scan algorithm.

In our experiment, vector selectivity was measured as a function of average number of bits per dimension, which actually reflects the quota for the total number of available bits b. Figure 3 (left) shows the results for 360-dimensional *Stockdata*. When the quota for bit allocation is increasing, the vector selectivity is quickly decreasing. The pruning rate during the first phase of similarity search is also shown as dotted line in this figure, and it is getting higher when the bit quota is increasing. For example, when the average number of bits per dimension is 4, the vector selectivity of the approximation file is only 8%. In contrast, the vector selectivity is always 100% for sequential scan since it needs to visit all the vectors in order to find the k nearest neighbors.

Page ratio was measured as a function of average number of bits per dimension too. Figure 3 (right) shows that the number of visited pages is decreasing quickly in vector approximation file when the number of available bits for allocation is increasing. When the average number of bits per dimension is 4.5, the number of visited pages in vector approximation file is only around 10% of that in sequential scan. Even when we consider the fact that sequential scan will not invoke any random access which might actually contribute to a factor of 5 for performance improvement [18], the vector approximation file approach still shows advantage.

To show the impact of window size and data size on the query performance, we also varied the window size in *Stockdata* and data size in *Satellite Image Data Set*. Figure 4 shows the results.

4.3   Experiments on Index Building

Previous section has demonstrated that the vector approximation file generated by the proposed approach can support efficient continuous queries in streaming database. We now want to show that the proposed approach can also support dynamic data streams in terms of building such a vector approximation file as an efficient index structure. A group of experiments was set up for this purpose. We

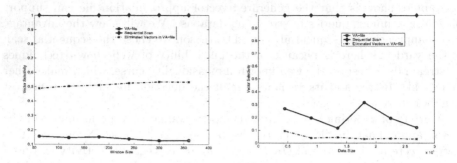

Fig. 4. Vector Selectivity versus Window Size in *Stockdata* (left) and Vector Selectivity versus Data Size in *Satellite Image Data Set*(right)

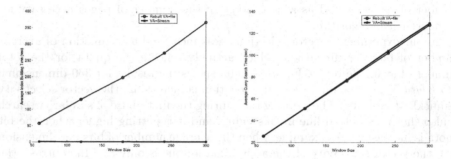

Fig. 5. Comparison of Index Building Time (left) and Query Response Time (right) between VA$^+$-file and VA$^+$-Stream for QUERY 1 (i.e. sliding windows) in *Stockdata*

compared the time of using VA$^+$-Stream to build an index structure incrementally against using VA$^+$-file technique to build an index structure from scratch. The reason we chose VA$^+$-file as the yardstick here is because of the following two reasons. First, both VA$^+$-file and VA$^+$-Stream can generate the vector approximation file which supports efficient k-NN search in high-dimensional space, while R-tree and its variants are suffering from the dimensionality curse and can not be used in streaming database. Secondly, to the best of our knowledge, there exists no specific techniques for targeting efficient k-NN search in streaming database, hence the possible approaches that can be used here for comparison purposes are just direct applications of existing efficient techniques for traditional high-dimensional databases to streaming databases.

The first group of experiments were set up for ALGORITHM 2b, which targets QUERY 1 with a fixed window size. To show the impact of window size on the performance of the approaches under test, the window sizes were chosen to be 60, 120, 180, 240, and 300 for *Stockdata* and *HighVariant*, respectively; the window sizes were set to be 30, 35, 40, 45, and 50 for *Satellite Image Data Set*.

The experiments were set up to process k-NN queries for the streaming database at any time positions after new dimension comes. The following two types of metrics were used here for performance evaluation: *average index building time* and *average query response time*.

In order to get the average index building time and query response time, for each different window size we processed 20 10-NN queries at each time position after the new dimension arrived. We recorded the index building time and the average query response time over 20 queries at each time position. For practical reasons, we actually sampled 10 continuous time positions for each different window size, and then computed the average index building time over 10 and the average query response time over 200 queries. Since for QUERY 1 and QUERY 2, the query points usually come from the database, the 20 10-NN queries issued at each time position in our experimental study were from the streaming data sets. These 20 queries were randomly chosen from the data set. For testing QUERY 1, *Stockdata*, *HighVariant* and *Satellite Image Data Set* are used. Since QUERY 3 can be treated as a special case of QUERY 1, no separate test was done for it. The algorithm to build the VA$^+$-file from scratch was used as one of the benchmarks with the same setup for the purpose of comparison.

At each sampled time position or dimension, we restructured the VA$^+$-file incrementally using ALGORITHM 2b. For a specific test instance of a certain window size, the total number of bits allocated to the feature vectors were always kept same. We also rebuilt a VA$^+$-file from scratch to make the comparison. The same k-NN search algorithm discussed before was used to search the result VA$^+$-file. As a result, the query response time only depended on the structure of VA$^+$-file. The search algorithm consists of a first-phase elimination, and a second-phase checkup. For all cases, the stated results are mean values.

Figure 5 (left) compares the index building time of two methods, for *Stockdata*. The index building time does not vary too much for VA$^+$-Stream technique, since it is an incremental method and works almost on only one dimension. But the index building time for completely rebuilding VA$^+$-file is skyrocketing with the window size increasing. This is because when we build a VA$^+$-file from scratch, the amount of efforts is proportional to the number of dimensions or the window size. When the window size is 300, VA$^+$Stream achieves a speedup of around 270. It is not surprising that Figure 5 (right) shows the average query response time of both methods is basically the same since the VA$^+$-files generated by them are actually the same. With the window size increasing, the query response time is getting longer. Similarly, Figure 6 shows the comparison of the index building time, for *HighVariant* and *Satellite Image Data Set*. For *HighVariant*, VA$^+$Stream achieves a speedup of 100 when the window size is 300. A speedup of around 28 is achieved when the window size is 50 for *Satellite Image Data Set*. It is also observed that the speedup of VA$^+$Stream is increasing with bigger window size for all three data sets.

We ran the test to compare the different implementations of VA$^+$-Stream. Figure 7 (left) shows the comparison of indexing building time of ALGORITHM 2b and ALGORITHM 2c for implementing VA+Stream. An experiment was also

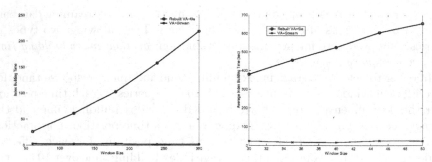

Fig. 6. Comparison of Index Building Time between VA$^+$-file and VA$^+$-Stream for QUERY 1 (i.e. sliding windows) in *High Variant* (left) and Satellite Image Data Set (right)

set up for testing ALGORITHM 3 over QUERY 2, which has an infinite window and needs to consider all the dimensions up to now. *Stockdata* was used here. For the purpose of testing the performance of algorithms, the experiment was set with an initial data set of 300 dimensions, i.e., we took the first 300 dimensions from *Stockdata* as our initial data set. Therefore each time new dimension comes, the proposed VA$^+$-Stream and the traditional VA$^+$ were run separately to build the index structure. Similarly, 20 10-NN queries were issued at each time position after new dimensions arrived. The index building time and the query response time were then recorded. Figure 7 (right) shows the comparison between VA$^+$-file and VA$^+$-Stream for processing QUERY 2. It is obvious there exists a huge difference between these two methods while the index building time is concerned. Especially, with the number of dimensions increasing in the data set, the index building time for traditional VA$^+$-files tends to increase a little bit, but the index building time for VA$^+$-Stream almost remains same since it is only dealing with one new dimension.

5   Conclusions

In this paper, we presented a scheme to efficiently build an index structure for streaming database, called VA-Stream and VA$^+$-Stream. We motivated the need for an effective index structure in streaming database. Our performance evaluation establishes that the proposed techniques can be in fact used to build the index structure for streaming database in a much shorter time than other available approaches, especially when the number of dimensions under consideration for building index structure is large.

To the best of our knowledge, the proposed technique is the first solution for building an index structure on multiple data streams. Our technique can work both as an update-efficient index and as a dynamic summary on stream data.

Although multi-dimensional index structure on multiple streams can significantly improve the performance of queries, dynamic nature of dimensions would

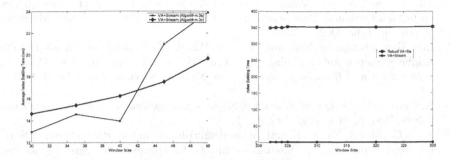

Fig. 7. Comparison of VA+Stream (ALGORITHM 2b) and VA+Stream (AL-GORITHM 2c) in Satellite Image Data Set (left) and Comparison of Index Building Time between VA$^+$-file and VA$^+$-Stream for QUERY 2 (i.e. no sliding window) in *Stockdata*

cause a significant restructuring on a tree-based index such as an R-tree. Neither an efficient method to restructure the tree nor whether the effort is worthwhile has been studied yet. The problem can be possibly attacked by a dual-based approach, e.g., a dual R-tree which is built on dimensions. Hence, when new dimension comes, we only need to consider an insertion problem instead of totally rebuilding the index tree. More investigation is needed to develop a more effective index for dynamic dimensionality.

References

[1] Brian Babcock, Shivnath Babu, Mayur Datar, Rajeev Motwani, and Jennifer Widom. Models and issues in data stream systems. In *Proceedings of the Twenty-First ACM SIGACT-SIGMOD-SIGART Symposium on Principles of Database Systems*, pages 1–16, Madison, Wisconsin, June 4–6 2002. 83, 87

[2] Shivnath Babu and Jennifer Widom. Continuous queries over data streams. *ACM SIGMOD Record*, 30:109–120, September 2001. 83

[3] N. Beckmann, H. Kriegel, R. Schneider, and B. Seeger. The R* tree: An efficient and robust access method for points and rectangles. In *Proc. ACM SIGMOD Int. Conf. on Management of Data*, pages 322–331, May 23-25 1990. 84

[4] Sirish Chandrasekaran and Michael J. Franklin. Streaming queries over streaming data. In *Proceedings of 28th VLDB Conference*, Hongkong, China, August 2002. 83

[5] H. Ferhatosmanoglu, E. Tuncel, D. Agrawal, and A. El Abbadi. Vector approximation based indexing for non-uniform high dimensional data sets. In *Proceedings of the 9th ACM Int. Conf. on Information and Knowledge Management*, pages 202–209, McLean, Virginia, November 2000. 89, 90

[6] Like Gao and X. Sean Wang. Continually evaluating similarity-based pattern queries on a streaming time series. In *Proc. ACM SIGMOD Int. Conf. on Management of Data*, Madison, Wisconsin, June 2002. 83, 84

[7] Like Gao and X. Sean Wang. Improving the performance of continuous queries on fast data streams: Time series case. In *SIGMOD/DMKD Workshop*, Madison, Wisconsin, June 2002. 83, 84

[8] Like Gao, Zhengrong Yao, and X. Sean Wang. Evaluating continuous nearest neighbor queries for streaming time series via pre-fetching. In *Proc. Conf. on Information and Knowledge Management*, McLean, Virginia, November 4-9 2002. 83, 84

[9] A. Gersho. *Vector Quantization and Signal Compression*. Kluwer Academic Publishers, Boston, MA, 1992. 89, 90, 91, 94

[10] Anna C. Gilbert, Yannis Kotidis, S. Muthukrishnan, and Martin J. Strauss. Surfing wavelets on streams: One-pass summaries for approximate aggregate queries. In *Proceedings of the 27th VLDB Conference*, Rome, Italy, September 2001. 94

[11] A. Guttman. R-trees: A dynamic index structure for spatial searching. In *Proc. ACM SIGMOD Int. Conf. on Management of Data*, pages 47–57, 1984. 84

[12] D.V. Kalashnikov, S. Prabhakar, W. G. Aref, and S. E. Hambrusch. Efficient evaluation of continuous range queries on moving objects. In *DEXA 2002, Proc. of the 13th International Conference and Workshop on Database and Expert Systems Applications*, Aix en Provence, France, September 2–6 2002. 83

[13] Y. Linde, A. Buzo, and R. M. Gray. An algorithm for vector quantizer design. *IEEE Transactions on Communications*, 28:84–95, January 1980. 90

[14] Xiaoyan Liu and H. Ferhatosmanoglu. Efficient k-nn search in streaming database. Technical Report OSU-CISRC-5/03-TR22, Dept. of Computer and Information Science, Ohio State University, 2003. 92

[15] S. P. Lloyd. Least squares quantization in pcm. *IEEE Transactions on Information Theory*, 28:127–135, March 1982. 90

[16] J. MacQueen. Some methods for classification and analysis of multivariate observations. In *Proceedings of the Fifth Berkeley Symposium on Math. Stat. and Prob*, volume 1, pages 281–196, 1967. 90

[17] Traderbot. http://www.traderbot.com. 87

[18] R. Weber, H.-J. Schek, and S. Blott. A quantitative analysis and performance study for similarity-search methods in high-dimensional spaces. In *Proceedings of the Int. Conf. on Very Large Data Bases*, pages 194–205, New York City, New York, August 1998. 88, 89, 96

On Query Processing and Optimality Using Spectral Locality-Preserving Mappings*

Mohamed F. Mokbel and Walid G. Aref

Department of Computer Sciences
Purdue University
{mokbel,aref}@cs.purdue.edu

Abstract. A locality-preserving mapping (LPM) from the multi-dimensional space into the one-dimensional space is beneficial for many applications (e.g., range queries, nearest-neighbor queries, clustering, and declustering) when multi-dimensional data is placed into one-dimensional storage (e.g., the disk). The idea behind a locality-preserving mapping is to map points that are nearby in the multi-dimensional space into points that are nearby in the one-dimensional space. For the past two decades, fractals (e.g., the Hilbert and Peano space-filling curves) have been considered the natural method for providing a locality-preserving mapping to support efficient answer for range queries and similarity search queries. In this paper, we go beyond the idea of fractals. Instead, we investigate a locality-preserving mapping algorithm (The Spectral LPM) that uses the spectrum of the multi-dimensional space. This paper provably demonstrates how Spectral LPM provides a globally optimal mapping from the multi-dimensional space to the one-dimensional space, and hence outperforms fractals. As an application, in the context of range queries and nearest-neighbor queries, empirical results of the performance of Spectral LPM validate our analysis in comparison with Peano, Hilbert, and Gray fractal mappings.

1 Introduction

An important consideration for multi-dimensional databases is how to place the multi-dimensional data into a one-dimensional storage media (e.g., the disk) such that the spatial properties of the multi-dimensional data are preserved. In general, there is no total ordering that fully preserves spatial locality. A mapping function f that maps the multi-dimensional space into the one-dimensional space provides a total ordering for the multi-dimensional data. A desirable property for the mapping function f is *locality-preservation*. Mapping data from the multi-dimensional space into the one-dimensional space is considered *locality-preserving* if the points that are nearby in the multi-dimensional space are nearby in the one-dimensional space.

Locality-preserving mappings from the multi-dimensional space into the one-dimensional space are used in many applications, for example:

---

* This work was supported in part by the National Science Foundation under Grants IIS-0093116, EIA-9972883, IIS-0209120, and by Purdue Research Foundation.

T. Hadzilacos et al. (Eds.): SSTD 2003, LNCS 2750, pp. 102–121, 2003.

- Range query processing [11, 14, 26, 37]: A locality-preserving mapping enhances the performance of multi-dimensional range queries. In a range query, it is preferable that the qualifying records be located in consecutive blocks rather than being randomly scattered in disk. A good locality-preserving mapping maps the records that lie in the query window in the multi-dimensional space into a consecutive set of blocks in disk.
- Nearest-neighbor finding and similarity search [14, 33, 44]: Multi-dimensional data is stored in disk using a locality-preserving mapping such that the nearest-neighbor for any point P can be retrieved by performing a sequential scan in the forward and backward directions from P. The quality of the locality-preserving mapping algorithms is determined by: (1) the amount of sequential data that needs to be accessed to find the nearest-neighbor and (2) the accuracy of the result.
- Spatial join of multi-dimensional data [38]: Multi-dimensional data is mapped into a one-dimensional domain using a locality-preserving mapping. The transformed data is stored in a one-dimensional data structure, e.g., the B^+-Tree [7], and a one-dimensional spatial join algorithm is applied.
- Spatial access methods [43]: Spatial objects located in disk storage are ordered according to the one-dimensional value of their central point, which is obtained from a locality-preserving mapping of the multi-dimensional space. This mapping minimizes the number of times a given page is retrieved from disk.
- R-Tree Packing [28]: The multi-dimensional central points of a set of rectangles are mapped into a one-dimensional domain using a locality-preserving mapping. Then, the rectangles are packed into the R-Tree [20] based on the one-dimensional value of their central points.
- Other uses of locality-preserving mappings include GIS Applications [5], declustering [12], multi-dimensional indexing [32], multimedia databases [35], disk scheduling [2], image processing [47], the traveling salesman problem [3], and bandwidth reduction for sampling signals [4].

These applications use space-filling curves (SFCs) [42], and fractals [34] to provide locality-preserving mappings. Examples of these curves are the Hilbert SFC [22], the Peano SFC [39], and the Gray SFC [10]. The Hilbert SFC is used for locality-preserving mapping in [13, 14, 26, 28, 32, 33, 43] while the Peano SFC is used for locality-preserving mapping in [5, 38, 47]. The Gray SFC is used for locality-preserving mapping in [10, 11].

In this paper, we go beyond the idea of using fractals as a means of a locality-preserving mapping. Instead, we develop a *Spectral Locality-Preserving Mapping* algorithm (Spectral LPM, for short) [36], that makes use of the spectrum of the multi-dimensional space. Although we focus on the effect of Spectral LPM in enhancing the performance of range queries and nearest-neighbor queries, we believe that Spectral LPM can efficiently replace any of the fractal locality-preserving mappings in the applications mentioned above. The contributions of this paper can be summarized as follows:

1. We argue against the use of fractals as a basis for locality-preserving mapping algorithms and give some examples and experimental evidence to show why the fractal-based algorithms produce a poor mapping (Section 2).
2. We introduce the Spectral LPM algorithm, an optimal locality-preserving mapping algorithm that depends on the spectral properties of the multi-dimensional points. As in the case of fractals, the Spectral LPM algorithm can be generalized easily to any multi-dimensional space (Section 3).
3. We define the notion of global optimality in locality-preserving mappings with respect to all multi-dimensional points, and prove that the Spectral LPM achieves this optimality (Section 4) while fractals do not. Also, we show that there are many cases that are infeasible to be mapped using fractals, while the same cases can be easily mapped optimally using Spectral LPM (Section 5).
4. As an application, in the context of range queries and nearest-neighbor queries, we provide empirical results of the performance of Spectral LPM using real data sets. The performance results validate our analysis in comparison with several fractal mappings. We demonstrate that Spectral LPM is superior to the fractal-based algorithms that have long been used for locality-preserving mappings (Section 6).

The rest of this paper is organized as follows: Section 2 provides the motivation for the spectral-based algorithm by showing the drawbacks of the fractal-based algorithms. Algorithm Spectral LPM is introduced in Section 3. Section 4 gives the proof of optimality of Spectral LPM. Section 5 demonstrates how Spectral LPM may incorporate additional requirements to the locality-preserving mapping. Experimental results comparing the performance of the spectral- and fractal-based mapping algorithms are presented in Section 6. Finally, Section 7 concludes the paper.

2   Locality-Preserving Mappings: The "Good", The "Bad", and The "Optimal"

In this section, we start by describing what properties an optimal locality-preserving mapping algorithm should have, and then discuss whether or not such a mapping is feasible. Next, we discuss the fractal locality-preserving mapping algorithms based on the Peano, Gray and Hilbert space-filling curves. We give examples that show why these algorithms produce a poor mapping. Finally, we discuss the idea of a spectral locality-preserving mapping that avoids the drawbacks of the fractal mapping.

2.1   The "Good" Mapping

An optimal locality-preserving mapping algorithm maps the multi-dimensional space into the one-dimensional space such that the distance between each pair of points in the multi-dimensional space is preserved in the one-dimensional space.

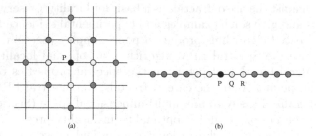

Fig. 1. The Optimal Locality-Preserving Mapping with respect to P

However, such a mapping is not feasible. For example, for any point P in the D-dimensional space, there are $2D$ neighboring points with Manhattan distance $M = 1$. Mapping P and its neighbors into the one-dimensional space allows only two neighbors to have $M = 1$. Thus, the distance between $2(D - 1)$ of the points cannot be preserved. The best we can do in this case is to divide the $2D$ neighbor points into two equal groups with D points in each group, and map the first group to the right of point P in the one-dimensional space, and the other D points to the left of P. The same argument is valid for points with Manhattan distance $M > 1$. The idea of such a mapping is that it guarantees that the points with Manhattan distance k from P in the multi-dimensional space will be nearer to P in the one dimensional space than the points with Manhattan distance $k + 1$.

Figure 1a gives an example of Point P in the two-dimensional space, where it has four neighbors with $M = 1$ (the white points) and eight neighbors with $M = 2$ (the gray points). Mapping P and its white neighbors into the one-dimensional space as in Figure 1b, results in only two points with $M = 1$ and another two points with $M = 2$. Mapping the eight gray neighbors results in placing four of them to the right of P and the other four to the left of P. Such a mapping is considered an optimal locality-preserving mapping with respect to P, since all the points that have $M = 1$ (the white points) in the two-dimensional space are nearer to P in the one-dimensional space than any of the points that have $M = 2$ (the gray points) in the two-dimensional space.

Although this locality-preserving mapping algorithm seems to be simple and optimal with respect to P, the mapping does not guarantee its optimality with respect to any other point. For example, consider the two white points Q, R that have $|P - Q| = 1$, $|P - R| = 2$ in the one-dimensional space as in Figure 1b. With respect to R, in the two-dimensional space, $|R - Q| = 2$ and $|R - P| = 1$. However, in the one-dimensional space, the situation is reversed where $|R - Q| = 1$ and $|R - P| = 2$. Thus, locality is not preserved from the two-dimensional space into the one-dimensional space with respect to R. This means that this mapping is not an optimal locality-preserving mapping for each individual point in the multi-dimensional space. In Section 4, we will define how a locality preserving mapping algorithm can be optimal with respect to all the points in the space.

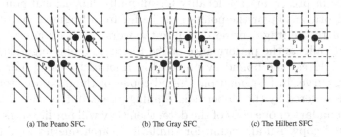

(a) The Peano SFC.   (b) The Gray SFC   (c) The Hilbert SFC

Fig. 2. The Fractal Locality-Preserving Mapping

2.2 The Fractal Mapping

For the past two decades, recursive space-filling curves, which are special cases of fractals [34], have been considered a natural method for locality-preserving mappings. Mandelbrot [34], the father of fractals, derived the term *fractal* from the Latin adjective *fractus*. The corresponding Latin verb *frangere* means "to break" or "to fragment". Thus, fractals divide the space into a number of fragments, visiting the fragments in a specific order. Once a fractal starts to visit points from a certain fragment, no other fragment is visited until the current one is completely exhausted. By dealing with one fragment at a time, fractal locality-preserving mapping algorithms perform a local optimization based on the current fragment.

Local optimization is the major drawback in fractal locality-preserving mapping algorithms. Consider the case of two points P_i and P_j that lie on the boundaries of two different fragments and $|P_i - P_j| = 1$. Although P_i and P_j are near to each other in the multi-dimensional space, they will be far from each other in the one-dimensional space because they lie in different fragments. Figure 2 gives an example of this boundary effect on three different fractal locality-preserving mapping algorithms, the Peano, Gray, and Hilbert space-filling curves. In each curve, the space is divided into four quadrants. Each quadrant is divided recursively into another four quadrants, as in the upper right quadrant. Notice that, in these fractals, a quadrant represents a fragment of the space. For points P_1 and P_2 in Figure 2, although $|P_1 - P_2| = 1$ in the two-dimensional space, the distance between P_1 and P_2 in the one-dimensional space will be 6, 5, 11 for the fractal mapping algorithms based on the Peano, Gray, and Hilbert space-filling curves, respectively. Things become even worse if we consider a finer resolution. For example, consider points P_3 and P_4 in Figure 2. $|P_3 - P_4| = 1$ in the two-dimensional space. The two points lie in two different quadrants and are far from each other in the one-dimensional space. The distance between P_3 and P_4 in the one-dimensional space will be 22, 47, 43 if we use the mapping algorithms based on the Peano, Gray, and Hilbert space-filling curves, respectively.

The boundary effect problem in fractal locality-preserving mapping algorithms is unavoidable, and results in non-deterministic results. Any application that uses a locality-preserving mapping algorithm would expect to have the same performance in preserving the locality for all multi-dimensional points. Fractal mapping algorithms favor the points that lie far from fragment borders. Points that lie near to the fragment borders fare the worst. In Section 6 we show how this property affects the performance of the fractal mapping algorithms.

[33, 44] address the boundary problem in fractals by using more than one space-filling curve. In [33], multiple shifted copies of the data are stored, where each copy is ordered by the Hilbert space-filling curve. In this case, if two points lie on the boundary of one copy of the data, then they will not lie on the boundary in the shifted copy. An algorithm for similarity search queries would search in all the shifted copies. A similar idea is proposed in [44], where multiple different space-filling curves are used for the same set of data. In this case, the set of candidate nearest neighbors is formed from the union of neighbors in accordance with the different space-filling curves. As can be observed, these are all heuristics for preserving the locality using fractals.

2.3   The Spectral Mapping

In this paper, we propose the use of the Spectral LPM, an optimal locality-preserving mapping with respect to all data points, to support multi-dimensional range queries and nearest-neighbor queries. The optimality proof is presented in Section 4. Spectral LPM avoids the drawbacks of the fractal algorithms by using a global optimization instead of a local one, where global optimization means that all multi-dimensional data points are taken into account when performing the mapping. Notice that the local optimization in fractals is achieved by considering only the points in the current fragment during the mapping process. Unlike fractals, Spectral LPM does not favor any set of points over the others; all points are treated in a similar way.

In general, spectral algorithms use the eigenvalues and eigenvectors of the matrix representation of a graph. Spectral algorithms are based on the spectral theory which relates a matrix to its eigenvalues and eigenvectors [46]. Spectral theory is attributed to David Hilbert, from a series of six papers collected and published as one volume in [23]. Although spectral algorithms are well known for

Table 1. Symbols used in the paper

P	A set of multi-dimensional points where $|P| = n$.
S	A linear order of all the points in P.
$G(V, E)$	A graph G with undirected edges E and vertices V, where $|V| = n$.
d_i	The degree of vertex $v_i \in V$.
$A(G)$	The *adjacency* matrix of G where $A(G)_{ii} = 0$, and $A(G)_{ij} = 1$ if the edge $(i, j) \in E$, o.w $A(G)_{ij} = 0$.
$D(G)$	The *diagonal* matrix of G where $D(G)_{ii} = d_i$, and $D(G)_{ij} = 0, \forall i \neq j$.
$L(G)$	The *Laplacian* matrix of G where $L(G)_{ii} = d_i$, and $L(G)_{ij} = -1$ if $(i, j) \in E$, o.w $L(G)_{ij} = 0$. For any graph G, $L(G) = D(G) - A(G)$.
λ_2	The second smallest eigenvalue for $L(G)$.
X_2	The eigenvector $(x_1, x_2, \cdots, x_n)$ that corresponds to the eigenvalue λ_2 (Also known as the Fiedler vector [16]).
e	The unary vector $(1, 1 \cdots, 1)$.

more than 90 years, their use in the computer science fields began in [9], where the eigenvectors of the adjacency matrix $A(G)$ of a graph G are used in graph partitioning. A milestone in spectral algorithms is due to Fiedler [15, 16] who proposed using the eigenvalues and eigenvectors of the *Laplacian* matrix $L(G)$ of a graph G instead of the adjacency matrix $A(G)$. Following Fiedler's work, all spectral algorithms turn out to use the *Laplacian* matrix $L(G)$. Spectral algorithms have been widely used in graph partitioning [40, 41], data clustering [29], linear labeling of a graph [27], and load balancing [21]. The optimality of the spectral order in many applications is discussed in [6, 19, 27, 29, 45]. To the authors' knowledge, the use of a spectral mapping in database systems to support range and similarity search queries is novel.

3   The Spectral Mapping Algorithm

For the remainder of this paper, we use the notations and definitions given in Table 1. Based on this notation, the pseudo code for the Spectral LPM algorithm is given in Figure 3.

Figure 4 gives an example of applying Spectral LPM to a set of two-dimensional points in a 3×3 grid. The main idea of Spectral LPM is to model the multi-dimensional points as a set of vertices V in an undirected, unweighted graph $G(V, E)$ with an edge $e \in E$ between two vertices if and only if the two vertices represent two points with Manhattan distance $M = 1$. Figure 4b gives the graph modeling of the multi-dimensional points in Figure 4a. Then, the *Laplacian* matrix is computed as in Figure 4c, where row i in $L(G)$ represents vertex $v_i \in V$. Note that the order used in numbering the vertices in G in Figure 4b is not important. Different orders result in different permutations of the rows in $L(G)$, which will yield the same result. The main step in Spectral LPM is to compute the second smallest eigenvalue λ_2, also known as the *alge-*

Algorithm Spectral LPM
   Input: *A set of multi-dimensional points P.*
   Output: *A linear order S of the set P.*

1. *Model the set of multi-dimensional points P as a graph $G(V, E)$ such that each point $P_i \in P$ is represented by a vertex $v_i \in V$, and there is an edge $(v_i, v_j) \in E$ if and only if $|P_i - P_j| = 1$.*
2. *Compute the graph Laplacian matrix $L(G) = D(G) - A(G)$.*
3. *Compute the second smallest eigenvalue λ_2 and its corresponding eigenvector X_2 of $L(G)$.*
4. *For each $i = 1 \to n$, assign the value x_i to v_i and hence to P_i*
5. *The linear order S of P is the order of the assigned values of P_i's.*
6. **return** *S.*
7. **End.**

Fig. 3. Pseudo code for the Spectral LPM

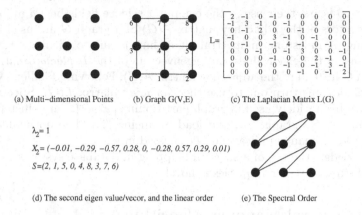

$$L = \begin{bmatrix} 2 & -1 & 0 & -1 & 0 & 0 & 0 & 0 & 0 \\ -1 & 3 & -1 & 0 & -1 & 0 & 0 & 0 & 0 \\ 0 & -1 & 2 & 0 & 0 & -1 & 0 & 0 & 0 \\ -1 & 0 & 0 & 3 & -1 & 0 & -1 & 0 & 0 \\ 0 & -1 & 0 & -1 & 4 & -1 & 0 & -1 & 0 \\ 0 & 0 & -1 & 0 & -1 & 3 & 0 & 0 & -1 \\ 0 & 0 & 0 & -1 & 0 & 0 & 2 & -1 & 0 \\ 0 & 0 & 0 & 0 & -1 & 0 & -1 & 3 & -1 \\ 0 & 0 & 0 & 0 & 0 & -1 & 0 & -1 & 2 \end{bmatrix}$$

(a) Multi–dimensional Points   (b) Graph G(V,E)   (c) The Laplacian Matrix L(G)

$\lambda_2 = 1$

$X_2 = (-0.01, -0.29, -0.57, 0.28, 0, -0.28, 0.57, 0.29, 0.01)$

$S = (2, 1, 5, 0, 4, 8, 3, 7, 6)$

(d) The second eigen value/vecor, and the linear order   (e) The Spectral Order

Fig. 4. The Spectral LPM algorithm

braic connectivity of the graph [15], and its corresponding eigenvector X_2, also known as the *characteristic valuation* of the graph [15] or Fiedler vector [16]. Figure 4d gives λ_2 and X_2 for $L(G)$ in Figure 4c. The eigenvalues and eigenvectors of a matrix can be determined by any of the well known general iterative methods, e.g., [8, 31]. More specific numerical methods to compute the Fiedler vector are proposed in [24, 30]. For a survey on iterative methods for computing eigenvalues, the reader is referred to [18]. Finally, the value $x_i \in X_2$ is assigned to each vertex $v_i \in V$ and point $p_i \in P$. The spectral order S is determined by ordering the vertices and hence the points according to their assigned values, as in Figures 4d and 4e.

4   The Optimality of the Spectral Mapping

An optimal mapping preserves the locality from the multi-dimensional space into the one-dimensional space. In Section 2, we showed how a mapping can be optimal with respect to a given point in the multi-dimensional space, and we called such mapping a *local* optimal mapping. We showed in Figure 1 that we can not have such *local* optimal mapping for each individual point in the multi-dimensional space. In this section, we show how a mapping can be considered *globally* optimal for all points in the space. Then, we prove that Spectral LPM achieves this optimality.

Definition 1. *A vector $X = (x_1, x_2, \ldots, x_n)$ that represents the n one-dimensional values of n multi-dimensional points represented as a graph $G(V, E)$ is considered to provide the globally optimal locality-preserving mapping from the* *multi-dimensional space into the one-dimensional space if X satisfies the following optimization problem:*

$$Minimize f = \sum_{(v_i,v_j)\in E} (x_i - x_j)^2 \quad S.t: \quad \sum_{i=1}^{i=n} x_i^2 = 1, \sum_{i=1}^{i=n} x_i = 0 \quad (1)$$

As in Figure 4, the locality-preserving mapping problem from the multi-dimensional space into the one-dimensional space is the same as the problem of embedding a graph G into a line L. A globally optimal mapping maps any two vertices $v_i, v_j \in V$ where $(v_i, v_j) \in E$ to the points x_i, x_j respectively such that $|x_i - x_j|$ is minimized. In other words, the points with Manhattan distance $M = 1$ in the multi-dimensional space are required to be near to each other in the one-dimensional space. By making this concept global over all the edges in the graph (recall that there is an edge in the graph between each pair of points with $M = 1$), we obtain the objective function: $Minimize f = \sum_{(v_i,v_j)\in E} |x_i - x_j|$. To avoid the absolute operation, we use the square for the difference between any two points. The objective function becomes $Minimize f = \sum_{(v_i,v_j)\in E} (x_i - x_j)^2$. However, the minimization problem is invariant under translation, yielding an infinite number of solutions for X. For example, the vectors X and $X + a$ give the same result for f. To force a unique solution to the optimization problem, we pick any valid solution $X^{'}$ and apply a transformation by $a = -Average(X^{'})$. Thus, the mapping vector X would be $X = X^{'} - Average(X^{'})$. The constraint $\sum_{i=1}^{i=n} x_i = 0$ forces a choice for X such that $\sum_{i=1}^{i=n} x_i = \sum_{i=1}^{i=n} x_i^{'} - \sum_{i=1}^{i=n} Average(X^{'}) = \sum_{i=1}^{i=n} x_i^{'} - n(\sum_{i=1}^{i=n} x_i^{'}/n) = 0$. Another problem for the objective function is the existence of a trivial solution where all x_i's are set to 0, and hence f will be 0. To find a non-trivial solution, we normalize X by dividing all x_i's by $\| x \| = \sqrt{x_1^2 + x_n^2 + \cdots + x_n^2}$. With this normalization, an additional constraint is added where $\sum_{i=1}^{i=n} x_i^2 = 1$.

Theorem 1. *The optimization problem in Definition 1 is equivalent to the following optimization problem:*

$$Minimize f = X^T L X \quad S.t: \quad X^T X = 1, X^T e = 0 \quad (2)$$

Proof. From the definition of the Laplacian matrix, we have $L(G) = D(G) - A(G)$. Therefore, the objective function can be rewritten as follows:

$$X^T L X = X^T D X - X^T A X \quad (3)$$

However, $X^T DX$ and $X^T AX$ can be rewritten in terms of x_i's as follows:

$$
X^T DX = X^T \begin{pmatrix} d_1 & 0 & \cdots & 0 \\ 0 & d_2 & \cdots & 0 \\ \vdots & \vdots & \ddots & \vdots \\ 0 & 0 & \cdots & d_n \end{pmatrix} \begin{pmatrix} x_1 \\ x_2 \\ \vdots \\ x_n \end{pmatrix} = \begin{pmatrix} x_1 & x_2 & \cdots & x_n \end{pmatrix} \begin{pmatrix} d_1 x_1 \\ d_2 x_2 \\ \vdots \\ d_n x_n \end{pmatrix} \tag{4}
$$

$$
= \sum_{i=1}^{n} d_i x_i^2 = \sum_{(v_i,v_j) \in E} (x_i^2 + x_j^2)
$$

and

$$
X^T AX = \begin{pmatrix} x_1 & x_2 & \cdots & x_n \end{pmatrix} \begin{pmatrix} \sum_{(v_1,v_j) \in E} x_j \\ \sum_{(v_2,v_j) \in E} x_j \\ \vdots \\ \sum_{(v_n,v_j) \in E} x_j \end{pmatrix} = \sum_{i=1}^{n} x_i \sum_{(v_i,v_j) \in E} x_j = 2 \sum_{(v_i,v_j) \in E} x_i x_j
$$

$$\tag{5}$$

substituting from 4, 5 into 3 results in:

$$
X^T LX = \sum_{(v_i,v_j) \in E} (x_i^2 + x_j^2) - 2 \sum_{(v_i,v_j) \in E} x_i x_j = \sum_{(v_i,v_j) \in E} (x_i - x_j)^2
$$

So, the objective function $f = \sum_{(v_i,v_j) \in E} (x_i - x_j)^2$ is equivalent to the objective function $f = X^T LX$. The two constraints $X^T X = 1$ and $X^T e = 1$ are just the vector form representation for the two constraints $\sum_{i=1}^{i=n} x_i^2 = 1$, $\sum_{i=1}^{i=n} x_i = 0$, respectively. Proving that these constraints are equivalent is trivial.

Theorem 2. *[15]: The solution of the optimization problem in Theorem 1 is the second smallest eigenvalue λ_2 and its corresponding eigenvector X_2.*

Proof. Given the first constraint, the objective function can be rewritten as $X^T LX = X^T X f = X^T f X \Rightarrow LX = f X$. Thus, X must be an eigenvector of L, with the corresponding eigenvalue f. Then, the solution of the optimization problem in Theorem 1 is the least non-trivial eigenvalue f, and its corresponding eigenvector X. Note that the eigenvector X is guaranteed to satisfy both constraints of the optimization problem with the transformation and normalization procedure discussed in Theorem 1. According to the Perron-Frobenius Theorem [17] , there is only **one maximum eigenvalue** for any non-negative irreducible[1] matrix M, which is $\rho(M)$ and is called the spectral radius of M. $\rho(M)$ is bounded by the minimum and maximum sum of all the rows in M. Applying this theorem on the non-negative irreducible matrix $M = (n-1)I - L(G)$,

---

[1] A matrix M is irreducible iff it represents a connected graph.

yields that $\rho(M) = n - 1$. Since, $\rho((n-1)I) = n - 1$, so $\rho(-L(G)) = 0$. This means that the matrix $L(G)$ has only **one minimum eigenvalue** with value 0, and therefore there is only one trivial eigenvalue for $L(G)$ [1]. This means that the first non-trivial eigenvalue for $L(G)$ is the second one. Thus, the minimization of $X^T L X$ is λ_2, the second smallest eigenvalue of L and its corresponding eigenvector X_2.

From Theorem 2, the eigenvector X_2 of the second smallest eigenvalue λ_2 (Step 3 in Spectral LPM) is the optimal solution of the optimization problems for Definition 1 and Theorem 1. Since the optimization problem in Definition 1 is modeled in the first step in Spectral LPM, then Spectral LPM guarantees the optimal result.

5   Extensibility of the Spectral Mapping

Additional requirements cannot be integrated in the fractal locality-preserving mapping algorithms. For example, assume that we need to map points in the multi-dimensional space into disk pages, and we know (from experience) that whenever point x in page P_x is accessed, there is a very high probability that point y in page P_y will be accessed soon afterwards. Assume that x and y lie very far from each other in the multi-dimensional space. A consistent mapping would result in pages P_x and P_y being far away from each other on disk. However, it is clear that we need to map x and y into nearby locations in the one-dimensional storage (disk), fractals cannot help with such an additional requirement (i.e., the requirement of taking the probability of access into consideration). Fractals deal only with the location of the multi-dimensional points in the space. In contrast, Spectral LPM provides an extensible environment that can incorporate any number of additional requirements. The flexibility of Spectral LPM comes from the degree of freedom it has in Step 1 of the Spectral LPM Algorithm, given in Figure 3. Step 1 is the graph modeling, where any requirement can be modeled as an edge in the graph G in Step 1 of Spectral LPM. Returning to the example of two disk pages P_x and P_y. To force mapping x and y into nearby locations in the one-dimensional space using Spectral LPM, we add an edge (x, y) to the graph G. By adding this edge, Spectral LPM learns that x and y need to be treated as if they have Manhattan distance $M = 1$ in the multi-dimensional space.

Another extensibility feature in Spectral LPM is that we can change the way we construct the graph G. For example, we can model the multi-dimensional points in a graph G such that there is an edge between any two points P_i and P_j if and only if the maximum distance over any dimension is one. In case of the two-dimensional space, this results in an eight-connectivity graph where each point P_i is connected to its eight neighbors (compare with the four-connectivity graph in Figure 4b). Figure 5 gives the modeling of two-dimensional points in a 4×4 grid with the resulting spectral order after applying Spectral LPM for four-connectivity (Figures 5a, 5b) and eight-connectivity graphs (Figures 5c, 5d).

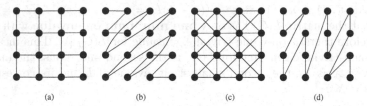

Fig. 5. Variation of the Spectral LPM algorithm. (a) Four-connectivity graph, (b) Its corresponding spectral order, (c) Eight-connectivity graph, (d) Its corresponding spectral order

More generally, points in the multi-dimensional space can be modeled as a weighted graph, where the weight w of an edge $e(v_1, v_2)$ represents the priority of mapping v_1 and v_2 to nearby locations in the one-dimensional space. In this case, the definition of $L(G)$ will be changed slightly to have $L(G)_{ii} = \sum_{(i,j) \in E} w_{ij}$, and $L(G)_{ij} = -w_{ij}$ if $(i,j) \in E$, o.w., $L(G)_{ij} = 0$. Also, the objective function of Definition 1 will be $f = \sum_{(v_i, v_j) \in E} w_{ij}(x_i - x_j)^2$. However, Theorems 1 and 2 will be the same.

Notice that the proof of optimality of Spectral LPM in Section 4 is valid regardless of the graph type. The idea of Spectral LPM is that it is optimal for the chosen graph type. For the rest of the paper, we choose to work with the four-connectivity graph in Figure 4b where it has a very sparse and symmetric matrix that results in efficient computation time.

6   Experimental Results

In this section, we give experimental evidence that Spectral LPM is superior to any of the fractal locality-preserving mapping algorithms. In the experiments, we focus on the effect of Spectral LPM on similarity search queries (e.g., nearest-neighbor queries) and range queries. However, due to its optimality, we believe that Spectral LPM will give similar superior performance when applied to other applications that require a locality-preserving mapping (e.g., the set of applications mentioned in Section 1).

We use the *Linear Span* for a given query selection (difference between the maximum and minimum linear coordinates in the selected region) as our measure of performance. The *Linear Span* measure is used in [26, 37, 38] to compare different fractal locality-preserving mappings. The lower the *Linear Span* of a given query, the better the locality-preserving mapping. The idea of the lower *Linear Span* is to have the ability to develop a single numeric index on a one-dimensional space for each point in a multi-dimensional space such that for any given object, the range of indices, from the smallest index to the largest, includes few points not in the object itself.

We evaluate Spectral LPM w.r.t. *Linear Span* by comparing Spectral LPM with three different fractal locality-preserving mapping algorithms based on the

Peano, Gray, and Hilbert space-filling curves. In addition, we consider a row-major method as a simple and straightforward solution for mapping the multi-dimensional space into the one-dimensional space. In the experiments, we refer to the row-major mapping by the Sweep space-filling curve (SFC) [35]. The motivation for choosing the Sweep SFC is that it provides another way of multi-dimensional mapping that is not based on fractals. A popular example that uses the Sweep SFC is storing the multi-dimensional matrices in memory.

For the implementation of Spectral LPM, we use the *conjugate gradient method* [30] to compute the Fiedler vector of $L(G)$. The *conjugate gradient method* is proved to have less iterations and efficient time processing over other algorithms. In addition, the conjugate gradient method directly gives the eigenvector associated with the second smallest eigenvalue (the Fiedler vector) without the need to compute any other eigenvectors. For the Hilbert SFC, we use the methodology in [4] to generate the Hilbert SFC for an arbitrary number of dimensions. The Peano and Gray SFCs can be easily implemented for the D-dimensional space as in [14]. The implementation of the Sweep SFC is straightforward.

We perform two sets of experiments; mesh-data and real-data experiments. In the mesh-data experiments, we assume that there exist a data point at every grid cell in the multi-dimensional space, and we exhaustively test all possible range and nearest-neighbor queries. In the real-data experiments, we use a real data set and generate a batch of range queries and nearest-neighbor queries. Both the mesh-data and real-data experiments show the superior performance of the Spectral LPM over any other locality-preserving mappings.

6.1   Range Query Performance Using Mesh-Data

In the first set of experiments, we run all possible four-dimensional range queries with sizes ranging from 2% to 64% of the multi-dimensional space. Figure 6a gives the maximum possible *Linear Span* of range queries. Spectral LPM outperforms all other locality-preserving mappings, while the Gray and Hilbert SFCs give the worst performance. For example, for a query that retrieves only 2% of the multi-dimensional space, in the worst case, the Gray and Hilbert SFCs can map this query to span 100% of the one-dimensional space. Although, the boundary effect in fractals is the main reason behind this bad performance, it does not have the same bad effect on the Peano SFC. The main reason is that the Gray and Hilbert SFCs visit the space fragments in the order imposed by the gray code while the Peano SFC visits the space fragments in the order imposed by the binary code. Spectral LPM has the smallest Linear Span. This demonstrates the notion of global optimality that Spectral LPM has. In other words, Spectral LPM optimizes over the entire space and treats the multi-dimensional space uniformly, and hence its worst-case Linear Span is much smaller than the other SFCs.

Figure 6b tests the stability of the locality-preserving mapping. A good locality-preserving mapping should provide the same performance for each query

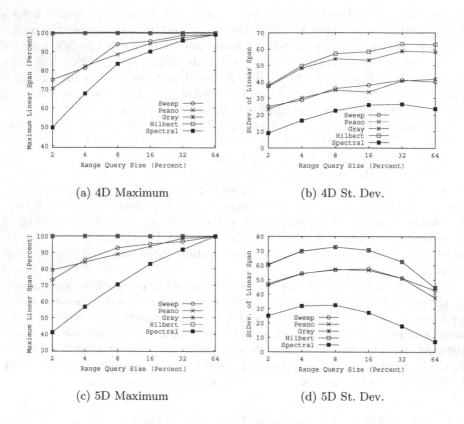

(a) 4D Maximum

(b) 4D St. Dev.

(c) 5D Maximum

(d) 5D St. Dev.

Fig. 6. The performance of range queries in 4D, 5D spaces

size, regardless of its location in the space. The standard deviation of the *Linear Span* is used as a measure of the stability of the locality-preserving mapping. Lower standard deviation indicates more stability. As expected (due to the boundary effect), the Gray and Hilbert SFCs gives the worst performance. Spectral LPM outperforms all other mappings for all range query sizes. The Peano and Sweep SFCs give an intermediate performance. Notice that although the Sweep SFC is not a fractal, it gives the same performance as the Peano fractal mapping. The main reason is that the Sweep SFC discriminates between the dimensions. For example, in the two-dimensional Sweep SFC, a range query that asks for all points with $y=1$ would result in an excellent performance, while the query that asks for all points with $x = 1$ would result in a very bad performance. For all cases, the Spectral LPM does not suffer from discriminating between dimensions, or boundary effect.

The same results are obtained when we perform the same experiments in the five-dimensional space. In general, the relative performance of the Spectral LPM over other mappings increases with the space dimensionality. Figures 6c,

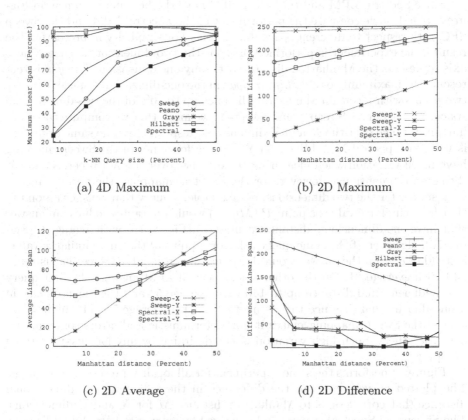

(a) 4D Maximum

(b) 2D Maximum

(c) 2D Average

(d) 2D Difference

Fig. 7. The performance of k-NN queries in 2D and 4D spaces using mesh data

and 6d give the maximum and standard deviation of the *Linear Span* in the five-dimensional space, respectively. Notice that the standard deviation of the *Linear Span* decreases with large query sizes for all locality-preserving mappings. This can be clarified if we consider the extreme case of a range query that covers 100% of the space. Clearly, there is only one range query with 100% space coverages. This results in zero standard deviation.

6.2   k-nearest-Neighbor Using Mesh-Data

Figure 7 gives the performance of k-nearest-neighbor (k-NN) queries. In the case of mesh data, we have data points in all space points. As a result, in the two-dimensional space, when setting $k = 4$, k-NN retrieves the four neighbors with Manhattan distance 1. Figures 7a gives the maximum *Linear Span* of all possible k-nearest-neighbor queries with query size up to 50% of the four-dimensional space. The spectral mapping gives much better performance than fractals with respect to the maximum linear span.

Since Spectral LPM and the Sweep SFC have the best performance, in Figures 7b and 7c we compare the performance of the Spectral LPM and the Sweep SFC with respect to different space dimensions. For simplicity in presenting the results, the experiment is performed only for the two-dimensional space. The x axis represents the Manhattan distance over only one dimension. The y axis represents the maximum possible *Linear Span* in the one-dimensional space for every two points with a certain Manhattan distance up to 50% of the two-dimensional space. By the curves Sweep-X and Sweep-Y, we mean that we compute the Manhattan distance over the X and Y dimensions, respectively. The same argument is valid for Spectral-X and Spectral-Y. The performance of the Sweep mapping have much variation when measuring the distance over the X (Sweep-X) and Y (Sweep-Y) dimensions. However, for the Spectral mapping, the performance is very similar for the two dimensions. For example, a query that asks for a point Q that have similar y value as point P ($M = 0$) would guarantee to have an answer that have one-dimensional distance at most 15 (Figure 7b) with average 6 (Figure 7c). However, if the same query asks for a point Q that has similar x value, instead of y, then the answer would have one-dimensional distance that is up to 240 with average 91. On the other side, Spectral LPM answers the first query in one-dimensional distance up to 146 with average 54 and the second query in a one-dimensional distance that is up to 173 with average 71. The high variation of the Sweep mapping makes it non-deterministic and favors some queries over the others. Such high variation is not desirable by any locality-preserving mapping.

Figure 7d performs the same experiment for all locality-preserving mappings. The plotted curves represent the difference in the maximum one-dimensional distance that corresponds to Manhattan distance M for X and Y dimensions. The Sweep and Spectral curves can be derived by getting the absolute difference $|SweepY - SweepX|$ and $|SpectralY - SpectralX|$ from Figure 7b, respectively. The Sweep mapping gives very bad performance. Spectral LPM almost gives an optimal result, where the difference is almost 0. Fractals, have a moderate performance that is not as good as Spectral LPM nor as bad as the Sweep mapping.

6.3   Performance Using Real-Data Sets

In this section, we use the North East data set that contains 123,593 postal addresses, which represent three metropolitan areas (New York, Philadelphia and Boston) [25]. The two-dimensional space is represented by a 128×128 grid. Each grid cell corresponds to a disk page. Data points are aligned to the nearest grid cell. Disk pages are stored in the order imposed by the underlying locality-preserving mapping. It is required that the locality-preserving mapping clusters the disk pages required to answer a specific query in a minimum *Linear Span*.

In the first experiment (refer to Figures 8a and 8b), we run 10,000 random range queries with sizes from 1% to 10% of the space. Figure 8a gives the average size of the *Linear Span* for each query size. Clearly, the Spectral LPM

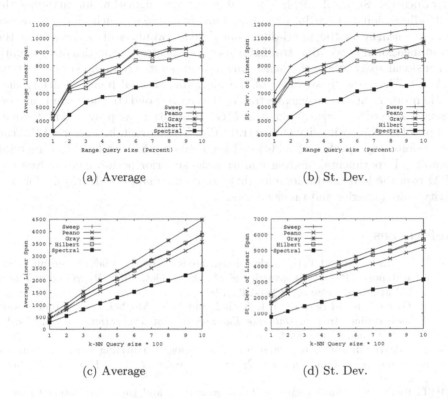

(a) Average

(b) St. Dev.

(c) Average

(d) St. Dev.

Fig. 8. The size of *Linear Span* of (a),(b) Range Queries, (c),(d) k NN Queries

outperforms all other mappings. As the query size increases, the relative performance of the Spectral LPM over other mappings increases. Figure 8b measures the stability of the locality-preserving mappings with regard to the location of the range query. The standard deviation of the *Linear Span* of range queries is used as an indication for the stability. The Spectral LPM outperforms all other mappings.

In the next experiment, (refer to Figures 8c and 8d), we run 10,000 random k-nearest-neighbor queries with k ranges from 100 to 1000. Figures 8c and 8d give the average and standard deviation of the *Linear Span*, respectively. Again, the results from the real data set agrees with the analytical results that the Spectral LPM outperforms all other locality-preserving mappings.

7   Conclusion

In this paper, we argue against the use of fractals as a basis for locality-preserving mapping algorithms by providing some examples and experimental evidence to show how fractal mapping algorithms produce a poor mapping. Then, we introduce the Spectral LPM; a provably optimal algorithm for mapping the multi-dimensional space into the one-dimensional space such that the points that are nearby in the multi-dimensional space would still be nearby in the one-dimensional space. Spectral LPM uses the spectral properties of the multi-dimensional space where the multi-dimensional points are mapped into a graph $G(V, E)$. Then, the linear order of the multi-dimensional points is determined by their order within the eigenvector X_2 that corresponds to the second smallest eigenvalue λ_2 of the *Laplacian* matrix $L(G)$. In addition, we provide a mathematical proof for the optimality of Spectral LPM. Unlike fractals, Spectral LPM can incorporate any number of additional requirements for the locality-preserving mapping. Experimental analysis confirms the superior performance of Spectral LPM over the long used fractal locality-preserving mapping algorithms for similarity search queries and range queries.

References

[1] W. N. Anderson and T. D. Morley. Eigenvalues of the laplacian of a graph. Technical Report TR-71-45, University of Maryland, Oct. 1971. Reprinted in Linear and Multilinear Algebra, 18:141-145, 1985. 112

[2] W. G. Aref, K. El-Bassyouni, I. Kamel, and M. F. Mokbel. Scalable qos-aware disk-scheduling. In *Intl. Database Engineering and Applications Symp., IDEAS*, Alberta, Canada, July 2002. 103

[3] J. J. Bartholdi and L. K. Platzman. An o(n log n) traveling salesman heuristic based on space filling curves. *Operation Research Letters*, 1(4):121–125, Sept. 1982. 103

[4] T. Bially. Space-filling curves: Their generation and their application to bandwidth reduction. *IEEE Transactions on Information Theory*, 15(6):658–664, Nov. 1969. 103, 114

[5] C. Bohm, G. Klump, and H.-P. Kriegel. xz-ordering: A space-filling curve for objects with spatial extension. In *Intl. Symp. on Advances in Spatial Databases, SSD*, pages 75–90, Hong Kong, July 1999. 103

[6] T. F. Chan, P. Ciarlet, and W. K. Szeto. On the optimality of the median cut spectral bisection graph partitioning method. *SIAM Journal on Scientific Computing*, 18(3):943–948, May 1997. 108

[7] D. Comer. The ubiquitous b-tree. *ACM Comp. Surveys*, 11(2):121–137, June 1979. 103

[8] E. Davidson. The iterative calculation of a few of the lowest eigenvalues and corresponding eigenvectors of large real-symmetric matrices. *Journal of Computational Physics*, 17:87–94, 1975. 109

[9] W. Donath and A. Hoffman. Algorithms for partitioning of graphs and computer logic based on eigenvectors of connection matrices. *IBM Technical Disclosure Bulletin*, 17:938–944, 1972. 108

[10] C. Faloutsos. Multiattribute hashing using gray codes. In *Intl. Conf. on Management of Data, SIGMOD*, pages 227–238, Washington D. C., May 1986. 103

[11] C. Faloutsos. Gray codes for partial match and range queries. *IEEE Transactions on Software Engineering, TSE*, 14(10):1381–1393, Oct. 1988. 103

[12] C. Faloutsos and P. Bhagwat. Declustering using fractals. In *Intl. Conf. on Parallel and Distributed Information Sys.*, pages 18–25, San Jose, CA, Jan. 1993. 103

[13] C. Faloutsos and Y. Rong. Dot: A spatial access method using fractals. In *Intl. Conf. on Data Engineering, ICDE*, pages 152–159, Japan, Apr. 1991. 103

[14] C. Faloutsos and S. Roseman. Fractals for secondary key retrieval. In *Symp. on Principles of Database Systems, PODS*, pages 247–252, Mar. 1989. 103, 114

[15] M. Fiedler. Algebraic connectivity of graphs. *Czechoslovak Math. Journal*, 23(98):298–305, 1973. 108, 109, 111

[16] M. Fiedler. A property of eigenvectors of nonnegative symmetric matrices and its application to graph theory. *Czechoslovak Math. Journal*, 25(100):619–633, 1975. 107, 108, 109

[17] F. G. Frobenius. Uber matrizen aus nicht negativen elementen. *Sitzungsberichte der Koniglich Preusischen Akademie der Wissenschaften zu Berlin*, 4:456–477, 1912. 111

[18] G. H. Golub and H. A. van der Vorst. Eigenvalue computation in the 20th century. *Jour. of Comp. and App. Math.*, 123(1-2):35–65, 2000. 109

[19] S. Guattery and G. L. Miller. On the quality of spectral separators. *SIAM Journal on Matrix Analalysis and Applications*, 19(3):701–719, July 1998. 108

[20] A. Guttman. R-trees: A dynamic index structure for spatial indexing. In *Intl. Conf. on Management of Data, SIGMOD*, pages 47–57, Boston, MA, June 1984. 103

[21] B. Hendrickson and R. Leland. Multidimensional spectral load balancing. In *SIAM Conf. on Parallel Processing*, pages 953–961, 1993. 108

[22] D. Hilbert. Ueber stetige abbildung einer linie auf ein flashenstuck. *Mathematishe Annalen*, pages 459–460, 1891. 103

[23] D. Hilbert. *Grundzuge einer allgemeinen Theorie der linearen Integralgleinhungen*. Teubner, Leipzig, 1912. 107

[24] M. Holzrichter and S. Oliveira. A graph based method for generating the fiedler vector of irregular problems. In *Parallel and Distributed Processing, LNCS*, volume 1586, pages 978–985. Springer Verlag, Apr. 1999. 109

[25] http://dias.cti.gr/ ytheod/research/datasets/spatial.html. 117

[26] H. V. Jagadish. Linear clustering of objects with multiple attributes. In *Intl. Conf. on Management of Data, SIGMOD*, pages 332–342, Atlantic City, NJ, June 1990. 103, 113

[27] M. Juvan and B. Mohar. Optimal linear labelings and eigenvalues of graphs. *Discrete Applied Mathematics*, 36:153–168, 1992. 108

[28] I. Kamel and C. Faloutsos. Hilbert r-tree: An improved r-tree using fractals. In *Intl. Conf. on Very Large Databases, VLDB*, pages 500–509, Chile, Sept. 1994. 103

[29] R. Kannan, S. Vempala, and A. Vetta. On clusterings - good, bad and spectral. In *Symp. on Foundations of Computer Science, FOCS*, pages 367–377, Redondo Beach, CA, Nov. 2000. 108

[30] N. P. Kruyt. A conjugate gradient method for the spectral partitioning of graphs. *Parallel Computing*, 22(11):1493–1502, Jan. 1997. 109, 114

[31] C. Lanczos. An iteration method for the solution of the eigenvalue problem of linear differential and integral operators. *Journal of Research of the National Bureau of Standards*, 45(4):255–282, 1950. 109

[32] J. K. Lawder and P. J. H. King. Querying multi-dimensional data indexed using the hilbert space filling curve. *SIGMOD Record*, 30(1), Mar. 2001. 103

[33] S. Liao, M. A. Lopez, and S. Leutenegger. High dimensional similarity search with space-filling curves. In *Intl. Conf. on Data Engineering, ICDE*, pages 615–622, Heidelberg, Germany, Apr. 2001. 103, 107

[34] B. B. Mandelbrot. *Fractal Geometry of Nature*. W. H. Freeman, New York, 1977. 103, 106

[35] M. F. Mokbel and W. G. Aref. Irregularity in multi-dimensional space-filling curves with applications in multimedia databases. In *Intl. Conf. on Information and Knowledge Managemen, CIKM*, Atlanta, GA, Nov. 2001. 103, 114

[36] M. F. Mokbel, W. G. Aref, and A. Grama. Spectral lpm: An optimal locality-preserving mapping using the spectral (not fractal) order. In *Intl. Conf. on Data Engineering, ICDE*, pages 699–701, Bangalore, India, Mar. 2003. 103

[37] B. Moon, H. Jagadish, C. Faloutsos, and J. Salz. Analysis of the clustering properties of hilbert space-filling curve. *IEEE Transactions on Knowledge and Data Engineering, TKDE*, 13(1):124–141, 2001. 103, 113

[38] J. A. Orenstein. Spatial query processing in an object-oriented database system. In *Intl. Conf. on Management of Data, SIGMOD*, pages 326–336, May 1986. 103, 113

[39] G. Peano. Sur une courbe qui remplit toute une air plaine. *Mathematishe Annalen*, 36:157–160, 1890. 103

[40] A. Pothen. Graph partitioning algorithms with applications to scientific computing. *Parallel Numerical Algorithms*, 4(8):888–905, Jan. 1997. 108

[41] D. Powers. Graph partitioning by eigenvectors. *Lin. Alg. Appl*, 101:121–133, 1988. 108

[42] H. Sagan. *Space Filling Curves*. Springer, Berlin, 1994. 103

[43] K. C. Sevcik and N. Koudas. Filter trees for managing spatial data over a range of size granularities. In *Intl. Conf. on Very Large Databases, VLDB*, pages 16–27, Bombay, India, Sept. 1996. 103

[44] J. Shepherd, X. Zhu, and N. Megiddo. A fast indexing method for multidimensional nearest neighbor search. *SPIE, Storage and Retrieval for Image and Video Databases*, 3656:350–355, 1998. 103, 107

[45] H. D. Simon and S.-H. Teng. How good is recursive bisection. *SIAM Journal on Scientific Computing*, 18(5):1436–1445, Sept. 1997. 108

[46] L. A. Steen. Highlights in the history of spectral theory. *American Math. Monthly*, 80(4):359–381, Apr. 1973. 107

[47] I. Witten and M. Neal. Using peano curves for bilevel display of continuous tone images. *IEEE Computer Graphics and Applications*, pages 47–52, 1982. 103

Categorical Range Queries in Large Databases

Alexandros Nanopoulos[1] and Panayiotis Bozanis[2]

[1] Dept. Informatics, Aristotle University
Thessaloniki, Greece
`alex@delab.csd.auth.gr`
[2] Dept. Computer Eng. and Telecom, University of Thessaly
Volos, Greece
`pbozanis@inf.uth.gr`

Abstract. In this paper, we introduce the categorical (a.k.a. chromatic) range queries (CRQs) in the context of large, disk-resident data sets, motivated by the fact that CRQs are conceptually simple and emerge often in DBMSs. On the basis of spatial data structures, and R-trees in particular, we propose a multi-tree index that follows the broad concept of augmenting nodes with additional information to accelerate queries. Augmentation is examined with respect to maximal/minimal points in subtrees, the properties of which are exploited by the proposed searching algorithm to effectively prune the search space. Detailed experimental results, with both real and synthetic data, illustrate the significant performance gains (up to an order of magnitude) due to the proposed method, compared to the regular range query (followed by the filtering w.r.t. categories) and to a naive R-tree augmentation method.

1 Introduction

Range queries, that find all tuples intersected (covered, etc.) by a query region, are commonplace in all kinds of database systems today. In a large number of applications, however, database objects can come aggregated in (disjoint) groups. Therefore, what becomes of interest is range queries searching for groups (instead of individual objects themselves) intersected by the query region. This type of query is denoted as *Categorical Range Query* (CRQ)[1] and the attribute that the grouping is based upon is called *categorical attribute*. CRQs have been comprehensively studied in the research fields of computational geometry and main-memory data structures [2, 9, 10, 11, 17, 18, 20, 23]. In contrast, much less attention has been given to supporting CRQs in large databases. Nevertheless, CRQs arise in many DBMSs. For instance: consider a set of locations, where each one is associated with its spatial coordinates and its soil type (a common case of thematic layers in GIS). A typical CRQ is to find all soil types of locations that are within a query window.

---

[1] Another common name is *Chromatic Range Query*, which corresponds to the same acronym.

T. Hadzilacos et al. (Eds.): SSTD 2003, LNCS 2750, pp. 122–139, 2003.

CRQs can be easily specified in any SQL-like language, including SQL extensions for spatial DBMSs. Nevertheless, the problem of query optimization for CRQs should be also taken into account. Despite their conceptual simplicity, CRQs present requirements for query optimization that are not addressed by current DBMSs. Considering the existing processing techniques, a CRQ will be processed by first executing the *regular range query*, i.e., the finding of individual objects (not categories) satisfying the range condition, followed by filtering its output set to select the distinct categories. The aforementioned approach does not take into account the difference between the selectivity (i.e., size of output set) of the CRQ and the one of the regular range query. In several real applications data tend to belong to categories and to be clustered along the categorical attributes. As a result, the selectivity of the CRQ can be much larger (i.e., smaller output size) than the one of the regular range query. By first processing the plain range query and then filtering with respect to the categorical attribute, a lot of cost is spent. Moreover, the domain size of the categorical attribute (i.e., the number of all its possible values) may be large enough, e.g., several hundreds or even thousands. This is prohibitive for a quick-fix solution that partitions objects based on their category (e.g., using independent indexes) and processes them separately.

The previously discussed issues have also been taken into account by approaches in computational geometry and main-memory data structures. Nevertheless, they have payed little attention to secondary memory, giving emphasis on worst-case asymptotic performance and requiring significant storage redundancy [19]. For large databases on secondary storage, high redundancy is prohibitive due to large space and update time overhead.

In this paper, we introduce the problem of categorical range queries in the context of large databases. Since CRQs find important applications in spatial data (e.g., GIS), we concentrate on this field, focusing, in such a way, on a concrete application framework. On the basis of spatial data structures, we develop a multi-tree index that integrates in an efficient way the spatial dimensions and the categorical attribute. This approach is based on the broad concept of the augmentation of nodes with additional information to accelerate queries [26]. The paper makes the following technical contributions:

- We develop novel techniques for spatial data structures and R-trees in particular (because they have been included in several commercial DBMSs [21]), which address the efficient query processing of CRQs in large databases.
- We provide a detailed experimental study, comparing the proposed method with two base-line algorithms: (i) the regular range query, and (ii) a naive method of incorporating the categorical attribute in the R-tree nodes. The results illustrate the significant gains (up to an order of magnitude) due to the proposed method.
- As another contribution, we discuss the issue of developing estimators for the selectivity of CRQs.

The rest of this paper is organized as follows. In Section 2 we give the related work. Section 3 describes the proposed approach, whereas Section 4 contains the experimental results. Finally, Section 5 presents the conclusions and directions of future work.

2   Related Work

Jarardan and Lopez [20] introduced this new type of problems that are of significant theoretical interest and rich in applications (e.g., document retrieval, internet packet categorization). Solutions for standard problems yield output-insensitive solutions for their generalized chromatic counterparts. For this reason they attracted a lot of research [2, 9, 10, 17, 18, 14, 23, 24]. These papers present a number of efficient, mainly theoretical, algorithms that are tailored to the main-memory context. Disk-resident data were considered in [15] for specific chromatic problems that are reductions of problems related to the indexing of 2-dimensional strings. However, [15] simply uses regular range queries, which are sufficient in their context, since the distribution of the resulting (transformed) data sets guarantee singleton categories with very high probability (greater than 0.9). As it will be described in the following, in the context of spatial data this assumption may not hold, and the regular range query can present significant limitations in several cases.

[17, 20] provided a uniform framework that yields efficient solutions for chromatic problems on iso-oriented objects. Their techniques consist of geometric transformations of generalized problems into equivalent instances of some standard problems and the use of persistence as a method for imposing range restrictions to static problems. New improved bounds, as also extensions to the non-iso-oriented geometrical objects case, were given in [9, 18, 11], whereas [10] treated the red-blue categorical reporting problem (we are given a set Q_1 of "red" categorical objects and a set Q_2 of "blue" ones and we want to report all intersecting pairs between "red" and "blue" objects). Recently, Agarwal et al. [2] presented solutions for chromatic objects with grid co-ordinates. [15, 24] considered the applications of colors in document retrieval and [14] studied the chromatic queries in the case of internet packet categorization. Also, approximate colored nearest neighbor search queries were studied in [23].

Finally, loosely related to this work can be regarded papers considering either the adaptation of main-memory data-structuring techniques to the disk (I/O) context (see, for example, [4, 5, 12, 16]) or following the node augmentation paradigm to solve geometric intersection query problems (e.g., [27, 29]).

3   Proposed Method

In this section, we describe our solution to the problem of processing CRQs in large databases. Since a number of commercial database systems have developed spatial extensions and R-tree indexes for the management of spatial data, the usefulness of any solution is increased if it is based on this infrastructure.

3.1   Maximal/Minimal Points

Assuming that the points of a data set are indexed with an R-tree, a straight-forward method to augment its nodes with information about categories is to store in the entries of intermediate nodes all categories that are present in the corresponding subtrees (using a bitmap, where each bit position corresponds to a category). Let q be a query rectangle. During a CRQ, we maintain an array A indicating the presence or absence of each category in rectangle q; initially, all categories are absent. Let also e be an entry in an intermediate node N. If q intersects e.MBR, then we find, through the bitmap of e, the categories that are present in the subtree of e. If the subtree contains any categories that are still absent from the result, then we descent to search in the subtree. Otherwise, we can prune the searching to this subtree. When reaching a leaf, we can determine the categories of its points that are covered by q, and, therefore, we can up-date A. Notice that analogous methods have been used in structures for regional data, e.g., quadtrees [22].

The aforementioned approach is simple and requires the addition of only one bitmap to each entry of intermediate nodes. It can avoid the searching to subtrees that are not going to contribute to the result, nevertheless it has the disadvantage that it can determine the actual existence of categories in the query rectangle only at the leaves. Due to this fact, one may not expect significant reductions in the I/O overhead, because the searching has to reach the leaf level many times. Also, the corresponding bitmaps will tend to be saturated and may indicate the presence of most of the categories. Henceforth, we denote the aforementioned approach as Naively Augmented R-tree (NAR).

To be able to determine the presence/absence of categories within the query rectangle at the upper levels as well, solutions in main-memory data structures and computational geometry are based on indexing schemes that, at each entry e of internal nodes, allow for the replication of all points stored at the subtree of e. Evidently, in the context of secondary storage and R-trees, such assumptions lead to prohibitive space and time overhead [19]. We, therefore, require a solution between these two extremes, i.e., the NAR approach, which does not store any points at internal nodes, and the aforementioned approaches which need to store all points of the subtrees. For this reason, we focus on the *maximal/minimal* points.

Definition 1 (Domination). *Let $p_1 = (x_1, \ldots, x_d)$ and $p_2 = (y_1, \ldots, y_d)$ be two d-dimensional points. We define that p_1 dominates maximally p_2 (denoted as $Dom_{\max}(p_1, p_2)$), when $x_i > y_i$, $\forall 1 \le i \le d$. We also define that p_1 dominates minimally p_2 (we denote $Dom_{\min}(p_1, p_2)$), when $x_i < y_i$, $\forall 1 \le i \le d$.*

Definition 2 (Maximal/Minimal Points). *Let S be a set of points. A point $p_i \in S$ is maximal (minimal, resp.), if there does not exist any other point $p_j \in S$ such that $Dom_{\max}(p_j, p_i)$ ($Dom_{\min}(p_j, p_i)$, respectively).*

Figure 1.a illustrates an example of a set of two-dimensional points and the corresponding maximal/minimal points. If the set S contains n points, then the

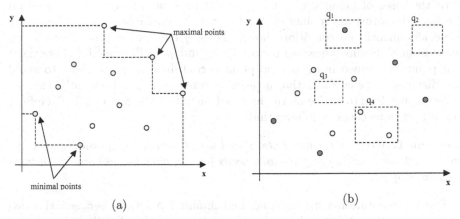

Fig. 1. Example of: (a) maximal/minimal points, (b) the different cases

calculation of maximal/minimal points can be done in $O(n \log n)$ time [8, 28]. Regarding the number of maximal (minimal, resp.) points, it is easy to see that in the worst case it is equal to n (for points placed in a diagonal line) and in the best case it is equal to one, i.e., a point at the upper-right (lower-left, resp.) corner. For the case of uniform placement, at random, of n points in a subset P of the plane, in [6] it was shown that the number of maximal points is normally distributed, with average value $\sim m\sqrt{\lambda}$, λ being the density and m a constant depending on P.[2]

For a set S of points, we denote as $S_{\max}$ and $S_{\min}$ the set of its maximal and minimal points respectively. $S_{\max}$ and $S_{\min}$ can be considered as a representation of S, which, given a rectangle q, allows for testing if q contains any points of S. Let q_{ll} and q_{ur} denote the lower-left and the upper-right corner of q. The following lemma is evident, since for each $p \in S_{\max}$ (equivalently, for each $p \in S_{\min}$) it also holds that $p \in S$.

Lemma 1. *If there exist a point p such that $p \in S_{\max}$ or $p \in S_{\min}$, and p is contained in a rectangle q, then q contains at least one point from S.*

For instance, see the case of rectangle q_1 in Figure 1.b, which contains a maximal point (maximal and minimal points are depicted as shaded). Due to the properties of maximal/minimal points, it is also easy to prove that:

Lemma 2. *If there does not exist any $p \in S_{\max}$ ($p \in S_{\min}$, resp.) such that $Dom_{\max}(p, q_{ll})$ ($Dom_{\min}(p, q_{ur})$, resp.), then there does not exist any point $s \in S$ such that s is contained in q.*

For an instance of the latter case regarding maximal points, see rectangle q_2 in Figure 1.b, where its lower-left corner dominates maximally all maximal points.

---

[2] The aforementioned results mainly focus on spaces with moderate dimensionality, which are the "target" of structures belonging to the R-tree family. In Section 5 we discuss the case of very high dimensionality.

In the cases of Lemmata 1 and 2, we get an exact answer to the question whether q contains any points of S. However, a third case exists, when none of the aforementioned conditions holds. Then, q may or may not contain any points from S. For instance, see rectangles q_3 and q_4 in Figure 1.b, where there exist points contained in q_4, but no point is contained in q_3. In order to avoid false-dismissals, we consider that q possibly contains points (evidently, this assumption may lead to a false-alarm, as it is depicted for the case of q_3). Therefore, from all previous cases, it follows that:

Theorem 1. *Given a set of points S and a rectangle q, S_{max} and S_{min} represent S without resulting to false-dismissals for the question whether q contains any points of S.*

The representation with the maximal/minimal points is between the two extreme cases (i.e., NAR and storing all points) and helps deciding about categories at internal nodes as well. Although in the worst case all points of a subtree may be maximal/minimal (leading to the second extreme), as explained, in the average case, only a small fraction of points are maximal/minimal. The details of how augmentation is applied with this type of representation are given in the following. Finally, we notice that the generalization for objects with spatial extent is immediate: after approximating them with iso-oriented geometrical objects (e.g., MBRs), one can work with the resulting upper and lower "corner" points; the choices can be made according to accuracy-time trade-offs.

3.2 The R-tree Augmentation Scheme

The proposed approach considers a multi-tree indexing scheme. It is based on a regular R-tree, which is augmented with auxiliary data structures that are maintained at each internal node entry. Each entry e in an internal R-tree node is of the form: $\langle e.\text{MBR}, e.\text{pointer}, e.\text{max\_btree}, e.\text{min\_btree}\rangle$, where $e.\text{max\_btree}$ and $e.\text{min\_btree}$ are pointers to the roots of B^+-trees that store the maximal and minimal, respectively, points in the subtree of e (the other two elements, $e.\text{MBR}$ and $e.\text{pointer}$, have their regular meaning). It has to be noticed that each present category in the subtree has its own maximal/minimal points (i.e., maximality and minimality is determined only between points of the same category).

Within the B^+-trees, the maximal and minimal points are ordered according to their category values, which comprise the search-keys in each B^+-tree. Therefore, the two B^+-trees of a node entry e are probed with respect to category values, and the maximal and minimal points can be retrieved. Figure 2.a illustrates a sample data set (the description of categories is also depicted) and Figure 2.b the corresponding multi-tree index (R-tree nodes are depicted with solid line whereas the B^+-tree ones with dashed). The points in the leaves of the R-tree are stored along with their category, however, there is no ordering with respect to the category values. In contrast, in the B^+-tree nodes the entries are the maximal/minimal points and they are ordered with respect to their category value. For instance, in node P, the maximal points for category 1 are points p_3

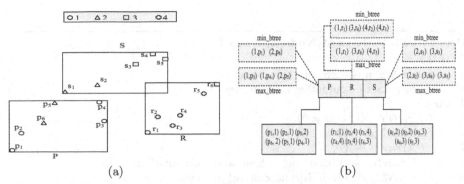

(a)   (b)

Fig. 2. (a) Example of a data set. (b) The corresponding augmented R-tree

and p_4, and for category 2 it is point p_5. For the same node, the minimal points are: p_1 for category 1 and p_6 for category 2.

Let Q be a query rectangle, where Q_{ll} and Q_{ur} denote its lower-left and upper-right corner. We maintain a boolean array $A[1..C]$, where C is the total number of categories (which, in general, is not constant). $A[i]$, $1 \le i \le C$, being true denotes that we need to search for category i in the currently visited node, otherwise we do not. The processing of a CRQ commences from the root of the R-tree, and initially all elements of A are set to true. When being at an internal node, we first find all its entries whose MBRs intersect Q. For each such entry e, we probe $e.max\_btree$ and $e.min\_btree$ to find the maximal and minimal points of all categories c for which $A[c]$ is true. According to the description in Section 3.1, we have to examine a set of cases for each such category c. The algorithm that processes CRQs with criteria based on the aforementioned cases is called M^2R (Maximal/Minimal R-tree) and is given in Figure 3 (the category of a point p is denoted as $p.category$, and the i-th entry of a node N is denoted as $N[i]$).

The categories included in Q are maintained in the global variable $outputSet$ (which is assumed to be empty before the execution of M^2R). An array A is separately used for each node entry $N[i]$ (step 7 of M^2R), since the absence of a category in an entry does not induce the absence in the other entries as well. When descending to a lower level, the contents of array A are passed from the father to the child node through argument FA. However, step 13 affects all other entries of node N, since we do not need to search for this category any more. For this reason FA is updated at step 16. It has to be noticed that it is necessary to test, at steps 21 and 8, if a category has been included in the output set of the CRQ, due to the depth-search manner that the searching proceeds. (We have also tried a breadth-first variation, but it performed purely because it results to many false-alarms.)

3.3 Management of B$^+$-trees

Firstly, we estimate the overall space complexity of B$^+$-trees. As previously mentioned, in [6] was proven that in the case of uniform placement at random

---

Procedure M^2R(**Rect** Q, **Node** N, **Array** FA)

1. **if** N is leaf
2.   **foreach** p in N such that Q contains p
3.   outputSet $\leftarrow$ outputSet $\cup$ p.category
4. **else**
5. $SI = \{N[i] \mid N[i] \cap Q \neq \emptyset\}$
6.   **foreach** N[i] $\in SI$
7.   **Array** $A \leftarrow$ FA
8.   **foreach** c such that $A[c] =$ **true** and $c \notin$ outputSet
9. $N^c_{\max}[i] = \{p$ in N[i].max_btree $\mid p$.category $= c\}$
10. $N^c_{\min}[i] = \{p$ in N[i].min_btree $\mid p$.category $= c\}$
11.   **if** $N^c_{\max}[i] = \emptyset$ **and** $N^c_{\min}[i] = \emptyset$
12. $A[c] \leftarrow$ **false**
13.   **else if** $\exists p \in N^c_{\max}[i] \cup N^c_{\min}[i]$ such that Q contains p
14.   outputSet $\leftarrow$ outputSet $\cup$ c
15. $A[c] \leftarrow$ **false**
16.   FA[c] $\leftarrow$ **false**
17.   **else if** $(\nexists p \in N^c_{\max}[i] : Dom_{\max}(p, Q_{||}))$**or**$(\nexists p \in N^c_{\min}[i] : Dom_{\min}(p, Q_{ur}))$
18. $A[c] \leftarrow$ **false**
19.   **end if**
20.   **end for**
21.   **if** $\exists c$ such that $A[c] =$ **true** and $c \notin$ outputSet
22. M^2R(Q, N[i].pointer, A)
23.   **end for**
24. **endif**
end M^2R

Fig. 3. The M^2R algorithm

of n points in a subset P of the plane, the number of maximal points is normally distributed, with average value $\sim \sqrt{\lambda}$, λ being the density. So, assuming w.l.o.g the normalized data space (where each coordinate is in the $[0, 1]$ range), one expects that the number of maximal points at level 0 (root) node is $O(\sqrt{n})$, at a level 1 node is $O(\sqrt{n/B})$ (B is the page capacity), at a level 2 node is $O(\sqrt{n/B^2})$, and generally, at a level i node is $O(\sqrt{n/B^i})$. Summing up we have the following lemma:

Lemma 3. *Let S be a set of n points stored in an augmented R-tree T. In case of uniformly distributed data, one expects that the B^+-trees of T demand $O(n/B^{1.5})$ pages.*

In the case of dynamic insertions/deletions of points, the proposed multi-tree indexing scheme can easily update the augmented information. For the insertion of a point p, it is initially inserted in the R-tree leaf N that is determined by the regular R-tree insertion algorithm. What has to be additionally taken into account is that some of the maximal or minimal points in the father-entry of N may no longer be valid. This happens only in the case when p is a new maximal or/and minimal point in N.[3] In this case, we have to probe the corresponding entries of the maximal/minimal B$^+$-trees, to find the ones that have to be removed, and to insert p. Since p may also invalidate maximal/minimal points at upper levels as well, the previous procedure is repeated for all R-tree nodes invoked during the insertion of p. Considering a deletion of a point p from a leaf N, if it is a maximal or a minimal point in N, then we have to remove it from all B$^+$-trees in the root-to-leaf path corresponding to N, and additionally to insert the possible new maximal or minimal points from N, which may result after deleting p.

The case of semi-dynamic data sets (when only insertions are permitted) can be analyzed by standard amortization arguments [26, 4].[4] Omitting the proof due to space constraints, we have:

Lemma 4. *In the case of a semi-dynamic data set, an update operation has* $O(\log_B^2 n)$ *amortized cost.*

When the underlying data set is fully dynamic, then one cannot prove better than $O(n)$ worst-case bounds. However, in the average case, is easy to see that only an $O(\sqrt{n})$ fraction of inserted/deleted points will require an update of the augmented information leading to an $O(\sqrt{n})$ worst-case average performance. In practice one can experience much better performance.

As an additional optimization, we consider the case where in a node N, the roots of the B$^+$-trees of N's entries tend to have low utilization (their minimum allowed utilization is two entries). Therefore, when possible, such roots with few entries are kept packed into a single node. This reduces the required space and the processing time. The packing is done separately for maximal and minimal B$^+$-trees. Moreover, we utilized a scheme of storing, when possible, these packed roots at consecutive pages with that of node N, by trying to pre-allocate consecutive space for the two B$^+$-tree roots. Experimenting with the aforementioned optimizations, we found that they result to significant performance improvements, thus they are incorporated in the proposed method.

3.4   Selectivity Estimation

The *relative selectivity* (RS) is defined as the ratio between the sizes of output sets of the CRQ and the regular range query, when both are performed with the same query rectangle (RS is in the range [0, 1]). Let us consider the processing of a CRQ by filtering the output set of the regular range query so as to select the distinct categories in it —this method is henceforth denoted as Plain Range query Filtering (PRF). The performance difference between M^{2}R and PRF depends on the value of RS. When RS is high, PRF does not waste much cost,

---

[3] A point p can be *both* maximal and minimal when it is the only point of p.category.

[4] This case corresponds to data warehousing applications, where data are historical (i.e., they are not deleted).

whereas the processing of the augmented structures for M^2R may not pay-off. In contrast, when RS is not high, PRF spends a large cost to first find many points that satisfy the regular range query but will be filtered out later on. In most cases of interest (see Section 4), data are clustered with respect to the categorical attribute, and RS does not have high values.

It follows that the optimization of CRQs can be advocated by the estimation of RS. Although several methods have been proposed for estimating the selectivity of regular range queries, e.g., [1], up to our knowledge, no results have been reported for estimating the selectivity of a CRQ. As an initial approach towards this direction, we used the approximation of spatial data with index partitionings [1], which exploits the division of data space achieved by the R-tree (an analogous approach can be found in [3, 25]). By keeping track of the distinct categories within each partition, we can process all partitions, find those intersected by Q, and determine how many categories from each of them will be assigned to the output set.[5] Experiments with the aforementioned approach resulted to estimation error less than 1% for CRQs with large query rectangles, and around 15-25% for small ones. We are currently working on the development of an algorithm for RS estimation based on the Min-Skew algorithm [1], considering the distribution of the values of the categorical attribute instead of the density alone. Clearly, by using such an approach, a more accurate estimation is expected to be achieved.

Based on the RS estimation, the query optimizer will be able to decide whether the use of augmented structures will pay-off compared to the PRF method. In the extreme cases where there exist no actual grouping of points with respect to the categorical attribute, and so RS is high, the optimizer can reduce the overhead resulting from the augmented structures. This can be done by adapting M^2R to: (i) either consider only a fraction of them, e.g., by selecting every k-th augmented structure in the node instead of each one; a technique denoted as *reduction*), or (ii) entirely avoid to use them —in this case M^2R and PRF become equivalent.

4   Experimental Results

This section describes the results on the experimental comparison of: (i) the proposed algorithm (M^2R); (ii) the algorithm that first performs a plain range query and then filters w.r.t. category values (PRF); and (iii) the algorithm that is based on the naive augmentation of R-trees (NAR). We also examine why independent R-trees, one for each category, are not a viable solution. Our experiments consider both synthetic and real data sets. We study the impact of: the relative selectivity (RS) values, the domain size, the query and buffer sizes.

---

[5] For instance, we can first find the ratio r ($0 < r \leq 1$) between the volume of the intersection and the volume of an intersected partition. Next, if t is the number of distinct categories in the partition, we can select $r \cdot t$ categories (uniformity assumption), and filter those that have already been included in the output. Nevertheless, further discussion on this issue is out of the scope of this paper.

In the remaining of this section, we first describe the experimental setting and then we give the results.

4.1 Experimental Setting

All examined methods were implemented in C using the same components. The experiments have been conducted on a computer with a Pentium III processor at 1.6 GHz. We used the R*-tree variant [7].

We used both synthetic and real data sets. The real data sets we consider are: Sequoia, Cover, and Census. The first one is from the Sequoia database[6] and contains 62,556 2-d points corresponding to California place names, along with their textual description. We cleaned the descriptions (e.g., by spell checking, removing empty ones, etc) and performed a grouping according to their type (e.g., a bar, beach, etc). This resulted to 180 distinct categories. The other two data sets belong to the UCI Machine Learning Repository[7]. The Cover data set contains 581,012 points and is used for predicting forest cover types from cartographic variables. From its 54 attributes, we used the spatial information to get the 2-d points corresponding to the locations. As categorical attribute we used the soil type information, which contains 40 distinct category values. Although Cover contains other possible categorical attributes, we selected soil because the others resulted to a much smaller number (less than ten) of distinct values. Finally, the Census-Income data set, denoted as Census, is a fragment of the US Census Bureau data and contains 199,523 records, from which we derived two separate sets: (i) the Census3d, having as dimensions the age, income and weeks worked; and (ii) the Census5d, having as additional dimensions the wage per hour and the dividends from stocks. As categorical attribute we selected, in both cases, the occupation type, that has 47 distinct values in total, because other possible ones would result to very small domains. Both the Cover and Census data sets have also been used elsewhere (e.g., in [13]).

To examine different characteristics of the data, we also considered synthetic data sets. Their generation was based on the following procedure. We specified a number of points that were the centers of overlapping 2-d normal (gaussian) distributions; since related work on main memory structures focused on the 2-d case, we use synthetic data sets of this dimensionality so as to examine the viability of the proposed method for this case, whereas we examine more dimensions with the Census data set. For each one of them, we generated a number of points that is given as a fraction of the total number of the points in the data set. This factor is called *replication factor* and corresponds to the size of each distribution. All points of a distribution are assigned to the same category. The total number of categories is pre-specified. We tested both the random (i.e., following uniform distribution) and skewed (i.e., following zipfian distribution) assignment of categories to points. However, both lead to qualitative similar results, thus we herein present results on the former. The coordinates in the data

---

[6] Available (also) at:

  http://dias.cti.gr/~ytheod/research/datasets/spatial.html

[7] Available at: http://www.ics.uci.edu/~mlearn/MLRepository.html

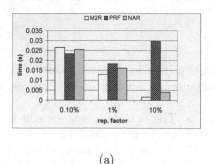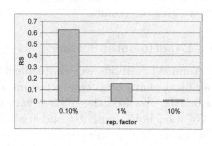

(a)   (b)

Fig. 4. Execution time (a) and RS (b) w.r.t. replication factor, for query size 0.05%

space were normalized in the range [0,1] and the standard deviation that was used in the normal distributions was equal to 5%.

The page size was set to 4 K and the default buffer size was set to the 20% of the data set size. For the queries we examined both uniform and biased workloads. With the former, queries corresponded to squares, the center of which follows a uniform distribution in the data set space. With the latter, the centers of the queries were points from the data set itself, thus they follow the data distribution. In our synthetic data sets we used uniform workloads, whereas for the real ones we used biased workloads. This is because the synthetic data have a good coverage of the entire data space, whereas the real ones are more skewed and the biased workload comprise a more realistic assumption. The query size is given as percentage of its size with respect to the size of the data space. The main performance metric was the total (wall-clock) execution time, measured in seconds, which includes I/O and CPU times for processing CRQs and the time to write the result.

4.2 Results

Our first experiment studies how the different values of RS affect CRQs. We used synthetic data sets with varying replication factor, that directly impacts RS. This happens because a larger replication factor results to a larger clustering with respect to the categorical value, therefore points that are close in space are more probable to belong to the same category. The data sets contained 100,000 points and 100 categories. Figures 4.a and 5.a depict the execution time (in seconds) with respect to replication factor, for query sizes 0.05% and 0.2% respectively. Figures 4.b and 5.b depict the corresponding RS values.

As expected, low values of replication factor result to large values of RS. In such cases, the PRF method performs well, since it does not spent too much extra cost. Nevertheless, the execution time of M^2R (also NAR) is similar to that of PRF, since it is not outperformed significantly by PRF for query size 0.05%,

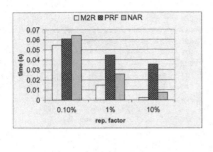 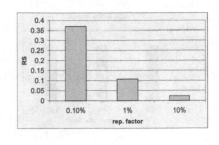

(a)   (b)

Fig. 5. Execution time (a) and RS (b) w.r.t. replication factor, for query size 0.2%

and is slightly better for query size 0.2%. The reason is that for these cases, M^2R exploits the reduction technique described in Section 3.4. When moving to medium and larger values of replication factor, RS reduces. The performance of PRF, however, is not affected —in some cases its execution time increases, whereas in others it reduces— since RS does not influence PRF. In contrast, as RS reduces, M^2R clearly outperforms PRF, whereas NAR comes second best. This is easily explained, since in these cases M^2R can perform a better pruning with respect to the categorical attribute. Another thing that can be noticed between Figures 4 and 5 is that in the latter, which corresponds to a larger query, RS values are relatively reduced. Although the output set of CRQ increases with increasing query size, the output set of the regular range query increases more rapidly with increasing query size. This results to the relative reduction in RS for the larger query size.

The aforementioned results verify the intuitive argument stated earlier in the paper, that the regular range query followed by filtering (i.e., PRF) is expected to waste a lot of cost in the cases when data are not randomly scattered along the categorical attribute, and that the performance gains due to M^2R are expected to be significant. Moreover, when RS values are high (random scattering), the results show that the overhead of M^2R is not significant. Fortunately, most of real data sets of interest (see the following) tend to be clustered along the categorical attributes. Therefore, in such cases the output size of the CRQ is a very small fraction of that of the regular range query.

Our next experiment examines the domain size of the categorical attribute, i.e., the total number of distinct values for the categorical attribute. We used synthetic data sets that were analogous to those used in the previous experiment. The replication factor was set to 5% and the query size was set to 0.1%. These values are selected so as to get a variety of different RS values w.r.t. the domain size. The execution time is depicted in Figure 6.a, whereas Figure 6.b illustrates the corresponding RS values.

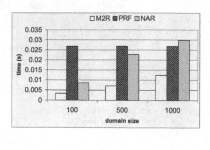

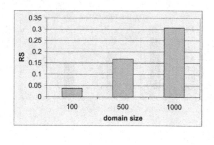

(a)   (a)

Fig. 6. Execution time (a) and RS (b) w.r.t. domain size of the categorical attribute

The increase in the domain size of the categorical attribute results to an increase in RS, since it increases the probability of more distinct categories to exist within the query region. As expected, PRF is independent from the domain size, because the result of the regular range query is the same in all cases. M^2R is only slightly affected by the increase in the domain size, and it outperforms the other two algorithms in all cases. In contrast, the impact is more clear on NAR, which for large domain sizes is outperformed by PRF. The aforementioned result indicates that M^2R scales well with respect to the domain size, even for very large values (in the order of thousand).

To validate the conclusions drawn with synthetic data, we also examined real ones. We first used the Sequoia data set. In this case, we also test the approach of having independent R-trees, each one storing separately the points of a category, which is denoted as IND. Figures 7.a and .b illustrate the execution time and RS, respectively, for varying query size, given as a percentage of the data set space. Similar to synthetic data sets, RS is decreased with increasing query size. It has to be noticed that the earlier stated argument, that the output of a CRQ is only a small fraction of the output of the regular range query, is verified by the values of RS in Figure 7.b. Regarding execution time, it is clearly noticed that IND presents the worst performance. This is because for every query it probes all categories although only few of them will belong to the output set. For this reason we do not examine IND in the following. Focusing on M^2R, NAR, and PRF, they perform similarly for very small query sizes. This is due to the higher RS values for these query sizes, and also due to the small size of the data set (about 62,000 thousand points) which renders all methods equivalent for such small query sizes. In contrast, for medium and large queries (0.5–1%), M^2R compares favorably to the other two methods.

As mentioned, the Sequoia data set is not large. To have a more clear comparison, we now move on to examine the Cover data set, that is much larger. Results on execution time for varying query size are depicted in Figure 8.a —RS values were similar to those in the previous experiment, thus they are omitted for

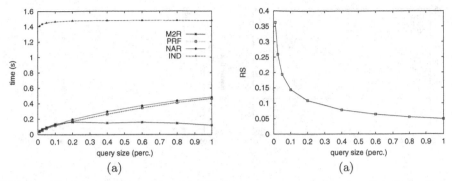

Fig. 7. Execution time (a) and RS (b) w.r.t. query size for the Sequoia real data set

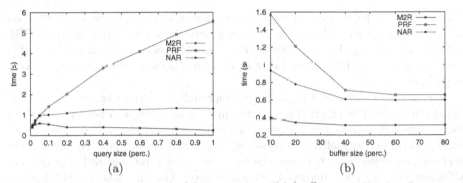

Fig. 8. Execution time w.r.t. (a) query size, (b) buffer size, for the Cover real data set

brevity. As shown, with increasing query size, PRF clearly looses out. Therefore, the large size of data sets like Cover, renders the performance of PRF impractical, since for larger query sizes (1%) its execution time is an order of magnitude larger than that of M^2R. In contrast, M^2R performs very well in all cases. NAR comes second best, whereas the performance difference between M^2R and NAR is significant. Also, it has to be noticed that with increasing query size, the size of the output set for a CRQ increases, because its selectivity reduces (i.e., more categories are included in larger queries). Nevertheless, M^2R is beneficial regardless of the selectivity, since it can better determine containment (or not) at the higher R-tree levels, thus avoiding visits to the lower levels. This is the reason for the relative decrease in the execution time of M^2R for large query sizes. This can also be noticed in Figure 7.a.

Evidently, the performance of all examined methods depends on the provided memory size that is used for buffering. For this reason, we examined the impact of buffer size on the execution time. We used the Cover data set, and the query size was set to 0.1%. Figure 8.b illustrates the results for varying buffer size,

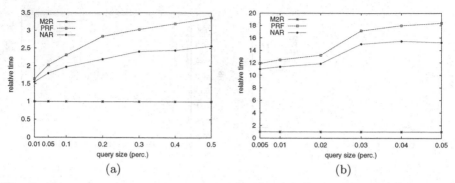

Fig. 9. Execution time w.r.t. query size for the: (a) Census3d and (b) Census5d real data sets

that is given as percentage of the data set size. Clearly, the execution time for all methods reduces with increasing buffer size. Since the performance of PRF is the worst among the three methods, it benefits more from increasing buffer size. Nevertheless, M^2R outperforms all other methods in all cases, even for very large buffer sizes.

Finally, we evaluated the proposed approach with the Census3d and Census5d data sets. The results for varying query size, given as a percentage of the data space, are depicted in Figure 9. The time axis corresponds to the relative execution times, normalized to those of M^2R, so as to more clearly present the performance differences between the two cases. For the Census3d (Figure 9.a), M^2R outperforms the other two methods by several factors, whereas NAR comes second best, performing similar to PRF for small query sizes and better for medium and larger ones. For the Census5d (Figure 9.b), the performance difference between M^2R and the other methods is much more pronounced. This is explained by the large skew that the additional two dimensions present, which result to a large cost paid by PRF even for small query sizes. In contrast, M^2R is not affected as much by the skewness, due to the early pruning with respect to categories.

5   Conclusions

This paper studied the problem of categorical range searching over large databases, that is, the finding of categories, instead of objects themselves, existing within the query region. We have developed M^2R, an algorithm that is based on the augmentation of R-trees with structures organizing the maximal/minimal points in subtrees. This approach follows the general paradigm of augmenting tree nodes in order to facilitate searching. M^2R is compared with the regular range query and with a naive method for augmenting R-tree nodes. Detailed experimental comparison with real and synthetic data illustrates the superiority of M^2R over the two base-line algorithms. Depending on the value of relative selectivity of the CRQ, M^2R attains performance improvements up to an order of magnitude, for large real data sets.

There exist several directions of future work, for instance, the examination of data sets of very high dimensionality and the development of more sophisticated estimators for the selectivity of CRQs. Regarding the first issue, a decomposition scheme, based on multi-level B^+-trees that first narrow down the search space of the high dimensional space and then apply the solution presented in this work for moderate dimensions, seems a good candidate, demanding polylogarithmic overhead [26]. It is also interesting to consider that research on CRQs can be extended to other analogous queries, like the categorical nearest-neighbor queries [23] or the counting queries [17]. Such extensions can find interesting applications in large databases and, therefore, we consider the problem examined in this paper as a first attempt towards this research direction.

References

[1] S. Acharya, V. Poosala, S. Ramaswamy: "Selectivity Estimation in Spatial Databases". *Int. Conf. on Management of Data (SIGMOD'99)*, pp. 13-24, 1999. 131

[2] P. Agarwal, S. Govindarajan, S. Muthukrishnan: "Range Searching in Categorical Data: Colored Range Searching on Grid". *European Symp. on Algorithms (ESA'02)*, pp. 17-28, 2002. 122, 124

[3] G. Antoshenkov: "Random Sampling from Pseudo-ranked B^+-trees". *Int. Conf. on Very Large Databases (VLDB'92)*, pp. 375-382, 1992. 131

[4] L. Arge, J. S. Vitter: "Optimal Dynamic Interval Management in External Memory". *Symp. on Foundations of Computer Science (FOCS'96)*, pp. 560-569, 1996. 124, 130

[5] L. Arge, V. Samoladas, J. S. Vitter: "On Two-Dimensional Indexability and Optimal Range Search Indexing". *Symp. on Principles of Database Systems (PODS'99)*, pp. 346-357, 1999. 124

[6] A. D. Barbour, A. Xia: "The number of two-dimensional maxima", *Advanced Applications on Probability (SGSA)*, vol. 33, pp. 727-750, 2001. 126, 128

[7] N. Beckmann, H.-P. Kriegel, R. Schneider, B. Seeger: "The R*-Tree: An Efficient and Robust Access Method for Points and Rectangles". *Int. Conf. on Management of Data (SIGMOD'90)*, pp. 322-331, 1990. 132

[8] M. de Berg, M. van Kreveld, M. Overmars, O. Schwarzkopf: *Computational Geometry*, Springer Verlag, 2nd ed., 2000. 126

[9] P. Bozanis, N. Kitsios, C. Makris, A. Tsakalidis: "New Upper Bounds for Generalized Intersection Searching Problems". *Int. Colloquium on Automata, Languages and Programming (ICALP'95)*, pp. 464-474, 1995. 122, 124

[10] P. Bozanis, N. Kitsios, C. Makris, A. Tsakalidis: "Red-Blue Intersection Reporting for Objects of Non-Constant Size". *The Computer Journal*, Vol. 39, No. 6, pp. 541-546, 1996. 122, 124

[11] P. Bozanis, N. Kitsios, C. Makris, A. Tsakalidis: "New Results on Intersection Query Problems". *The Computer Journal*, vol. 40, No. 1, pp. 22-29, 1997. 122, 124

[12] P. Bozanis, A. Nanopoulos, Y. Manolopoulos: "LR-tree: a Logarithmic Decomposable Spatial Index Method", *The Computer Journal, to appear*, 2003. 124

[13] N. Bruno, S. Chaudhuri, L. Gravano: "Top-k selection queries over relational databases: Mapping strategies and performance evaluation". *ACM Transactions on Database Systems*, Vol. 27, No. 2, pp. 153-187, 2002. 132

[14] D. Eppstein, S. Muthukrishnan: "Internet packet filter management and rectangle geometry". *Symp. on Discrete Algorithms (SODA'01)*, pp. 827-835, 2001. 124

[15] P. Ferragina, N. Koudas, S. Muthukrishnan, D. Srivastava: "Two-dimensional Substring Indexing". *Symp. on Principles of Database Systems (PODS'01)*, pp. 282-288, 2001. 124

[16] S. Govindarajan, P. K. Agarwal, L. Arge: "CRB-Tree: An Efficient Indexing Scheme for Range-Aggregate Queries". *Intl. Conf. on Database Theory (ICDT'03)*, pp. 143-157, 2003. 124

[17] P. Gupta, R. Janardan, M. Smid: "Further Results on Generalized Intersection Searching Problems: Counting, Reporting, and Dynamization". *Journal of Algorithms*, Vol. 19, No. 2, pp. 282-317, 1995. 122, 124, 138

[18] P. Gupta, R. Janardan, and M. Smid: "Efficient Algorithms for Generalized Intersection Searching on Non-Iso-oriented Objects". *Computational Geometry: Theory & Applications*, Vol. 6, No. 1, pp. 1-19, 1996. 122, 124

[19] J. Hellerstein, E. Koutsoupias, D. Miranker, C. Papadimitriou, V. Samolodas: "On a Model of Indexability and Its Bounds for Range Queries". *Journal of the ACM*, Vol. 19, No. 1, pp. 35-55, 2002. 123, 125

[20] R. Janardan, M. Lopez: "Generalized intersection searching problems". *Int. Journal on Computational Geometry and Applications*, Vol. 3, pp. 39-69, 1993. 122, 124

[21] K. Kanth, S. Ravada, D. Abugov. "Quadtree and R-tree indexes in oracle spatial: a comparison using GIS data". *Int. Conf. on Management of Data (SIGMOD'02)*, pp. 546-557, 2002. 123

[22] Y. Manolopoulos, E. Nardelli, G. Proietti, E. Tousidou: "A generalized comparison of linear representations of thematic layers". *Data and Knowledge Engineering*, Vol. 37, No. 1, pp. 1-23, 2001. 125

[23] D. Mount, N. Netanyahu, R. Silverman, A. Wu: "Chromatic nearest neighbor searching: A query sensitive approach". *Computational Geometry*, Vol. 17, No. 3-4, pp. 97-119, 2000. 122, 124, 138

[24] S. Muthukrishnan: "Efficient algorithms for document retrieval problems". *Symp. on Discrete Algorithms (SODA'02)*, pp. 657-666, 2002. 124

[25] A. Nanopoulos, Y. Theodoridis, Y. Manolopoulos: "An Efficient and Effective Algorithm for Density Biased Sampling". *Int. Conf. on Information and Knowledge Management (CIKM'02)*, pp. 63-68, 2002. 131

[26] M. H. Overmars: *The Design of Dynamic Data Structures*, Springer-Verlag, Berlin, Heidelberg, 1983. 123, 130, 138

[27] D. Papadias, Y. Tao, P. Kalnis, J. Zhang: "Indexing Spatio-Temporal Data Warehouses". *Int. Conf. on Data Engineering (ICDE'02)*, 2002. 124

[28] J. R. Sack, J. Urrutia (Eds.): *Handbook of Computational Geometry*, North-Holland, 2000. 126

[29] Y. Tao, D. Papadias: "The MV3R-Tree: A Spatio-Temporal Access Method for Timestamp and Interval Queries". *Intl. Conf. on Very Large Data Bases (VLDB'01)*, pp. 431-440, 2001. 124

Probabilistic Spatial Database Operations

Jinfeng Ni[1], Chinya V. Ravishankar[1], and Bir Bhanu[2]

[1] Department of Computer Science & Engineering
[2] Department of Electrical Engineering
University of California, Riverside
Riverside, CA 92521, USA

Abstract. Spatial databases typically assume that the positional attributes of spatial objects are precisely known. In practice, however, they are known only approximately, with the error depending on the nature of the measurement and the source of data. In this paper, we address the problem how to perform spatial database operations in the presence of uncertainty. We first discuss a probabilistic spatial data model to represent the positional uncertainty. We then present a method for performing the probabilistic spatial join operations, which, given two uncertain data sets, find all pairs of polygons whose probability of overlap is larger than a given threshold. This method uses an R-tree based probabilistic index structure (PrR-tree) to support probabilistic filtering, and an efficient algorithm to compute the intersection probability between two uncertain polygons for the refinement step. Our experiments show that our method achieves higher accuracy than methods based on traditional spatial joins, while reducing overall cost by a factor of more than two.

1 Introduction

The past decade has witnessed a significant increase in work on spatial database management systems. The field has gained significance both in traditional applications such as urban planning, as well as in emerging areas such as mobile ad-hoc networks. The increase in GPS-based has also been a significant boost to this field. A standard assumption in the spatial database domain has been that the positional attributes of spatial objects are known precisely. Unfortunately, this is often not the case, and various kinds of uncertainty may be associated with spatial data. GIS researchers, in particular, have long recognized that spatial data are rarely error-free [8, 30]. Five important components of spatial data quality are categorized in the National Standard for Spatial Data Accuracy(NSSDA) [6]: positional accuracy, attribute accuracy, logical consistency, completeness and lineage.

In this paper, we focus on positional accuracy. The positional accuracy represents how closely the coordinate descriptions of spatial objects match their actual positions (or ground truth). The term *positional uncertainty* or *positional error* is often used to refer the difference between the digital representations of spatial objects and the actual locations. Numerous factors may contribute

T. Hadzilacos et al. (Eds.): SSTD 2003, LNCS 2750, pp. 140–159, 2003.

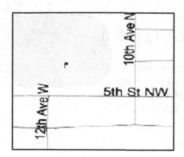

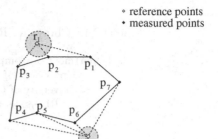

Fig. 1. Data problems: Overlay places building (flag) within lake (grey area), instead of on 5th Street [18]

Fig. 2. A surveying network with 2 reference points

to the positional uncertainty in spatial data. In practice, there are a variety of ways to capture spatial data, each having its own sources of errors. Several widely used data sources are land surveys, GPS information, photography, remotely sensed satellite images, and digitizing or scanning a paper map. As indicated in [18], errors may be introduced during these processes by the digitizing methods used, the source material characteristics, generalizations, symbol interpretations, specifications for aerial photography, aerotriangulation techniques, ground control reliability, photogrammetric characteristics, scribling precision, resolution, processing algorithms, printing limitations, and so on.

Traditional techniques for querying spatial data need to be revised, since uncertainties in spatial data may affect the accuracy of the answers to queries. It is in fact possible for traditional database queries to produce wildly incorrect or invalid results based on the measured data. To illustrate this point, consider the example in Figure 1, taken from a document by Minnesota Planning [18]. In this example, the locations of buildings, shown as the black flag, are measured by GPS receivers, and then overlaid over a digital base map containing roads, and lakes. However, this operation results in some buildings being located in the middle of lakes! The error in this case arises from the differences in data sources and their differing accuracies. The base map was accurate to 167 feet, while the GPS data was accurate only to 300 feet.

1.1 Managing Uncertainty

It is generally agreed that positional uncertainties should be reported along with data, so that users may evaluate the suitability of the data for specific applications during decision making. One recent attempt is the widely-accepted standard by NSSDA [6]. NSSDA provides a well-defined statistical method and promotes the use of root-mean-square error (RMSE) to estimate and report the positional accuracy. RMSE is the square root of the average of the set of squared differences between dataset coordinate values and "ground truth" values of coordinates from an independent source of higher accuracy for the same points. For example, [18] shows how to apply NSSDA to report the positional accuracy in a variety of data. A typical positional accuracy statement is *using the National Standard for Spatial Data Accuracy, the data set tested 0.181meters horizontal accuracy at 95% confidence level.*

Unfortunately, RMSE is merely a gross, global measure of uncertainty, averaged over all points in a given data set. It therefore fails to characterize the local or spatial structure of uncertainty [7], and is inadequate for analysis of uncertainty. It remains a research issue to find an appropriate model to estimate and report the spatial structure of positional uncertainty.

From the perspective of spatial database systems, there are two important issues to address: modeling and reporting the positional uncertainty, and evaluating spatial queries over uncertain spatial data. In our work, we develop a probabilistic spatial data model (PSDM) for polygon data that associates probability distributions with the positional attributes. In PSDM, each polygon is partitioned into k disjoint independent *chunks*. Vertices from the same chunk have fully correlated uncertainties, while vertices from different chunks are independent. Furthermore, each chunk's uncertainty is assumed to follow a circular normal distribution.

Given the inherent positional uncertainties in the spatial data, exact match responses to queries are not meaningful, but probabilistic statements about query results are appropriate. Probabilistic answers to range and nearest-neighbor queries over moving point objects with uncertain locations were used in [29, 25]. In contrast, our work is concerned with probabilistic responses to queries when positional uncertainty exists over polygon boundaries. We also consider how to perform spatial operations in the presence of uncertainty.

In particular, we focus on evaluating *probabilistic spatial joins*. The response to a probabilistic spatial join consists of object pairs and the intersection probability between each pair. For example, consider the set R of state parks in California, and the set S of burned areas from recent forest fires. An example of a probabilistic spatial join query between R and S is: *Find all burned areas that overlap state parks in California with a probability of at least 0.8, and compute their overlap probability.*

As with traditional spatial joins, we evaluate probabilistic spatial join in two steps: filtering and refinement [5]. We propose the Probabilistic R-tree (PrR-tree) index, which supports a probabilistic filter step. We also propose an efficient algorithm to obtain the intersection probability between two candidate polygons for the refinement step.

This paper is organized as follows. Section 2 discusses related work. Section 3 presents PSDM, a probabilistic spatial data model for polygon's uncertainty. Section 4 presents our filtering and refinement algorithms for evaluating probabilsitc spatial joins. Experimental results are given in Section 5. Section 6 concludes the paper.

2   Related Work

Much work has been done on spatial databases, especially on the evaluation of spatial joins. Typically, spatial objects are approximated and indexed using their minimal bounding rectangle (MBR). A spatial join query is processed in two steps: *filtering*, where all the MBR pairs satisfying the join predicative are retrieved, and *refinement*, where the exact geometry of the objects is used to determine whether the object pair is a true hit or a false hit.

Consequently, previous work on spatial join has focussed on either the filtering or refinement step. For example, [5] proposed an algorithm to perform spatial join of two datasets indexed by the R-tree and its variations [2, 21]. Similarly, [15, 17] proposed algorithms to join one pre-indexed dataset with one unindexed dataset, and [16, 12, 23] proposed algorithms for the cases where neither dataset has existing indices. Other work focuses on how to improve the performance of the refinement step, which is much more expensive than the filtering step in terms of both I/O and computation costs. A common approach for the refinement is to approximate the spatial objects with a better approximation than MBR provides. For instance, [4] proposed a multi-step framework for processing spatial join, using approximations such as convex hulls, and minimum bounding m-corner boxes. In contrast, [9] proposed the Symbolic Intersect Detection (SID) technique to reduce the expensive computation cost of exact geometry test. Raster approximations are proposed for refinement step in [31].

In contrast, little work exists on query evaluation for spatial objects with uncertain position. In [13], the ϵ-*band* model is used to model the probabilistic distribution of polygon boundaries, and the upper bound of the probability for the point-in-polygon query is derived. The ϵ-band model requires one parameter to describe the uncertainty of a database, and simply assumes that all points, including the intermediate points between two vertices have the same uncertainty. However, as [26] indicates, this assumption may not be valid. The work in [26] found that the uncertainty of the middle points is lower than that of the two vertices. Also, [13] showed no experimental results for their approach, so it is unclear how well their approach works. Furthermore, point-in-polygon queries are very simple, and are not be applicable to spatial join in any direct way. The *G-Band* was proposed in [27] to describe the positional uncertainty of line segments, assuming that the uncertainties of the endpoints follow two-dimensional Normal distributions. One good feature of G-Band model is that it accounts for the dependence between the two end-points of segments. However, it may impose high computation cost when being applied to query evaluation.

Due to the complexity of spatial uncertainty, Openshaw [22] recommended the use of *Monte Carlo* techniques to evaluate the spatial uncertainty inherited in the spatial dataset. With this approach, a set of equally probable realizations of the spatial objects are generated, and these realizations can be used to evaluate the uncertainty associated with the spatial data. Although this is a computation-intensive method, Openshaw argued that due to the improvement of computer technology, this approach would find its way in more and more applications. For instance, [10, 7] demonstrated how to evaluate point-in-polygon queries using

Table 1. Summary of notation

Notation	Description
p_i	Vertex i
(x_i, y_i)	The x and y coordinates of vertex p_i
σ_i	The standard dviation of the circular normal associated with p_i
$\langle P \rangle$	A polygon P.
$\langle P : j \rangle$	The j-th *chunk* of polygon P
$\langle p_k, p_{k+1}, \cdots, p_{k+l} \rangle$	Chunk with vertices $p_k, p_{k+1}, \cdots, p_{k+l}$ (numbered anti-clockwise)
$[\![x^\vdash, y^\vdash, x^\dashv, y^\dashv]\!]$	MBR with lower left corner at $(x^\vdash, y^\vdash)$ and upper right corner $(x^\dashv, y^\dashv)$
$\sigma_x^\vdash, \sigma_y^\vdash, \sigma_x^\dashv, \sigma_y^\dashv$	The standard deviations of respective MBR corners X and Y axes.
γ	Confidence threshold for probabilistic queries

a Monto Carlo method. Despite great improvements in computer technology, Monte Carlo method is still not usable in large spatial databases. One possible use of this approach, suggested by Openshaw, is to serve as a benchmark for the evaluation of new techniques. Indeed, we use the result of Monte Carlo method to generate the ground truth values in our experiments.

The notion of probabilistic answers to queries over uncertain data was introduced in [29, 25] for range queries and nearest-neighbor queries when handling with the uncertainty associated with the location of moving point objects. Each query returns a set of tuples in the form of (O, p), where O is the object, and p is the probability that O satisfies the query predicate. The uncertainty of moving objects also was discussed in [28], where the uncertainty of object locations was modeled as a 3D cylindrical body along the trajectory, and semantics *sometime, always, everywhere, somewhere, possibly* and *definitely* were added into the traditional range queries. In [24], Pfoser et. al reported how to represent the uncertainty of moving objects introduced by the sampling technique and interpolation, and presented a filter-and-refine approach for probabilistic range queries.

3   Probabilistic Spatial Data Model

Traditional spatial databases typically use three primitives to represent spatial extent: points, lines, and polygons. Consequently, the uncertainty of the spatial extent can be described via the probability distributions of the vertices defining these three primitive objects. We recognize three requirements for an ideal probabilistic spatial data model: *simplicity, accuracy*, and *efficiecny*. Simplicity dictates that few parameters must be needed to describe the uncertainty, making it easier to incorporate probabilistic spatial data models into current spatial databases. Accuracy requires that the model should characterize the uncertainty with the greatest fidelity. Efficiency dictates that cost of processing the uncertainty during query execution should be reasonable.

In this section, we will present a probabilsitc spatial data model (PSDM) which meets these requirements. Table 1 is the list of notations used in this paper.

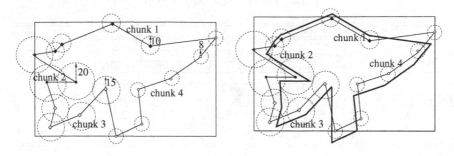

(a) A polygon with four chunks

(b) A possible realization of the uncertain polygon

Fig. 3. An uncertain polygon with 4 chunks, and a possible realization for this polygon

3.1 Positional Uncertainty Model

Our model begins with a partitioning of polygons into contiguous series of vertices called *chunks*. The positions of vertices from the same chunk are perfectly correlated, and positions of vertices from different chunks are independent. This model is reasonable in many practical scenarios since positions of vertices on polygons defining features are frequently assigned locations with respect to some standard reference points.

Consider Figure 2, in which a surveyor is mapping out a polygonal region with seven vertices. Because of site characteristics such as landmark visibility and distance, the surveyor has chosen to obtain the positions of vertices p_1, p_2, p_3 with respect to a reference point r_1, and the positions of p_4, p_5, p_6, p_7 with respect to a different reference point r_2. One approach is to obtain the locations of vertices relative to reference points via trigonometric calculations using measurements of distances and angles, the accuracy associated with which approach can be quite high. It is therefore reasonable to assert that the positional uncertainties in the locations of these vertices is largely determined by the uncertainties in the locations of the reference points. In this case, our chunks are $\langle p_1, p_2, p_3 \rangle$ and $\langle p_4, p_5, p_6, p_7 \rangle$. The errors in the postions of these chunks are uncorrelated as long the positions of r_1 and r_2 are.

Errors can occur both systematically and randomly [11, 3]. Generally, systematic errors, in the form of outliers, biases, blunders, do not follow a distribution function, and can be removed through a posteriori techniques such as calibration. Random errors commonly arise during measurement and tend to be distributed Normally [3]. We consider only random errors, and assume that the positional uncertainty of a point follows a circular Normal distribution, as in previous work [13, 14].

Definition 1. *Uncertainty of point: Let p be a point in 2 dimensional space whose position is uncertain. If σ is the uncertainty parameter associated with p, then the probability that p is located within a circle of radius r centered at p is given by the circular Normal distribution* $\Pr_p(r) = 1 - e^{-\frac{r^2}{2\sigma^2}}$.

Now, consider the uncertainty associated with a polygon $\langle P \rangle$ with n vertices $p_1, p_2, \ldots, p_n$. If we partition these vertices into the k disjoint chunks $\langle P : 1 \rangle$, $\langle P : 2 \rangle, \ldots, \langle P : k \rangle$, all the vertices in any chunk move as a unit. That is, if chunk $\langle P : j \rangle$ comprises the contiguous vertices $\langle p_{s_j}, p_{s_{j+1}}, \cdots, p_{s_{j+l}} \rangle$, the positions of any two of these vertices are perfectly correlated. Consequently, if any vertex in this set has associated uncertainty parameter σ, every other vertex in the chunk also has uncertaintly σ. On the other hand, the vertices from different chunk are independent.

Figure 3(a) shows a polygon $\langle P \rangle$ with four chunks, where the dotted circles have radius σ, the uncertainty parameter of the corresponding chunk. In Figure 3(b) the dark polyon is a possible realization for $\langle P \rangle$. Notice that all the vertices in a chunk move in tandem.

Various types of queries over the uncertain spatial data can be defined under this model. It is also natural to assign a probability value to each query result. A similar approache is adopted in [29, 25], where methods are presented for evaluating probabilistic range queries and nearest neighbour queries over moving points with location uncertainty. Probabilistic range, distance, and spatial join queries may now be defined as follows.

Definition 2. *Probabilistic Range Query: Given a rectangular region R, a set of uncertain polygons S, and a constant γ, $0 \leq \gamma \leq 1$, a Probabilistic Range Query (PRQ) returns a set of pairs of the form (s_i, π_i), where $s_i \in S$, and $\pi_i \geq \gamma$ is the intersection probability between s_i and R. We call γ the confidence threshold for the range query.*

Definition 3. *Probabilistic Distance Query: Given a query point q, a query distance d, a set of uncertain polygons S, and a constant γ, $0 \leq \gamma \leq 1$, a Probabilistic Distance Query (PDQ) returns a set of pairs of the form (s_i, π_i), where $s_i \in S$ is within distance d from q with probability $\pi_i \geq \gamma$. We call γ the confidence threshold for the distance query.*

Definition 4. *Probabilistic Spatial Join: Given two sets of uncertain polygons S_1, S_2, a query distance d, and a constant γ, $0 \leq \gamma \leq 1$, a Probabilistic Spatial Join (PSJ) returns a set of triples of the form (s_i, s_j, π_i), where $s_i \in S_1$ and $s_j \in S_2$ are within distance d of each other with probability $\pi_i \geq \gamma$. We call γ the confidence threshold for the join query.*

A question common to such queries is how to compute the intersection probability between two polygons, given that at least one of them has an uncertain boundary. In the following sections, we will focus on PSJ and show how to evaluate it for the case when $d = 0$, that is for overlap queries. The other queries are answerable using the resulting methods.

4   Query Evaluation for PSJ

As the shapes of spatial objects are rarely regular, they are usually approximated by their Minimum Bounding Rectangles (MBR). Traditional spatial joins are executed in two steps [5]. In the first or *filtering step*, the join predicate is evaluated on the set of MBRs, and a result set of candidate pairs is produced. The MBRs are indexed with indices such as the R-tree and its variations [2, 21], or Seeded Trees [15], and a *tree matching* algorithm is used to find matching pairs of MBRs. In the second or *refinement step*, the actual spatial objects are matched using the join predicate.

This filtering-and-refinement strategy can also be applied to evaluate probabilistic spatial joins. However, traditional spatial indices do not support any notion of uncertainty or probabilistic matching. We must hence modify the MBR approximations and index structures to support probabilistic filtering. In this section, we present the PrR-tree, an R-tree based index structure for uncertain polygons.

4.1   PrR-Tree and Probabilistic Filtering

The PrR-tree is a disk-based, balanced and multi-way tree with the structure of an R-tree. To support probabilistic filtering, we augment the MBR approximation with the probability distribution of MBR's boundary. As in an R-tree, the entry in a leaf node has the form (MBR, oid) tuples, and contains an object's MBR and a pointer to its exact representation. Intermediate node entries have the form (MBR, ptr), where ptr points to a lower level node, and MBR *covers* all the MBRs in this node in the sense explained below.

Consider a polygon $\langle P \rangle$, as in Figure 4, and let its MBR be defined by the lower-left and upper-right vertices being $(x^\vdash, y^\vdash)$ and $(x^\dashv, y^\dashv)$, respectively. We will represent this MBR as $[\|x^\vdash, y^\vdash, x^\dashv, y^\dashv\|]$. Observe that $x^\vdash$ is determined by the vertex of $\langle P \rangle$ with the lowest X-coordinate, and that $y^\vdash$ is determined by the vertex with the lowest Y-coordinate. These may be different vertices, so the uncertainty distribution of the lower-left corner is not a circular Normal, even when the vertices of $\langle P \rangle$ are associated with uncertainties that are circular Normals.

We could, in principle, apply the techniques of *Order Statistics* [20] to derive the probability distribution of $x^\vdash$, from the probability distributions of the individual vertices. However, these derived distributions tend to have very complicated forms, and would impose a high computation cost during the filter step. Instead, we obtain approximations for the distributions for $x^\vdash, y^\vdash, x^\dashv, y^\dashv$ in terms of Normal distributions. This approach is reasonable since the means for the vertex positions are likely to be large compared to their variances.

Therefore, the parameters for the MBR $[\|x^\vdash, y^\vdash, x^\dashv, y^\dashv\|]$ implicitly include both the mean positions $x^\vdash$, $y^\vdash$, $x^\dashv$, $y^\dashv$ as well as the corresponding variances $\sigma_x^\vdash, \sigma_y^\vdash, \sigma_x^\dashv, \sigma_y^\dashv$. One obvious benefit of this approach is that the representation of MBR is quite simple, since we only need add four more values to the traditional representation of MBRs.

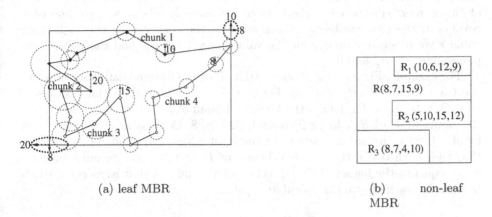

	R$_1$ (10,6,12,9)
R(8,7,15,9)	
	R$_2$ (5,10,15,12)
R$_3$ (8,7,4,10)	

(a) leaf MBR   (b)   non-leaf
                                          MBR

Fig. 4. The MBR at leaf node and the MBR at intermediate node

Specifically, we order the vertices of $\langle P \rangle$ by the mean values of their X and Y coordinates, and take lowest of the X-coordinates to be the mean position of $x^{\vdash}$. The value of $\sigma_x^{\vdash}$ is the maximum σ value among all vertices whose mean positions coincide with the MBR's left edge. For example, Figure 4 (a) shows a polygon with four chunks, whose sigma values are 10, 20, 15, 8, respectively. The left edge of the MBR is defined by one vertex from chunk 2, so that the mean value of $x^{\vdash}$ is defined by the mean position of this vertex, and $\sigma_x^{\vdash}$, the sigma value for $x^{\vdash}$, is equal to the sigma value of chunk 2, that is, $\sigma_x^{\vdash} = 20$. We can similarly obtain the mean values for $y^{\vdash}$, $x^{\dashv}$ and $y^{\dashv}$, and the sigma values $\sigma_y^{\vdash} = 8$, $\sigma_x^{\dashv} = 8$, and $\sigma_y^{\dashv} = 10$.

Covering MBRs. The MBR at the intermediate level of the PrR-Tree can be derived as follows. We represent MBRs as $[|x^{\vdash}, y^{\vdash}, x^{\dashv}, y^{\dashv}|]$, and use $\sigma_x^{\vdash}$, $\sigma_y^{\vdash}$, $\sigma_x^{\dashv}$, $\sigma_y^{\dashv}$ to represent the standard deviation of $x^{\vdash}$, $y^{\vdash}$, $x^{\dashv}$, $y^{\dashv}$, respectively.

We say MBR $[|x^{\vdash}, y^{\vdash}, x^{\dashv}, y^{\dashv}|]$ *covers* the MBRs at an intermediate node in the PrR-tree if it overlays these MBRs tightly. First, the mean position of $x^{\dashv}$ must correspond to the farthest left of the lower-left corners of the covered MBRs.

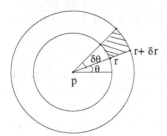

Fig. 5. Shadow area is $\triangle_p(r, \theta)$ for vertex p

Also, the value of $\sigma_x^\vdash$ of the covered MBR must also correspond to the $\sigma_x^\vdash$ value of this corner. (In the case where several covered MBRs have their lower-left corners at the extreme left position, we pick the corner with the highest $\sigma_x^\vdash$ value.) We proceed similarly for the values of $y^\vdash$, $x^\dashv$, $y^\dashv$, and the uncertainty parameters $\sigma_y^\vdash$, $\sigma_x^\dashv$ and $\sigma_y^\dashv$.

For example, Figure 4 (b) shows a MBR R at the intermediate node covering the three MBRs R_1, R_2, and R_3. For simplicity, we only show the σ values of these MBRs. Since R_3 defines the lower X-bound of R, the $\sigma_x^\vdash$ for R is equal to the sigma value of R_3's lower X-bound, that is, 8. Computing $\sigma_x^\dashv$ is a bit more involved, since the mean positions of the right edges of R_1 and R_2 coincide, so that they both define the upper X-bound of R. In this case, we must take R's $\sigma_x^\dashv$ as equal to the higher of the $\sigma_x^\dashv$ values of R_1 and R_2, that is, as equal to 15. In a similar fashion, we can calculate $\sigma_y^\vdash$ and $\sigma_y^\dashv$.

Insertion and Deletion. The insertion and deletion algorithm of the R-tree can be directly applied to the PrR-tree, as the mean positions of MBRs are used to compute their areas, intersection areas, and margins. However, we must maintain the σ values for the MBRs as described above during insertions, deletions, or node split processing.

Filtering Algorithm. The basic idea behind the filtering step for PSJ is to simultaneously traverse the two PrR-trees, checking whether the intersection probabilities between pairs of MBRs exceeds γ. If the intersection probability of two MBRs is less than γ, there can be no PSJ candidate pairs among the MBRs covered by them. Otherwise, there could be candidate pairs whose intersection probability equals or exceeds γ, in the corresponding subtrees.

While our algorithm is similar to the traditional tree-matching algorithm for spatial join in [5], it is also different since it must compute the intersection probability between two MBRs. Given two MBRs $R_1 = [|x_1^\vdash, y_1^\vdash, x_1^\dashv, y_1^\dashv|]$, and $R_2 = [|x_2^\vdash, y_2^\vdash, x_2^\dashv, y_2^\dashv|]$, the intersection probability between them can be computed as follows:

$$\Pr[R_1 \cap R_2] = (1 - \Pr[x_2^\dashv \leq x_1^\vdash] - \Pr[x_1^\dashv \leq x_2^\vdash]) \times (1 - \Pr[y_2^\dashv \leq y_1^\vdash] - \Pr[y_1^\dashv \leq y_2^\vdash]). \tag{1}$$

If X, Y are two independent Normal random variables, then $X - Y$ is also Normal. Therefore, it is quite easy to get $Pr(X \leq Y)$ by computing $Pr(X - Y <= 0)$. Since $x_1^\vdash$, $y_1^\vdash$, $x_1^\dashv$, $y_1^\dashv$, $x_2^\vdash$, $y_2^\vdash$, $x_2^\dashv$ all follow Normal distributions, we can easily compute $Pr(x_2^\dashv \leq x_1^\vdash)$, $Pr(x_1^\dashv \leq x_2^\vdash)$, $Pr(y_2^\dashv \leq y_1^\vdash)$, and $Pr(y_1^\dashv \leq y_2^\vdash)$, and thus derive $\Pr[R_1 \cap R_2]$.

Heuristic Adjustment of the Threshold γ. In Figure 4(b), let the lower bounds along the X-axis for R, R_1, R_2, and R_3 be $x^\vdash$, $x_1^\vdash$, $x_2^\vdash$, and $x_3^\vdash$. Since we have approximated the distribution of $x^\vdash$ with the distribution of $x_1^\vdash$, we risk missing some true hits if we simply used γ as the threshold in the filtering step.

To minimize this risk, we heuristically adjust γ by estimating the probability that our approximation is correct.

Let $\delta_x^\vdash$ be the probability that $x_1^\vdash$ is less than both $x_2^\vdash$ and $x_3^\vdash$. Let $\delta_x^\dashv$, $\delta_y^\vdash$, and $\delta_y^\dashv$ be similarly defined, and let δ be the highest of these values. (Since $x_1^\vdash$, $x_2^\vdash$ and $x_3^\vdash$ follow Normal distributions, these probabilities are easy to compute.) We store δ in R, and use the value $(\delta \times \gamma)$ as the threshold during the filtering step. Our experiments show that this adjustment reduces the number of false negatives at the cost of some increase in false positives. However, the total number of errors is also reduced in the process. Since our problem definition inherently involves uncertainty, not exact matching, this is a reasonable tradeoff.

4.2   The Refinement Step

The filtering step returns a set of candidate pairs whose MBRs intersect with probability at least $(\delta \times \gamma)$. This set, however, may contain false hits which do not satisfy the join predicate. The refinement step must retrieve the exact representations of polygons, compute the intersection probability between two polygons, and evaluate the join predicate. We now consider this problem in greater detail.

Consider two polygons $\langle P_1 \rangle$ and $\langle P_2 \rangle$. To get the intersection probability between $\langle P_1 \rangle$ and $\langle P_2 \rangle$, we first compute the probability that at least one vertex of $\langle P_1 \rangle$ is located inside $\langle P_2 \rangle$, and the probability that at least one vertex of $\langle P_2 \rangle$ is located inside $\langle P_1 \rangle$. We then use the larger of these values as the intersection probability between $\langle P_1 \rangle$ and $\langle P_2 \rangle$.

Denote the event that at least one vertex of $\langle P_1 \rangle$ is located inside $\langle P_2 \rangle$, by $[\langle P_1 \rangle \succ \langle P_2 \rangle]$. We now consider how to compute the probability $\Pr[\langle P_1 \rangle \succ \langle P_2 \rangle]$. The exact representations of $\langle P_1 \rangle$ and $\langle P_2 \rangle$ are retrieved. Since the uncertainties of any two chunks are independent, the event that the vertices of $\langle P_1 : i \rangle$ are outside of $\langle P_2 \rangle$ is independent of the event that the vertices of $\langle P_1 : j \rangle$ are outside of $\langle P_2 \rangle$. It therefore follows that

$$\Pr[\langle P_1 \rangle \succ \langle P_2 \rangle] = 1 - \Pr[\langle P_1 \rangle \nsucc \langle P_2 \rangle] = 1 - \prod_{j=1}^{k}(1 - \Pr[\langle P_1 : j \rangle \succ \langle P_2 \rangle]). \quad (2)$$

Now, given the chunk $\langle P_1 : j \rangle$, it remains to show how to compute $\Pr[\langle P_1 : j \rangle \succ \langle P_2 \rangle]$, the probability that any vertex in $\langle P_1 : j \rangle$ is located inside $\langle P_2 \rangle$.

Computing Intersection Probabilities. In Figure 5, let $\triangle_p(r, \theta)$ denote the shaded area between the circles of radii r and $r + \delta r$ at angles θ and $\theta + \delta\theta$ centered around the mean position of p, here p is any vertex from the chunk $\langle P_1 : j \rangle$. From Definition 1, the probability that p is located within a circle of radius r centered at its mean is given by the distribution $\Pr(r) = 1 - e^{-\frac{r^2}{2\sigma^2}}$, where σ is the uncertainty parameter of p and the other vertices in $\langle P_1 : j \rangle$. The corresponding density function is $\mathrm{pr}(r) = \frac{r}{\sigma^2}e^{-r^2/(2\sigma^2)}$. Then, the probability

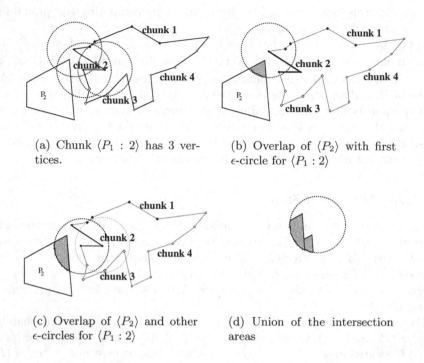

(a) Chunk $\langle P_1 : 2 \rangle$ has 3 vertices.

(b) Overlap of $\langle P_2 \rangle$ with first ϵ-circle for $\langle P_1 : 2 \rangle$

(c) Overlap of $\langle P_2 \rangle$ and other ϵ-circles for $\langle P_1 : 2 \rangle$

(d) Union of the intersection areas

Fig. 6. Computing $\Pr[\langle P_1, 2 \rangle \succ \langle P_2 \rangle$

that p is located inside $\triangle_p(r, \theta)$ is obtained from the corresponding density function as $\mathrm{pr}(r) * \delta r * \frac{\delta\theta}{2\pi}$.

Recall that our aim is to get the probability that *any* vertex from the chunk $\langle P_1 : j \rangle$ is located inside $\langle P_2 \rangle$. That is, we don't really care if more than one such vertex is located inside $\langle P_2 \rangle$. We therefore define an indicator function $I(r, \theta)$, such that $I(r, \theta) = 1$ if and only if there is a vertex from $\langle P_1 : j \rangle$, for which $\triangle_p(r, \theta)$ is inside $\langle P_2 \rangle$ for some values of r and θ. Now, we can obtain $\Pr[\langle P_1 : j \rangle \succ \langle P_2 \rangle]$ by integrating over all possible r and θ to get

$$\Pr[\langle P_1 : j \rangle \succ \langle P_2 \rangle] = \int_0^\infty dr \int_0^{2\pi} \frac{1}{2\pi} \mathrm{pr}(r) * I(r, \theta) d\theta. \qquad (3)$$

ϵ-Circles and Efficient Computation of the Integral. In practice, it is unnecessary to integrate from 0 to ∞, since the Gaussian distribution is concentrated near its mean. For instance, the probability that p is inside a circle of radius $r = 3\sigma$ is more than 0.99. We can simplify the integral by choosing a probability ϵ, and then finding the r_ϵ such that $\Pr[r_\epsilon] = 1 - \epsilon$. In this case, the probability that p is beyond radius r_ϵ is no more than ϵ. Now, we are safe in computing the above integral by integrating from 0 to r_ϵ. For a given value of ϵ, this resulting circle of radius r_ϵ is called the ϵ-*circle*.

Table 2. Characteristics of the Data Sets Used in the Experiments

Set	Description	Size	Density	Vsize	Csize	CV_{area}	CV_{dist}
LAB	Los Angeles block groups	6357	0.79	35.2	6.9	0.17	
LAL	Los Angeles landmark polygons	5135	0.45	31.8	6.2	0.27	0.0023
UM1	Uniformly distributed monotone polygons	10000	0.34	30.0	5.9	0.35	
UM2	Uniformly distributed monotone polygons	10000	0.31	30.0	5.9	0.35	0.0018
UM3	Uniformly distributed monotone polygons	50000	0.39	29.9	5.9	0.35	
UM4	Uniformly distributed monotone polygons	50000	0.39	30.0	5.9	0.35	0.0010

We simplify the computation of the integral $\int_0^{r_\epsilon} dr \int_0^{2\pi} \frac{1}{2\pi} pr(r) * I(r, \theta) d\theta$. Consider Figure 6 (a), where we need compute $\Pr[\langle P_1 : 2\rangle \succ \langle P_2\rangle]$, the probability that some vertex of the chunk $\langle P_1 : 2\rangle$ of $\langle P_1\rangle$ is located inside $\langle P_2\rangle$. First, we pick a constant ϵ, and for each vertex p in chunk $\langle P_1 : 2\rangle$, we compute the overlap area between $\langle P_2\rangle$ and an ϵ-circle around p (see Figure 6 (b), (c)). If the union of these intersection areas is A (see Figure 6 (d)), we simply compute $\int \int_A \frac{1}{2\pi} pr(r) dr d\theta$.

5 Experimental Evaluation

We conducted experiments to examine the performance of PSJ with both synthetic and real-life datasets, to determine the accuracy, efficiency, and the scalability of our Probabilistic Spatial Join method.

5.1 Data Sets

In our experiments, we used *quasi-real* and *synthetic* datasets. The quasi-real datasets were generated using real map information as follows. We used the TIGER/LINE data from the U.S Bureau of the Census [19] to determine the mean position of the polygons. We then randomly generated chunks and associated uncertainties (standard deviations σ for the circular normal distribution in our case). For synthetic datasets, both the polygons and chunks with uncertainties were generated randomly.

Table 2 describes several *quasi-real* and synthetic datasets used in the experiments. We use *density*, defined as the total area of the polygons' MBR divided by the total area of the workspace, to measure the coverage of the datasets. The metric *Vsize* represents the average number of vertices per polygon, while *Csize* represents the average number of chunks per polygon. Also, we use the coefficient of variation for the polygons' area(CV_{area}) and the coefficient of variation for the distance between two polygons (CV_{dist}) to measure the degree of uncertainty of the datasets.

The data set LAB contains the block groups in Los Angeles, while LAL contains the landmark polygons in Los Angeles. The synthetic dataset UM1, UM2,UM3,UM4 are created according to a uniformly distributions with 100 clusters. As in [16], we first generated 100 cluster rectangles, whose centers were randomly distributed in the map area. Once the cluster rectangles are generated, we can randomly generate the MBRs of the polygons, which fixes the size and location of the random polygons.

Given the MBRs, we use the method in [1] to generate random *monotone polygons*, a very common class of polygons, as follows. First, a set of random points is chosen inside the MBR, and a random horizontal line is drawn through them. The points above and below the line are sorted by their x coordinates and connected in the sorted order. The leftmost and rightmost points are moved vertically to the splitting line, and are connected to the other points to form a polygon. Finally, this horizontally aligned polygon is rotated by a random angle.

The ground truth in our experiments is computed using *Monte Carlo* approach. Given two datasets associated with uncertainty, n equally probable realizations are generated and spatial join is applied to these n realizations. Based on the results from n runs, the intersection probability between any polygons are computed. These experimentally obtained intersection probabilities are assumed to be the ground truth and used to measure the accuracy of different approaches. In our experiment, we set $n = 1000$.

5.2 Competing Methods

To demonstrate the efficiency and accuracy of PSJ, we compare it with two other competitors: *Mean Spatial join (MSJ)* and *Random Spatial Join (RSJ)*. PSJ is our algorithm, as described in Section 4. It has two PrR-trees before evaluating join operations. MSJ is the normal R-tree based spatial join using the mean positions of the polygons. Both the two datasets have pre-existing R^*-tree indices and the query is executed using the algorithm in [5]. RSJ is same as the *Monte Carlo Simulation* approach used to get the ground truth, except that RSJ uses much fewer random samples. The notations RSJ3, RSJ5, RSJ10 indicate that the number of random realizations were 3, 5, and 10, respectively.

Each run of RSJ executes the following four steps. First, the the uncertain polygons are read in, and a random sample is generated. Next, we build two R^*-tree for this random sample. The third step is to run the filter step using these two R^*-tree . The final step is to run the refinement step using plane sweep algorithm.

As indicated in [16], it is much more expensive to perform spatial join for two non-indexed datasets using R^*-tree based approach, compared with other approaches like spatial hash join [16], size separation spatial join [12] and PBSM [23]. To make our comparisons with RSJ reasonable, we ignore the costs of tree construction and the costs of the filter step. That is, we counted the CPU and I/O costs of only the first and fourth steps described above. No matter which filtering technique is used, those two steps are essential. In other words, for RSJ, the measured CPU and I/O costs are underestimates, and the real costs should be larger than our measurements.

Table 3. Space and overall construction costs of PrR-tree, normalized to those costs of R^*-tree

Dataset	Ratio of space cost	Ratio of overall construction cost
LAL	1.89	1.90
UM1	1.84	2.04
UM3	1.93	1.85

5.3   Experimental Setup

The experiments were conducted on a Pentium IV 1.7GHz machine with 512MBytes of RAM, running Mandrake Linux 8.2. All the algorithms were implemented in C++ using GNU compilers. To measure I/O costs, we assumed a buffer page size of 8K. The buffer size is set to be 10% of the total size of two datasets. In our experiments, the datasets used have size of 8M, 11M, 55M, respectively. Therefore, the buffer size is set to be 800K(100 pages), 1112K(139 pages), 5536K(692 pages). To compute the I/O cost more precisely, it is desirable to distinguish sequential I/O access from random I/O access. We assumed the ratio of the cost of accessing one disk block randomly to that of accessing one disk block sequentially to be 5 [16], and measured the I/O cost as the number of weighted disk access. The CPU cost can be accurately measured during the program is running. The overall cost is obtained by charging 10ms each random disk access, charging 2ms each sequential access.

5.4   Performance Metrics and Evaluation

The first set of experiments is to evaluate the space and overall construction cost of PrR-tree, compared with those of R^*-tree . Table 3 presents the ratio of the size of PrR-tree to the size of R^*-tree for the three groups of datasets, and the ratio of the overall cost of building PrR-tree to the overall cost of building R^*-tree . Note here the buffer size is set to be 10% of the size of PrR-trees.

We then evaluate the accuracy of the three methods. Accuracy covers two aspects: *completeness*, or how well the method is able to find the object pairs that should be found, and *fidelity*, which measures how close the returned probability is to the actual probability defined by ground truth.

Two metrics are used to measure the completeness aspect of the accuracy of the three methods: *ratio of false negative*(R_{fn}) and *ratio of false positive*(R_{fp}). Let GT represent the ground true result, QR represents the query result. R_{fn} is defined as $|GT - QR|/|QT|$, and R_{fp} is defined as $|QR - GT|/|QR|$. The accuracy of competing methods is compared in terms of *errorRatio*, defined as the sum of R_{fn} and R_{fp}. The comparisons are shown in Figure 7(a) - (c).

As for fidelity, we use the root mean square error (square root of the average of the set of squared differences) between the returned probability and the actual probability (RMSE). These comparisons are shown in Figure 7(d)-(f).

Finally, we evaluate the efficiency of the three methods, in terms of CPU cost, weighted I/O cost and overall cost. The results are shown in Figure 8.

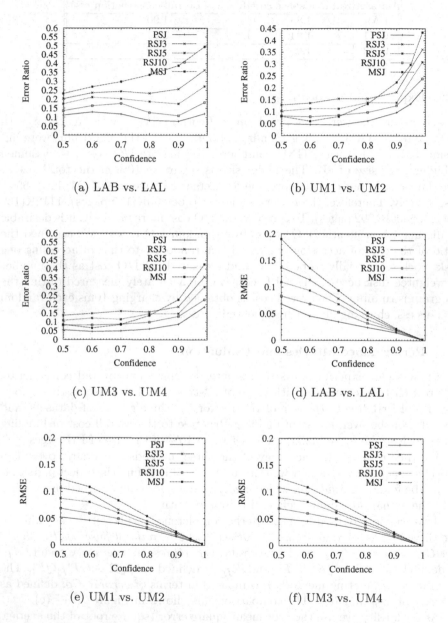

(a) LAB vs. LAL

(b) UM1 vs. UM2

(c) UM3 vs. UM4

(d) LAB vs. LAL

(e) UM1 vs. UM2

(f) UM3 vs. UM4

Fig. 7. Experimental comparison of error ratio and RMSE

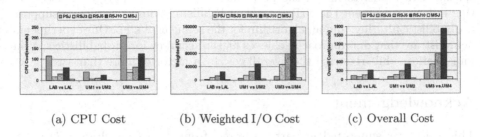

(a) CPU Cost　　　　　(b) Weighted I/O Cost　　　　　(c) Overall Cost

Fig. 8. Experimental comparison of Evaluation Cost

5.5　Comparisons

As Table 3 shows, the space and construction costs for PrR-tree is roughly 80% - 100% higher than that of R^*-tree . This is expected, since each entry of PrR-tree records the mean positions as well as the standard deviations, and the insertion procedure must maintain both these values.

Figures 7 and 8 show that MSJ has the lowest CPU cost, weighted I/O cost and overall cost for all of the datasets. However, MSJ's *errorRatio* is among one of the highest. In particular, when the confidence threshold ranges between 0.85 - 0.99, its *errorRatio* increased dramatically to about 0.3 - 0.5. We conclude that MSJ does not make much sense when the confidence threshold is relatively high, although it has low CPU cost and I/O cost.

RSJ has lower CPU cost than PSJ, but much higher I/O cost. RSJ's I/O costs and accuracy increase with the number of samples since it must retrieve the representations of uncertain polygons and generate random samples for each run. Also, RSJ's I/O cost dominates the overall cost. With the gap between computation speed and I/O speed continuing to increase, the overhead of RSJ's I/O cost makes it unsuitable for large spatial databases.

In contrast, PSJ achieves the lowest *errorRatio* and RMSE among the three competitors, with the overall cost being reduced by a factor of 2.4–5.3 over RSJ10, which has the highest accuracy among the three variations of RSJ. PSJ has the highest CPU cost, since it must compute integrals during the refinement step. However, this drawback is compensated for by its weighted I/O cost, which is much lower than RSJ's. It is worth noting that PSJ outperforms RSJ10 in proportional to dataset size, since RSJ10 has much higher I/O overhead. We believe that with the continuing increases in CPU speed, PSJ's computation overhead will not be a great problem.

6　Conclusions

The modeling of spatial objects with uncertain boundaries and evaluating spatial queries over them is an open issue. We have presented a method for performing spatial joins over uncertain spatial data. We have also proposed a probabilistic spatial data model to model the positional uncertainty of polygons. Based on this model, we present the PrR-tree, a probabilisitc index structure to support probabilistic filtering, and an algorithm for the refinement step. Our experiments demonstrate that our approach achieves higher accuracy for probabilistic spatial join queries, while reducing the overall cost by a factor of more than two.

Acknowledgement

This work was supported in part by grants from Tata Consultancy Services, Inc., the Digital Media Innovations program of the University of California, the National Science Foundation under contract 0114036, and by the Fault-Tolerant Networks program of the Defense Advanced Research Projects Agency, under contract F30602-01-2-0536. Thanks are due to M. Hadjieleftheriou for providing the R^*-tree library, and to Sandeep Gupta for helpful discussions.

References

[1] A. Aboulnaga and J.F. Naughton. Accurate estimation of the cost of spatial selections. In *Proceedings of International Conference on Data Engineering(ICDE)*, pages 123–134, San Diego, California, March 2000. 153

[2] A. Guttman. R-trees: A dynamic index structure for spatial searching. In *Proceedings of the 1984 ACM-SIGMOD Conference*, pages 47–57, Boston, Massachusetts, June 1984. 143, 147

[3] M. Azouzi. Introducing the concept of reliability in spatial data. In Kim Lowell and Annick Jaton, editors, *Spatial Accuracy Assessment: land information uncertainty in Natural Resources*, pages 139–144. Ann Arbor Press, 1999. 145

[4] T. Brinkhoff, H. Kriegel, R. Schneider, and B. Seeger. Multi-step processing of spatial joins. In *Proceedings of the 1994 ACM-SIGMOD Conference*, pages 197–208, Minneapolis, Minnesota, May 1994. 143

[5] T. Brinkhoff, H. Kriegel, and B. Seeger. Efficient processing of spatial joins using r-trees. In *Proceedings of the 1993 ACM-SIGMOD Conference*, pages 237–246, Washington, D.C., May 1993. 142, 143, 147, 149, 153

[6] FGDC. National standard for spatial data accuracy, fgdc-std-007.3-1998. http://www.fgdc.gov/standards/status/sub1_3.html, March 1998. 140, 141

[7] M.F. Goodchild, A.M. Shortridge, and P. Fohl. Encapsulating simulation models with geospatial data sets. In Kim Lowell and Annick Jaton, editors, *Spatial Accuracy Assessment: land information uncertainty in Natural Resources*, pages 123–129. Ann Arbor Press, 1999. 142, 143

[8] G.B.M. Heuvelink. *Error Propagation in Environmental Modeling with GIS*. Taylor & Francis, London, UK, 1998. 140

[9] Y.W. Huang, M. Jones, and E. A. Rundensteiner. Symbolic intersect detection: A method for improving spatial intersect joins. *GeoInformatica*, 2(2):149–174, June 1998. 143

[10] G. Hunter and M.F. Goodchild. Application of new model of vector data uncertainty. In Kim Lowell and Annick Jaton, editors, *Spatial Accuracy Assessment: land information uncertainty in Natural Resources*, pages 203–208. Ann Arbor Press, 1999. 143

[11] J.P. King. Modeling boundaries of influence among positional uncertainty fields. Master's thesis, University of Maine, December 2002. 145

[12] N. Koudas and K. C. Sevcik. Size separation spatial join. In *Proceedings of the 1997 ACM-SIGMOD Conference*, pages 324–335, Tucson, Arizona, May 1997. 143, 153

[13] Y. Leung and J. Yan. Point-in-polygon analysis under certainty and uncertainty. *GeoInformatica*, 1(1):93–114, Apr 1997. 143, 145

[14] Y. Leung and J. Yan. A locational error model for spatial features. *Int. J. Geographical Information Science*, 12(6):607–620, Nov 1998. 145

[15] M.L. Lo and C. V. Ravishankar. Spatial joins using seeded trees. In *Proceedings of the 1994 ACM-SIGMOD Conference*, pages 209–220, Minneapolis, Minnesota, June 1994. 143, 147

[16] M.L. Lo and C. V. Ravishankar. Spatial hash join. In *Proceedings of the 1996 ACM-SIGMOD Conference*, pages 247–258, Montreal, Canada, June 1996. 143, 152, 153, 154

[17] N. Mamoulis and D. Papadias. Slot index spatial join. *IEEE Transaction on Knowledge and Data Engineering*, 15(1):211–231, Jan 2003. 143

[18] Minnesota Planning. Positional accuracy handbook. http://www.mnplan.state.mn.us/press/accurate.html, October 1999. 141, 142

[19] U.S. Bureau of the Census. *Census 2000 TIGER/Line Data*. Washington DC, 2000. 152

[20] N. Balakrishnan and C.R. Rao. *Order statistics: theory and methods*. Elsevier, New York, 1998. 147

[21] N.Beckmann, R. Schneider H.P. Kriegel, and B. Seeger. The r*-tree: An efficient and robust access method for points and rectangles. In *Proceedings of the 1990 ACM-SIGMOD Conference*, pages 322–331, Atlantic City, NJ, May 1990. 143, 147

[22] S. Openshaw. Learning to live with errors in spatial databases. In M. Goodchild and S. Gopal, editors, *Accuracy of Spatial Databases*, pages 263–276. Taylor & Francis, 1989. 143

[23] J. M. Patel and D. J. DeWitt. Partition based spatial-merge join. In *Proceedings of the 1996 ACM-SIGMOD Conference*, pages 259–270, Montreal, Canada, June 1996. 143, 153

[24] D. Pfoser and C. S. Jensen. Capturing the uncertainty of moving-object representations. In *Proceeding of the 6th International Symposium on Large Spatial Databases(SSD)*, pages 111–132, Hongkong, China, July 1999. 144

[25] R. Cheng, D.V. Kalashnikov, and S. Prabhakar. Querying imprecise data in moving object environments. Poster Session, International Conference on Data Engineering(ICDE), 2003. To appear. 142, 144, 146

[26] W. Shi. A generic statistical approach for modeling error of geometric features in gis. *Int. J. Geographical Information Science*, 12(2):131–143, March 1998. 143

[27] W. Shi and W. Liu. A stochastic process-based model for the positional error of line segments in gis. *Int. J. Geographical Information Science*, 14(1):51–66, Jan 2000. 143

[28] G. Trajcevski, O. Wolfson, F. Zhang, and S. Chamberlain. The geometry of uncertainty in moving object databases. In *Proceedings of the 8th International Conference on Extending Database Technology(EDBT)*, pages 233–250, Prague, Czech Republic, March 2002. 144

[29] O. Wolfson, P.A. Sistla, S. Chamberlain, and Y. Yesha. Updating and querying databases that track mobile units. *Distributed and Parallel Databases*, 3(7):257–387, July 1999. 142, 144, 146

[30] J.X. Zhang and M.F. Goodchild. *Uncertainty in Geographical Information System*. Taylor & Francis, Erewhon, NC, 2002. 140

[31] G. Zimbrao and J.M. Souza. A raster approximation for the processing of spatial joins. In *Proceedings of the 24th VLDB Conference*, pages 311–322, New York City, New York, August 1998. 143

Validity Information Retrieval for Spatio-Temporal Queries: Theoretical Performance Bounds

Yufei Tao[1], Nikos Mamoulis[2], and Dimitris Papadias[3]

[1] Department of Computer Science
Carnegie Mellon University, USA, 15213-3891
taoyf@cs.cmu.edu
[2] Department of Computer Science and Information Systems
University of Hong Kong , Hong Kong
nikos@csis.hku.hk
[3] Department of Computer Science
Hong Kong University of Science and Technology, Hong Kong
dimitris@cs.ust.hk

Abstract. The results of traditional spatial queries (i.e., range search, nearest neighbor, etc.) are usually meaningless in spatio-temporal applications, because they will be invalidated by the movements of query and/or data objects. In practice, a query result R should be accompanied with *validity information* specifying (i) the (future) time T that R will expire, and (ii) the change C of R at time T (so that R can be updated incrementally). Although several algorithms have been proposed for this problem, their worst-case performance is the same as that of sequential scan. This paper presents the first theoretical study on validity queries, and develops indexes and algorithms with attractive I/O complexities. Our discussion covers numerous important variations of the problem and different query/object mobility combinations. The solutions involve a set of non-trivial reductions that reveal the problem characteristics and permit the deployment of existing structures.

1 Problem Formulation

Traditional spatial query processing is insufficient in spatio-temporal applications, where the data and/or query objects change their locations. Consider, for example, a moving user who asks for the nearest hotel; the result (e.g., hotel a) of a conventional nearest neighbor query is by itself meaningless because it may be invalidated as soon as the user moves. In practice, the query result R should be accompanied by additional validity information: (i) the *expiry time T* of R, i.e., the future time when a ceases to be the nearest hotel (based on the user's moving direction and speed), and (ii) the result change C at T (e.g., the next nearest hotel after a expires). This problem is not specific to nearest neighbor search, but actually exists in all query types [TP02].

T. Hadzilacos et al. (Eds.): SSTD 2003, LNCS 2750, pp. 159–178, 2003.

In this paper, we discuss validity information retrieval for the most common spatial queries, namely, (orthogonal) range search (RS) and nearest neighbor (NN) queries, considering one- or two- dimensional objects with linear movements. Following the common modeling in the literature [SJLL00, GBE+00], a moving point p is represented using its location $\mathbf{p}(0)$ at the system reference time 0, and its current velocity $\mathbf{v}$ ($\mathbf{p}(0)$ and $\mathbf{v}$ are 1D/2D vectors), such that its location $\mathbf{p}(t)$ at any future time t can be computed as $\mathbf{p}(t)=\mathbf{p}(0)+\mathbf{v}\cdot t$. Similarly, we represent a moving rectangle with two moving points that decide its opposite corners, under the constraint that they have identical velocity vectors (i.e., the extent of the rectangle remains fixed at all times). Static objects are trivially captured with zero velocities. Without loss of generality, we assume (unless specifically stated) that the system reference time 0 coincides with the current time.

The result R of a spatial query is invalidated when some object "influences" it in the future, namely, (i) an object currently not in R starts qualifying the query predicate, or (ii) an object originally in R incurs predicate violation. A natural way to define validity retrieval is through the concept of "influence time" introduced in [TP02]. Specifically, given a RS (range search) query q with result R (containing all the objects currently covered by q), the *influence time* T_p of data point p in R, equals the earliest time that p falls out of q; on the other hand, for a point p not in R, T_p corresponds to the first timestamp that p lies in q. The concept of influence time also applies to NN (nearest neighbor) search. In this case, the influence time of a data point is the time when it will come closer to q than its current NN. Here the influence time should be interpreted as the time that the object will invalidate the query result R, only if it has not changed earlier. Now we are ready to formulate the problem of validity information retrieval.

Problem (Validity Information Retrieval): Given a set of points $S=\{p_1, p_2, ..., p_N\}$ and a spatial query at the current time 0, the corresponding *validity query* q returns (i) the expiry time $T=\min\{T_{p_i} (1 \leq i \leq N)\}$, and (ii) the result change (at time T) $C=\{p_i \in S: T_{p_i}=T\}$, where T_{p_i} is the influence time of point p_i. $\Rightarrow$

This paper presents the first study on the theoretical complexity of validity queries, aiming at solutions with good worst case performance. Our discussion is based on the popular memory-disk hierarchy [ASV99, AAE00], where each I/O access transfers a page of B (i.e., page size) units of information from the disk to the main memory, which contains at least B^2 pages (a reasonable assumption in practice). The query cost is measured as the number of disk pages visited. Our objective is to achieve fast query time with small space consumption.

1.1   Previous Results

A study of validity queries appear in [TP02] which deploys branch-and-bound algorithms on R*-trees [BKSS90] (for static objects) and TPR-trees [SJLL00] (for dynamic objects). In the worst case, these algorithms perform $O(N/B)$ I/Os (i.e., the complexity of a simple sequential scan), where N is the number of objects in the dataset. All the other attempts [SR01, TPS02, BJKS02] addressing variations of the problem, incur the same complexity. On the other hand, there is a significant amount of theoretical results on conventional spatial queries for static and moving objects.

For *orthogonal range search* on static points, Kanth and Singh [KS99] prove that the best possible query time using any structure consuming linear $O(N/B)$ space is $O((N/B)^{1/2}+K/B)$ I/Os, where K is the number of objects retrieved. This bound is tight and has been realized by the *O-tree* [KS99] and the *cross-tree* [GI99]. Applying the theory of indexability [HKP97], Arge et al. [ASV99] show that a structure achieving optimal query cost $O(\log_B(N/B)+K/B)$ must occupy $\Omega((N/B)\log_B(N/B)/\mathrm{loglog}_B(N/B))$ space. They propose the *external range tree* that achieves these bounds. A special RS is the so-called *3-sided query*, where an edge of the query rectangle lies on the boundary of the data space. Arge et al. [ASV99] design the *external priority search tree* that answers such queries optimally (i.e., logarithmic query cost and linear space consumption). Earlier, non-optimal structures for RS and 3-sided queries can be found in [IKO87, KRVV96, RS94, SR95].

The first study on RS queries for moving objects [KGT99a] deals with only 1D data. Agarwal et al. [AAE00] present several interesting results in the 2D space following the *kinetic approach* [BGH97]. In particular, they show that if queries arrive in chronological order, a RS can be answered with the same time complexity as the static case (i.e., optimally) using the kinetic external range tree. They also give two time-responsive indexing schemes (later refined in [AAV01]) where the query cost depends on the difference between the query issue time and the current time.

Fewer results exist for nearest neighbor search in secondary memory. For static data, a Voronoi diagram can be constructed in $O(N\log N)$ time [BKOS97], after which a NN query is reduced to a point-location problem (i.e., identifying the Voronoi cell that contains the query point), which can be solved optimally using linear space and logarithmic I/O overhead [ADT03]. Agarwal et al. [AAE+00] design another solution that avoids computing the Voronoi diagram, and answers a NN query in $O(\log_B(N/B))$ time, but uses non-linear $(N/B)\log(N/B)$ space. Little work has been done for NN retrieval on moving objects in external memory. Kollios et al. [KGT99b] develop various schemes, but do not prove any performance bound. Finally, several solutions exist for the different but related problem of approximate nearest neighbor search [CGR95, GLM00, AAE00]. In this paper we focus on exact NN queries.

1.2   Our Results

For static data (and moving queries), we show that a validity RS query can be answered optimally in $O(\log_B(N/B))$ I/Os using $O(N/B)$ space, for a constant number of query sizes and directions. Then, we discuss the problem where the query has arbitrary size but its movement is restricted to be axis-parallel, and develop a structure that consumes $O((N/B)\log_B(N/B))$ space and answers a query in $O(\log_B(N/B))$ I/Os. Based on the external range tree, we present another solution that occupies $O((N/B)\log_B(N/B)/\mathrm{loglog}_B(N/B))$ space and solves a query in $O(\log_B^2(N/B)/\mathrm{loglog}_B(N/B))$ I/Os. The persistent version of this structure answers a query with arbitrary size and moving direction with the same cost but higher space complexity $O((N^2/B)\log_B(N/B)/\mathrm{loglog}_B(N/B))$. All the above problems can also be solved using a modified partition tree with linear space and query overhead $O((N/B)^{1/2+\varepsilon})$, where ε is an arbitrarily small positive number. For moving data and static RS, a validity query can be answered with optimal $O(\log_B(N/B))$ I/O cost, using an index with $O((N^2/B)\log_B(N/B))$ space. If both objects and queries move on a linear space, we propose a solution that achieves $O(\log_B(N/B))$ query time and requires $O(N/B)$ space. Further, given a Voronoi diagram on static data, a validity NN query can be answered in $\log(N/B)$ time based on an optimal external memory structure for point location queries. The same complexity can also be achieved for one-dimensional dynamic queries and objects.

The rest of the paper is organized as follows. Section 2 reviews the previous indexes fundamental to our discussion, and elaborates the problems solved together with the corresponding query time and space complexities. Section 3 presents our results for validity RS queries, while Section 4 focuses on nearest neighbor search. Section 5 concludes the paper with a set of open problems.

2   Preliminary Structures

The *persistent* (also known as *multi-version*) B-tree [BGO+96] is an efficient storage scheme for a set of B-trees B_1, B_2, ..., B_β. The idea is to store in B_i ($2 \leq i \leq \beta$) only the "changes" from the previous version B_{i-1}, while sharing the index nodes that contain their common records. Particularly, in each node, there is either none or at least $\Theta(B)$ records for any B_i ($1 \leq i \leq \beta$), which guarantees that querying each B_i has the same complexity as a normal B-tree. As proven in [BGO+96], if the total number of distinct records in all B-trees (i.e., the total number of "changes" between consecutive trees) is $O(N)$, a persistent B-tree uses linear space $O(N/B)$ and can be constructed in $O((N/B)\log_B(N/B))$ I/Os [A94]. A range-query in any B-tree B_i ($1 \leq i \leq \beta$) is answered in $O(\log_B(N_i/B)+\log_B(\beta/B)+K/B) = O(\log_B(N/B)+K/B)$ I/Os, where N_i is the number of records in B_i, β the total number of B-trees, and K is the number of records retrieved. Both the space and query time complexities are optimal. As shown shortly, the persistent structure constitutes a powerful tool for our problem.

The *partition tree* [AAE00] is a popular 2D structure for the *simplex range query*, which specifies a constant number of half-planes and retrieves the set of points in their intersection (i.e., the search region). Given a set S with N points, the idea is to construct a *balanced simplicial partition* $\Lambda = \{\Lambda_1, \Lambda_2, ..., \Lambda_r\}$, where $r = O(B)$ and all points in Λ_i ($1 \leq i \leq r$) are covered by a triangle Δ_i. The partitions have the following properties: (i) $\Lambda_1 \cup \Lambda_2 \cup ... \cup \Lambda_r = S$, (ii) for any i, j in $[1,r]$, $\Lambda_i \cap \Lambda_j = \varnothing$ (i.e., the first two properties guarantee that any data point belongs to a unique partition), (iii) each Λ_i ($1 \leq i \leq r$) contains at most $2N/r$ points, and (iv) the number of triangles Δ_i crossed by *any* line l in the data space is $O(\sqrt{r}) = O(\sqrt{B})$. Δ_1, Δ_2, ..., Δ_r constitute the entries in the root node of the partition tree. The next level is created by constructing balanced simplicial partitions for each Λ_i ($1 \leq i \leq r$), and this process is repeated until each partition contains $O(B)$ points, in which case all points in it are stored collectively as a leaf node. Since every point appears in a unique leaf node, the whole tree consumes $O(N/B)$ disk pages. A simplex range query is answered by visiting those nodes whose bounding triangles intersect its search region. Agarwal et al. [AAE+00] show that the query cost is bounded by $O((N/B)^{1/2+\varepsilon}+K/B)$ I/Os, where ε is an arbitrarily small positive number.

The *external priority search tree* [ASV99] answers a *3-sided query q* optimally. Specifically, given a set S of N 2D points, this tree consumes $O(N/B)$ space, and answers q in $O(\log_B(N/B)+K/B)$ I/Os, where K is the number of points retrieved. Interestingly, it also optimally solves *stabbing* queries on 1D intervals. Specifically, given a set of N 1D intervals $\{i_1, i_2, ..., i_N\}$ where $i_j=[i_{sj},i_{ej}]$ ($1{\leq}j{\leq}N$), a stabbing query specifies a value q and retrieves all intervals i_j ($1{\leq}j{\leq}N$) such that $i_{sj}{\leq}q{\leq}i_{ej}$. To solve the problem with the external priority search tree, each interval $i_j=[i_{sj},i_{ej}]$ is converted to a 2D point (i_{sj},i_{ej}); the intervals satisfying q correspond to those points in the 3-sided rectangle with x-projection $[0, q]$ and y-projection $[q, \infty)$.

3   Validity Information Retrieval for Range Search

The result of a RS query q changes (as q or data move) when the boundary of q hits a data point p. Thus, we can retrieve, for each edge e_i ($1{\leq}i{\leq}4$) of q, the first point p_i that will be hit by e_i, together with the time t_i when this happens. The expiry time T of the current result then equals the smallest t_i ($1{\leq}i{\leq}4$), and the result change C is due to the point p_i with $t_i=T$ (i.e., T is the influence time of p_i). Therefore, a validity RS query can be reduced to four *dragging queries*[1] each specifying a moving horizontal/vertical line segment (the direction of movement can be arbitrary), and finds the first point it crosses. Consider, for example, Figure 3.1a with static data points $p_1, p_2, ..., p_7$ (similar observations also hold for dynamic objects). The validity RS query q is reduced to dragging queries e_1, e_2, e_3, e_4 as in Figure 3.1b, for which the first points hit are $\varnothing, p_4$, $\varnothing, p_6$, respectively (the result of the validity query is p_4 since it is crossed earlier than p_6). In the sequel we focus on the vertical dragging query q (the same solutions apply to horizontal queries by symmetry), whose initial position is a vertical line segment at $x=q_x$ with y-projection $[q_{sy},q_{ey}]$ (represented as $q_x:[q_{sy},q_{ey}]$). A query is characterized using two parameters: (i) *query length* $q_L=q_{ey}-q_{sy}$, and (ii) *tilting angle* q_θ between the query's moving direction and the x-axis, as shown in Figure 3.1c using e_4 as an example. The subsequent sections solve vertical dragging queries in various problem settings, covering both static data points (Sections 3.1-3.3) and the dynamic ones (Sections 3.4, 3.5).

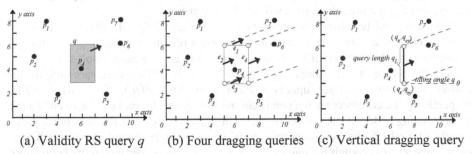

(a) Validity RS query q (b) Four dragging queries   (c) Vertical dragging query

Fig. 3.1. Reducing RS validity retrieval to dragging queries

---

[1] The term "dragging query" was first used in [C88] for orthogonal line segments with axis-parallel movements. Here, we use this term for queries with arbitrary moving directions.

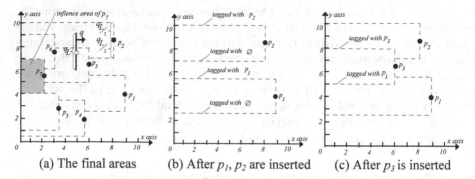

Fig. 3.2. Computing the influence areas

3.1   Static Data and Predictable Queries

We first present an optimal solution that consumes linear space $O(N/B)$ and answers a "predictable" dragging query q in $O(\log_B(N/B))$ I/Os, namely, the query's length and tilting angle (of its movement) are chosen from a *constant* number of combinations[2]. Our solution consists of a set of structures, each one targeting a specific combination. For simplicity, we use queries with length q_L moving towards the positive direction of the x-axis; the extension to the other directions is straightforward.

As shown in Figure 3.2a, our goal is to divide the space into disjoint *influence areas* according to the data points. Specifically, the influence area $A(p)$ of a point $p=(p_x,p_y)$ is a 3-sided rectangle whose projections on the x- and y- axes are $(-\infty, p_x)$ and $[p_y-q_L/2, p_y+q_L/2]$ respectively, where q_L is the targeted query length (e.g., the shaded area in Figure 3.2a represents $A(p_7)$). Furthermore, for two data points p_i, p_j such that $p_{ix}<p_{jx}$ (i.e., p_{ix} is to the "left" of p_{jx}), $A(p_i)$ "overwrites" $A(p_j)$ if they overlap (e.g., part of $A(p_6)$ is obstructed by $A(p_7)$). The crucial observation is that, given a dragging query $q=q_x:[q_{sy},q_{ey}]$, the first point p hit by q is the one whose influence area $A(p)$ covers the query center $(q_x,(q_{sy}+q_{ey})/2)$. As an example, the result of the query $q=5:[6,9]$ in Figure 3.2a is p_3 because its center (the white point) at coordinates (5,7.5) falls into $A(p_3)$. Note that, if such an influence area does not exist, the query result is empty, namely, the dragging query will not hit any point.

We use a persistent B-tree to index the influence areas. Specifically, the persistent B-tree contains a (logical) B-tree at each x-coordinate x, which stores the y-coordinates of the horizontal boundaries of the influence areas spanning x. For instance, the B-tree at $x=5$ stores 5 values {0.5, 3.5, 5, 8, 10}, corresponding to the (lower, upper, lower, upper, upper) boundaries of $A(p_4)$, $A(p_4)$, $A(p_3)$, $A(p_3)$, $A(p_2)$, respectively. To construct such a persistent tree, we insert the influence areas of points in descending order of their x-coordinates. In Figure 3.2b, p_1 is the first point processed, after which the persistent tree consists of a single logical B-tree (at the x-coordinate 9 of p_1) containing entries 3.5, 5.5 (i.e., the y-coordinates of the boundaries of $A(p_1)$). Entry 5.5 is "tagged" with p_1 (using constant space), indicating that the

---

[2]   Note that, in practice where query's actual length and moving direction can be measured only discretely, the number of such combinations is indeed constant.

region below it belongs to $A(p_1)$), while entry 3.5 is tagged with $\varnothing$, meaning that the region below it is not in any influence area. Similarly, the next point p_2 inserts two entries 7, 10 (tagged with $\varnothing$, p_2 respectively) in the B-tree at $x=8$ (all the B-trees in the x-range (8,10] have the same content as the one at $x=9$). Handling the next point p_3 is more complex since its influence area overlaps $A(p_1)$ and $A(p_2)$. In this case, two entries 5.5 and 7 are removed from the B-tree at x=6, "terminating" the upper and lower boundaries of $A(p_1)$ and $A(p_2)$ respectively. Then, two entries 5, 8 (for the boundaries of $A(p_3)$) are inserted into the same tree, after which the tree contains 4 entries 3.5, 5, 8, 10 tagged with $\varnothing$, p_1, p_3, p_2 respectively. The remaining points are inserted in the same way. A dragging query $q=q_x:[q_{sy},q_{ey}]$ is directed to the B-tree at $x=q_x$, and finds the smallest entry larger than $(q_{sy}+q_{ey})/2$ (i.e., the y-coordinate of the query center). In Figure 3.2a, for example, the B-tree inspected is at $x=5$, and the entry returned has value 8. Then, the result (i.e., the point first hit by q) is the point tagged with the retrieved entry (p_3 in the case). The whole processing incurs $O(\log_B(N/B))$ I/Os.

Theorem 3.1: Given a dataset S of N static 2D points, we can pre-process S into a set of persistent B-trees that occupy totally $O(N/B)$ space and can be constructed in $O((N/B)\log_B(N/B))$ I/Os, such that a validity RS query q can be answered in $O(\log_B(N/B))$ I/Os, provided that the query rectangle's size and movement direction are decided from a constant number of combinations. $\Rightarrow$

3.2   Static Data and Axis-Parallel Moving Queries

In this section, we consider (vertical) dragging queries with arbitrary lengths but horizontal movements (i.e., zero tilting angles). It suffices to discuss queries moving towards the positive direction of the x-axis (by symmetry those towards the negative side can be solved in the same way). The first point hit by such a query $q_x:[q_{sy},q_{ey}]$ is the one with the smallest x-coordinate in the 3-sided rectangle $[q_x,\infty]:[q_{sy},q_{ey}]$. In Figure 3.3, for example, $q=5:[1,8]$ and its 3-sided rectangle $[5,\infty]:[1,8]$ covers points p_1, p_3, p_4, among which p_4 has the smallest x-coordinate and hence, is the result of q. Next, we propose two solutions with different tradeoffs between query time and space.

Using the Persistent Aggregate Tree

We maintain an aggregate B-tree (aB-tree) at every x-coordinate x, indexing the y-coordinates of all the points whose x-coordinates are larger than x. In addition to the search key, each non-leaf entry of the aB-tree also stores, using $O(1)$ space, the point with the smallest x-coordinate among all the points in its subtree. Figure 3.3b demonstrates the aB-tree at $x=5$, where the first root entry $<p_4, 2>$, for example, indicates that the smallest y-coordinate of all the data points (i.e., p_4, p_1) in its subtree is 2, and p_4 has the smallest x-coordinate. We store all the aB-trees in a *persistent aB-tree*, which as shown [TPZ02][3] consumes $O((N/B)\log_B(N/B))$ space and can be constructed in $O((N/B)\log_B(N/B))$ I/Os.

---

[3]   The structure in [TPZ02] is slightly different from the aB-tree in our case, but the complexity analysis still applies.

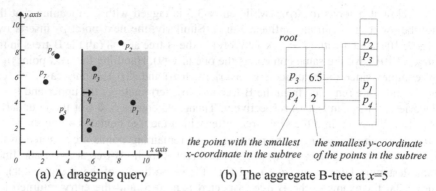

(a) A dragging query   (b) The aggregate B-tree at $x=5$

Fig. 3.3. Dragging queries with arbitrary lengths

Given a query $q_x:[q_{sy},q_{ey}]$, the aB-tree at $x=q_x$ allows us to answer it in $O(\log_B(N/B))$ I/Os. To illustrate this, consider the query $(5:[1,8])$ in Figure 3.3a and the tree in Figure 3.3b. The algorithm starts from the root and descends a non-leaf entry if its "y-range" (enclosing the y-coordinates of points in its subtree) intersects, but is not totally contained in, that of the query ([1,8] in this case). For example, the y-range [2,6.5] of the first root entry in Figure 3.3b (where 6.5 is obtained from the second entry) is contained in [1,8], in which case we simply take point p_4 (stored in this entry) as the candidate result. The subtree of the second entry must be explored because its y-range [6.5,∞] partially intersects [1,8]. In its child node, we examine every data point and update our candidate result accordingly. In this case, p_3 has larger x-coordinate than p_4 (our current candidate) while p_2 does not fall in the 3-sided rectangle [5,∞]:[1,8] of the query; hence, no result update is necessary and the algorithm terminates by returning p_4. At each level of the aB-tree, the query y-range *partially* intersects those of at most two entries (notice that the y-ranges of the entries at the same level are disjoint); thus, the algorithm accesses (at most) two complete paths of the tree, i.e., incurring the same complexity as the tree height $O(\log_B(N/B))$.

Theorem 3.2: Given a dataset S of N static 2D points, we can pre-process S into a set of persistent aB-trees that consume totally $O((N/B)\log_B(N/B))$ space, and can be constructed in $O((N/B)\log_B(N/B))$ I/Os, such that a validity RS query can be answered in $O(\log_B(N/B))$ time, provided that the moving direction of the query rectangle is axis-parallel.   ⇒

Using the External Range Tree

To decrease the space complexity, we present another solution based on a simplified version of the external range tree. Specifically, as shown in Figure 3.4 (for the data points in Figure 3.3a), the primary structure is a B-tree with fanout $O(\log_B(N/B))$ built on the y-coordinates of the data points (the height of the tree is thus $O(\log_B(N/B)/\log\log_B(N/B))$). Let $v_1, v_2, ..., v_r$ ($r=3$ in Figure 3.4) be the subtrees of an intermediate node v of the tree (e.g., the root of the B-tree). For each branch v_i ($1 \le i \le r$), let $|v_i|$ be the number of points it contains, and $p_{i_1}, p_{i_2}, ..., p_{i|v_i|}$ be these points sorted in ascending order of their x-coordinates $p_{i_1x}, p_{i_2x}, ..., p_{i|v_i|x}$. In Figure 3.4, the sorted lists for the root entries 2, 4, 7.5 are $\{p_5, p_4\}$, $\{p_7, p_3, p_1\}$, $\{p_6, p_2\}$, respectively. We define the *interval set* of v_i as $\{[-\infty, p_{i,1x}], [p_{i,1x}, p_{i,2x}], \ldots, [p_{i|v_i|x}, \infty]\}$, namely, the intervals produced by the projections of points in v_i on the x-axis.

For example, the interval sets for root entries 2, 4, 7.5 in Figure 3.4 are, $\{[-\infty, 3.5]$, [3.5, 5.5], [5.5, \infty]\}$, $\{[-\infty, 2], [2, 6] [6, 9], [9, \infty]\}$ and $\{[-\infty, 2.5], [2.5, 8], [8, \infty]\}$. The intervals in the interval sets of *all* v_i are indexed using a priority search tree associated with v. Note that, for the non-leaf nodes at the same level of the B-tree, their priority search trees index *disjoint* sets of intervals, the total number of which is $O(N)$. Given that the height of the primary B-tree is $O(\log_B(N/B)/\log\log_B(N/B))$, the total size of the priority search trees (at all B-tree levels) is $O((N/B)\log_B(N/B)/\log\log_B(N/B))$, which dominates the B-tree size $O(N/B)$ and constitutes the overall space complexity. This simplified external range tree can be constructed with $O((N/B)\log_B(N/B))$ I/Os, same as the complete external range tree [ASV99].

A right-moving dragging query $q=q_x:[q_{sy}, q_{ey}]$ is answered as follows. At the root of the B-tree, we search its associated priority search tree for all the 1D intervals containing value q_x, which is a stabbing query as reviewed in Section 2. Given the query $q=5:[1,8]$ (Figure 3.3a), for example, this search in the tree of Figure 3.4 returns intervals [3.5, 5.5], [2, 6], [2.5, 8] (containing $q_x=5$). It is important to note that, each of these intervals comes from the interval sets of *distinct* subtrees ([3.5, 5.5], [2, 6], [2.5, 8] are from root entries 2, 4, 7.5, respectively). Now, let us consider the data points corresponding to the second numbers of these intervals, namely, p_4, p_3, and p_2 (5.5, for example, is the x-coordinate of p_4). It is safe to conclude that p_3 is the point first hit by q, among all the points in the subtree of entry 4, whose y-range [4, 7.5) is contained in that [1,8] of q. Similar conclusions, however, cannot be made for p_4 (p_2), originating from the subtree of root entry 2 (7.5), because its y-range [2,4) ([7.5, \infty)) partially intersects [1,8]. In this case, we must visit the child nodes of these entries, where we discover point p_4 that is hit earlier than p_3, and becomes the final result.

In general, the above algorithm visits the nodes of the B-tree whose y-ranges *partially* intersect that of the query. Similar to the case of Figure 3.3b, the number of such nodes has the same complexity as the tree height, i.e., $O(\log_B(N/B)/\log\log_B(N/B))$. At each node visited, a stabbing query is performed in its associated priority search tree, which returns as many intervals as the node fanout, i.e., $O(\log_B(N/B))$, incurring $O(\log_B(N/B)+\log_B(N/B)/B)=O(\log_B(N/B))$ I/Os (see the performance of the priority search tree in Section 2). As a result, the total query cost is bounded by $O(\log_B^2(N/B)/\log\log_B(N/B))$ I/Os.

Theorem 3.3: Given a dataset S of N static 2D points, we can pre-process S into a set of simplified external search trees that consume $O((N/B)\log_B(N/B)/\log\log_B(N/B))$ space and can be constructed in $O((N/B)\log_B(N/B))$ I/Os, such that a validity RS query q can be answered in $O(\log_B^2(N/B)/\log\log_B(N/B))$ time, provided that the moving direction of the query rectangle is axis-parallel. $\Rightarrow$

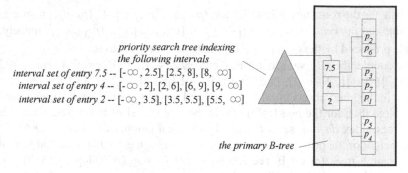

priority search tree indexing
the following intervals
interval set of entry 7.5 -- [-∞, 2.5], [2.5, 8], [8, ∞]
interval set of entry 4 -- [-∞, 2], [2, 6], [6, 9], [9, ∞]
interval set of entry 2 -- [-∞, 3.5], [3.5, 5.5], [5.5, ∞]

the primary B-tree

Fig. 3.4. A simplified external range tree (for the dataset in Figure 3.3a)

3.3   Static Data and Arbitrary Queries

This section focuses on dragging queries with arbitrary lengths and tilting angles q_θ. Figure 3.5 shows an example query q_x:$[q_{sy}, q_{ey}]$ whose moving direction has slope[4] q_s=tg(q_θ). Similar to Figure 3.3a, the goal is to find the point (i.e., p_3) with the smallest x-coordinate among the points in the shaded *3-sided parallelogram*. In the sequel, we present two solutions with different characteristics. It is worth mentioning that, these solutions also apply to the problems in the previous two sections, which are special instances of the queries discussed here.

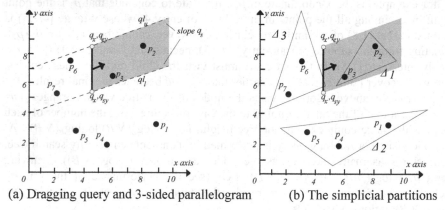

(a) Dragging query and 3-sided parallelogram   (b) The simplicial partitions

Fig. 3.5. Handling dragging queries with non-axis-parallel movement

Using the Partition Tree

As mentioned in Section 2, given a set of N data points, the partition tree answers a simplex query in $O((N/B)^{1/2+\varepsilon}+K/B)$ I/Os (where ε is an arbitrary positive number, and K is the number of points retrieved). Note that, the parallelogram produced by the dragging query (Figure 3.5a) is indeed a "simplex" shape, i.e., the intersection of three

---

[4]   The slope is not defined for tilting angle q_θ=π/2 and 3π/2, namely, the movement of the query is vertical. This special case is solved in Section 3.2.

half planes. Applying the partition tree in this case, however, requires solving the following problem: since the goal is to find only one point in the parallelogram, we should avoid paying the extra cost K/B of reporting the other points.

We solve this problem with a slight modification to the partition tree. In each non-leaf node Λ of the tree, we store, using $O(1)$ space for each child Λ_i (which, as described in Section 2, corresponds to a triangular simplicial partition Δ_i), the point with the smallest x-coordinate in its subtree. Figure 3.5b shows an example where the data points are divided into three simplicial partitions Δ_1, Δ_2, Δ_3, whose extents are stored in the root of the tree. The points stored for these partitions are p_7, p_3, p_5, respectively. This modification does not affect the space and building time complexities of the tree, which, however, can now solve the dragging query in $O((N/B)^{1/2+\varepsilon})$ I/Os. Specifically, the search starts from the root, and visits the subtrees whose simplicial partitions partially intersect the 3-sided parallelogram decided by the query. In Figure 3.5b, for example, Δ_1 is not accessed because it lies completely in the parallelogram, in which case the data point p_7 with the smallest x-coordinate is obtained directly from the corresponding root entry. Δ_2, on the other hand, must be visited because it partially intersects the shaded region (even though it does not contain any data point inside the parallelogram). Following an analysis similar to that in [AAE+00], we can derive the following theorem.

Theorem 3.4: Given a dataset S consisting of N 2D points, we can pre-process S into a modified partition tree that consumes $O(N/B)$ space such that a validity RS query can be answered in $O((N/B)^{1/2+\varepsilon})$ I/Os, for arbitrarily small $\varepsilon > 0$. The partition tree can be constructed in $O((N/B)\log_B(N/B))$ expected I/Os. $\Rightarrow$

Using the Dual Transformation

We present another solution that reduces general dragging queries (with arbitrary tilting angles) to those with axis-parallel movements, using the dual transformation which converts (i) a point (p_x, p_y) in the original space to a line $y = p_x \cdot x - p_y$ in the dual space, and (ii) a line $y = a \cdot x - b$ to a dual point (a, b). Figure 3.6a illustrates the *dual data lines* for the points in Figure 3.5a. Given a dragging query q, let ql_l and ql_u be the lines representing the movements of the query segment's upper and lower end-points, respectively (see Figure 3.5a). Since they have the same slope q_s, their dual points qp_l and qp_u have the same x-coordinate q_s. The vertical line segment (we also refer to it as the *query segment*) in the dual space $q_s:[qp_{ly}, qp_{uy}]$ connecting qp_l and qp_u has the following important property: it intersects a dual data line (in Figure 3.6a, the intersected lines are l_2, l_3, l_6, l_7) *if and only if* the corresponding data point (i.e., p_2, p_3, p_6, p_7) lies between ql_l and ql_u in the original space.

As shown in Figure 3.5a, the result (i.e., p_3) of the original dragging query $q_x:[q_{sy}, q_{ey}]$ is the point with the smallest x-coordinate among those (i) that lie between lines ql_l and ql_u, and (ii) whose x-coordinates are larger than q_x. In the dual space, this is equivalent to finding the dual data line with the smallest slope among those (i) that intersect the vertical segment $q_s:[qp_{ly}, qp_{uy}]$, and (ii) whose slopes are larger than q_x. For this purpose, we perform yet another transformation, which converts a dual data line to a point in the *slope-rank space*. Specifically, the *ranks* of dual lines are defined according to their topological ordering at certain x-coordinate (lines may have different ranks at different x-coordinates). In Figure 3.6a, for example, the rank of l_2 (with slope 8) at $x=q_s$ is 1, because its intersection with $x=q_s$ is the lowest among the intersection points of all the lines; thus, it is mapped to (8,1) in the slope-rank space. Following the same idea, Figure 3.6b shows the converted points in the slope-rank space of all the lines (with respect to $x=q_s$) in Figure 3.6a.

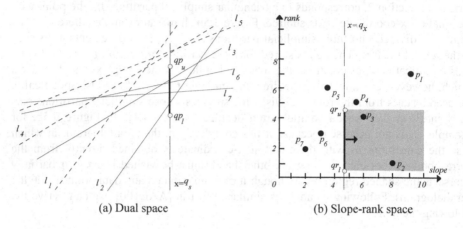

(a) Dual space   (b) Slope-rank space

Fig. 3.6. Using two transformations to solve queries with non-axis-parallel movement

Accordingly, the query segment q_s:[qp_{ly},qp_{uy}] in the dual space is converted into another vertical line segment q_x:[qr_l,qr_u] in the slope-rank space, where q_x is the x-coordinate of the original dragging query (in Figure 3.5a, q_x=3.5), and qr_l (qr_u) is the rank of point qp_l (qp_u) at $x=q_s$ in the dual space. In Figure 3.6, qr_l is set to 0.5, indicating that qp_l is below all lines at $x=q_s$; similarly qr_u is assigned to 4.5, meaning that qp_u is between l_4 and l_3 at this x-coordinate. Note that, the values of qr_l and qr_u are not unique; for example, qr_l can be any number between 4 (the rank of l_4) and 5 (the rank of l_3), while qr_u can be any number below 1 (the rank of l_2). The merit of this transformation is that, now it remains to find, in the slope-rank space, the point first hit by the right-moving vertical dragging query q_s:[qr_l,qr_u] (i.e., p_3, which as in Figure 3.5a is the correct answer to the original dragging query). This problem was solved in Section 3.2; we use the solution based on the simplified external range tree (Figure 3.4).

We have shown that a dragging query whose moving direction has *specific* slope q_s, can be solved using an external range tree at $x=q_s$ in the dual space. In order to support all slopes, we must maintain such a tree at every x-coordinate. Fortunately, since we only care about the topological ordering of the dual lines, a new tree is necessary only when the ranks of two lines change. Motivated by this, we adopt the persistent version of the (simplified) external range tree, where a new tree is created at the x-coordinates where two dual lines cross each other. Towards this, the first step is to obtain the intersection points of all pairs of dual lines, using an I/O optimal algorithm for *line arrangement* computation [GTVV93]. Then the second step constructs the persistent tree in the ascending order of the intersections' x-coordinates. Since there are totally $O(N^2)$ intersections, the space occupied by the persistent tree is $O((N^2/B)\log_B(N/B)/\log\log_B(N/B))$ and its construction incurs $O((N^2/B)\log_B(N/B))$ I/Os.

Further, in order to efficiently assign ranks to the end points of the query segment in the dual space (see Figure 3.6a), we maintain another persistent B-tree where each logical B-tree indexes the ranks of the lines at each x-coordinate in the dual space. This tree consumes $O(N^2/B)$ space, and can be built in $O((N^2/B)\log_B(N/B))$ I/Os. The query ranks can be assigned in $O(\log_B(N/B))$ I/Os, by searching the B-tree at x=q_s (i.e., the query slope). The total query cost, however, is dominated by that of searching the external range tree, which, as shown in Theorem 3.3, has complexity $O(\log_B^2(N/B)/\log\log_B(N/B))$.

Theorem 3.5: Given a dataset S of N static 2D points, we can pre-process S into a set of index structures that consume $O((N^2/B)\log_B(N/B)/\log\log_B(N/B))$ space and can be constructed in $O((N^2/B)\log_B(N/B))$ expected I/Os, such that a validity RS query q (with arbitrary window size and moving direction) can be answered in $O(\log_B^2(N/B)/\log\log_B(N/B))$ time. $\Rightarrow$

3.4   Dynamic Data and Static Queries

Having solved dragging queries on static objects, in this section, we discuss dynamic data points assuming, however, static queries. As before, the goal is to find the first point that crosses the (static) query segment $q=q_x:[q_{sy},q_{ey}]$. For this purpose, we separate points moving towards the positive/negative direction of the x-axis, and process them independently. Due to the symmetry, it suffices to elaborate our solution for right-moving points. Figure 3.7a shows an example with 5 points $p_1, p_2, ..., p_5$ whose trajectories are represented as rays $l_1, l_2, ..., l_5$. For simplicity, assume that all points move at the same speed. Consider two dragging queries q_1, q_2 in Figure 3.7a, both of which intersect rays l_2 and l_3, but in different order. Specifically, for q_1, the first point hit is p_3, while for q_2 the first point is p_2. Such ordering determines the corresponding query result, and can be described using the concept of "arrival time". Specifically, for each data point p with x-coordinate p_x, its *arrival time* $at_p(x)$ for any $x \geq p_x$ is the future timestamp such that $p_x=x$. Then, a dragging query $q=q_x:[q_{sy},q_{ey}]$ is reduced to finding the point p with the smallest arrival time $at_p(q_x)$, among those whose trajectories intersect the query line segment. As an example, q_1 intersects p_2 and p_3, while p_3 is the final result since $at_{p_3}(q_{1x}) < at_{p_2}(q_{1x})$.

Based on this idea, we solve a dragging query using a persistent aggregate tree in logarithmic query cost. Specifically, the persistent tree maintains a logical aggregate B-tree at every x-coordinate x indexing all the data trajectories spanning x (e.g., in Figure 3.7 the logical tree at x=9 stores all rays), which are sorted according to their ranks (i.e., the topological ordering, similar to Figure 3.6) at x (e.g., at x=9, l_4, l_3 have ranks 1, 5 respectively). Furthermore, in each non-leaf entry (of the aggregate tree at x) we store the ray with the smallest arrival time at x among those in its subtree. In Figure 3.7b, the first root entry $<p_5,l_4,l_5>$, for example, indicates that at x=9, the point with the lowest (highest) rank in its subtree has trajectory l_4 (l_5), and the point with the minimal arrival time is p_5. Given a query $q_x:[q_{sy},q_{ey}]$, the problem now is reduced to finding the point, in the aggregate tree at x=q_x, with the minimal arrival time among those intersecting the query segment which, using the same algorithm given in Section 3.2, can be solved in $O(\log_B(N/B))$ I/Os.

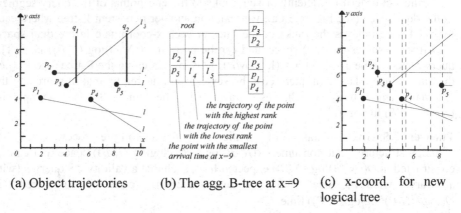

(a) Object trajectories   (b) The agg. B-tree at x=9   (c) x-coord. for new
                                                                       logical tree

Fig. 3.7. Handling dynamic data

Constructing the persistent aggregate tree deserves further discussion. We deploy a plane-sweep that creates the logical trees from left to right. Specifically, a new logical tree is necessary at the x-coordinates where one of the following *events* occurs: (i) a new data point appears, (ii) the rays of two points intersect (i.e., the ranks of the rays change), and (iii) the arrival time of two points becomes equal. Figure 3.7c (i.e., the dashed lines) demonstrates all the events for the example of Figure 3.7a. Notice that the x-coordinate e_x of the last event (i.e., the right-most dashed line) is due to the fact that the arrival time of p_2 equals that of p_3, i.e., $at_{p_2}(e_x)= at_{p_3}(e_x)$. In general, any pair of points (p_i, p_j) defines an event (based on their arrival time), if $p_{ix}>p_{jx}$ and the speed of p_i is larger than that of p_j. It is easy to see that the number of all events is bounded by $O(N^2)$, and they can be obtained using an algorithm similar to the line arrangement computation given in [GTVV93].

Theorem 3.6: Given a dataset S of N moving 2D points (with arbitrary velocity), we can pre-process S into a set of aggregate B-trees that consume $O((N^2/B)\log_B(N/B))$ space and can be constructed in $O((N^2/B)\log_B(N/B))$ expected I/Os, such that a static validity RS query q (with arbitrary window size) is answered in $O(\log_B(N/B))$. $\Rightarrow$

3.5   Dynamic Data and Dynamic Queries

We discuss the general case where both the data and query are dynamic in the 1D space, and leave the 2D case for future work. Figure 3.8 shows the trajectories ($l_1, l_2,$ ..., l_5) of 5 points $p_1, p_2, ..., p_5$ in the x-time space, and an RS query q with interval $[q_{sx},q_{ex}]$ at the current time t_c moving as indicated by the arrows. In this case, the corresponding (1D) dragging queries are two "rays" (i.e., ql_s and ql_e the figure) shooting from the end points of q, and each of them finds the point that is first encountered (p_2 and p_3 respectively). The final answer is the one hit earlier (i.e., p_3).

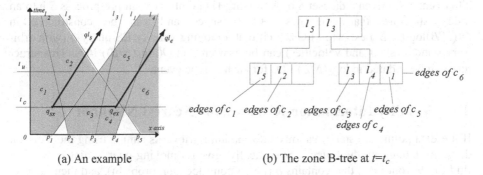

(a) An example   (b) The zone B-tree at $t=t_c$

Fig. 3.8: Handling moving data and queries

To solve the 1D dragging query, we only need to maintain the *zone at the current time* t_c, which consists of all the cells, intersecting line $t=t_c$, in the arrangement of the data points' trajectories. Figure 3.8 demonstrates the zone with shaded polygons c_1, c_2, ..., c_5. The zone has complexity $O(N)$ [BKOS97], meaning that the polygons that generate it have $O(N)$ edges (although a single polygon can have $O(N)$ edges in the worst case, the number of such polygons is $O(1)$). To answer a dragging query (e.g., ql_s in Figure 3.8), we first find the cell c_1 of the zone that covers the source $(q_{sx}, q_t=t_c)$ of the query ray, which can be achieved in $O(\log_B(N/B))$ I/Os, by searching, with value q_{sx}, a B-tree (called the *zone B-tree* in the sequel) that indexes the topological ordering of the data trajectories at $t=t_c$. In Figure 3.8b, for example, the zone B-tree stores lines l_2, l_1, l_3, l_5, l_4, whose ranks at time t_c are in this order. Each trajectory is associated with a pointer to the cell (of the zone) to its left. In this example, the cell c_1 containing (q_{sx},q_t) is identified through the pointer stored in l_2. Then, a second search is performed to identify the (unique) edge in c_1 that is hit by ql_s. Since c_1 contains $O(N)$ edges, this can be accomplished in $O(\log_B(N/B))$ I/Os through, for example, a binary search. Thus, the total query time is $O(\log_B(N/B))$ I/Os.

The zone at the current time may become useless as the time progresses. Particularly, the zone changes at discrete timestamps (i.e., events) when the trajectories of two data points cross each other. Following the kinetic approach [BGH97], we manage these events in an event queue, and dynamically maintain the zone at the next event removed from the queue. In Figure 3.8, the next event is at timestamp t_u, at which time lines l_5 and l_1 change their ranks (i.e., ordering). To reflect this, we perform two deletions from the zone B-tree, corresponding to the old ranks of l_5 and l_1, and then two insertions for their new ranks. Furthermore, we also need to maintain the cells in the zone, specifically as shown in the figure, removing cell c_3 that is no longer in the zone, and inserting a new one which is enclosed only by l_5 and l_1. Finally, we must insert two new events in the event queue, which correspond to the (future) intersection time of l_2 and l_5, l_1 and l_3, respectively. In general, a new event is created as a pair of lines become adjacent in the zone B-tree for the first time. Using an external priority queue [A94] as the event queue, handling an event incurs totally $\log_B(N/B)$ I/Os.

Theorem 3.7: Given a dataset S of N moving 1D points, we can pre-process S into an index structure that consumes $O(N/B)$ space and can be constructed in $O((N/B)\log_B(N/B))$ expected I/Os, such that a moving validity RS query q (with arbitrary window sizes and velocities) can be answered in $O(\log_B(N/B))$ I/Os. This structure can be updated in $\log_B(N/B)$ I/Os for each kinetic event. $\Rightarrow$

4   Validity Information Retrieval for Nearest Neighbor

If the data points are static, validity information retrieval is simple using the Voronoi diagram defined by the objects. Specifically, given a moving query point q, we first find the Voronoi cell that contains q (i.e., a point location problem), and then identify the edge of the cell hit by the movement of q (discussed in Section 3.5). The point location problem in the secondary memory can be solved in $O(\log_B(N/B))$ I/Os, using a persistent B-tree, which (given that the Voronoi cell has complexity $O(N)$) consumes $O(N/B)$ space, and can be constructed in $O((N/B)\log_B(N/B))$ I/Os [ADT03].

Theorem 4.1: Given a dataset S of N static 2D points and its Voronoi diagram, we can pre-process S into an index structure that consumes $O(N/B)$ space and can be constructed in $O((N/B)\log_B(N/B))$ expected I/Os, such that a moving validity NN query q (with arbitrary moving direction) can be answered in $O(\log_B(N/B))$ I/Os. $\Rightarrow$

Next, we consider the problem with moving objects in the 1D space (the 2D problem is left for future work). Figure 4.1a shows the trajectories l_1, l_2, l_3, l_4, l_5 of 5 points and a moving query q, whose current nearest neighbor is p_3. In order to find the point that will become the next nearest neighbor of q, we *mirror* l_3 to l_3' (i.e., the dotted line) such that the horizontal distance between l_3', q is the same as that between l_3, q for any future time t. In this example, the first points crossed by p_3 and p_3' (after the query time) are p_1 and p_5 respectively, among which p_5 is the next NN of q. Figure 4.1b shows another example, where the trajectories of q and its current NN p_3 do not intersect. We mirror l_3 to l_3' in the same way, and the first point hit by these two lines is p_1, the next NN of q. The following lemma states that the next NN of q always come from the first points hit by its current NN and its mirror.

Lemma 4.1: Given a set S of 1D moving points, let q be the query point whose nearest neighbor is $\rho \in S$. Let ρ' be the *mirror* of ρ with respect to q, such that $\forall t>0$, $dist(\rho(t),q(t)) = dist(\rho'(t),q(t))$, where $x(t)$ denotes the position of point x at time t. Assume that p_1, p_2 are the first points in S that are crossed by ρ and ρ' respectively, and let t_1, t_2 be the time when these "crossings" occur. Then the next nearest neighbor of q is p_1 if $t_1<t_2$, or p_2 otherwise. $\Rightarrow$

This lemma permits answering a validity NN query using logarithmic time in the same way as we solved the (1D) dragging query on dynamic data. Specifically, we maintain the zone B-tree as in Figure 3.8b so that, given a query point q at the current time, we can efficiently find the cell (in the zone of the current time) that contains q (the shaded polygons in Figures 4.1a, 4.1b). Then, its current NN is decided from its neighboring points in the zone B-tree (in both examples of Figure 4.1, p_2, p_3 are the neighboring points, among which p_3 is the NN). Then, deciding the first points hit by the NN and its mirror involves inspecting at most two cells, e.g., two (one) cells in Figure 4.1a (4.1b) (note that the cell containing q is always visited). The zone B-tree and the cells of the zone at the current time can be updated using the kinetic approach as discussed in Section 3.5, with the same query time and space complexities.

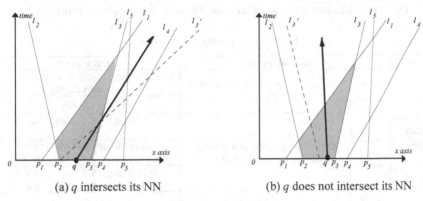

(a) q intersects its NN   (b) q does not intersect its NN

Fig. 4.1. Validity NN query

Theorem 4.2: Given a dataset S of N moving 1D points, we can pre-process S into an index structure that consumes $O(N/B)$ space and can be constructed in $O((N/B)\log_B(N/B))$ I/Os, such that a moving validity RS query q (with arbitrary moving direction) can be answered in $O(\log_B(N/B))$ I/Os. This structure can be updated in $\log_B(N/B)$ I/Os for each kinetic event.   ⇒

5   Summary and Open Problems

Validity information retrieval aims at accompanying with expiry information the result of a traditional spatial query in a dynamic environment. Therefore, a validity query is usually executed together with the corresponding spatial query and the overall complexity is dominated by the more expensive of these two queries. Table 6.1 summarizes the results in this paper and illustrates the best performance for the corresponding traditional queries. Each cell includes the space complexity, followed by the query time. Using this table, we identify the following open problems:

- For validity RS queries on static data, is there a method which consumes linear space and answers a query in $O((N/B)^{1/2})$ I/Os? This would eliminate the extra $O((N/B)^{\varepsilon})$ query overhead and make the validity query as expensive as the traditional RS, achieving optimal performance using linear space.
- For validity RS queries on static data, is there a method which consumes space $O((N/B)\log_B(N/B)/\log\log_B(N/B))$ and answers an axis-parallel-moving query in $O(\log_B(N/B))$ I/Os? Such a method would achieve logarithmic query time using the minimal space.
- For static validity RS queries on dynamic data, devise a method which achieves logarithmic query cost with less space consumption than the current solution.

- Develop index structures for dynamic validity RS queries on dynamic 2D data with good worst case bounds.
- Design a solution that answers NN, and validity NN queries on dynamic 2D data.
- Determine the lower (space/query cost) bounds for the above problems.

Table 6.1. Summary of the results

query		traditional queries	validity queries
range search on static data	linear space	$O(N/B)$, $O((N/B)^{1/2}+K/B)$ [KS99, GI99]	$O(N/B)$, $O(\log_B(N/B))$ for constant query size and velocities
			$O(N/B)$, $O((N/B)^{1/2+\varepsilon})$
	non-linear space	$O((N/B)\log_B(N/B)/\log\log_B(N/B))$, $O(\log_B(N/B)+K/B)$ [ASV99]	$O((N/B)\log_B(N/B))$, $O(\log_B(N/B))$ for APM*
			$O((N/B)\log_B(N/B)/\log\log_B(N/B))$, $O(\log_B^2(N/B)/\log\log_B(N/B))$ for APM
			$O((N^2/B)\log_B(N/B)/\log\log_B(N/B))$, $O(\log_B^2(N/B)/\log\log_B(N/B))$
range search on dynamic data	linear space	$O(N/B)$, $O((N/B)^{1/2}+K/B)$ [ASV99]	NA
	non-linear space	$O((N/B)\log_B(N/B)/\log\log_B(N/B))$, $O(\log_B(N/B)+K/B)$ [ASV99]	$O((N^2/B)\log_B(N/B))$, $O(\log_B(N/B))$ for static queries
			$O(N/B)$, $O(\log_B(N/B))$ for 1D data
			NA for 2D data
NN on static data		$O(N/B)$, $O(\log_B(N/B))$ (Voronoi diagram plus point location queries)	$O(N/B)$, $O(\log_B(N/B))$
NN on dynamic data		$O(N/B)$, $O(\log_B(N/B))$ for 1D	$O(N/B)$, $O(\log_B(N/B))$ for 1D
		NA for 2D	NA for 2D

*APM= axis-parallel-moving queries

Acknowledgements

This work was supported from grants HKUST 6081/01E, HKUST 6197/02E and HKU 7380/02E from Hong Kong RGC.

References

[A94]   Arge, L. The Buffer Tree: A New Technique for Optimal I/O Algo rithms. WADS, 1994.

[AAE+00]   Agarwal, P., Arge, L., Erickson, J., Franciosa, P., Vitter, J. Efficient Searching with Linear Constraints. Journal of Computer and System Sciences, 61(2): 194-216, 2000.

[AAE00]   Agarwal, P., Arge, L., Erickson, J. Indexing Moving Points. ACM PODS, 2000.

[AAV01]   Agarwal, P., Arge, L., Vahrenhold, J. A Time Responsive Indexing Scheme for Moving Points. Workshop on Algorithms and Data Struc tures, 2001.

[ADT03]   Arge, L., Danner, A., Teh, S. I/O Efficient Point Location Using Persistent B-Trees. ALENEX, 2003.

[ASV99]   Arge, L., Samoladas, V., Vitter, J. On Two-Dimensional Indexability and Optimal Range Search Index. ACM PODS, 1999.

[BGH97]   Basch, J., Guibas, L., Hershberger, J. Data Structures for Mobile Data. ACM SODA, 1997.

[BGO+96]   Becker, B., Gschwind, S., Ohler, T., Seeger, B. Widmayer, P. An Asymptotically Optimal Multiversion B-trees. VLDB Journal, 5(4): 264-275, 1996.

[BJKS02]   Benetis, R., Jensen, C., Karciauskas, G., Saltenis, S. Nearest Neighbor and Reverse Nearest Neighbor Queries for Moving Objects. IDEAS, 2002.

[BKOS97]   de Berg, M., van Kreveld, M., Overmars, M., Schwarzkopf, O. Computational Geometry. Springer, 1997.

[BKSS90]   Beckmann, N., Kriegel, H., Schneider, R., Seeger, B. The R*-tree: An Efficient and Robust Access Method for Points and Rectangles. ACM SIGMOD, 1990.

[C88]   Chazelle, B. An algorithm for segment-dragging and its implementation. Algorithmica, 3: 305-221, 1988.

[CGR95]   Callahan, P., Goodrich, G., Ramaiyer, K. Topology B-Trees and Their Applications. Workshop on Algorithms and Data Structures, 1995.

[GBE+00]   Guting, R., Böhlen, M., Erwig, M., Jensen, C., Lorentzos, N., Schneider, M., Vazirgiannis, M. A Foundation for Representing and Querying Moving Objects. ACM TODS, 25(1): 1-42, 2000.

[GI99]   Grossi, R., Italiano, G. Efficient Splitting and Merging Algorithms for Order Decomposable Problems. Information and Computation, 154(1): 1-33, 1999.

[GLM00]   Govindarajan, S., Lukovszki, T., Maheshwari, A., Zeh, N. I/O-Efficient Well-Separated Pair Decomposition and Its Applications. Annual European Symposium on Algorithms, 2000.

[GTVV93]   Goodrich, M., Tsay, J., Vengroff, D., Vitter, J. External Memory Computational Geometry. IEEE FOCS, 1993.

[HKP97]   Hellerstein, J., Koutsoupias, E., Papadimitriou, C. On the Analysis of Indexing Schemes. ACM PODS, 1997.

[IKO87]   Icking, C., Klein, R., Ottmann, T. Priority Search Trees in Secondary Memory. GTCCS, 1987.

[KGT99a]   Kollios, G., Gunopulos, D., Tsotras, V. On Indexing Mobile Objects. ACM PODS, 1999.

[KGT99b]   Kollios, G., Gunopulos, D., Tsotras, V. Nearest Neighbor Queries in Mobile Environment. STDBM, 1999.

[KRVV96]   Kanellakis, P., Ramaswamy, S., Vengroff, D., Vitter, J. Indexing for Data Models with Constraints and Classes. Journal of Computer and System Sciences, 52(3): 589-612, 1996.

[KS99]   Kanth, K., Singh, A. Optimal Dynamic Range Searching in Non-Replicating Index Structures. ICDT, 1999.

[RS94]   Ramaswamy, S., Subramanian, S. Path Caching: A Technique for Optimal External Searching. ACM PODS, 1994.

[SJLL00]   Saltenis, S., Jensen, C., Leutenegger, S., Lopez, M. Indexing the Positions of Continuously Moving Objects. ACM SIGMOD, 2000.

[SR01]   Song, Z., Roussopoulos, N. K-Nearest Neighbor Search for Moving Query Point. SSTD, 2001.

[SR95]   Subramanian, S., Ramaswamy, S. The P-Range Tree: A New Data Structure for Range Searching in Secondary Memory. ACM SODA, 1995.

[TPZ02]   Tao, Y., Papadias, D., Zhang, J. Aggregate Processing of Planar Points. EDBT, 2002.

[TP02]   Tao, Y., Papadias, D. Time-Parameterized Queries for Spatio-Temporal Databases. ACM SIGMOD, 2002.

[TPS02]   Tao, Y., Papadias, D., Shen, Q. Continuous Nearest Neighbor Search. VLDB, 2002.

Exploiting
the Multi-Append-Only-Trend Property
of Historical Data in Data Warehouses*

Hua-Gang Li[1], Divyakant Agrawal[1], Amr El Abbadi[1], and Mirek Riedewald[2]

[1] University of California
Santa Barbara, CA 93106, USA
{huagang,agrawal,amr}@cs.ucsb.edu
[2] Cornell University
Ithaca, NY 14853, USA
mirek@cs.cornell.edu

Abstract. Data warehouses maintain historical information to enable
the discovery of trends and developments over time. Hence data items
usually contain time-related attributes like the time of a sales transaction
or the order and shipping date of a product. Furthermore the values of
these time-related attributes have a tendency to increase over time. We
refer to this as the Multi-Append-Only-Trend (MAOT) property. In this
paper we formalize the notion of MAOT and show how taking advantage
of this property can improve query performance considerably. We focus
on range aggregate queries which are essential for summarizing large data
sets. Compared to MOLAP data cubes the amount of pre-computation
and hence additional storage in the proposed technique is dramatically
reduced.

1 Introduction

The notion of *time* has received considerable attention in data warehouses during
the past few years due to the accumulation of large amounts of time evolving
data. Data items often contain time-related attributes such as the time of a sales
transaction or the order and shipping date of a product. This enables analysts
to extract interesting information over a certain period of time, e.g., observing
a sales trend or analyzing revenue and expense trends over time. The importance
of time even resulted in a separate branch of research specifically concerned with
temporal databases [13].

A main characteristic of data collections is that the data grows very often
rapidly over time. To make these massive data collections digestible for human
analysts, support for efficient aggregation and summarization is vital. An important tool for analyzing data is the orthogonal range aggregate query, for instance,
"what is the total value of all orders in California which were ordered in the first

---

* This research was supported by the NSF under IIS98-17432, EIA99-86057, EIA00-
80134, and IIS02-09112.

T. Hadzilacos et al. (Eds.): SSTD 2003, LNCS 2750, pp. 179–198, 2003.

half of July 2002 and shipped in August or later?". This query selects ranges on some of the attributes and computes aggregates over the selected data items. Besides, roll-up and drill-down queries [4] that aggregate on different levels of granularity are often collections of related range queries. In this paper, we concentrate on the most prevalent aggregation operation SUM in OLAP applications. Note that the aggregation operator COUNT is a special case of SUM, and AVG can be obtained through a tuple (*sum,count*).

In [20], Riedewald et al. developed a new framework supporting efficient aggregation over *append-only* data sets. An append-only data set refers to a collection of data items with one of the describing attributes being a *transaction time dimension* (TT-dimension). Typically there is a correlation between the value of the transaction time attribute and when the data item is incorporated into the data collection. For instance, sales transactions and phone calls are recorded in a timely manner and hence the earlier a sales event or phone call takes place, the earlier it will be recorded in the data warehouses. Intuitively, a *d*-dimensional data set is append-only, if updates can only affect data items with the latest or a greater transaction time coordinate.

In practice we observe that there are many data sets with multiple time-related attributes whose values increase over time. For example, the retail data set from an online shop has an order date, a shipping date, and may be even a delivery date to describe data items. Hence the data space grows along multiple dimensions which introduces a high degree of sparseness. For that reason data cubes like *prefix sum cube* and its variations [12, 3, 10, 18] which are based on array structures will not be space efficient for supporting aggregation. A "diagonal line" of data points (when looking only at the time-related dimensions with growing values) is also difficult to index with popular bounding-shape based trees like R-tree [9] and SS-tree [21]. On the other hand if there is truly a diagonal line, i.e., the data is *Multi-Append-Only* (MAO) in time-related dimensions, we can just reduce the multiple time-related dimensions to one-dimensional aggregation.

In real applications one will rarely find multiple dimensions such that newly inserted data items have increasing values in all these dimensions. For instance, once an order for a product is placed, the retailer processes it and ships the product to the customer within a certain amount of time. Typically given a later order date, there will be a later shipping date. However, varying order processing speed will cause exceptions from the rule. On the other hand such exceptions are not arbitrarily bad. In the order example most outliers will be off by at most 1 or 2 days. Hence such data sets with multiple time-related dimensions may exhibit a non-decreasing trend in some time-related dimensions while in others may maintain this trend *approximately*. That is to say, some data points in the data sets are slightly off, but still within a certain bound. We refer to this as the *Multi-Append-Only-Trend* (MAOT) property and data sets with such property are the focus of this paper. Intuitively in a MAOT data set the data points are within a narrow diagonal band (when considering only the time-related dimensions), hence we want to be able to deal with aggregation in MAOT data

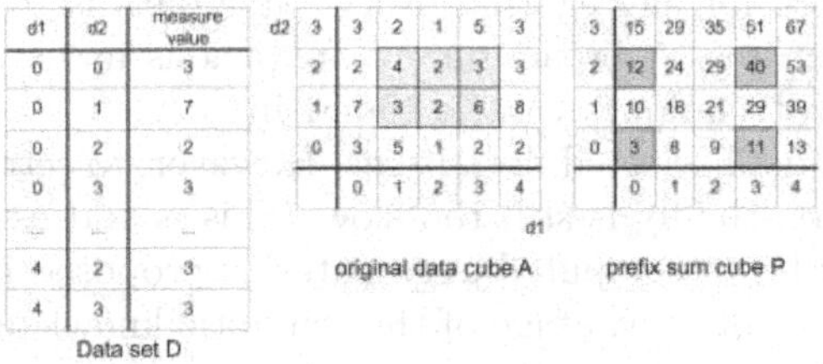

Fig. 1. The original array and prefix sum array

sets as efficiently as in MAO data sets. This idea is at the heart of our novel aggregation technique.

The rest of the paper is organized as follows. Section 2 gives an overview of related work. In Section 3, motivation of our research work is stated. In Section 4, we discuss and empirically evaluate our proposed technique for two-dimensional MAOT data sets. Conclusions and future research work are given in Section 5.

2   Related Work

Some of the most efficient OLAP aggregation techniques maintain a d-dimensional data set $\mathcal{D}$ in a d-dimensional array-like data cube structure. For Example, Fig. 1 shows a two-dimensional data set with its corresponding data cube. Ho et al. [12] introduced an elegant technique for computing range aggregate queries on general data sets, which is referred to as the *Prefix Sum* technique (PS). The basic idea is to compute the prefix sums of the original data cube (see Fig. 1). In particular, each cell indexed by (x_1, x_2) in the prefix sum cube P maintains the sum of all cells (c_1, c_2) of the original data cube A that satisfy $0 \leq c_1 \leq x_1$ and $0 \leq c_2 \leq x_2$. The PS technique ensures constant query time, more precisely at most 2^d cell accesses per query. In Fig. 1, the range sum query shown by the shaded area can be computed by accessing cells (3,2), (0,2), (3,0) and (0,0) in the prefix sum data cube P, i.e. $P[3,2] - P[0,2] - P[3,0] + P[0,0] = 40 - 11 - 12 + 3 = 20$. The storage cost for pre-aggregated information is $O(n^d)$ assuming each dimension size of n without loss of generality. Other array-based techniques [3, 10, 18] provide a variety of different tradeoffs between query and update costs. Similar to PS their storage requirement is in the order of $O(n^d)$. Unfortunately array-based techniques are not feasible for very sparse and high-dimensional data sets. For instance constructing the PS cube for a sparse data set will result in a high degree of redundancy.

A number of highly sophisticated aggregation techniques for sparse data have been proposed for computational geometry applications [6, 5, 22]. However, typically the storage overhead is super-linear, e.g., $O(N \log^{d-1} N)$ for a data set of size N, which is infeasible for large multidimensional data sets in data warehousing applications. Also, since the data structures are fairly involved, they are rarely used in practice.

Another approach for aggregating over sparse data is to take advantage of existing index structures. A broad survey on various index structures is given in [11]. More recent techniques can be found in [1, 2, 8, 16, 17]. Indexing can provide fast access to all selected data items. However, to retrieve and aggregate each selected item on-the-fly is still too slow. This is addressed by augmenting index structures with pre-computed aggregates as proposed in [19, 14]. None of these techniques can take advantage of the semantic knowledge provided by the time-related attributes.

The only previous aggregation framework that explicitly takes advantage of properties of time-related attributes was introduced by Riedewald et al. [20]. Their approach reduced the complexity of the aggregation problem by making query and update costs independent of the time dimension. However, taking advantage of multiple time-related dimensions was not supported.

3   Technique for Multi-Append-Only Data

Assume that all dimensions are time-related and that inserted data items have the MAO property, i.e., in each dimension the coordinate value of a newly inserted data point is at least as high as for all previously inserted points. In the following we describe a simple yet efficient aggregation approach for this setup.

As discussed in Section 1, the data space of an MAO data set grows along multiple time-related dimensions and hence high sparseness will be introduced due to the infinite domain of time-related dimensions. To apply the PS technique and its variations directly on an MAO data set will cause high storage overhead as illustrated in Example 1.

Example 1. Fig. 2 shows the data cube of a two-dimensional MAO data set. The original data cube has a high degree of sparseness, therefore the corresponding PS cube contains a high amount of redundant information. Applying any of the other array-based aggregation techniques would have a similar effect.

As the data set in Fig. 2 has the MAO property, we can conceptually map all MAO dimensions to a single dimension and then apply a technique similar to [20] as follows. Let R denote a data structure such that for each pair of time coordinates (t_1, t_2), a R-*instance* $R(t_1, t_2)$ maintains the cumulative information of all data points whose time1 attribute value is less than or equal to t_1 and time2 attribute value is less than or equal to t_2. Fig. 3 shows the R-instances

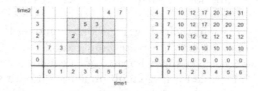

Fig. 2. An MAO data set and its prefix sum cube

constructed for the two-dimensional MAO data set in Fig. 2. For instance, $R(2, 2)$ maintains the cumulative knowledge of data points $(2, 2), (1, 1), (0, 1)$.

This cumulative knowledge enables us to reduce a two-dimensional range query to finding two R-instances as follows. For example, a range aggregate query is specified as $2 \leq \mathtt{time1} \leq 5$ and $1 \leq \mathtt{time2} \leq 3$ (shaded area in Fig. 2). We first get $R(4, 3)$ with the greatest time values, in both dimensions, which are less than or equal to the upper values of the selected time ranges. $R(4, 3)$ maintains the sum of all data points whose $\mathtt{time1}$ coordinate is less than or equal to 4 and $\mathtt{time2}$ coordinate is less than or equal to 3, which is 20. To answer the actual range query, we have to remove all the data points whose $\mathtt{time1}$ coordinate is less than 2 and $\mathtt{time2}$ coordinate is less than 1. Hence, we refer to $R(1, 1)$ to get the sum of those data points, which is 10. Then we subtract the result from the initial value, obtaining the correct result of 10.

So far we have not described how to find the appropriate R-instances needed to answer range aggregate queries. In order to do that, we need a directory that maintains the correspondence between time coordinates and instances of R, called R-*instance directory*. For example, Fig. 3 also shows the R-instance directory maintained for the given two-dimensional MAO data set. For any given range aggregate query, we have to perform two lookups of the R-instance directory, one for the lower and one for the upper end of the range query. The time coordinates of data points are ordered in non-decreasing order, therefore we can perform a 'binary-search-like' lookup. The actual procedure is shown in Fig. 3. The cost of a lookup is at most logarithmic in the number of data points. Thus the total query cost is $O(\log N)$ where N is the total number of data points in the data set. Also it is obvious that the storage cost for additional information is $O(N)$. When compared with the existing techniques, this technique achieves significant reduction in storage cost while maintaining efficient query processing time. Note that our approach easily generalizes to higher dimensionality and to data sets with both time-related and "general" dimensions. In the latter case our technique reduces the complexity for queries and updates to that of a data set which is the projection of the original set to the lower-dimensional data space defined by the general dimensions only.

However, the MAO property imposes a very strict condition on time-related attributes of historical data sets. In real applications, data sets with multiple time-related attributes very often only exhibit the weaker MAOT property. In this paper, we propose a space-efficient technique to handle range aggregate queries in MAOT data sets and our goal is to treat the data sets as if there were no outliers and to correct for possible mistakes by paying a small cost, which depends on the deviation of the outlier.

4   A Technique for Two-Dimensional MAOT Data Sets

4.1   Notation

Let $\mathcal{D}$ denote a **data set** with d dimensional attributes $\delta_1, \ldots, \delta_d$, and a single measure attribute m. Let (X^d, v), $X^d = (x_1, \ldots, x_d)$, refer to a **data point**

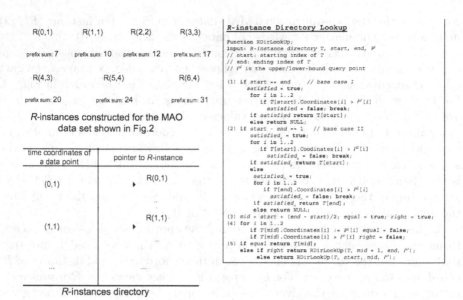

Fig. 3. R-instances, R-instance directory and searching

in $\mathcal{D}$ and its measure value is v. A data point exists in the data set, if and only if its measure value is not NULL. A multi-dimensional range aggregate query specifies a range (L_i, U_i) in each dimension δ_i, the selection possibly being a single value or the entire domain. The query selects all data points X^d that satisfy $L_i \leq x_i \leq U_i$ for all dimensions δ_i and applies aggregate operator (e.g. SUM) over these cells. $L^d = (L_1, \ldots, L_d)$ and $U^d = (U_1, \ldots, U_d)$ are referred to as the **lower-bound query point** and the **upper-bound query point** of a multi-dimensional range aggregate query.

The d-dimensional data set $\mathcal{D}$ is a data set with **Multi-Append-Only-Trend** (MAOT) property if and only if it satisfies the following conditions:

1. one of its dimensions, say δ_1, is a *transaction time dimension* (TT-dimension).
2. d_t of its dimensions, say $\delta_2, \ldots, \delta_{d_t+1}$, are *valid time dimensions* (VT-dimensions).
3. the TT-coordinate of the latest update u always follows a non-decreasing trend, i.e., if an update to a data point X^d arrives at the data set before another update to a data point Y^d, then $x_1 \leq y_1$.
4. if the ith VT-coordinate of the latest update u does not follow a non-decreasing trend, it should be at most ε time units earlier than the ith VT-coordinate of the previous data point, which has the greatest TT-coordinate and whose i^{th} VT-coordinate follows a non-decreasing trend. We refer to this preceding point as the *Sentinel Data Point* (SDP) for i^{th} VT-dimension (ε-bound).

To simplify the following discussion we will further on assume no two data points have the same coordinate in the TT-dimension δ_1. The generalization is straightforward.

4.2   Illustration of the Technique

For simplicity, the technique is illustrated for a two-dimensional MAOT data set $\mathcal{D}$ with $\varepsilon = 1$ and the operator SUM, which is shown in Fig. 4. Let the dimensions be time1, time2. New points arrive in the strict order of time1, i.e., time1 dimension is a TT-dimension. The time2 dimension is a VT-dimension, i.e., if the VT-coordinate of the latest update u does not follow a non-decreasing trend, it should be at most $\varepsilon = 1$ time unit earlier than the corresponding VT-coordinate of its SDP for time2 dimension.

Adjustment of Outlier Data Points. Like the technique proposed for MAO data sets, we can capture the information of the MAOT data set $\mathcal{D}$ in a collection of instances of a data structure I (defined later in this subsection) such that there is an I-instance for each pair of time coordinates (t_1, t_2) for which a data point exists. The information in these data structures is cumulative. The TT-dimension property ensures that an update u in $\mathcal{D}$ either affects the existing I-instance with the greatest TT-coordinate or appends a new I-instance with a greater TT-coordinate. Furthermore, if the VT-coordinate of the newly appended I-instance does not follow a non-decreasing trend (*an outlier data point*), we adjust it by increasing its value by at most ε time units to ensure its new value is at least as large as that of its SDP for time2 dimension.

After adjustment, the data set $\mathcal{D}$ appears as though there were no outlier data points. Thus the technique proposed for MAO data sets can be applied to the MAOT data set. However, to correct for possible mistakes, we need to store additional information. For each pair of time coordinates (t_1, t_2) (t_2 may be an adjusted VT-coordinate), the corresponding I-instance $I(t_1, t_2)$ maintains not only cumulative knowledge of all the data points $X^2 = (x_1, x_2)$ where $x_1 \leq t_1, x_2 \leq t_2$, but also some other auxiliary information which is not required for MAO data sets.

Example 2. In Fig. 4, we can observe that there are two outlier data points in the data set $\mathcal{D}$. The VT-coordinate of data point $(3, 4)$ does not follow a non-decreasing trend, thus we adjust it to ensure its VT-coordinate is at least as large as that of its SDP for time2 dimension $(2, 5)$, i.e., 5 (as shown from circle to star in the figure). Similarly, we increase the VT-coordinate of data point $(8, 9)$ to that of its SDP for time2 dimension $(7, 10)$, i.e., $(8, 9) \rightarrow (8, 10)$.

Classification of Data Points. Recall that the R-instance constructed for each pair of time coordinates in a two-dimensional MAO data set maintains

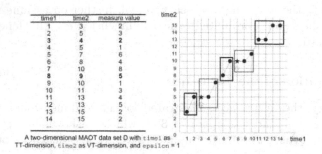

Fig. 4. A 2-dimensional MAOT data set (time1: TT-dimension, time2: VT-dimension, $\varepsilon = 1$)

the same kind of cumulative information. However, we cannot deal with two-dimensional MAOT data sets likewise as we need additional information in I-instances with adjusted VT-coordinates to correct for the possible errors introduced by VT-coordinate adjustment. Thus it is necessary to classify data points into groups according to the characteristics of their original VT-coordinates and each group is either of the following two kinds of groups:

1. *Normal group*: a group in which the VT-coordinates of all data points always follow a non-decreasing trend;
2. *Outlier group*: a group starting at a data point s whose original VT-coordinate does not follow a non-decreasing trend and ending at a data point e whose VT-coordinate is later than that of s by at least ε time units; in order to keep the outlier group as small as possible, e is selected such that e has a VT-coordinate at most ε time units greater than that of s and the least TT-coordinate.

Intuitively an outlier group is the smallest group that begins with an outlier and "advances the clock" in the VT-dimension by at least ε.

Example 3. In the example of Fig. 4 we can divide all the data points into groups as shown by rectangles. Solid rectangles represent normal groups and dashed rectangles represent outlier groups. For instance $[(6,8),(7,10)]$ is a normal group and $[(8,10),(9,10),(10,11)]$ is an outlier groups. Note that the first outlier group starts at the data point $(3,5)$ whose original VT-coordinate (4) does not follow a non-decreasing trend and ends at the data point $(5,7)$ whose VT-coordinate (7) is later than that of $(3,5)$ by 2 time units, which is greater than $\varepsilon = 1$ time unit(s).

From the definition and the example above, one may notice that there are some data points in the outlier group which are not outlier data points. We now briefly motivate why we extend outlier groups to an ending data point whose VT-coordinate is later than that of the starting data point by at least ε time units. The ε difference is chosen to ensure that for each range query there is at most one outlier group which is intersected by the query and which could contain data points whose VT-coordinates are less than that of the lower-bound query point. This leads to the efficient query algorithm presented later on which only has to deal with different cases for a single outlier group.

Cumulative and Auxiliary Information. In this subsection, we define the data structure I such that for each pair of time coordinates, $I(t_1, t_2)$ maintains cumulative and auxiliary information which exploits the MAOT property of data set $\mathcal{D}$. All I-instances maintain the following common information:

1. Similar to the technique for MAO data sets, in each I-instance $I(t_1, t_2)$ we maintain the cumulative values of data points $X^2 = (x_1, x_2)$ in data set $\mathcal{D}$ whose time coordinates satisfy $x_1 \leq t_1$ and $x_2 \leq t_2$, denoted as PSum;
2. Original measure value of the data point (t_1, t_2) denoted as OVal;
3. The group type (normal, outlier) to which the data point (t_1, t_2) belongs, denoted as GRP.

In addition, for an I-instance constructed for a data point (t_1, t_2) of an outlier group, we need to maintain extra information as follows which is used to correct for the possible errors introduced by the VT-coordinate adjustments of outlier data points.

1. A one-dimensional array EPSum of size ε. The cell $EPSum[i](0 \leq i \leq \varepsilon - 1)$ maintains the sum of measure values of data points $X^2 = (x_1, x_2)$ where $x_1 \leq t_1, x_2 \leq t_2$, but excludes those data points in the same outlier group with original VT-coordinates earlier than $s - i$ where s is the VT-coordinate of the starting data point of its group;
2. A pointer to the I-instance for the starting data point of the outlier group, denoted as SIns;
3. A pointer to the I-instance for the ending data point of the outlier group, denoted as EIns; if there is no ending data point yet for the group, it is set to NULL;
4. A pointer to the I-instance for the data point arriving immediately after data point (t_1, t_2), denoted IIns, if data point (t_1, t_2) is the ending data point of its outlier group;
5. A boolean variable indicating whether the VT-coordinate of a data point (t_1, t_2) is adjusted or not, denoted as ADJUSTED;
6. Original time coordinates, if data point (t_1, t_2) is an adjusted one, denoted as ORC. Otherwise it is set to NULL;

Example 4. Referring to Fig. 4 again, we can construct the I-instances of data set $\mathcal{D}$ as shown in Fig. 5. Note that the I-instance $I(3, 5)$ belongs to an outlier group, so its group information is 'outlier'; PSum stores the sum of measure values of data points whose TT-coordinate is less than or equal to 3 and VT-coordinate is less than or equal to 5, i.e., $2+3+2 = 7$; OVal stores the original measure value of data point $(3, 5)$. EPSum[0] stores the sum of measure values of data points whose TT-coordinate is less than or equal to 3 and VT-coordinate is less than

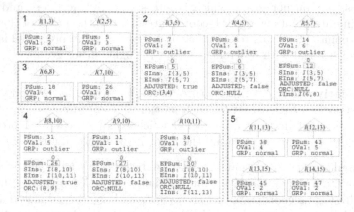

Fig. 5. I-instances constructed for the two-dimensional MAOT data set $\mathcal{D}$ shown in Fig. 4

or equal to 5, but excludes those data points which are in the same group and whose original VT-coordinate is less than $5 - 0 = 5$, i.e., EPSum[0] $= 2 + 3 = 5$.

Answering Range Aggregate Queries. Now we illustrate how to use the cumulative and auxiliary information to speed up range aggregate (SUM) queries. Consider a range query represented as $\mathtt{Query}(L^2 = (3,5), U^2 = (8,9))$, which corresponds to the lighter grey area in Fig. 6. We observe that the outlier data point $(8,9)$ is actually inside the given query range, but due to the adjustment of its VT-coordinate, it appears to be outside. In order to guarantee that no point is missed, we have to expand the query range by increasing the VT-coordinate of the upper-bound query point by $\varepsilon = 1$. Then we obtain $\mathtt{Query}_{\mathrm{expand}}(L^2 = (3,5), U^2 = (8,10))$, as shown by the lighter and darker grey areas together. A natural question is why an analogous correction is not necessary at the bottom (for data points that move up into the query region). The reason is that we can

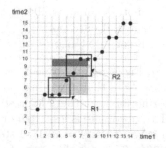

Fig. 6. Ranges selected on time1 and time2 dimensions

use the EPSum array for correction instead of examining the ε stripe at the query bottom.

After query range expansion, some data points which are not inside the given query range may now appear in the expanded query range. For example, data point $(7, 10)$ is not inside the given range query, but now appears in the expanded query range, which is shown as a darker gray region in Fig. 6. Such points must be excluded from the final answer. Hence, the original range query is transformed into two sub-queries: $\mathtt{subQuery_{expand}}(L^2 = (3,5), U^2 = (8,10))$ and $\mathtt{subQuery_{surplus}}(L^2 = (3,9), U^2 = (8,10))$, i.e., the query result is equal to $\mathtt{subQuery_{expand}} - \mathtt{subQuery_{surplus}}$.

Therefore, given any range aggregate query, we expand the original query such that it is guaranteed that all selected points are included. Since data points can only move "up", we do not need to expand the bottom part of the query. After expanding, all we need to do is filter out the effect of false hits by using the pre-computed information.

Both sub-queries can be processed similarly. Here we only use $\mathtt{subQuery_{expand}}$ as an example to show how to process the sub-query. We start by defining two I-instances LB_{ins}, UB_{ins} where LB_{ins} is the I-instance with the least time coordinates which is greater than or equal to the lower values of the selected time ranges and UB_{ins} is the I-instance with the greatest time coordinates which is less than or equal to the upper values of the selected time ranges. For our example, we get $LB_{ins} = I(3,5)$ and $UB_{ins} = I(8,10)$.

As LB_{ins} is an I-instance for a data point of an outlier group ($R1$ in Fig. 6), we can locate the I-instance for the ending data point of the outlier group through $LB_{ins}.\mathtt{EIns}$, which is $I(5,7)$. Recall that the VT-coordinate of the ending data point of the outlier group is greater than that of the starting data point of the outlier group by at least ε time units. Thus the VT-coordinate of all data points after $I(5,7)$ can not fall below the query range. Thus we can simply use the cumulative information stored in $I(8,10)$ and $I(5,7)$ to compute the sum of data points remaining in the query($R2$ in Fig. 6), i.e., $I(8,10).\mathtt{PSum} - I(5,7).\mathtt{PSum} = 31 - 14 = 17$.

$R1$ only contains data points of an outlier group and not all of them are inside the query range due to the VT-coordinate adjustment. To exclude those data points whose original VT-coordinates are not within the selected range on $\mathtt{time2}$ dimension, we can use the EPSum maintained in the I-instances $I(3,5)$ and $I(5,7)$ to compute the sum of data points in $R1$. The lower bound of the selected range in $\mathtt{time2}$ dimension is 5, so we have to exclude those data points in the outlier group whose original VT-coordinate is earlier than 5. From the definition of EPSum, we know that EPSum[0] will exclude those data points, i.e., sum of data points in $R1$ can be computed through $I(5,7).\mathtt{EPSum}[0] - I(3,5).\mathtt{EPSum}[0]$, which is $12 - 5 = 7$. Thereby we can get the result for $\mathtt{Query_{expand}}$, which is $17 + 7 = 24$. Likewise, we can get the result for $\mathtt{Query_{surplus}}$, which is 8. Thus the query result for $\mathtt{Query}(L^2 = (3,5), U^2 = (8,9))$ is $24 - 8 = 16$.

4.3 Algorithm and Time Complexity Analysis

We now present a formal description of how sub-queries such as $\mathtt{subQuery_{expand}}$ or $\mathtt{subQuery_{surplus}}$ are processed. Recall that we get the final answer to any given range aggregate query by subtracting $\mathtt{subQuery_{surplus}}$ from $\mathtt{subQuery_{expand}}$, hence both sub-queries by themselves may include false hits. Also note that data points in the following refer to data points after VT-coordinate adjustment unless otherwise specified:

1. If both LB_{ins} and UB_{ins} are NULL, the sub-query range does not contain any data point and consequently we return 0 as the sub-query result.
2. If LB_{ins} is equal to UB_{ins} (an example sub-query shown in Fig. 7(a)), the sub-query range contains only one I-instance. If it is not an adjusted data point (by checking ADJUSTED) or the original time coordinates of its data point (by checking ORC) are inside the range, we return LB_{ins}.OVal as the sub-query result; otherwise we return 0 as the sub-query result.
3. If LB_{ins} and UB_{ins} are two different I-instances and the VT-coordinate of LB_{ins} is greater than that of the lower-bound query point L^2 by at least ε time units (an example sub-query shown in Fig. 7(b)), every data point between LB_{ins} and UB_{ins} must be inside the sub-query range. PSum maintained in UB_{ins} gives the sum of all data points whose time coordinates are less than or equal to those of UB_{ins}. To answer the actual sub-query, we have to remove all data points whose time coordinates are

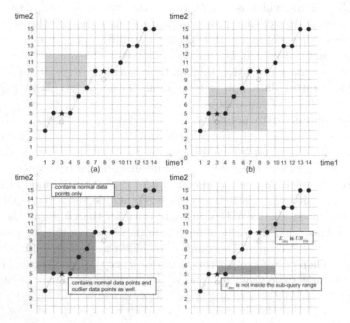

Fig. 7. Processing a sub-query: case 2, 3, 4.i, 4.ii

less than those of LB_{ins}. The sum of such data points can be obtained by subtracting LB_{ins}.OVal from LB_{ins}.PSum. Hence, the correct answer is UB_{ins}.PSum $- (LB_{ins}$.PSum $- LB_{ins}$.OVal$)$.

4. If LB_{ins} and UB_{ins} are two different I-instances, and the difference between the VT-coordinate of LB_{ins} and that of L^2 is less than ε time units, then there might be data points between LB_{ins} and UB_{ins} which are not inside the sub-query range because of the VT-coordinate adjustments. In this case, the sub-query will be processed differently according to the characteristics of LB_{ins}, i.e., depending on LB_{ins} being the I-instance for a data point of a normal group, the starting data point of an outlier group, or the middle data point (including the ending data point) of an outlier group. The corresponding cases are called normalQuery, outlierSQuery, outlierMQuery respectively.

CASE i normalQuery (example sub-queries shown in Fig. 7(c)): If LB_{ins} is the I-instance for a data point of a normal group, an I-instance O_{ins} will be obtained such that its data point is the starting data point of the outlier group which is immediately after LB_{ins}'s group. If O_{ins} is NULL or not inside the sub-query range, then the sub-query range only contains data points from a normal group and the processing is the same as described in case 3; otherwise, we divide the data points covered by the sub-query into two parts such that the first part contains data points arriving before the data point of O_{ins} and the second part contains the remaining data points. The second part can be processed by calling outlierSQuery because it starts with the data point of O_{ins} which is the starting data point of an outlier group. Thus we return $(O_{ins}$.PSum $- LB_{ins}$.PSum $+ LB_{ins}$.OVal $- O_{ins}$.OVal$) +$ outlierSQuery(O_{ins}, UB_{ins}) as the sub-query result.

CASE ii outlierSQuery (example sub-queries shown in Fig. 7(d)): If LB_{ins} is the I-instance for the starting data point of an outlier group, an I-instance E_{ins} is obtained through LB_{ins}.EIns, whose data point is the ending data point of the outlier group. If E_{ins} is NULL or not inside the sub-query range or E_{ins} is equal to UB_{ins}, then all the data points between LB_{ins} and UB_{ins} are in the same group, i.e., the outlier group. If LB_{ins} aligns with the bottom line of the range, we return UB_{ins}.EPSum$[0] - LB_{ins}$.EPSum$[0]$ as the sub-query result; otherwise, we return UB_{ins}.PSum $- LB_{ins}$.PSum $+ LB_{ins}$.OVal as the sub-query result. If E_{ins} is inside the range (as the query example in Section 4.2), then every data point between E_{ins} and UB_{ins} is inside the sub-query. Similarly, if LB_{ins} aligns with the bottom line of the range, we return $(E_{ins}$.EPSum$[0] - LB_{ins}$.EPSum$[0]) + (UB_{ins}$.PSum $- E_{ins}$.PSum$)$ as the sub-query result; otherwise, we return $(E_{ins}$.PSum $- LB_{ins}$.PSum $+ LB_{ins}$.OVal$) + (UB_{ins}$.PSum $- E_{ins}$.PSum$)$ as the sub-query result.

CASE iii outlierMQuery: This covers the remaining possibility of LB_{ins} being the I-instance for a data point in an outlier group which is not the starting point of the outlier group. If LB_{ins} is not the ending data point of the outlier group, the processing is similar to the outlierSQuery;

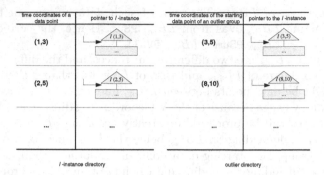

Fig. 8. I-instance directory and outlier directory

otherwise, an I-instance I_{ins} is obtained through LB_{ins}.IIns, whose data point arrives immediately after LB_{ins}. We return E_{ins}.OVal + normalQuery(I_{ins}, UB_{ins}) as the sub-query result if I_{ins} is the I-instance for a data point of a normal group; otherwise return LB_{ins}.OVal + outlierSQuery(I_{ins}, UB_{ins})

So far we have not discussed how to find the appropriate I-instances LB_{ins}, UB_{ins} and O_{ins}. We need two directories: One directory, referred to as I-*instance directory*, maintains the correspondence between the time coordinates of data points and their I-instances and is used to search for LB_{ins} and UB_{ins}. The other directory, referred to as *outlier directory*, maintains the correspondence between the time coordinates of the starting data points of outlier groups and their I-instances. It is used to search for O_{ins}.

Example 5. For the two-dimensional MAOT data set shown in Fig. 4, we maintain the I-instance directory and outlier directory as shown in Fig. 8.

We now analyze the query and storage costs of the proposed approach. For any range query, two sub-queries are executed to compute the result, i.e., subQuery$_{\text{expand}}$ and subQuery$_{\text{surplus}}$. For either sub-query, we first need to find the appropriate I-instances for the lower and upper-bound query points of the

Fig. 9. Modify EPSum filed for two-dimensional MAOT data sets with $\varepsilon > 1$

query range. The cost of a lookup is logarithmic in the number of data points N of a data set $\mathcal{D}$ as it performs a 'binary-search-like' search in the I-instance directory. Then according to the characteristics of LB_{ins} and UB_{ins}, the sub-query is processed in four cases as discussed above. Cases 1, 2 and 3, take constant time. For case 4, a `normalQuery`, requires another lookup in the outlier directory and the lookup cost is logarithmic in the number of outlier groups, which is no more than N; if it is an `outlierSQuery`, it takes constant time; an `outlierMQuery`, on the other hand, may be reduced to another `normalQuery` and thus the worst cost is logarithmic in the number of outlier groups. Therefore the query cost for any range aggregate query is $O(\log N)$ in the worst case.

We maintain a historical I-instance for each data point, an I-instance directory and an outlier directory. The storage cost for the cumulative and auxiliary information maintained in a historical I-instance is constant and thus the storage cost for the historical I-instances is $O(N)$. The storage cost of the I-instance directory is also $O(N)$ since we maintain the correspondence between the time coordinates of data points and the pointers to their I-instances. Likewise, the storage cost of the outlier directory is $O(N)$ in the worst case. Consequently the storage cost of additional information is $O(N)$.

Since two-dimensional MAOT data sets with $\varepsilon = 1$ are special cases of two-dimensional MAOT data sets, when dealing with range aggregate queries on data sets with $\varepsilon > 1$, we need to apply some minor changes to the above-mentioned technique for two-dimension MAOT data sets with $\varepsilon = 1$. The changes are described as follows.

For convenience, we denote a two-dimensional MAOT data set with $\varepsilon > 1$ as $\mathcal{D}^2_{\varepsilon>1}$ and a two-dimensional MAOT data set with $\varepsilon = 1$ as $\mathcal{D}^2_{\varepsilon=1}$. Let I_e denote a data structure which extends I (as defined in Section 4.2) in the field of `EPSum` only such that for each pair of time coordinates in $\mathcal{D}^2_{\varepsilon>1}$, there is an I_e-instance of I_e which maintains cumulative and auxiliary information.

From Fig. 9, we observe that the characteristics of an outlier group in $\mathcal{D}^2_{\varepsilon>1}$ is different from that of an outlier group in $\mathcal{D}^2_{\varepsilon=1}$. Once a data point whose VT-coordinate is greater than that of the starting data point of the outlier group, the outlier group will be ending for $\mathcal{D}^2_{\varepsilon=1}$ according to the definition of an outlier group. However, that is not the case for $\mathcal{D}^2_{\varepsilon=1}$. Even after some data point whose VT-coordinate is greater than that of the starting data point of the outlier group, there are still possibly some outlier data points and the outlier group will be ending at a data point whose VT-coordinate is later than that of the starting data point of the outlier group by at least ε time units. Thus it is enough for $\mathcal{D}^2_{\varepsilon=1}$ to keep `EPSum` sized of ε to correct for the possible errors introduced due to the VT-coordinate adjustments. However it is not enough for $\mathcal{D}^2_{\varepsilon>1}$. For example, for data point P in Fig. 9, if we maintain `EPSum` sized of ε, i.e., the information of outlier data points on lines l_1, l_2 and l_3, then we are missing the information of outlier data points on line l_4.

Therefore, we redefine the `EPSum` of $I(t_1, t_2)$ for a data point (t_2, t_2) (excluding the ending data point) of an outlier group as a one-dimensional array structure with dimension size $\varepsilon + t_2 - s$ (s is the VT-coordinate of the starting data point of the outlier group), in which a cell EPSum$[i]$($0 \le i \le \varepsilon + t_2 - s - 1$) maintains the sum of measure values of data points $X^2 = (x_1, x_2)$ where $x_1 \le t_1, x_2 \le t_2$ but excludes those data points in the same outlier group with original VT-coordinate earlier than $t_2 - i$.

If $I(t_1, t2)$ is the I_e-instance for the ending data point of an outlier group, the EPSum maintains a one-dimensional array structure with dimension size $\varepsilon + t_{be} - s$ (s is the VT-coordinate of the starting data point of its group and t_{be} is the VT-coordinate of the data point immediately before the ending data point), in which a cell EPSum$[i]$($0 \le i \le \varepsilon + t_{be} - s - 1$) maintains the sum of measure values of data points $X^2 = (x_1, x_2)$ where $x_1 \le t_1, x_2 \le t_2$ but excludes those data points in the same outlier group with original VT-coordinate earlier than $t_{be} - i$. As we know t_2 of a non-ending data point is at most $s + \varepsilon - 1$ and so is t_{be}, thus we know that the size of EPSum of any time instance within an outlier group is at most $2\varepsilon - 1$, which still promises the maintained information finite.

As the algorithm for two-dimensional MAOT data sets with $\varepsilon > 1$ is very similar to that for two-dimensional MAOT data sets with $\varepsilon = 1$ and also due to the space limit, we do not present it here and more details can be found in [15]. Furthermore, we generalized our technique to d-dimensional data sets with two MAOT dimensions, i.e., data sets having two MAOT dimensions as well as other non-temporal "general" attributes, e.g., location. The details of this generalization can also be found in [15].

4.4   Experimental Results

We empirically evaluated the performance of our technique for two-dimensional MAOT data sets and also compared it with R-tree technique. We implemented both techniques in Java and all experiments were performed on a Pentium IV PC with 2.4GHZ CPU and 1GB of main memory which runs Linux RedHat 8.0. We generated synthetic two-dimensional MAOT data sets as data source by varying epsilon (ε) and data set size. The ratio of the outlier data points over total data points of each data set is about 10%. We compared our proposed technique with the R-Tree technique in three settings and the metrics we used are average query time and average number of disk I/Os per query. For the purpose of a fair comparison, we cached part of the R-tree in main memory during searching for a query answer and the cache size is the same as that of the I-instance directory (It is maintained in main memory for our proposed technique when answering range queries). Moreover we used Least Recently Used (LRU) cache algorithm.

The first setting is to evaluate the effect of data set size on the performance. We generated MAOT data sets by fixing the epsilon (ε) and varying the data set size from 10^4 to 10^6. We executed about 5000 uniformly generated range queries on every data set to compute the average query time and average number of disk I/Os. The experimental results of this setting are shown in Fig. 10. We can observe that changing the data set size does not change the performance of our technique too much while the performance of R-tree technique degrades actually grows linearly with respect to the data set size. As the dominant query time is the hard disk access time and our technique just requires a few number of hard disk accesses, thus even a large data set size will not affect overall query time too much, which comprises hard disk access time and I-instance directory searching time.

The second setting is to evaluate the effect of epsilon (ε) on the performance. We generated MAOT data sets by fixing the data set size (10^5) and varying epsilon (ε) from 3 to 10. Likewise, we executed about 5000 uniformly generated range queries on every data set to compute the average query time and average number of disk I/Os. As both techniques' searching algorithms are independent of the size of epsilon, thus changing epsilon size do not affect the performance of both techniques which coincides the experimental results shown in Fig. 11. Besides we can observe that our proposed technique still outperforms the R-tree technique. However a larger epsilon definitely results in more storage space needed for outlier instances.

The third setting is to evaluate the effect of query selectivity on the performance. In this setting, we ran queries on a two-dimensional MAOT data set with epsilon $= 3$ and data set size $= 10^5$. We then generated range queries by enforcing the selectivity constraint $k\%$ on time dimensions and then examined how they affected query time and disk I/Os. The selectivity constraint $k\%$ means that the length of any queried ranged is less than or equal to $k \times dom(i)/100$ where $dom(i)$ represents the length of the domain. When generating the range queries, the start points of the ranges is selected uniformly from the domain of the dimensions and then the range is determined randomly according to the selectivity. Note that the range in every dimension is independently selected. The experimental results of about 40000 range queries are reported in Fig. 12. We can observe that the performance of our technique does not change too much as the query selectivity decreases while the performance of R-tree technique degrades. Our technique requires at most a few number of hard disk accesses per query and thus query size do not really matter a lot when searching the query

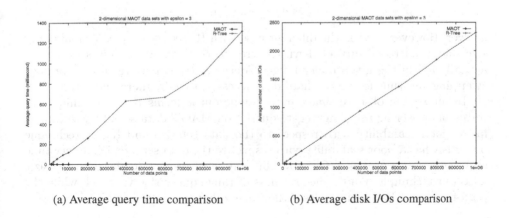

(a) Average query time comparison   (b) Average disk I/Os comparison

Fig. 10. Effect of *data set size* on performance

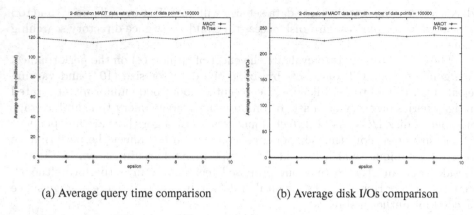

(a) Average query time comparison   (b) Average disk I/Os comparison

Fig. 11. Effect of *epsilon* on performance

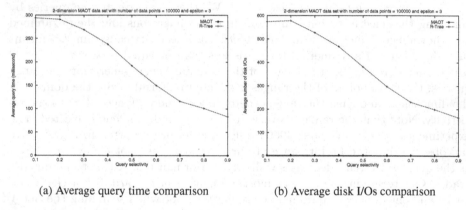

(a) Average query time comparison   (b) Average disk I/Os comparison

Fig. 12. Effect of *query selectivity* on performance

answer. However, that is the different case with R-tree technique, a small query size may need to go further down the tree to trace the data points which are actually are in the given query range. Consequently it may require more page swapping and thus lead more hard disk accesses, thereby more query time.

In all we can observe that our technique outperforms R-tree techniques in terms of answering range aggregate queries on MAOT data sets. Our technique has a good scalability with respect to the data set size and R-tree technique obviously has a poor scalability with respect to the data set size, i.e., query time and the number of disk I/Os grows linearly with respect to the data set size. Also our technique handle the skewness of range query size very well while the performance of R-tree degrades if the range query size is too small.

5   Conclusion and Future Work

Append-only data sets are increasing in popularity due to the increasing demand for both archival data as well as trend analysis of such data sets. OLAP applications that need aggregate support for different ranges for such data sets need to be efficient. In this paper, we formalize the notion of Multi-Append-Only-Trend (MAOT) property of historical data sets in data warehousing. Due to the sparsity of MAOT data sets, application of existing techniques leads to significant storage explosion. Thus, we propose a new technique for handling range aggregate (SUM) queries efficiently on MAOT data sets. This paper is thus a continuation of our development of techniques for managing large append-only data sets. In [20], we proposed a framework for efficient aggregation over data sets with a single append-only dimension. In this paper, we extended our development to data sets with multi-append-only-trend property. Data sets would benefit significantly if such dimensions are recognized and efficiently incorporated into analysis tools. The technique proposed in this paper essentially allows us to process a d-dimensional data set with two time-related dimensions as efficient as if it was only a $(d-2)$-dimensional data set. In particular a data set of size N that only has TT- and VT-dimensions can be searched and updated in $O(\log N)$ time, while requiring storage linear in N.

We are currently extending this approach to d-dimensional data set with arbitrary number of MAOT dimensions. Part of our future work is also to examine how to choose the ε parameter for data sets where the value is not known in advance.

References

[1] C. Böhm and H.-P. Kriegel. Dynamically Optimizing High-Dimensional Index Structures. In *Proc. Int. Conf. on Extending Database Technology (EDBT)*, pages 36-50, 2000. 182

[2] C.-Y. Chan and Y. E. Ioannidis. An Efficient Bitmap Encoding scheme for selection Queries. In *Proc. Int. Conf. on Management of Data (SIGMOD)*, pages 215-216, 1999. 182

[3] C.-Y. Chan and Y. E. Ioannidis. Hierarchical Cubes for Range-Sum Queries. In *Proc. Int. Conf. on Very Large Data Bases (VLDB)*, pages 675-686, 1999. 180, 181

[4] S. Chaudhuri and U. Dayal. An Overview of Data Warehousing and OLAP Technology. *SIGMOD Record*, 26(1):65-74, 1997. 180

[5] B. Chazelle. A Functional Approach to Data Structures and its Use in Multidimensional Searching. *SIAM Journal on Computing*, 17(3):427-462, 1988. 181

[6] M. de Berg and M. van Kreveld and M. Overmars and O. Schwarzkopf. *Computational Geometry*. Springer Verlag, 2 edition, 2000. 181

[7] J. R. Driscoll and N. Sarnak and D. D. Sleator and R. E. Tarjan. Making Data Structures Persistent. *Journal of Computer and System Sciences (JCSS)*, 38(1):86-124, 1989.

[8] M. Ester and J. Kohlhammer and H.-P. Kriegel. The DC-Tree: A Fully Dynamic Index Structure for Data Warehouses. In *Proc. Int. Conf. on Data Engineering (ICDE)*, pages 379-388, 2000. 182

[9] A. Guttman. R-Trees: A Dynamic Index Structure for Spatial Searching. In *Proc. ACM SIGMOD Int. Conf. on Management of Data*, pages 47-57, 1984. 180

[10] S. Geffner and D. Agrawal and A. El Abbadi. The Dynamic Data Cube. In *Proc. Int. Conf. on Extending Database Technology (EDBT)*, pages 237-253, 2000. 180, 181

[11] V. Gaede and O. Günther. Multidimensional access methods. *ACM Computing Surveys*, 30(2):170-231, 1998. 182

[12] C. Ho and R. Agrawal and N. Megiddo and R. Srikant. Range Queries in OLAP Data Cubes. In *Proc. Int. Conf. on Management of Data (SIMGMOD)*, pages 73-88, 1997. 180, 181

[13] C. S. Jensen et al. *Temporal Databases - Research and Practice*, volume 1399 of *LNCS*, chapter The Consensus Glossary of Temporal Database Concepts, pages 367-405, Springer Verlag, 1998. 179

[14] I. Lazaridis and S. Mehrotra. Progressive Approximate Aggregate Queries with a Multi-Resolution Tree Structure. In *Proc. ACM SIGMOD Int. Conf. on Management of Data*, pages 401-412, 2001. 182

[15] H.-G. Li and D. Agrawal and A. El Abbadi and M. Riedewald. Exploiting the Multi-Append-Only-Trend Property of Historical Data in Data Warehouses. *Technical Report*, Computer Science Department, University of California, Santa Barbara, 2003. http://www.cs.ucsb.edu/research/trcs/docs/2003-09.ps. 194

[16] V. Markl and F. Ramsak and R. Bayer. Improving OLAP Performance by Multidimensional Hierarchical clustering. In *Proc. Int. Conf. on Database Engineering and Applications Symp. (IDEAS)*, pages 165-177, 1999. 182

[17] P. E. O'Neil and D. Quass. Improved Query Performance with Variant Indexes. In *Proc. Int. Conf. on Management of Data (SIGMOD)*, pages 38-49, 1997. 182

[18] M. Riedewald and D. Agrawal and A. El Abbadi. Flexible Data Cubes for Online Aggregation. In *Proc. Int. Conf. on Database Theory (ICDT)*, pages 159-173, 2001. 180, 181

[19] M. Riedewald and D. Agrawal and A. El Abbadi. pCube: Update-Efficient Online Aggregation with Progressive Feedback and Error Bounds. In *Proc. Int. Conf. on Scientific and Statistical Database Management (SSDBM)*, pages 95-108, 2000. 182

[20] M. Riedewald and D. Agrawal and A. El Abbadi. Efficient Integration and Aggregation of Historical Information. In *Proc. ACM SIGMOD Int. Conf. on Management of Data*, pages 13-24, 2002. 180, 182, 197

[21] D. A. White and R. Jain. Similarity Indexing with the SS-tree. In *Proc. Int. Conf. on Data Engineering (ICDE)*, pages 516-523, 1996. 180

[22] D. E. Willard and G. S. Lueker. Adding Range Restriction Capability to Dynamic Data Structures. *Journal of the ACM*, 32(3):597-617, 1985. 181

Cross-Outlier Detection*

Spiros Papadimitriou and Christos Faloutsos

Computer Science Department
Carnegie Mellon University
5000 Forbes Ave, Pittsburgh, PA, USA
{spapadim,christos}@cs.cmu.edu

Abstract. The problem of outlier detection has been studied in the context of several domains and has received attention from the database research community. To the best of our knowledge, work up to date focuses exclusively on the problem as follows [10]: "given a *single* set of observations in some space, find those that deviate so as to arouse suspicion that they were generated by a different mechanism."
However, in several domains, we have more than one set of observations (or, equivalently, as single set with class labels assigned to each observation). For example, in astronomical data, labels may involve types of galaxies (e.g., spiral galaxies with abnormal concentration of elliptical galaxies in their neighborhood; in biodiversity data, labels may involve different population types, e.g., patches of different species populations, food types, diseases, etc). A single observation may look normal both within its own class, as well as within the entire set of observations. However, when examined with respect to other classes, it may still arouse suspicions.
In this paper we consider the problem "given a set of observations with class labels, find those that arouse suspicions, taking into account the class labels." This variant has significant practical importance. Many of the existing outlier detection approaches cannot be extended to this case. We present one practical approach for dealing with this problem and demonstrate its performance on real and synthetic datasets.

1 Introduction

In several problem domains (e.g., surveillance and auditing, stock market analysis, health monitoring systems, to mention a few), the problem of detecting rare events, deviant objects, and exceptions is very important. Methods for finding

---

* This material is based upon work supported by the National Science Foundation under Grants No. IIS-9817496, IIS-9988876, IIS-0083148, IIS-0113089, IIS-0209107 IIS-0205224 by the Pennsylvania Infrastructure Technology Alliance (PITA) Grant No. 22-901-0001, and by the Defense Advanced Research Projects Agency under Contract No. N66001-00-1-8936. Additional funding was provided by donations from Intel. Any opinions, findings, and conclusions or recommendations expressed in this material are those of the author(s) and do not necessarily reflect the views of the National Science Foundation, DARPA, or other funding parties.

T. Hadzilacos et al. (Eds.): SSTD 2003, LNCS 2750, pp. 199–213, 2003.

such outliers in large data sets are drawing increasing attention [1, 3, 5, 8, 11, 13, 16, 14, 17, 18].

As noted in [10], "the intuitive definition of an outlier would be 'an observation that deviates so much from other observations as to arouse suspicions that it was generated by a different mechanism'." The traditional and—to the best of our knowledge—exclusive focus has been on the problem of detecting deviants in a single set of observations, i.e.,

Problem 1 (Outlier detection—single set). Given a set of objects, find these that deviate significantly from the rest.

However, there are several important practical situations where we have two collections of points. Consider the following illustrative example: Assume we have the locations of two types of objects, say vegetable patches and rabbit populations. If we consider, say, rabbit populations in isolation, these may be evenly distributed. The same may be true for food locations alone as well as for the union of the two sets.

Even though everything may look "normal" when we ignore object types, there is still the possibility of "suspicious" objects when we consider them in relation to objects of the other type. For example, a group of patches with far fewer rabbits present in the vicinity may indicate a measurement error. A population away from marked food locations may hint toward the presence of external, unaccounted-for factors.

The above may be considered a "toy" example that only serves illustrative purposes. Nonetheless, in several real-world situations, the spatial relationship among objects of two different types is of interest. A few examples:

- Situations similar to the one above actually do arise in biological/medical domains.
- In geographical/geopolitical applications, we may have points that represent populations, land and water features, regional boundaries, retail locations, police stations, crime incidence and so on. It is not difficult to think of situations where the correlations between such different objects are important.
- In astrophysics, it is well known that the distributions of different celestial objects follow certain laws (for example, elliptical and exponential galaxies form small clusters of one type and these clusters "repel" each other). There are *vast* collections of astrophysical measurements and even single deviant observations would potentially be of great interest.

In brief, we argue that the following outlier detection problem is of practical importance:

Problem 2 (Cross-outlier detection). Given two sets (or classes) of objects, find those which deviate with respect to the other set.

In this case we have a primary set $\mathbb{P}$ (e.g., elliptical galaxies) in which we want to discover *cross-outliers* with respect to a reference set $\mathbb{R}$ (e.g., spiral galaxies). Note that the single set case is always a special case, where $\mathbb{R} = \mathbb{P}$.

However, the converse is *not* true. That is, approaches for the single-set problem are not immediately extensible to cross-outlier detection. First off, several outlier definitions themselves cannot be extended (see also Section 5.1 let alone the corresponding methods to apply the definitions and compute the outliers. In summary, the contributions of this paper are two-fold:

- We identify the problem of cross-outlier detection. To the best of our knowledge, this has not been explicitly studied in the past, even though it is of significant practical interest. In general, an arbitrary method for the single-set problem cannot be easily extended to cross-outlier detection (but the opposite is true).
- We present a practical method that solves the problem. The main features of our method are:
  - It provides a meaningful answer to the question stated above, using a statistically intuitive criterion for outlier flagging (the local neighborhood size differs more than three standard deviations from the local averages), with no magic cut-offs.
  - Our definitions lend themselves to fast, single-pass estimation using box-counting. The running time of these methods is typically linear with respect to both dataset size and dimensionality.
  - It is an important first step (see also Section 5.3) toward the even more general problem of multiple-class cross-outliers (where the reference set $\mathbb{R}$ may be the union of more than one other class of objects).

The rest of the paper is organized as follows: Section 2 briefly discusses related work for the single class case, as well as more remotely related work on multiple dataset correlations and clustering. Section 3 presents our definition of a cross-outlier and briefly discusses its advantages. Section 4 demonstrates our approach on both synthetic and real datasets. Section 5 discusses some important issues and possible future directions. Finally, Section 6 gives the conclusions.

2 Background and Related Work

In this section we present prior work on the problem of single class outlier detection. To the best of our knowledge, the multiple class problem has not been explicitly considered.

2.1 Single Dataset Outlier Detection

Previous methods for single dataset outlier detection broadly fall into the following categories.

Distribution Based Methods in this category are typically found in statistics textbooks. They deploy some standard distribution model (e.g., normal) and flag as outliers those points which deviate from the model [5, 10, 21].

For arbitrary data sets without any prior knowledge of the distribution of points, we have to perform expensive tests to determine which model fits the data best, if any.

Clustering Many clustering algorithms detect outliers as by-products [12]. However, since the main objective is clustering, they are not optimized for outlier detection. Furthermore, the outlier-ness criteria are often implicit and cannot easily be inferred from the clustering procedures.

An intriguing clustering algorithm using the fractal dimension has been suggested by [4]; however it has not been demonstrated on real datasets.

Depth Based This is based on computational geometry and finds different layers of k-d convex hulls [13]. Points in the outer layer are potentially flagged as outliers. However, these algorithms suffer from the dimensionality curse.

Distance Based This was originally proposed by E.M. Knorr and R.T. Ng [16, 14, 17, 18]. A point in a data set $\mathbb{P}$ is a *distance-based outlier* if at least a fraction β of the points in $\mathbb{P}$ are further than r from it.

This outlier definition is based on a single, global criterion determined by the parameters r and β and cannot cope with local density variations.

Density Based This was proposed by M. Breunig, et al. [8]. It relies on the *local outlier factor* (*LOF*) of each point, which depends on the local density of its neighborhood. The neighborhood is defined by the distance to the *MinPts*-th nearest neighbor. In typical use, points with a high LOF are flagged as outliers.

This approach was proposed primarily to deal with the local density problems of the distance based method. However, selecting *MinPts* is non-trivial; in order to detect outlying clusters, *MinPts* has to be as large as the size of these clusters.

2.2   Multiple Class Outlier Detection

To the best of our knowledge, this problem has not received explicit consideration to this date. Some single class approaches may be modified to deal with multiple classes, but the task is non-trivial. The general problem is open and provides promising future research directions. In this section we discuss more remotely related work.

Multi-dimensional Correlations The problem of discovering general correlations between two datasets has been studied to some extent, both in the context of data mining, as well as for the purposes of selectivity estimation of spatial queries. However, none of these approaches deal with single points and identification of outlying observations.

[22] deals with the problem the general relationship of one multi-dimensional dataset with respect to another. This might be a good first step when exploring correlations between datasets. However, even when two datasets have been found to be correlated as a whole and to some extent co-located in space, this method cannot identify single outlying points.

Prior to that, [9] considers the problem of selectivity estimation of spatial joins across two point sets. Also, [6, 7] consider the selectivity and performance of nearest neighbor queries within a single dataset.

Non-spatial Clustering Scalable algorithms for extracting clusters from large collections of spatial data are presented in [19] and [15]. The authors also combine this with the extraction of characteristics based on non-spatial attributes by using both spatial dominant and non-spatial dominant approaches (depending on whether cluster discovery is performed first or on subsets derived using non-spatial attributes). It is not clear if these results can be extended to deal with the multiple class outlier detection problem. In the single class case, clusters of one or very few points can be immediately considered as outliers. However, this is not necessarily the case when dealing with multiple classes.

3 Proposed Method

In this section we introduce our definition of an outlier and discuss its main properties. Our approach is based on the distribution of distances between points of the primary set and a reference set with respect to which we want to discover outliers. We use an intuitive, probabilistic criterion for automatic flagging of outliers.

3.1 Definitions

We consider the problem of detecting outlying observations from a primary set of points $\mathbb{P}$, with respect to a reference set of points $\mathbb{R}$. We want to discover points $p \in \mathbb{P}$ that "arouse suspicions" with respect to points $r \in \mathbb{R}$. Note that single-set outliers are a special case, where $\mathbb{R} = \mathbb{P}$.

Table 1 describes all symbols and basic definitions. To be more precise, for a point $p \in \mathbb{P}$ let $\hat{n}_{\mathbb{P},\mathbb{R}}(p, r, \alpha)$ be the average, over all points $q \in \mathbb{P}$ in the r-neighborhood of p, of $n_{\mathbb{R}}(q, \alpha r)$. The use of two radii serves to decouple the neighbor size radius αr from the radius r over which we are averaging.

We eventually need to *estimate* these quantities (see also Fig. 1). We introduce the following two terms:

Definition 1 (Counting and Sampling Neighborhood). *The* counting neighborhood *(or αr-neighborhood) is the neighborhood of radius αr, over which each $n_{\mathbb{R}}(q, \alpha r)$ is estimated. The* sampling neighborhood *(or r-neighborhood) is the neighborhood of radius r, over which we collect samples of $n_{\mathbb{R}}(q, \alpha r)$ in order to estimate $\hat{n}_{\mathbb{P},\mathbb{R}}(p, r, \alpha)$. The* locality parameter *is α.*

The locality parameter α determines the relationship between the size of the sampling neighborhood and the counting neighborhood. We typically set this value to $\alpha = 1/2$ (see also Section 5.1).

Our outlier detection scheme relies on the standard deviation of the αr-neighbor count of points in the reference set $\mathbb{R}$. Therefore, we also define the quantity $\hat{\sigma}_{\mathbb{P},\mathbb{R}}(p, r, \alpha)$ to be precisely that, for each point $p \in \mathbb{P}$ and each sampling radius r.

Table 1. Symbols and definitions

Symbol	Definition
$\mathbb{P}$ p_i	Primary set of points $\mathbb{P} = \{p_1, \ldots, p_i, \ldots, p_N\}$.
$\mathbb{R}$ r_i	Reference set of points $\mathbb{R} = \{r_1, \ldots, r_i, \ldots, r_M\}$.
N, M	Point set sizes.
k	Dimension of the data sets.
$d(p,q)$	Distance between points p and q.
$R_\mathbb{P}, R_\mathbb{R}$	Range (diameter) of each point set—e.g., $R_\mathbb{P} := \max_{p,q \in \mathbb{P}} d(p,q)$.
$\mathcal{N}_P(p,r)$	The set of r-neighbors of p from the point set P, i.e., $$\mathcal{N}(p,r) := \{q \in P \mid d(p,q) \leq r\}$$ Note that p does not necessarily belong to P.
$n_P(p,r)$	The number of r-neighbors of p_i from the set P, i.e., $n_P(p,r) := |\mathcal{N}_P(p,r)|$. Note that if $p \in P$, then $n_P(p,r)$ cannot be zero.
α	Locality parameter.
$\hat{n}_{\mathbb{P},\mathbb{R}}(p,r,\alpha)$	Average of $n_\mathbb{R}(p, \alpha r)$ over the set of r-neighbors of $p \in \mathbb{P}$, i.e., $$\hat{n}_{\mathbb{P},\mathbb{R}}(p,r,\alpha) := \frac{\sum_{q \in \mathcal{N}_\mathbb{P}(p,r)} n_\mathbb{R}(q, \alpha r)}{n_\mathbb{P}(p,r)}$$ For brevity, we often use $\hat{n}$ instead of $\hat{n}_{\mathbb{P},\mathbb{R}}$.
$\hat{\sigma}_{\mathbb{P},\mathbb{R}}(p,r,\alpha)$	Standard deviation of $n_\mathbb{R}(p, \alpha r)$ over the set of r-neighbors of $p \in \mathbb{P}$, i.e., $$\hat{\sigma}_{\mathbb{P},\mathbb{R}}(p,r,\alpha) := \sqrt{\frac{\sum_{q \in \mathcal{N}_\mathbb{P}(p,r)} (n_\mathbb{R}(q, \alpha r) - \hat{n}_{\mathbb{P},\mathbb{R}}(p,r,\alpha))^2}{n_\mathbb{P}(p,r)}}$$ where $p \in \mathbb{P}$. For brevity we often use $\hat{\sigma}$ instead of $\hat{\sigma}_{\mathbb{P},\mathbb{R}}$.
k_σ	Determines what is *significant* deviation, i.e., a point $p \in \mathbb{P}$ is flagged as an outlier with respect to the set $\mathbb{R}$ iff $$|\hat{n}_{\mathbb{P},\mathbb{R}}(p,r,\alpha) - n_\mathbb{R}(p,\alpha r)| > k_\sigma \hat{\sigma}_{\mathbb{P},\mathbb{R}}(p,r,\alpha)$$ Typically, $k_\sigma = 3$.

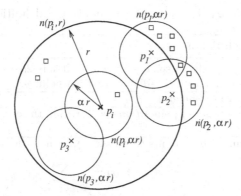

Fig. 1. Definitions for n and $\hat{n}$. Points in the primary set $\mathbb{P}$ are shown with "×" and points in the reference set $\mathbb{R}$ with "□". For instance, $n_{\mathbb{P}}(p_i, r) = 4$ (including itself), $n_{\mathbb{R}}(p_i, \alpha r) = 1$, $n_{\mathbb{R}}(p_1, \alpha r) = 6$ and $\hat{n}_{\mathbb{P},\mathbb{R}}(p_i, r, \alpha) = (1+5+4+0)/4 = 3.25$

Definition 2 (Cross-Outlier Criterion). *A point* $p \in \mathbb{P}$ *is a* cross-outlier *at scale (or radius)* r *with respect to the reference set* $\mathbb{R}$ *if*

$$|\hat{n}_{\mathbb{P},\mathbb{R}}(p, r, \alpha) - n_{\mathbb{R}}(p, \alpha r)| > k_\sigma \hat{\sigma}_{\mathbb{P},\mathbb{R}}(p, r, \alpha)$$

Finally, the average and standard deviation with respect to radius r can provide very useful information about the vicinity of a point.

Definition 3 (Distribution Plot). *For any point* $p \in \mathbb{P}$, *the plot of* $n_{\mathbb{R}}(p, \alpha r)$ *and* $\hat{n}_{\mathbb{P},\mathbb{R}}(p, r, \alpha)$ *with* $\hat{n}_{\mathbb{P},\mathbb{R}}(p, r, \alpha) \pm 3\hat{\sigma}_{\mathbb{P},\mathbb{R}}(p, r, \alpha)$, *versus* r *(for a range of radii of interest), is called its* (local) distribution plot.

3.2   Advantages of Our Definitions

Among several alternatives for an outlier score (such as $\max(\hat{n}/n, n/\hat{n})$, to give one example), our choice allows us to use probabilistic arguments for flagging outliers.

The above definitions and concepts make minimal assumptions. The only general requirement is that a distance is defined. Arbitrary distance functions are allowed, which may incorporate domain-specific, expert knowledge, if desired.

A final but very important point is that distance distributions can be quickly estimated in time that is linear with respect both to dataset sizes and dimensionality. Therefore, the above definitions lend themselves to fast, single-pass estimation algorithms, based on box-counting [20]. The only further constraint imposed in this case is that all points must belong to a k-dimensional vector space (either inherently, or after employing some embedding technique).

Table 2. Box-counting symbols and definitions

Symbol	Definition
$\mathcal{C}(p, r, \alpha)$	Set of cells in some grid, with cell side $2\alpha r$, each fully contained within $\mathcal{L}^\infty$-distance r from point p.
C_i	Cell in some grid.
$c_{P,i}$	The count of points *from set P* within the corresponding cell C_i.
$S_P^q(p, r, \alpha)$	Sum of box counts (from set P) to the q-th power, i.e.,

$$S_P^q(p, r, \alpha) := \sum_{C_i \in \mathcal{C}(p,r,\alpha)} c_{P,i}^q$$

$P_{P,R}^q(p, r, \alpha)$	Sum of box count products (from sets P and R); in particular,

$$P_{P,R}^q(p, r, \alpha) := \sum_{C_i \in \mathcal{C}(p,r,\alpha)} c_{P,i} c_{R,i}^q$$

Note that, $S_P^q = P_{P,P}^{q-1}$.

The main idea is to approximate the r-neighbor counts for each point p with pre-computed counts of points within a cell[1] of side r which contains p.

In a little more detail, in order to quickly estimate $\hat{n}(p, r, \alpha)$ for a point $p_i \in \mathbb{P}$ (from now on, we assume $\mathcal{L}^\infty$ distances), we can use the following approach. Consider a grid of cells with side $2\alpha r$ over both sets $\mathbb{P}$ and $\mathbb{R}$. Within each cell, we store separate counts of points it contains from $\mathbb{P}$ and $\mathbb{R}$. Perform a *box count* on the grid: For each cell C_j in the grid, find the counts, $c_{\mathbb{R},j}$ and $c_{\mathbb{P},j}$, of the number of points from $\mathbb{R}$ and $\mathbb{P}$, respectively, in the cell. There is a total number of $c_{\mathbb{P},j}$ points $p \in \mathbb{P} \cap C_j$ (counting p itself), each of which has $c_{\mathbb{P},j}$ neighbors from $\mathbb{R}$. So, the total number of $\mathbb{R}$ neighbors over all points from $\mathbb{P}$ in C_j is $c_{\mathbb{P},j} c_{\mathbb{R},j}$. Denote by $\mathcal{C}(p, r, \alpha)$ the set of all cells in the grid such that the entire cell is within distance r of p_i. We use $\mathcal{C}(p, r, \alpha)$ as an approximation for the r-neighborhood of p_i. Summing over all these cells, we get a total number of $\mathbb{P}$-$\mathbb{R}$ pairs of $P_{\mathbb{P},\mathbb{R}}(p, r, \alpha) := \sum_{C_j \in \mathcal{C}(p,r,\alpha)} c_{\mathbb{P},j} c_{\mathbb{R},j}$. The total number of objects is simply the sum of all box counts for points in $\mathbb{P}$, i.e., $S_{\mathbb{P}}^1(p, r, \alpha)$

$$\hat{n}_{\mathbb{P},\mathbb{R}}(p, r, \alpha) = \frac{P_{\mathbb{P},\mathbb{R}}^1(p, r, \alpha)}{S_{\mathbb{P}}^1(p, r, \alpha)}$$

---

[1] In practice, we have to use multiple cells in a number randomly shifted grids and use some selection or voting scheme to get a good approximation; see [20] for more details.

A similar calculation can be done to estimate

$$\hat{\sigma}_{\mathbb{P},\mathbb{R}}(p,r,\alpha) = \sqrt{\frac{P^2_{\mathbb{P},\mathbb{R}}(p,r,\alpha)}{S^1_{\mathbb{P}}(p,r,\alpha)} - \left(\frac{P^1_{\mathbb{P},\mathbb{R}}(p,r,\alpha)}{S^1_{\mathbb{P}}(p,r,\alpha)}\right)^2}$$

4 Experimental Results

In this section we give examples of our method and discuss some important observations related to our approach, as well as the problem in general.

Gap In this case (see Fig. 2, top row) the primary set consists of 340 points with a uniformly random distribution within a square region. In single-set outlier detection ($\mathbb{R} = \mathbb{P}$) some fringe points are flagged with a positive deviation (i.e., at some scale, their neighbor count is below the local average). Also, a few interior points in locally dense regions are flagged with a negative deviation.

In cross-outlier detection, we use a reference set $\mathbb{R}$ of 1400 points, again uniformly random in a slightly larger square region, but with a central square gap. As expected, the points of $\mathbb{P}$ that fall within well within the gap of $\mathbb{R}$ are detected as cross-outliers with a positive deviation. Also, very few[2] other points are flagged.

Core In this case (see Fig. 2, middle row), the primary set again consists of 300 points with a uniformly random distribution within a square region. The single-set outliers are similar to the previous case.

In cross-outlier detection, we use a reference set $\mathbb{R}$ of 250 points uniformly random within a central square "core." As expected again, the points of $\mathbb{P}$ that fall within the reference "core" are all detected as outliers. Also, some fringe points are still detected as outliers (see Section 4.1).

Lines The primary set $\mathbb{P}$ consists of 100 points regularly spaced along a line (Fig. 2, bottom row). The single-set outliers ($\mathbb{P} = \mathbb{R}$) consist of eight points, four at each end of the line. Indeed, these points are "special," since their distribution of neighbors clearly differs from that of points in the middle of the line.

In cross outlier detection, the reference set $\mathbb{R}$ consists of two lines of 100 points each, both parallel to $\mathbb{P}$ and slightly shifted downward along their common direction. As expected, the points at the bottom-left end of $\mathbb{P}$ are no longer outliers, with respect to $\mathbb{P}$. Note that the *same* four points along the top-right end are flagged (see discussion in Section 4.1).

Galaxy The primary set consists of a section with 993 spiral galaxies and the reference set of a section with 1218 elliptical galaxies, both from the Sloan Digital Sky Survey (Fig. 3). Although not shown in the figure, all cross-outliers are flagged with a *negative* deviation (except two at the very edge of the dataset).

---

[2] Since $\mathbb{R}$ is significantly denser than $\mathbb{P}$, this is expected.

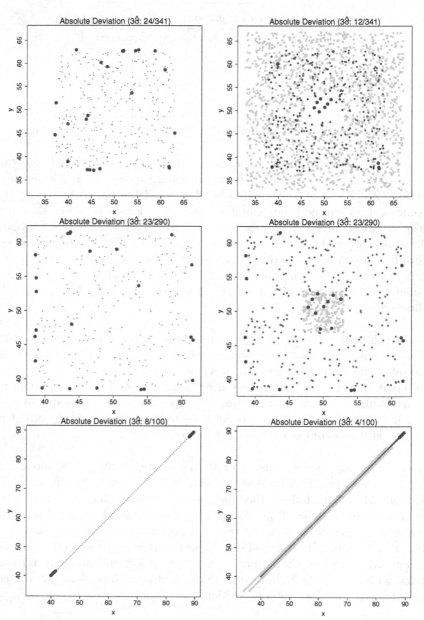

Fig. 2. "Plain" outliers (left, $\mathbb{R} = \mathbb{P}$) and cross-outliers (right). The reference set is shown with square, gray points in the right column. Outliers are marked with larger, red points in each case. In all cases, $\alpha = 1/4$

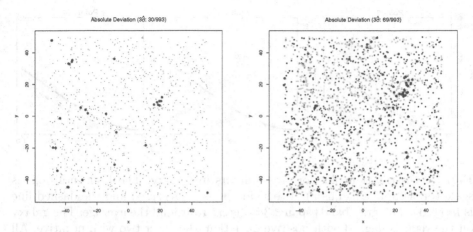

Fig. 3. "Plain" outliers (left, $\mathbb{R} = \mathbb{P}$) and cross-outliers (right) for the galaxy datasets. In all cases, $\alpha = 1/4$

Also (see Fig. 4 and Section 4.1) all are flagged by a narrow margin. This is indeed expected: elliptical galaxies form clusters, intertwined with clusters of spiral galaxies. The distribution is overall even (as evidenced by the consistently wide standard deviation band); however, a few of the elliptical galaxies are within unusually dense clusters of spiral galaxies.

4.1 Observations

Fringe Points The points located along the fringes of a data set are clearly different from the rest of the points.

One could argue that outlier definitions such as the one of the depth-based approach [13] rely *primarily* on this observation in order to detect outliers. Our method goes beyond that and can also capture isolated central points (as can be seen, for example, from the Gap example), but can still distinguish fringe points.

With respect to pairwise distances upon which our approach is based, the first observation is that fringe points have fewer neighbors than interior points. More than that, however, all neighbors of fringe points lie on the *same* half-plane. It is a consequence of this *second* fact that the standard deviation of neighbor counts is (comparatively) smaller at certain scales for fringe points.

This explains why in the Core example more fringe points are detected as cross-outliers than in Gap. The reference set in Gap is chosen to cover a slightly larger region than the primary set in order to illustrate this point. The fringe points of $\mathbb{P}$ in Gap are not fringe points *with respect to* $\mathbb{R}$: they have $\mathbb{R}$-neighbors on all sides of the plane. However, the fringe points of $\mathbb{P}$ in Core have $\mathbb{R}$-neighbors only on one half-plane. Thus, the fringe points of $\mathbb{P}$ in Core are indeed different than the interior points (always *with respect to* $\mathbb{R}$).

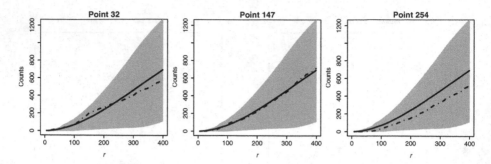

Fig. 4. Distribution plot for cross-outliers in `Galaxy`. The horizontal axis is scale (or, sampling radius r). The solid line is $\hat{n}_{\mathbb{P},\mathbb{R}}(p, r, \alpha)$ and the dashed line is $n_{\mathbb{R}}(p, \alpha)$. The gray bands span $\pm 3\hat{\sigma}_{\mathbb{P},\mathbb{R}}(p, r, \alpha)$ around the average. The galaxy on the right is flagged with positive deviation, the other two with negative. All are flagged at small scales by a narrow margin

Role of Each Distribution In this paragraph we further discuss the sampling and counting neighborhoods. In particular, the former contains points of the primary set $\mathbb{P}$, while the latter of the reference set $\mathbb{R}$. Thus, the distribution of points in *both* sets plays an important role in cross-outlier detection (but see also Section 5.1).

This explains the fact that in `Lines` the same four endpoints are flagged as cross-outliers. We argue that this is a desirable feature. First, the points near the top-right end that are closer to $\mathbb{R}$ are indeed less "distinct" than their neighbors at the very end. This fact depends on the distribution of $\mathbb{P}$, not $\mathbb{R}$! Furthermore, consider extending $\mathbb{P}$ toward the top-right: then, neither of the endpoints are suspicious (whether surrounded or not by points of $\mathbb{R}$). This, again, depends on the distribution of $\mathbb{P}$! Indeed, in the latter case, our method does not detect any outliers.

Digging Deeper As hinted in the discussion of the results, the sign of the deviation can give us important information. However, we can go even further and examine the *distribution plots*, which we discuss very briefly here. Fig. 5 is included as an example. We can clearly see that a point within the gap belongs to a sparse region (with respect to $\mathbb{R}$). Moreover, we can clearly see that the point within the gap is flagged by a much wider margin and at a wider range of scales, whereas a fringe point is marginally flagged. Thus, the distribution plots provide important information about *why* each point is an outlier, as well as its vicinity.

5   Discussion

In this section we first discuss why the problem of cross-outlier detection is different from the single-set case, even though the two may, at first, seem almost

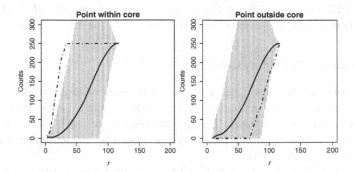

Fig. 5. Distribution plot for cross-outliers in `Core`. Again, the horizontal axis is scale (or, sampling radius r). The solid line is $\hat{n}_{\mathbb{P},\mathbb{R}}(p, r, \alpha)$ and the dashed line is $n_{\mathbb{R}}(p, \alpha)$. The gray bands span $\pm 3 \hat{\sigma}_{\mathbb{P},\mathbb{R}}(p, r, \alpha)$ around the average

identical. We also discuss some directions for future research. These relate to the fast, single-pass estimation algorithms that our definitions admit.

5.1 Differences to Single Class Outlier Detection

The intuitive definition of [10] implies two important parts in any definition of an outlier: *what* is considered a deviation (i.e., where or how we look for them) and *how* do we determine *significant* deviations. Therefore, all outlier definitions employ a model for the data and a measure of correlation, either explicitly or implicitly.

The first difference in the case of cross-outliers follows directly from the problem definition. What we essentially estimate is not a single probability distribution or correlation, but either some (conditional) probability with respect to the reference set or the covariance among sets. However, several of the existing definitions do not make their model assumptions clear or employ a model that cannot be easily extended as described above. These outlier detection approaches are hard to modify.

It should be noted that our definition employs a very general and intuitive model which is based on pairwise distanced and makes minimal assumptions.

The second major difference again follows from the fact that we are dealing with two *separate* sets. Simply put, in the "classical" case ($\mathbb{R} = \mathbb{P}$), we can obviously assume that a point set is co-located in space with respect to itself. However, this need not be the case when $\mathbb{R} \neq \mathbb{P}$. This assumption is sometimes implicitly employed in outlier definitions.

Tools such as that of [22] are useful here as a first step to determine the *overall* spatial relationship between the two sets. It must further be noted that, in our approach, the locality parameter α is tunable and typically two values should be sufficient: $\alpha \approx 1/2$ (or 1) and any $\alpha \leq r_{min}/\max\{R_{\mathbb{P}}, R_{\mathbb{R}}\}$ where r_{min} is the smallest distance between any two points (irrespective of type)[3].

5.2 Efficiency Considerations

Our definitions are based on pairwise distance distributions. As demonstrated in [22, 20], these can be estimated very quickly with a single pass over the data, in time that is practically linear with respect to both data set size and dimensionality. The only minor restriction imposed by these algorithms is that $\alpha = 1/2^k$ for some integer k.

Furthermore, if we have more than two classes of points, the pre-processing step for box counting can be modified to keep separate counts for each class. This does not increase computational cost (only space in proportion to the number of classes) and allows fast outlier detection where the reference set $\mathbb{R}$ is the *union* of points from several classes (rather than a single class).

5.3 Generalizations

The observation in the last paragraph of the previous section naturally leads to the problem of multi-class outlier detection. As pointed out, the fast algorithms can easily detect outliers when the reference set $\mathbb{R}$ is any *given* combination of classes, without incurring any extra computational cost.

An interesting future research direction is to extend these algorithms with heuristic pruning approaches (e.g., similar to those in association rule[4] algorithms [2]; in our case, items correspond to point classes) to efficiently search the entire space of all class combinations (i.e., pointset unions) in the place of $\mathbb{R}$.

6   Conclusions

In this paper we present the problem of *cross-outlier* detection. This is the first contribution; we argue that this is a non-trivial problem of practical interest and certainly more than an immediate generalization. We discuss several aspects of the problem that make it different from "classical" outlier detection. The former is a special case of cross-outliers (with $\mathbb{R} = \mathbb{P}$) but the converse is not true.

Beyond introducing the problem, we present a method that can provide an answer. Furthermore, our definitions use a statistically intuitive flagging criterion and lend themselves to fast, single-pass estimation. We demonstrate our approach using both synthetic and real datasets.

---

[3] The second choice for α formally implies that, at every scale, the sampling neighborhood completely covers both datasets.

[4] This is one potential approach; regions with *no* co-located classes can probably be ignored. Of course, this far from exhausts all possible pruning techniques.

References

[1] C.C. Aggarwal and P.S. Yu. Outlier detection for high dimensional data. In *Proc. SIGMOD*, 2001. 200

[2] R. Agrawal and R. Srikant. Fast algorithms for mining association rules in large databases. In *Proc. VLDB*, pages 487–499, 1994. 212

[3] A. Arning, R. Agrawal, and P. Raghavan. A linear method for deviation detection in large database. In *Proc. KDD*, pages 164–169, 1996. 200

[4] Daniel Barbará and Ping Chen. Using the fractal dimension to cluster datasets. In *Proc. KDD*, pages 260–264, 2000. 202

[5] V. Barnett and T. Lewis. *Outliers in Statistical Data*. John Wiley, 1994. 200, 201

[6] A. Belussi and C. Faloutsos. Estimating the selectivity of spatial queries using the 'correlation' fractal dimension. In *Proc. VLDB*, pages 299–310, 1995. 202

[7] S. Berchtold, C. Böhm, D.A. Keim, and H.-P. Kriegel. A cost model for nearest neighbor search in high-dimensional data space. In *Proc. PODS*, pages 78–86, 1997. 202

[8] M.M. Breunig, H.P. Kriegel, R.T. Ng, and J. Sander. Lof: Identifying density-based local outliers. In *Proc. SIGMOD Conf.*, pages 93–104, 2000. 200, 202

[9] C. Faloutsos, B. Seeger, C.Traina Jr., and A. Traina. Spatial join selectivity using power laws. In *Proc. SIGMOD*, pages 177–188, 2000. 202

[10] D.M. Hawkins. *Identification of Outliers*. Chapman and Hall, 1980. 199, 200, 201, 211

[11] H.V. Jagadish, N. Koudas, and S. Muthukrishnan. Mining deviants in a time series database. In *Proc. VLDB*, pages 102–113, 1999. 200

[12] A.K. Jain, M.N. Murty, and P.J. Flynn. Data clustering: A review. *ACM Comp. Surveys*, 31(3):264–323, 1999. 202

[13] T. Johnson, I. Kwok, and R.T. Ng. Fast computation of 2-dimensional depth contours. In *Proc. KDD*, pages 224–228, 1998. 200, 202, 209

[14] E. M. Knorr and R.T. Ng. Algorithms for mining distance-based outliers in large datasets. In *Proc. VLDB 1998*, pages 392–403, 1998. 200, 202

[15] E.M. Knorr and R.T. Ng. Finding aggregate proximity relationships and commonalities in spatial data mining. *IEEE TKDE*, 8(6):884–897, 1996. 203

[16] E.M. Knorr and R.T. Ng. A unified notion of outliers: Properties and computation. In *Proc. KDD*, pages 219–222, 1997. 200, 202

[17] E.M. Knorr and R.T. Ng. Finding intentional knowledge of distance-based outliers. In *Proc. VLDB*, pages 211–222, 1999. 200, 202

[18] E.M. Knorr, R.T. Ng, and V. Tucakov. Distance-based outliers: Algorithms and applications. *VLDB Journal*, 8:237–253, 2000. 200, 202

[19] R.T. Ng and J. Han. Efficient and effective clustering methods for spatial data mining. In *Proc. VLDB*, pages 144–155, 1994. 203

[20] S. Papadimitriou, H. Kitagawa, P.B. Gibbons, and C. Faloutsos. LOCI: Fast outlier detection using the local correlation integral. In *Proc. ICDE*, 2003. 205, 206, 212

[21] P.J. Rousseeuw and A.M. Leroy. *Robust Regression and Outlier Detection*. John Wiley and Sons, 1987. 201

[22] A. Traina, C. Traina, S. Papadimitriou, and C. Faloutsos. Tri-Plots: Scalable tools for multidimensional data mining. In *Proc. KDD*, pages 184–193, 2001. 202, 211, 212

Accessing Scientific Data: Simpler is Better*

Mirek Riedewald[1], Divyakant Agrawal[2], Amr El Abbadi[2], and Flip Korn[3]

[1] Cornell University
Ithaca, NY.
mirek@cs.cornell.edu
[2] University of California
Santa Barbara, CA,
{agrawal,amr}@cs.ucsb.edu
[3] AT&T Labs-Research
Florham Park, NJ,
flip@research.att.com

Abstract. A variety of index structures has been proposed for supporting fast access and summarization of large multidimensional data sets. Some of these indices are fairly involved, hence few are used in practice. In this paper we examine how to reduce the I/O cost by taking full advantage of recent trends in hard disk development which favor reading large chunks of consecutive disk blocks over seeking and searching. We present the Multiresolution File Scan (MFS) approach which is based on a surprisingly simple and flexible data structure which outperforms sophisticated multidimensional indices, even if they are bulk-loaded and hence optimized for query processing. Our approach also has the advantage that it can incorporate a priori knowledge about the query workload. It readily supports summarization using distributive (e.g., count, sum, max, min) and algebraic (e.g., avg) aggregate operators.

1 Introduction

Modern scientific databases and data warehouses reach sizes in the order of terabytes [7] and soon even petabytes [4]. Hence fast aggregation techniques and efficient access to selected information play a vital role in the process of summarizing and analyzing their contents. The complexity of the problem grows with increasing dimensionality, i.e., number of attributes describing the data space. For instance the cloud data in [12] is defined by 20 attributes.

Despite the availability of high-capacity memory chips, rapidly growing amounts of information still require maintaining and accessing large data collections on hard disk. Hence the I/O cost, i.e., the time it takes to retrieve relevant information from hard disk, dominates the query cost. Our goal is to reduce this cost factor. There is a variety of indices which try to address this problem (see for instance [8] for an overview). Unfortunately, except for the R-tree [11] and its

---

* This work was supported by NSF grants IIS98-17432, EIA99-86057, EIA00-80134, and IIS02-09112.

T. Hadzilacos et al. (Eds.): SSTD 2003, LNCS 2750, pp. 214–232, 2003.

relatives (e.g., R*-tree [1] and X-tree [3]) few have ever gained wide acceptance in practice. Hence, instead of developing another sophisticated index, our goal is to examine how efficiently queries can be supported using the *simplest possible* data structure—a collection of flat files.

Notice that indices typically concentrate on *what* is accessed, that is, the *number* of accessed index pages during search. In this paper, we demonstrate that it is at least as important to optimize *how* the data is accessed since the disk geometry supports data streams (sequential I/O) rather than random accesses [24, 25]. Over the last decade, improvements in disk transfer rates have rapidly outpaced seek times. For example, the internal data rate of IBM's hard disks improved from about 4 MB/sec to more than 60 MB/sec. At the same time, the positioning time only improved from about 18 msec to 9 msec [30]. This implies that reading and transferring large chunks of data from sequentially accessed disk sectors became about 15 times faster, while the speed for moving to a "random" position only improved by a factor of 2. The disk can reach its peak performance only if large chunks of consecutive sectors are accessed. Hence, it is often more efficient to read data in large chunks, even if the chunks contain irrelevant sectors.

A naive way to take advantage of the disk geometry in answering queries is by reading the whole data set using fast sequential I/O. While this approach, known as *sequential scan*, may make sense when much of the data must be accessed, it is not efficient for very selective range queries. We propose the Multiresolution File Scan (MFS) technique to address this issue. MFS is based on a selection of flat files ("views") that represent the data set at multiple resolutions. Its simple structure and low storage overhead (typically below 5% of the data size) allow it to scale with increasing dimensionality. Each of the files is accessed using a pseudo-optimal schedule which takes transfer and positioning time of the disk into account. Our experiments show that for processing range queries MFS achieves up to two orders of magnitude speedup over the sequential scan and is on average a factor of 2-12 times faster than the X-tree.

The simple structure of MFS makes it easy to model its performance. It also allows the incorporation of a priori knowledge about the query workload. Another benefit is the flexibility in choosing the sort order of the data set, which is particularly useful for temporal data. Often there is a strong correlation between the value of a temporal attribute and the time when the corresponding data point is inserted into the database [21]. For instance environmental measurements and sales transactions are recorded in a timely manner. Later analysis then is concerned with discovering trends, hence also involves the temporal attribute(s). MFS enables grouping of points with similar time values in neighboring disk blocks. Hence queries and updates observe a high locality of access. Similarly, removing chunks of old (and hence less relevant) data from disk to slower mass storage only affects a small portion of the data structure.

The outline of this paper is as follows. In Section 2 we motivate the design of MFS and then present its data structures and algorithms in Section 3. The selection of the files for MFS is discussed in Section 4, including a discussion on file selection for temporal data. Section 5 shows how MFS design principles can improve the query cost of standard indices. Detailed experimental results are presented in Section 6. Related work is discussed in Section 7. Section 8 concludes this article.

2   Problem Definition and Motivation

Scientific and warehouse data is often conceptualized as having multiple logical *dimensions* (e.g., `latitude`, `longitude`) and *measure attributes* (e.g., `temperature`, `cloud cover`). Complex phenomena like global warming can be analyzed by summarizing measure attribute values of points which are selected based on predicates on the dimensions. A typical and important query in scientific and business applications is the *multidimensional range aggregate*. It computes an aggregate over range selections on some (or all) of the dimension attributes. Suppose we have geographical data with schema (`latitude`, `longitude`, `temperature`). An example of a range aggregate on this data is, "Find the minimum and maximum temperatures in the region of Santa Barbara County."

In the following we will concentrate on the `count` operator. Other aggregate operators can be handled in a similar way. Note that applying the `null` "aggregate" operator is equivalent to *reporting* all selected data points without performing any aggregation. While MFS can efficiently answer such reporting queries, the focus of this paper is on its performance for range aggregates. For the sake of simplicity we will further on assume that the data set has d *dimension* attributes and a single *measure* attribute (for the `null` operator no measure attribute is necessary). Our technique can be easily generalized.

Hard Disk Geometry. Here we only provide a high-level view of relevant disk features; the interested reader might consult [24, 23] for more details. A disk read request is specified by its *start sector* and the *number of bytes* to be transferred. Unless the requested data is already in the disk cache, this request incurs two major access costs. First *positioning time*, more exactly seek time and rotational latency, is spent to move the disk head above the start sector. Once the head is correctly positioned the start sector and all following sectors are read and transferred until the specified amount of data is read. This cost is referred to as *transfer time* (for the sake of simplicity we omit a discussion of head and track switch times). Depending on the actual seek distance, modern hard disks are able to transfer 50 or more sectors during a time frame equivalent to the positioning time. Hence it is often faster to issue a single large read request which might contain irrelevant sectors, instead of using multiple small reads which each incur positioning time. Figure 1 shows a schematic illustration of this process.

To be able to find the best access strategy, the set of target sectors must be known in advance. The *pre-fetching* option of modern disk drives only partially addresses this problem by automatically reading several sectors *after* the requested target sectors and keeping them in the disk cache for future requests.

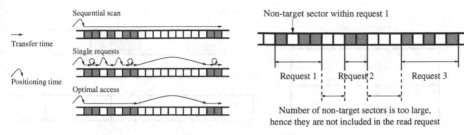

Fig. 1. Reading disk sectors (relevant sectors are shaded

Fig. 2. Pseudo-optimal access schedule for $R = 2$

However, pre-fetching is not effective if requests are not accessing sectors in order or if there is a large "gap" between groups of target sectors.

Dimensionality Curse for Indexing and Aggregation. There is an inherent dimensionality curse in indexing and computing range aggregates. The best known algorithms whose runtime is provably sub-linear in the size of the data set, e.g., [6], have polylogarithmic query cost and storage overhead. However, for dimensionality $d \geq 9$ a polylogarithmic cost is practically worse than a linear cost. Let n denote the number of data points. Then for $d = 9$ the polylogarithmic value $\log^d n$ is only less than n if $n > 10^{15}$. This means that polylogarithmic performance does not guarantee a practically better cost than a simple sequential scan of the whole data set. A storage explosion by a factor of $\log^d n$, i.e., a total storage cost of $O(n \log^d n)$ is clearly unacceptable for large data sets.

A similar dimensionality curse has also been observed for popular practical indexing techniques [3]. Other empirical studies for nearest neighbor queries have also shown that balanced tree structures can be outperformed by a sequential scan of the complete data set [5, 32].

Another possibility to speed up aggregate queries is to materialize pre-computed values and to use them to reduce on-the-fly computation and access costs, e.g., as has been proposed for the data cube operator [10]. Unfortunately for a d-dimensional data set any pre-computed value is contained in at most about one out of 2^d possible range queries (proof omitted due to space constraints). Hence the effectiveness of materializing pre-computed aggregates is very sensitive to changes in the query workload.

3 The MFS Technique

The discussion in the previous section shows that even the most sophisticated index cannot *guarantee* good query performance for multidimensional data sets with 8 or more dimensions. Together with the limited practical impact complex indices have had in the past, there is a strong motivation to try the opposite direction—supporting queries using the *simplest* possible data structure.

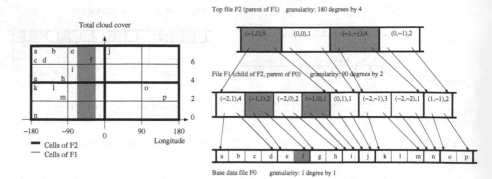

Fig. 3. Data set and query (shaded)

Fig. 4. Basic structure of MFS (tuples intersected by query are shaded)

3.1 Overview of MFS

MFS consists of a collection of flat files and pointers. Each file represents the data set at a different level of resolution. The file with the finest resolution contains the exact information. The next coarser file partitions the data space into regions and stores for each region the number of data points in the region.[1] The next coarser file in turn stores the count value over regions of regions, etc.

Figure 3 shows an example for a data set with the two dimensions `longitude` and `total cloud cover` [12]. The letters indicate weather stations that measure the cloud cover for certain locations (projected to their longitudes for presentation purposes). The user is interested in finding out how many stations measured a given cloud cover range for a given longitude range. Note that in practice there are far more dimensions.

The original data set is at the granularity of single degrees by 1 cloud intensity level. Figure 4 shows a possible MFS where the coarser files are at 90 degrees by 2 levels and 180 degrees by 4 levels resolution, respectively. The tuples in the files are shown as (`longitude`,`cloud cover`),measure and correspond to the cells indicated in Figure 3. For instance the first tuple in top file F_2 corresponds to the upper left quarter of the whole data space, i.e., to range $[-180, -90)$ by $[4, 8]$ in `longitude` and `total cloud cover` dimension, respectively. Note that coarser granularity enables a more efficient encoding of the dimension values since less bits are necessary to distinguish between the values.

The granularities establish a conceptual hierarchy among the files. Figure 4 illustrates this hierarchy by placing the file with the coarser resolution above the file with the next finer one. We will therefore refer to the file with the coarsest resolution as the *top* file. Also, a file and the next coarser file are referred to as child and parent. Let F_i be the file at level i, level 0 containing the base

---

[1] Recall that we describe MFS for the `count` operator, other operators are handled similarly.

Algorithm Query
Input: MFS-file; query
Output: progressively refined approximate results with absolute error bounds

1. Scan top file to find tuples intersected by query;
2. Compute approximate query result with error bounds and output it;
3. While (the file has a child file of finer resolution)
   Compute pseudo-optimal schedule to access all relevant sectors in child file;
   Access child file according to schedule to find tuples intersected by query;
   Output new approximate result when all child tuples of a parent are read;

Fig. 5. Querying MFS ("breadth-first")

data. Knowledge about the workload can be taken into account by selecting the appropriate file granularities.

An example for a query that selects the longitude range from -22 to -66 degrees and the whole cloud cover range is indicated in Figure 3. In Figure 4 the tuples that intersect the query at the different granularities are shaded. To allow efficient pruning during range query processing, each non-base tuple has two pointers **first** and **last**. They point to the first and last sector on disk that contains information that refines the aggregate information of a high-level aggregate tuple.

3.2 Processing Queries

The query procedure is similar to a breadth-first tree traversal. The main contribution of MFS are the emphasis on file organization and access order rather than on the number of accessed "index" pages alone. Another main aspect is the use of a simple and fast, yet very efficient disk access scheduler.

A query is processed by first sequentially scanning the (small) top file. Then the relevant tuples in its child file are read using a pseudo-optimal access schedule that takes the disk parameters into account. Then the next child file is pseudo-optimally accessed and so forth. This way the query proceeds breadth-first, file by file in increasing order of resolution. The **first** and **last** pointers provide the information for computing the pseudo-optimal schedule. The overall algorithm is shown in Figure 5. Approximate output is generated similar to [20].

The **pseudo-optimal disk access schedule** is computed using a very fast approximation algorithm which assumes a simple disk model. This algorithm is a simplified version of a scheduler proposed in [25], nevertheless the experimental results in Section 6 show that it is very effective. Let $R = \frac{t_{positioning}}{t_{transfer}}$ denote the ratio between the "average" positioning time and the transfer time per sector. Given a set of target sectors, the pseudo-optimal schedule is generated as follows. The first read request starts at the target sector with the lowest number and contains all target sectors with higher numbers such that the number of non-target sectors between any neighboring target sectors in the request is less than R. The second read request starts at the target sector with the lowest number which is not in the first request and contains all following sectors such that there are no gaps of R or more sectors between neighboring target sectors, and so on. The motivation for allowing gaps of less than R consecutive non-target sectors in a read request is that it is faster to read and transfer the non-target sectors instead of issuing smaller reads which each incur positioning time. Figure 2 shows an example for $R = 2$.

3.3   File Organization

In general the tuples in a file could be sorted in *any* order. However note that during query processing for an intersected tuple in file F_i all child tuples in the next file F_{i-1} are accessed to refine the result. In order to increase locality of access these "sibling" tuples should be stored in neighboring disk sectors. Hence each file (except for the top file) consists of chunks of sibling nodes which could be stored in any order on disk, e.g., Z- or Hilbert order.

The requirement of clustering tuples that share the same parent tuple establishes a *partial order* which is determined by the selected file granularities. Tuples in a file therefore can be stored in any order which is consistent with this partial order.

3.4   Bulk-Loading MFS

For now assume the granularities for the files of MFS are known. As discussed in Section 3.3 the tuples in a file can be stored in any order that is consistent with the partial order established by the file granularities. For bulk-loading a consistent *total order* "$\leq$" is selected which has the following property. For any two base tuples t_i and t_j it holds that if $t_i \leq t_j$ then for all ancestors a_i and a_j of t_i and t_j it also holds that $a_i \leq a_j$. Such an order trivially exists (just group descendent tuples together recursively).

The bulk-loading algorithm first sorts the input file according to the total order. Then all files of MFS are constructed simultaneously by scanning the sorted file only *once*. This is possible because of the ancestor order ensured by "$\leq$". The algorithm only needs little memory to hold the currently processed tuple with all its ancestors. The values of the pointers first and last are generated during the scan as well. In Figure 6 the algorithm is shown in pseudo code. The total bulk-loading cost is equivalent to the cost of one sort and one scan of the data set. Both operations take advantage of the disk geometry by transferring large chunks of sequentially stored data. Note that the bottom file of MFS is already complete after the sorting step, therefore during step 3 only tuples of the small coarse-resolution files are written to disk. The write cost thus is negligible compared to the cost of scanning the sorted base data file.

3.5   Updating MFS

In the following discussion the term *update* denotes any change to the base data set, including insertion and deletion of tuples. Processing updates on MFS

Algorithm Bulk-load
Input: File containing input data; total order $\leq$ of input tuples
Output: Files of MFS

1. Sort input file `baseFile` according to total order $\leq$;
2. Read first tuple from `baseFile` and generate list `Ancestors` of
   its ancestor tuples in the coarse-resolution files;
3. While (there are more tuples in `baseFile`)
       Read `tuple` from `baseFile`; `currentFile` = `baseFile`;
       Do
           If (`tuple` is a child of the corresponding parent tuple `parent` in `Ancestors`)
               Update aggregate value of `parent`; `continue` = false;
           Else
               Create new parent tuple `newParent` of `tuple`;
               Set `first` pointer of `newParent`;
               Replace `parent` by `newParent` in `Ancestors`;
               Set `last` pointer of `parent` and append it to the corresponding file;
               `tuple` = `newParent`; `currentFile` = parent of `currentFile`;
               `continue` = true;
       while (`continue`);
4. Append tuples from `Ancestors` to the respective files;

Fig. 6. Bulk-loading MFS (writes are buffered)

is simple and inexpensive. As discussed in Section 3.3 the files only have to maintain a partially ordered set. Hence whenever an update leads to overflowing sibling chunks or gaps within the file, selected sibling chunks can be moved to a different location in the file. A standard garbage collection algorithm can maintain the gaps within a file at a low cost [5]. Details are omitted due to space constraints. Updates to the dimensions, e.g., inserting a new product, can be processed in the same way.

MFS's regular structure also simplifies batch updates. First a small delta-MFS is built for the updates (using MFS' granularities). If MFS is maintained according to the total order "$\leq$", both MFS and delta-MFS can be merged in a single scan. Otherwise the sub-"trees" of common top-level tuples are merged using pseudo-optimal accesses.

Note that one can leave "gaps" of empty sectors within the files of MFS to enable fast single updates with very low re-organization cost. Thanks to the use of the pseudo-optimal scheduler these gaps have virtually no effect on the query cost (cf. Section 6).

4   Selecting the Granularities for the MFS Files

The main design challenge for MFS is to select the right number of files and their granularities. We show how MFS can take workload information into account and discuss how to construct it if no such knowledge exists.

4.1   Notation

Let the data set $\mathcal{D}$ have d dimensions and n tuples. Each dimension i has $l(i)$ hierarchy levels. The levels are numbered $0, 1, \ldots, l(i) - 1$; 0 being the level with the finest resolution and $l(i) - 1$ corresponding to the artificial ALL value that stands for the whole domain of attribute i (cf. [10]). For instance time could have the 3 levels month ($=0$), year ($=1$), and ALL ($=2$). If no natural attribute hierarchy exists, any hierarchical partitioning, e.g., according to the decimal system, can be used. We use N_i to denote the size of the domain of dimension i. We assume that MFS has l files $F_0, F_1, \ldots, F_l$ in decreasing order of their resolution. Let n_k denote the number of tuples in F_k.

The smallest unit of measurement in the data set is a tuple of the original data set. We can conceptually view such a base tuple as a cell of side length 1 that contains a value. Notice that our model can also be applied to continuous domains by assuming that a point has a size of 1 as well. Tuples of coarser resolution files correspond to hyper-rectangular regions of base level cells. We will use $x_i^{(k)}$ to denote the side length in dimension i for the region of a tuple in file F_k.

4.2   Estimating Query Performance for a Given MFS

Given a certain MFS configuration we evaluate its expected query performance by using a fast and lightweight analytical solution. As described in Section 3.2 a query first completely scans the top file F_l and then reads all child tuples of those tuples in F_l which intersect the query, and so forth. Hence the selectivity of the query in file F_{k-1}, $1 \le k \le l$, is affected by the granularity of its *parent* file F_k. Let query q select a multidimensional range that has size q_i in dimension i. The expected selectivity of q in file F_{k-1} ($0 < k \le l$) can then be computed as $\prod_{i=1}^d \frac{q_i + x_i^{(k)} - 1}{N_i}$ (proof omitted due to space constraints). Based on the selectivity, the average number of accessed bits can be estimated as $n_{k-1} s_{k-1} \prod_{i=1}^d \frac{q_i + x_i^{(k)} - 1}{N_i}$. Here s_{k-1} denotes the number of bits required to encode a tuple of file F_{k-1}, including the measure value and the two pointers to the child tuples.

The overall query cost for MFS is the sum of the cost for scanning F_l and the query cost for reading relevant tuples in each file below. With the above formula this cost is estimated as

$$n_l s_l \quad + \quad \sum_{k=l}^{1} n_{k-1} s_{k-1} \prod_{i=1}^d \frac{q_i + x_i^{(k)} - 1}{N_i}.$$

This formula provides an estimate for the average time it takes to read the data from disk. Note that we are actually not interested in the absolute value. All we need to find is the MFS configuration with the lowest cost *relative* to all other examined configurations.

To compute the result we have to determine all n_k, the number of tuples in file F_k. One can either materialize the files to obtain the exact values, or use efficient approximation techniques like the one proposed by Shukla et al. [26]. For *fractal* data sets (cf. [17]) there is an even faster purely analytical way of determining the n_k. Let D_0 be the Hausdorff fractal dimension. Then n_k can be accurately estimated as $n_k = n \left(\frac{\sqrt{d}}{d_k}\right)^{D_0}$ where d_k denotes the diameter of the region that corresponds to a tuple of file F_k.

4.3   Addressing the Complexity

So far we have a formula that computes the cost for a certain MFS configuration. However, the number of possible MFS configurations is exponential in the number of dimensions. We therefore use a greedy heuristic to explore this space.

The algorithm first selects the granularity for F_1 assuming MFS only consists of F_0 and F_1. It greedily reduces the resolution of F_1 in that dimension which leads to the greatest reduction in query cost. Once a local minimum is reached, the algorithm adds a new top level file F_2 with F_1's resolution and greedily decreases F_2's resolution, and so on until adding a new top level file does not result in any improvement.

This greedy process over-estimates the cost for non-top level files during the search. When a new candidate for the top file is examined, the cost of a scan is assumed for it. Later, when a file with coarser resolution is added above it, the actual cost contribution is much lower. To correct for this problem we use a second bottom-up process which greedily *increases* the resolution of the files. This process iterates over all files until no improvements are possible.

The overall process in the worst case examines a number of MFS configurations which is linear in $\sum_{i=1}^{d} l(i)$, the total number of hierarchy levels of the dimensions.

4.4   Taking the Query Workload into Account

The formula derived in Section 4.2 computes the average cost given a certain query specification. A workload containing several of these query specifications with their respective probabilities can be taken into account by computing the cost for each query type and weighting it with its probability.

Often there exists less specific information about the most likely queries, e.g., "the majority of the queries selects on product categories rather than single products". Such knowledge about queries aligning in some dimensions can be incorporated by correcting the query volume enlargement caused by the coarser parent file.

Knowledge about the *location* of a query can also be taken into account, e.g., for density-biased queries. One simply needs to partition the data space into smaller regions and then perform the cost analysis using the appropriate query workload and weight for each region. Similar to multidimensional histograms [18] there is a tradeoff between accuracy of estimation and storage and maintenance costs. Examining this tradeoff is beyond the scope of this paper.

4.5 Default Configuration

So far we have discussed how to select the file granularities when a query work-load is given. If there is no such knowledge, one could choose any typical mix of range queries. During the experimental evaluation we noted that choosing very selective queries to configure MFS resulted in best overall performance. Choosing such queries generated a larger number of coarse-resolution files, allowing efficient pruning during search. Queries that select large ranges typically access a large number of disk blocks in any MFS-configuration and are well supported by the pseudo-optimal disk scheduling anyway. In the experiments (cf. Section 6) MFS was simply configured assuming each query selects 10% of the domain in each dimension. The resulting data structure performed very well for queries with varying selectivity, indicating the robustness of MFS.

4.6 MFS for Temporal Data

MFS's flexible tuple order enables it to efficiently support management of real-time observations. Such observations could be measurements of environmental factors (e.g., temperature, amount of clouds), experimental data, or sales transactions in retail stores. All these applications have in common that the observations are time stamped in order to be able to discover *trends* like global warming or unusual sales patterns. As discussed in [21], there is a strong correlation between the time of the observation and the time when a tuple is inserted into the database. In other words, the data set consists of a *current* part which is heavily updated and a much larger *historical* part which is mainly queried and rarely updated.

MFS can explicitly support such applications by choosing a tuple order which groups tuples with similar time stamps into neighboring disk blocks. This is done by selecting a sufficiently fine resolution for the temporal attribute at the top file. For instance, if the temporal attribute is at granularity month in the top file, all tuples belonging to the same month are automatically clustered together. Newly arriving observations therefore only affect the small part of MFS which corresponds to the current month, guaranteeing a high locality. Parts that contain the previous months are rarely updated and hence can be packed without leaving empty space into disk blocks. Queries that search for trends and hence compare aggregate values for different time periods observe similar locality since the values are essentially clustered by time periods.

The same benefits apply to *data aging* processes in data warehouses which manage rapidly growing amounts of data by retiring old information from hard disk to slower mass storage.

5 Improving Indices

New indexing techniques proposed in the literature only rarely address the exact layout of the structure on disk and the scheduling of node accesses taking this layout into account. Our experiments indicate that these aspects should become integral parts of index structure proposals since they considerably affect the performance.

Figure 9 shows how the query cost of the X-tree index can be reduced by applying MFS' design principles. The first graph shows the query cost distribution for the standard depth-first (DFS) traversal of a dynamically generated X-tree. The second graph indicates the improvement obtained for exactly the same index structure, now using breadth-first (BFS) traversal and our pseudo-optimal scheduler for accessing the next tree levels. Finally the curve for the bulk-loaded X-tree was obtained by clustering the tree level-wise and making sure that the children of an inner node are stored in neighboring disk blocks. The experimental setup is explained in detail in Section 6.

6   Experimental Results

We evaluated the performance of MFS for several real and synthetic data sets. To allow a fair and detailed comparison, we report the I/O costs measured with the DiskSim 2.0 simulation environment [9]. This tool is publicly available at http://www.ece.cmu.edu/~ganger/disksim and was shown to model the real access times very accurately. In our experiments we used the settings for the most detailed and exact simulation.

We compare MFS to the *dynamic* X-tree [3] and a *bulk-loaded* X-tree [2]. The latter has a high page utilization (in the experiments it was 90% and higher) and there is generally no overlap of page extents (except, if page boundaries touch). Furthermore the bulk-loaded tree also is given the advantage of having all its non-leaf nodes in fast cache. The leaf nodes also are laid out such that they are traversed in order, i.e., the disk arm does not have to move forth and back while processing a query. For both indices the page size was set to 8 KB. MFS works at the level of single disk sectors since its approach is not based on index pages.

We initially also compared MFS to *augmented* index structures that maintain pre-computed aggregates in their inner nodes [20, 16]. However, due to the fairly high dimensionality of the data, the results were virtually identical to the non-augmented indices, sometimes even worse, and hence are not included. Similarly the performance comparison for indexing, i.e., for *reporting* all selected points rather than computing an aggregate, led to almost identical results and therefore is omitted as well.

6.1   Experimental Setup

The results presented here were obtained for the Seagate Cheetah 9LP hard disk (9.1 GB, 10045 rpm, 0.83–10.63 msec seek time, 4.65MB/sec max transfer rate). All parameters, including a detailed seek time lookup table for different seek distances, are part of the simulation tool and set to match the exact performance of the real disk. The results for other disks are similar.

Table 1. Quantiles of the query selectivity for the experiments

Figure	20%	40%	60%	80%	100%
7, 8	1.5e-9	3.5e-7	3.3e-5	4.1e-3	0.91
9, 10					

We compared the different approaches for a variety of data sets. Due to lack of space only the results obtained for two real data sets are discussed here. Experiments with other data, e.g., the TPC benchmark [31] and synthetic skewed data consisting of Gaussian clusters, were similar.

Weather is a real data set which contains 1,036,012 cloud reports for September 1986 [12]. We selected the 9 dimensions Day, Hour, Brightness, Latitude, Longitude, Station-ID, Present-weather, Change-code, and Solar-Altitude. For Day the natural hierarchy (ALL, year, month, day) was selected. For the other dimensions we recursively partition the domain by 10 (large domains), by 4 (medium domains) or by 2 (small domains). Data set *WeatherL* has the same attributes, but contains 4,134,221 cloud reports for four months of 1986 (September till December).

We measured the performance for several workloads of multidimensional aggregate range queries. The results discussed here were obtained for a workload that was constructed as follows. For a query for each dimension one of the four range predicates $min \leq x \leq A$ (prefix range), $A \leq x \leq B$ (general range), $x = A$ (point range), and $min \leq x \leq max$ (complete range) is chosen with probability 0.2, 0.4, 0.2, and 0.2, respectively. Values A and B are uniformly selected. This way of generating queries models realistic selections and ensures a wide variety of selectivities. Table 1 shows the 20 percent quantiles for the selectivity distribution of the queries that were used to produce the figures. For instance, the value for the 60% quantile and Figure 7 indicates that 60% of the queries in this experiment had a selectivity of 3.3e-5 or below, and that the other 40% had a higher selectivity.

Note that the queries as generated above are the most expensive for MFS because they do not take hierarchies into account. In practice users often query according to hierarchies. For example it is more likely that a query selects the 31-day period from May 1 till May 31 (i.e., the month May), than from say

Table 2. Average query costs (in seconds)

Data set	MFS	Bulk X-tree	Dyn. X-tree	Scan
Weather (fast controller)	0.18	0.33	1.83	0.91
Weather	0.40	0.79	2.80	3.91
WeatherL	1.36	2.82	9.07	15.52

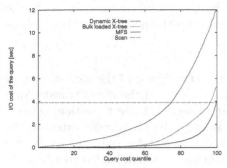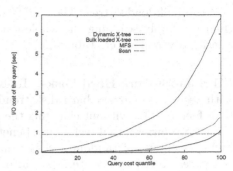

Fig. 7. Query cost distribution for *Weather* (slow controller)

Fig. 8. Query cost distribution for *Weather* (fast controller)

May 5 till June 5. MFS benefits from such hierarchy-aligned queries because its "grid" structure is based on hierarchies, therefore the query intersects less tuples (cf. cost formula in Section 4.2).

MFS Properties. MFS did *not* take the real query workload into account during construction. The file selection algorithm simply assumed that each query selects a range of 10% of the domain in each dimension (cf. Section 4.5). The resulting MFS configurations had between 4 and 5 files. The overall storage overhead was below 2.4% compared to the base data set.

6.2 Performance of MFS

We report results obtained for 10,000 range queries. Notice that for the indices the disk's pre-fetching feature was enabled. Without it the average query cost increased from 2.8 to 5.1 sec (dynamic X-tree) and from 0.79 to 2.0 sec (bulk-loaded X-tree).

The results are presented in Figures 7 and 8 for a slow and fast disk controller, respectively. The figures show the query cost distribution over *all* queries. The numbers on the x-axis are the cost quantiles, the y-axis shows the corresponding I/O cost in seconds. We report all quantiles, hence the graphs show the *exact* cost distribution.

The graphs of Figure 7 were obtained for the original configuration of the hard disk. MFS clearly outperforms the competitors, virtually never exceeding the cost of a sequential scan. Note that the 50% fastest queries on the bulk-loaded index are faster than the fastest 50% of the queries on MFS. However, the absolute I/O-cost difference there is between 10 and 30 msec and mostly caused by not counting the inner node accesses for the index. MFS on the other hand shows clear performance advantages for the expensive queries that take 500 msec and longer and cause noticeable delays for the user. For instance, 78.4% of the queries on MFS take less than 500 msec, compared to only 65.8% on the bulk-loaded index. The dynamic X-tree performs much worse than both MFS and the bulk-loaded tree. About 25% of the queries take longer on the X-tree than by simply scanning the whole data set even though the selectivity of the queries is very low (cf. Table 1).

MFS and Future Hard Disks. To examine the fitness of the data structures with respect to current hard disk trends, we increased the disk's transfer rate by a factor of 4.3 without changing the parameters that affect positioning time. Figure 8 shows that all techniques benefit from the higher transfer rate, but the high percentage of random accesses limits the benefit for the dynamic X-tree compared to the competitors (see also Table 2). The bulk-loaded tree benefits similarly to MFS. The reason is that most of its disk positionings are actually masked thanks to the pre-fetching. Recall that the pre-fetching is only effective because we made sure that the leaf pages are laid out and accessed on disk in the right order, i.e., following the principles established for MFS.

Scalability with Data Size. The cost distribution for the larger *WeatherL* is almost identical to *Weather*, hence the graphs are omitted. The average query costs are reported in Table 2. It turned out that the worst case cost for the dynamic X-tree increased from 12 to 63 sec, i.e., by a factor of 5. For the other techniques the worst case cost increased almost exactly by a factor of 4, the size ratio of the two weather sets.

Support for Single Updates. We examined the effect of leaving empty space in the MFS files to enable incorporation of single updates. We constructed MFS by leaving k empty sectors in between chunks of j non-empty sectors. An update would sequentially read the appropriate chunk of j non-empty sectors and write the updated chunk back. The variables j and k determine the query-update cost tradeoff. Larger j and smaller k increase the update cost, but avoid query overhead caused by reading empty sectors (or seeking over a chunk of empty sectors). Figure 10 shows the query cost distribution for the same set of queries we used in Section 6.2. Variables j and k were such that the storage utilization of MFS was only 75%. We examined the combinations (j=2000,k=500), (j=400,k=100), and (j=80,k=20). As expected, the larger the absolute values, the lower the effect of leaving empty space. Note that for j=2000 and j=400 the cost distribution is almost identical to MFS without empty sectors. The experiment shows that moderate amounts of single updates (up to 25% of the data size) can be supported with virtually no effect on the queries.

7   Related Work

The DABS-tree [5] and the VA-file [32] (including its variants) explicitly address high-dimensional data spaces, but focus on nearest neighbor queries. The underlying idea is to have simple two-level schemes where the first level is sequentially scanned and then the relevant data in the second level is accessed. MFS extends

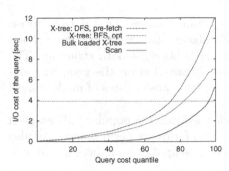
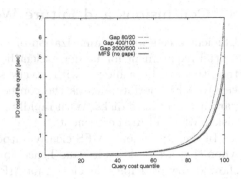

Fig. 9.   Index   performance   for
Weather (slow controller)

Fig. 10.   Query cost distribution for
MFS with empty space for single updates

these approaches and addresses range queries. It is more general by allowing
multiple "levels" depending on the query workload.

Roussopoulos et al. [14, 22] use packed R-trees to store tuples of multiple
views of the base data in a single data structure. The techniques were shown to
be effective for low to medium dimensionality. With increasing dimensionality
the R-tree performance is expected to degrade as shown in this paper for the
X-tree. Note that the packing requires the tuples to be sorted in row-major order
(alphabetically) which was shown to be inferior to lattice path clustering in [13].
MFS supports lattice path clustering.

Seeger et al. [25, 24] propose algorithms for determining the fastest way of
retrieving a set of disk pages when this set is known a priori. Our technique to
select the pseudo-optimal schedule is similar to the approach of [25] for limited
gaps and unlimited buffer.

Previous work regarding the prediction of range query performance focused
on B-trees and the R-tree family [28, 29, 19]. Our cost model arrives at similar
results regarding the selectivity estimation of a query. However, it is specific to
our technique and can take advantage of the regular and simple structure of
MFS. For data structures like B-trees and R-trees the shape of the bounding
box of a tree node can only be approximated which leads to high errors with
increasing dimensionality [15].

Recent work by Tao and Papadias [27] improves index performance by adap-
tively changing the number of pages assigned to index nodes. Their motivation,
like for MFS, is to reduce the number of disk positioning operations (seeks). Since
the technique is based on detailed cost models, its effectiveness will rapidly decrease with less accurate cost prediction in medium to high dimensions. MFS
takes a more radical approach away from improving indices and using complex
(and hence fragile) cost models.

8   Conclusions and Future Work

Efficient access and summarization of massive multidimensional data is an essential requirement for modern scientific databases. The MFS technique shows that this can be achieved with a very simple lightweight data structure. The key to MFS' performance is the consequent orientation on the geometry and parameters of hard disks. With rapidly increasing transfer rates of modern hard disks, MFS will further benefit.

In the experiments MFS clearly outperformed existing popular indices, even when they are bulk-loaded and hence optimized for query performance. We also showed how principles developed for MFS can be applied to indices in order to increase their performance.

MFS' simple and flexible structure enables it to take query workloads into account. By choosing an appropriate tuple order, timestamped data (e.g., experimental measurements, sales transactions) and data aging can be managed with guaranteed locality of access. For the same reason provably efficient clustering strategies like snaked lattice paths [13] are supported as well. Thanks to its use of simple flat files, MFS can also be combined with popular secondary indices like B+-trees. Examining the actual tradeoffs involved in choosing certain tuple orders and secondary indices is part of our future work.

References

[1] N. Beckmann, H.-P. Kriegel, R. Schneider, and B. Seeger. The R*-tree: An efficient and robust access method for points and rectangles. In *Proc. ACM SIGMOD Int. Conf. on Management of Data*, pages 322–331, 1990. 215

[2] S. Berchtold, C. Böhm, and H.-P. Kriegel. Improving the query performance of high-dimensional index structures by bulk-load operations. In *Proc. Int. Conf. on Extending Database Technology (EDBT)*, pages 216–230, 1998. 225

[3] S. Berchtold, D. A. Keim, and H.-P. Kriegel. The X-tree: An index structure for high-dimensional data. In *Proc. Int. Conf. on Very Large Databases (VLDB)*, pages 28–39, 1996. 215, 217, 225

[4] P. A. Bernstein et al. The Asilomar report on database research. *SIGMOD Record*, 27(4):74–80, 1998. 214

[5] C. Böhm and H.-P. Kriegel. Dynamically optimizing high-dimensional index structures. In *Proc. Int. Conf. on Extending Database Technology (EDBT)*, pages 36–50, 2000. 217, 221, 228

[6] B. Chazelle. A functional approach to data structures and its use in multidimensional searching. *SIAM Journal on Computing*, 17(3):427–462, 1988. 217

[7] Winter Corporation. Database scalability program. http://www.wintercorp.com, 2001. 214

[8] V. Gaede and O. Günther. Multidimensional access methods. *ACM Computing Surveys*, 30(2):170–231, 1998. 214

[9] G. R. Ganger, B. L. Worthington, and Y. N. Patt. *The DiskSim Simulation Environment Version 2.0 Reference Manual*, 1999. 225

[10] J. Gray, S. Chaudhuri, A. Bosworth, A. Layman, D. Reichart, M. Venkatrao, F. Pellow, and H. Pirahesh. Data cube: A relational aggregation operator generalizing group-by, cross-tab, and sub-totals. *Data Mining and Knowledge Discovery*, pages 29–53, 1997. 217, 222

[11] A. Guttman. R-trees: A dynamic index structure for spatial searching. In *Proc. ACM SIGMOD Int. Conf. on Management of Data*, pages 47–57, 1984. 214

[12] C. J. Hahn, S. G. Warren, and J. London. Edited synoptic cloud reports from ships and land stations over the globe, 1982-1991. http://cdiac.esd.ornl.gov/ftp/ndp026b, 1996. 214, 218, 226

[13] H. V. Jagadish, L. V. S. Lakshmanan, and D. Srivastava. Snakes and sandwiches: Optimal clustering strategies for a data warehouse. In *Proc. ACM SIGMOD Int. Conf. on Management of Data*, pages 37–48, 1999. 229, 230

[14] Y. Kotidis and N. Roussopoulos. An alternative storage organization for RO-LAP aggregate views based on cubetrees. In *Proc. ACM SIGMOD Int. Conf. on Management of Data*, pages 249–258, 1998. 229

[15] C. A. Lang and A. K. Singh. Modeling high-dimensional index structures using sampling. In *Proc. ACM SIGMOD Int. Conf. on Management of Data*, pages 389–400, 2001. 229

[16] I. Lazaridis and S. Mehrotra. Progressive approximate aggregate queries with a multi-resolution tree structure. In *Proc. ACM SIGMOD Int. Conf. on Management of Data*, pages 401–412, 2001. 225

[17] B.-U. Pagel, F. Korn, and C. Faloutsos. Deflating the dimensionality curse using multiple fractal dimensions. In *Proc. Int. Conf. on Data Engineering (ICDE)*, pages 589–598, 2000. 223

[18] V. Poosala and Y. E. Ioannidis. Selectivity estimation without the attribute value independence assumption. In *Proc. Int. Conf. on Very Large Databases (VLDB)*, pages 486–495, 1997. 223

[19] G. Proietti and C. Faloutsos. I/O complexity for range queries on region data stored using an R-tree. In *Proc. Int. Conf. on Data Engineering (ICDE)*, pages 628–635, 1999. 229

[20] M. Riedewald, D. Agrawal, and A. El Abbadi. pCube: Update-efficient online aggregation with progressive feedback and error bounds. In *Proc. Int. Conf. on Scientific and Statistical Database Management (SSDBM)*, pages 95–108, 2000. 219, 225

[21] M. Riedewald, D. Agrawal, and A. El Abbadi. Efficient integration and aggregation of historical information. In *Proc. ACM SIGMOD Int. Conf. on Management of Data*, pages 13–24, 2002. 215, 224

[22] N. Roussopoulos, Y. Kotidis, and M. Roussopoulos. Cubetree: Organization of and bulk updates on the data cube. In *Proc. ACM SIGMOD Int. Conf. on Management of Data*, pages 89–99, 1997. 229

[23] C. Ruemmler and J. Wilkes. An introduction to disk drive modeling. *IEEE Computer*, 27(3):17–28, 1994. 216

[24] B. Seeger. An analysis of schedules for performing multi-page requests. *Information Systems*, 21(5):387–407, 1996. 215, 216, 229

[25] B. Seeger, P.-A. Larson, and R. McFayden. Reading a set of disk pages. In *Proc. Int. Conf. on Very Large Databases (VLDB)*, pages 592–603, 1993. 215, 219, 229

[26] A. Shukla, P. Deshpande, J. F. Naughton, and K. Ramasamy. Storage estimation for multidimensional aggregates in the presence of hierarchies. In *Proc. Int. Conf. on Very Large Databases (VLDB)*, pages 522–531, 1996. 223

[27] Y. Tao and D. Papadias. Adaptive index structures. In *Proc. Int. Conf. on Very Large Databases (VLDB)*, pages 418–429, 2002. 229

[28] Y. Tao, D. Papadias, and J. Zhang. Cost models for overlapping and multi-version structures. In *Proc. Int. Conf. on Data Engineering (ICDE)*, pages 191–200, 2002. 229

[29] Y. Theodoridis and T. K. Sellis. A model for the prediction of R-tree performance. In *Proc. Symp. on Principles of Database Systems (PODS)*, pages 161–171, 1996. 229

[30] D. A. Thompson and J. S. Best. The future of magnetic data storage technology. *IBM Journal of Research and Development*, 44(3):311–322, 2000. 215

[31] Transaction Processing Performance Council. TPC benchmarks. http://www.tpc.org. 226

[32] R. Weber, H.-J. Schek, and S. Blott. A quantitative analysis and performance study for similarity-search methods in high-dimensional spaces. In *Proc. Int. Conf. on Very Large Databases (VLDB)*, pages 194–205, 1998. 217, 228

Optimization of Spatial Joins on Mobile Devices

Nikos Mamoulis[1], Panos Kalnis[2], Spiridon Bakiras[3], and Xiaochen Li[2]

[1] Department of Computer Science and Information Systems
University of Hong Kong
Pokfulam Road, Hong Kong
nikos@csis.hku.hk
[2] Department of Computer Science
National University of Singapore
{kalnis,g0202290}@nus.edu.sg
[3] Department of Electrical and Electronic Engineering
University of Hong Kong
Pokfulam Road, Hong Kong
sbakiras@eee.hku.hk

Abstract. Mobile devices like PDAs are capable of retrieving information from various types of services. In many cases, the user requests cannot directly be processed by the service providers, if their hosts have limited query capabilities or the query combines data from various sources, which do not collaborate with each other. In this paper, we present a framework for optimizing spatial join queries that belong to this class. We presume that the connection and queries are ad-hoc, there is no mediator available and the services are non-collaborative. We also assume that the services are not willing to share their statistics or indexes with the client. We retrieve statistics dynamically in order to generate a low-cost execution plan, while considering the storage and computational power limitations of the PDA. Since acquiring the statistics causes overhead, we describe an adaptive algorithm that optimizes the overall process of statistics retrieval and query execution. We demonstrate the applicability of our methods with a prototype implementation on a PDA with wireless network access.

1 Introduction

The rapid development of mobile gadgets with computational, storage, and networking capabilities, has made possible for the user to connect to various distributed services and process information from them in an ad-hoc manner. In the common distributed data/service model there exist several services and global information is distributed to them based on theme and/or location. Spatial information is not an exception; spatial data are distributed and managed by various services depending on the location and the service type. For example, there could be a specialized service for querying census data from Long Beach county and a separate service for querying tourist data from the same area. This decentralized model is cheap, efficient, easily maintainable, and avoids integration constraints (e.g., legacy constraints).

T. Hadzilacos et al. (Eds.): SSTD 2003, LNCS 2750, pp. 233–251, 2003.

In many practical cases, complex queries need to combine information from multiple sources. As an example, consider the spatial join between two datasets which are hosted on two different servers. Server A hosts a database with information about hotels and other tourist services. Server B is a GIS server, providing information about the physical layers in a region (e.g., rivers, urban areas, forests, etc.). The user is a visitor and a nature lover who wants to find hotels which are close to forests. The query can be formed as a *distance join*: "find all hotels which are at most 2 km from a forest".

Since information about hotels and forests are provided by different services, the query cannot be processed by either of them. Typically, queries to multiple, heterogeneous sources are handled by mediators which communicate with the sources and integrate information from them via wrappers. Mediators can use statistics from the sources to optimize the queries. However, there are several reasons why this architecture may not be appropriate or feasible. First, the services may not be collaborative; they may not be willing to share their data with other services or mediators, allowing only simple users to connect to them. Second, the user requests may be ad-hoc and not supported by existing mediators. Third, the user may not be interested in using the service by the mediator, if she has to pay for this; retrieving the information directly from the sources may be less expensive.

Thus, we assume that the query should be evaluated at the client's side, on the mobile device. In this communication model, the user is typically charged by the bulk of transferred data (e.g., transferred bytes/packets), rather than by the time she stays connected to the service. We are therefore interested in minimizing the downloaded information from the services, instead of the processing cost at the servers. Another (realistic) assumption is that the services are not willing to share their statistics or indexes with the user. Therefore, information can only be downloaded by means of queries (which are supported by the service), like window queries, for instance.

In this paper, we describe MobiHook[1], a framework for optimizing complex distributed spatial operations on mobile devices such as wireless PDAs. As a special case, we consider the evaluation of spatial joins [3, 7], where the joined information is retrieved by two different services. We provide an evaluation algorithm that aims to minimize the transferred information instead of the processing time of the queries. Indeed, the user is typically willing to sacrifice a few seconds in order to minimize the query cost in dollars.

For efficient processing, we propose a query evaluation paradigm, which *adapts* to the data characteristics. First, the device downloads some statistical information, which is dynamically computed at the servers by submitting aggregate queries to them. With the help of these summaries, the mobile client is then able to minimize the data that have to be downloaded in order to process the query. For the distance join example we first retrieve some statistics which describe the distribution of data in each dataset. Based on these, we can avoid downloading information which cannot possibly participate in the result. For

---

[1] MobiHook is an acronym for MOBIle, ad-HOc hoOKing on distributed services.

instance, by applying a cheap (in terms of transferred data) query to the forests server, we can conclude that in some (e.g., urban or desert) areas there are no forests. This information will later help us avoid downloading any hotels in these areas.

Every partition of the data space is examined independently and the query optimizer decides the physical operator that will be applied. Therefore, depending on the retrieved statistics, different fragments can be processed by different physical operators (*adaptivity*). The optimizer may also choose to *recursively* obtain more statistics for some partitions, if the overhead is justified, based on a detailed cost model. Retrieving and processing summaries prior to actual data has the additional advantage of facilitating interactive query processing. By processing summary information we are able to provide estimates about the query result and the cost of transferring the actual data in order to process it. The user may then choose to restrict the query to specific regions, or tighten the constraints in order to retrieve more useful results.

The rest of the paper is organized as follows. Section 2 defines the problem formally, describes types of spatial queries that fit in the framework, and discusses related work. Section 3 presents the spatial join algorithm and the cost model which is used by the query optimizer. The proposed techniques are experimentally evaluated in Section 4. Finally, Section 5 concludes the paper with a discussion about future work.

2   Problem Definition

Let q be a spatial query issued at a mobile device (e.g., PDA), which combines information from two spatial relations R and S, located at different servers. Let b_R and b_S be the cost per transferred unit (e.g., byte, packet) from the server of R and S, respectively. We want to minimize the cost of the query with respect to b_R and b_S. Here, we will focus on queries which involve two spatial datasets, although in a more general version the number of relations could be larger.

The most general query type that conforms to these specifications is the *spatial join*, which combines information from two datasets according to a spatial predicate. Formally, given two spatial datasets R and S and a spatial predicate θ, the spatial join $R \bowtie_\theta S$ retrieves the pairs of objects $\langle o_R, o_S \rangle$, $o_R \in R$, and $o_S \in S$, such that $o_R \, \theta \, o_S$. The most common join predicate for objects with spatial extent is *intersects* [3].

Another popular spatial join operator is the *distance* join [9, 7, 16]. In this case the object pairs $\langle o_R, o_S \rangle$ that qualify the query should be within distance ε. The Euclidean distance is typically used as a metric. Variations of this query are the *closest pairs query* [4], which retrieves the k object pairs with the minimum distance, and the *all nearest neighbor* query [19], which retrieves for each object in R its nearest neighbor in S.

In this paper we deal with the efficient processing of intersection and distance joins under the transfer cost model described above. Previous work (e.g., [3, 7]) has mainly focused on processing the join using hierarchical indexes (e.g., R–trees [6]). Since access methods cannot be used to accelerate processing in our setting, we consider hash-based techniques [14].

Although the distance join is intuitively a useful operator for a mobile user, its result could potentially be too large. Large results are usually less interpretable/useful to the user and they are potentially more expensive to derive. She might therefore be interested in processing queries of high selectivity with potentially more useful results. A spatial join query of this type is the *iceberg distance semi-join* operator. This query differs from the distance join in that it asks only for objects from R (i.e., semi-join), with an additional constraint: the qualifying objects should 'join' with at least m objects from S. As a representative example, consider the query "find the hotels which are close to *at least* 10 restaurants". In pseudo-SQL the query could be expressed as follows:

```
SELECT H.id
FROM Hotels H, Restaurants R
WHERE dist(H.location,R.location)≤ε
GROUP BY H.id
HAVING COUNT(*)≥m ;
```

2.1   Related Work

There are several spatial join algorithms that apply to centralized spatial databases. Most of them focus on the *filter* step of the spatial *intersection* join. Their aim is to find all pairs of object MBRs (i.e., *minimum bounding rectangles*) that intersect. The qualifying candidate object pairs are then tested on their exact geometry at the final *refinement* step. Although these methods were originally proposed for intersection joins, they can be easily adapted to process distance joins, by extending the objects from both relations by $\varepsilon/2$ on each axis [9, 12].

The most influential spatial join algorithm [3] presumes that the datasets are indexed by hierarchical access methods (i.e., R–trees). Starting from the roots, the trees are synchronously traversed, following entry pairs that intersect. When the leaves are reached, intersecting object MBRs are output. This algorithm is not directly related to our problem, since server indexes cannot be utilized, or built on the remote client. Another class of spatial join algorithms applies on cases where only one dataset is indexed [13]. The existing index is used to guide hashing of the non-indexed dataset. Again, such methods cannot be used for our settings.

On the other hand, spatial join algorithms that apply on non-indexed data could be utilized by the mobile client to join information from the servers. The Partition Based Spatial Merge (PBSM) join [14] uses a regular grid to hash both datasets R and S into a number of P partitions $R_1, R_2, \ldots, R_P$ and $S_1, S_2, \ldots, S_P$, respectively. Objects that fall into more than one cells are replicated to multiple buckets. The second phase of the algorithm loads pairs

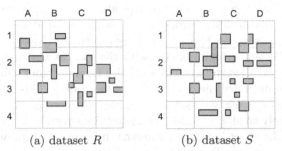

(a) dataset R	(b) dataset S

Fig. 1. Two datasets to be joined

of buckets R_x with S_x that correspond to the same cell(s) and joins them in memory. To avoid ending up with partitions with significant differences in size, in case the datasets are skewed, a tiling scheme paired with a hash function is used to assign multiple cells to the same hash bucket.

Figure 1 illustrates an example of two hashed datasets. Notice that MBRs that span grid lines are hashed to multiple cells (i.e., the cells that they intersect). The side-effect is that the size of hashed information is larger than the original datasets. Moreover, a duplicate removal technique is required in order to avoid reporting the same pair of objects twice, if they happen to be hashed to more than one common buckets. For instance, the objects than span the border of cells B2 and B3 could be reported twice, if no duplicate removal is applied. Techniques that avoid redundancy in spatial joins are discussed in [5, 12]. Finally, PBSM is easily parallelizable; a non-blocking, parallel version of this algorithm is presented in [12]. The data declustering nature of PBSM makes it attractive for use for the problem studied in this paper. Details are discussed in Section 3. Alternative methods for joining non-indexed datasets were proposed in [11, 2].

The problem of evaluating nearest neighbor queries on remote spatial databases is studied in [10]. The server is assumed to evaluate only window queries, thus the client has to estimate the minimum window that contains the query result. The authors propose a methodology that estimates this window progressively or approximates it using statistics from the data. However, they assume that the statistics are available at the client's side. In our work, we deal with the more complex problem of spatial joins from different sources, and we do not presume any statistical information at the mobile client. Instead, we generate statistics by sending aggregate queries, as explained in Section 3.

Distributed processing of spatial joins has been studied in [17]. Datasets are indexed by R-trees, and the intermediate levels of the indices are transferred from the one site to the other, prior to transferring the actual data. Thus, the join is processed by applying semi-join operations on the intermediate tree level MBRs in order to prune objects, minimizing the total cost. Our work is different, since we assume that the sites do not collaborate with each other, and they do not publish their index structures.

Many of the issues we are dealing here also exist in distributed data management with mediators. Mediators provide an integrated schema for multiple heterogeneous data sources. Queries are posed to the mediator, which constructs the execution plan and communicates with the sources via custom-made wrappers. The HERMES [1] system tracks statistics from previous calls to the sources and uses them to optimize the execution of a new query. This method is not applicable in our case, since we assume that the connections are ad-hoc and the queries are unlikely to share modules with previous retrievals from the services. DISCO [18], on the other hand, retrieves cost information from wrappers during the initialization process. This information is in the form of logical rules which encode classical cost model equations. Garlic [15] also obtains cost information from the wrappers during the registration phase. In contrast to DISCO, Garlic poses simple aggregate queries to the sources in order to retrieve the statistics. Our statistics retrieval method is closer to Garlic. Nevertheless, both DISCO and Garlic acquire cost information during initialization and use it to optimize all subsequent queries, while we optimize the entire process of statistics retrieval and query execution for a single query. The Tuckila [8] system also combines optimization with query execution. It first creates a temporary execution plan and executes only parts of it. Then, it uses the statistics of the intermediate results to compute better cost estimations, and refines the rest of the plan. Our approach is different, since we optimize the execution of the current (and only) operator, while Tuckila uses statistics from the current results to optimize the subsequent operators.

3 Spatial Joins on a Mobile Device

As discussed already, we cannot use potential indexes on the servers to evaluate spatial join queries. On the other hand, it is a realistic assumption that the hosts can evaluate simple queries, like spatial selections. In addition, we assume that they can provide results to simple *aggregate* queries, like for example "find the number of hotels that are included in a spatial window". Notice that this is not a strong assumption, since the results of a window query may be too many to be accommodated in the limited resources of the PDA. Therefore, it is typical for the mobile client to first wait for an acknowledgment about the *size* of the query result, before retrieving it.

Since the price to pay here is the communication cost, it is crucial to minimize the information transferred between the PDA and the servers during the join; the time length of connections between the PDA and the servers is free in typical services (e.g., mobile phones), which charge users based on the traffic. There are two types of information interchanged between the client and the server application: (i) the queries sent to the server and (ii) the results sent back by the server. The main issue is to minimize this information for a given problem.

The simplest way to perform the spatial join is to download both datasets to the client and perform the join there. We consider this as an infeasible solution in general, since mobile devices are usually lightweight, with limited memory and processing capabilities. First, the relations may not fit in the device which makes join processing infeasible. Second, the processing cost and the energy consumption on the device could be high. Therefore we have to consider alternative techniques.

3.1 A Divisive Approach

A divide-and-conquer solution is to perform the join in one spatial region at a time. Thus, the dataspace is divided into rectangular areas (using, e.g. a regular grid), a window query is sent for each cell to both sites, and the results are joined on the device using a main memory join algorithm (e.g., plane sweep [2]). Like PBSM [14], a hash-function can be used to bring multiple tiles at a time and break the result size more evenly. However, this would require multiple queries to the servers for each partition. The duplicate avoidance techniques of [5, 12] can also be employed here to avoid reporting a pair more than once.

As an example of an intersection join, consider the datasets R and S of Figure 1 and the imaginary grid superimposed over them. The join algorithm applies a window query for each cell to the two servers and joins the results. For example, the hotels that intersect A1 are downloaded from R, the forests that intersect A1 are downloaded from S, and these two window query results are joined on the PDA. In the case of a distance join, the cells are extended by $\varepsilon/2$ at each side before they are sent as window queries. A problem with this method is that the retrieved data from each window query may not fit in memory. In order to tackle this, we can send a memory limit constraint to the server together with the window query and receive either the data, or a message alarming the potential memory overflow. In the second case, the cell can be recursively partitioned to a set of smaller window queries, similar to the recursion performed by PBSM [14].

3.2 Using Summaries to Reduce the Transfer Cost

The partition-based technique is sufficiently good for joins in centralized systems, however, it requires that all data from both relations are read. When the distributions in the joined datasets vary significantly, there may be large empty regions in one which are densely populated in the other. In such cases, the simple partitioning technique potentially downloads data that do not participate in the join result. We would like to achieve a sublinear transfer cost for our method, by avoiding downloading such information. For example, if some hotels are located in urban or coastal regions, we may avoid downloading them from the server, if we know that there are no forests close to this region with which the hotels could join. Thus, it would be wise to retrieve a distribution of the objects in both relations before we perform the join. In the example of Figure 1, if we know that cells C1 and D1 are empty in R, we can avoid downloading their contents from S.

The intuition behind our join algorithm is to apply some cheap queries first, which will provide information about the distribution of objects in both datasets. For this, we pose aggregate queries on the regions before retrieving the results from them. Since the cost on the server side is not a concern[2], we first apply a COUNT query for the current cell on each server, before we download the information from it. The code in pseudo-SQL for a specific window w (e.g., a cell) is as follows (assuming an *intersection* join):

```
Send to server H:
SELECT COUNT(*) as c1
FROM Hotels H
WHERE H.area INTERSECTS w
If (c1>0) then
Send to server F:
SELECT COUNT(*) as c2
FROM Forests F
WHERE F.area INTERSECTS w
If (c2>0) then
SELECT * FROM
(SELECT * FROM Hotels H AS HW WHERE H.area INTERSECTS w),
(SELECT * FROM Forests F AS FW WHERE F.area INTERSECTS w)
WHERE HW.area INTERSECTS FW.area
```

Naturally, this implementation avoids loading data in areas where some of the relations are empty. For example, if there is a window w where the number of forests is 0, we need not download hotels that fall inside this window. The problem that remains now is to set the grid granularity so that (i) the downloaded data from both relations fit into the PDA, so that the join can be processed efficiently, (ii) the empty area detected is maximized, (iii) the number of queries (messages) sent to the servers is small, and (iv) data replication is avoided as much as possible.

Task (i) is hard, if we have no idea about the distribution of the data. Luckily, the first (aggregate) queries can help us refine the grid. For instance, if the sites report that the number of hotels and forests in a cell are so many that they will not fit in memory when downloaded, the cell is recursively partitioned. Task (ii) is in conflict with (iii) and (iv). The more the grid is refined, the more dead space is detected. On the other hand, if the grid becomes too fine, many queries will have to be transmitted (one for each cell) and the number of replicated objects will be large. Therefore, tuning the grid without apriori knowledge about the data distribution is a hard problem.

To avoid this problem, we refine the grid recursively, as follows. The granularity of the first grid is set to 2×2. If a quadrant is very sparse, we may choose not to refine it, but download the data from both servers and join them on the PDA. If it is dense, we choose to refine it because (a) the data there may not fit in our memory, and (b) even when they fit, the join would be expensive. In the example of Figure 1, we may choose to refine quadrant AB12, since the

---

[2] In fact, this query may not be expensive, if the server maintains precomputed aggregates or employs aggregate spatial indexes.

aggregate query indicates that this region is dense (for both R and S in this case), and avoid refining quadrant AB34, since this is sparse in both relations.

3.3   Handling Bucket Skew

In some cells, the density of the two datasets may be very different. In this case, there is a high chance of finding dead space in one of the quadrants in the sparse relation, where the other relation is dense. Thus, if we recursively divide the space there, we may avoid loading unnecessary information from the dense dataset. In the example of Figure 1, quadrant CD12 is sparse for R and dense for S; if we refined it, we would be able to prune cells C1 and D1.

On the other hand, observe that refining such partitions may have a counter-effect in the overall cost. By applying additional queries to very sparse regions we increase the traffic cost by sending extra window queries with only a few results. For example, if we find some cells where there is a large number of hotels but only a few forests, it might be expensive to draw further statistics from the hotels database, and at the same time we might not want to download all hotels. For this case, it might be more beneficial to stop drawing statistics for this area and *perform the join as a series of selection queries*, one for each forest. Recall that a potential (nested-loops) technique for $R \bowtie S$ is to apply a selection to S for each $r \in R$. This method can be fast if $|R| << |S|$. Thus, the join processing for quadrant CD12 proceeds as follows (a) download all forests intersecting CD12, (b) for each forest apply a window query on the hotels. This method will yield a lot of savings if the hotels from that cell that participate in the join are only a few.

The point to switch from summary retrieval to window queries depends on the cost parameters and the size of the smallest partition (e.g., forests). In the next section, we provide a methodology that recursively partitions the dataspace using statistical information terminating at regions where it is more beneficial to download the data from both sites and perform the join on the PDA or download the objects from one server only and process the join by sending them as queries to the other.

3.4   A Recursive, Adaptive Spatial Join Algorithm

By putting everything together, we can now define the proposed algorithm for spatial joins on a mobile device. We assume that the servers support the following queries:

- WINDOW query: return all the objects intersecting a window w.
- COUNT query: return the number of objects intersecting a window w.
- ε-RANGE query: return all objects within distance ε from a point p.

The *MobiJoin* algorithm is based on the divisive approach and it is *recursive*; given a rectangular area w of the data space (which is initially the MBR of the joined datasets) and the cardinalities of R and S in this area, it may choose to perform the join for this area, or recursively partition the data space to smaller windows, collect finer statistics for them, and postpone join processing. Therefore, the algorithm is *adaptive* to data skew, since it may follow a different policy depending on the density of the data in the area which is currently joined.

Initially, the algorithm is called for datasets R and S, considering as w the intersection of their MBRs. For this, we have to apply two queries to each server. The first is an aggregate query (easily expressed in SQL) asking for the maximum and minimum coordinates of the objects, which define the MBR of the dataset. The intersection w of the MBRs of R and S defines the space the joined results should intersect. If the distribution of the datasets is very different, w can be smaller than the map window that encloses them and many objects can be immediately pruned. The second query retrieves the number of objects from each dataset intersecting w (i.e., a COUNT query).

Let $R_w.count$ and $S_w.count$ be the number of objects from R and S, respectively, intersected by w. The recursive MobiJoin algorithm is shown in Figure 2. If one of the $R_w.count$ and $S_w.count$ is 0, the algorithm returns without elaborating further on the data. Else, the algorithm employs a cost model to estimate the cost for each of the potential actions in the current region w: (1) download the objects that intersect w from both datasets and perform the join on the PDA, (2) download the objects from R that intersect w and *send them* as *selection queries* to S, (3) download the objects from S that intersect w and *send them* as *selection queries* to R, and (4) divide w into smaller regions $w' \in w$, retrieve refined statistics for them, and apply the algorithm recursively there.

Action (1) may be constrained by the resource constraints on the PDA. Actions (2) and (3) may have different costs depending on which of the $R_w.count$ and $S_w.count$ is the smallest and the communication costs with each of the sites. Finally, the cost of action (4) is the hardest to estimate; for this we use probabilistic assumptions for the data distribution in the refined partitions, as explained in the next section.

3.5 The Cost Model

In this section, we describe a cost model that can be used in combination with MobiJoin to facilitate the adaptivity of the algorithm. We provide formulae, which estimate the cost of each of the four potential actions that the algorithm may choose. Our formulae are parametric to the characteristics of the network connection to the mobile client. For simplicity, we consider distance joins between point sets instead of intersection joins. However, the formulae can be easily adapted for intersection joins.

The largest amount of data that can be transferred in one physical frame on the network is referred to as MTU (Maximum Transmission Unit). The size of the MTU depends on the specific protocol; Ethernet, for instance, has $MTU = 1500$ bytes, while dial-up connections usually support $MTU = 576$ bytes. Each transmission unit consists of a header and the actual data. The largest segment of TCP data that can be transmitted is called MSS (Maximum

// R and S are spatial relations located at different servers
// w is a window region
// $R_w.count$ (resp. $S_w.count$) is the number
// of objects from R (resp. S), which intersect w
MobiJoin($R,S,w,R_w.count,S_w.count$)
1.   if $R_w.count = 0$ or $S_w.count = 0$ then terminate;
2. $c_1(w)$ = cost of downloading $R_w.count$ objects from R
            and $S_w.count$ objects from S and joining them on the PDA;
3. $c_2(w)$ = cost of downloading $R_w.count$ objects from R, send them
            as window queries to server that hosts S and receive the results;
4. $c_3(w)$ = cost of downloading $S_w.count$ objects from S, send them
            as window queries to server that hosts R and receive the results;
5. $c_4(w)$ = cost of applying recursive counting in $R_w.count$ and $S_w.count$,
            retrieve more detailed statistics, and apply MobiJoin recursively;
6. $c_{min} = \min\{c_1(w), c_2(w), c_3(w), c_4(w)\}$;
7.   if $c_{min} = c_4$ then
8.   impose a regular grid over w;
9.   for each cell $w' \in w$
10.   retrieve $R_{w'}.count$ and $S_{w'}.count$;
11.   MobiJoin($R,S,w',R_{w'}.count,S_{w'}.count$);
12.   else follow action specified by c_{min};

Fig. 2. The recursive MobiJoin algorithm

Segment Size). Essentially, $MTU = MSS + B_H$, where B_H is the size of the TCP/IP headers (typically, $B_H = 40$ bytes).

Let D be a dataset. The size of D in bytes is $B_D = |D| \cdot B_{obj}$, where B_{obj} is the size of each object in bytes. For point objects $B_{obj} = 4 + 2 \cdot 4 = 12$ bytes (i.e., point ID plus its coordinates). Thus, when the whole D is transmitted through the network, the number of transferred bytes is:

$$T_B(B_D) = B_D + B_H \cdot \left\lceil \frac{B_D}{MSS} \right\rceil, \tag{1}$$

where the second component of the equation is the overhead of the TCP/IP headers.

The cost of sending a window query q_w to a server is $B_H + B_{qtype} + B_w$, i.e., transferring the query type B_{qtype} and the coordinates of the window B_w. Let $R_w.count$ and $S_w.count$ be the number of objects intersecting window w at site R and S respectively. Let b_R and b_S be the per-byte transfer cost (e.g., in dollars) for sites R and S respectively. The total cost of downloading the objects from R and S and joining them on the PDA is:

$$c_1(w) = (b_R + b_S)(B_H + B_{qtype} + B_w)$$
$$+ b_R T_B(R_w.count \cdot B_{obj}) + b_S T_B(S_w.count \cdot B_{obj}) \tag{2}$$

Now let us consider the cost c_2 of downloading all $R_w.count$ objects from R and sending them as *distance selection* queries to S. Each of the $R_w.count$ objects is transformed to a *selection region* and sent to S. For each query point p, the expected number of point from S in w within distance ε from p is $\frac{\pi \cdot \varepsilon^2}{w_x \cdot w_y} \cdot S_w.count$, assuming uniform distribution in w, where w_x and w_y are the lengths of the window's sides.[3] In other words, the *selectivity* of a *selection* query q over a region w with uniformly distributed points is probabilistically defined by $area(q)/area(w)$. The query message consists of the query type, p and ε (i.e., $S_q = S_{qtype} + S_p + S_\varepsilon$).Therefore, the cost of sending the query is $B_H + S_q$. The total number of transferred bytes for transmitting the distance query and receiving the results is:

$$T_B(w, \varepsilon) = (B_H + S_q) + T_B \left(\frac{\pi \cdot \varepsilon^2}{w_x \cdot w_y} \cdot S_w.count \cdot B_{obj} \right) \tag{3}$$

Therefore the total cost of downloading the objects from R intersecting w and sending them one by one as distance queries to S is:

$$c_2(w) = b_R(B_H + B_{qtype} + B_w) + b_R T_B(R_w.count \cdot B_{obj}) + b_S R_w.count \cdot T_B(w, \varepsilon) \tag{4}$$

The cost c_3 of downloading the objects from S and sending them as queries to R is also given by Equation 4 by exchanging the roles of R and S. Finally, in case of an intersection join, we can use the same derivation, but we need to know statistics about the average area of the object MBRs intersecting w for R and S. These can be obtained from the server when we retrieve $R_w.count$ and $S_w.count$ (i.e., we can post an additional aggregate query together with the COUNT query).

The final step is to estimate the cost c_4 of repartitioning w and applying MobiJoin recursively for each new partition w'. In order to retrieve the statistics for a new partition w', we have to send an aggregate COUNT query to each site ($B_H + B_{qtype} + B_w$ bytes) and retrieve ($B_H + 4$ bytes) from there. Thus, the total cost of repartitioning and retrieving the refined counters is:

$$c_{CQ(w)} = N_p(b_R + b_S)(B_H + B_{qtype} + B_w + B_H + 4), \tag{5}$$

where N_p is the number of new partitions over w. Now we can define:

$$c_4(w) = c_{CQ(w)} + \sum_{\forall w'} \min\{c_1(w'), c_2(w'), c_3(w'), c_4(w')\} \tag{6}$$

Without prior knowledge about how the objects are distributed in the new partitions, it is impossible to predict the actions of the algorithm when run at the next level for each w'. The minimum value for $c_4(w)$ is just $c_{CQ(w)}$, i.e., the cost of refining the statistics, assuming that the condition of line 1 in Figure 2 will hold (i.e., one of the $R_{w'}.count$, $S_{w'}.count$ will be 0 for all w'). This will happen if the data distribution in the two datasets is very different. On the other

---

[3] For the sake of readability, we ignore boundary effects here.

hand, $c_4(w)$ is maximized if the distribution is uniform in w for both R and S. In this case, $c_4(w) = c_{CQ(w)} + \sum_{\forall w'} \min\{c_1(w'), c_4(w')\}$, i.e., case 1 will apply for all w', unless the data for each w' does not fit in the PDA, thus the algorithm will have to be recursively employed.

In practice, we expect some skew in the data, thus some partitions will be pruned or converted to one of the cases 2 and 3. For the application of our model, we consider $c_4(w) = c_{CQ(w)}$, i.e., an *optimistic* approach that postpones join processing, as long as refining the statistics is cheaper. While this estimation was effective for most of the tested cases, we are currently working on a more accurate model.

3.6   Iceberg Spatial Distance Semi-joins

Our framework is especially useful for iceberg join queries. As an example, consider the query "find all hotels which are close to at least 20 restaurants", where closeness is defined by a distance threshold ε. Such queries usually have few results, however, when processed in a straightforward way they could be as expensive as a simple spatial join. The grid refinement method can be directly used to prune areas where the restaurant relation is sparse. In this case, the condition $R_w.count = 0$ in line 1 of Figure 2 will become $R_w.count < k_{min}$, where k_{min} is the minimum number of objects from R that must join with an object in S. Therefore, large parts of the search space could potentially be pruned by the cardinality constraint early. In the next section, we show that this method can boost performance by more than one order of magnitude, for moderate values of k_{min}.

4   Experimental Evaluation

In this section, we study the performance of the MobiJoin algorithm described in Figure 2 and compare it against two simpler techniques. The fist one, called *Nested Loop Spatial Join* (NLSJ), is a naïve algorithm which resembles cases 2 and 3 of MobiJoin. The PDA receives in a stream all the objects from server R and sends them one by one as distance queries to server S, which returns the results. For fairness, we first check the number of objects in each server, and set R to be the one with the smallest dataset. The second algorithm is *Hash Based Spatial Join* (HBSJ), and consists of cases 1 and 4 of MobiJoin. The PDA retrieves statistics from the servers and recursively decomposes the data space, until the partitions of the two datasets fit in memory. The corresponding fragments are downloaded and the join is performed in the PDA.

We implemented our algorithms in Visual C++ for Windows Pocket PC. Our prototype run on an HP-IPAQ PDA with a 400MHz RISC processor and 64MB RAM. The PDA was connected to the network through a wireless interface. The servers for the spatial datasets resided on a 2-CPU Ultra-SPARC III machine with 4GB RAM. In all experiments, we set $b_R = b_S$, i.e., the transfer cost is the same for both servers. We used synthetic datasets consisting of 1000 to 10000

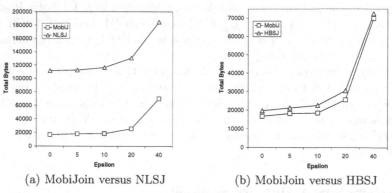

(a) MobiJoin versus NLSJ   (b) MobiJoin versus HBSJ

Fig. 3. Transferred bytes as a function of the distance threshold ε

points, in order to simulate typical windows of users' requests. The points were clustered around n randomly selected centers, and each cluster was following a Gaussian distribution. To achieve different levels of skew, we varied n from 1 to 128. We also employed two real-life datasets, namely the road and railway segments of Germany. Each of these sets had around 35K points.

In the first set of experiments, we compare the three algorithms in terms of the total number of bytes sent and received, including the overhead due to the TCP/IP headers, as a function of the joining distance ε. We used two datasets if 1000 points and set the PDA's memory size to 100 points. In Figure 3 we present the average values of the results over 10 runs with different datasets. Figure 3a compares MobiJoin with NLSJ. It is obvious that MobiJoin easily outperforms the naïve NLSJ by almost an order of magnitude. This is due to two reasons. First, NLSJ transmits a huge number of queries to the largest dataset, which have a high cost (including the cost of the packet headers for each query). Second, MobiJoin avoids downloading any data from regions where at least one dataset is empty. Clearly, performing the join on the mobile device comes with significant cost savings. The results also demonstrate that the overhead of identifying such regions (i.e., the additional aggregate queries) is justified.

Figure 3b compares MobiJoin with HBSJ. MobiJoin is better than HBSJ, but the difference is small (i.e., 22% in the best case). The performance gain is due to cases 2 and 3 of the algorithm, which apply Nested Loop Join for some partitions. If a space partition w contains many points in (say) S but only a few points in R, MobiJoin executes Nested Loop Join in w, which is cheaper than hashing (i.e., downloading both fragments). Note that as ε increases, the cost of each algorithm increases, but for different reasons. In the case of NLSJ it is due to the larger number of solutions that must be transferred. For HBSJ, on the other hand, it is due to the enlargement of the query window by $2 \cdot \varepsilon$ at each side, while for MobiJoin it is a combination of the two reasons.

The distribution of the data is crucial for the performance of our algorithms. Intuitively, MobiJoin performs very well on skewed data. If, for example, all data

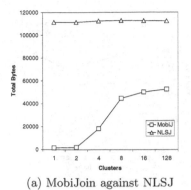
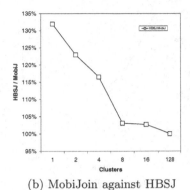

(a) MobiJoin against NLSJ   (b) MobiJoin against HBSJ

Fig. 4. Total number of bytes transferred vs. the number of clusters in the dataset

of R are near the lower left corner and all data of S are near the upper right corner, then the algorithm will terminate after one step, since no combination of quadrants produces any result. On the other hand, if the datasets are uniform there is a lower probability of successful pruning; therefore MobiJoin reduces to HBSJ. In the following experiment, we test the algorithm under varying data skew. We employ a 1000 points dataset and vary the number of clusters from 1 to 128. Fewer clusters result in more skewed data and vice-versa. The comparison between our algorithm and NLSJ is shown in Figure 4a.

For very skewed data, MobiJoin can be as much as two orders of magnitude better than NLSJ. When the data are more uniform, however, the performance of MobiJoin drops, while NLSJ is stable.[4] Still, MobiJoin is two times better in the worst case. This is due to the fact that MobiJoin behaves like hash join when data are uniformly distributed. In such case, it only has to transfer $|R|+|S|$ objects in bulk to the PDA, while NLSJ transfers $|R|$ objects in bulk, then sends $|R|$ objects one by one to server S, and finally receives the results.

The fact that MobiJoin reduces to hash join is further investigated in Figure 4b. There, we present the total number of bytes transferred by HBSJ over the bytes transferred by MobiJoin. When data is skewed, HBSJ is 32% worse, since MobiJoin joins some of the fragments using the nested loops approach. For uniform data, however, the two algorithms are identical.

We also investigated the effect of varying the buffer size which is available in the PDA and present the results in Figure 5. The size of the buffer is presented as a percentage of the total size of the two datasets and varies from 0.3% to 4%. Each dataset contains 1000 points in 4 clusters. In Figure 5a we compare MobiJoin with HBSJ in terms of the total packets transferred. As expected, if more memory is available in the PDA, less packets are transferred. This is especially true for HBSJ; since larger windows can be joined in the PDA, more data are transferred in bulk. MobiJoin, on the other hand, is not affected much,

---

[4] The small fluctuation of NLSJ is due to the different number of solutions

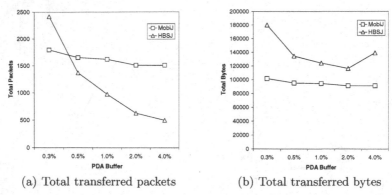

(a) Total transferred packets   (b) Total transferred bytes

Fig. 5. Transferred data vs. the PDA's memory size (% of the total size of the datasets)

since some fragments are joined by the nested loop approach which transfers many small packets. In Figure 5b, we present the total number of transferred data for the same settings. Observe that MobiJoin transfers less data in total. Since most services charge the user by the amount of transferred data, the behavior of MobiJoin is preferable.

Notice also the strange trend of the cost in terms of bytes for HBSJ. When the size of the buffer grows from 0.3% until 2%, the cost drops, as expected. However, for larger buffer sizes the cost increases again. This can explained by the stopping condition of the recursive algorithm; data are partitioned recursively until the partitions fit in memory. If the buffer is small, many queries are transmitted and the cost is high. If the buffer is large, on the other hand, the recursion stops early and HBSJ fails to prune sub-partitions that are empty in either of the datasets. There is a range of memory sizes, where a good trade-off between these two cases is achieved.

In the final set of experiments, we tested our algorithms for the case of iceberg queries. We employed the Germany Roads and Railways datasets, and we joined them with synthetic datasets of 1000 points, which represent locations of interest (e.g., hotels). We varied the minimum support threshold k_{min} from 2 to 32. Since we wanted to test the efficiency of pruning due to space partitioning, we compared the HBSJ algorithm against NLSJ. Notice that the settings of the experiment are favorable for nested loop join, since we join a small dataset with a large one. The results are presented in Figures 6a and 6b. In the first figure, the hotels dataset is uniform. This is the worst case for our algorithm, which is 3 times worse than NLSJ, for small values of k_{min}. However, when k_{min} increases, more partitions are pruned, and HBSJ can be as much as one order of magnitude better than NLSJ. Observe that the cost of NLSJ is stable, since it must always transfer the data from the smaller set, regardless of the value of the support threshold k_{min}. Figure 6b presents the results in the case where the hotels dataset is skewed. NLSJ does not change, since its performance depends

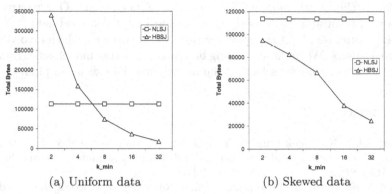

(a) Uniform data (b) Skewed data

Fig. 6. Iceberg queries for real datasets. Transferred data vs. the threshold k_{min}

mostly on the size of the hotels dataset, and not on the distribution. HBSJ, on the other hand, takes advantage of the skewed distribution and performs better that NLSJ in all cases. In summary, our technique of obtaining statistics information, decreases considerably the cost when k_{min} is sufficiently large and is especially suitable for skewed data.

5 Conclusions

In this paper, we dealt with the problem of evaluating spatial joins on a mobile device, when the datasets reside on separate remote servers. We assume that the servers support three simple query types: (i) *window* queries, (ii) *aggregate* queries, and (iii) *distance-range* queries. We also assume that the servers are non-collaborative, they do not wish to share their internal indices, and no mediator can perform the join of these two sites. These assumptions are valid for many practical situations, where users apply ad-hoc joins. For instance, consider two services which provide maps and hotel locations, and a user who requests an unusual combination like "Find all hotels which are at most 200km away from a rain forest". Executing this query on a mobile device must address two issues: (i) the limited resources of the device and (ii) the fact that the user is charged by the amount of transferred information, instead of the processing cost on the servers.

We developed MobiJoin, an algorithm that partitions recursively the data space and retrieves statistics in the form of simple aggregate queries. Based on the statistics and a detailed cost model, MobiJoin can either (i) prune a partition, (ii) join its contents in hash join or nested loop fashion, or (iii) request further statistics. In contrast to the previous work on mediators, our algorithm dynamically optimizes the entire process of retrieving statistics and executing the join, for a single ad-hoc query.

We developed a prototype on a wireless PDA and tested our method for a variety of synthetic and real datasets. Our experiments reveal that MobiJoin outperforms the naïve approach by an order of magnitude. Our partitioning method is also suitable for iceberg queries, especially for skewed data.

In the future, we plan to support complex spatial queries, which involve more than two datasets. We are also working on refining our cost model, since accurate estimations are crucial for selecting the most beneficial execution plan.

References

[1] Sibel Adali, K. Selçuk Candan, Yannis Papakonstantinou, and V. S. Subrahmanian. Query caching and optimization in distributed mediator systems. In *Proc. of ACM SIGMOD Int'l Conference*, 1996. 238

[2] Lars Arge, Octavian Procopiuc, Sridhar Ramaswamy, Torsten Suel, and Jeffrey Scott Vitter. Scalable sweeping-based spatial join. In *Proc. of VLDB Conference*, 1998. 237, 239

[3] Thomas Brinkhoff, Hans-Peter Kriegel, and Bernhard Seeger. Efficient processing of spatial joins using r-trees. In *Proc. of ACM SIGMOD Int'l Conference*, 1993. 234, 235, 236

[4] Antonio Corral, Yannis Manolopoulos, Yannis Theodoridis, and Michael Vassilakopoulos. Closest pair queries in spatial databases. In *Proc. of ACM SIGMOD Int'l Conference*, 2000. 235

[5] Jens-Peter Dittrich and Bernhard Seeger. Data redundancy and duplicate detection in spatial join processing. In *Proc. of Int'l Conf. on Data Engineering (ICDE)*, 2000. 237, 239

[6] A. Guttman. R-trees: a dynamical index structure for spatial searching. In *Proc. of ACM SIGMOD Int'l Conference*, 1984. 236

[7] Gisli R. Hjaltason and Hanan Samet. Incremental distance join algorithms for spatial databases. In *Proc. of ACM SIGMOD Int'l Conference*, 1998. 234, 235

[8] Zachary G. Ives, Daniela Florescu, Marc Friedman, Alon Y. Levy, and Daniel S. Weld. An adaptive query execution system for data integration. In *Proc. of ACM SIGMOD Int'l Conference*, 1999. 238

[9] Nick Koudas and Kenneth C. Sevcik. High dimensional similarity joins: Algorithms and performance evaluation. In *Proc. of Int'l Conf. on Data Engineering (ICDE)*, 1998. 235, 236

[10] Danzhou Liu, Ee-Peng Lim, and Wee Keong Ng. Efficient k nearest neighbor queries on remote spatial databases using range estimation. In *Proc of Int'l Conference on Scientific and Statistical Database Management (SSDBM)*, 2002. 237

[11] Ming-Ling Lo and Chinya V. Ravishankar. Spatial hash-joins. In *Proc. of ACM SIGMOD Int'l Conference*, 1996. 237

[12] Gang Luo, Jeffrey F. Naughton, and Curt Ellmann. A non-blocking parallel spatial join algorithm. In *Proc. of Int'l Conf. on Data Engineering (ICDE)*, 2002. 236, 237, 239

[13] Nikos Mamoulis and Dimitris Papadias. Integration of spatial join algorithms for processing multiple inputs. In *Proc. of ACM SIGMOD Int'l Conference*, 1999. 236

[14] Jignesh M. Patel and David J. DeWitt. Partition based spatial-merge join. In *Proc. of ACM SIGMOD Int'l Conference*, 1996. 236, 239

[15] Mary Tork Roth, Fatma Ozcan, and Laura M. Haas. Cost models do matter: Providing cost information for diverse data sources in a federated system. In *Proc. of VLDB Conference*, 1999. 238

[16] Hyoseop Shin, Bongki Moon, and Sukho Lee. Adaptive multi-stage distance join processing. In *Proc. of ACM SIGMOD Int'l Conference*, 2000. 235

[17] Kian-Lee Tan, Beng-Chin Ooi, and David J. Abel. Exploiting spatial indexes for semijoin-based join processing in distributed spatial databases. *IEEE Trans. on Data and Knowledge Engineering*, 12(2):920–937, 2000. 237

[18] Anthony Tomasic, Louiqa Raschid, and Patrick Valduriez. Scaling access to heterogeneous data sources with disco. *IEEE Trans. on Data and Knowledge Engineering*, 10(5):808–823, 1998. 238

[19] Jun Zhang, Nikos Mamoulis, Dimitris Papadias, and Yufei Tao. All-nearest-neighbors queries in spatial databases. Technical Report CS07-02, HKUST, Hong Kong, 2002. 235

On Spatial-Range Closest-Pair Query*

Jing Shan, Donghui Zhang, and Betty Salzberg

College of Computer and Information Science
Boston, MA 02115
{jshan,donghui,salzberg}@ccs.neu.edu

Abstract. An important query for spatial database research is to find the closest pair of objects in a given space. Existing work assumes two objects of the closest pair come from two different data sets indexed by R-trees. The closest pair in the whole space will be found via an optimzed R-tree join technique. However, this technique doesn't perform well when the two data sets are identical. And it doesn't work when the search range is some area other than the whole space. In this paper, we address the closest pair problem within the same data set. Further more, we propose a practical extension to the closest pair problem to involve a query range. The problem now becomes finding the closest pair of objects among those inside a given range. After extending the existing techniques to solve the new problem, we proposed two index structures based on augmenting the R-tree and we also give algorithms for maintaining these structrures. Experimental results show that our structures are more robust than earlier approaches.

1 Introduction

Spatial databases have received more and more attention recently. Some major database vendors have provided spatial database support, e.g. Oracle Spatial Cartridge [1] and IBM Informix Spatial DataBlade [2]. Examples of spatial database applications include mapping, urban planning, transportation planning, resource management, geomarketing, archeology and environmental modelling [6].

One important spatial database query is the *closest pair (CP)* query, which is to find the closest pair of objects among two data sets. One may be interested in finding the closest middle school and bar, the closest supermarket and apartment building, etc. This topic has good solutions in the computational geometry area [17, 7]. However, only recently has this problem received interest in the environment of spatial databases [10, 5, 6, 21]. All of these focus on two disjoint data sets. In fact, Corral et al. have studied the effect of overlapping between two data sets and found out that "a small increase in the overlap between the data sets may cause performance deterioration of orders of magnitude" [5, 6]. Obviously, when two data sets are identical, there is extensive overlapping. Although in their technical report [5], Corral et al. introduced a way to extend

---

* This work was partially supported by NSF grant IIS-0073063.

T. Hadzilacos et al. (Eds.): SSTD 2003, LNCS 2750, pp. 252–270, 2003.
© Springer-Verlag Berlin Heidelberg 2003

their algorithms to solve the case when two data sets are the same, they also pointed out that "this case still deserves careful attention".

Furthermore, to the best of our knowledge, none of the existing work has addressed the *Range-CP* problem, i.e. *Given a spatial range R, find the closest pair of objects located within R.* For example, one may be interested in finding, within Massachusetts, the closest (high school, bar) pair. The CP problem is a special case of the Range-CP problem when the query range is the whole space. The Range-CP problem is more interesting for the following reason. In the original CP problem, the pair of closest objects is fixed. Thus we can perform the query once and store the answer and we need only perform the query again after there are inserts or deletes of objects. The Range-CP problem, however, is more difficult. The query range can be arbitrary. To maintain a closest pair of objects for every possible spatial range is not practical.

The contributions of the paper are as follows:

- We propose a practical extension to the Closest Pair problem to involve a query range. We address this new Range-CP problem in the case when the two data sets are identical. An example query is: "what are the closest pair of post offices in Boston?" If the City Hall wants to move some post office to a new location, this query result may help decision making. The query also applies to finding closest pairs of different types of objects, e.g. between high schools and bars, when both are indexed in the same R-tree.
- We discuss how to extend existing CP solutions to solve the Self Range-CP problem.
- We propose two versions of the SRCP-tree, a new index structure, to solve this problem.
- We identify a practical issue not addressed in the most recent solution for CP problem [21] and provide solutions, thus improving the algorithm.
- Experimental results are provided which demonstrate the efficiency of our approaches.

The rest of the paper has the following organization: Section 2 formally defines the problem to be addressed and provides related work. Section 3 presents our extension to existing techniques to solve the new problem. Our new solutions appear in section 4. We provide experimental results in section 5. Finally, section 6 contains our conclusions and future directions.

2 Problem Definition and Related Work

2.1 Problem Definition

The CP query finds a pair of objects from two data sets with minimum distance between them. If there are more than one pairs with this distance. The CP query returns one of them. The formal definition is given below:

Definition 1. *Given two spatial data sets S and T, the* **Closest Pair (CP) query** *finds the pair of objects (s, t) such that $s \in S$, $t \in T$, and $\forall s' \in S$ and $t' \in T$, $distance(s, t) \leq distance(s', t')$.*

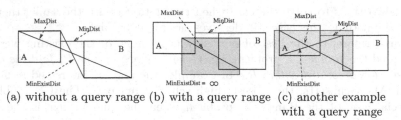

(a) without a query range (b) with a query range (c) another example
with a query range

Fig. 1. Two MBRs and their *MinDist*, *MaxDist* and *MinExistDist*

Here $distance(s, t)$ corresponds to the Euclidean distance of two objects s and t. A practical variation which we do not see in the literature is the *Range-CP* problem, where a spatial range R is involved and we are interested in finding the closest pair of objects inside R. The SRCP query finds the closest pair of objects from a subset of objects in one data set, where the subset of objects are those whose locations are in a given spatial range. More formally,

Definition 2. *Given a spatial data set S, the* **Self Range Closest Pair (SRCP) query** *regarding to a spatial range R finds the pair of objects (s, t) such that $s, t \in S$, $s \neq t$, R contains s and t, and $\forall s', t' \in S$ such that $s' \neq t'$ and R contains s' and t', $distance(s, t) \leq distance(s', t')$.*

Both these problems have a variation of finding k closest pairs instead of only one. Here $k \geq 1$ is given at run time.

2.2   The R-Tree and Some Useful Metrics

Spatial database index structures have received a lot of attention from researchers. Various indexing techniques have been proposed, e.g. the R-tree family [9, 3]. An review of spatial index structures appears in [8]. In an R-tree, every node has an *minimum bounding rectangle (MBR)* and the MBR of a higher-level tree node contains the MBRs of all its children. Thus when performing a range query, we only need to browse the sub-trees whose root-level MBRs intersect with the query range.

Given two MBRs A, B of R-tree nodes, following [15], we define some useful metrics. $MinDist(A, B)$ is the smallest distance between A and B boundaries. It is a lower bound of the distance between an object enclosed in A and an object enclosed in B. Similarly, $MaxDist(A, B)$ is the largest distance between A and B boundaries and it is a upper bound of the distance between an object enclosed in A and an object enclosed in B. Another metric is $MinExistDist(A, B)$, which is the minimum distance which guarantees that there exists a pair of objects, one in A and the other in B, with distance closer than the metric. In other words, $MinExistDist$ expresses an upper bound for the solution of the closest pair problem, since the closest pair in the collection will be closer or equal in distance to that of any $MinExistDist$ for any pair A, B of R-tree nodes. An example illustrating these metrics is shown in Figure 1a, which is borrowed from [6]. To summarize, the following hold:

$$\forall o_1 \in A, o_2 \in B, MinDist(A, B) \leq dist(o_1, o_2) \leq MaxDist(A, B)$$

$$\exists o_1 \in A, o_2 \in B, dist(o_1, o_2) \leq MinExistDist(A, B)$$

The papers [6, 15], although using these metrics, did not consider query ranges. We extend these metrics to the case when there is a query range R involved, as shown in the shadowed rectangle in Figure 1b and 1c. As we can see in both figures, the value of $MinDist$ remains the same, and the value of $MaxDist$ changes. We can prove that $MaxDist(A, B, R) = MaxDist(A \cap R, B \cap R)$. Intuitively, the $MaxDist$ with a query range R is equal to the $MaxDist$ of the following MBRs without any query range: the intersection of A with R, and the intersection of B with R.

The case of $MinExistDist(A, B, R)$ is tricky. It can be $+\infty$ as shown in Figure 1b. This is because it is possible that there is no object from at least one MBR that is in this range. In this case, however large a distance is, we cannot guarantee that there exists a pair of objects in this range. However, in Figure 1c, $MinExistDist$ is not ∞. The reason is that the query range contains (at least) one edge from each MBR.

2.3 Related Work

The closest pair query has been studied in computational geometry [17, 7]. More recently, this problem has been approached in the environment of spatial databases [10, 5, 6, 21]. As far as we know, Hjaltason and Samet [10] were the first to address this issue. Their paper proposed an incremental join algorithm between two R-tree indices. The idea is to maintain a priority queue which contains pairs of index entries and objects, and pop out the closest pair and process it.

Later, Corral et al. [6] proposed an improved version known as the *heap algorithm*. One improvement, which was also proposed simultaneously by Zhang et al. [23, 24], is the *virtual height optimization* which can be applied when joining two R-trees with different height. A benefit of this optimization is that we can avoid pushing a pair of objects (from the shorter tree) and internal node (from the higher tree) into the queue. Another improvement is that there is no need to push any pair of objects into the queue at all. Rather, we remember a threshold value T as the distance of the closest pair of objects we have seen. Instead of pushing a pair of objects into the queue, we use it to update T if the distance is smaller than T.

The most important optimization is that we can use the value T as a filter to shrink the size of the queue dynamically. If the $MinDist$ of a pair of nodes is no smaller than T, there is no way the closest pair of objects can be found by processing the pair of nodes, and thus there is no need to maintain it in the queue. Another important optimization is that if $MinExistDist$ of a pair of nodes is smaller than T, we can reduce T without actually seeing the pair of objects with distance equal to or smaller than T.

However, both the above algorithms are not efficient when the two R-trees have extensive overlapping. In the case when two nodes intersect, their $MinDist$ is 0. Both algorithms need to process all pairs of intersecting nodes. If the two R-trees are identical, since the distance between every page and itself is 0, the query algorithm has to at least check every tree page.

Recently, Yang and Lin [21] proposed a new structure called the *b-Rdnn tree* which has a better solution to the CP problem when there is overlap between the two data sets. The idea is to find k objects from each data set which are the closest to the other data set. Here the distance between an object and a data set is the minimum distance between the object and all objects in the data set. The paper proves that the closest pairs can be found by examining these $2k$ objects. In order to efficiently find these $2k$ objects, along with each object, the distance dnn to its nearest neighbor in the other data set is maintained. Also, along with each index entry, a value min_dnn (max_dnn) is maintained which is the minimum (maximum) dnn value of all objects in the sub-tree.

However, this approach does not apply to our new query where there is a query range involved. The thing is, the object with the smallest distance to the data set may not be inside the query range. Even if it is, its nearest neighbor of it may not be in the query range.

Also related are papers [15, 4, 12, 16, 11] on nearest neighbor queries and papers [22, 14, 19] on reverse nearest neighbor queries. In addition, there are nearest neighbor algorithms for moving object databases [13, 18].

2.4   Improvement on an Existing CP Problem Solution

In this section, we identify a very practical issue not addressed in the most recent solution to the CP problem proposed by Yang and Ling [21]. The paper contains a theorem: "for any pair of objects (o_1, o_2), which is one of the k closest pairs between S and T, $o_1 \in kNN(S,T)$ and $o_2 \in kNN(T,S)$". Here $kNN(S,T)$ is the k objects from S that are the closest to T.

We argue that the theorem and the algorithm based on it are valid only when no two pairs of objects have the same distance. In a practical scenario, it is quite possible that different pairs of objects may have the same distance. If so, the algorithm there may not be correct. Figure 2 shows an example. Objects s_1, s_2 belong to set S, while objects t_1, t_2 belong to set T. Assume $Dist(s1,t1) = Dist(s2,t2)$ is the minimum distance between any object in S and any object in T. Consider the case when $k=1$, i.e. we want to find only one closest pair between S and T. It is possible that the algorithm uses the bRdnn-tree on S to find s_1 (since the distance between s_1 and T is minimal), while it uses the bRdnn-tree on T to find t_2. Now, the only candidate for the closest pair is (s_1, t_2), which leads to an error.

We propose two solutions to this problem. One solution works as follows. In order to find the k closest pairs, instead of finding k objects from S which are the closest to T (as in [21]), we find also all objects whose distance to T

Fig. 2. When different pairs of objects can have the same distance, the algorithm of [21] may not be correct

is equal to the distance between the kth object and T. Similarly, we find more than k objects from T which are the closest to S. Let's say we find $k + x$ objects from S and we find $k + y$ objects from T. These two sets of objects form a set of $(k + x)(k + y)$ pairs, and we can prove that the k closest pairs of objects must belong to this set.

For the other solution, we only find k objects from each data set which are the closest to the other set. They form a set of k^2 pairs. However, along with each object thus found, we also find its nearest neighbor in the other data set. If we union the k^2 pairs with the $2k$ NN pairs, we get a set of $k^2 + 2k$ pairs. We can prove that the k closest pairs of objects must come from this set.

3   Straightforward Solutions

In this section, we extend existing solutions to the CP problem to solve the Self Range Closest Pair (SRCP) problem.

3.1   Range Query Followed by Plane Sweep

We know that spatial access methods like the R-tree support range queries. We also know that when all objects are in memory, there are computational geometry solutions to the CP problem. So one straightforward approach, assuming the range query result is not too big, is to perform a range query on the data set and then perform some computational geometry method, e.g. the well-know *sweeping* technique, on the range query result.

To find the closest pair, the sweeping technique works as follows. Read objects in increasing x order, while maintaining the closest pair found so far. Whenever an object is read into the buffer, compare it with all objects that are already in the buffer to determine if the distance is smaller than the currently maintained closest pair. If no object is ever removed from the buffer, this is obviously an $O(n^2)$ algorithm. However, objects which can be determined not to be close to any non-read objects can be dynamically removed from the buffer. Here we use the distance of the currently maintained closest pair as a threshold, and any object whose distance in the x dimension to the currently sweep line is larger than this threshold, can be removed from the buffer.

3.2   Extending the Incremental Join Algorithm and Heap Algorithm

Both the incremental join algorithm of [10] and the heap algorithm of [6] can be extended to solve the SRCP problem. To extend to the Self-CP case, we just assume there are two copies of the same data set and apply the original algorithm to the two copies. A minor modification is that the pair of an object and itself should not be counted as a closest pair.

The extension to the Range-CP case is as follows. Whenever a pair of internal nodes are about to be pushed into the queue, we check to make sure that both nodes intersect with the query range. Whenever a pair of objects are about to be compared, we check to make sure that both of them are inside the query range. Also, an important thing is that we have extended the definition of $MinExistDist$ to include a query range, as discussed in section 2.2.

4   Our Solutions

There are two motivations to our solutions to the SRCP problem.

- Suppose we maintain the closest pair of objects in a system table outside the R-tree used for the general SRCP problem. Upon a query where $k = 1$, if it turns out that both these two objects fall in the query range, we can immediately determine that this pair is the SRCP query result without accessing any tree node. None of the existing solutions in section 3 has this ability.
- When applying the incremental join algorithm or the heap algorithm (section 3.2) to the SRCP problem, the distance of every "self-pair" of nodes is zero and thus every self-pair of tree nodes intersecting the query range must be pushed into the processing queue and processed. However, if along with each index node, we store the shortest distance of objects in the sub-tree, we can then use this value instead of zero as the priority of the self-pair. This increases the chance that a pair can be eliminated from the queue and improves performance.

Based on these two motivations, we develop two versions of the SRCP-tree, which is presented in section 4.1 and 4.2. We then analytically compare them with the straightforward approaches in section 4.3. For simplicity, we focus on finding a single closest pair, and we discuss how to extend to finding k closest pairs in section 4.4.

4.1   SRCP-Tree (Version One)

In this section, we define the first version of the SRCP tree. We first define some notation. Let e be an index entry pointing to some node in the R-tree. We use $Node(e)$ to represent the node that e points to. We use $Subtree(e)$ to represent the sub-tree rooted by $Node(e)$.

Tree Structure The SRCP-tree (version one) is an R-tree augmented with "local" closest pair information. Each index entry e of the R-tree is augmented with a triple $(o_1, o_2, dist)$. Here o_1 and o_2 are the closest pair of objects in the sub-tree rooted by $Node(e)$. The value $dist$ is the distance between o_1 and o_2. (Since it can always be computed from o_1 and o_2, we could choose not to store $dist$.) In a small auxiliary tree descriptor, we store the closest pair of objects in the whole tree. We can think of this pair as being associated with the entry pointing to the root node of the tree.

Closest Pair Computation Given an R-tree, we discuss here how to compute the augmented closest pair information to be stored along with an entry e.

Case 1: $Node(e)$ is a leaf page. We can use a plane-sweep algorithm to compute the closest pair of objects among the objects in $Node(e)$.

Case 2: $Node(e)$ is an index page. Suppose the index entries stored in $Node(e)$ are $e_1, \ldots, e_t$, and the augmented information for these entries is computed already. Our task is to find the closest pair (p, q) in the sub-tree rooted by $Node(e)$. Without loss of generality, assume among pairs of objects stored in $e_1, \ldots, e_t$, the pair in e_i has the smallest distance. We know that $distance(p, q) \leq e_i.dist$, and that if $distance(p, q) \neq e_i.dist$, p and q are in different sub-trees. So, we can perform an incremental join on every pair of (e_x, e_y) such that $MinDist(e_x, e_y) < e_i.dist$. Note that here we use a threshold $T = e_i.dist$ to determine whether we join a pair of nodes or not. In fact, the threshold T can be dynamically reduced by: (a) when joining e_x and e_y, if $MinExistDist(e_x, e_y) < T$, set $T = MinExistDist(e_x, e_y)$; and (b) when a pair of objects is found with a smaller distance than T, assign that distance to T.

Insertion Suppose we want to insert a new object o. First, we follow the regular R-tree insertion algorithm to insert the object. We can prove that, among all entries stored in the tree, only those pointing to tree nodes along the insertion path may need to be updated. Let $e_1, \ldots, e_h$ be the index entries pointing to the tree nodes that are along the insertion path. Here e_1 points to the root node, e_h points to the leaf node where the new object o was inserted, and $Node(e_i)$ is a parent node of $Node(e_{i+1})$.

The closest pair stored at e_i needs to be updated if and only if there exists an object o' in the sub-tree rooted by $Node(e_i)$ such that $Distance(o, o') < e_i.dist$. So, we can perform a range search on $Subtree(e_i)$ to see if there exists any object whose distance to o is less than $e_i.dist$. If we find such an object o', we update the closest pair stored at e_i as (o, o'). Otherwise, e_i does not need to be updated.

Notice that these range searches have overlap. For instance, when determining the new closest pair for e_i, we may check $Subtree(e_{i+1})$, since it is part of $Subtree(e_i)$. However, when determining the new closest pair for e_{i+1}, we may check $Subtree(e_{i+1})$ again. These searches can be combined in the following algorithm: (a) Perform a range search on $Subtree(e_1)$ with radius $e_1.dist$ around the new object o, ignoring $Subtree(e_2)$. If any object is found, update the closest pair stored at e_1. (b) Perform a range search on $Subtree(e_2)$ with radius $e_2.dist$ around o, ignoring $Subtree(e_3)$. If any object o' is found, update e_2. If $distance(o, o') < e_1.dist$, update e_1 as well. Extending this method to lower levels of the tree is straightforward.

Now we discuss node splitting. If a node N is split into two, N and N', we need to update the local closest pair information stored at the entries pointing to the two nodes. This can be done by the close-pair computation algorithm given above.

Deletion Similar to the insertion case, after we delete an object o using the R-tree deletion algorithm, in order to maintain the augmented information, only the entries pointing to nodes on the deletion path need to be updated. Let e_i be an entry on the deletion path. The closest pair stored at e_i needs to be updated if and only if the closest pair stored at e_i contains o. Further, we differentiate two cases.

Case 1: $Node(e_i)$ is a leaf node. We perform a plane-sweep algorithm to find the new closest pair of objects in $Node(e_i)$.

Case 2: $Node(e_i)$ is an index node. We perform the closest pair computation algorithm above. But before we do that, there is an optimization. Suppose there exists an index entry se stored in $Node(e_i)$ where $se.dist = e_i.dist$, and the closest pair stored at se does not contain o. In this case, we can simply copy the closest pair stored at se to e_i.

If two tree nodes merge into one, we update the closest pair stored at the new node by performing the closest pair computation algorithm.

Query The query algorithm for the SRCP-tree is given below.

Algorithm _SRCPQuery_(SRCP-tree S, Range R): Given a SRCP-tree S and a spatial range R, find the closest pair of objects of S that are inside R.
1. If both $S.o_1$ and $S.o_2$ are inside R, return $(S.o_1, S.o_2)$.
2. Push $(S, S, S.dist)$ into a priority queue Q, ordered by the third value of each triple.
3. Initialize threshold $T = \infty$ and the query result $(res_1, res_2) = NULL$.
4. **while** (Q is not empty)
   (a) Pop the triple $(e_1, e_2, dist)$ from Q which has the smallest $dist$ value.
   (b) **if** ($Node(e_1)$ is a leaf node)
       for (every object $o_1 \in Node(e_1)$ and $o_2 \in Node(e_2)$ that are inside R and $o_1 \neq o_2$)
           If $distance(o_1, o_2) < T$, update $(res_1, res_2) = (o_1, o_2)$, $T = distance(o_1, o_2)$, then optimize Q.
       end for
       Goto step 4.
       end if
   (c) /* $Node(e_1)$ is an index node */
       for (every entry $se_1 \in Node(e_1)$ and $se_2 \in Node(e_2)$ that both intersect R)

     i. **if** $(se_1 = se_2)$

       A. If $se_1.dist \geq T$, continue the for loop.

       B. If both $se_1.o_1$ and $se_1.o2$ are inside R, update $(res_1, res_2) = (se_1.o_1, se_1.o_2)$, $T = se_1.dist$, then optimize Q, and then continue the for loop.

       C. Push $(se_1, se_1, se_1.dist)$ into Q.

    ii. **else** /* $se_1 \neq se_2$ */

       A. If $MinExistDist(se_1, se_2, R) < T$,

         update $T = MinExistDist(se_1, se_2, R)$ and optimize Q;

       B. If $MinDist(se_1, se_2) < T$,

         push $(se_1, se_2, MinDist(se_1, se_2))$ into Q;

    end if

   end for

  end while

5. return (res_1, res_2);

We explain the algorithm in a little detail. Let S denote both the SRCP-tree and the index entry pointing to the root node of the SRCP-tree S. Since the closest pair of objects (without a range) is stored along with S, step 1 of the algorithm checks to see if both objects in the closest pair are inside the query range R. If yes, we have already found the result and the algorithm finishes. Otherwise, we initialize the processing queue Q by pushing the pair of root entries into Q.

Each element in Q contains a pair of index entries and a distance value. For a pair of two different entries, the value is their $MinDist$. For a pair of the same entry, the value is the closest-pair distance stored in the entry. This distance is a lower bound of the distance of any pair of objects to be found by examining the pair. Thus if during execution of the algorithm, a pair of objects is found with distance smaller than or equal to this distance of some triple in Q, the triple can be safely erased from Q. In fact, this is what we mean when we say "optimize Q" later in the algorithm.

The major task is done in step 4, which pops from Q one triple at a time and processes it. Let the triple be $(e_1, e_2, dist)$. Step 4(b) handles the case when e_1 points to a leaf node (e_2 points to a leaf node as well). We examine every pair of objects, one from each node, that are inside R. If the distance between the two objects is smaller than the currently maintained threshold T, we remember this pair and update T. Note that at this step, we also optimize Q as follows: we remove all triples from Q where $dist$ is no smaller than T.

Step 4(c) handles the case when e_1 and e_2 point to index nodes. In this case, we check every child entry of $Node(e_1)$ against every child entry of $Node(e_2)$. Of course, we only consider the child entries that intersect the query range R. Let the pair of child entries be (se_1, se_2).

A subcase, as shown in step 4(c)i, is when se_1 and se_2 are actually the same entry. Existing algorithms always push such self-pairs into Q, since the distance of a self-pair is regarded to be zero. As shown in step 4(c)iA, our algorithm may avoid pushing this pair into Q, since we already know the minimum distance of any two objects in the sub-tree. Even if the distance of the closest pair stored along with se_1 is smaller than the current threshold T, it is still possible that our algorithm avoids pushing the pair into Q. This case is shown in step 4(c)iB, when both objects in the closest pair stored at se_1 are inside R.

Another subcase, as shown in step 4(c)ii, is when entries se_1 and se_2 point to different nodes. This case is the same as the heap algorithm. First, we check to see if their $MinExistDist$ is smaller than threshold T. If yes, since it is guaranteed that by joining this pair, we can find a pair of objects with distance no larger than that, we can go ahead and update threshold T. After that, we compare the $MinDist$ of the two entries with T and we can avoid pushing this pair into Q if the $MinDist$ is no smaller than T.

4.2   SRCP-Tree (Version Two)

Tree Structure Instead of storing "local" closest pair information $(o_1, o_2, dist)$ in each index entry e as discussed in the previous section, in version two of our structure we store "*local-parent*" closest pair information $(o_c, o_p, dist)$ along with each index entry e. If $Node(e)$ is not the tree root, (o_c, o_p) is the closest pair of objects where o_c comes from objects indexed by $Subtree(e)$ and o_p comes from objects indexed by the subtree rooted by the parent of $Node(e)$. If $Node(e)$ is the tree root, (o_c, o_p) is the closest pair of objects for the whole tree. In both cases, $dist$ is the distance of the two corresponding objects and we could choose not to store it but compute it when in need.

Insertion The insertion algorithm is similar to that of version one. Besides the R-tree insertion algorithm, we need to update the local-parent closest-pair information. We start with the entry S pointing to the root node. Since at the root entry, both versions of the SRCP-tree maintain the same information: the closest pair for the whole tree, to update the information in the second version is the same as in version one.

Now let's go one level down. Suppose the child entries stored inside of $Node(S)$ are A, B and C. Assume the new object o is inserted into $Subtree(B)$. We need to update B if there exists an object in $Subtree(S)$ whose distance to o is smaller than $B.dist$. We can find such an object by performing a range search on $Subtree(S)$. The insertion of o may also affect the information stored at A, if the distance between o and some object in $Subtree(A)$ is smaller than $A.dist$. In order to find such an object, we perform a range search on $Subtree(A)$. The case for C is similar. Notice that this does not mean the whole tree needs to be updated. For instance, the information stored at the children of $Node(A)$ and the children of $Node(C)$ do not need to be updated. Basically, we check the insertion path, and for each entry along the insertion path, we check its sibling entries as well.

Deletion

The deletion algorithm needs to be modified from version one of the structure accordingly. Basically, for each index entry e along the deletion path, we need to modify the information stored at e and the sibling entries of e.

Query The query algorithm here is similar to that of the first version. The difference lies in step 4(c), i.e. when a pair of entries (e_1, e_2) pointing to index nodes are popped from Q and are to be processed. We differentiate two subcases. Case one is when e_1 and e_2 are different entries. In this case, we process every pair of child entries, one from $Node(e_1)$ and the other from $Node(e_2)$, in the same way as step 4(c)ii of the version-one query algorithm does. In the rest, we focus on the other subcase, when an entry e is to be joined with itself.

Let A, B be sibling index entries. If $A.dist \leq B.dist$ and both objects in the closest pair stored at A are inside the query range R, we can determine that there is no need to process any pair consisting of B and a sibling. The reason is that the minimum distance of an object in $Subtree(B)$ and an object in the sub-tree rooted by any of its siblings (including B itself) is $B.dist$, which is no better than the pair stored with A, which we already found.

The above observation motivates our algorithm. To process the pair (e, e), we first determine, among all child entries in $Node(e)$ where both objects in the maintained closest pair are inside R, which one has the smallest $dist$. This smallest distance is defined as $\boldsymbol{SmallestExistDist}(e, R)$. If this smallest distance is smaller than the current threshold T, we can safely update T and update the currently found closest pair, then optimize Q.

Next, we consider another concept: $\boldsymbol{SmallestDist}(e) = min\{se.dist | se$ is a child entry in $Node(e)\}$. This is the smallest $dist$ among those maintained along with every child entry in $Node(e)$, independent to any query range. Obviously, we have: $SmallestDist(e) \leq SmallestExistDist(e, R)$. If the two values are equal, there is no need to push any pair of child entries of e to the processing queue Q at all. This is because, by examining sub-trees of $Node(e)$, the best we can get is a pair of objects with distance being $SmallestDist(e)$, and we have already found such an object with distance $SmallestExistDist(e, R)$.

Now, the only case left is when $SmallestDist(e) < SmallestExistDist(e, R)$. In this case, we examine every pair of child entries (se_1, se_2) of $Node(e)$ that intersect range R. We push this pair into Q if all the following three conditions holds: (a) $MinDist(se_1, se_2) < T$, (b) $se_1.dist < SmallestExistDist(e, R)$, and (c) $se_2.dist < SmallestExistDist(e, R)$. In this case, we push $(se_1, se_2, max\{se_1.dist, se_2.dist\})$ into Q.

4.3   Analytical Comparison of the Algorithms

Our SRCP-trees are obviously better than the straightforward approach of performing a range query and then finding the closest pair on the query result, especially if the query range is large. When there are many objects in the range query result, to maintain them in memory and process them is costly.

Our SRCP-trees should have better query performance than both the incremental join algorithm [10] and the heap algorithm [6]. The main reason is that the two algorithms join every intersecting pair. In particular, in our addressed problem, the two data sets being joined are identical, which leads to extensive overlapping. For instance, every node has zero distance with itself and thus every self pair must be joined. Our algorithms improve on this. In version one, for example, each index entry stores the minimum distance between two objects in the sub-tree. Thus it is quite likely that self pairs do not need to be joined.

Now we compare the two versions of our SRCP-tree. In our previous version, we can get a better performance than incremental join algorithm because it is likely that we can avoid self pair comparison. For example, assume the node pointed by entry S is the parent node of nodes pointed by entries A, B and C. When joining S with itself, in incremental join algorithm, six pairs need to be considered. They are AA, BB, CC, AC, AB, and BC. Version one of our structure is good in that we might eliminate AA, BB and CC according to the local closest pair information they stored. However, we can not eliminate AB, AC and BC, assuming $MinExistDist$ of each of the three pairs is larger than threshold T. The second version of our SRCP-tree can improve in this case. For instance, if $A.dist < B.dist$, and both objects in the closest pair stored at A are inside query range R, we can determine that there is no need to examine any pair involving B. This means we instantly avoid three pairs BB, AB, BC. Thus we believe the second version of the SRCP-tree has better query performance.

The other thing is, even though the two versions of the structure have exactly the same index size, the update cost for the second version is more expensive than the first version, since the second version needs to the sibling entries of every entry along the update path.

4.4   Extensions to Finding k Closest Pairs between Different Types of Objects

In order to find k closest pairs, we can use the same structure, but we modify the query algorithm as follows. We maintain an array of up to k different object pairs instead of one. The threshold we use to optimize the priority queue is the distance of the largest pair in the array.

In a practical scenario, we can have a data set which contains two different types of objects, e.g. high schools and primary schools, and we have an R-tree built on top of the data set. In this case, the query to find the closest pairs of high schools with primary schools is also supported by our techniques. We still augment the R-tree with some closest pair information, with the extension that each closest pair should contain one primary school and one high school, not the same type of schools.

5   Experimental Result

5.1   Experimental Setup

Since we know for sure that the range query followed by plane-sweep is not good especially when the query range is large, we implemented the heap algorithm [6], and the two versions of our SRCP trees. The query algorithm for each structure is implemented as we discussed in section 3 and section 4.

We implemented all of these structures in Java using XXL Library [20]. Our experiments were run on a PC with a 2.66-GHz Pentium 4 processor. Each tree node capacity is set to be between $m = 10$ and $M = 20$.

We test our experiments on two different data sets.

(1) We randomly generated data sets of size 20k, 40k, 60k, 80k with uniform-like distribution.

(2) We also use a real data set from US National Mapping Information web site (URL: http://mappings. usgs.gov/www/gnis/). We use the longitude and latitude of 26700 sites from Massachusetts as a 2D point data set. Notice that in the original file, some sites have the same position. We consider them as the same point. Here the 26700 is the number of total points.

For each data set, we test each structure with query range 1%, 5%, 10%, 20%, 40%, 60%, 80% and 100% of the total area that the data set covers. We randomly generated 20 queries for each query range and the average running time is calculated.

(3) Furthermore, we experimented with objects with extents. For simplicity, we assume square objects. We use the 40K data set described in case (1) as the center of each object, while each object is extended as a square of fixed size. The object size is described as *area ratio*, which is defined as $\frac{O}{T} * 100\%$, where O is the area of an object and T is the area covered by the whole data set. Given a fixed query range 40% of T, we test each structure with area ratio 0.001%, 0.01%, 0.1%, 1% and 10%. For each ratio, 20 queries are randomly generated and the average running time is given.

5.2   Performance Comparison

We first compare the algorithms when the query range is small, between 1% and 10% of the space. As shown in Figure 3(a), the query time increases for all three structures. But both versions of SRCP outperform the heap algorithm. As the query range increases, more nodes will intersect the query range. Hence the comparison numbers and query times will increase. But due to the pre-computed information stored in both versions of SRCP trees, some branch can be eliminated before any calculation. That's why SRCP tree gains a better query performance in this situation. We also observe that the second version of the SRCP-tree has better performance.

When the query range is large, as shown in Figure 3(b), the query time for heap algorithm increases as it does for a small query range due to the same reason. However, the query time of SRCP trees decrease dramatically. This is

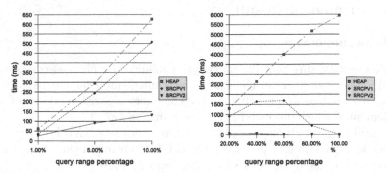

(a) Small query range comparison (b) Large query range comparison

Fig. 3. Different query range comparion for a 40K data set

because when the query range gets larger, the probability that a CP pair is in the query range also increases. The special case is when the query range is the same as the root node MBR. In this situation, we know for sure that the closest pair stored along with the root entry will be the desired pair. Hence the query time for it is almost zero.

We also compare the same query area ratio (10% of space) with different data sets. As we can see in Figure 4, when the size of a data set increases, the query time for the same area ratio will also increase, which is reasonable. When the data set contains more objects, the number of objects in the query range will be bigger. So there are more calculations. This causes the increase of query time when the data set size gets larger. However, we still observe that our approaches are much better than the existing approach, and that the second version of our structure is more robust.

Figure 5 shows the query result in the real data set (the Massachusetts sites). In this experiment, SRCP trees outperform the heap algorithm even more than it does in the randomly generated data case. This is because in the real data

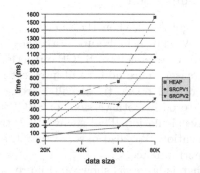

Fig. 4. Varying the number of objects

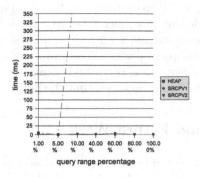

Fig. 5. Range query comparison for a real data set

set, many sites are very close to each other, especially some pairs has a distance almost zero. So in each page, one can always find a pair with very small distance. It is more like for SRCP query algorithm to stop when such a pair is found.

Our structure works for not only point data but also non-point data. Figure 6 is the query result of objects with extents. In this experiment, SRCP trees again have a better performance than heap algorithm. Notice that when the object area is enlarged, the performance of SRCP trees keeps almost unchanged while the query time of heap algorithm increases dramatically. In other words, SRCP trees outperform heap algorithm more when the object area gets larger.This is due to the fact that when object becomes larger, the MBR of the leaf node that contains this object is also augmented. The enlargement of the leaf node MBR will then cause the MBR of its parent node to be increased. The augmentation will be propogated till the root node. This senario makes the overlap between sibling MBRs happen more often. As we have seen, overlap is the key reason that gives the heap algorithm a poor performance while SRCP trees doesn't sacrifice too much from overlap.

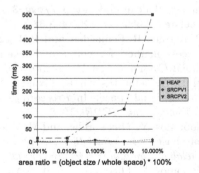

Fig. 6. Non-point data sets with different area ratio. A fixed value is used for the space covered by the data set

Generally speaking, SRCP tree gains a much better performance on CP range query problem and index maintenance (the update algorithm is around three times slower) than heap algorithm with limited additional cost in space usage . That's a tradeoff between query performance and index maintainable time. Here we assume the maintenance is less often than range query, which is a practical assumption. Due to space limitations, we omit the performance for index update.

6   Conclusions and Future Work

In this paper, we have extended the spatial closest-pair problem to involve a query range. This problem, although practical, has not been addressed in the literature. In particular, we consider the case where the closest pairs are supposed to come from a single index. We have proposed two versions of a new index structure (the SRCP-tree) to solve this new problem. We compare our approaches with straightforward approaches, both analytically and experimentally. Performance results show that our methods are more robust than existing approaches. Among the two versions of our structures, the second version has overall the best query performance.

As for future directions, we are working on supporting the closest pair queries for multiple types of objects. For instance, the data set may maintain schools, bars, supermarkets, etc. The query may ask for k closest pairs of any two types of objects. One way to solve this problem by extending our solutions is that each index entry maintains, for each pair of different types, some local closest pair information. However, this is costly if there are many different types. We are seeking for more efficient solutions.

References

[1] Oracle8 spatial cartridge.
http://technet.oracle.com/products/oracle8/ info/sdods/xsdo7ds.htm.
252

[2] IBM informix spatial datablade module. http://www-3.ibm.com/software/data/
informix/pubs/specsheets/SWSEC27152000D.pdf. 252

[3] N. Beckmann, H.-P. Kriegel, R. Schneider, and B. Seeger. The R*-Tree: an efficient and robust access method for points and rectangles. In *Proceedings of ACM/SIGMOD Annual Conference on Management of Data*, 1990. 254

[4] S. Berchtold, B. Ertl, D. A. Keim, H.-P. Kriegel, and T. Seidl. Fast nearest neighbor search in high-dimensional space. In *Proceedings of the 14th International Conference on Data Engineering (ICDE)*, 1998. 256

[5] A. Corral, Y. Manolopoulos, Y. Theodoridis, and M. Vassilakopoulos. Closest pair queries in spatial databases. *Technical Report, Aristotle Univ. of Thessaloniki, Greece, url=http://delab.csd.auth.gr/~michaliz/cpq.html*, 1999. 252, 255

[6] A. Corral, Y. Manolopoulos, Y. Theodoridis, and M. Vassilakopoulos. Closest pair queries in spatial databases. In *Proceedings of ACM/SIGMOD Annual Conference on Management of Data*, 2000. 252, 255, 258, 264, 265

[7] M. Dietzfelbinger, T. Hagerup, J. Katajainen, and M. Penttonen. A reliable randomized algorithm for the closest-pair problem. *Journal of Algorithms*, 25(1), 1997. 252, 255

[8] V. Gaede and O. Günther. Multidimensional access methods. *ACM Computing Surveys*, 30(2), 1998. 254

[9] A. Guttman. R-trees: a dynamic index structure for spatial searching. In *Proceedings of ACM/SIGMOD Annual Conference on Management of Data*, 1984. 254

[10] G. R. Hjaltason and H. Samet. Incremental distance join algorithms for spatial databases. In *Proceedings of ACM/SIGMOD Annual Conference on Management of Data*, Seattle, WA, USA, 1998. 252, 255, 258, 264

[11] G. R. Hjaltason and H. Samet. Distance browsing in spatial databases. *ACM Transactions on Database Systems (TODS)*, June 1999. 256

[12] N. Katayama and S. Satoh. The SR-tree: An index structure for high-dimensional nearest neighbor queries. In *Proceedings of ACM/SIGMOD Annual Conference on Management of Data*, 1997. 256

[13] G. Kollios, D. Gunopulos, and V. J. Tsotras. Nearest neighbor queries in a mobile environment. In *Proceedings of the International Workshop on Spatio-Temporal Database Management*, pages 119–134, 1999. 256

[14] F. Korn and S. Muthukrishnan. Influence sets based on reverse nearest neighbor queries. In *Proceedings of ACM/SIGMOD Annual Conference on Management of Data*, 2000. 256

[15] N. Roussopoulos, S. Kelly, and F. Vincent. Nearest neighbor queries. In *Proceedings of ACM/SIGMOD Annual Conference on Management of Data*, 1995. 254, 255, 256

[16] T. Seidl and H.-P. Kriegel. Optimal multi-step k-nearest neighbor search. In *Proceedings of ACM/SIGMOD Annual Conference on Management of Data*, 1998. 256

[17] M. Smid. Closest point problems in computational geometry. In J.-R. Sack and J. Urrutia, editors, *Handbook on Computational Geometry*. Elsevier Science Publishing, 1997. 252, 255

[18] Z. Song and N. Roussopoulos. K-nearest neighbor search for moving query point. In *Proceedings of the 7th International Symposium on Spatial and Temporal Databases*, pages 79–96, 2001. 256

[19] I. Stanoi, D. Agrawal, and A. E. Abbadi. Reverse nearest neighbor queries for dynamic databases. In *Proceedings of the ACM SIGMOD Workshop on Research Issu in Data Mining and Knowledge Discovery*, 2000. 256

[20] J. van den Bercken, J.-P. Dittrich B. Blohsfeld, J. Krämer, T. Schäfer, M. Schneider, and B. Seeger. XXL- a library arrproach to supporting efficient implementations of advanced database queries. In *Proceedings of the 27th VLDB Conference*, 2001. 265

[21] C. Yang and K. Lin. An index structure for improving closest pairs and related join queries in spatial databses. In *Proceedings of the International Database Engineering and Applications Symposium (IDEAS'02)*, 2002. 252, 253, 255, 256, 257

[22] C. Yang and K.-I. Lin. An index structure for efficient reverse nearest neighbor queries. In *Proceedings of the 14th International Conference on Data Engineering (ICDE)*, 01. 256

[23] D. Zhang, V. J. Tsotras, and B. Seeger. A comparison of indexed temporal joins. *Tech Report, UCR-CS-00-03, CS Dept., UC Riverside*, http://www.cs.ucr.edu/~donghui/publications/tempjoin.ps, 2000. 255

[24] D. Zhang, V. J. Tsotras, and B. Seeger. Efficient temporal join processing using indices. In *Proceedings of the 14th International Conference on Data Engineering (ICDE)*, 2002. 255

Evaluation of Iceberg Distance Joins

Yutao Shou[1], Nikos Mamoulis[1], Huiping Cao[1],
Dimitris Papadias[2], and David W. Cheung[1]

[1] Department of Computer Science and Information Systems
University of Hong Kong
Pokfulam Road, Hong Kong
{ytshou,nikos,hpcao,dcheung}@csis.hku.hk
[2] Department of Computer Science
Hong Kong University of Science and Technology
Clear Water Bay, Hong Kong
dimitris@cs.ust.hk

Abstract. The iceberg distance join returns object pairs within some distance from each other, provided that the first object appears at least a number of times in the result, e.g., "find hotels which are within 1km to at least 10 restaurants". The output of this query is the subset of the corresponding distance join (e.g., "find hotels which are within 1km to some restaurant") that satisfies the additional cardinality constraint. Therefore, it could be processed by using a conventional spatial join algorithm and then filtering-out the non-qualifying pairs. This approach, however, is expensive, especially when the cardinality constraint is highly selective. In this paper, we propose output-sensitive algorithms that prune the search space by integrating the cardinality with the distance constraint. We deal with cases of indexed/non-indexed datasets and evaluate the performance of the proposed techniques with extensive experimental evaluation covering a wide range of problem parameters.

1 Introduction

The most common types of spatial joins involve *intersection* (e.g., "find all pairs of roads and rivers that intersect") or *distance* predicates (e.g., "find all hotels that are within 100 meters from the coastline"). A large amount of research work has been devoted to spatial joins due to their applicability in various GIS operations (e.g., map overlay) and high execution cost, which, in the worst case, is quadratic to the size of the data. Several algorithms have been proposed to minimize the cost, considering cases where both [6], one [18, 21], or neither [23, 19, 2] dataset is indexed. Even though these methods were originally developed for intersection joins, they can be easily adapted for distance joins (i.e., by extending the object boundaries by $\epsilon/2$ [17, 20]). Nevertheless, spatial join operators are optimized for queries that require *all* join results.

For typical geographic layers (e.g., rivers with road-lines), the size of the join result is linear to the size of the data. However, users who want to analyze spatial data often impose additional constraints that restrict the output size.

T. Hadzilacos et al. (Eds.): SSTD 2003, LNCS 2750, pp. 270–288, 2003.

Such a query is the *iceberg distance join*, which, given two relations R, S, a distance threshold ϵ, and a cardinality threshold t, returns object pairs $\langle r, s \rangle$, $(r \in R,\ s \in S)$ within distance ϵ from each other, provided that r appears at least t times in the join result. An example of a semi-join query in this class is "find hotels which are close to *at least t* restaurants". In pseudo-SQL it could be expressed as follows:

```
SELECT H.id
FROM Hotels H, Restaurants R
WHERE dist(H.location,R.location) <= ε
GROUP BY H.id
HAVING COUNT(*) >= t ;
```

A spatial DBMS would evaluate this query by (i) processing the spatial join using some existing algorithm and (ii) sorting/hashing the qualifying $\langle r, s \rangle$ pairs by $r.id$ to output all $r \in R$ which appear more than t times in the joined pairs. The spatial join operator itself may produce many results before filtering out the ones that do not qualify the cardinality constraint t. In other words, the methodology above is not *output sensitive*, i.e., its cost does not depend on the result size, which is affected by t.

In this paper we propose output sensitive algorithms, by "pushing" the cardinality constraint t into the spatial join operators in order to filter out large parts of the search space. We study the cases of both indexed and both non-indexed joined datasets, by extending efficient algorithms for each case. The rest of the paper is organized as follows. Section 2 provides background and related work. In Section 3 we describe and optimize techniques for iceberg distance joins. Section 4 evaluates the proposed techniques with comprehensive experiments. Finally, Section 5 concludes the paper with a discussion about related work.

2 Background and Related Work

Although our methods are applicable to any space-partitioning access method, we only consider R–trees [11] due to their simplicity and popularity. The R–tree indexes minimum bounding rectangles (MBRs) of objects and processes fast the filter step of the most important query types, i.e., range queries, nearest neighbors [14], and spatial joins. Section 2.1 provides background on intersection join algorithms, while section 2.2 discusses distance join processing. Section 2.3 reviews related work on iceberg queries and motivates the problem studied in this paper.

2.1 Spatial Joins

The R–tree join (RJ) [6] is the most influential algorithm for spatial joins when both datasets are indexed by R–trees. Starting from the two roots, it synchronously traverses the trees, following entry pairs that intersect. Upon reaching

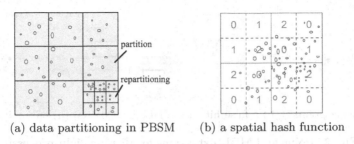

(a) data partitioning in PBSM   (b) a spatial hash function

Fig. 1. Example of PBSM

the leaves, pairs of intersecting object MBRs are output. RJ employs two heuristics that greatly reduce its computational cost. Given two nodes n_R and n_S to be joined, if an entry e_R in node n_R does not intersect the MBR of node n_S (i.e., the MBR of all entries contained in n_S), then there can be no entry $e_S \in n_S$, such that e_R and e_S overlap. Using this observation, RJ performs two linear scans in the entries of both nodes before applying intersection tests, and prunes from each node the entries that do not intersect the MBR of the other node. The second technique (*forward sweep* [2]), is based on plane sweep and applies sorting on one dimension in order to reduce the quadratic number of comparisons for candidate entry pairs. A breadth-first version of RJ with improved I/O cost was proposed in [15].

The Partition Based Spatial Merge join (PBSM) [23] is based on the relational hash join operator and applies on two non-indexed sets. The space is regularly partitioned using an orthogonal grid and objects from both datasets are hashed into the partitions, replicating the ones that span boundaries. Figure 1a illustrates a regular space partitioning incurred by PBSM and some data hashed into the partitions. Data hashed into the same partitions are then joined in memory using plane sweep. If two buckets to be joined do not fit in memory, the algorithm is recursively applied for their contents. Since data from both datasets may be replicated, the simple version of the algorithm may produce duplicates; however, these can be avoided by a simple check [9, 20]. When the data to be joined are skewed, some partitions may contain a large percentage of the hashed objects, whereas others very few objects, rendering the algorithm inefficient. To handle skewed data, the cells of the grid are distributed to partitions according to a hash function and the space covered by a partition is no longer continuous, but consists of a number of scattered tiles. Figure 1b shows such a (round-robin like) spatial hash function, where tiles with the same number are assigned to the same bucket. A parallel, non-blocking version of PBSM was proposed in [20].

Koudas and Sevcik [16] proposed a hierarchical partitioning that avoids data replication, by assigning each object to the topmost layer where it does not span any grid line. The Spatial Hash Join (SHJ) algorithm [19] defines hash-buckets with irregular extents (which may overlap), such that each object from the inner dataset is hashed to exactly one bucket and only objects from the outer one may be replicated. Finally, the method proposed in [2] applies external plane sweep

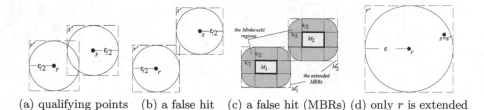

(a) qualifying points   (b) a false hit   (c) a false hit (MBRs) (d) only r is extended

Fig. 2. Point and MBR extensions for distance join processing

after sorting both datasets on an axis. This method was later extended in [1] to a unified technique for indexed and non-indexed inputs.

Another class of algorithms aims at joining a non-indexed dataset with an R–tree. The Seeded Tree Join algorithm (STJ) [18] builds a second R–tree using the existing one as a seed and then applies RJ. Slot Index Spatial Join (SISJ) [21] is a hybrid of STJ and SHJ, which uses the existing R–tree in order to determine the bucket extents. If H is the desired number of hash buckets, SISJ finds the topmost level of the tree such that the number of entries is larger or equal to H. These entries are then grouped into H (possibly overlapping) partitions called *slots*, which define the bucket extents. Each slot contains the MBR of the indexed R–tree entries, along with a list of pointers to these entries. The grouping policy used by SISJ is based on the the the splitting heuristic of the R*–tree [3]. The hashing and joining phase of SISJ is similar to the corresponding phases of SHJ; all data from the R–tree indexed by a slot are loaded and joined with the corresponding hash-bucket.

2.2   Distance Joins and Related Queries

Research on the *distance join* operator has mainly focused on point datasets, because they are more relevant in applications of higher dimensionality (e.g., image processing, data mining), where the data are points. If two points r and s are within distance ϵ, then the circles d_r, d_s with centers r, s and radii $\epsilon/2$ intersect, implying that their MBRs r' and s' intersect, as illustrated in Figure 2a. Therefore, given two point sets R and S that fit in memory, we can reduce the $O(|R||S|)$ distance join cost, by applying a plane-sweep algorithm on the MBRs of their circles. Then, we remove any false hits (like the one in Figure 2b) by exact distance calculations. Notice that point extension can be performed dynamically and on-demand for each value of ϵ, without any pre-computations. Figure 2c shows how this method can be generalized for R–tree MBRs (i.e., for the RJ algorithm), which are extended to *Minkowsky* regions and approximated by rectangles. An alternative method, which simplifies the join, is to extend by ϵ and approximate only the points (and MBRs) of one dataset. Figure 2d illustrates the extension and approximation of r only, in the configuration of Figure 2a. Distance joins are closely related to *similarity retrieval* in high-dimensional spaces. [25] present the dynamic construction of a tree that indexes the points using one dimension per level, and can efficiently find point pairs within distance ϵ. [17] develop a generalization of the algorithm in [16] and compare it with an extension of RJ. Finally, an optimized method for problems of medium dimensionality (e.g., 5–10 dimensions) is proposed in [5]. In summary, these techniques are suitable for high dimensional problems without cardinality constraints and for the case when the qualifying pairs are retrieved from the same dataset.

For the spatial (i.e., 2-dimensional) domain, the algorithms of the previous section are still applicable with some modifications. Furthermore, related work has been proposed in the context of *closest pairs* (CP) queries. Given a threshold k, a CP query retrieves the k closest pairs $\langle r, s \rangle$, $r \in R$, $s \in S$. CP queries have been studied only for the case, where both R and S are indexed by R–trees. [13] present an *incremental* algorithm (for unknown k), which is optimized in [26]. [8] show that a depth-first join algorithm, adapted from RJ, can minimize random I/Os in the presence of a buffer.

2.3   Iceberg Queries

The term *iceberg* query was defined in [10] to characterize a class of relational queries that retrieve aggregate values above some specified threshold (defined by a HAVING clause). An example of an iceberg query in SQL is shown below:

```
SELECT part, region, sum(quantity)
FROM Sales
GROUP BY part, region
HAVING sum(quantity) >= l;
```

The motivation is that the data analyst is interested in retrieving only exceptional aggregate values that may be helpful for decision support. In this example, we want to find $\langle part, region \rangle$ pairs with many sales, in order to organize advertisement campaigns there. A typical query optimizer would first perform the aggregation for each $\langle part, region \rangle$ group and then find the ones whose aggregate value exceeds the threshold. In order to avoid useless aggregations for the pairs which disqualify the query, [10] present several hash-based methods with output-sensitive cost. Similar techniques for data cubes and On-Line Analytical Processing are proposed by [4, 12].

The efficient processing of iceberg queries is also relevant to Spatial Databases. We focus on iceberg distance joins, since joins are hard by nature and potential improvements are very beneficial. Our proposal includes extensions, which can be easily integrated to existing spatial join algorithms by the Spatial DBMS developer. Notice that the algorithms in [10] are not applicable for our problem, since they consider aggregate queries (not joins) on relational data.

3   Algorithms for Iceberg Distance Joins

Figure 3 illustrates an iceberg distance join example. The user is interested in retrieving hotels and the restaurants within ϵ distance from them, provided that the number of such restaurants is at least $t = 3$. The result of the iceberg join should be $\{\langle h_2, r_2\rangle, \langle h_2, r_3\rangle, \langle h_2, r_4\rangle\}$. On the other hand, h_1 and h_3 are also close to some restaurants (i.e., they belong to the result of the conventional distance join) but they do not qualify the cardinality threshold t.

The iceberg distance join is an asymmetric operator, since the cardinality constraint t applies only on the occurrences of values from R. In other words, $R \bowtie S \neq S \bowtie R$, in general. Due to this property we have to distinguish between the four cases (i) R and S are not indexed, (ii) R and S are indexed, (iii) only R is indexed, or (iv) only S is indexed. For each of the above cases we discuss how to process the cardinality constraint t together with the join. For joined inputs that fall into case (i), we propose extensions of PBSM [23]. For case (ii), we extend RJ [6] and we discuss adaptations of SISJ [21] for cases (iii) and (iv). Finally, we show how our methods can be applied for variations of the iceberg distance join query.

3.1 R and S Are Not Indexed

When neither dataset is indexed, we can process the join, using a hash algorithm based on PBSM [23], called *Partitioned Iceberg Distance Join* (PIDJ). In this section, we present a number of progressively more optimized variations of this method.

Avoiding Duplication of Results and Sorting. In order to avoid sorting the results for validating the cardinality constraint, and at the same time eliminate duplicates, we extend only the objects in S by ϵ. In other words, each point in R is hashed to *exactly one* bucket, based on the cell that contains it. On the other hand, points from S are extended to circles and hashed to multiple partitions (for each cell they intersect). For instance, point $s \in S$ depicted in Figure 4 is hashed to buckets corresponding to cells C_2, C_4, and C_5. Finding these cells is a two-step process. First, we locate the cells, which intersect the circle-bounding

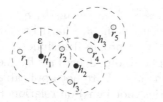

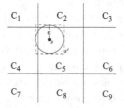

Fig. 3. Iceberg distance join example   **Fig. 4.** Replication of points from S

rectangle s' (i.e., C_1, C_2, C_4, and C_5). Then, the distance to the qualifying cell boundaries is computed and used to prune false alarms (i.e., C_1).

The second phase of the algorithm, loads for each cell C_x the corresponding buckets R_x and S_x and joins them. If the buckets are too large to be joined in memory, their contents are repartitioned using a finer grid and PIDJ is applied recursively. Here, we have to note that in most cases at least R_x will fit in memory, since only points from S_x are replicated. In such cases repartitioning can be avoided, by building for example a main-memory R–tree for R_x, as suggested by [19, 21]. Because the points from R are not duplicated, we can immediately count their occurrences in the joined pairs. Thus, after obtaining the results for the bucket pair $\langle R_x, S_x \rangle$, we sort them in memory on $r.id$ and report the pairs for those $r.id$ that appear at least t times.

Filtering out Small Buckets. If the distance threshold ϵ is small and the cardinality threshold t is large, we can expect that some joined buckets will not return any results. This can happen, when the number of objects in S_x is smaller than t, in which case, it is obvious that no $r \in R_x$ qualifies the query. Therefore, we can use the cardinalities of the buckets, which are already tracked, to prune bucket pairs.

Although this method already avoids loading some bucket pairs, we can still do better by re-scheduling the hashing process. Thus, we first hash S and then R. By doing so, we can immediately spot the cells, which may not contain any results, and mark them. This approach has two benefits. First, all data from R which fall into disqualifying cells are filtered out immediately; hashing them to a bucket (i.e., writing them) is avoided. Second, pages from the memory buffer, which would normally be allocated for disqualified partitions, are now free for use by the remaining partitions.

Filtering out Uniform, Sparse Buckets. Filtering cells that contain fewer than t points from S can reduce the join cost significantly if t is large, but it can still leave many buckets S_x which provide no result. Can we do better? The answer is yes, if we have knowledge about the distribution of points inside each bucket. The rationale is that if the points from S_x are uniformly distributed and the cell extent is much larger than ϵ, we can prune the bucket, or parts of the bucket that may not give any results.

To illustrate the idea, consider the shaded cell C_x of Figure 5a, and assume for simplicity that the length of each side of the cell is $4 \times \epsilon$. While hashing S, we construct a *fine* grid $\mathcal{F}$ with *microcells* of length ϵ at each side, which captures the distribution of objects in S. The dashed cells in Figure 5a show the part of this grid that *influence* cell C_x, i.e., the distribution of points whose extended circle intersects C_x. A counter for each microcell indicates the number of points from S which fall there.

Let us assume that $t = 50$ and have a closer look to the points in S_x that fall into and around the individual microcells of length ϵ in C_x. Observe that the points from R that fall into the microcell c_1 shown in Figure 5b can only

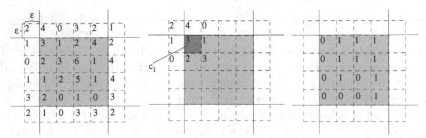

(a) a fine statistical grid (b) the influence cells of c_1 (c) the filtering bitmap

Fig. 5. Pruning buckets or data space using an ϵ-length grid

join with objects in S_x that fall into c_1 and its surrounding microcells (i.e., the numbered ones in Figure 5b). The total number of objects in these microcells is just $16 < t$, indicating that *no object from R that falls into c_1 can participate in the iceberg join result.* All microcells in C_x are eliminated by this process, thus we can prune the whole C_x. Observe that C_x cannot be pruned by considering only the total number of points in this partition, since $|S_x| = 75 \geq t$.

In addition, this method can also save us I/Os even when C_x is not pruned. Assume for example that $t = 20$. Figure 5c shows a bitmap for C_x, indicating which microcells may contain qualifying points from R. The bitmap can be constructed by adding to a microcell's counter the counters of the surrounding ones. We use this (lightweight) bitmap as a replacement of the fine grid $\mathcal{F}$, to prune points from R, while hashing the dataset; if a point $r \in R$ falls into a microcell with a 0, it can be immediately eliminated, reducing the size of R_x on disk. The generation, computation and management of $\mathcal{F}$ and its associated bitmap comes with little overhead, assuming that $|S|$ is much larger than the total number of microcells. For instance, if $\epsilon = 1\%$ of the map's length, we need space for 10,000 integers, or just 40Kb of memory. If ϵ is much smaller, we can use as length a multiple of ϵ, trading memory space with accuracy. The speedup improvement due to this technique is significant, as demonstrated in Section 4.

Figure 6 shows a pseudocode of PIDJ with all optimizations we have discussed. Before join processing, the space is partitioned at two levels, by the regular grid $\mathcal{G}$ which defines the buckets and by the fine grid $\mathcal{F}$ (lines 1–2). A counter for the number of points from S that fall in each microcell, is initialized (lines 3–4). Then, S is read and each $s \in S$ is hashed to the buckets that correspond to the cells intersected by its extended area (lines 5–9). After hashing S, cells with fewer objects than t are pruned. For each cell C_x that is not pruned, a bitmap like the one in Figure 5c is defined (using $\mathcal{F}$) to mark regions, in which points from R can potentially participate in the result. If there are no such regions, we can prune the whole cell (lines 10–16). The next phase of the algorithm hashes each point from R to exactly one cell C_r that contains it, provided that neither this cell nor the corresponding microcell c_r from $\mathcal{F}$ have been pruned (lines 17–21). Finally, the algorithm loads all bucket pairs that cor-

Algorithm $PIDJ$(Objectset R, Objectset S, real e, int t)
1.   define the regular grid $\mathcal{G}$ according to the available memory; /* like PBSM */
2.   define the *fine* grid $\mathcal{F}$ according to ϵ;
3.   **for each** microcell $c_x \in \mathcal{F}$
4. $c_x.count := 0$;
5.   **for each** object $s \in S$
6.   extend s to a circle s_c with center s and radius ϵ;
7.   **for each** cell $C_s \in \mathcal{G}$ intersected by s_c
8.   hash s to the corresponding partition S_s;
9. $c_s :=$ microcell in $\mathcal{F}$ containing s; $c_s.count$++;
10.   **for each** cell $C_x \in \mathcal{G}$
11.   **if** $|S_x| < t$ /*size of corresponding partition of S is small */
12.   prune C_x;
13.   **else**
14.   use fine grid $\mathcal{F}$ to compute $c_y.bit, \forall c_y \in C_x$ (and $C_x.bitmap$);
15.   **if** $C_x.bitmap$ has no 1's
16.   prune C_x;
17.   **for each** object $r \in R$
18. $C_r :=$ cell in $\mathcal{G}$ containing r;
19. $c_r :=$ microcell in $\mathcal{F}$ containing r;
20.   **if** C_r has not been pruned and $c_r.bit = 1$
21.   hash r into partition R_r that corresponds to C_r;
22.   **for each** cell $C_x \in \mathcal{G}$
23.   **if** C_x has not been pruned
24.   load R_x and S_x and perform the distance join in memory;
25.   **for each** $r \in R_x$ in the join result
26.   **if** r appears at least t times in the result;
27.   output all join pairs that contain r;

Fig. 6. Partitioned Iceberg Distance Join

respond to active cells, performs the distance join in memory, and applies the cardinality constraint t to output the qualifying pairs (lines 22–27).

3.2 R and S Are Indexed

In this section we propose extensions of the R–tree join algorithm [6] for the iceberg join query. The join can be evaluated by (i) applying RJ to get all object pairs $\langle r, s \rangle$ within distance ϵ, and (ii) sorting them by $r.id$ to bring together pairs with the same $r.id$ in order to validate the threshold constraint t. Sorting (or hashing) in step (ii) is essential, since RJ does not produce the pairs clustered by $r.id$. In the next section we propose a modification of RJ that employs a priority queue to produce the join results clustered. In section 3.2 we propose an improved version of this algorithm that can save I/Os by pruning nodes in the R–tree of R, which may not point to qualifying $r \in R$.

Avoiding Sorting. RJ is a *depth-first* search algorithm, since after joining a pair of nodes, it solves the subproblems created by their intersecting entries one by one. Thus it holds in memory only two paths p_R and p_S from the R–trees that index R and S, respectively. On the other hand, our adapted *R–tree based Iceberg Distance Join* (RIDJ) algorithm traverses the trees in a fashion between *depth-first* search and *breadth-first* search. We use a priority queue PQ, which organizes qualifying entry pairs $\langle e_R, e_S \rangle$ with respect to the lower x-coordinate e_R's MBR. Ties are broken by using e_R's node level as a second priority key; higher level entries get higher priority. In case of an additional tie, we use $e_R.id$ as a second key to prevent interleaving of entry pairs at the same level with the same lower x-coordinate. Initially, PQ contains the roots of the trees (i.e., their MBRs and pointers to them). At each step of the algorithm, the first pair is fetched from PQ and the distance join algorithm is applied for the corresponding nodes. When joining a pair of nodes n_R and n_S, the qualifying entry pairs $\langle e_R, e_S \rangle$ are enqueued in PQ. By continuing this way, the algorithm guarantees that the distance join results $\langle r, s \rangle$ will be clustered by $r.id$. The trade-off is that more memory might be required compared to the original RJ. A similar technique that employs a priority queue to traverse data in sorted order was proposed in [1].

A pseudocode of the algorithm is shown in Figure 7. At each step it gets the next pair $\langle e_i, e_j \rangle$ from PQ, which can be either a pair of intermediate node entries or a pair of objects. In the first case, it applies the main-memory distance join algorithm for the R–tree nodes pointed by e_i and e_j and enqueues the qualifying entry pairs (lines 7–8). In the second case, it continuously removes pairs from PQ as long as they contain the same entry e_i. These correspond to the results of the distance join algorithm. Since they are clustered by $r.id$, we can count them immediately in order to validate the cardinality constraint t (lines 10–14) and output potential pairs that qualify the iceberg join. The pseudocode assumes that the two R–trees have the same height, but it can be easily extended for the general case. Details are omitted for the sake of readability.

Pruning R-Tree Nodes Early. The only benefit of the RIDJ algorithm described above compared to RJ, is that it avoids sorting the distance join results for validating the cardinality constraint t. However, it does not consider t during the R–tree join process. In this section, we propose an improved version that prunes R–tree nodes early, considering t. The motivation is that, due to PQ, the node pairs to be joined are produced clustered on R. In other words, if $\langle e_i, e_j \rangle$ is the pair currently first in PQ, we know that if there are any other pairs containing e_i, these will be the next ones in the queue.

We can exploit this property to prune node pairs as follows. Whenever we retrieve a pair $\langle e_i, e_j \rangle$ from PQ, we continue fetching more pairs $\langle e_R, e_S \rangle$ as long as $e_i.id = e_R.id$ (just like we do for the leaf level). Now for the current $e_i \in R$ we have a list $L(e_i) = \{e_{S1}, e_{S2}, \ldots, e_{Sk}\}$ that join with it and we know that these are the only ones (at the same level in the R–tree indexing S) that join with e_i. If the total number of points indexed by entries in $L(e_i)$ is smaller than t, no object in R indexed by the subtree rooted at e_i can participate in the result.

Algorithm $RIDJ$(Objectset R, Objectset S, real e, int t)
1. $e_R := \langle$MBR of R, ptr to root node of R's R–tree $\rangle$;
2. $e_S := \langle$MBR of S, ptr to root node of S's R–tree $\rangle$;
3.   Initialize PQ and enqueue $\langle e_R, e_S \rangle$;
4.   **while** PQ is not empty
5.   get next $\langle e_i, e_j \rangle$ from PQ;
6.   **if** e_i and e_j are non-leaf node entries
7.   distance-join nodes n_i, n_j pointed by e_i and e_j; /* same as in RJ */
8.   add qualifying entry pairs $\langle e_R, e_S \rangle$, $e_R \in n_R$, $e_S \in n_S$ to PQ;
9.   **else** /* e_i and e_j are leaf node entries */
10. $counter := 1$;
11.   **while** $e_i.id = e_R.id$ of the first pair $\langle e_R, e_S \rangle$ in PQ
12.   get next $\langle e_R, e_S \rangle$ from PQ and put it in a memory-buffer B;
13. $counter := counter + 1$;
14.   **if** $counter > t$ output $\langle e_i, e_j \rangle$ and the results in B; /* found results */

Fig. 7. R–tree based Iceberg Distance Join

Thus we do not have to join the node pairs indexed by e_i and the entries in $L(e_i)$. Using this observation, we can prune early many R–tree node pairs if t is large enough. Since the exact number of objects indexed by an intermediate entry is not known, we use an upper bound based on the fanout of the tree nodes.[1] Alternatively we could employ the *aggregate R–tree* [22], which stores for each intermediate entry the number of objects in its sub-tree.

3.3   Only one Dataset Is Indexed

In this section, we discuss an adaptation of SISJ that borrows ideas from PIDJ (discussed in Section 3.1). Let us first assume that only dataset R is indexed. While hashing S, we construct the fine grid $\mathcal{F}$ and create a bitmap for each slot, similar to the one depicted in Figure 5c. If all bits in this bitmap are 0, we can prune the corresponding slot, which means (a) we avoid loading the part of the tree indexed by this slot, (b) we avoid loading the corresponding bucket from S. Naturally, we expect this technique to work best for small values of ϵ, large values of t, and uniform data from S in the pruned buckets.

The case where S is indexed is harder to handle. The reason is that objects $r \in R$ are now replicated to multiple buckets. Therefore it is possible that some r

---

[1] When e_i points to a leaf node, we perform an additional optimization. The entries in $L(e_i)$ are clustered to sets, such that no two entries in different sets are within distance ϵ from each other. Then, we initially use an upper bound for the total number of objects in each set using the fanout of the nodes. Finally, we visit the nodes pointed by the entries one-by-one, and replace the contribution of each of them to the upper bound by the actual number of objects in them. If at some point the upper bound becomes smaller than t, we can prune this set of entries. We do the same for the remaining sets, until e_i is pruned, or we are forced to perform the distance join.

within distance ϵ of objects $s \in S$ may belong to different slots. In that case, it will be impossible to prune a slot, unless it does not overlap with any other slots. Therefore, we can only process the iceberg join using the conventional two-step processing, i.e., (i) apply SISJ to evaluate the distance join, (ii) sort the pairs $\langle r, s \rangle$ to count the occurrences of each r and report the iceberg join result. Alternatively, we can ignore the R–tree for S and employ PIDJ. Since PIDJ does not require sorting, it can be faster than the two-step, conventional technique.

3.4 Adaptation to Special Types of Iceberg Distance Joins

Our algorithms can be easily adapted for other forms of iceberg join queries. One is the iceberg semi-join, discussed in the introduction. In this case, we are interested only in the objects $r \in R$, which qualify the iceberg distance join constraints. A straightforward way to process the semi-join is to evaluate the iceberg distance join, and output only the distinct r which appear in the resulting pairs $\langle r, s \rangle$. However, we can do better by exploiting statistical information. Consider for instance the grid $\mathcal{F}$, as depicted in Figure 5a. This grid has granularity ϵ and captures the number of $s \in S$ that fall into each cell, as explained in Section 3.1. Observe that while reading (and hashing) R, if point $r \in R$ falls into a microcell c_x with $c_x.count \geq t$, we can *immediately* output r, without hashing or joining it, because we know for sure that it will participate in the semi-join result (since there are at least t objects from S in the same microcell, i.e., within distance ϵ from it[2]).

In another iceberg distance join query, the cardinality constraint t may not provide a lower threshold for the occurrences of $r \in R$ in the distance join pairs, but an upper threshold. For instance, in this case we might be interested in hotels which are close to *at most t* restaurants. Again, for this query we can use the fine grid $\mathcal{F}$ to detect early pruned regions for R; if $c_x.count \geq t$ for a microcell c_x, we can prune the microcell, since we know that every r that falls there joins with at least t $s \in S$. Therefore, the bit-mapping technique now uses the counters in the microcells instead of adding to them the ones of the influence microcells around them. Finally, the proposed techniques can be easily adapted for the iceberg join, when the number of appearances should be in the range between t_{low} and t_{up} times. For each c_x, its counter provides a *lower* bound of the join results and the counters in its influence region an *upper bound*. These bounds can be used in combination with t_{low} and t_{up} to prune disqualifying cells.

4 Experimental Evaluation

We evaluated the performance of the proposed techniques for a wide range of settings, using synthetic and real data of various cardinalities and skew. The real datasets, which were originally line segments, were converted to points, by taking

---

[2] Actually for defining the microcells here we use a value smaller than ϵ, which is the side of the *minimum enclosed square* in a circle with radius $\epsilon/2$. We skip the details for the sake of readability.

the center of the segments. Files T1 and T2 [7] contain 131,461 roads and 128,971 rivers, respectively, from an area in California. AS and AL [24] contain 30,674 roads and 36,334 railroads, respectively, from Germany. The buffer size was set to 20% of the total size both joined datasets occupy on disk. As a measure of performance, we counted random I/Os. The sequential I/Os were normalized to random ones according to current disk benchmarks (e.g., a random page access costs as much as 10 sequential ones, if the page size is 8Kb). The experiments were run using a 700MHz Pentium III processor.

4.1 Evaluation of PIDJ

In this section we evaluate the performance of PIDJ under various experimental settings. We compare the three progressively more optimized versions of the algorithm. The baseline implementation (referred to as $PIDJ_1$) avoids duplication and sorting. In addition to these, $PIDJ_2$ filters out buckets using their cardinalities without applying the fine grid $\mathcal{F}$ refinement. Finally $PIDJ_3$ includes all the optimizations described in Section 3.1. For these experiments the page size was set to 8Kb.

In the first experiment, we compare the I/O performance of the three PIDJ versions for several pairs of joined datasets, by setting the distance threshold ϵ to 2% of the data-space projection, and varying the value of the cardinality threshold t. Figures 8 and 9 plot the I/O cost of the algorithms as a function of t for the joins AS ⋈ AL and AL ⋈ AS, respectively; in the first case the relation R where t applies is AS and in the second it is AL (notice that the join is asymmetric, therefore it is possible to have different results and performance in these two cases). Observe that the improvement of $PIDJ_2$ over $PIDJ_1$ is marginal for the tested values of t. This is because the number of buckets in this case is small (only 25 in this example) and the regions that they cover are quite large. $PIDJ_2$ cannot prune buckets, since all of them contain a large number of points from R. On the other hand, the fine grid $\mathcal{F}$ employed by $PIDJ_3$ manages to prune a large percentage of R; as t increases more cells are pruned by the bit-mapping method and less data from R are hashed.

For the Tiger files T1 and T2, on the other hand, $PIDJ_2$ reduces significantly the cost of the baseline implementation (especially for the T1 ⋈ T2 pair). Figures 10 and 11 plot the I/O cost of the three versions of PIDJ. The improvement of $PIDJ_3$ is significant also in this case. The large improvement of $PIDJ_2$ is due to the large values of t tested, and due to the fact that now grid $\mathcal{G}$ is finer than for the AS ⋈ AL joins.[3] The sparse areas of the map are usually pruned using $\mathcal{G}$ and the rest are very dense this is why $PIDJ_3$ adds little improvement.

In the next set of experiments we compare the three versions of PIDJ for joins on synthetic data. For this purpose we generated four synthetic datasets G1, G2, U1, and U2, as follows. All datasets contain 200K points. G1 and G2 were created according to a Gaussian distribution with 10 clusters. The centers of

---

[3] The datasets are larger, thus more memory (20% of the total size) is allocated for the join and more buckets are defined.

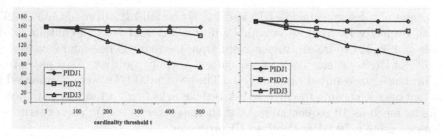

Fig. 8. I/O cost, AS ⋈ AL, $\epsilon = 2\%$ **Fig. 9.** I/O cost, AL ⋈ AS, $\epsilon = 2\%$

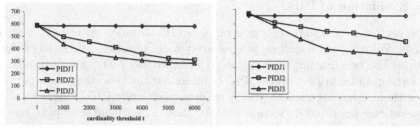

Fig. 10. I/O cost, T1 ⋈ T2, $\epsilon = 2\%$ **Fig. 11.** I/O cost, T2 ⋈ T1, $\epsilon = 2\%$

the clusters for both files were randomly generated. The sigma value of the data distribution around the clusters in G1 was set to a random value between $1/5$ and $1/10$ of the data space. Thus, all clusters are similar, they spread around the whole data-space, and the resulting dataset has little skew. On the other hand, the sigma value of the clusters in G2 has high variance; half of the clusters are very skewed, with sigma between $1/10$ and $1/20$ of the data space, and the other half have little skew (sigma is between $1/3$ and $1/5$). In this way we wanted to simulate the case where both datasets are non-uniform, but one of them has higher skew in some regions. U1 and U2 contain uniformly distributed points.

Figures 12 and 13 plot the I/O cost for G1 ⋈ G2 and G2 ⋈ G1, respectively. In both joins, PIDJ$_3$ achieves significant improvement over the baseline version of the algorithm. Notice that for G2 ⋈ G1 the improvement is larger. This is due to the fact that G1 is more uniform than G2, so if it is taken as S, the probability that PIDJ$_3$ prunes a microcell increases. We also experimented with other combinations of skewed data with similar results. In general, the improvement of PIDJ$_3$ over PIDJ$_2$ increases with the uniformity of the data, since more regions corresponding to the microcells $c_i \in \mathcal{F}$ are pruned. The experiment plotted in Figure 14 validates this argument. This time we joined two uniform datasets U1 and U2. Note that uniformity is normally the worst setting for an iceberg join algorithm, since buckets cannot be pruned using their global statistics. As expected, here PIDJ$_2$ has no improvement over PIDJ$_1$, since the number of data from U2 in each bucket is the same and larger than t (unless t becomes very large). On the other hand, PIDJ$_3$ for $t > 200$ starts pruning many cells in $\mathcal{F}$, sharply until it converges to the cost of just reading and hashing S.

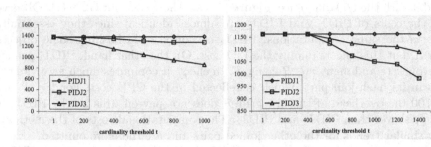

Fig. 12. I/O cost, G1 ⋈ G2, $\epsilon = 2\%$ **Fig. 13.** I/O cost, G2 ⋈ G1, $\epsilon = 2\%$

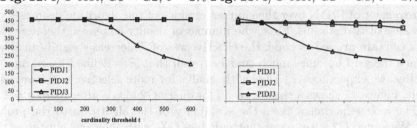

Fig. 14. I/O cost, U1 ⋈ U2, $\epsilon = 2\%$ **Fig. 15.** CPU time (sec), G2 ⋈ G1, $\epsilon = 2\%$

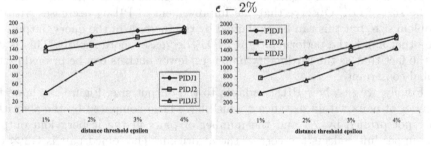

Fig. 16. I/O cost, AL ⋈ AS, $t = 400$ **Fig. 17.** I/O cost, G2 ⋈ G1, $t = 1400$

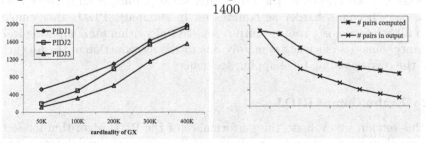

Fig. 18. I/O cost, G2 ⋈ GX, $\epsilon = 2\%$,   **Fig. 19.** I/O cost, G2 ⋈ G1, $\epsilon = 2\%$ $t = 1400$

We have also tracked the computational cost of the three versions and compared it with the I/O difference. Figure 15 plots these costs for $G2 \bowtie G1$. Observe that the costs of $PIDJ_1$ and $PIDJ_2$ are almost identical since they essentially perform the same computations. $PIDJ_2$ can only avoid hashing some objects from R, but this affects mainly the I/O cost. On the other hand, $PIDJ_3$ prunes more buckets and many $r \in R$ using $\mathcal{F}$. In effect, it computes much fewer joined pairs in its hash-join part, which is reflected in the CPU cost. For $t = 1$ and $t = 100$ the overhead of the fine grid $\mathcal{F}$ does not pay-off, this is why $PIDJ_3$ is slightly slower than $PIDJ_1$ and $PIDJ_2$. The computational costs of the methods show similar trends for the other joined pairs and are therefore omitted.

In the next experiment, we study the effects of ϵ in the three versions of PIDJ. Figure 16 plots the I/O cost of $AL \bowtie AS$ as a function of ϵ when $t = 400$. The improvement of $PIDJ_3$ over the simpler versions of the algorithm decreases with ϵ because of two reasons. First, the number of results increases, therefore much fewer cells are pruned. Second, the effectiveness of $\mathcal{F}$ decreases significantly with ϵ, since the grid becomes much coarser (recall that $\mathcal{F}$ is defined based on ϵ). In practice, we expect iceberg joins with small ϵ for more selective and more useful result. Figure 17 shows a similar trend for query $G2 \bowtie G1$, after fixing $t = 1400$.

The next experiment tests the scalability of the algorithm to the problem size. We joined G2 with many synthetic files GX, with the same cluster settings as G1, but varying size from 50K objects to 400K objects. In these experiments $\epsilon = 2\%$ and $t = 1400$. Figure 18 shows the performance of PIDJ as a function of the size of GX. Observe that the improvement of $PIDJ_3$ decreases with the problem size, but this can be explained by the increase of the query output. On the other hand, the performance of $PIDJ_2$ decreases more rapidly. This is due to the fact that as the cardinality increases, fewer buckets can be pruned by the global constraint.

Finally, we test how $PIDJ_3$ adapts to the output size. Figure 19 shows the number of pairs within distance ϵ which have been computed by the algorithm (i.e., not pruned by $\mathcal{F}$) and the number of pairs in the iceberg join output. The upper line reflects the cost of the algorithm. The joined pair is $G2 \bowtie G1$, $\epsilon = 2\%$, and t varies. Indeed, the cost of the algorithm drops as its output decreases, however, not at the same rate, since pruning a large percentage of false pairs becomes harder as t increases. In summary, PIDJ, after employed with all heuristics, is a robust, output sensitive algorithm for computing iceberg distance joins. Its efficiency is mainly due to the introduction of the fine grid $\mathcal{F}$ and the corresponding bit-mapping technique.

4.2   Evaluation of RIDJ

In this section we evaluate the performance of the RIDJ algorithm for iceberg distance join queries. For this, we built two R–trees for the real datasets AS and AL, with node size 1Kb. We used a small node size, since this facilitates pruning in RIDJ; the fanout of the nodes is not very large and for values of t which return results (i.e., in the range 100–1000) it becomes possible for the algorithm to prune R–tree node pairs early.

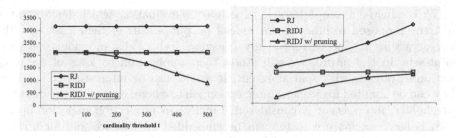

Fig. 20. I/O cost, AL ⋈ AS, $\epsilon = 2\%$ **Fig. 21.** I/O cost, AL ⋈ AS, $t = 400$

The following experiment validates this assertion. We performed the join AL ⋈ AS for different values of t and ϵ and compared the performance of three algorithms; RJ, RIDJ and RIDJ employed with the pruning heuristic. Figures 20 shows the performance of the algorithms for $\epsilon = 2\%$ and various values of t. Observe that the cost difference between RJ and the basic version of RIDJ is the same for all values of t. It translates to the overhead of RJ to sort a large number of pairs that qualify the distance join (around 3.6 million for this join) in order to validate the cardinality threshold t. Most page accesses are sequential, this is why the normalized cost difference is not extreme. On the other hand, the version of RIDJ with pruning is output sensitive. Many node pairs are pruned as t increases (and the result decreases).

In the experiment of Figure 21, the cardinality threshold is fixed to $t = 400$ and ϵ varies. Observe that the cost of RJ increases with ϵ, since more pairs qualify the distance join as ϵ is relaxed. On the other hand, the cost of the basic RIDJ algorithm remains constant, since the algorithm exploits the buffer to avoid incurring more I/O accesses than the total number of nodes in both trees. The efficiency of the pruning heuristic diminishes with the increase of ϵ, because the lists $L(e_i)$ increase significantly due to the increase of the extended MBRs by $\epsilon/2$ while processing the distance join. Nevertheless, at the same time, the number of the iceberg query results increases significantly with ϵ. In summary, RIDJ, when employed with the pruning heuristic, is an output sensitive algorithm that manages to prune the search space, by exploiting gracefully the query constraints.

5   Conclusions

In this paper we have shown how spatial join algorithms can be adapted for the interesting class of iceberg distance join queries. The proposed methods exploit data density and distribution statistics, obtained while processing the query, to shrink the search space according to the cardinality constraint t. In an attempt to cover all possible indexing presumptions for the joined data we have extended a hash-based algorithm (PBSM) and a index-based method (RJ). We have also described adaptations for single-index algorithms. Finally, we have discussed how our methods can be used to process special types of iceberg distance joins.

We conducted a comprehensive experimental evaluation, which demonstrates that the proposed techniques are indeed output sensitive; their cost steadily decreases with t. The current study considers iceberg distance joins between point-sets. In the future, we will study their application to joins of datasets containing objects with spatial extent. It would also be interesting to see how they can be adapted for iceberg intersection joins, where, instead of the distance threshold ϵ, intersection is considered. Finally, an interesting issue for future work is how *ranking* predicates can be embedded in distance join algorithms (e.g., output the top-k hotels with the largest number of nearby restaurants).

References

[1] Lars Arge, Octavian Procopiuc, Sridhar Ramaswamy, Torsten Suel, Jan Vahrenhold, and Jeffery Scott Vitter. A unified approach for indexed and non-indexed spatial joins. In *Proc. of EDBT Conference*, 2000. 273, 279

[2] Lars Arge, Octavian Procopiuc, Sridhar Ramaswamy, Torsten Suel, and Jeffrey Scott Vitter. Scalable sweeping-based spatial join. In *Proc. of VLDB Conference*, 1998. 270, 272

[3] Norbert Beckmann, Hans-Peter Kriegel, Ralf Schneider, and Bernhard Seeger. The R*-tree: An efficient and robust access method for points and rectangles. In *Proc. of ACM SIGMOD Int'l Conference*, 1990. 273

[4] Kevin S. Beyer and Raghu Ramakrishnan. Bottom-up computation of sparse and iceberg cubes. In *Proc. of ACM SIGMOD Int'l Conference*, 1999. 274

[5] Christian Böhm, Bernhard Braunmüller, Florian Krebs, and Hans-Peter Kriegel. Epsilon grid order: an algorithm for the similarity join on massive high-dimensional data. In *Proc. of ACM SIGMOD Int'l Conference*, 2001. 274

[6] Thomas Brinkhoff, Hans-Peter Kriegel, and Bernhard Seeger. Efficient processing of spatial joins using R-trees. In *Proc. of ACM SIGMOD Int'l Conference*, 1993. 270, 271, 275, 278

[7] Bureau of the Census, TIGER/Line Precensus files: 1990 Technical Documentation, 1989. 282

[8] Antonio Corral, Yannis Manolopoulos, Yannis Theodoridis, and Michael Vassilakopoulos. Closest pair queries in spatial databases. In *Proc. of ACM SIGMOD Int'l Conference*, 2000. 274

[9] Jens-Peter Dittrich and Bernhard Seeger. Data redundancy and duplicate detection in spatial join processing. In *Proc. of Int'l Conf. on Data Engineering (ICDE)*, 2000. 272

[10] Min Fang, Narayanan Shivakumar, Hector Garcia-Molina, Rajeev Motwani, and Jeffrey D. Ullman. Computing iceberg queries efficiently. In *Proc. of VLDB Conference*, 1998. 274

[11] A. Guttman. R-trees: a dynamical index structure for spatial searching. In *Proc. of ACM SIGMOD Int'l Conference*, 1984. 271

[12] Jiawei Han, Jian Pei, Guozhu Dong, and Ke Wang. Efficient computation of iceberg cubes with complex measures. In *Proc. of ACM SIGMOD Int'l Conference*, 2001. 274

[13] Gisli R. Hjaltason and Hanan Samet. Incremental distance join algorithms for spatial databases. In *Proc. of ACM SIGMOD Int'l Conference*, 1998. 274

[14] Gisli R. Hjaltason and Hanan Samet. Distance browsing in spatial databases. *TODS*, 24(2):265–318, 1999. 271

[15] Yun-Wu Huang, Ning Jing, and Elke A. Rundensteiner. Spatial joins using R-trees: Breadth-first traversal with global optimizations. In *Proc. of VLDB Conference*, 1997. 272

[16] Nick Koudas and Kenneth C. Sevcik. Size separation spatial join. In *Proc. of ACM SIGMOD Int'l Conference*, 1997. 272, 274

[17] Nick Koudas and Kenneth C. Sevcik. High dimensional similarity joins: Algorithms and performance evaluation. In *Proc. of Int'l Conf. on Data Engineering (ICDE)*, 1998. 270, 274

[18] Ming-Ling Lo and Chinya V. Ravishankar. Spatial joins using seeded trees. In *Proc. of ACM SIGMOD Int'l Conference*, 1994. 270, 273

[19] Ming-Ling Lo and Chinya V. Ravishankar. Spatial hash-joins. In *Proc. of ACM SIGMOD Int'l Conference*, 1996. 270, 272, 276

[20] Gang Luo, Jeffrey F. Naughton, and Curt Ellmann. A non-blocking parallel spatial join algorithm. In *Proc. of Int'l Conf. on Data Engineering (ICDE)*, 2002. 270, 272

[21] Nikos Mamoulis and Dimitris Papadias. Integration of spatial join algorithms for processing multiple inputs. In *Proc. of ACM SIGMOD Int'l Conference*, 1999. 270, 273, 275, 276

[22] Dimitris Papadias, Panos Kalnis, Jun Zhang, and Yufei Tao. Efficient OLAP operations in spatial data warehouses. In *Proc. of SSTD*, 2001. 280

[23] Jignesh M. Patel and David J. DeWitt. Partition based spatial-merge join. In *Proc. of ACM SIGMOD Int'l Conference*, 1996. 270, 272, 275

[24] Penn State University Libraries, Digital Chart of the World, http://www.maproom.psu.edu/dcw/, 1997. 282

[25] Kyuseok Shim, Ramakrishnan Srikant, and Rakesh Agrawal. High-dimensional similarity joins. In *Proc. of Int'l Conf. on Data Engineering (ICDE)*, 1997. 273

[26] Hyoseop Shin, Bongki Moon, and Sukho Lee. Adaptive multi-stage distance join processing. In *Proc. of ACM SIGMOD Int'l Conference*, 2000. 274

Indexing Objects Moving on Fixed Networks

Elias Frentzos

Department of Rural and Surveying Engineering
National Technical University of Athens, Zographou
15773, Athens, Hellas, Greece
efrentzo@central.ntua.gr

Abstract. The development of a spatiotemporal access method suitable for objects moving on fixed networks is a very attractive challenge due to the great number of real-world spatiotemporal database applications and fleet management systems dealing with this type of objects. In this work, a new indexing technique, named Fixed Network R-Tree (FNR-Tree), is proposed for objects constrained to move on fixed networks in 2-dimensional space. The general idea that describes the FNR-Tree is a forest of 1-dimensional (1D) R-Trees on top of a 2-dimensional (2D) R-Tree. The 2D R-Tree is used to index the spatial data of the network (e.g. roads consisting of line segments), while the 1D R-Trees are used to index the time interval of each object's movement inside a given link of the network. The performance study, comparing this novel access method with the traditional R-Tree under various datasets and queries, shows that the FNR-Tree outperforms the R-Tree in most cases.

1   Introduction

Most recently developed spatiotemporal access methods (3D R-Tree [16], HR-Tree [6, 7], TB-Tree, STR-Tree [10], TPR-Tree [13], Mv3R-Tree [14], PPR-Tree [3]) are designed to index objects performing any kind of movement in a two-dimensional space. These methods are general and do not take into consideration the special requirements of the application in which they are used. However, in real-world applications several conditions having to do with the demanded level of generalization and the way of perception of data, can improve the performance of the spatiotemporal indexes. For example, in a research for the emigrational habits of some animal population (dolphins, whales e.t.c.), more likely is that the precise position of each separate animal is not of interest, but the region in which is contained the population. This can lead to dramatic reduction of the number of moving objects that should be indexed by an indexing technique, and to the consequently increase of its performance.

Another condition that can be used to improve the performance of spatiotemporal indexes is the existence of restrictions in the space in which moving objects realize their movement. Although the vast majority of spatiotemporal access methods index objects moving in the whole of the two dimensional space, in most real-world applications the objects are moving in a constrained space: planes fly in air-paths, cars and

T. Hadzilacos et al. (Eds.): SSTD 2003, LNCS 2750, pp. 289–305, 2003.

pedestrians move on road networks, while trains have fixed trajectories on railway networks. These kind of special conditions (moving restrictions) have recently been subject of the researching interest [5, 8, 9, 11].

As it is obvious, the development of a spatiotemporal access method suitable for objects moving on fixed networks is a very attractive challenge because a great number of real-world spatiotemporal database applications have to do mainly with objects (e.g. cars) moving on fixed networks and fleet management systems. In the next sections of this paper, we focus on the movement of such objects constrained to move on a fixed urban network and we study how we can use this restriction in order to develop alternative access methods to index those data.

Specifically, we develop and evaluate the performance of a new index, named Fixed Network R-Tree (FNR-Tree), proposed for objects constrained to move on fixed networks in a two dimensional space; an extension of the well-known R-Tree [2]. The general idea that describes the FNR-Tree is a forest of 1 dimensional (1D) R-Trees on top of a 2 dimensional (2D) R-Tree. The 2D R-Tree is used to index the spatial data of the network (e.g. roads consisting of line segments), while the 1D R-Trees are used to index the time interval of each object's movement inside a given link of the network.

The outline of this paper is as follows. Section 2 focuses on the motivation for the development of a new access method and summarizes the related work. Section 3 presents the structure and the algorithms of the FNR-Tree. Section 4 provides a performance study for the FNR-Tree and compares it with the conventional 3D R-Tree [16]. Finally, section 5 presents conclusions and directions for future work.

2   Motivation

Much work has been recently conducted in the domain of indexing spatiotemporal data and several spatiotemporal access methods have been proposed, which can be separated into two major categories: those indexing the past positions of moving objects (3D R-Tree [16], HR-Tree [6], TB-Tree, STR-Tree [10]), and those indexing the current and predicted movement of objects [12, 13]. Because our interest is in recording the past positions of moving objects in order to use them for post-processing purposes, we will only consider access methods of the first type.

According to [8], there are three scenarios about the movement of objects in a two dimensional space: the unconstrained movement (e.g., vessels at sea), the constrained movement (e.g., pedestrians on an urban environment), and the movement in transportation networks (e.g., trains and, typically, cars). Generalizing the second two categories, we can say that the way in which an urban network is handled depends of the required precision of the application. For example, if the application requires the precise knowledge of the position of each moving object, then the network can be faced as in Figure 1(a), where the existing infrastructure (building squares in gray regions) restricts the movement of objects. On the contrary, if the application does not require the precise knowledge of the position of each moving object, the same area can be represented by a set of connected line segments forming a road network.

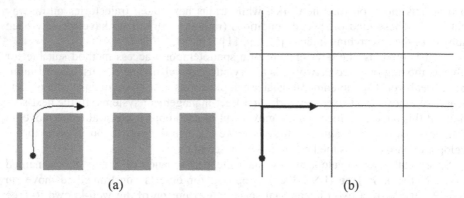

Fig. 1. (a) Movement of object restricted by the infrastructure in urban area, (b) Movement of object on fixed network representing the same urban area

Pfoser et al. [9] use the restrictions placed in the movement of objects by the existing infrastructure, in order to improve the performance of spatiotemporal queries executed against a spatiotemporal index. The strategy followed does not affect the structure of the index itself. Instead, they adopt an additional preprocessing step before the execution of each query. In particular, provided that the infrastructure is rarely updated, it can be indexed by a conventional spatial index such as the R-Tree. TB-Tree [10] or 3D R-Tree [16] can be used to index the pure spatiotemporal data. Then, a preprocessing step of the query, divides the initial query window in a number of smaller windows, from which the regions covered by the infrastructure have been excluded. Each one of the smaller queries is executed against the index returning a set of candidate objects, which are finally refined with respect to the initial query window.

In the same paper, an algorithm is provided for the implementation of the query-preprocessing step, based on the work presented in [4]. According to that, the number of node accesses required by an R-tree-based index to answer a window query, depends not only by the window area as well as from its dimensions. Consequently, what concerns is not only the minimization of the query area (which is achieved by removing the section containing the infrastructure from the initial window) but also the minimization of the perimeter of the query window. In the corresponding evaluation, the performance of two spatiotemporal indexes (TB and 3D R-tree) was compared, using or not the described query preprocessing step (i.e., dividing the initial window in smaller windows), and it was shown that the query performance was improved for both indexes.

As previously reported, there exist applications that do not require to keep track of each moving object's exact position, by terms of coordinates (Figure 1(b)); it is enough to project the object's position onto a fixed network constituted by a set of connected line segments. This type of application is very common, for example, management of vehicles moving in an urban road network (fleet-management applications) does not require each vehicle's precise position but its relative location inside the road network. Thus, the trajectory of a vehicle could be represented by a set

$\{[route_1, t_1], [route_2, t_2], ... [route_i, t_i]\}$, where each pair denotes the time of entry of a given vehicle in network's line segment $route_i$.

According to Kollios et al. [5], the domain of the object's trajectories moving in a network is not the 2+1 dimensional space, but a space with 1.5 dimensions, as line segments consisting the network can be stored in a conventional index of spatial data (such as the R-tree). Then, indexing of objects moving in such a network is a problem with only one dimension. Though [5] consider the indexing of objects moving on fixed networks from the theoretical aspect, they do not propose any access method that could be used in real-world applications.

Recently, Papadias et al. [11] adopted the same assumption of movement on fixed networks, in order to create a structure that answers spatiotemporal aggregate queries of the form "*find the total number of objects in the regions intersecting some window q_s during a time interval q_t*". The Aggregate R-B-Tree (aRB-Tree) is a combination of R- and B-trees and is based on the following idea: the lines of the network are stored only one time and indexed by an R-tree. Then, in each internal and leaf node of the R-Tree, a pointer to a B-tree is placed, which stores historical aggregate data about the particular spatial object (e.g. the MBB of the node).

Pfoser in [8] proposes a method for simplifying the trajectory data obtained by objects moving on fixed networks. A two-dimensional network is transformed to a one-dimensional set of segments and the trajectory data is mapped accordingly. Consequently, a simple two-dimensional access method (such as R-Tree) can be used in order to index the positions of objects moving on a fixed network. Although this is an easy to implement approach, one may argue that it has disadvantages such as the modification of line segments distribution in space and the modification in general of the distance and the topological relations between spatial objects (i.e. connections between network's line segments).

On the contrary, the proposed FNR-Tree does not have these disadvantages because it is not based in any transformation technique. Moving objects' positions are recorded each time an object passes a node of the network. It assumes that moving parameters do not change between two network nodes, and therefore, linear interpolation can be used in order to calculate each object's position on a given time instance. In the following section, we will present the structure and the algorithms of the FNR-Tree and then we will show that it outperforms the 3D R-Tree for a wide palette of queries.

3   The Fixed Network R-Tree (FNR-Tree)

The FNR-Tree is based on the well-known R-Tree [2]. The general idea is that for a road network consisting of n links, the FNR-Tree can be considered as a forest of several 1D R-Trees on top of a single 2D R-Tree. The 2D R-Tree is used to index the spatial data of the network (e.g. roads consisting of line segments), while each one of the 1D R-Trees corresponds to a leaf node of the 2D R-Tree and is used to index the time intervals that any moving object was moving on a given link of the network. Therefore, the 2D R-Tree remains static during the lifetime of the FNR-Tree – as long as there are no changes in the network.

3.1 The FNR-Tree Structure

Before we describe in detail the structure of the proposed index, let us recall the structure of the original R-Tree. It is a height-balanced tree with the index records in its leaf nodes containing pointers to the actual data objects. Leaf node entries are in the form (id, MBB), where id is an identifier that points to the actual object and MBB (Minimum Bounding Box) is a n-dimensional interval. Non-leaf node entries are of the form (ptr, MBB), where ptr is a pointer to a child node, and MBB the bounding box that covers all child nodes. A node in the tree corresponds to a disk page and contains between m and M entries.

The 2D R-Tree inside the FNR-Tree, is slightly different: Since the only spatial objects that are inserted in the 2D R-Tree are line segments, leaf node entries can be modified in the form (*MBB, orientation*), where "*orientation*" is a flag that describes the exact geometry of the line segment inside the MBB and takes values from the set {0,1} (Figure 2(a)). A similar approach was followed in [10] to represent segments of trajectories in a 3D R-tree-based technique. The structure of each leaf node entry of the 2D R-Tree inside the FNR-Tree is of the form *(Line Id, MBB, Orientation)*, and the structure of each non-leaf (internal) node of the 2D R-Tree inside the FNR-Tree, is of the form *(Pointer to child Node, MBB)*. Each leaf node of the 2D R-Tree contains a pointer that points to the root of a 1D R-Tree; consequently, for each leaf node of the 2D R-Tree, there is a corresponding 1D R-Tree.

Each leaf entry of an 1D R-Tree contains the time intervals that a moving object was moving on a line segment included in the MBB of the corresponding leaf of the 2D R-Tree, the *ID* of the moving object, the *ID* of the corresponding line segment and the *direction* of the moving object. The *direction* is another flag that describes the direction of the moving object and takes values from the set {0, 1} (Figure 3). Specifically, the *direction* becomes 0 when the moving object inserted in the line segment from the left-most node, and 1 when the moving object inserted from the right-most node. In the special case where the line segment is vertical, the *direction* becomes 0 for object inserted in the line segment from the bottom-most node and 1 for objects inserted from the top-most node. The structure of each leaf node entry of the 1D R-Trees inside the FNR-Tree is of the form *(Moving Object Id, Line Segment Id, $T_{entrance}$, T_{exit}, Direction)*. The structure of each internal (non-leaf) node entry of the 1D R-Trees inside the FNR-Tree is of the form *(Pointer to child Node, $T_{entrance}$, T_{exit})*.

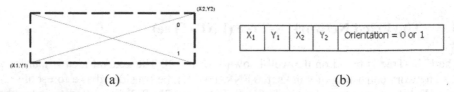

(a)   (b)

Fig. 2. (a) Ways that a line segment can be contained inside a MBB and the orientation flag, (b) The corresponding leaf node entry of the 2D R-Tree inside the FNR-Tree

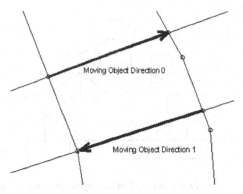

Fig. 3. The direction flag

3.2   The FNR-Tree Algorithms

The insertion algorithm of the FNR-Tree is executed each time a moving object leaves a given line segment of the network. It takes as arguments the 3-dimensional interval defined by the coordinates of the start and the end of the line segment (X_{Start}, X_{End}, Y_{Start}, Y_{End}), the direction of the moving object according to what was previously reported, as well as the time interval while the moving object was moving inside the given line segment ($T_{Entrance}$, T_{Exit}). The insertion algorithm is illustrated in figure 4.

For the insertion algorithm of the 1D R-Tree, a choice could be Guttman's insertion algorithm, which is executed in three steps: ChooseLeaf algorithm selects a leaf node in which to place a new index entry. In case an insertion causes a node split, one of three alternatives split algorithms (Exhaustive, QuadraticSplit, LinearSplit) is executed. Finally, changes in the leaf MBB are propagated upwards by the AdjustTree algorithm. ChooseLeaf and Split are based upon the least enlargement criterion and are designed to serve spatial data that are inserted in the R-Tree in random order. Trees formed using these algorithms usually have small overlap between nodes as well as small space utilization.

FNR-Tree Insertion Algorithm

---

1.   Execute Guttmann's search algorithm in the 2D R-Tree in order to find the line segment, which leaves the moving object. Locate the leaf node that contains the given line segment and the corresponding 1D R-Tree.

2.   Execute insertion algorithm in the 1D R-Tree.

Fig. 4. FNR-Tree Insertion Algorithm

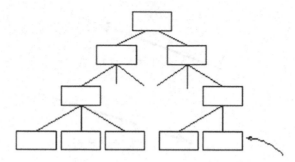

Fig. 5. New entries are always inserted in the right-most node of each 1D R-Tree

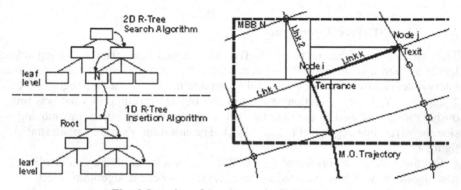

Fig. 6. Insertion of a new entry in the FNR-Tree

However, considering the 1D R-Trees of the FNR-Tree, the 1-dimensional time intervals are inserted in the tree in increasing order for the reason that time is monotonic. This fact leads us to the following modification of the insert algorithm of the 1D R-Tree as shown in Figure 5. Every new entry is simply inserted in the most recent (right-most) leaf of the 1D R-Tree. In case this leaf node is full, a new node is created and the entry is inserted in it. The new leaf node is inserted in the father node of the last leaf. Then, changes are propagated upwards using the conventional AdjustTree algorithm of the R-Tree. In general, this is the same technique that was used by Pfoser et al. [10] in the insertion algorithm of the TB-Tree.

This insertion technique results to 1D R-Trees with full leaves and very low overlapping. The space utilization of the FNR-Tree using the conventional insertion technique in the 1D R-Trees was 65% while, after the illustrated modification, it reached 96%.

As shown in figure 6, the insertion algorithm is executed when the moving object reaches a node (*Node j*) of the network. The first step requires a spatial search among the 2D R-tree (with arguments, the coordinates of *Node i* and *Node j*) in order to find the line segment *Link k* that is contained in the *MBB N* of the 2D R-tree *leaf node N*. Next, we follow the pointer to the 1D R-tree, in which is inserted the *one dimensional interval* (T_{entry}, T_{exit}), together with the *Moving Object Id*, the *Link Id* and the *Direction flag*. The newly inserted entry is always placed in the right-most 1D R-tree leaf node.

If it is required, changes in the MBB of the leaf node (or a newly created leaf node), are propagated upwards until the 1D R-tree *Root*.

The FNR-Tree search algorithm with a spatiotemporal window (3D interval) as an argument is illustrated in figure 7.

Suppose we would search the FNR-Tree with a spatiotemporal query window (X_1, Y_1, X_2, Y_2, T_1, T_2) (Figure 8). The first step requires a spatial search (with arguments the 2D interval (X_1, Y_1, X_2, Y_2)) among the 2D R-Tree in order to locate the line segments and the corresponding 2D R-Tree leaves (in particular, *leaf node N with MBB N*) which cross the spatial query window. Next, a search (with arguments the 1D interval (T_1, T_2)) is executed in each one of the 1D R-Trees that correspond to the leaf nodes of the 1st step. In our example, the search led us to the 1D R-Tree leaf nodes *T1* and *T2* that (among others) contain *link k*, *link l* and *link o*. In the final step we retrieve from the main memory the coordinates of each link selected in the 2nd step and we reject those, which are fully outside the spatial query window (in particular, *link o*).

FNR-Tree Search Algorithm

---

1.   Execute Guttman's search algorithm in the 2D R-Tree in order to find the line segments of the network contained in the spatial query window. Locate the corresponding 2D R-Tree leaves. Store these line segments in main memory.

2.   Execute Guttman's search algorithm in each one of the 1D R-Trees that correspond to the leaf nodes of the 1st step.

3.   For each entry in every leaf of the 1D R-Trees that were retrieved from the 2nd step, locate – via the line segment id stored in main memory – the corresponding line segment among those of the 1st step. Reject those entries that correspond to a line segment that is fully outside the spatial window of the spatiotemporal query.

Fig. 7. FNR-Tree Search Algorithm

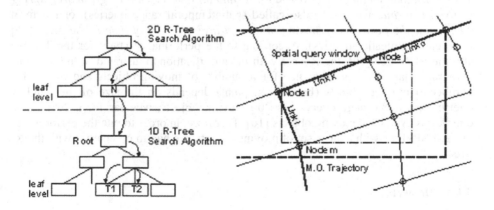

Fig. 8. Searching in the FNR-Tree

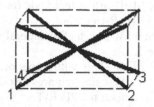

Fig. 9. Alternative ways that a 3D line segment can be contained inside a MBB

4   Performance Study

In order to determine in which conditions, the FNR-Tree is efficient, we conducted a set of experiments using a Visual Basic implementation that simulates the behavior of the FNR-Tree. We have chosen the page size for the leaf and non-leaf nodes to be 1024 bytes, which lead to a fanout of 50 for the leaf and non-leaf nodes of the 2D R-Tree. The fanout for the 1D R-Trees inside the FNR-Tree was 73 for the leaf, and 85 for the non-leaf nodes.

So as to have a direct comparison with another spatiotemporal access method, we have chosen the conventional 3D R-Tree [16]. It was also implemented in Visual Basic and (in order to provide an as fair as possible performance comparison) was modified as described in the [10]: a MBB can contain a given 3d line segment in 4 different ways only (figure 9). Taking, therefore, into consideration that the 3D R-Tree can contain only simple line segments, we can replace the pointer to the actual object with a flag that takes values from the domain {1,2,3,4}. Consequently, the entry format of the leaf nodes of the 3D R-Tree is of the form *(Id, MBB, Orientation)*. The fanout for the 3D R-Tree was 36 for both leaf and non-leaf nodes.

The reason that the 3D R-Tree was chosen instead of another spatiotemporal access method (e.g. TB-Tree) is explained below: The FNR-Tree is designed to efficiently answer spatiotemporal queries of the form *"find all objects within a given area during a given time interval"* [15] (also called spatiotemporal range queries), or the form *"determine the positions of moving objects at a given point of time in the past"* [16] (also called timeslice queries). According to the performance study for the TB-tree and the STR-Tree [10], the R-Tree with the modifications illustrated in the previous paragraph, has better performance for a number of moving objects and over. This number of moving objects (break-even point) depends on the size of the window query: for a 10% range query it is 200 moving objects, whereas for a 20% range query, it is over 1000 moving objects [10]. Therefore, in order to rate the performance of the FNR-Tree with a large set of moving objects, we had to compare it with the R-Tree.

4.1   Datasets

While there are several real spatial datasets for the conduction of experiments, real moving-object datasets are not widespread. Owing to this lack of real spatiotemporal data, our performance study was based upon synthetic datasets created using a network-based data generator [1] and the real-world road networks of Oldenbourg and San Jose. For each of the two networks we produced trajectory datasets of 200, 400, 800, 1200, 1600 and 2000 moving objects, where each object's position was sampled 400 times. While the output of the generator was of the form {id, t, x, y}, the FNR-Tree can utilize those data only if (x, y) are the coordinates of a *node* of the network. Therefore, the generator was modified in order to produce a record of the form {id, t, x, y} each time a moving object was passing through each node of the network. The maximum volume of line segments inserted in the FNR and the 3D R-Tree was approximately 1000K and came up for the 2000 objects of San Jose.

4.2   Results on Tree Size and Insertion Cost

The size of the created index structures is shown in the Table 1. As shown, the size of the FNR-Tree is in any case much smaller than the 3D R-Tree. The ratio between the index size of FNR and 3D R-Tree varies between 0.30 and 0.45 for large number of moving objects. For example, the size of the FNR-Tree for 2.000 moving objects in the network of Oldenbourg is about 11 MB, while the size of the respective 3D R-Tree is 38 MB.

The results for the space utilization are similar. As shown in table 1, the space utilization of the 3D R-Tree is about 65% and remains steady regardless of the volume of moving objects. On the contrary, the space utilization of the FNR-Tree grows, as the number of moving objects is growing. Thus, the space utilization of the FNR-Tree with 200 moving objects on the network of Oldenburg is 80%, while, for 1200 objects and over, and for the same network, reaches the 96%. Similar – but not identical - are the results for the network of San Jose: the space utilization for a small number of moving objects (200) is 66%, while for 1200 and over it reaches 92%.

Table 1. Index Size and Space Utilization

	Oldenburg		San Jose	
	FNR-Tree	3D R-Tree	FNR-Tree	3D R-Tree
Index Size	~6 KB per object	~19 KB per object	~9 KB per object	~23 KB per object
Space Utilization	96%	65%	92%	65%

Table 2. Node accesses per insertion

	Oldenburg		San Jose	
	FNR-Tree	3D R-Tree	FNR-Tree	3D R-Tree
Node Accesses per insertion	~8	~4.5	~12	~4.5

The results on nodes accesses per insertion are illustrated in Table 2. Each insertion of a 3D line segment in the FNR-Tree of Oldenbourg and San Jose requires 8 and 12 node accesses respectively, while an insertion in the 3D R-Tree requires an average of 4.5 node accesses for both networks. This demerit of FNR-Tree can be explained if we have in mind its insertion algorithm: The algorithm requires a pre-searching of the top 2D R-Tree in order to find the 1D R-Tree in which to place the newly inserted line segment. Consequently, for each insertion there is a (stable) number of node accesses which correspond to the spatial search of the 2D R-Tree. This also explains the significant difference between Oldenbourg's and San Jose's node accesses per insertion: San Jose's road network is much larger than Oldenbourg's (~24000 vs. ~7000 line segments), consequently, the spatial search in the corresponding 2D R-Tree requires more node accesses.

4.3   Results on Search Cost

Range queries are very important for spatiotemporal data. They are usually of the form *"find all objects within a given area during a given time interval"* and can be expressed by a 3D query window. Range queries can be divided in two sub-categories: those having the same size in each dimension (spatial and temporal), and those with different size in the temporal and the spatial dimensions. Of special interest are queries belonging to the second subcategory having the temporal dimension set to 100% as such a query can answer questions of the form *"find all moving objects having ever passed through given area"*, or, *"When the moving object x passed through a given area"*. Timeslice queries are of the form *"Determine the positions of moving objects at a given point of time in the past"* and they are also subclass of the range queries having the temporal dimension of the 3D window equal to 0.

Range and timeslice queries were used in order to evaluate the performance of the FNR-Tree. Both were executed against the FNR-Tree and the 3D R-Tree having the same data, at the same time, so as to direct compare the performance of those access methods. In particular, we used sets of 500 queries with the following query windows:

- 3 query windows with equal size in all three dimensions and a range of 1%, 10% and 20% in each dimension, resulting on 0.0001%, 0.1% and 0.8% of the total space respectively.
- 2 query windows with a range of 1% in each spatial dimension and 10% and 100% in the temporal dimension and, 1 with a range of 10% in each spatial dimension and 100% in the temporal dimension, resulting on 0.001%, 0.01% and 1% of the total space respectively.

We also used sets of 500 timeslice queries, using spatial window with range 1%, 10%, and 100% in each dimension.

Range Queries with Equal Spatial and Temporal Extent. Figures 10 and 11 show the average number of node accesses per query for various ranges and datasets. In particular, figure 10 shows the average number of node accesses for range queries with a window of 1%, 10% and 20% in each dimension for objects moving on the network of Oldenbourg, while figure 11 shows the same for objects moving on the network of San Jose. As it is clearly illustrated, the FNR-Tree has superior range query performance over the 3D R-Tree, for a number of moving objects and above, in all query sizes, on both networks.

The break-even point at which the FNR-Tree has better range query performance depends on the network and the query size. Specifically, in the network of Oldenbourg for small query size (1% in each dimension), the break-even point is at about 300 moving objects, while for larger query sizes (20% in each dimension), the FNR-Tree shows better range query performance in all data sizes. The corresponding break-even point for the network of San Jose is at about 500 moving objects for 1% and 10% query size, while for 20% query size it decreases to 350. The main reason for the difference in the break-even point is that San Jose's road network is much larger than Oldenbourg's and consequently, the spatial search in the corresponding 2D R-Tree requires more node accesses - which remain stable regardless of the number of moving objects.

It is worth to note that on both networks, the ratio between node accesses of the FNR and the 3D R-Tree is conversely relative to the query size and the data size: as much as the data size grows, the ratio between the FNR and the 3D R-Tree node accesses gets smaller. In Oldenbourg, for 1% query size the ratio is 1.22 for 200 moving objects and 0.55 for 2000 moving objects. As the query window increases to 10% and 20%, the ratio decreases to 0.44 and 0.40 respectively. The same trend is illustrated in the results for San Jose, where the ratio from 1.31 for 1% query size and 200 moving objects, decreases to 0.15 for 2000 objects and for larger query size (20%).

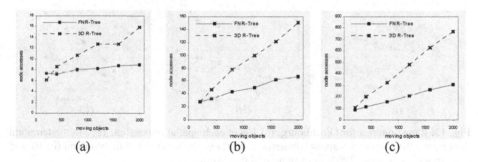

Fig. 10. Range queries for Oldenbourg: (a) 1%, (b) 10% and (c) 20% in each dimension

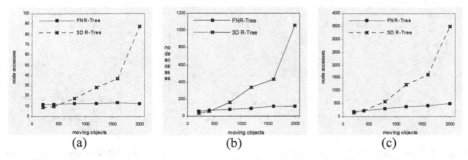

Fig. 11. Range queries for San Jose: (a) 1%, (b) 10% and (c) 20% in each dimension

Range Queries with Larger Temporal Extent. Figures 12 and 13 show the average number of node accesses for several datasets and queries having larger temporal extent. In all datasets and query sizes that we used on both networks, the FNR-Tree shows superior performance over the 3D R-Tree. Furthermore, if we compare the performance of the FNR-Tree in queries having larger temporal extent, with queries of equal spatial and temporal extent, we could see that its performance is much better on the first query type. Specifically, for 2000 moving objects and a query size of 1% in the two spatial dimensions and 10% in the temporal dimension, the ratio between the FNR and the 3D R-Tree node accesses is 0.49 for Oldenbourg's road network. As the temporal extent grows, this ratio gets smaller: for 2.000 moving objects, 1% query size in each spatial dimension and 100% in the temporal dimension, the ratio decreases to 0.36. The same trend is shown in the network of San Jose where the performance of the FNR-Tree is much better in all query and data sizes (Figure 13).

The fact that the FNR-Tree shows better performance in the queries with larger temporal extent can be explained below: When a query is executed against the FNR-Tree, the search algorithm starts with the spatial search in the 2D R-Tree. Then, having located the corresponding 1D R-Trees inside the FNR-Tree, the performance of a searching among them, requires minimum node accesses, because the inserted data have been already sorted in ascending order (a consequence of the monotonicity of time) and the formed 1D R-Trees have very low overlap and high space utilization.

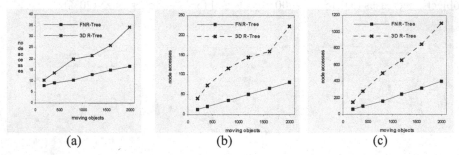

(a)   (b)   (c)

Fig. 12. Range queries for Oldenbourg: (a) 1% in each spatial dimension, 10% in the temporal dimension, (b) 1% in each spatial dimension, 100% in the temporal dimension and (c) 10% in each spatial dimension, 100% in the temporal dimension

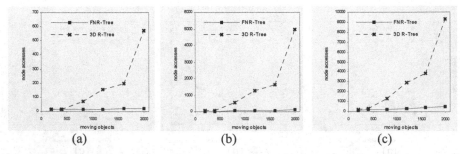

(a)   (b)   (c)

Fig. 13. Range queries for San Jose: (a) 1% in each spatial dimension, 10% in the temporal dimension, (b) 1% in each spatial dimension, 100% in the temporal dimension and (c) 10% in each spatial dimension, 100% in the temporal dimension

Time Slice Queries. On the contrary, the performance of the FNR-Tree in time slice queries is not that good. Figures 14 and 15 show the average number of node accesses for time slice queries with several datasets and spatial extents. In the road network of Oldenbourg, the FNR-Tree shows better performance for a number of moving objects and over; the break-even point depends on the query size and is at about 300 for 1% and 900 for 100% query size in each spatial dimension. In the road network of San Jose, the 3D R-Tree shows better performance in most cases, except for less than 600 moving objects and 1% query size in each spatial dimension.

The main reason for this shortcoming of the FNR-Tree is that searching in a large spatial window leads searching many 1D R-Trees in the forest. Even if the cost of each search is the minimum of 2 node accesses (i.e., a typical height of the 1D R-tree), for a spatial window of 100% the minimum number of node accesses could not be less than *2*(Number of 1D R-Trees) + (Number of 2D R-Tree Nodes) = 2*(Number of 2D R-Tree Leaves) + (Number of 2D R-Tree Nodes)*. This formula in the case of Oldenbourg results to *2*212+230=664* node accesses.

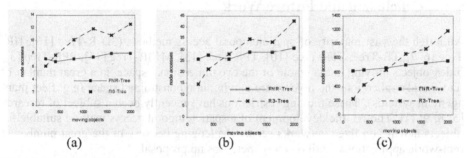

(a)   (b)   (c)

Fig. 14. Timeslice queries for Oldenbourg: (a) 1%, (b) 10% and (c) 100% in each spatial dimension

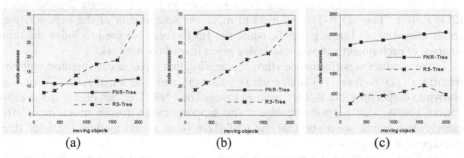

(a)   (b)   (c)

Fig. 15. Timeslice queries for San Jose: (a) 1%, (b) 10% and (c) 100% in each spatial dimension

4.4   Summary of the Experiments

The experiments that were conducted in order to evaluate the performance of the FNR-Tree showed that it supports range queries much more efficiently than the 3D R-Tree. We found additionally, that in a special case of range query, where the temporal extent of the query is much larger than the spatial extent, the performance of the FNR-Tree increases significantly. On the contrary, in time slice queries the performance depends on the road network: For a relatively small network (Oldenbourg) the FNR-Tree shows better performance from a number of moving objects and over, while for a larger network (San Jose), the 3D R-Tree outperforms the FNR-Tree in most cases. Regarding the size of the FNR-Tree, its space utilization – depending on the network and the number of moving objects – can reach the 96%, and the average size per moving object can be 2 to 3 times less than the respective size of a 3D R-Tree. However, the average node accesses per insertion in the FNR-Tree can be 2 to 3 times more than the respective accesses for an insertion in the 3D R-Tree.

5   Conclusion and Future Work

Although the vast majority of spatiotemporal access methods (3D R-Tree [16], HR-Tree [6, 7], TB-Tree, STR-Tree [10], TPR-Tree [13], Mv3R-Tree [14], PPR-Tree [3]) index objects moving in the whole of the two dimensional space, in a great number of real-world applications the objects are moving in a constrained space (e.g. fleet management systems). These moving restrictions have recently been a subject of research [5, 8, 9, 11]. Though the development of a spatiotemporal access method suitable for objects moving on fixed networks seems challenging because of the great number of real-world applications, until recently there was no proposal.

For this purpose, we present a new indexing technique, called Fixed Network R-Tree (FNR-Tree); an extension of the R-Tree [2] designed to index moving objects constrained to move on fixed networks. The general idea that describes the FNR-Tree is a forest of several 1-dimensional (1D) R-Trees on top of a single 2-dimensional (2D) R-Tree. The 2D R-Tree is used to index the spatial data of the network (e.g. roads consisting of line segments), while the 1D R-Trees are used to index the time interval of each object's movement inside given link of the network.

In the conducted performance study, comparing this novel access method with the traditional 3D R-Tree [16] under various datasets and queries, the FNR-Tree was shown to outperform the R-Tree in most cases. The FNR-Tree has higher space utilization, smaller size per moving object and supports range queries much more efficiently. In general, we argue that the FNR-Tree is an access method ideal for fleet management applications.

The FNR-Tree showed a weakness in time-slice queries and, in general, is inefficient to retrieve object trajectories that intersect with a time interval without any spatial extend, because this would result to a search among all the 1D R-Trees contained in the FNR-Tree. Another shortcoming is the inability of the FNR-Tree to answer topological (trajectory-based) queries [10]. This kind of queries requires the preservation of each moving object's trajectory. Therefore, future work has to include the integration of the trajectory preservation as well as the improvement of the access method in order to efficient answer queries without spatial extent.

Acknowledgements

Part of this work was in a MSc. dissertation under the supervision of Professor Timos Sellis, for the MSc. program on GEOINFORMATICS at the National Technical University of Athens (NTUA). The author would like to thank his supervisor Timos Sellis, Yannis Theodoridis for discussions on the subject, and Thomas Brinkhoff for providing his network-based data generator and support. The author is a scholar under the Greek State Scholarship's Foundation.

References

[1]   Brinkhoff, T.: Generating Network-Based Moving Objects. In *Proceedings of the 12th Int'l Conference on Scientific and Statistical Database Management*, SSDBM'00, Berlin, Germany, 2000.

[2]   Guttman, A.: R-Trees: a dynamic index structure for spatial searching, *In Proceedings of the 13th Association for Computing Machinery SIGMOD Conference*, 1984, 47-57.

[3]   Hadjieleftheriou, M., Kollios, G., Tsotras, V.J., Gunopulos, D.: Efficient Indexing of Spatiotemporal Objects. *In Proceedings of 8th International Conference on Extending Database Technology (EDBT)*, Prague, Czech Republic, 2002.

[4]   Kamel, I., and Faloutsos, C.: On Packing R-trees. In Proceedings of the 2nd Conference on Information and Knowledge Management, 490-499, 1993.

[5]   Kollios, G., Gunopulos, D., and Tsotras, V.: On Indexing Mobile Objects. *In Proceedings of the 18th ACM Symposium on Principles of Database Systems*, Philadelphia, PA, USA, 261-272, 1999.

[6]   Nascimento, M.A., and Silva, J.R.O.: Towards historical R-trees. *In Proceedings of the 13th ACM Symposium on Applied Computing (ACM-SAC'98)*, 1998.

[7]   Nascimento, M.A., Silva, J.R.O., and Theodoridis, Y.: Evaluation for access structures for discretely moving points. *In Proceedings of the International Workshop on Spatio-Temporal Database Management (STDBM'99)*, Edinburgh, Scotland, 171-188, 1999.

[8]   Pfoser, D: Indexing the Trajectories of Moving Objects. *IEEE Data Engineering Bulletin*, 25(2):2-9, 2002.

[9]   Pfoser, D., and Jensen, C.S.: Querying the Trajectories of On-Line Mobile Objects. TIMECENTER Technical Report, TR-57, 2001.

[10] Pfoser D., Jensen C.S., and Theodoridis, Y.: Novel Approaches to the Indexing of Moving Object Trajectories. *In Proceedings of the 26th International Conference on Very Large Databases*, Cairo, Egypt, 2000.

[11] Papadias, D., Tao, Y., Kalnis., P., and Zhang, J.: Indexing Spatio-Temporal Data Warehouses. *In Proceedings of IEEE International Conference on Data Engineering (ICDE)*, 2002.

[12] Saltenis, S., and Jensen, C.S.: Indexing of Moving Objects for Location-Based Services. TIMECENTER Technical Report, TR-63, 2001.

[13] Saltenis, S., Jensen, C.S., Leutenegger, S.T., and Lopez, M.A.: Indexing the Positions of Continuously Moving Objects. TIMECENTER Technical Report, TR-44, 1999.

[14] Tao, Y., and Papadias, D.: Mv3R-tree: a spatiotemporal access method for time-stamp and interval queries. *In Proceedings of the 27th International Conference on Very Large Databases*, 2001.

[15] Theodoridis, Y., Sellis, T., Papadopoulos, A.N., Manolopoulos, Y.: Specifications for Efficient Indexing in Spatiotemporal Databases. *In Proceedings of the 10th International Conference on Scientific and Statistical Database Management*, Capri, Italy, 1998.

[16] Theodoridis, Y., Vazirgiannis, M., and Sellis, T.: Spatio-temporal Indexing for Large Multimedia Applications. *In Proceedings of the 3rd IEEE Conference on Multimedia Computing and Systems*, Hiroshima, Japan, 1996.

On-Line Discovery of Dense Areas in Spatio-temporal Databases[*]

Marios Hadjieleftheriou[1], George Kollios[2], Dimitrios Gunopulos[1], and Vassilis J. Tsotras[1]

[1] Computer Science Department, University of California, Riverside
{marioh,dg,tsotras}@cs.ucr.edu
[2] Computer Science Department, Boston University
gkollios@cs.bu.edu

Abstract. Moving object databases have received considerable attention recently. Previous work has concentrated mainly on modeling and indexing problems, as well as query selectivity estimation. Here we introduce a novel problem, that of addressing density-based queries in the spatio-temporal domain. For example: "Find all regions that will contain more than 500 objects, ten minutes from now". The user may also be interested in finding the time period (interval) that the query answer remains valid. We formally define a new class of density-based queries and give approximate, on-line techniques that answer them efficiently. Typically the threshold above which a region is considered to be dense is part of the query. The difficulty of the problem lies in the fact that the spatial and temporal predicates are not specified by the query. The techniques we introduce find all candidate dense regions at any time in the future. To make them more scalable we subdivide the spatial universe using a grid and limit queries within a pre-specified time horizon. Finally, we validate our approaches with a thorough experimental evaluation.

1 Introduction

Databases that manage moving objects have received considerable attention in recent years due to the emergence and importance of location-aware applications like intelligent traffic management, mobile communications, sensor-based surveillance systems, etc. Typically the location of a moving object is represented as a function of time and the database stores the function parameters [2, 1, 17, 9, 22, 21, 16, 24, 15, 27, 23, 10]. This results into a tractable update load. The system is updated only when an object changes any of its moving parameters (e.g., speed, direction, etc). The alternative of storing the object's continuously changing location is practically infeasible since it would correspond to one update per object for each time instant [23]. A database that maintains the moving functions can compute and thus answer interesting

---

[*] This work was partially supported by NSF grants IIS-9907477, EIA-9983445, IIS-0220148 and Career Award 0133825.

T. Hadzilacos et al. (Eds.): SSTD 2003, LNCS 2750, pp. 306–325, 2003.

queries about the locations of the moving objects *in the future*. Examples include range queries: "Find which objects will be in area A, ten minutes from now" [10, 2, 17, 9, 22, 21, 20], nearest neighbor queries: "Find the closest object(s) to a given location within the next five minutes" [24], etc. The answer to such queries is based on the knowledge about the object movements at the time the query is issued [25, 26].

In this paper we present a framework for answering *density*-based queries in moving object databases. An area is dense if the number of moving objects it contains is above some threshold. Discovering dense areas has applications in traffic control systems, bandwidth management, collision probability evaluation, etc. In these environments users are interested in obtaining fast and accurate answers.

We identify two interesting versions of the problem: Snapshot Density Queries (SDQ) and Period Density Queries (PDQ). In SDQ the user is interested in finding the dense areas at a specified time instant in the future. Given a collection of objects moving on a 2-dimensional space, an SDQ example is: "find all regions that will have more than 1000 vehicles per square mile at 3:30pm". On the other hand, a PDQ query finds the dense areas along with the time periods (intervals) that the answers remain valid. For example, a basic operation in a cellular communication network is the identification of all cells that will become dense and for how long.

For the static version of the problem (i.e., where objects are not moving) a number of density based clustering methods have been proposed in recent years. The most relevant is the STING [29] algorithm that uses a hierarchical structure to store statistical information about the dataset. However, this method cannot be used directly for the moving objects environment since the update and space overhead will be large. Another algorithm is CLIQUE [3], suited best for high dimensional static datasets. The basic idea is to find dense areas in lower dimensions first and continue recursively for higher dimensions.

Discovering arbitrary dense areas inside the universe is a rather difficult problem. Both STING and CLIQUE are grid-based approaches. They divide the universe uniformly into a number of disjoint *cells*. The problem is thus simplified to that of finding all the *dense cells*. We use the same approach for two reasons: For most cases (e.g., traffic management) the granularity and arrangement of the grid can be set according to user needs. In other applications (e.g., cellular networks) all cells are already available.

For many practical applications the *exact* density of a region is not of critical importance. For example, a query about potential traffic jams may tolerate a small approximation error. Our approach is to keep a small summary of the moving object dataset in main memory that can be used to answer queries quickly. Also, due to high update rates, the data structures must be easy to maintain in an on-line fashion. To achieve these goals we use spatio-temporal grids and propose techniques based on Dense Cell Filters and Approximate Frequency Counting (Lossy Counting). These methods guarantee against false negatives but have a few false positives. In applications where false positives cannot be ignored our techniques can be used as a pre-filtering step. Our estimators can quickly identify the (typically few) candidate dense regions which must then be passed through a post-filtering step.

To the best of our knowledge this is the first work that addresses density-based queries in a spatio-temporal environment. Previous work has dealt with range, join and nearest neighbor queries. Related to density queries is recent work on *selectivity estimation* for spatio-temporal range queries [27, 8]. Spatio-temporal estimators compute the number of objects that will cross a user defined spatial region at a user defined time instant in the future. However, a density query is "orthogonal" in nature since the user does not specify the spatial and temporal query predicates. One straightforward way to use a spatio-temporal estimator to identify dense areas is by computing the selectivity estimate for *each* cell in the spatio-temporal grid. While simplistic, this approach is clearly inefficient due to its large computational cost (the spatio-temporal grid typically contains too many cells).

To summarize our contributions:

- We identify two novel query types for spatio-temporal databases based on the notion of density in space and time. We concentrate on tractable versions of the problem based on a regular spatio-temporal grid.
- We propose solutions that provide fast *approximate* answers by building main memory summaries that can accommodate large update rates and deliver fast query responses.
- We present an extensive experimental study that validates the accuracy and efficiency of our methods. The proposed Dense Cell Filter approach has the most robust performance requiring limited space and yielding a very small number of false positives.

2   Problem Definition

2.1   General Framework

In this section we define the general density-based query framework and our notation. We assume that a database stores a set of N objects moving on a 2-dimensional plane. We model these objects as points represented by tuples of the form: (x, y, v_x, v_y), where (x, y) is the current location and $v = (v_x, v_y)$ the velocity vector. In our setting, objects can follow *arbitrary* trajectories in the future (represented by generic functions of time). For illustration purposes and simplicity, in the rest of the paper we refer to linear trajectories only.

The objective is to find regions in space and time that with high probability will satisfy interesting predicates. For 2-dimensional movements an interesting property is finding areas where objects tend to be very close to each other. We formalize this notion with the following definition:

Region Density. *The density of region R during time interval ΔT is defined as: $Density(R, \Delta T) = \frac{\min_{\Delta T} N}{Area(R)}$, where $\min_{\Delta T} N$ is the minimum number of objects inside R during ΔT and $Area(R)$ is the total area of R.*

Hence, we define region density as the minimum concentration of objects inside the region during the time interval of interest. An important observation is that regions with high density are not necessarily interesting. For example, two objects arbitrarily close to each other define a region with arbitrarily high density. Therefore, we allow the user to define both the level of density and the minimum and maximum area that a qualifying region must have. Given the above definition we can now state the following density based queries:

Period Density Query. *Given a set of N moving objects in space, a horizon H and thresholds α_1, α_2 and ξ, find regions $R = \{r_1, \ldots, r_k\}$ and maximal time intervals $\Delta T = \{\delta t_1, \ldots, \delta t_k | \delta t_i \subset [T_{now}, T_{now} + H]\}$ such that: $\alpha_1 \leq Area(r_i) \leq \alpha_2$ and $Density(r_i, \delta t_i) > \xi$ (where T_{now} is the current time, $i \in [1, k]$ and k is the query answer size).*

Notice that in the above query we do not specify time or spatial predicates. Any method for answering this query must find not only the dense regions but also the time periods that these regions appear to be dense inside the specified horizon H. Typically, we require the area to be within some size (α_1, α_2) since the most interesting cases are when a large number of objects are concentrated in a small region of space. Also, the reported time periods are required to be maximal. The time interval associated with a dense region should include all time instants between the time the region will first become dense (with respect to threshold ξ) until it seizes to be so.

A special case of the period density query is:

Snapshot Density Query. *Given a set of N moving objects in space, a horizon H, a time instant T_q ($T_q \in [T_{now}, T_{now} + H]$) and thresholds α_1, α_2 and ξ, find regions $R = \{r_1, \ldots, r_k\}$ such that: $\alpha_1 \leq Area(r_i) \leq \alpha_2$ and $Density(r_i, T_q) > \xi$ (where $i \in [1, k]$ and k denotes the query answer size).*

In Figure 1 we show an example of objects moving on a 2-dimensional surface. The current time is 1. The answer to a PDQ with $H = 3, \xi = 3$ and $\alpha_1 = \alpha_2 = 1$ (i.e., we are looking for regions 1 square unit in size), is $R = \{A, B\}$ and

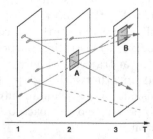

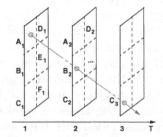

Fig. 1. An example of objects moving linearly in 2-dimensional space over time

Fig. 2. The space-time grid for $H_f = 3$. The trajectory of the object will cross cells $\{A_1, B_2, C_3\}$

$\Delta T = \{[2,2],[3,3]\}$. It should be clear that by increasing $\alpha_{1,2}$ or decreasing ξ, increases the size of the answer. Meaningful values for $\alpha_{1,2}$ and ξ are, of course, application dependent.

The requirement for arbitrary region sizes along with the need for discovering maximal time periods render the general density-based queries very difficult to answer and hint at exhaustive search solutions. In addition, the horizon is not restricted and its upper boundary advances continuously as the current time increases. We proceed with the simplified versions of density-based queries, based on spatio-temporal grids and *fixed* horizons.

2.2   Simplified Queries

We partition the universe using a number of disjoint cells (buckets) and consider the problem of finding the most dense cells. Assuming that the partitioning of space is done according to user requirements, fast on-line discovery of the most dense cells is the first, most important step for answering general density queries. The solutions we propose are orthogonal to the partitioning process. For simplicity we consider only uniform grids of cells but the techniques work for general partitions also, as long as the cells are disjoint and their sizes remain fixed inside the horizon. The emphasis in our treatment is in handling a very large number of cells efficiently.

We also choose a *fixed* horizon during which user queries can be answered. Instead of letting the boundary of the horizon advance as the current time advances, a fixed horizon provides answers only inside a fixed time interval $[T_{now}, H_f]$ (the upper boundary remains constant). Simplified fixed horizons apply to most practical moving object applications [22, 27, 8]; the user is typically interested in the near future for which the current information holds. When the horizon expires the estimators should be rebuilt [27, 8]. It is reasonable to assume that the user can decide in advance the time period during which most queries will refer to. A problem that arises with fixed horizons is that as T_{now} advances closer and closer to the horizon boundary, inevitably, queries will refer to an ever decreasing time period into the future. One way to avoid this situation is by rebuilding the estimators halfway through the horizon. For example, if T_{now} is 1:00pm and H_f is set to 2:00pm, after half an hour (at 1:30pm) we can rebuild the estimator for another 30 minutes, until 2:30pm. Essentially, we can answer queries for at least 30 minutes into the future at all times.

Using the spatio-temporal partitioning and the fixed horizons the queries we answer have the following two forms:

Simple Period Density Query. *Given a fixed partitioning $\mathcal{P}$ of space into a number of disjoint cells, find the cells that contain a number of objects larger than a user specified threshold ξ inside the fixed horizon, along with the time periods that the answers remain valid.*

Simple Snapshot Density Query. *Given a fixed partitioning $\mathcal{P}$ of space into a number of disjoint cells, find the cells that contain a number of objects larger* *than a user specified threshold ξ, at a user specified time T_q inside the fixed horizon.*

Assuming uniform grids of cells from now on (without loss of generality), first a grid granularity and an appropriate horizon length are decided. Conceptually we create a spatial grid for every time instant inside the horizon. For example, assume a horizon of three time instants and let the 2-dimensional spatial universe be 100 miles long in each direction, with a grid granularity of 1 square mile. This will divide the space-time grid into $3 \times 100 \times 100 = 30,000$ cells. All cells are enumerated with unique IDs (Figure 2). One straightforward approach to address the problem is as follows. Since the speed and direction of a moving object are known at insertion time, we can extrapolate its trajectory and find all the cells that the object will cross in the space-time grid. Every object update is thus converted into a set of cell IDs, one ID (at most) per time instant of the horizon. By maintaining the number of crossings per cell we know each cell's density at any time instant in the horizon. The same technique is used for handling deletions and updates (by adjusting the appropriate cells).

While simplistic, this approach has a major disadvantage. In any practical application the total number of cells of the space-time grid is expected to be very large (millions of cells). Keeping a density counter for each cell consumes unnecessary space. We could reduce space by keeping only the cells that have been crossed so far and discard cells with zero density. However, for real datasets this will not decrease space substantially since most cells will be crossed at least once. Other techniques, like concise and counting samples [13], can be used to compress the density information. Counting samples would keep only a random sample of cell $< ID, count >$ pairs in a straightforward way. This approach offers many advantages, but still, it is probabilistic and does not guarantee against false negatives.

It is apparent that the granularity and arrangement of the chosen partitioning $\mathcal{P}$ directly affects the performance of any solution, for a given application. A very fine grained (and a very coarse) grid might fail to produce any dense cells. A very large number of cells will have a negative impact on answer speed, etc. We postulate, though, that for most practical applications the partitioning is already (at least vaguely) defined thus limiting available choices.

We propose several techniques that compress the density information by building estimators that identify only the most dense cells and discard the rest. The penalty of using estimators is two fold. First, the reported densities are approximations. Second, in order to guarantee no false dismissals a number of false positives will be reported along with the correct answers.

3 Grid-Based Techniques

We first describe a simple improvement based on *coarse grids*. We then present an *Approximate Frequency Counting* algorithm (termed Lossy Counting) that appeared in [18] and can be modified and used in our setting. Finally, we introduce another approach, the *Dense Cell Filter*.

3.1   Coarse Grids

Coarse grids are a general technique that can be utilized by all subsequent estimators for decreasing their size. Instead of keeping one density counter per cell
for the whole space-time grid (Figure 2), multiple consecutive cells in time are
combined into a single bucket associated with only one counter (Figure 3). The
granularity of the coarse grid is defined as the number of consecutive cells in
time that belong to the same bucket. By making the buckets larger (decreasing the granularity) we can decrease the size of the original grid substantially.
It should be noted that coarse grids compress the grid in the time dimension
only. Combining cells in the spatial dimensions is not applicable since it would
invalidate the application dependent partitioning.

Figure 3 shows an example of a coarse grid with granularity 2 (buckets are
illustrated by the shaded regions). Essentially, the number of total counters is
reduced by half. An object trajectory crosses buckets $A_{1,2}$ and $B_{3,4}$, and thus
these counters should be adjusted.

The coarse grid guarantees no
false dismissals but may introduce false positives. For example,
the reported density for cell A_2 is
the value of counter $A_{1,2}$, which
increases once for every crossing
of any cell (A_1 or A_2) that belongs to that bucket. If the number of crosses of either A_1 or A_2
exceeds threshold ξ, $A_{1,2}$ will also
exceed ξ, hence no false negatives
are created. On the other hand,

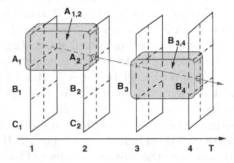

Fig. 3.   A coarse grid of granularity 2

very fast moving objects may introduce false positives. If the slope of a trajectory is large, the object might pass through a bucket without crossing all the
cells that belong to it. In such cases the densities of some cells are overestimated.
Obviously, the larger the bucket width (and the faster the objects) the more false
positives may be created.

Answering an SDQ is straightforward. We locate the cells that correspond
to time instant T_q and report the ones that belong to dense buckets. To answer a PDQ we scan the grid that corresponds to the beginning of the horizon
(assume T_{now} for simplicity) and locate all the dense buckets. For every dense
bucket B, we check later time instants to find how many consecutive buckets are
also dense.

3.2   Lossy Counting

Lossy counting is a deterministic algorithm introduced in [18] for computing
item frequencies over a stream of transactions. It guarantees an upper bound of
$\frac{1}{\epsilon} \log \epsilon L$ space, where L is the current length of the stream. The input to the
algorithm is an error threshold ϵ. The output is a set containing the most frequent

items. The estimated frequencies differ from the actual frequencies by at most ϵL. The algorithm calculates the frequency of the items as a percentage of L and detects the ones that appear with the highest rate (as L continuously increases). For example, a query has the following form: "Find items that appeared until now in the stream for more than 70% of the time". The answer to this query would be all items with frequency $f \geq 0.7L$.

The actual algorithm appears in Figure 4. The incoming stream is divided into consecutive buckets. Every bucket B consists of w items, where $w = \frac{1}{\epsilon}$ is the width of each bucket. The algorithm maintains a set $\mathcal{F}$ of the most frequent items. Every entry in $\mathcal{F}$ has the form $E = < id, f, \Delta >$, where id is the item identifier, f the estimated frequency and Δ the maximum possible error in f. Initially $\mathcal{F}$ is empty and $B = 1$. Whenever a new item I arrives, the algorithm checks whether I is in $\mathcal{F}$. If it is, the entry is updated by increasing its frequency $(E_I.f)$. If it is not, a new entry is inserted in $\mathcal{F}$. Every w items the bucket boundary is reached and $\mathcal{F}$ is updated by removing the items that are not frequent anymore. At any point, the estimator can return all items that appeared more than pL times (where $p \in [0, 1]$ and is specified by the query) by outputting all entries in $\mathcal{F}$ for which $E.f \geq (p - \epsilon)L$.

This technique works well for finding the most frequent items. Once such items are inserted into $\mathcal{F}$ their frequency is being calculated and, most probably, they will never be deleted from $\mathcal{F}$. Items that are not as frequent will be inserted and later removed from $\mathcal{F}$. We can apply the Lossy Counting approach for density queries with some *modifications*. Instead of a stream of items we have a sequence of object insertions and deletions. Every insertion is converted into a set of cell IDs (Figure 2). We input the IDs that are being crossed by the object trajectories as the streaming values of the Lossy Counting algorithm. The dense

---

Input: Stream of items $\{I_1, I_2, \ldots\}$. Error ϵ.
Output: Set $\mathcal{F}$ of entries $E = < id, f, \Delta >$ representing the most frequent items in the stream.

$\mathcal{F} = \emptyset, w = \frac{1}{\epsilon}, B = 1, L = 0$
New item I appears in stream:
  // Check for bucket boundary first.
  If $L > 0$ and L mod $w = 0$:
    For all $E \in \mathcal{F}$: If $E.f + E.\Delta \leq B$: remove E from $\mathcal{F}$
    $B+ = 1$
  // Process the new item.
  $L+ = 1$
  If $I \in \mathcal{F}$: $E_I.f+ = 1$
  Else: Add $E = < I.id, 1, B - 1 >$ in $\mathcal{F}$
Return the most frequent items:
  For all $E \in \mathcal{F}$: If $E.f \geq (p - \epsilon)L$: return $E.id$

Fig. 4. The Lossy Counting algorithm

cells, whose IDs appear more frequently, are kept in $\mathcal{F}$. Less interesting cells are omitted. A deletion is straightforward. For a cell C crossed by the old trajectory, if $C \in \mathcal{F}$ we decrease $C.f$ by one. Cells that become non-frequent will be deleted at the bucket boundary.

This algorithm can find the cells that have been crossed by more than pL trajectories, where $L \approx NH$ is the number of IDs that have appeared on the stream, a number roughly as large as the number of object updates N times the remaining horizon length H. Since not all trajectories cross one cell per time instant of the horizon but some extend outside of the universe, L might be smaller than the above product. However, user queries have a pre-specified density threshold ξ that represents an absolute number of objects, while Lossy Counting can only produce entries that are frequent with respect to L. Thus, we have to express ξ as a percentage of L. In particular, in order to retrieve all the answers we need to find p such that $pL \leq \xi$. However, since $p \leq \frac{\xi}{L} \Rightarrow \lim_{L \to \infty} p = 0$, as L increases no p may satisfy the query. To prove this suppose we return all cells with frequencies: $\mathcal{A} = \{C | C.f \geq \xi - \epsilon L\}$, while the correct answer is: $\mathcal{CA} = \{C | C.f \geq pL - \epsilon L\}$. Since $pL \leq \xi$, we get: $Cardinality(\mathcal{A}) \leq Cardinality(\mathcal{CA})$. This means that we might miss some of the answers. Unfortunately, this pitfall cannot be avoided unless the estimator is rebuilt more frequently such that L does not become too large (so that a p exists that satisfies the query).

Regarding implementation, set $\mathcal{F}$ can be organized as a collection of hash tables, one for every time instant of the horizon. To answer an SDQ with time T_q and threshold ξ we find all cells with density larger than ξ in the appropriate hash table. To answer a PDQ we scan the hash table that corresponds to the beginning of the horizon (assume T_{now} for simplicity) and locate all the dense cells. For every dense cell $C_{T_{now}}$, we probe the hash table at time instant $T_{now}+1$ to see if the corresponding cell $C_{T_{now}+1}$ is also dense, and continue as long as the cell remains dense.

An interesting observation about Lossy Counting is that cells that may be false positives have densities in the interval $[(p - \epsilon)L, pL]$. All cells with larger densities definitely belong to the correct answer. However, in the worst case all reported cells may have densities in the aforementioned interval. That is, the method does not provide any guarantees on the number of false positives, neither this number can be estimated.

3.3   Dense Cell Filter

To overcome some of the above limitations we introduce the Dense Cell Filter approach. This novel solution uses a modification of a basic Bloom Filter to create a small summary of the dense cells. A Bloom Filter [5] is a simple randomized data structure for representing a set in order to support membership queries and it is very space efficient.

Given a set $\mathcal{S} = \{C_1, \ldots C_E\}$ of E elements the problem is to find if item X belongs to $\mathcal{S}$ (membership query). A basic Bloom Filter is a hashing scheme that uses a bit-vector array with M bits (initialized to zero) and a set of K independent hash functions $\mathcal{H} = \{h_1, \ldots, h_K\}$, that produce values in the range

$[1, M]$. For every C_e ($e \in [1, E]$) all K hash functions $h_k(C_e)$ ($k \in [1, K]$) are computed, producing K numbers. Each number maps to a bit in the bit vector hence the corresponding bits are *set*. To find if X belongs to S the hash functions are applied on X to produce K values. If all K values map to bits that are set, X is in S with some probability. If at least one bit is not set, then X is not in S.

Figure 5 shows an example. The filter has $M = 10$ bits and uses $K = 2$ hash functions. Initially all bits are *reset* (set to zero and depicted as white boxes). During the insertion stage we insert set $S = \{C_1, C_2\}$. Hash functions $h_1(C_1) = 1, h_2(C_1) = 5$ and $h_1(C_2) = 5, h_2(C_2) = 9$ are computed and the resulting bits are set (shaded boxes). During the query stage three membership queries are performed. For C_1 and C_3 the result-

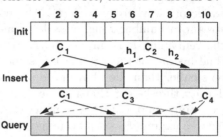

Fig. 5. A Bloom Filter using $K = 2$ hash functions and $M = 10$ bits

ing bits are already set thus these items might be in S or not. It is apparent that C_3 is a false positive since the item was never inserted in the filter. On the other hand, C_4 certainly does not belong to S since $h_1(C_4) = 7$ is not set.

Assuming perfect hash functions it can be shown that the probability of a false positive is $(1 - e^{-\frac{KE}{M}})^K$. By knowing the values of E and M, the number K of hash functions that minimize the number of false positives can be computed. This is achieved for $K = \ln 2(\frac{M}{E})$ [6]. By increasing M we decrease the probability of false positives, but at the same time the size of the Bloom Filter increases.

A variation of the basic Bloom filter, directly related to our approach, is the *counting Bloom Filter* [12]. Each bit of the bit vector is replaced with a small counter (for example 2 bytes). Every time a new element is inserted, the corresponding counters are incremented (instead of the bits just being set). When an element is deleted, the counters are decremented. In our environment we have a spatio-temporal grid $S = \{C_1, \ldots, C_E\}$ of E distinct cells (or buckets in case of coarse grids) and we want to store the density of each cell using as little space as possible. We also want to identify the most dense cells quickly. We thus build a counting Bloom Filter that stores S, and maintain it on-line. Every time an object update is performed, we convert it into a sequence $U \subset S$ of cell IDs and insert them into the filter. If the counter of a cell C_i becomes larger than ψ (specified at construction time), we insert C_i into the list of dense cells (DCL). From that point, the frequency of C_i is updated in the DCL only, without affecting the filter. Deletions are straightforward. They just reverse the effect of the corresponding insertion. The algorithm is shown in Figure 6.

One improvement would be to keep a separate Bloom Filter per time instant of the horizon. As time progresses, Bloom Filters that refer to the past can be discarded to save space. Also, since fewer cells are associated with each filter, we expect to have fewer false positives. Since the DCL list can grow very large, it should be organized as a set of in memory hash tables, one for every time instant of the horizon.

An interesting issue is that the DCL contains all cells that exceed threshold ψ, specified at construction time. If the user poses a query with $\xi < \psi$, the DCL cannot report an answer. There are two solutions for such queries. Either the filter has to be rebuild with a full database scan or it has to adapt to the lower threshold ξ gradually, while postponing the answer to the query. With the adaptive threshold approach the filter cannot guarantee anymore that some dense cells will not be missed. Nevertheless, the Dense Cell Filter is still a valuable approach since for most applications the lower possible threshold can be decided at construction time.

In contrast to Lossy Counting the Dense Cell Filter can provide certain probabilistic guarantees on the number of false positives introduced. Below we show that the probability of a cell with density $c < \xi$ being reported is small and depends on the number of objects, the number of counters, c and ξ.

Lemma 1. *Given N moving objects, a query threshold ξ and a Bloom Filter with one stage of M counters per time instant of the horizon, the probability that cell C with density $c < \xi$ is being reported by the filter is in the worst case $P \leq \frac{1}{M} \frac{N-c}{\xi-c}$ (the proof can be found in the full paper).*

Note that the lemma provides an upper bound and the probability of false positives is much smaller in practice. Nevertheless, from the formula we can infer

---

Input: Set of cells $\mathcal{S} = \{C_1, \ldots, C_E\}$. Number of stages K and hash functions $h_{1,\ldots,K}$. Counters per stage M. Threshold ψ. Horizon H.
Output: A dense cell list (DCL).

$DCL = \emptyset$, $V_{1,\ldots,K}$ = vectors of M counters
For $k = 1 \to K, m = 1 \to M : V_k[m] = 0$
Object insertion:
$U \subset \mathcal{S}$ = set of cell IDs crossed by object during H
For all $C_i \in U$:
  If $C_i \in DCL : C_i.density+ = 1$
  Else:
    For $k = 1 \to K : V_k[h_k(C_i)]+ = 1$
    If all $V_k[h_k(C_i)] \geq \psi$: add C_i in DCL
Object deletion:
$U \subset \mathcal{S}$ = set of cell IDs crossed by object during H
For all $C_i \in U$:
  If $C_i \in DCL$:
    $C_i.density- = 1$
    If $C_i.density < \psi$: remove C_i from DCL
  Else: For $k = 1 \to K : V_k[h_k(C_i)]- = 1$

Fig. 6. The Dense Cell Filter algorithm

that be increasing the number of counters M or the threshold ξ, the probability for false positives decreases. It is also apparent that increasing the number of stages K per filter will have a negative impact. Both observations are validated by our experimental results (refer to Section 5).

4 Discussion

First we comment on the advantages and disadvantages of each of the three grid-based techniques. Then, we consider methods for eliminating false positives.

4.1 Comparison of Grid-Based Algorithms

The coarse grid uses a simple idea to compress the space-time grid. Since the compression process is independent of the actual cell densities, the number of false positives will increase substantially for large granularities. Furthermore, since only one density counter is kept per bucket, the estimated densities will not be very accurate either.

An advantage of Lossy Counting is that (if certain conditions are met) it computes the estimated densities with great accuracy, since the most dense cells are always stored in memory. However, it provides no guarantees about the number of false positives in the answer. Moreover, the estimator needs to be rebuilt frequently so that it does not miss actual dense cells. Since a large number of cells are added and dropped at the bucket boundaries continuously (i.e., these cells are considered by the algorithm to be almost frequent but not frequent enough) their estimated frequencies have a higher error. If the user threshold is small enough to be close to the density of these cells, the algorithm will yield a higher number of false positives with an increased estimation error. Finally, the algorithm has a substantial computational overhead since it has to perform one linear scan of the in memory list per bucket boundary. The cost will increase, of course, when the list is larger (for smaller user thresholds or a multitude of dense cells).

In contrast, the Dense Cell Filter provides strong guarantees on the number of false positives and can be easily adjusted according to space requirements. Moreover, when dense cells are identified they are added in the DCL and their estimated densities are computed with high accuracy. Another benefit is that the algorithm is very efficient with an expected small computational overhead. A drawback of Dense Cell Filter is that the threshold cannot be dynamically set (the lowest possible threshold has to be decided at construction time).

4.2 False Positives

One approach for minimizing false positives is by using a spatio-temporal histogram. Such histograms provide an estimate of the selectivity of each reported cell. Unfortunately, recently proposed techniques [27, 8] do not provide any guarantees on the selectivity estimates they report. An alternative is the use of *sketching* (proposed in [14] and based on the seminal work of [4]). Sketches can be used to approximate the spatio-temporal grid by summarizing the information associated with the cells. The advantage of sketching is that the estimation is highly accurate with high probability. The disadvantage is that they are computationally expensive.

If the objective is the full elimination of false positives the user may run a spatio-temporal range query using the spatial range of each cell being reported by the estimators. Such a query finds the actual objects in that cell (i.e., an exact answer). Indexing techniques for moving points can be used for that purpose (the TPR-tree [22, 21], the duality indexing of [17] or the partitioning schemes in [11]). Those indices are dynamically updated and index the whole moving dataset. While a range query provides the exact answer, it runs at time proportional to the number of objects in the cell (and since these are the denser cells, they will contain a lot of objects).

5   Experimental Results

All experiments were run on an Intel Pentium(R) 4 1.60Ghz CPU with 1Gb of main memory. We generated various synthetic datasets of moving objects. For the first dataset we initially pick a random number of dense locations and place a large number of objects around them (a snapshot is shown in Figure 7(a)). We distribute the rest of the objects uniformly in space and let them move freely on the plane. The dataset tries to simulate vehicles that disperse from dense areas. For example, the downtown L.A. area at 3:00pm or a stadium after the end of a game. In the rest, we refer to this dataset as DENSE. The second dataset represents a network of highways and surface streets (denoted as ROAD, Figure 7(b)). Each road is represented by a set of connected line segments (231 line segments were generated in total). The 2-dimensional universe for both datasets is 100 miles long in each direction. Every simulation lasts for 100 time instants. We generated 1 million moving objects per dataset. Every time instant at least 1% of the objects issue an update (which changes the speed and/or direction of the object). The velocities of the vehicles are generated using a skewed distribution, between 10 and 110 miles per hour.

For our measurements we used a 250×250 uniform grid; this gives 62,500 cells in total, while every cell is 0.4 miles wide. The horizon was fixed at the start of each simulation. As time proceeds, queries refer to time instants that fall inside the horizon interval. For example, if the horizon was set to $H_f = 20$ and the current time is $T_{now} = 9$, the estimators provide answers for queries that refer to time instants between 9 and 20. When the current time reaches halfway through the horizon, all estimators are automatically rebuild.This is typical for horizon-based solutions [22, 27, 8].

We also created synthetic query workloads. For each experiment we set a fixed density threshold, both for period and snapshot queries. Each experiment is run multiple times varying the density threshold from 1000 to 2500 objects. For snapshot queries the time predicate is uniformly distributed inside the remaining period of the current horizon. For every simulation we run 200 queries in total.

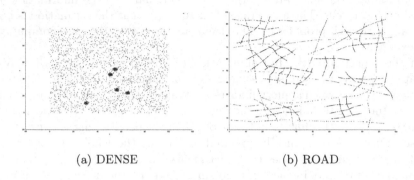

(a) DENSE   (b) ROAD

Fig. 7. Datasets

We compare 3 techniques: Dense Cell Filters (denoted as DCF), Lossy Counting (LC), and coarse grids (CG). We tested every technique using several configurations in order to "optimally" tune their performance. We run DCF with several different combinations of stages and counters, LC with varying bucket widths and CG with decreasing granularities. In the rest of this section for every technique we plot the best result given among all configurations with similar size. To compare the efficiency of our techniques we use the *answer size* as a measure. We define the answer size as the total number of false positives plus the actual dense cells reported by each estimator. In addition, we compute the answer size as a percentage of the total number of cells in the spatio-temporal grid. The answer size is an important indication of an estimator's robustness since it gives a good feeling about the reduced processing cost required for finding an exact answer, after the estimator has produced a result superset (compared with calculating the exact answer exhaustively, without the help of the estimator). In addition, since false positives tend to dominate the result set, the smaller the answer size the better the estimator. Thus, a direct comparison between estimators is realistic.

The efficiency of the techniques as a function of the estimator size for snapshot queries is shown in Figure 8. The size of the estimators is computed as a percentage of the size of the entire spatio-temporal grid. For this graph we used a density threshold equal to 1500 objects and a fixed horizon of 50 time instants (i.e., 3,125,000 cells). Assuming 4 bytes per cell, the 5% estimator uses only 600KB of main memory. We can deduce that for DCF and LC a 5% estimator size yields very few false positives (less than 2% answer size). Increasing their size beyond 5% does not yield substantial improvements, especially for DCF. On the other hand, CG benefits even for sizes greater than 10%. The CG estimator in order to reduce the grid to 5% of its original size has to become very coarse thus its performance deteriorates due to very large bucket lengths. For the rest of the graphs we compare all techniques using estimators with 5% size (to be fair we used 2 bytes per counter for DCF since this is enough to represent a maximum reasonable threshold).

Figure 9 shows a scale-up experiment for increasing horizon lengths. We tested all estimators with an SDQ set using horizons of 10, 20 and 50 time instants, while keeping the estimator sizes within 5% of the total number of cells. The DCF performance remains unaffected; since a separate filter is kept per time instant of the horizon, the horizon length should not affect the accuracy in general. It is apparent that LC is robust for uniform data (DENSE), but its performance deteriorates for highly skewed distributions (ROAD). Also, a much larger bucket size was needed in order to keep the estimator within the 5% limit, without loosing some of the correct answers. For CG there is a noticeable performance penalty for both datasets. In order to keep the estimator size within our space requirements the grid granularity has to become very coarse. Moreover, this technique is very fluctuant, which makes it even less attractive.

In Figure 10 we plot efficiency as a function of density threshold. For this experiment we used an SDQ set and a horizon length of 50 time instants. As expected, the larger the density threshold the fewer false positives are reported. If there is only a small number of dense cells at a specific time instant, the estimators identify them with great accuracy. The problem becomes more difficult as the number of cells that have densities around that threshold becomes larger. For thresholds larger than 2000 objects all estimators report very few false positives. For the DENSE dataset DCF and LC give the best results (almost no false positives are reported) while CG does not perform well. Performance deteriorates though for LC, especially for smaller thresholds. For the ROAD dataset DCF gives again the best results; it reports less than 1% of the total number of cells in all cases. Even when exact density answers are required, it is obvious that there is a substantial benefit when using this technique as a pre-filtering step to reduce the amount of cells that need to be checked.

Figure 11 plots the relative error in computing the exact density for the dense cells (averaged over all queries), as a function of density thresholds. All techniques report the densities of the dense cells with less than 1% error (over the exact density of that cell). The results reported by DCF and LC were very close to the actual densities. CG was considerably worse, but still below 1% error.

Figure 12 shows the update cost of the techniques as a function of horizon length. For DCF and CG the update cost does not grow substantially (CG is almost two times more expensive than DCF). The cost for LC increases proportionally for larger horizon lengths due to the larger bucket widths needed. Moreover, LC is about three times slower than DCF.

Figure 13 plots the estimator performance for period queries (PDQ) as a function of density threshold. We observe the same trends as with snapshot queries. DCF is the best compromise between accuracy, speed and robustness for increasing density thresholds and highly skewed data (less than 3% answer size for all cases). LC works very well for the DENSE dataset, but its performance

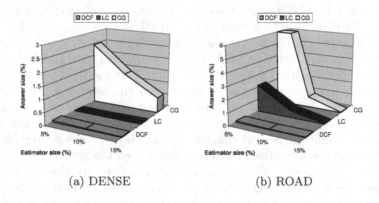

(a) DENSE   (b) ROAD

Fig. 8. Performance evaluation as a function of estimator size for snapshot queries

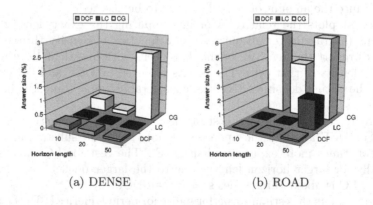

(a) DENSE   (b) ROAD

Fig. 9. Performance evaluation as a function of horizon length for snapshot queries

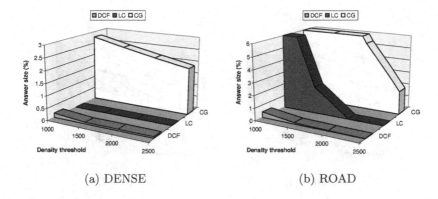

(a) DENSE   (b) ROAD

Fig. 10. Performance evaluation as a function of density threshold for snapshot queries

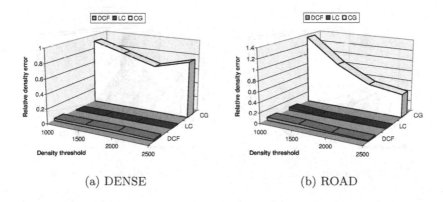

(a) DENSE   (b) ROAD

Fig. 11. Relative density error as a function of density threshold for snapshot queries

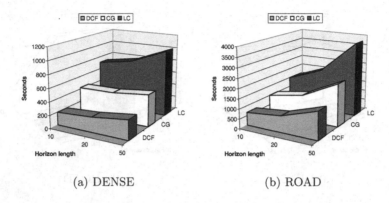

(a) DENSE   (b) ROAD

Fig. 12. Estimator update cost as a function of horizon length

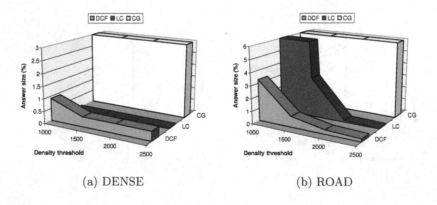

(a) DENSE   (b) ROAD

Fig. 13. Performance evaluation as a function of density threshold for period queries

deteriorates for the ROAD dataset and small density thresholds. CG, on the other hand, reported more than 8% false positives for all cases.

From our extensive experimental evaluation DCF presented the most robust performance making it a quite accurate, fast and reliable density estimation technique. LC gives very good density estimates but has much higher update cost and does not work well for highly skewed environments.

6   Conclusions

We addressed the problem of on-line discovery of dense areas in spatio-temporal environments. We simplified the problem by dividing the spatial universe into a uniform grid of cells and considering a fixed horizon in the time domain. We proposed efficient solutions that provide fast answers with high accuracy. Our solutions are based on Dense Cell Filters and Approximate Frequency counting algorithms. They guarantee no false dismissals (but few false positives), provide fast updates and are space efficient. An extensive experimental evaluation was also presented, showing that the Dense Cell Filter was the most robust solution. It gave fast and accurate answers, with a minimal number of false positives. In future work we will address Top-K density-based queries. Instead of specifying a density threshold the query must report the k most dense cells. Methods based on histograms [19, 28] or sampling [13, 7] should be considered.

References

[1] P. Agarwal, L. Arge, and J. Vahrenhold. Time responsive indexing schemes for moving points. In *Proc. of WADS*, 2001.   306
[2] P. K. Agarwal, L. Arge, and J. Erickson. Indexing moving points. *In Proc. of the 19th ACM Symp. on Principles of Database Systems (PODS)*, pages 175–186, 2000.   306, 307
[3] R. Agrawal, J. Gehrke, D. Gunopulos, and P. Raghavan. Automatic Subspace Clustering of High Dimensional Data for Data Mining Applications. *In Proc. of ACM SIGMOD Conference*, pages 94–105, June 1998.   307
[4] N. Alon, Y. Matias, and M. Szegedy. The space complexity of approximating the frequency moments. In *Journal of Computer and System Sciences*, volume 58(1), pages 137–147, 1999.   317
[5] B. H. Bloom. Space/time trade-offs in hash coding with allowable errors. *Communications of the ACM*, 13(7):422–426, 1970.   314
[6] A. Broder and M. Mitzenmacher. Network Applications of Bloom Filters: A Survey. In *To appear in Allerton 2002*.   315
[7] C.-M. Chen and Y. Ling. A sampling-based estimator for Top-k query. In *Proc of IEEE ICDE*, 2002.   324
[8] Yong-Jin Choi and Chin-Wan Chung. Selectivity estimation for spatio-temporal queries to moving objects. In *Proc. of ACM SIGMOD*, 2002.   308, 310, 317, 318
[9] H. D. Chon, D. Agrawal, and A. El Abbadi. Storage and retrieval of moving objects. In *Mobile Data Management*, pages 173–184, 2001.   306, 307
[10] C. Jensen (editor). Special issue on indexing moving objects. *Data Engineering Bulletin*, 2002.   306, 307

[11] K. Elbassioni, A. Elmasry, and I. Kamel. An efficient indexing scheme for multi-dimensional moving objects. *9th International Conference on Database Theory, Siena, Italy (to appear)*, 2003. 318

[12] L. Fan, J. Almeida P. Cao, and A. Broder. Summary cache: a scalable wide-area web cache sharing protocol. *IEEE/ACM Transactions on Networking*, 8(3):281–293, 2000. 315

[13] P. Gibbons and Y. Matias. New sampling-based summary statistics for improving approximate query answers. In *Proc. of ACM SIGMOD*, April 1998. 311, 324

[14] A. C. Gilbert, Y. Kotidis, S. Muthukrishnan, and M. Strauss. Surfing Wavelets on Streams: One-Pass Summaries for Approximate Aggregate Queries. In *The VLDB Journal*, September 2001. 317

[15] O. Ibarra H. Mokhtar, J. Su. On moving object queries. In *Proc. 21st ACM PODS Symposium on Princeples of Database Systems, Madison, Wisconsin*, pages 188–198, 2002. 306

[16] G. Kollios, D. Gunopulos, and V. Tsotras. Nearest Neighbor Queries in a Mobile Environment. *In Proc. of the Spatio-Temporal Database Management Workshop, Edinburgh, Scotland*, pages 119–134, 1999. 306

[17] G. Kollios, D. Gunopulos, and V. Tsotras. On Indexing Mobile Objects. *In Proc. of the 18th ACM Symp. on Principles of Database Systems (PODS)*, pages 261–272, June 1999. 306, 307, 318

[18] G. S. Manku and R. Motwani. Approximate Frequency Counts over Data Streams. In *Proc. of 28th VLDB*, pages 346–357, August 2002. 311, 312

[19] S. Chaudhuri N. Bruno and Luis Gravano. Top-k selection queries over relational databases: Mapping strategies and performance evaluation. *ACM TODS*, 27(2), 2002. 324

[20] K. Porkaew, I. Lazaridis, and S. Mehrotra. Querying mobile objects in spatio-temporal databases. In *Proc. of 7th SSTD*, July 2001. 307

[21] S. Saltenis and C. Jensen. Indexing of Moving Objects for Location-Based Services. *Proc. of IEEE ICDE*, 2002. 306, 307, 318

[22] S. Saltenis, C. Jensen, S. Leutenegger, and Mario A. Lopez. Indexing the Positions of Continuously Moving Objects. *In Proceedings of the ACM SIGMOD*, pages 331–342, May 2000. 306, 307, 310, 318

[23] A. P. Sistla, O. Wolfson, S. Chamberlain, and S. Dao. Modeling and Querying Moving Objects. *In Proceedings of the 13th ICDE, Birmingham, U.K*, pages 422–432, April 1997. 306

[24] Z. Song and N. Roussopoulos. K-nearest neighbor search for moving query point. In *Proc. of the SSTD*, pages 79–96, 2001. 306, 307

[25] Y. Tao and D. Papadias. Time-parameterized queries in spatio-temporal databases. *Proc. of ACM SIGMOD*, 2002. 307

[26] Y. Tao, D. Papadias, and Q. Shen. Continuous nearest neighbor search. In *Proc. of VLDB*, 2002. 307

[27] Y. Tao, J. Sun, and D. Papadias. Selectivity estimation for predictive spatio-temporal queries. *Proceedings of 19th IEEE International Conference on Data Engineering (ICDE), to appear*, 2003. 306, 308, 310, 317, 318

[28] M. Wang, J. S. Vitter, L. Lim, and S. Padmanabhan. Wavelet-based cost estimation for spatial queries. In *Proc. of SSTD*, pages 175–196, 2001. 324

[29] W. Wang, J. Yang, and R. Muntz. STING: A statistical information grid approach to spatial data mining. In *The VLDB Journal*, pages 186–195, 1997. 307

Accuracy and Resource Consumption in Tracking and Location Prediction*

Ouri Wolfson and Huabei Yin

Department of Computer Science
851 S. Morgan (M/C 152), Chicago, IL 60607, USA
{wolfson, hyin}@cs.uic.edu

Abstract. Tracking is an enabling technology for many location based services. Given that the location of a moving object changes continuously but the database cannot be updated continuously, the research issue is how to accurately maintain the current location of a large number of moving objects while minimizing the number of updates. The traditional approach used in existing commercial transportation systems is for the moving object or the cellular network to periodically update the location database; e.g. every 2 miles. We introduce a new location update policy, and show experimentally that it is superior to the simplistic policy currently used for tracking; the superiority is up to 43% depending on the uncertainty threshold. We also introduce a method of generating realistic synthetic spatio-temporal information, namely *pseudo trajectories* of moving objects. The method selects a random route, and superimposes on it speed patterns that were recorded during actual driving trips.

1   Introduction

Miniaturization of computing devices, and advances in wireless communication and sensor technology are some of the forces that are propagating computing from the stationary desktop to the mobile outdoors. Some important classes of new applications that will be enabled by this development include location-based services, tourist services, mobile electronic commerce, and digital battlefield. Tracking, i.e. continuously maintaining in a database the transient location of a moving object, is an enabling technology for these application classes. Other application classes that will benefit from tracking include transportation and air traffic control, weather forecasting, emergency response, mobile resource management, and mobile workforce.

Often, tracking enables tailoring the information delivered to the mobile user in order to increase relevancy; for example delivering accurate driving directions, instant

* Research supported by NSF Grants ITR-0086144, NSF-0209190, CCR-0070738, and EIA-0000516.

T. Hadzilacos et al. (Eds.): SSTD 2003, LNCS 2750, pp. 325-343, 2003.

coupons to customers nearing a store, or nearest resource information like local restaurants, hospitals, ATM machines, or gas stations.

In addition to enabling applications, tracking is also a fundamental component of other technologies such fly-through visualization (visualized terrain changes continuously with the location of the user), context awareness (location of the user determines the content, format, or timing of information delivered), and augmented reality (location of both the viewer and the viewed object determines the types of information delivered to viewer).

As defined, tracking involves continuously maintaining in a database the current location of moving objects. The location of a moving object is sensed either by the cellular network using techniques of triangulation among the cellular towers, or by a Global Positioning System (GPS) receiver on board the moving object. In either case, for tracking the location is transmitted to the database. Given that the location of a moving object changes continuously, but the database cannot be updated continuously, the research issue is how to accurately maintain the current location of a large number of moving objects while minimizing the number of updates.

The traditional approach used in all existing commercial transportation systems (see for example [19, 20]) is for the moving object or the cellular network to periodically update the location database; e.g. every 2 miles, or every 5 minutes. The advantage of the <u>distance</u> update policy, which updates the database every x distance units, is that it provides a bound on the error in response to database queries. Specifically, in response to a query: "what is the current location of m?" the answer is: within a circle of radius x, centered at location l (provided in the last database update). Similarly, in an augmented reality or context awareness application, if a Personal Digital Assistant (PDA) can hold images or graphics that pertain to an interval of 20 meters, then the moving object will provide its location every 20 meters, and get the next set of images from the database.

In this paper we introduce and evaluate an alternative to the commonly used distance update policy. It pertains to motion on the road network given by a map, and it improves the performance of tracking by location prediction. In this sense it is a location *prediction* policy as much as a location *update* policy, but we will still use the term update for uniformity. It called the <u>deviation</u> policy, and it predicts that following a location update, the moving object will continue moving on the same street. This assumption provides an *expected* location at any point in time after each location update, and thus in response to future queries it will provide the expected location. The moving object or the network will update the database whenever the *actual* location deviates from the expected location by more than a given threshold x. Thus, in terms of accuracy, the deviation policy is identical to the distance policy in the sense that both allow for a maximum location error; in other words, given the same *threshold x,* both methods have the same location uncertainty. Thus one can compare how many updates are required by each policy to maintain a given uncertainty threshold x. This is a measure of the location prediction power of the deviation policy. We discover that the deviation policy is up to 43% more efficient than the distance policy (which is currently the state of the art) in the sense that to maintain an uncertainty threshold of 0.05 miles the distance policy uses 43% more updates than the deviation policy. The advantage of the deviation policy decreases as the uncertainty threshold increases, but it is always better than the distance policy.

Now consider a data streaming application in virtual or augmented reality, or fly through visualization. Suppose that a vehicle is driving through a city and at any point in time it needs to show on the passenger's handheld computer the objects (buildings, stores, mountains) within r miles of the vehicle's current location. Suppose that the computer has a limited amount of memory that allows it to store objects within R miles of the vehicle's location, and the data is streamed to the mobile computer by a server that tracks the vehicle. Then if the server makes a tracking error of more than $R-r$ miles, then the mobile computer will have to update its database location at the server and request an up-to-date chunk of data (interrupting the display flow while waiting for that chunk). In this sense $R-r$ corresponds to the error threshold mentioned above, and the distance policy will generate up to 43% more location updates/requests than the deviation policy.

Another way to view these results is as follows. There are quite a few works that examine the efficiency of indexing methods in moving objects databases (see for example [16, 21]). In other words, these works examine how to make updates (and also retrievals) more efficient. However, efficiency can be addressed not only by making each update more efficient, but also by reducing the number of required updates. And this is the approach we take in this paper, i.e. we examine which location update policy will minimize the total number of location updates for each given uncertainty threshold.

In addition to the new location update policy, another major contribution of this paper is a method of generating realistic synthetic spatio-temporal information, namely *pseudo trajectories* of moving objects. Observe that in order to compare the above location update policies for a given uncertainty threshold, one needs to know how the speed of a vehicle changes during a trip. This can be recorded by driving and using a GPS RECEIVER, however, but for an accurate comparison one would have to use traces of hundreds of trips. We solve this problem by tracing three trips of about 24 miles each, thus generating three real trajectories. Pseudo trajectories are trajectories that are not generated by driving, but by selecting a random route, and superimposing on it speed patterns that were generated along the real trajectories.

In Summary, the Main Contributions of this Paper Are: (1) We introduce the deviation location update policy, and show experimentally that it is superior to the simplistic policy currently used for tracking; the superiority is up to 43% depending on the uncertainty threshold. (2) We introduce a method of generating realistic synthetic spatio-temporal information, namely *pseudo trajectories* of moving objects. The method selects a random route, and superimposes on it speed patterns that were recorded during actual driving trips.

The rest of this paper is organized as follows. The data model and two update policies are introduced in section 2. In section 3, we first present the test databases and a method of generating pseudo trajectories of moving objects; and then the experimental comparison of the update policies is discussed. Section 4 discusses the related work. Finally we conclude the paper and propose the future work in section 5.

2   Location Update Policies

In this section we first introduce the database model used for tracking (subsection 2.1), and then in each one of the following two subsections we introduce an update policy.

2.1   The Data Model

In this section we define the main concepts used in this paper. We define a map, and what tracking means in database terminology. We also define the notion of a trajectory.

An *object-class* is a set of attributes. Some object classes are designated as *spatial*. Each spatial object class is either a point class, or a polygonal line (or *polyline* for short) class.

Definition 1. *A __map__ is a spatial object class represented as a relation, where each tuple corresponds to a block with the following attributes:*

- *Polyline: Each block is a polygonal line segment in 2D. Polyline gives the sequence of the endpoints: (x_1, y_1), (x_2, y_2), ..., (x_n, y_n). Where (x_1, y_1) is the start point of this polyline, and (x_n, y_n) is the end point.*
- *Street Name: The street name of this block.*
- *Street Category: six categories, from major highway, to undivided local road.*
- *Bid: The block id number.*
- *Speed: The average driving speed on this block*
- *One_way: (boolean) One way indicator*

Plus, among others, a set of geo-coding attributes which enable translating between an (x, y) coordinate and an address, such as "*2222 W Taylor St.*" (e.g. R_f_add and R_t_add: the from and to street numbers on the right side, respectively.)

The start point (x_1, y_1) of a block is the end point (x_n, y_n) of the preceding block, and an intersection of two streets is the endpoint of the four blocks – polylines. A *street-polyline* is the concatenation of the polylines belonging to all the blocks of the street. Thus each map is a graph, with the tuples representing edges of the graph. Such maps are provided by, among the others, Geographic Data Technology[1] Co (GDT).

Point object classes are either mobile or stationary. A point object class O has a *location attribute L*. If the object class is *stationary*, its location attribute has two sub-attributes *L.x*, and *L.y*, representing the x and y coordinates of the object. If the object class is *mobile*, its location attribute has six sub-attributes, *L.street*, *L.location*, *L.time*, *L.direction*, *L.speed*, and *L.uncertainty*. The attribute represents the location of the object at the last location update.

The semantics of the sub-attributes are as follows.

L.street is (the pointer to) street polyline indicating the street on which an object in the class O is moving.

---

[1]   www.geographic.com

L.location is a point (x, y) on *L.street*; it is the location of the moving object at time *L.time*. In other words, *L.time* is the time when the moving object was at location *L.location*. We assume that whenever the system updates the *L* attribute of a moving object it updates at least the *L.location* sub-attribute; thus at any point in time *L.time* is also the time of the last location-update. We assume in this paper that the database updates are instantaneous, i.e. valid- and transaction-times (see [18]) are equal. Therefore, *L.time* is the time at which the location was sensed in the real world system being modeled, and also the time when the database installs the update. In practice, if the difference between these two times is not negligible, then all our results still hold by simply including the location-sensing time in the update message to the server.

L.direction is a binary indicator having a value 0 or 1 (these values may correspond to north-south, east-west, or the two endpoints of the street). *L.speed* is a function of time that represents the expected speed of the object after the last update, *L.time*. It enables computing the distance of the moving object from *L.location* as a function of the number t of time units elapsed since that last location-update, namely since *L.time*. In its simplest form (which is the only form we consider in this extended abstract) *L.speed* represents a constant speed v, i.e. this distance is $v \times t$.

We define the *street-distance* between two points on a given street to be the distance along the street polyline between the two points. The street distance between two points can be easily computed in linear time (in the size of the street polyline), and so can the point at a given street-distance from another given point. The *database location* of a moving object at a given point in time is defined as follows. At time *L.time* the database location is *L.location*; the database location at time *L.time+t* is the point (x, y) which is at street-distance *L.speed·t* from the point *L.location*.

Loosely speaking, the database location of a moving object m at a given time point *L.time+t* is the location of m at that time, as far as the DBMS knows; it is the location that is returned by the DBMS in response to a query entered at time *L.time+t* that retrieves m's location. Such a query also returns the uncertainty defined below.

Intuitively, the difference among the update policies discussed in this paper is that they treat differently the time until which the database location is computed in this fashion. Remember that the server computer does not know the destination or the future location of the object. Thus the distance policy assumes that the database location does not change until the next location-update received by the DBMS. In contrast, the deviation policies assume that following a location update, the object moves on the same street with a speed given by *L.speed*, until the object reaches the end of the street; after that time, the database location of the object is the point at the end of the street until the next location update.

Now we discuss when the next update occurs. *L.uncertainty* is a constant, representing the threshold on the location deviation (the deviation is formally defined below); when the deviation reaches the threshold, the moving object (or the network sensing its location) sends a location update message. Thus, in response to a query entered at time *L.time+t* that retrieves m's location, the DBMS returns an answer of the form: m is within a circle with radius *L.uncertainty* centered at the point which is the database location of m.

Since between two consecutive location updates the moving object does not travel at exactly the speed *L.speed*, the actual location of the moving object deviates from its database location. Formally, for a moving object, the *deviation* d at a point in time t, denoted *d(t)*, is the straight-line Euclidean distance between the moving object's actual location at time *t* and its database location at time *t* (notice that the deviation is not computed using the street distance). The deviation is always nonnegative. At any point in time the moving object (or the network sensing its location) knows its current location, and it also knows all the sub-attributes of its location attribute. Therefore at any point in time the computer onboard the moving object (or the network) can compute the current deviation. Observe that at time *L.time* the deviation is zero.

At the beginning of the trip the moving object updates[2] all the sub-attributes of its location (L) attribute. Subsequently, the moving object periodically updates its current *L.location*, *L.speed*, and *L.street* stored in the database. Specifically, a *location update* is a message sent by the moving object to the database to update some or all the sub-attributes of its location attribute. The moving object sends the location update when the deviation exceeds the *L.uncertainty* threshold. The location update message contains at least the value for *L.location*. Obviously, other sub-attributes can also be updated, and which ones will be updated when will become clear when we describe the policies. The sub-attribute *L.time* is written by the DBMS whenever it installs a location update; it denotes the time when the installation is done.

When an update message is received, before the L attribute is updated, the previous values are used in order to extend the current trajectory (see the next definition below). This trajectory is used in order to answer queries about the location of the moving object in the past.

Representing the (*location, time*) information of the moving object as a trajectory is a typical approach (see [10, 11, 12]) and we use the definition introduced in [11]:

Definition 2. *A trajectory Tr of a moving object is a piece-wise linear function from time T to 2D space Tr: T→(X,Y), represented as a sequence of points (x_1, y_1, t_1), (x_2, y_2, t_2), ..., (x_n, y_n, t_n) $(t_1 < t_2 < ... < t_n)$. The projection of Tr on the X-Y plane is called the route of Tr.*

A trajectory defines the location of a moving object as a function of time. The object is at (x_i, y_i) at time t_i, and during each segment $[t_i, t_{i+1}]$, the object moves along a straight line, at constant speed, from (x_i, y_i) to (x_{i+1}, y_{i+1}). Thus,

Definition 3. *Given a trajectory Tr, the expected location of the object at a point in time t between t_i and t_{i+1} $(1 \leq i < n)$ is obtained by a linear interpolation between (x_i, y_i) and (x_{i+1}, y_{i+1}).*

---

[2] For the rest of the paper we will assume for simplicity of presentation that the location updates are generated by the moving object itself. However, as explained above, the updates can also be generated by the network that continuously senses the moving object location.

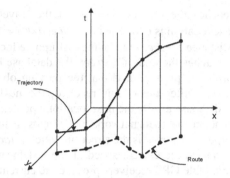

Fig. 1. A trajectory and its two dimensional route

An illustration of trajectory and its route is shown in Fig. 1.We can obtain the real trajectory of a moving object by using an on board GPS receiver while it moves on the road network, or simply generate it by some algorithms, such as our pseudo trajectory generation algorithm that is described in Section 3.

It should be clear that the trajectory can be extended in linear time (in the number of straight line segments of the map, traversed since the last update) at each update.

Finally, let us observe that all our concepts and results are presented for motion in two dimensions, but they can be extended for 3D motion.

2.2   The Distance Policy

The distance location update policy is widely used in moving objects database applications due to its simplicity. It dictates that the moving object m sends an update message to the database server if the *Euclidean*-distance or the *route*-distance[3] between the current location and *L.location* exceeds the *L.uncertainty* threshold. *L.location* is simply the point on the road network that is closest to the GPS point that generated the last location update. Remember that m knows its current location from its on-board GPS receiver.

In other words, when a location update is generated, this policy "snaps" the GPS point that caused the location update onto the road network, and stores the snapped point in the sub-attribute *L.location*. Snapping is necessary since, although GPS receivers are accurate to within a couple of meters most of the time, sometimes the GPS receiver on board a vehicle traveling on the road network senses a location that is off the road.

2.3   The Deviation Policy

The deviation update policy proposed in this paper is as follows. The moving object m still updates the database when the deviation between the current location and the database location exceeds the *L.uncertainty* threshold. However, the database location is computed differently. At any time point t between the time point *L.time* and the

---

[3]   The *route-distance* between two points x and y on the road network is the length of the shortest path between x and y in the network represented by the map.

time point when m reaches the end of $L.street$ (in the travel direction given by $L.direction$), the database location is computed by $L.speed \times t$; i.e. the database location is on $L.street$ at street distance $L.speed \times t$ from the last update location, i.e. $L.location$. After the time when m reaches the end of $L.street$, the database location is the end of the street. In other words, the prediction is that the moving object continues on the current street until its end; after the end is reached, the next location cannot be predicted; therefore the database awaits the next location update.

$L.location$ is the point on the road network that is closest to the GPS point that generated the location update. $L.street$ is the street on which $L.location$ lies. $L.speed$ is the predicted speed. It can be the current speed at the last location-update from the object (commercially available GPS receivers provide the current speed in addition to the current location), or, more generally, it can be the average of the speed-readings during the latest x time units. Thus, for the deviation policy, the location update message also includes the value for the $L.speed$ sub-attribute.

Next we discuss how the value of $L.direction$ is determined. The two possible values of $L.direction$ are the two endpoints of the street $L.street$. The value for $L.direction$ is determined at each location update as follows. If the previous location update was on the same street, it is easy to get the value for the sub-attribute $L.direction$. It is simply the endpoint that is closer to the last update than to the previous one. For example consider street ST_1 in Fig. 2. Its endpoints are E and F. If A and B are two consecutive location updates on the street ST_1, then the $L.direction$ computed at the second one is E (in other words the direction is FE). Otherwise, i.e. if the last two location updates are on two different streets, $L.direction$ is computed as follows. Let C be the current location update, and let B the previous one. Let D be the closest point on the current $L.street$ to the location B (i.e., the shortest path (in terms of travel time) in the map graph from B to D is not longer than the path from B to some other intersection on $L.street$). Then the endpoint of $L.street$ that is closer to C than to D determines the current $L.direction$. For example, assume that B and C are two consecutive location updates on two different streets ST_1 and ST_2 respectively (see again Fig. 2). Assume further that C is on the street ST_2 with endpoints G and H. Then the value of $L.direction$ computed at C-update time is H, where D is the closest intersection to B among all intersections on ST_2.

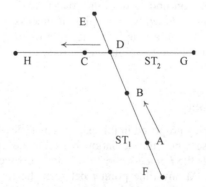

Fig. 2. The direction of the movement of the moving object

Finally, we make two observations. First, we discussed how the L sub-attributes are computed, but we did not discuss whether the computation is performed by the DBMS or the client on the moving object. If both the client and the DBMS server store the map, then the computation can be performed in either. If the map is stored only in the server, then the computations are performed in the server, which downloads to the client the street polyline from $L.location$ until the endpoint, and the sub-attributes $L.direction$ and $L.speed$.

The second observation is that the computation of $L.street$ and $L.direction$ may produce errors. Specifically, the GPS point may be snapped onto the wrong street, and even if the street is right, the computed direction may be wrong. The only implication of such errors is an increase in the number of updates. In other words, if travel is assumed on one street but actually occurs on another, then the deviation will grow faster, and the next update will occur sooner.

3 Experiments

In this section we present our experimental setup. In subsection 3.1 we describe the data (i.e. trajectories) used in our experiments. In subsection 3.2 we describe the experiments and the results of comparing the three location update policies.

3.1 Test Data

First let us point out the difficulty in generating realistic data for comparing the update policies. Observe that the number of updates generated by the distance based policy per mile can be easily generated as follows. A random route can be generated by selecting two random points on the map, and connecting them by the shortest path. For each route, the number of updates for a given threshold th can be easily computed by finding the first point that is at Euclidean- or route- distance th from the beginning of the route, then the next point, that is at Euclidean- or route- distance th from the previous one, etc. Thus, by generating hundreds of random routes, the average number of updates per mile, per threshold th, can be computed. However, the problem is computing the number of updates for the deviation policy, because this depends on the way the speed of the moving object varies over time. Thus the method outlined above for the distance policy will not work. In other words, we need to generate trajectories which reflect a realistic variation of speed over time. This is the procedure described precisely in this subsection. Intuitively, we do so as follows. First we generate a few real trajectories by actual driving on routes that include streets of the various categories, and recording the speed every two seconds. Then, the set of recorded speeds is used to generate pseudo trajectories that have a realistic speed-change pattern. In the first subsection we describe the generation of three real trajectories by actual driving on roads, and then, in the next subsection we describe the generation of 80 pseudo trajectories.

Table 1. Meta data about the real trajectories

trajectory id	length	number of 3D points
1	24.6469	1318
2	23.441	2276
3	24.9924	3183
average	24.3601	2259

3.1.1   Real Trajectories Database

We actually drove in the Chicago metropolitan area and collected 3 real trajectories over routes that cover all street categories. Each trajectory describes a trip of average length 24.36 miles from a source to a destination. The driving conditions included both, heavy and light traffic. Information related to the real (i.e. driven) trajectories is shown in Table 1.

For each trip, a real trajectory is generated. The *real* trajectory of a moving object is obtained by repeatedly reading the (*longitude, latitude, time*) from a Differential GPS device (which has an accuracy of a couple meters; see [13]) connected to a laptop. A reading is taken every two seconds. The sequential file of DGPS readings is used to generate a trajectory that has an (x_i, y_i, t_i) point for every two seconds. So, we obtain a sequence of points (x_1, y_1, t_1), (x_2, y_2, t_2), ..., (x_n, y_n, t_n) $(t_1 < t_2 < ... < t_n)$, that is a trajectory representing the speed changes over time during an actual trip. Based on each straight line segment in a trajectory, the average speed during the respective two-second interval can be computed.

3.1.2   Pseudo Trajectories Database

Pseudo trajectories are trajectories that are not generated by driving, but by selecting a random route, and superimposing on it speed patterns that were generated along the real trajectories. More precisely, the procedure of generating a pseudo trajectory is as follows:

Randomly pick an integer m between 3 and 6 as the number of source and intermediate destinations. Then randomly generate a sequence of m locations in the map (see Definition 1). Then find the shortest path that travels this sequence (for example, if m is 3, then the pseudo trajectory starts at location l_1, moves to location l_2, and from there to the final location l_3. This corresponds to, for example, a delivery route that starts at l_1, and drops off at l_2 and from there it goes and drops off at l_3). Thus the shortest path is a polyline consisting of the concatenation of block polylines (see Definition 1). It is also the route R of the pseudo trajectory. The size of the route is the number of points of that route.

Generate a sequence of speeds for the route R.

In order to explain how we execute step (2) above, we first need to define the notion of a Speed Pattern of a real trajectory:

Definition 4. *A speed pattern is a sequence of consecutive 2-second speeds in a real trajectory, for a given street category.*

Where the street category is defined by electronic maps (see Definition 1). There are six street categories in electronic maps (see for example [2]):

A1, LIMITED ACCESS HIGHWAYS
A2, PRIMARY or MAJOR HIGHWAYS
A3, SECONDARY or MINOR HIGHWAYS
A4, LOCAL ROADS
A5, VEHICULAR (4WD) TRAIL
A6, ROADS WITH SPECIAL CHARACHTERISTICS

There are several subcategories in each category. However, for our classification purposes, the subcategories do not matter. In the Chicago metropolitan area map used in our experiments, A6 streets are the entrance ramps and the exits of the expressways, and there are no streets of category A5. Since A5 is a slow road, and in general there are very few roads of this type on maps, A5 is classified as a minor road for the hybrid policy. Thus we use five different street categories for classifying the street categories into major and minor classes. The street categories analyzed are shown as in the Table 2, along with the average travel speed on each. Observe that, for highways for example, the maximum speed is 55, but the average speed given in the map is 45.

To obtain the speed patterns we first calculate the average speed for every two consecutive real trajectory points. A sequence of consecutive speeds that belong to (i.e. were taken on) the same street category forms a speed pattern. For example, suppose that for a real trajectory T we have a set of points on an A3 street, as shown in Table 3; the time t is relative from the start of the trajectory, in seconds. Suppose further that after the 20th second, during the trip that generated T, the moving object entered a different street category. Then we obtain a speed pattern for street category A3, as shown in the right table of Table 3(corresponding to the left table of Table 3); the unit of speed is miles per hour, and each speed in table 4 is called a *speed-item* of the speed pattern.

Table 2. Categories of streets in a major U.S. metropolitan area, along with the average speed in miles/hour

Category	A1	A2	A3	A4	A6
SPEED	45	35	25	25	20

Table 3. Left Table: A set of trajectory points on an A3 street; Right Table: a speed pattern calculated from the left table

x	y	t		speed_id	speed
221.311	358.893	0		1	1.8
221.311	358.892	2		2	1.8
221.31	358.892	4		3	1.8
221.309	358.892	6		4	3.6
221.307	358.892	8		5	25.4558
221.293	358.89	10		6	30.6529
221.276	358.889	12		7	34.2473
221.257	358.888	14		8	36.0450
221.237	358.887	16		9	37.8
221.216	358.887	18		10	37.8428
221.195	358.886	20			

Table 4. The speed pattern set for A3

pattern_id	1	1	...	1	...	1	1	...
speed id	1	2	...	1	...	1	2	...
speed	14.5121	16.0997	...	1.8	...	19.2996	17.9999	...

The length of one speed pattern is the number of speeds of that pattern. All the speed patterns of the same street category form the *Speed Pattern Set (SPS)* of that street category. Thus a speed pattern set of a street category represents the patterns (collected during our real trajectory generation trips) of speed changes while for that street category. The size of one *SPS* is the sum of the lengths of its speed patterns. Table 4 is an example of the speed pattern set for the street category A3. There are 5 speed patterns in Table 4 whose pattern_id's are 1, 2, 3, 4, and 5 respectively. For the street categories A1, A2, A4 and A6, we have 2, 4, 5 and 3 speed patterns in our SPS repository, respectively. Overall, the average length of a speed pattern is 355.526.

Now we are ready to describe the details of step (2) above, namely the generation of a pseudo trajectory based on a route R and the SPS's for the various street categories. Intuitively, we do so as follows. Suppose that we generated the pseudo trajectory up to a location *l* on route *R*. Suppose further that *l* is on a category A1 street. Then we select from the A1 SPS a random speed from all the speeds that are equal (or, if no such exists, closest) to the speed of the moving object at *l* (see further discussion of this in the next paragraph). Then "run" the moving object with the pattern to which the speed belongs, starting at the location of the speed within the pattern; do so until the end of the current sequence of A1 streets on R, or until the end of the speed pattern, whichever occurs first. The reached location is the new *l* location, and the speed at this location is the speed of the pattern. The process repeats until the end of the route R.

Observe that the speeds that are equal to the speed at location *l* may belong to different speed patterns; and if they belong to the same pattern, they will appear at different sequential locations from the start of the pattern. For example, consider Fig. 3. Suppose that *a* in speed pattern 1, and *b, c* in speed pattern 2, are the speeds that are equal to the speed at location *l*. Then, if the random selection picks *a*, then speed pattern 1 is run for 5 2-second intervals (assuming that the end of the street category is not reached beforehand). If *b* is picked, then speed pattern 2 is run for 5 2-second intervals; and if *c* is picked then it is run for one interval (the last one of speed pattern 2).

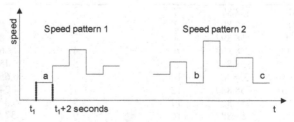

Fig. 3. Selection of the speed pattern

Observe additionally that when a speed pattern is "run", then trajectory points are generated at the end of each 2-second interval, and also at the end of each straight line segment of the route. Formally the trajectory generation algorithm is as follows:

Algorithm 1 Generate Pseudo Trajectory Algorithm

Input: Map M, Route given as a sequence of points (see step (1) at beginning of this subsection) $R = (r_1, r_2, ..., r_n)$, Speed Pattern Sets SPS of all street categories.
Output: Trajectory Tr.
1.   i = 1, current_category = the street category of r_1, current_time = 0, current_speed = 0, current_p = (r_1, current_time).
2.   **Append** current_p to Tr.
3.   **while** i ≤ n
4.   Randomly select a speed pattern from the SPS labeled by current_category such that the selected speed pattern has a speed item sp_j that is closest to current_speed in the SPS.
5.   Use the speed sp_j to compute the next location p where street-distance between r_i and p is $sp_j \times 2/3600$, and the direction of the motion is from r_i to r_{i+1}.
6.   **If** p exceeds the r_{i+1} (i.e. the street-distance between the location of current_p and p is larger than the street-distance between the location of current_p and r_{i+1})
            Then compute the traveling time t' from the location of current_p to r_{i+1} by the speed sp_j. current_p = (r_{i+1}, current_time + t'), current_time = current_time + t', and append current_p to Tr. i = i + 1, current_category = the street category of r_i, and goto step 8.
            Else current_p = (p, current_time + 2), and current_time = current_time + 2, and append current_p to Tr.
7.   **If** the location of current_p = r_{i+1}
            Then i = i + 1, current_category = the street category of r_i.
            Else, j = j + 1.
8.   **If** the current_category is changed
            Then current_speed = sp_j, and goto step 4
            Else j = j + 1
9.   **If** the end of selected speed pattern is reached
            Then current_speed = the last speed-item of the selected speed pattern, and goto step 4
            Else goto step 5
10.   **end while**

Fig. 4. Algorithm 1

All points (x_i, y_i, t_i) appended in order by Algorithm1 form a pseudo trajectory. The worst case time complexity of the algorithm is $O(k \lg m + n \lg m + m \lg m)$ where k is the length of the route divided by the minimum nonzero speed (i.e. the maximum number of 2-second intervals that it takes to traverse the route), n is number of vertices on the route, and m is the number of speeds in the speed patterns. The reason for this is that for every 2-seconds or for every point on the route, the equal speeds in the speed pattern set have to be found; and if the speeds in each pattern have been sorted (takes $O(m \lg m)$), then this can be done in $O(\lg m)$.

Example 1. Suppose that r_i's are the points of the route, and p_i's are the points of the trajectory (see Fig. 5). Observe that according to the algorithm, every point of the route is also a point of the trajectory. The number in parentheses next to a r_i or p_i is time (in seconds) of the trajectory at the r_i or p_i location, for example, it takes the moving object 7 seconds to reach p_4. Suppose that the street category of r_1 and r_2 is A3, that's the route from r_1 to r_3 is of category A3, and the street category of r_3, r_4, r_5, and r_6 is A4, that's the route from r_3 to r_6 is of category A4. First $(r_1, 0)$ is appended to Tr in step 2. A speed pattern from A3 SPS is chosen in step 4, and suppose that it is $(0, 2, 2, 15, 20, 21, 23, 25.5, 26, 27, 30, 31, 26, 23, 22, 27)$. We use the speeds starting from 0 miles/hour to compute the locations p_1 to p_4 in four iterations of step 5; and find out in step 6 that p_4 exceeds r_2. So we re-compute the traveling time t' from p_3 to r_2; it is 1 second, hence the r_2 with its arrival time $(7 = 6 + 1)$ becomes the next point p_4 of the trajectory. At p_4 the street category doesn't change, thus we continue the same speed pattern to compute p_5 and p_6 in the next two iterations of step 5. In step 7, we find out that p_6 equals to r_3, and in step 8 we find out that the street category changes to A4. So we select a speed pattern from A4 SPS in step 4 which has a speed item closest to 21 miles/hour (we end up with 21 miles/hour of the previous selected speed pattern), suppose that it's $(27, 26, 21, 26, 27, 30, 31, 29, 27, 24, 27, 30, 33, 35)$. Then we use the speeds starting from 21 miles/hour to compute p_7 and p_8 in the next two iterations of step 5; in step 7 we find out that p_8 equals to r_4. At p_8 the street category doesn't change, thus we continue the same speed pattern to compute p_9 to p_{11} in the next three iterations of step 5. Since in step 6 we find out that that p_{11} exceeds r_5, we re-compute the traveling time t' from p_{10} to r_5; it is 1 second, hence the r_5 with its arrival time $(20 = 19 + 1)$ becomes the next point p_{11} of the trajectory. At p_{11} the street category is still A4, thus we continue the same speed pattern to compute p_{12} and p_{13} in the next two iterations of step 5. In step 7, we find out that p_{13} equals to r_6. Finally, in step 3 we find out that the end of the route is reached. The generated trajectory Tr is $((r_1, 0), (p_1, 2), (p_2, 4), (p_3, 6), (p_4, 7), (p_5, 9), (p_6, 11), (p_7, 13), (p_8, 15), (p_9, 17), (p_{10}, 19), (p_{11}, 20), (p_{12}, 22), (p_{13}, 24))$ (see Fig. 5).

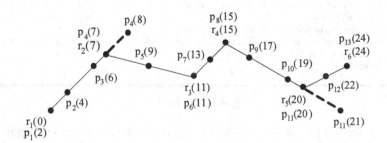

Fig. 5. Example 1

3.2   Experimental Comparison of Policies

In this subsection we discuss the experimental results. We simulated the distance and deviation policies on a database of 80 pseudo trajectories. The total length of the routes traversed is 6290.325 miles, and the total number of 3D points of the trajectories is 516111. The threshold was considered in terms of both, the Euclidean distance and the route-distance. The variant of the distance policy that we used establishes the predicted speed as the average of the speeds of each time unit since the last update. In other words, the predicted speed is obtained at location-update time by taking the speed of each time unit (2 seconds) since the last location update, and averaging them. Intuitively, the motivation for this is that the predicted speed depends on the expected period of time until the next update. And assuming that the length of the time interval between consecutive location updates does not vary much, this method (called *adaptive speed prediction*) naturally adapts the number of time units to the time interval between updates.

Fig. 6 and Fig. 7 present the number of updates per mile, as a function of *th* which ranges from 0.05 to 5 miles. The four curves correspond to the two policies, with each one evaluated for the route- and Euclidean- distances. The number of updates per mile UPM is expressed as the following formula:

$$UPM = \text{the total number of updates/the total length of the routes} \qquad (1)$$

We observe that the deviation policy is at least as good as the distance policy, for both Euclidean- and route- distance thresholds. The advantage of the deviation policy starts at 43% for *th* = 0.05, and it decreases as the threshold increases. The reason for the decrease is that the likelihood that the vehicle stays on the same street decreases as the threshold (and therefore the time interval between consecutive updates) increases.

Next we wanted to determine to the speed-prediction power of the adaptive speed prediction method mentioned above at the beginning of the section. Thus we compared it with the naïve method that simply predicts that the speed will be the same as during the last time unit (last 2 seconds). The results of this experiment are that surprisingly to us, the difference between the two methods is not very significant.

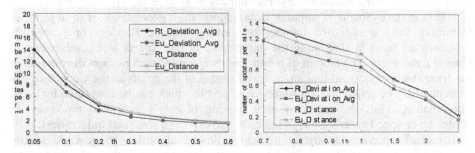

Fig. 6 and **Fig. 7** The number of updates per mile with *th* = 0.05 − 5.0

4   Related Work

As mentioned in the introduction, this paper makes contributions in update policies and synthetic spatio-temporal database generation, thus the relevant work applies to two these categories.

In the area of update policies, several works have been published [1, 17]. In [1] we propose dead-reckoning update policies to reduce the update cost. However these policies are only applicable when the destination and motion plan of the moving objects is known a priori. In other words, inherent in the policies is that the route is fixed and known to both the moving object and the server, and the update policy is used to revise the time at which the moving object is expected to be at various locations on the fixed route. However, often the destination or future route of a tracked object is not known. For example, the wireless service provider tracks every cellular phone, but it does not know the future route or destination. The user may simply not be willing to enter this information into the computer and provide it to the tracking server, or this information may change too often to make it practical.

In [17], Lam et al. propose two location update mechanisms for increasing the level of "correctness" of location-dependent continuous query results returned to clients, while reducing the location update cost of moving objects. Their methods are based on the assumption that the moving objects "covered" by the answers of the queries need more updates. In fact, their idea can be used in the present work in the sense that moving objects that are covered by continuous queries have a lower threshold, resulting in a higher location accuracy. In other words, their work discusses the selection of uncertainty thresholds for each moving object for continuous queries, whereas our work addresses the selection of update policies after the thresholds are decided.

The performance of update policies on moving objects databases with secondary access methods, for instance, R-tree or Quad-tree, is quite an interesting research issue. [21] examines the techniques that make updates more efficient: 1) by processing the individual updates more efficiently, and 2) by reducing the number of updates. Consistent with the second point, our approach seeks heuristics for future movement prediction.

In the area of synthetic spatio-temporal database generation, four methods have been published. First method is by Theodoridis et al. (see [3, 4]). They propose the GSTD (Generate_Spatio_ Temporal_Data) algorithm. It generates a set of trajectories stemming from a specified number of moving objects. Random or probability functions are used in simulating the movements of the objects as a combination of several parameters. The motion of points are always ruled by a random distribution of the form random(x, y), so that an unbiased spread of the points in the workspace can be achieved. The trajectory is a sequence of points which can be connected by linear interpolation. Thus the speed of each moving object is generated randomly. In contrast, our speed generation is based on actual driving traces (real trajectories).

Brinkhoff proposes a strictly network-followed algorithm to generate spatio-temporal databases which can simulate the moving behaviors of the real world [5, 6]. He stresses many user-defined factors which affect the behaviors of moving objects. One of these factors is "the number of moving objects influences the speed of the objects if a threshold is exceeded". The route is generated on the network by the A* algorithm, a modification of Dijkstra's shortest path algorithm. The speed is influenced by many factors, i.e. the max speed of the class of vehicles which the moving objects belongs to, the max speed of the route on which the object moves, traffic jams, and special weather conditions. However, the speed of a moving object is fixed for relatively large periods of time (for example, the model will not capture slowing down to avoid a pedestrian or a patch of ice on the road). This makes Brinkhoff's algorithm inapplicable to comparing our update policies, since the number of updates of the deviation policy critically depends on fine speed variations.

In [7], Saglio and Moreira propose an interesting approach to model the moving objects behaviors, i.e. according to their present environment instead of randomly. They argue that "a generator producing completely random data will not fulfill the principle of representativeness", since the surrounding environment affects their behaviors, e.g. seeking food and avoiding danger. They choose as the objects fishing boats that move in the direction of the most attractive shoals of fish while trying to avoid storm areas. During the period of generation, the objects of one class may be attracted or repulsed by other classes of objects in the evolution. The drawbacks of this generator are: (1) Attracting and repulsing relationship is hard to define; (2) It is a limited application scenario; and (3) It is not applicable to road networks, which is the focus of our work.

The spatio-temporal database used in [14] is generated by CitySimulator, a scalable, three-dimensional model city that enables the creation of dynamic spatial data simulating the motion of up to 1 million objects. It can simulate any mobile objects moving about in a city, driving on the streets, walking on the sidewalks and even entering buildings, where they can go up and down the floors and stay on a floor and then leave for the streets. For the motion on the streets, an optional traffic flow model which causes traffic jams (or shock waves) is included in the simulator. However the users of CitySimulator have to provide some simulation control parameters, such as enter or exit probability (in a building), up/down probability (in a building), drift probability (on the streets), scatter probability (on intersections), etc. Furthermore, CitySimulator is designed for evaluation of database algorithms for indexing (see [15]). From the documentation it is not clear if it is possible to generate patterns of speed change for moving objects. Again, such patterns are critical in our case in order to compare update policies.

5   Conclusion and Future Work

In this paper we addressed tracking of moving objects, i.e. the continuous representation of their location in the database. We introduced the deviation database update policy for this purpose, and compared it with the straightforward policy currently used by commercial tracking systems, namely the distance policy. Using the distance policy the moving object updates the database every x distance units, and thus x is the maximum location uncertainty of a moving object. We showed that for any given location accuracy (i.e. location uncertainty threshold) the deviation policy outperforms the distance policy by up to 43% in the sense that it uses less updates for enabling the same accuracy. The advantage of the new policy depends on the location accuracy, and it decreases as the accuracy decreases, i.e. the uncertainty threshold increases.

We also introduced a method of generating realistic synthetic (maybe a better term is "semi-synthetic") spatio-temporal information, namely *pseudo trajectories* of moving objects. The method selects a random route, and superimposes on it speed patterns that were recorded during actual driving trips.

The deviation policy is aimed at vehicles moving on road networks. It predicts that following a location update the moving object will continue at the current speed until the end of the street. There are variants of this policy with which we have experimented, without great improvement. One variant is the hybrid policy. It uses the deviation policy on major streets and the distance policy on minor streets. The idea behind the hybrid was that a vehicle is likely to continue on a major street but not necessarily on a minor one. Actually, the policy used depended on both the category of street, and the location accuracy. The optimal policy for each (street category, uncertainty) pair was found experimentally; i.e. we constructed a matrix that gives the best policy for each pair, and defined the hybrid policy to behave according to the matrix. It turns out that the hybrid policy slightly improves over the deviation policy, but the change is relatively small, thus we did not report on it in the present paper. Anyway, one of the advantages of the hybrid policy is that it points in a direction for further improvement in the future.

In terms of future work, observe that some variations on the hybrid policy may improve its resource- consumption/accuracy tradeoff. For example, suppose that we introduce another class of streets, medium, in addition to major and minor. And suppose further that on this class of streets, the moving object is assumed to continue at the current speed until the next major intersection, i.e. intersection with a street in a higher category. Observe that this is a middle-ground between the assumption for a minor street (the moving object stops at the last location update) and a major street (the object continues until the end of the street). It is interesting to determine experimentally whether this variation improves on the policy analyzed in this paper. For this purpose, the experimental methodology can be the same as the one used in this paper.

Another direction for future work is a better speed-prediction for the deviation policy. More generally, how does the future speed of a moving object depend on its past speed behaviour? The pseudo trajectory generation algorithm will come in handy for answering this question.

Another direction of future work is to determine whether our results hold for trajectories generated in rural areas and in foreign countries.

References

[1]   Ouri Wolfson, A.Prasad Sistla, Sam Chamberlain, and Yelena Yesha, Updating and Querying Databases that Track Mobile Units. Special issue of the Distributed and Parallel Databases Journal on Mobile Data Management and Applications, 7(3), 1999.
[2]   GDT: www.geographic.com/support/docs/D20_101.pdf
[3]   Theodoridis Y., Silva J.R.O., Nascimento M.A., On the Generation of Spatiotemporal Datasets. SSD1999, July 20-23, 1999. LNCS 1651, Springer, pp. 147-164.
[4]   Pfoser D., Theodoridis Y., Generating Semantics-Based Trajectories of Moving Objects. Intern. Workshop on Emerging Technologies for Geo-Based Applications, Ascona, 2000.
[5]   Brinkhoff Thomas, Generating Network-Based Moving Objects. In Proc. of the 12th Inter. Conf. on Scientific and Statistical Database Management, July 26-28, 2000.
[6]   Brinkhoff Thomas, A Framework for Generating Network-Based Moving Objects. Tech. Report of the IAPG, http://www2.fh-wilhelmshaven.de/oow/institute/iapg/personen/brinkhoff/paper/TBGenerator.pdf

[7]   Jean-Marc Saglio and José Moreira, Oporto: A Realistic Scenario Generator for Moving Objects. In Proc. of 10th Inter. Workshop on Database and Expert Systems Applications, IEEE Computer Society, Florence, Italy, 1999, pp. 426-432, ISBN 0-7695-0281-4.

[8]   Kollios, G., Gunopulos, D., Tsotras, V., Dellis, A., and Hadjieleftheriou, M. Indexing Animated Objects Using Spatiotemporal Access Methods. IEEE Transactions on Knowledge and Data Engineering, Sept/Oct 2001, Vol.13, No.5, p 758-777.

[9]   Tao, Y., and Papadias, D. The MV3R-tree: A Spatio-Temporal Access Method for Timestamp and Interval Queries. VLDB 2001.

[10]   Dieter Pfoser, Christian S. Jensen, and Yannis Theodoridis. Novel Approaches to the Indexing of Moving Object Trajectories. VLDB'00, Cairo, Egypt, September 2000.

[11]   G. Trajcevski, O. Wolfson, F. Zhang, and S. Chamberlian, The Geometry of Uncertainty in Moving Objects Databases. EDBT 2002.

[12]   M. Vlachos, G. Kollios, and D. Gunopulos, Discovering Similar Multi-dimensional Trajectories. ICDE 2002.

[13]   Trimble Navigation Limited. Differential GPS Sources: www.trimble.com/gps/dgps.html

[14]   Jussi Myllymaki and James Kaufman, LOCUS: A Testbed for Dynamic Spatial Indexing. In IEEE Data Engineering Bulletin 25(2), p48-55, 2002.

[15]   CitySimulator:http://alphaworks.ibm.com/tech/citysimulator

[16]   Zhexuan Song, and Nick Roussopoulos, Hashing Moving Objects. MDM 2001.

[17]   Kam-Yiu Lam, Ozgur Ulusoy, Tony S. H. Lee, Edward Chan and Guohui Li, Generating Location Updates for Processing of Location-Dependent Continuous Queries. DASFAA 2001, Hong Kong.

[18]   Richard T. Snodgrass and Ilsoo Ahn, The Temporal Databases. IEEE Computer 19(9), p35-42, September, 1986.

[19]   QUALCOMM Inc.: http://www.qualcomm.com

[20]   At Road Inc.: http://www.atroad.com/

[21]   Christian S. Jensen and Simonas Saltenis, Towards Increasingly Update Efficient Moving-Object Indexing. Bulletin of the IEEE on Data Engineering, 2002.

Region-Based Query Languages for Spatial Databases in the Topological Data Model

Luca Forlizzi[1], Bart Kuijpers[2], and Enrico Nardelli[1,3]

[1] University of L'Aquila
Dipartimento di Informatica
Via Vetoio, 67010 L'Aquila, Italy
{forlizzi,nardelli}@univaq.it
[2] University of Limburg
Dept. of Mathematics, Physics and Computer Science
3590 Diepenbeek, Belgium
bart.kuijpers@luc.ac.be
[3] IASI–CNR
Viale Manzoni 30, 00185 Roma, Italy

Abstract. We consider spatial databases in the topological data model, i.e., databases that consist of a finite number of labeled regions in the real plane. Such databases partition the plane further into *elementary regions*. We propose a first-order language, which uses elementary-region variables and label variables, to query spatial databases. All queries expressible in this first-order logic are *topological* and they can be evaluated in polynomial time. Furthermore, the proposed language is powerful enough to distinguish between any two spatial databases that are not topologically equivalent. This language does not allow the expression of all computable topological queries, however, as is illustrated by the connectivity query. We also study some more powerful extensions of this first-order language, e.g., with a while-loop. In particular, we describe an extension that is sound and computationally complete for the topological queries on spatial databases in the topological data model.

1 Introduction and Motivation

We consider planar spatial databases in the topological data model, i.e., databases that consist of a finite number of labeled regions in the real plane. Egenhofer and his collaborators, who were among the first to consider this model, have studied the possible topological relationships between regions in the plane and proposed a number of predicates (the so-called 9-intersection model) to express topological properties of pairs of regions [7, 8, 9]. Independently, in the area of spatial reasoning, these topological relations were studied by Randell, Cui and Cohn [30]. Later on, the topological data model was investigated further and given a theoretical foundation by Papadimitriou, Segoufin, Suciu, and Vianu [25, 32], who considered first-order languages, built on the predicates of

T. Hadzilacos et al. (Eds.): SSTD 2003, LNCS 2750, pp. 344–361, 2003.

the 9-intersection model, to express topological properties of spatial data (for an overview and a general discussion on topological spatial data and topological queries see also [24]). In these languages the input databases as well as the variables range over some infinite class of regions.

Recently, the advantages of region-based models over point-based models (e.g., [23, 25, 32]) or coordinate-based models (as are found in the constraint database model for spatial databases [26, 31]) have been investigated by Pratt and his collaborators [27, 28, 29]. Although Pratt *et al.* have concluded that in some non-topological contexts the power of languages in these three models coincides, they show that a region-based approach is more efficient and parsimonious in a topological setting both from a logic and an AI point of view.

Inspired by one of the languages of Papadimitriou, Suciu, and Vianu [25], namely FO(*Alg, Alg*), in which both the variables and the inputs range over the set of labeled semi-algebraic disks, we propose, in this paper, an alternative region-based first-order language, named $\mathcal{RL}$, which is less expressive but which does have a semantics that is computable. Query evaluation has polynomial time complexity (in the size of the input database). The language $\mathcal{RL}$, just like the one of Papadimitriou, Suciu, and Vianu, is a two-sorted logic. Variables of a first type range over region labels. The labeled regions of a database in the topological data model partition the plane further into a finite number of *elementary regions*. In $\mathcal{RL}$, a second sort of variables range over elementary regions. Apart from some set-theoretical predicates, the only topological predicates available in $\mathcal{RL}$ express in which order elementary regions appear around an elementary region.

First, we show that all queries, expressible in $\mathcal{RL}$, are *topological*. Furthermore, the proposed language is shown to be powerful enough to distinguish between any two spatial databases that are not topologically equivalent. Although our first-order language can express all the predicates of the 9-intersection model, it does not allow the expression of all computable topological queries, however, as is illustrated by the connectivity query. Also Papadimitriou, Suciu and Vianu [25] have shown that their logic is not powerful enough to express all computable topological queries and they study an extension with infinitary recursive disjunctions. The latter language is shown to be complete for the topological queries. The topological connectivity query can be viewed as the spatial analogue of the standard relational query of graph connectivity, which is also not expressible in the standard relational calculus [1, 35]. To be able to express queries such as graph connectivity, one typically uses a more powerful query language such as Datalog [35], an extension of the relational calculus with recursion.

Also in the constraint model for spatial data [26, 31], various people have proposed and studied extensions of first-order logic over the reals with tractable recursion mechanisms to obtain more expressive languages. For example, Datalog versions with constraints have been proposed [14, 20]; a programming language extending first-order logic over the reals with assignments and a while-loop has been shown to be a computationally complete language for constraint databases [26, Chapter 2]; extensions of first-order logic over the reals with topological predicates have been proposed and studied [2, 13]; and various extensions of first-order logic over the reals with various transitive-closure operators have been proposed [12, 14, 18]. These extensions are more expressive, in particular, they allow the expression of connectivity and reachability queries and some are even computationally complete (in general or for what concerns topological queries).

Motivated by these results, we also study an extension of the first-order language $\mathcal{RL}$, with ad-hoc predicates, with a transitive-closure operator and with *while-loop*. Of the latter languages we can show different kinds of completeness with respect to certain complexity classes. In particular, we describe an extension of $\mathcal{RL}$ with while-loop and some set-theoretic operators that is sound and computationally complete for the topological queries on spatial databases in the topological data model.

This paper is organized as follows. In the next section, we define spatial databases in the topological data model, topological equivalence of spatial databases and spatial database queries. In Section 3, we define the region-based first-order query language $\mathcal{RL}$ and investigate its expressive power. The different extensions of $\mathcal{RL}$ their completeness are discussed in Section 4. We end this paper with a discussion of the obtained results and future work.

2   Definitions and Preliminaries

In this section, we define spatial databases, topological equivalence of spatial databases and spatial database queries. We denote the set of real numbers by $\mathbf{R}$ and the real plane by $\mathbf{R}^2$.

2.1   Spatial Databases

We adopt the well-known *topological data model* for spatial data in which a spatial database consists of labeled regions in the plane [7, 9, 24, 25, 32]. We assume the existence of an infinite set **Names** of *region labels*.

Definition 1. A *spatial database (instance)* Δ consists of a finite subset $names_\Delta$ of **Names** and a mapping ext_Δ from $names_\Delta$ to semi-algebraic regions in $\mathbf{R}^2$ that are homeomorphic[1] to the open unit disk.   □

We remark that semi-algebraic regions can be finitely described as a Boolean combination of polynomial constraint expressions of the form $p(x, y) > 0$, where $p(x, y)$ is a polynomial in the real variables x, y with integer coefficients. The upper half of the open unit disk, that can be described by the polynomial constraint formula $x^2 + y^2 < 1 \wedge y > 0$ is an example of a semi-algebraic region.

Spatial databases are therefore within the framework of constraint databases [26, 31] in which spatial data is modeled as semi-algebraic sets. Figure 1 (a) gives an example of a spatial database instance with four regions, labeled

---

[1] Two sets A and B in $\mathbf{R}^2$ are called *homeomorphic* if there exists an homeomorphism h of the plane, i.e., a continuous bijective mapping from $\mathbf{R}^2$ to $\mathbf{R}^2$ with a continuous inverse, such that $h(A) = B$.

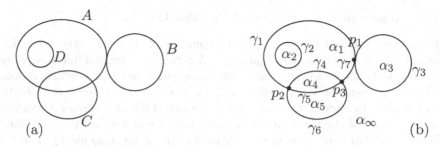

Fig. 1. In (a), an example of a spatial database with four labeled regions (remark that the regions are actually the interiors of the curves) and its elementary points, curves, and regions (b)

with A, B, C and D. All these regions are homeomorphic to the open unit disk. Remark that the region labeled D is a subset of the region labeled A.

In the remainder of this paper, we denote the topological interior, the topological border, and the topological closure of a set S respectively by $S°$, ∂S, and $\bar{S}$.

Definition 2. Let Δ be a spatial database instance.

- We refer to the union of the bordering curves of the labeled regions of Δ, i.e.,

$$\bigcup_{A \in names_\Delta} \partial(ext_\Delta(A)),$$

as the *frame of* Δ, and denote this set by $Frame(\Delta)$;
- We call the points of the frame where the frame is locally not homeomorphic to a straight line, the *elementary points of* Δ, and denote the set of these points by P_Δ;
- We call the connected components of $Frame(\Delta) \setminus P_\Delta$ the *elementary curves of* Δ and denote this set of curves by C_Δ;
- We call the connected components of $\mathbf{R}^2 \setminus Frame(\Delta)$ the *elementary regions of* Δ, and denote the set of elementary regions by R_Δ. □

For the spatial database instance depicted in Figure 1 (a), these sets are illustrated in Figure 1 (b). There are three elementary points: p_1, p_2 and p_3 (the frame has four branches locally around these points). There are seven elementary curves: $\gamma_1, ..., \gamma_7$ in Figure 1 (b). The complement of the frame has six connected components: $\alpha_1, ..., \alpha_5$, and α_∞ in Figure 1 (b).

From well-known properties of semi-algebraic sets it follows that P_Δ, C_Δ and R_Δ are always finite sets and that there is exactly one unbounded elementary region, which we denote by the constant α_∞ [3]. Throughout the remainder of this paper, we use $p_1, p_2, ...$ to denote elementary points, $\gamma_1, \gamma_2, ...$ to denote elementary curves, and $\alpha_1, \alpha_2, ...$ to denote elementary regions.

2.2 Topological Equivalence of Spatial Databases

It is well-known that the homeomorphisms of $\mathbf{R}^2$ are either orientation-preserving or orientation-reversing [33]. A reflection around a line is an example of an orientation-reversing homeomorphism. Orientation preserving homeomorphisms are commonly referred to as *isotopies* [33]. To increase readability, we will work with isotopies in this paper. We can think of isotopies as continuous deformations of the plane that take place completely within the plane (for a reflection around a line, we need to leave the plane for a moment). The results presented in this paper can be easily extended to homeomorphisms, however.

Definition 3. We call two spatial databases Δ_1 and Δ_2 *topologically equivalent* if $names_{\Delta_1} = names_{\Delta_2}$ and if there exists an isotopy i of $\mathbf{R}^2$ such that $i(ext_{\Delta_1}(A)) = ext_{\Delta_2}(A)$ for all A in $names_{\Delta_1}$. □

We denote the fact that Δ_1 and Δ_2 are topologically equivalent by an isotopy i, by $i(\Delta_1) = \Delta_2$. Topological equivalence of spatial databases can be decided in polynomial-time [19, 21].

2.3 Spatial Database Queries

We now turn to spatial database queries. In this paper, we are mainly interested in Boolean queries. We consider a *spatial database query* to be computable mapping on spatial database instances with a one-bit output. Furthermore, we are especially interested in topological queries.

Definition 4. We say that a spatial database query Q is *topological*, if for any topologically equivalent spatial databases Δ_1 and Δ_2, $Q(\Delta_1) = Q(\Delta_2)$. □

"Is the union of the labeled regions in Δ connected?" is an example of a (Boolean) topological query. "Are there more than four labeled regions of Δ that are above the x-axis?" is *not* topological, however.

The restriction to Boolean queries is not fundamental, however. Indeed, for instance by reserving specific labels for input database regions and others labels for output regions, we can simulate a spatial database query Q that on input Δ_1 returns output Δ_2, by a Boolean query Q' that takes as input the disjoint union $\Delta_1 \cup_d \Delta_2$ and that is such that $Q(\Delta_1) = \Delta_2$ if and only if $Q'(\Delta_1 \cup_d \Delta_2)$ is true.

3 $\mathcal{RL}$: An Elementary-Region Based First-Order Query Language

In this section, we describe the two-sorted first-order logic $\mathcal{RL}$, a spatial query language which uses label variables and elementary-region variables. We also study its expressive power as a topological query language.

3.1   Syntax and Semantics of the Language $\mathcal{RL}$

Syntax of $\mathcal{RL}$. The language $\mathcal{RL}$ is a two-sorted first-order logic with label variables (typically denoted by a with or without accents and subscripts) and elementary-region variables (typically denoted by r with or without accents and subscripts). The logic $\mathcal{RL}$ has α_∞ as an elementary-region constant and all A, for $A \in$ **Names**, as name constants.

A *query* in the language $\mathcal{RL}$ is expressed by a first-order formula

$$\varphi(a_1, \ldots, a_m, r_1, \ldots, r_n),$$

with free label variables $a_1, \ldots, a_m$ and free elementary region variables $r_1, \ldots, r_n$. Such first-order formulas are built with the connectives $\wedge, \vee, \neg, \rightarrow$ and $\leftrightarrow$, quantification $(\exists r)$ and $(\forall r)$ over elementary regions, and quantification $(\exists a)$ and $(\forall a)$ over labels, from atomic formulas of the form

- $r \subseteq a$,
- $a = a'$, $a = A$, for $A \in$ **Names**,
- $r = r'$, $r = \alpha_\infty$, and
- $\mathsf{cw}^{d_1 d_2 d_3}(r, r'_1, r'_2, r'_3)$, for $d_1, d_2, d_3 \in \{0, 1\}$,

where r, r', r'_1, r'_2, and r'_3 are elementary-region variables and a and a' are label variables. $\square$

Further on, we will also use expressions like $r \subseteq A$. These abbreviate the formulas $(\exists a)(r \subseteq a \wedge a = A)$. We now turn to the semantics of $\mathcal{RL}$ queries.

Semantics of $\mathcal{RL}$. The truth value of an $\mathcal{RL}$ query $\varphi(a_1, \ldots, a_m, r_1, \ldots, r_n)$, when evaluated on an input database Δ and with the instantiations $A_1, \ldots A_m$ for $a_1, \ldots, a_m$, and $\alpha_1, \ldots, \alpha_n$ for $r_1, \ldots, r_n$ is defined as follows (in terms of logic, we are going to define the meaning of what is usually denoted as $\Delta \models \varphi[A_1, \ldots, A_m, \alpha_1, \ldots, \alpha_n]$). The elementary region variables appearing in $\varphi(a_1, \ldots, a_m, r_1, \ldots, r_n)$ are interpreted to range over the finite set R_Δ of elementary regions of Δ and the label variables are interpreted to range over the elements of the set $names_\Delta$. The expression $r \subseteq a$ means that the elementary region r is contained in the labeled region with label a. The formula $a = a'$ expresses equality of labels, and $a = A$ express the equality of the label variable a and the constant label A. The expressions $r = r'$ and $r = \alpha_\infty$ express respectively equality of elementary regions and the equality with the unbounded elementary region in Δ. Finally, the formula $\mathsf{cw}^{d_1 d_2 d_3}(r, r'_1, r'_2, r'_3)$ means that the elementary regions r'_1, r'_2 and r'_3 (possibly, some or all of these are the same) appear consecutively in clockwise order around the bounded elementary region r such that the intersection of the closure of r and the closure of r'_i is d_i-dimensional ($i = 1, 2, 3$). A 0-dimensional intersection is a point, and a 1-dimensional intersection is a curve segment. If r is an elementary region, surrounded by a single elementary region r', we agree that $\mathsf{cw}^{111}(r, r', r', r')$ holds. We agree that $\mathsf{cw}^{d_1 d_2 d_3}(\alpha_\infty, r', r'', r''')$ evaluates to *false* for any values of r', r'' and r'''. $\square$

For examples of the latter expressions, we turn to the database of Figure 1 (a). Both the expressions $\text{cw}^{101}(\alpha_1, \alpha_\infty, \alpha_3, \alpha_\infty)$, $\text{cw}^{010}(\alpha_4, \alpha_\infty, \alpha_5, \alpha_\infty)$ and $\text{cw}^{111}(\alpha_2, \alpha_1, \alpha_1, \alpha_1)$ hold but $\text{cw}^{000}(\alpha_1, \alpha_\infty, \alpha_3, \alpha_\infty)$ does not hold.

When evaluated on the database shown in Figure 1 (a), the sentence $(\exists r)(\exists a)$ $(r \subseteq a \wedge a = A)$ evaluates to *true*, since there is an elementary region within the region labeled A. The sentence $(\exists r)(\exists r')(\exists a)(\neg r = r' \wedge r \subseteq a \wedge r' \subseteq a \wedge a = D)$ evaluates to *false* on this database instance, however. Indeed, the region labeled D contains only one elementary region.

In the above definition, we allow an $\mathcal{RL}$ query to be expressed by a formula $\varphi(a_1, \ldots, a_m, r_1, \ldots, r_n)$ with free variables. As stated in the previous section, we are mainly interested in Boolean queries, i.e., queries expressed by formulas without free variables.

The following proposition says that $\mathcal{RL}$ queries can be efficiently computed.

Proposition 1. $\mathcal{RL}$ *queries can be evaluated in polynomial time (in the size of the constraint formulas that describe the input database).*

PROOF SKETCH. Let $\varphi(a_1, \ldots, a_m, r_1, \ldots, r_n)$ be an $\mathcal{RL}$ formula. To evaluate this formula on a given input database Δ, we can proceed as follows. Firstly, the sets of elementary points, curves and regions of Δ are computed. The sets P_Δ, C_Δ and R_Δ have sizes that are bounded polynomially in the size of Δ (more precisely, in the size of the constraint formulas describing Δ) and they can be computed in polynomial time. The set P_Δ can be computed from the polynomial constraint formulas of the labeled regions in Δ in first-order logic over the reals (see, e.g., [22]). The computation of C_Δ and R_Δ from the given polynomial constraint formulas also requires polynomial time (in the number of polynomials used to describe Δ and their degrees) [15].

Subformulas of $\varphi(a_1, \ldots, a_m, r_1, \ldots, r_n)$ of the form $(\exists r)\psi(a_1, \ldots, a_k, r, r_1, \ldots, r_l)$ can be equivalently replaced by

$$\bigvee_{\alpha \in R_\Delta} \psi(a_1, \ldots, a_k, \alpha, r_1, \ldots, r_l),$$

and subformulas of the form $(\exists a)\psi(a, a_1, \ldots, a_k, r_1, \ldots, r_l)$ can be equivalently replaced by

$$\bigvee_{A \in names_\Delta} \psi(A, a_1, \ldots, a_k, r_1, \ldots, r_l).$$

These formulas are polynomially long in the size of Δ. (Remark that strictly speaking the latter formulas are not in $\mathcal{RL}$. But we write them in an $\mathcal{RL}$-like fashion to show how their evaluation can be performed). After these replacements, we obtain a quantifier-free expression, that equivalently expresses the original query, to be evaluated.

To compute the output set of all of $(A_1, \ldots, A_m, \alpha_1, \ldots, \alpha_n) \in (names_\Delta)^m \times (R_\Delta)^n$ for which $\Delta \models \varphi[A_1, \ldots, A_m, \alpha_1, \ldots, \alpha_n]$, we can then proceed as follows. We generate all possible candidate outputs $(A_1, \ldots, A_m, \alpha_1, \ldots, \alpha_n) \in (names_\Delta)^m \times (R_\Delta)^n$ and test each of them. Since, for the given formula

$\varphi(a_1, \ldots, a_m, r_1, \ldots, r_n)$, m and n are fixed, the number of possible outputs is again polynomial in the size of Δ. The latter test can be done because when all variables are instantiated, the atomic formulas can be evaluated. Indeed, the formulas $r \subseteq A_i$, $r = r'$ and $r = \alpha_\infty$ can be checked in first-order logic over the reals (in polynomial time again), whereas, $\mathsf{cw}^{d_1 d_2 d_3}(r, r_1', r_2', r_3')$ can be verified by computing adjacency information on the elements of P_Δ, C_Δ and R_Δ. Also the adjacency information can be computed in time polynomial in the size of Δ.

In conclusion, we can say that for a fixed $\mathcal{RL}$ expression $\varphi(a_1, \ldots, a_m, r_1, \ldots, r_n)$, this expression can be evaluated on each input database Δ in time polynomial in the size of Δ.   □

We remark that, even for a fixed number of labeled regions, the number of elementary regions is not bounded. So, $\mathcal{RL}$ is by no means equivalent to a propositional logic.

3.2 Some First Observations on Expressing Topological Queries in $\mathcal{RL}$

Here, we start by observing that the language $\mathcal{RL}$ is powerful enough to express the relations of the 9-intersection model. We also state that all queries expressible in $\mathcal{RL}$ are topological.

The 9-Intersection Model. So, firstly we show that $\mathcal{RL}$ is expressive enough to allow the formulation of the predicates of the 9-intersection model. Consider these spatial predicates on labeled regions that were investigated in depth by Egenhofer and his collaborators [7, 8, 9]:

- disjoint(A, B), meaning that the topological closure of A is disjoint with that of B;
- overlap(A, B), meaning that A and B have intersecting interiors;
- meet$_{Line}(A, B)$, meaning that A and B have disjoint interiors and that part of their borders have a 1-dimensional intersection;
- meet$_{Point}(A, B)$, meaning that A and B have disjoint interiors and that part of their borders have a zero-dimensional intersection;
- contain(A, B), meaning that $B \subseteq A$ and that their borders are disjoint;
- cover(A, B), meaning that $B \subset A$ and their borders touch;
- equal(A, B), meaning that $A = B$.

Proposition 2. *The predicates* disjoint, overlap, contain cover, equal, meet$_{Line}$, *and* meet$_{Point}$ *of the 9-intersection model are expressible in* $\mathcal{RL}$.

PROOF. The formula

$$\psi(A, B) \equiv (\forall r)(\forall r')\Big(r \subseteq A \wedge r' \subseteq B \rightarrow (\forall r'')(\forall r''')\big(\bigwedge_\delta \neg \mathsf{cw}^\delta(r, r', r'', r''')\big)\Big),$$

where δ ranges over $\{0,1\}^3$, expresses that the borders of A and B are disjoint. Now, disjoint(A,B) can be equivalently expressed in $\mathcal{RL}$ by the sentence $\neg(\exists r)(r \subseteq A \wedge r \subseteq B) \wedge \psi(A,B)$. The fact meet$_{Line}(A,B)$ is expressed as

$$\neg(\exists r)(r \subseteq A \wedge r \subseteq B) \wedge$$
$$(\exists r)(\exists r')(\exists r'')(\exists r''')(r \subseteq A \wedge r' \subseteq B \wedge \bigvee_{(d_1,d_3)\in\{0,1\}^2} \mathsf{cw}^{d_1 1 d_3}(r,r'',r',r''')).$$

And meet$_{Point}(A,B)$ is expressed as

$$\neg(\exists r)(r \subseteq A \wedge r \subseteq B) \wedge$$
$$(\exists r)(\exists r')(\exists r'')(\exists r''')(r \subseteq A \wedge r' \subseteq B \wedge \bigvee_{(d_1,d_3)\in\{0,1\}^2} \mathsf{cw}^{d_1 0 d_3}(r,r'',r',r''')).$$

The formula overlap(A,B) is expressed as $(\exists r)(r \subseteq A \wedge r \subseteq B)$, contains$(A,B)$ is expressed as $(\forall r)(r \subseteq B \rightarrow r \subseteq A) \wedge \psi(A,B)$, covers$(A,B)$ is expressed as $(\forall r)(r \subseteq B \rightarrow r \subseteq A) \wedge \neg\psi(A,B)$, and finally equal$(A,B)$ is expressed as $(\forall r)(r \subseteq A \leftrightarrow r \subseteq B)$.   □

Topological Queries in $\mathcal{RL}$. In Section 2.3 we have given the definition of a topological query (Definition 4). As already remarked, $\mathcal{RL}$ also allows the expression of queries that produce a non-Boolean output. Using the remark made at the end of Section 2.3, we can generalize the definition of a topological query to situations where queries can produce an arbitrary output as follows.

Definition 5. We say that a formula $\varphi(a_1,\ldots,a_m,r_1,\ldots,r_n)$ in $\mathcal{RL}$ is *topological* if and only if for any spatial databases Δ_1 and Δ_2 that are topologically equivalent by some isotopy i, we also have that $\{(A_1,\ldots,A_m,\alpha_1,\ldots,\alpha_n) \in (names_{\Delta_1})^m \times (R_{\Delta_1})^n \mid \Delta_1 \models \varphi[A_1,\ldots,A_m,\alpha_1,\ldots,\alpha_n]\}$ is mapped to $\{(A_1, \ldots,A_m,\alpha_1,\ldots,\alpha_n) \in (names_{\Delta_2})^m \times (R_{\Delta_2})^n \mid \Delta_2 \models \varphi[A_1,\ldots,A_m,\alpha_1,\ldots,\alpha_n]\}$ by the function $(id,\ldots,id,i,\ldots,i)$, where id is the identity mapping.   □

Using this more general definition of topological query, the following proposition can be proven straightforwardly by induction on the syntactic structure of $\mathcal{RL}$ formulas.

Proposition 3. *All queries expressible in $\mathcal{RL}$ are topological.*   □

3.3   Further Results on Expressing Topological Queries in $\mathcal{RL}$

Here, we discuss lower and upper bounds on the expressive power of $\mathcal{RL}$ as a language to express topological properties of spatial databases.

Lower Bound on the Expressiveness of $\mathcal{RL}$. First, we give the definition of elementarily equivalent spatial databases. The notion of elementary equivalence of a language captures the power of this language to distinguish different databases.

Definition 6. We denote the fact that two spatial databases Δ_1 and Δ_2 cannot be distinguished by any Boolean $\mathcal{RL}$ query (i.e., for every $\mathcal{RL}$ sentence ψ, $\Delta_1 \models \psi$ if and only if $\Delta_2 \models \psi$) by $\Delta_1 \equiv_{\mathcal{RL}} \Delta_2$, and we say that Δ_1 and Δ_2 are *elementarily equivalent.*   □

The following result gives a lower bound for the expressive power of $\mathcal{RL}$.

Theorem 1. *We have that*

(i) if two spatial databases Δ_1 and Δ_2 are topologically equivalent then they are elementarily equivalent, i.e., then $\Delta_1 \equiv_{\mathcal{RL}} \Delta_2$;

(ii) if two spatial databases Δ_1 and Δ_2 are elementarily equivalent, i.e., if $\Delta_1 \equiv_{\mathcal{RL}} \Delta_2$, then they are topologically equivalent;

(iii) for every database instance Δ there exists a $\mathcal{RL}$ sentence χ_Δ such that for every database instance Δ', $\Delta' \models \chi_\Delta$ if and only if Δ and Δ' are topologically equivalent.   □

Item (iii) states that for every spatial database there is a *characteristic formula* that exactly describes the topology of the spatial database.

Whereas (i) of this Theorem follows immediately from Proposition 3, (ii) and (iii) require more work.

We first prove the following technical lemma.

Lemma 1. *Two spatial database instances Δ_1 and Δ_2 are topologically equivalent if and only if there exists a bijection between R_{Δ_1} and R_{Δ_2} that maps the unbounded elementary region to the unbounded elementary region, that maps elementary regions within certain labeled regions to elementary regions in regions with the same region label and that preserves for any d_1, d_2, $d_3 \in \{0, 1\}$ the eight relations $\mathrm{cw}^{d_1 d_2 d_3}(r, r_1, r_2, r_3)$.*

PROOF SKETCH. The only-if direction is obvious. For the if-direction, we first observe that two spatial database instances Δ_1 and Δ_2 are topologically equivalent if and only if their frames are isotopic[2] by an isotopy that respects the labels. So, we proceed with their frames. We first remark that the frame of a spatial database can be constructed by applying the following two operations Op_1 and Op_2 a finite number of times starting from the empty plane:

Op_1 : add a closed curve in the unbounded region;

Op_2 : add a curve in the unbounded region between two points of already existing curves such that a new region is created.

This can be proven easily by induction on the number of elementary curves in the spatial database.

---

[2] We call two subsets of $\mathbf{R}^2$ isotopic if there is an isotopy (i.e., an orientation-preserving homeomorphism) of $\mathbf{R}^2$ that maps one to the other.

We prove the if-direction by induction on the number of elementary curves in the frame of Δ_1. If the number of elementary curves is zero, Δ_1 only has one elementary region, namely α_∞. By assumption, also Δ_2 has only one elementary region and therefore the identity mapping is the desired isotopy.

Assume that the number n of elementary curves of Δ_1 is strictly positive. Let b be the bijective mapping between R_{Δ_1} and R_{Δ_2} that we assume to exist. Because any frame can be constructed using operations Op_1 and Op_2, it follows that Δ_1 has an elementary curve γ that is adjacent to α_∞ with contact of dimension 1 (since a frame can be constructed using Op_1 and Op_2, γ can be either an isolated curve or a curve that connects two points of some other curves). Suppose γ separates α_∞ from the elementary region α_0 in Δ_1 and let γ' correspond in Δ_2 to γ. So, γ' separates α_∞ from $b(\alpha_0)$. If we remove γ and γ' from Δ_1 and Δ_2 respectively this results in two spatial database frames F_1 and F_2 such that α_0 and $b(\alpha_0)$ are identified with α_∞. It is not difficult to show that hereby the bijection b induces a bijection between the elementary regions of F_1 and F_2 that preserves the clockwise appearance of elementary regions around each elementary region. By the induction hypothesis, there exists an isotopy i of the plane that maps F_1 to F_2, and that respects the labeling. This isotopy maps the curve γ to $i(\gamma)$ which is not necessarily equal to γ'. We remark that $i(\gamma)$ creates a new elementary region. We can make sure that the labeling is respected. A "local" isotopy can be constructed however that locally maps $i(\gamma)$ to γ' and that leaves the remainder of the frame F_1 unaltered. Since by assumption, the labels of the elementary regions are respected, the composition of this local isotopy with i gives the desired isotopy that maps Δ_1 to Δ_2. $\qquad\square$

PROOF SKETCH OF THEOREM 1. If two databases Δ_1 and Δ_2 are isotopic, they cannot be distinguished by any $\mathcal{RL}$ sentence because of Proposition 3. This proves (i). To prove (ii), it suffices to prove (iii). We show that any spatial database Δ can be characterized up to isotopy by an $\mathcal{RL}$ sentence χ_Δ. This formula is of the form

$$(\exists r_1)\cdots(\exists r_n)\left(\left((\forall r)\bigvee_{i=1}^{n} r = r_i\right) \wedge \bigwedge_{i<j} r_i \neq r_j \wedge \bigwedge_i r_i \neq \alpha_\infty \wedge\right.$$
$$\left.\bigwedge_{i,j_i} r_i \subseteq A_{j_i} \wedge \bigwedge_{i,(i_1,i_2,i_3)} \mathsf{cw}^{d_{i_1} d_{i_2} d_{i_3}}(r_i, r_{i_1}, r_{i_2}, r_{i_3})\right)$$

which expresses that there are exactly n bounded elementary regions, says to which of the labeled regions these n elementary regions belong, and completely describes the clockwise appearance of elementary regions around all elementary regions.

Suppose that another database Δ' satisfies χ_Δ. Then there exists an assignment of the variables $r_1, \ldots, r_n$ to distinct bounded elementary regions of Δ' that makes χ_Δ true. This variable assignment then determines a bijection between the elementary regions of Δ and of Δ'. Because both databases satisfy χ_Δ, the

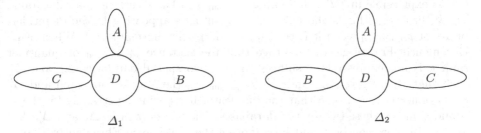

Fig. 2. Two databases Δ_1 and Δ_2 that cannot be distinguished using the less powerful predicate $cw^{d_1 d_2}(r, r_1, r_2)$ alone

corresponding bounded elementary regions have the same clockwise appearance of areas around them. By Lemma 1, Δ and Δ' are therefore isotopic. This proves the theorem.   □

We remark that a predicate $cw^{d_1 d_2}(r, r_1, r_2)$, that expresses that r_1 and r_2 appear clockwise around r with contact of dimension d_1 and d_2 respectively is not sufficient to obtain Theorem 1. This is illustrated by the two databases in Figure 2. They cannot be distinguished using $cw^{d_1 d_2}(r, r_1, r_2)$ alone. This is the reason why the more powerful $cw^{d_1 d_2 d_3}(r, r_1, r_2, r_3)$ is used in $\mathcal{RL}$.

Upper Bound on the Expressiveness of $\mathcal{RL}$. The following result shows that not all topological queries can be expressed in $\mathcal{RL}$. With $connect(r_1, r_2)$ we denote that the elementary regions r_1 and r_2 can be connected by a connected path that completely belongs to union of the closure of the labeled regions.

Proposition 4. *The predicate* connect *is not expressible in* $\mathcal{RL}$.

This result can be proven using a classical Ehrenfeucht-Fraïssé game argument. The proof of the above proposition would be too technical to give here in full, but the idea is outlined below.

PROOF IDEA. An Ehrenfeucht-Fraïssé game is a game played over a certain number of rounds on two databases by two players; the first player is usually called the spoiler and the second the duplicator. (For the technical details of Ehrenfeucht-Fraïssé games we refer to theoretical database books [1] or logic texts [6].)

Assume that the predicate $connect(r_1, r_2)$ is expressible in $\mathcal{RL}$. The sentence $\varphi_{connected}$ given as

$$(\forall r_1)(\forall r_2)(((\exists a_1)(\exists a_2)(r_1 \subseteq a_1) \wedge (r_2 \subseteq a_2)) \to connect(r_1, r_2))$$

expresses that the spatial database is *topologically connected.*[3] So, if the predicate $connect(r_1, r_2)$ is expressible in $\mathcal{RL}$, then also the topological connectivity

---

[3] More precisely, we call a spatial database here *topologically connected* if the union of the closure of the labeled regions in the spatial database is a path-connected subset of the plane.

test is expressible in $\mathcal{RL}$. The sentence $\varphi_{\text{connected}}$ has a certain quantifier rank, say k (basically, this is the number of quantifiers appearing in the quantifier-prefix of $\varphi_{\text{connected}}$ when it is transformed in prenex normal form). When using Ehrenfeucht-Fraïssé games to prove that the sentence $\varphi_{\text{connected}}$ of quantifier rank k is not expressible it suffices to give two spatial databases Δ_k and Δ'_k such that $\Delta_k \models \varphi_{\text{connected}}$ and $\Delta'_k \not\models \varphi_{\text{connected}}$ (i.e., Δ_k is connected and Δ'_k is disconnected), and such that the duplicator has a winning strategy for the k-round game on these two spatial databases. The two databases Δ_k and Δ'_k that are needed here can be found by adapting the well-known Ehrenfeucht-Fraïssé games that show that graph-connectivity is not expressible in the relational calculus (see, for instance, the proof of Proposition 17.2.3 in [1]) to this situation. Roughly, Δ_k would consist of an exponentially (in k) long chain of regions in which two neighboring regions are connected and Δ'_k would consist of two disjoint such chains. Using similar arguments as in the relational case [1], it can be shown that the duplicator has a winning strategy on these databases for the k-round game. □

We remark that there is a variety of examples of computable topological queries that are not expressible in $\mathcal{RL}$. For instance, the parity queries "Is the number of elementary regions in the database even?" and "Is the number of connected components of the database even?" are both not expressible in $\mathcal{RL}$.

4   More Powerful Query Languages: Extensions of $\mathcal{RL}$

Although many interesting properties of spatial databases in the topological data model can be expressed in $\mathcal{RL}$, an important deficiency of $\mathcal{RL}$ is that for practical applications important queries such as the connectivity test and reachability are not expressible in this first-order language, as we have seen in the previous section. In this section, we will briefly study a number of extensions of $\mathcal{RL}$: $\mathcal{RL}$ augmented with connect; $\mathcal{RL}$ augmented with a transitive closure operator and $\mathcal{RL}$ augmented with a while-loop (and some set-theoretic operators).

4.1 $\mathcal{RL}$ Augmented with Connect or Transitive Closure

An obvious approach to obtain the expressibility of the connectivity test is simply to augment $\mathcal{RL}$ with the predicate $\text{connect}(r_1, r_2)$. Then connectivity of a database is expressible, as shown above, by the formula $(\forall r_1)(\forall r_2)(((\exists a_1)(\exists a_2) (r_1 \subseteq a_1) \wedge (r_2 \subseteq a_2)) \rightarrow \text{connect}(r_1, r_2)$. However, it is not clear if the language $\mathcal{RL}$ + connect is complete in the sense that all computable topological queries are expressible in it. In the constraint model, for instance, when first-order logic over the reals is augmented with a predicate that expresses connectivity of two-dimensional sets, then parity of a set of real numbers is expressible. For $\mathcal{RL}$ + connect we conjecture the opposite, however.

A transitive-closure operator can be added to $\mathcal{RL}$ in several ways. One possibility is that we add to $\mathcal{RL}$ expressions of the form

$$[\text{TC } \varphi(r'_1, r'_2)](r_1, r_2),$$

where $\varphi(r'_1, r'_2)$ is a $\mathcal{RL}$ formula with two free elementary-region variables. The meaning of $[\text{TC } \varphi(r'_1, r'_2)](r_1, r_2)$ is that the couple (r_1, r_2) of elementary regions belongs to the transitive closure of the binary relation defined by the $\mathcal{RL}$ formula $\varphi(r'_1, r'_2)$, i.e., the set $\{(r'_1, r'_2) \mid \varphi(r'_1, r'_2)\}$. Various more powerful extensions of $\mathcal{RL}$ could be thought of, but this one is strong enough to express the topological connectivity test. Indeed,

$$(\forall r_1)(\forall r_2)(((\exists a_1)(\exists a_2)((r_1 \subseteq a_1) \wedge (r_2 \subseteq a_2))) \rightarrow$$

$$[TC \ (\exists a_1)(\exists a_2)((r'_1 \subseteq a_1) \wedge (r'_2 \subseteq a_2) \wedge \text{meet}(r'_1, r'_2))](r_1, r_2))$$

where $\text{meet}(r'_1, r'_2)$ abbreviates $\text{meet}_{Line}(r'_1, r'_2) \vee \text{meet}_{Point}(r'_1, r'_2) \vee r'_1 = r'_2$ (the predicates meet_{Line} and meet_{Point} are defined as in Section 3.2), expresses that every pair of elementary regions that are in a labeled region are also in the transitive closure of the binary relation defined by meet (which contains all pairs of elementary regions which are adjacent). The computation of the transitive closure is guaranteed to terminate because the number of elementary regions is finite for any input database. This expresses that the union of the closure of the labeled regions in the spatial database is a connected subset of the plane. It is not clear what the expressive power of this extension of $\mathcal{RL}$ exactly is, however.

4.2 $\mathcal{RL}$ Augmented with a While-Loop

In the final part of this section, we introduce the language $\mathcal{RL} + $ While. This language is essentially the extension of the first-order logic $\mathcal{RL}$ with a while-loop and some set-theoretic operations. This extension of $\mathcal{RL}$ is a sound and complete language for the computable topological queries on spatial databases in the topological data model.

Definition 7. An $\mathcal{RL} + $ While-*program* is a finite sequence of *statements* and *while-loops*.

A statement is either an $\mathcal{RL}$-definition of a relation, based on previously defined relations or the result of a set-theoretic operation on previously defined relations. An $\mathcal{RL}$-definition of a relation has the form

$$R := \{(a_1, \ldots, a_m, r_1, \ldots, r_n) \mid \varphi(a_1, \ldots, a_m, r_1, \ldots, r_n)\};$$

where R is a relation variable of arity $m+n$ and φ is a formula in $\mathcal{RL}$ augmented with expressions $S(a_1, \ldots, a_k, r_1, \ldots, r_l)$ where S is some previously introduced relation variable of arity $k+l$. The other (set-theoretic) form of defining relations is one of the following: $R := S \cap S'$; $R := \neg S$; $R := S\!\downarrow$; $R := S\!\uparrow^a$; $R := S\!\uparrow^r$; and $R := S\!\sim$, where S and S' are some previously introduced relation variables.

A while-loop has the form

$$\textbf{while } \varphi \textbf{ do } \{P\};$$

where P is a program and φ is a sentence in $\mathcal{RL}$ augmented with expressions $S(a_1, \ldots, a_k, r_1, \ldots, r_l)$ where S is some previously introduced relation variable of arity $k+l$. □

In this definition, it is assumed that there is a supply of untyped relation variables (this is important because relations in the while-language can grow arbitrarily wide). Semantically, a program in the query language $\mathcal{RL}$ + While allows the creation of relations and in a loop like **while** φ **do** P , P is executed until φ becomes false. A program therefore expresses a query in the obvious way as soon as one of its relation variables has been designated as the output variable (e.g., R_{out}). The semantics of the set-theoretic operations needs some further clarification. An assignment $R := S \cap S'$ simply expresses the intersection. The assignment $R := \neg S$ expresses the complement with respect to the appropriate domains. The assignment $R := S\downarrow$ is projecting out the first dimension or coordinate. The assignment $R := S\uparrow^a$ is projecting in on the right with a extra label-dimension. And $R := S\uparrow^r$ is similar for a region-dimension. Finally, $R := S\sim$ exchanging the two right-most coordinates of S.

Obviously, the while-loops of $\mathcal{RL}$ + While can be non-terminating. However, if a while-loop terminates (or a $\mathcal{RL}$ + While-program for that matter), then all computed relations are $\mathcal{RL}$-definable.

As an example, we give an $\mathcal{RL}$ + While-program that expresses that the input spatial database is connected (i.e., that the union of all the labeled regions in the input is a connected subset of the plane). In the following $\text{meet}(r, r')$ abbreviates $\text{meet}_{Line}(r, r') \vee \text{meet}_{Point}(r, r') \vee r = r'$, where meet_{Line} and meet_{Point} are in turn the abbreviations introduced in Section 3.2.

$$R := \{(r, r') \mid (\exists a)(\exists a')(r \subseteq a \wedge r' \subseteq a' \wedge \text{meet}(r, r'))\};$$
$$R_1 := R;$$
$$R_2 := \{(r, r') \mid (\exists r'')(R_1(r, r'') \wedge R(r'', r'))\};$$
$$\textbf{while } R_1 \neq R_2 \textbf{ do } \{$$
$$\qquad R_1 := R_2;$$
$$\qquad R_2 := \{(r, r') \mid (\exists r'')(R_1(r, r'') \wedge R(r'', r'))\};$$
$$\qquad \};$$
$$R_{\text{out}} := \{() \mid (\forall r)(\forall r')((\exists a)(\exists a')(r \subseteq a \ \wedge r' \subseteq a' \rightarrow R_2(r, r')))\};$$

Here, an expression like $R_1 := R$ is an abbreviation of $R_1 := \{(r, r') \mid R(r, r')\}$. In this program, first a binary relation consisting of all adjacent elementary regions that are in a labeled region is computed. Next, the transitive closure of this binary relation is computed. The computation of the transitive closure is guaranteed to terminate because the number of elementary regions is finite for any input database. Finally, the relation R_{out} is defined. This relation is empty for a disconnected input and non-empty for a connected input database.

The main result of this section is the following.

Theorem 2. *The language $\mathcal{RL}$ + While is sound and computationally complete for the topological queries on spatial databases in the topological data model.*

PROOF IDEA. Using the results in Section 3, it is easy to show soundness. To prove completeness, we first observe that Cabibbo and Van den Bussche [36] have shown that many-sorted logics, like $\mathcal{RL}$ can be equivalently expressed in an untyped logic that is augmented with unary type-predicates (here ER and L). So, we can consider untyped variants of $\mathcal{RL}$ and $\mathcal{RL}$ + While: $\mathcal{RL}^u$ and $\mathcal{RL}^u$ + While. The proof of the theorem is then in two steps. For what concerns the first step we observe that the relations $R_L = \{x \mid L(x)\}$, $R_{ER} = \{x \mid ER(x)\}$, $R_{\text{label}} = \{(x,y) \mid ER(x) \wedge L(y) \wedge x \subseteq y\}$, and $R_{d_1 d_2 d_3} = \{(x, x_1, x_2, x_3) \mid \text{cw}^{d_1 d_2 d_3}(x, x_1, x_2, x_3) \wedge ER(x) \wedge ER(x_1) \wedge ER(x_2) \wedge ER(x_3)\}$ (with $d_1, d_2, d_3 \in \{0, 1\}$) contain the complete topological information of the input spatial database (this follows directly from Lemma 1). For a given input spatial database Δ, the relational database Δ_{fin}, consisting of these eleven relations is therefore definable in $\mathcal{RL}^u$, as just shown.

Secondly, we observe that by adding the set-theoretic operations to $\mathcal{RL}$ + While we have obtained a language powerful enough to express all generic Turing computable functions on Δ_{fin} (we can do this by showing that the query language QL of Chandra and Harel [4] can be simulated in $\mathcal{RL}^u$ + While).   □

Finally, we remark that if we extend $\mathcal{RL}$ with while as in Chandra and Harel [5] (also [1, Chapter 17]) and if we assume an ordering on the (elementary) regions, that then, using a well-known result, this extension of the language $\mathcal{RL}$ captures the PSPACE topological queries on spatial databases in the topological data model.

5   Conclusion and Discussion

In this paper, we have continued the search for effective, convenient and expressive languages for querying topological properties of spatial databases in the topological data model. In searching for such languages we face a number of challenges. We typically want languages to be natural in the sense that the primitives appearing in it express natural concepts such as intersection, adjacency and connectivity. We also want that queries are computable and have a complexity that belongs to a nice class such as PSPACE or PTIME. A third issue is completeness: all topological queries from preferably some suitable computational class should be captured.

To deal with these issues we propose the two-sorted logic $\mathcal{RL}$ and a number of extensions of it. In the language $\mathcal{RL}$ variables range over regions from the active domain of a spatial database instance, as opposed to an infinite universe of regions in previously discussed languages [25]. This logic, by the predicate cw, is descriptive enough to characterize the topological information of a spatial database instance. As we have shown in this paper, with $\mathcal{RL}$ and its extensions we meet some of the above set challenges. Especially on the level of naturalness improvement should be expected.

The topological data model allows a representation where a prominent role is given to the spatial containment relation [10, 11, 16, 17]. This is interesting from a practical point of view since it allows to use efficient data structures for the management of (partial) order relations [34]. Future work will focus on the translation of $\mathcal{RL}$ queries in terms of operations on suitably enriched order-based data structures.

References

[1] S. Abiteboul, R. Hull, and V. Vianu. *Foundations of Databases*. Addison-Wesley, 1995. 345, 355, 356, 359

[2] M. Benedikt, M. Grohe, L. Libkin, and L. Segoufin. Reachability and connectivity queries in constraint databases. In *Proceedings of the 19th ACM SIGMOD-SIGACT-SIGART Symposium on Principles of Database Systems (PODS'00)*, pages 104–115, 2000. 345

[3] J. Bochnak, M. Coste, and M. F. Roy. *Géométrie Algébrique Réelle*. Springer-Verlag, 1987. 347

[4] A. Chandra and D. Harel. Computable queries for relational database systems. *Journal of Computer and System Sciences*, 21(2):156–178, 1980. 359

[5] A. Chandra and D. Harel. Structure and complexity of relational queries. *Journal of Computer and System Sciences*, 25:99–128, 1982. 359

[6] H.-D. Ebbinghaus, J. Flum, and W. Thomas. *Mathematical Logic*. Undergraduate Texts in Mathematics. Springer-Verlag, 1984. 355

[7] M. Egenhofer. Reasoning about binary topological relations. In *Advances in Spatial Databases, Second International Symposium (SSD'91)*, volume 525 of *Lecture Notes in Computer Science*, pages 143–160. Springer-Verlag, 1991. 344, 346, 351

[8] M. Egenhofer. Topological relations between regions in $\mathbf{R}^2$ and $\mathbf{Z}^2$. In *Advances in Spatial Databases, Third International Symposium (SSD'93)*, volume 692 of *Lecture Notes in Computer Science*, pages 316–336. Springer-Verlag, 1993. 344, 351

[9] M. Egenhofer and R. Franzosa. On the equivalence of topological relations. *International Journal Geographical Information Systems*, pages 523–542, 1994. 344, 346, 351

[10] L. Forlizzi and E. Nardelli. Some results on the modelling of spatial data. In *Proceedings of the 25th Conference on Current Trends in Theory and Practice of Informatics (SOFSEM'98)*, pages 332–343, 1998. 359

[11] L. Forlizzi and E. Nardelli. Characterization results for the poset based representation of topological relations-I: Introduction and models. *Informatica (Slovenia)*, 23(2):332–343, 1999. 359

[12] F. Geerts and B. Kuijpers. Linear approximation of planar spatial databases using transitive-closure logic. In *Proceedings of the 19th ACM SIGMOD-SIGACT-SIGART Symposium on Principles of Database Systems (PODS'00)*, pages 126–135, 2000. 346

[13] Ch. Giannella and D. Van Gucht. Adding a path connectedness operator to FO+poly (linear). *Acta Informatica*, 38(9):621–648, 2002. 345

[14] S. Grumbach and G. Kuper. Tractable recursion over geometric data. In *Proceedings of Principles and Practice of Constraint Programming (CP'97)*, volume 1330 of *Lecture Notes in Computer Science*, pages 450–462. Springer-Verlag, 1997. 345, 346

[15] J. Heintz, M.-F. Roy, and P. Solernó. Description of the connected components of a semialgebraic set in single exponential time. *Discrete and Computational Geometry*, 6:1–20, 1993. 350

[16] W. Kainz. Spatial relationships-topology versus order. In *Proceedings of the 4th International Symposium on Spatial Data Handling*, volume 2, pages 814–819, 1990. 359

[17] W. Kainz, M. Egenhofer, and I. Greasley. Modelling spatial relations and operations with partially ordered sets. *International Journal of Geographical Information Systems*, 7(3):215–229, 1993. 359

[18] S. Kreutzer. Fixed-point query languages for linear constraint databases. In *Proceedings of the 19th ACM SIGMOD-SIGACT-SIGART Symposium on Principles of Database Systems (PODS'00)*, pages 116–125, 2000. 346

[19] B. Kuijpers. *Topological Properties of Spatial Databases in the Polynomial Constraint Model*. PhD thesis, University of Antwerp (UIA), 1998. 348

[20] B. Kuijpers, J. Paredaens, M. Smits, and J. Van den Bussche. Termination properties of spatial Datalog programs. In D. Pedreschi and C. Zaniolo, editors, *International Workshop on Logic in Databases (LID'96)*, volume 1154 of *Lecture Notes in Computer Science*, pages 101–116. Springer-Verlag, 1996. 345

[21] B. Kuijpers, J. Paredaens, and J. Van den Bussche. Lossless representation of topological spatial data. In *Proceedings of the 4th International Symposium on Spatial Databases*, volume 951 of *Lecture Notes in Computer Science*, pages 1–13. Springer-Verlag, 1995. 348

[22] B. Kuijpers, J. Paredaens, and J. Van den Bussche. Topological elementary equivalence of closed semi-algebraic sets in the real plane. *The Journal of Symbolic Logic*, 65(4):1530–1555, 2000. 350

[23] B. Kuijpers and J. Van den Bussche. On capturing first-order topological properties of planar spatial databases. In *7th International Conference on Database Theory (ICDT'99)*, volume 1540 of *Lecture Notes in Computer Science*, pages 187–198, 1999. 345

[24] B. Kuijpers and V. Vianu. Topological queries. In J. Paredaens, G. Kuper, and L. Libkin, editors, *Constraint databases*, chapter 2, pages 231–274. Springer-Verlag, 2000. 345, 346

[25] Ch. H. Papadimitriou, D. Suciu, and V. Vianu. Topological queries in spatial databases. *Journal of Computer and System Sciences*, 58(1):29–53, 1999. An extended abstract appeared in PODS'96. 344, 345, 346, 359

[26] J. Paredaens, G. Kuper, and L. Libkin, editors. *Constraint databases*. Springer-Verlag, 2000. 345, 346

[27] I. Pratt. First-order qualitative spatial representation languages with convexity. *Spatial Cognition and Computation*, 1:181–204, 1999. 345

[28] I. Pratt and O. Lemon. Ontologies for plane, polygonal mereotopology. *Notre Dame Journal of Formal Logic*, 38(2):225–245, Spring 1997. 345

[29] I. Pratt and D. Schoop. A complete axiom system for polygonal mereotopology of the real plane. *Journal of Philosophical Logic*, 27(6):621–661, 1998. 345

[30] D. A. Randell, Z. Cui, and A. G. Cohn. A spatial logic based on regions and connection. In *Principles of Knowledge Representation and Reasoning: Proceedings of the 3rd International Conference (KR'92)*, pages 165–176. Morgan Kaufmann, 1992. 344

[31] P. Revesz. *Introduction to Constraint Databases*. Springer-Verlag, 2002. 345, 346

[32] L. Segoufin and V. Vianu. Querying spatial databases via topological invariants. *Journal of Computer and System Sciences*, 61(2):270–301, 2000. An extended abstract appeared in PODS'98. 344, 345, 346

[33] J. Stillwell. *Classical Topology and Combinatorial Group Theory*, volume 72 of *Graduate Texts in Mathematics*. Springer-Verlag, 1980. 348

[34] M. Talamo and P. Vocca. A data structure for lattice representation. *Theoretical Computer Science*, 175(2):373–392, 1997. 359

[35] J. Ullman. *Principles of Database and Knowledge-Base Systems, volumes I and II*. Computer Science Press, 1989-1990. 345

[36] J. Van den Bussche and L. Cabibbo. Converting untyped formulas to typed ones. *Acta Informatica*, 35(8):637–643, 1998. 358

Query Pre-processing of Topological Constraints: Comparing a Composition-Based with Neighborhood-Based Approach*

M. Andrea Rodríguez[1], Max J. Egenhofer[2,3], and Andreas D. Blaser[4]

[1]Department of Information Engineering and Computer Science, University of Concepción
Edmundo Larenas 215, Concepción, Chile
andrea@udec.cl
[2]National Center for Geographic Information and Analysis,
University of Maine,
Orono, ME 04469-5711, USA
[3]Department of Information Science, University of Maine,
Orono, ME 04469-5711, USA
max@spatial.maine.edu
[4] Environmental Systems Research Institute,
380 New York Street, Redlands, CA 92373-8100, USA
abl@esri.com

Abstract. This paper derives and compares two strategies for minimizing topological constraints in a query expressed by a visual example: (1) elimination of topological relations that are implied uniquely by composition and (2) restriction to topological relations that relate near-neighbor objects, as determined by a Delaunay triangulation. In both cases, the query processing approach is to solve a constraint satisfaction problem over a graph of binary topological relations. Individuals and the combination of the composition- and neighborhood-based strategies were implemented and compared with respect to their ability to reduce topological constraints, and with respect to the quality of the results obtained by a similarity-based searching that uses these pre-processing strategies. The main conclusion of this work is that similarity queries that are formulated in a visual language should exploit the metric characteristics of the configuration, even if only topological constraints are considered for making matches.

* This work was partially funded by FONDECYT 1010897 and 7010897 and the National Imagery and Mapping Agency under grant number NMA202-97-1-1023. Max Egenhofer's work is further support by grants from the National Science Foundation under grant numbers IIS-9970123 and EPS- 9983432, the National Imagery and Mapping Agency under grant numbers NMA201-01-1-2003, NMA201-00-1-2009, NMA401-02-1-2009, and National Institute of Environmental Health Sciences, NIH, under grant number 1 R 01 ES09816-01.

T. Hadzilacos et al. (Eds.): SSTD 2003, LNCS 2750, pp. 362-379, 2003.

1   Introduction

Query evaluation in geographic databases is often expensive, because the spatial data stored are more complexly structured and data sets are larger than their non-spatial counter parts. Spatial queries are usually expressed as a set of spatial objects and a set of spatial constraints among the objects. The spatial constraints may be topological (e.g., *overlap* or *inside*), metric (e.g., *within 2 miles* or *near*), and directional (e.g., *north*). The goal of a query evaluation is to match the query constraints among the related objects with binary spatial relations between objects that are stored in a spatial database. Since the spatial objects are embedded in the same space, the set of binary spatial relations—and, therefore, also the number of possible constraints—grows exponentially with the number of spatial objects in the query. This is the case, for example, if the goal is to find spatial scenes that are similar to a given configuration or if a spatial query is derived from a sketch [1], where the user specifies a query by drawing an example that is composed of objects and implicit spatial constraints. For n objects drawn, the sketch—and, therefore, the derived query—contains n^2 topological relations, n^2 direction relations, and n^2 metric relations. Such a type of query implies very hard combinatorial computations [2-4] and, therefore, presents a challenging problem for spatial information retrieval.

The evaluation of a spatial query is typically composed of a sequence of steps (Figure 1) [5]. Starting with the semantic analysis, a *consistency checker* evaluates whether or not query constraints contain self-contradictions [6]. The *optimizer* aims at speeding up the query processing by generating an evaluation plan according to optimization rules and access path selections. Finally, the *query processor* is in charge of carrying out the evaluation. This paper focuses on spatial query optimization involving binary topological relations.

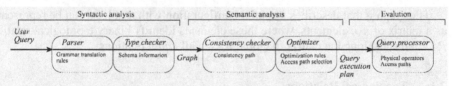

Fig. 1. Sequence of tasks in a query evaluation (based on [5]).

Most approaches to spatial query optimization have pursued an efficient search process by defining an optimal evaluation plan [7-11]. In these approaches, the complexity of spatial operators and the size of the search space become the basis for defining the best sequence of tasks in answering a query. This paper pursues a complementary approach that is independent of the data collection in the spatial database and, therefore, can be performed as part of query optimization in a pre-processing step. Query pre-processor aims at reducing the number of spatial constraints by analyzing the content of a spatial query with the goal to find a subset of constraints that will satisfy the query. A subset of constraints does not lose information if the results of the query process obtained with this subset satisfy the constraints that were not evaluated.

This study considers two strategies for reducing the number of topological relations that describe a spatial configuration: (1) composition-based and (2) neighborhood-based approaches. The composition-based approach considers the spatial reasoning concept of composition, where topological relations can be derived from a subset of given topological relations [12]. It is, therefore, based purely on the algebraic properties of the set of topological relations. The neighborhood-based strategy considers semantics of the space by emphasizing that non-disjoint topological relations are more relevant than disjoint relations, since they indicate physical connection between objects [13, 14]. Thus, what matters are the relations between objects that are physically close to each other. Although some level of composition-based or neighborhood-based query pre-processing has been used in the past [13, 15, 16], no study has described the background, and the advantages and disadvantages of pre-processing the query with such strategies.

The organization of the remainder of this paper is as follows: Section 2 presents the representation of spatial configurations and definitions associated with topological relations. Section 3 and 4 develop composition-based and neighborhood-based pre-processing strategies, respectively. Experimental results that compare both pre-processing strategies are given in Section 5. Section 6 draws conclusions and discusses future research directions.

2   Representing Topological Relations

A configuration C is a set of objects O and a set of constraints R expressed by the binary topological relations between two objects (Equation 1). This configuration can be seen as a graph, where nodes are the objects and directed edges are the binary topological relations [15, 18].

$$C = \left\{ (O, R) : O = \{ o_1 ... o_n \} \wedge R = \{ (o_i, o_j) : o_i, o_j \in O \} \right\} \quad (1)$$

The graph g that describes a spatial configuration with n objects can be represented as a matrix of $n{\times}n$ elements, where these elements identify binary topological relations R_{ij}. Elements along the matrix diagonal $R_{i,i}$ are all *equal* relations.

2.1   Topological Relations

Topological relations are binary spatial relations that are preserved under topological transformations such as rotation, translation, and scaling. This work concentrates on topological relations between regions. Figure 2 shows the eight topological relations that can be found between two regions [19, 20], organized in a graph that connects conceptual neighbors derived from the concept of *gradual changes* [21]. For example, *disjoint* and *meet* are two neighboring relations in this graph and, therefore, they are conceptually closer than *disjoint* and *overlap*. Only regions are considered here, because objects are usually indexed based on their Minimum Bounding Rectangles (MBRs) [10, 22]. Searching for MBRs is a first filter in solving a query and is usually sufficient for finding a spatial object.

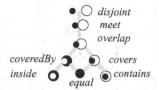

Fig. 2. Eight topological relations between regions, arranged by their conceptual neighborhoods [12]

Refinements of these topological relations can be also introduced in order to differentiate relations by taking into account metric characteristics of objects, such as relative size and distances [23, 24]. Thus, a pair of objects can be seen as further disjoint than another pair if the distance between the first pair is larger than the distance between the second pair.

2.2   Relation Algebra

Topological relations are usually defined as a *relation algebra* [25]. A *relation algebra* (with universe $\mathfrak{R}$) is defined as a ten-tuple $\langle \mathfrak{R}, +, \bullet, -, 0, 1, ;, 1', 0', \overline{} \rangle$, where $\langle \mathfrak{R}, +, \bullet, -, 0, 1 \rangle$ is a Boolean algebra, 0 is the *empty* relation, 1 is the *universal* relation, ; is a binary operation called *composition*, 1' is the *identity* relation, 0' is the *diversity* relation, and $\overline{}$ is a unary operator forming the *converse* of a given relation [25]. The composition operation (;) allows us to make inferences about the relation between two objects, o_i and o_k, by combining the relations, R and S, over a common object, o_j (Equation 2).

$$R ; S \equiv . o_i, o_k) \mid \exists o_j \text{ such that } (o_i, o_j) \in R \text{ and } (o_j, o_k) \in S \qquad (2)$$

1.3   Composition of Topological Relations

The composition may result in a set of relations that is composed of one or more than one element and whose number of elements increases as less precise information is obtained from the inference. For example, if the composition of two operations yields the set with all possible relations (i.e., the universal relation 1), no information at all is obtained from this inference. The composition table for topological relations between regions (Figure 3) shows that out of the 64 compositions, 27 compositions have a unique result, three compositions yield the universal relation, and 34 compositions have between two and six relations in their results.

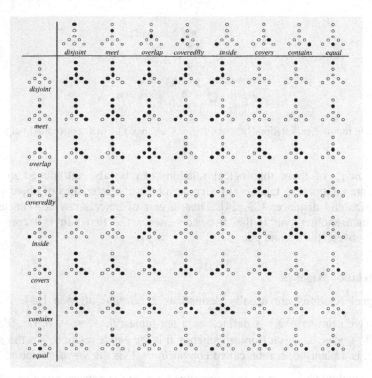

Fig. 3. Composition able of topological relations between regions [12]

3   Composition-Based Pre-processing

The composition-based approach for query pre-processing is solely based on the algebraic properties of composition. It does not require or exploit any metric descriptions of the objects in a configuration. The composition-based approach starts with a consistent graph and finds a smallest subgraph, from which one can derive the complete, original graph. The strategy for finding this subgraph follows the principles of topological consistency in a graph [26]. There is a comprehensive method for analyzing the consistency of spatial configuration based on the logical consistency expressed by the composition of relations. Given a configuration expressed as a graph, topological consistency is formulated as a constraint satisfaction [16,17] problem over a network of binary topological relations [18, 27]:

- Each node must have a self-loop, denoting the identity relation (Equation 3).

$$\forall_i\ r_{ii} = 1'$$

(3)

- For each directed edge from N to M, there must be an edge in the reverse direction, denoting the converse topological relation (Equation 4).

$$\forall_{i,j}\ r_{i,j} = \overline{r_{j,i}}$$

(4)

- Although a variety of paths can lead from one node to another, in order to infer the path consistency of a relation it is sufficient to consider all compositions of path length 2 that connect the relation's two nodes [26]. Having a consistent graph, a topological relation must coincide with its induced relation determined by the intersection of all possible composition path of length 2 (Equation 5).

$$\forall_{i,j} \; r_{i,j} = \bigcap_{k=A}^{N} r_{i,k} ; r_{k,j} \tag{5}$$

Following the principle of path consistency, a relation could be completely derived if and only if it is the unique possible relation that results from the intersection of different path compositions in the query graph.

Having an initial graph that is consistent and complete, we must prove that the minimum subgraph is unique. Otherwise, the algorithm that determines the subgraph would need to choose between different paths. The analysis of the uniqueness of this minimum subgraph is done exhaustively using an algorithm that checks possible composition-based derivations.

Consider each single composition with a crisp result, that is, all compositions whose results have a single relation. To obtain a unique subgraph with three objects, no permutation of the relations of compositions with crisp results should produce another crisp result.

Antecedent: $r_{i,j} = r_{i,k} ; r_{k,j}$, where "=" implies a crisp result.

Hypothesis: $(r_{i,k} \neq r_{i,j} ; r_{j,k}) \wedge (r_{k,j} \neq r_{k,i} ; r_{i,j})$.

Without considering the fifteen trivial compositions with *equal*, there exist twelve crisp results of the topological compositions (Table 1). By checking exhaustively all twelve compositions, we accept the hypothesis. Thus, for single compositions, the derived relation is the only relation that can be derived from the combinations of the three relations involved in the composition (i.e., *R*, *S*, and *T*). An important observation is that *overlap* is the only relation whose participation in a composition operation does not result in a non-trivial crisp result.

Table 1. Crisp results for single composition

Crisp Result	disjoint	inside	contains
Number of Occurrences	6	3	3

For path consistency it is known that a relation can be derived if the intersection of all possible composition paths of length 2 results in this unique relation (Equation 5). The foundation for this assessment is the set of permutations that can be created by exchanging the derived relation with any of the two composition components in all possible composition paths of length 2. To check the uniqueness of the minimum graph then requires the analysis of whether or not the intersections of all permutations result in a crisp relation.

Antecedent: $r_{i,j} = \underset{\forall k,k \neq i \wedge k \neq j}{\cap} r_{i,k}; r_{k,j}$.

Hypothesis: $\left(r_{i,k} \neq \underset{\forall l, l \neq i \wedge l \neq k}{\cap} r_{i,l}; r_{l,k} \right) \wedge \left(r_{k,j} \neq \underset{\forall l, l \neq j \wedge l \neq k}{\cap} r_{k,l}; r_{l,j} \right)$

Using an exhaustive approach we consider, in a first instance, intersections of two paths of length 2. For example, given that $r_{i,j}$ follows from the intersection of $r_{i,k}; r_{k,j} \cap r_{i,l}; r_{l,j}$, the approach is to check whether or not $r_{i,k} = r_{i,j}; r_{j,k} \cap r_{i,l}; (r_{l,k}; r_{j,k})$.

In this process we considered all possible pairs of compositions that do not involve the *equal* relation (i.e., 49 different compositions). There are 1,176 possible combinations, created by the combination of two compositions over the set of 49 possible compositions. Ninety-eight different intersections create crisp results and do not include a single composition with crisp result. Among these 98 crisp intersections, only ten combinations derive a relation other than *overlap* (Table 2). The permutation of the derived relation by any of the components of the combination proves to give no crisp result. Thus, for configurations with four elements there is just one unique minimum graph, since no exchangeable relation could be derived with the same set of objects.

Table 2. Crisp results for intersections of two compositions with path length 2

Intersections of Two Compositions with Path Length 2 Yielding Crisp Results	Crisp Result	Number of Occurrences
	overlap	88
	covers	4
	coveredBy	4
	meet	2

Subsequently, crisp results could be derived from the intersection of three paths of length 2. In such a case, there are 162 intersections of three paths with crisp results. This number does not include double paths of compositions or single compositions with crisp results (Table 3). All these intersections produce the relation *overlap*. An exhaustive analysis shows that for configurations with five objects there exists only one unique minimum graph.

Table 3. Crisp results for the 162 intersections of three compositions with path length 3

Intersections of Three Compositions with Path Length 2 Yielding Crisp Results	Number of Occurrences
(diagrams)	128
(diagrams)	32
(diagrams)	2

Subsequently, the analysis found no further combinations of composition paths whose intersection would produce a crisp result. Indeed, after the intersection of two compositions of length 2, no crisp results other than *overlap* were found. This *overlap* relation does not produce any crisp result when it is composed with other topological relation. So, if we have a configuration with a given set of spatial objects, where one topological relation exists that is completely derivable from the intersection of all possible path of length 2 (Equation 5), we have proved that no permutations of relations that participate in these intersections produce another crisp result. Consequently, no other relation within this configuration can be derivable, and the minimum graph that represents the configuration is unique.

4   Neighborhood-Based Pre-processing

Pre-processing techniques that concentrate on closely related spatial objects follow Tobler's *First Law of Geography*: "Everything is related to everything else, but nearby things are more related than distant things" [29]. Neighborhood-based pre-processing keeps only the relations in a query graph that represent physically connected objects and near-disjoint relations, but eliminates medium- and far-disjoint. An object is physically connected to another objects if their boundaries are neighbors. There exist different algorithms to establish the neighborhood of spatial objects. Some graph structures that consider the spatial distribution of objects are the Minimum Spanning Tree and the Relative Neighborhood Graph [30, 31].

One of the most widely used methods to connect points in the space is the *Delaunay Triangulation* [32]. It partitions the Euclidean space, composed of a set of points, into triangles such that no four points of this set are co-circular. The dual of the Delaunay Triangulation, the *Voronoi Diagram*, represents a partition of space into regions where points of the Delaunay Triangulation are the nuclei of specific areas. These areas are bounded by the perpendicular bisectors of the nucleus and the set of its neighboring points [33].

A Delaunay Triangulation is based on a set of points. Spatial configurations, however, may be composed of points, lines, or regions. To qualify as neighbors, the boundaries of two objects must share one or more Voronoi edges. Because of the dual

characteristics of the Voronoi and Delaunay Triangulation, a shared Voronoi edge is
the same as one or more connecting edges in the Delaunay Triangulation [13]. Figure
4 illustrates two constrained Delaunay Triangulations. They capture the spatial
neighborhood at different levels of detail using either the objects' boundaries (Figure
4a) or the objects' MBRs (Figure 4b).

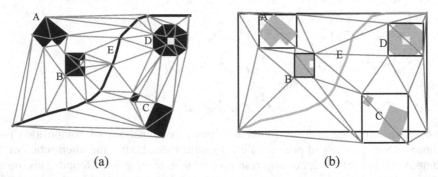

(a)   (b)

Fig. 4. Delaunay triangulation of a spatial configuration represented by (a) its objects' edges
and (b) its objects' MBRs

Since the detail in the boundary representations affects the space partition, the
Delaunay Triangulation may change depending on the geometric representation of
objects. This effect is even clearer as objects are represented by their MBRs using two
or four extreme points. This work addresses query pre-processing using the objects'
MBRs that are defined by four extreme points. Based on these triangulations we
obtained two different subgraphs (Figure 5), where the graph determined based on
objects' boundaries represents a subgraph of the graph determined based on objects'
MBR. Consequently, although from a theoretical point of view there is a unique
minimum subgraph derived from the Delaunay Triangulation, this subgraph may not
be the one that is obtained with the Delaunay Triangulation implemented. The
implementation, however, is deterministic in the sense that it always finds the same
subgraph for a spatial configuration with a given representation.

(a)   (b)

Fig. 5. Subgraphs obtained with Delaunay triangulation of a spatial configuration represented
by (a) its objects' edges and (b) its objects' MBRs

Euler's Equation (Equation 6) [33] can be applied for every convex polyhedron
with m_v nodes (vertices), m_f faces, and m_e edges. Each edge in a Delaunay
Triangulation bounds exactly two vertices. Therefore, if all vertices of a Delaunay
Triangulation were substituted with objects and all edges with binary relations, we

can deduce that for a *very large graph* the average number of neighbors (av_ng) of an object is less than six (Equation 7). Since in this work four points represented the geometry of an object, and in the extreme case all four points connect to different objects, the number of neighbors of an objects in a *very large graph* is less than 24, that is, it grows linearly by $O(n)$, with n being the number of objects. This upper bound of the number of relations in the final subgraph contrasts the theoretical bound of $O(n^2)$ of a query without pre-processing.

$$m_e \leq 3 \cdot m_v - 6 \tag{6}$$

$$av\_ng = \frac{2m_e}{m_v} \leq 6 - \frac{12}{m_v} \tag{7}$$

5   Experimental Comparison

In this experiment, queries are sketches that provide topological relations as well as metric characteristics of objects. The experiment involves the implementation of a searching mechanism that is based on a content measure. We also used an experimental database that could include regular and extreme cases of realizable configurations, to test whether such cases have an impact on the composition-based or the neighborhood-based pre-processing techniques.

5.1   Experimental Setting

Our analysis applied three different strategies for pre-processing: (1) pre-processing using topological composition $S(g)$, (2) pre-processing using Delaunay triangulation $V(g)$, and (3) pre-processing using Delaunay triangulation followed by composition-based pre-processing ($S(V(g))$).

While composition-based $S(g)$ pre-processing acts over relations (i.e., constraints), neighborhood-based pre-processing $V(g)$ acts over spatial objects. Thus, while eliminating a constraint affects subsequent eliminations when using composition-based pre-processing, eliminating a constraint does not affect the subsequent elimination by the neighborhood-based strategy. This work eliminates only constraints, so $V(S(...())$ will not differ from $V(g)$. On the other hand, although it is known that $S(S(...S(g)...)$ is the same as $S(g)$, it is impossible to eliminate a priori $S(V())$.

This study evaluates the quality of the pre-processing techniques by using a searching process. This evaluation analyzes whether or not by eliminating constraints through the different pre-processing strategies, the query process can still give good results. The experiment evaluates queries using a *forward checking algorithm* [34] and a *content-based* similarity evaluation of configurations [4]. The content of topological relations in a configurations is defined by a quantitative content measure (Equation 8), which distinguishes the eight topological relations between regions in a plane and introduces metric refinements to differentiate among sizes and distances between objects [24]. This content measure is independent of rotation and horizontal or vertical flipping of configurations.

$$F_m(A, B) = \frac{area(A) - 2area(A \cap B)}{area(A)} + \frac{distance(\delta A, \delta B)}{diagonal(A)},$$

$$F_m(B, A) = \frac{area(B) - 2area(A \cap B)}{area(B)} + \frac{distance(\delta B, \delta A)}{diagonal(B)} \quad \text{whe}$$

$$distance(\delta A, \delta B) = \begin{cases} d_e(\delta A, \delta B) & \text{if } A \cap B = \varnothing \\ -d_i(\delta A, \delta B) & \text{if } A \cap B \neq \varnothing \end{cases}$$

(8)

We define a similarity value between configurations as the inverse of the distances between content-measure values of pair of objects in the first and second configuration (Equation 9).

$$D(Q, S) = \sum_{v_i, v_j \in Q; u_i, u_j \in S} \sqrt{\left(F_m(v_i, v_j) - F_m(u_i, u_j)\right)^2 + \left(F_m(v_j, v_i) - F_m(u_j, u_i)\right)^2}$$

(9)

The forward checking strategy takes the constraints one-by-one and searches for pairs of objects that satisfy this constraint [22]. Then, it performs a *join operation* to combine the results of the search of objects that satisfy individual constraints. A constraint is considered satisfied if the difference between the content measure of the objects in a query and the content measure of the objects in the solution is less than or equal to a threshold (0.01 in this case).

5.2   Data Domain

To perform the experiment we created a database of 2,025 elements from all possible objects that fit in a 9x9 box, considering objects whose edge lengths vary from 1 to 9. From this database of 2,025 objects we created a domain of topological relations with a total of 758,614 *disjoint*, 192,464 *meet*, 851,328 *overlap*, 25,200 *coveredBy*, 2,024 *inside*, 173,620 *covers*, and 44,100 *contains* relations. In order to speed up the searching process, binary relations, which are defined as tuples of the content measure $(F(o_i, o_j), F(o_j, o_i))$, were indexed using an R-Tree-like structure [4]. Unlike the traditional use of the R-Tree structure, which organizes objects by their physical locations, the R-tree structure is used here for organizing content values of topological relations [4]. In this experiment, 98 queries with five objects were randomly created, 52 configurations when the pre-processing based on composition reduces the number of constraints, and 46 configurations when pre-processing based on composition does not change the initial configurations.

Table 4 presents six of the total of queries (*g*) analyzed by using $S(g)$, $V(g)$, and $S(V(g))$ pre-processing. Queries represent different combinations of results after applying the pre-processing strategies. The first two queries do not have any change after $S(g)$ pre-processing, while they have one or six less relations after $V(g)$ pre-processing. In particular, the second query is an extreme case by using neighborhood-based preprocessing with six eliminations. The opposite situation occurs for the third query, where $V(g)$ composition has no changes and $S(g)$ pre-processing eliminates five relations. The last tree queries have fewer relations after both $S(g)$ and $V(g)$ pre-processing; however, they differ in how $S(g)$, $V(g)$, and $S(V(g))$ are related.

Table 4. Topological queries and their pre-processing results with relations *disjoint* (d), *meet* (m), *overlap* (o), *inside* (i), *contains* (c), *covers* (cv), *coveredBy* (cb), and *equal* (e)

G	Query	S(g)	V(g)	S(V(g))

a — S(g):

-	d	d	d	o
-	-	d	m	m
-	-	-	d	o
-	-	-	-	cb
-	-	-	-	-

$S(a) \supset S(V(a))$

a — V(g):

-	d	d	d	o
-	-	-	m	m
-	-	-	d	o
-	-	-	-	cb
-	-	-	-	-

$V(a) \subset S(a)$

a — S(V(g)):

-	d	d	d	o
-	-	-	m	m
-	-	-	d	o
-	-	-	-	cb
-	-	-	-	-

$S(V(a)) = V(a)$

b — S(g):

-	d	d	d	d
-	-	d	d	d
-	-	-	d	o
-	-	-	-	d
-	-	-	-	-

$S(b) \supset S(V(b))$

b — V(g):

-	d	-	-	-
-	-	d	-	-
-	-	-	d	-
-	-	-	-	d
-	-	-	-	-

$V(b) \subset S(b)$

b — S(V(g)):

-	d	-	-	-
-	-	d	-	-
-	-	-	d	-
-	-	-	-	d
-	-	-	-	-

$S(V(b)) = V(b)$

c — S(g):

-	-	d	o	-
-	-	i	-	cv
-	-	-	cb	-
-	-	-	-	-
-	-	-	-	-

$S(c) = S(V(c))$

c — V(g):

-	d	d	o	d
-	-	i	i	cv
-	-	-	cb	c
-	-	-	-	c
-	-	-	-	-

$V(c) \supset S(c)$

c — S(V(g)):

-	-	d	o	-
-	-	i	-	cv
-	-	-	cb	-
-	-	-	-	-
-	-	-	-	-

$S(V(b)) \subset V(c))$

d — S(g):

-	-	d	m	-
-	-	cb	-	-
-	-	-	d	-
-	-	-	-	c
-	-	-	-	-

$S(d) \supset S(V(d))$

d — V(g):

-	-	d	m	d
-	-	cb	-	-
-	-	-	-	-
-	-	-	-	c
-	-	-	-	-

$V(d) \neq S(d)$

d — S(V(g)):

-	-	d	m	-
-	-	cb	-	-
-	-	-	-	-
-	-	-	-	c
-	-	-	-	-

$S(V(d)) \subset V(d)$

e — S(g):

-	-	d	m	-
-	-	i	-	c
-	-	-	-	-
-	-	-	-	cv
-	-	-	-	-

$S(e) \neq S(V(e))$

e — V(g):

-	d	m	-	-
-	-	i	o	c
-	-	-	o	-
-	-	-	-	cv
-	-	-	-	-

$V(e) \neq S(e)$

e — S(V(g)):

-	-	d	-	-
-	-	i	-	c
-	-	-	o	-
-	-	-	-	cv
-	-	-	-	-

$S(V(e)) \subset V(e)$

f — S(g):

-	-	d	o	cb
-	-	d	i	d
-	-	-	i	m
-	-	-	-	-
-	-	-	-	-

$S(f) \neq S(V(f))$

f — V(g):

-	d	d	o	cb
-	-	d	i	-
-	-	-	i	-
-	-	-	-	o
-	-	-	-	-

$V(f) \neq S(f)$

f — S(V(g)):

-	d	d	o	cb
-	-	d	i	-
-	-	-	i	-
-	-	-	-	o
-	-	-	-	-

$S(V(f)) = V(f)$

5.3   Results

With respect to the sets of constraints obtained after the query pre-processing, the experiment shows that $S(V(a))$ can reduce the number of edges more than $S(a)$ and $V(a)$ do (Query *d*). For all three strategies, the maximum number of eliminated edges in a query with five objects was six. For all pre-processing strategies, *converse* and *identity* operators over topological relations were applied, such that the experiment considers topological relations only in one direction (upper half of the matrix that represents the graph). Six association rules were derived from the analysis of the results (Equations 10-15).

$$(S(g) = g) \rightarrow (V(g) = S(V(g))) \tag{10}$$

$$(V(g) = g) \rightarrow (S(g) = S(V(g))) \tag{11}$$

$$(S(g) \subset V(g)) \rightarrow ((S(g) = S(V(g))) \wedge (S(V(g)) \subset V(a))) \tag{12}$$

$$(S(g) = V(g)) \rightarrow ((V(g) = S(V(g))) \wedge (S(g) = S(V(g)))) \tag{13}$$

$$(V(g) \subset S(g)) \rightarrow ((V(g) = S(V(g))) \wedge (S(V(g)) \subset S(g))) \tag{14}$$

$$(V(g) \neq S(g)) \rightarrow \neg(S(g) = S(V(g))) \tag{15}$$

With respect to the results of the search process, for all six queries the algorithm with or without query pre-processing finds the right solutions, that is, configurations that are equal to the queries (i.e., optimal solutions). Since the content measure considers the relative size and position of objects, while it disregards differences due to rotation and flipping, the algorithm finds more than one optimal solution. These additional optimal solutions are equivalent to the query if configurations are rotated or flipped over the horizontal or vertical axis.

Results of the search process vary among queries (Table 5). The number of solutions in each query increases as pre-processing eliminates constraints. This increment depends not only on the number of constraints eliminated, but on the type of these constraints. *Disjoint* and *overlap* relations are far more frequent and, therefore, constraints based on these relations will have more candidate solutions. In terms of the satisfaction of topological constraints, while composition-based pre-processing guarantees that topological constraints are satisfied, neighborhood-based cannot guarantee this satisfaction. In the worst case, neighborhood-based pre-processing obtains solutions where 4 of the constraints were not satisfied and, in the worst average, 2 constraints where not satisfied. It is important to note that although neighborhood-based pre-processing may loose information of the query, the algorithm will always find the optimal solutions, if they exist, and the ranking of the solutions will place optimal solutions first.

In terms of performance, there is no clear relationship between time and number of constraints. Since queries are of small number of objects, time pre-processing does not affect the overall time. Although in most cases, neighborhood-based pre-processing tends to reduce the CPU time of query evaluation, composition-based pre-processing is not always efficient in doing so. In all cases CPU time is strongly influenced by the number of constraints in the query and the frequency of relations in the database. As the number of candidate relations in the database that correspond to a query constraint increases, the computational cost grows, since more candidate objects have to be combined. In addition, less constrained queries may also increase the CPU Time. This is the case, for example, of Query *a*, where the CPU time for the original query was less than the reduced query ($V(a)$), since an elimination of a constraint (i.e., *disjoint*) may increases the domain of search.

Table 5. Search results in terms of number and similarity values (distance 0 stands for an optimal solution)

	Query	G	S(g)	V(g)	S(V(g))
a	Solutions	45	45	45	45
	Solutions with constraint	0	0	0	0
	Maximum constraint	0	0	0	0
	Average Distance	0	0	0	0
	CPU time [seconds]	399.24	399.24	406.57	406.57
b	Solutions	876	876	45,648	45,648
	Solutions with constraint	0	0	0	0
	Maximum constraint	0	0	0	0
	Average Distance	0	0	1.45	1.45
	CPU time [seconds]	25.35	25.35	4.66	4.66
c	Solutions	24	720	24	720
	Solutions with constraint	0	0	0	0
	Maximum constraint	0	0	0	0
	Average Distance	0	0.08	0	0.08
	CPU time [seconds]	0.16	0.08	0.16	0.08
d	Solutions	5	1,024	982	65,996
	Solutions with constraint	0	0	790	501.88
	Maximum constraint	0	0	4	4
	Average Distance	0	0.32	0.96	1.13
	CPU time [seconds]	594.22	591.71	596.61	587.49
e	Solutions	94	244	450	594
	Solutions with constraint	0	0	300	416
	Maximum constraint	0	0	1	1
	Average Distance	0	0.06	0.24	0.27
	CPU time [seconds]	0.44	0.76	0.11	0.01
f	Solutions	48	96	96	96
	Solutions with constraint	0	0	48	48
	Maximum constraint	0	0	1	1
	Average Distance	0	0.001	0.07	0.07
	CPU time [seconds]	19.72	79.03	8.78	8.78

In terms of performance, there is no clear relationship between time and number of constraints. Since queries are of small number of objects, time pre-processing does not affect the overall time. Although in most cases, neighborhood-based pre-processing tends to reduce the CPU time of query evaluation, composition-based pre-processing is not always efficient in doing so. In all cases CPU time is strongly influenced by the number of constraints in the query and the frequency of relations in the database. As the number of candidate relations in the database that correspond to a query constraint increases, the computational cost grows, since more candidate objects have to be combined. In addition, less constrained queries may also increase the CPU Time. This is the case, for example, of Query *a*, where the CPU time for the original query was less than the reduced query ($V(a)$), since an elimination of a constraint (i.e., *disjoint*) may increases the domain of search.

The metric refinements make further distinctions among topological relations that allow us to reduce the time needed to find a candidate solution. For example, since *disjoint* relations are more frequent in the database, one could think that queries based on this relation will need more processing time. The metric refinements of topological constraints, however, differentiate among types of *disjoint* relations, reducing candidate solutions of query constraints and, therefore, reducing the processing time (e.g., Query *b*).

Table 6. Best and worst results of six test queries

Query	Result with Best Match	Worst Result
a		
b		
c		
d		
e		
f		

A possible explanation for the better performance with the neighborhood-based pre-processing—when both strategies eliminate constraints—is that objects may have many *disjoint* relations; however, *closely disjoint* objects are less frequent than *far apart* objects. Neighborhood-based pre-processing will always keep *closely disjoint* objects, while it eliminates *far apart* objects. Composition-based pre-processing, on the hand, will not distinguish between *far* or *closely disjoint* objects. So, while for many queries neighborhood-based preprocessing keeps *disjoint* relations, these *disjoint* relations are less common and, therefore, they tend to keep the evaluation cost low.

Table 6 shows the results of the searching process. We selected a random solution among the optimal solutions and a random solution among the solutions with worst confidence (i.e., larger number of constraints violated when they occur, or larger distance with respect to the query when no violation occur). A visual analysis of the results shows good matches, confirming that the forward-checking algorithm, which enforces that all constraints evaluated must be satisfied, is an appropriate choice for this experiment. The performance of this algorithm, however, decreases drastically depending on the number of occurrences of topological relations in the database.

6   Conclusions

This paper derived and compared composition-based and neighborhood-based pre-processing strategies for reducing the number of topological constraints that need to be satisfied in spatial query processing. The setting is tailored for similarity-based retrieval where a target configuration is either given by an existing spatial scene or derived from a sketch. Results of this study are that neighborhood-based ($V(g)$) pre-processing provides a good mechanism for reducing topological constraints that tends to reduce the computational cost of query evaluation. Although neighborhood-based pre-processing does not guarantee that topological constraints will be satisfied, solutions ranked by a similarity measure place optimal solutions first. Thus, similarity queries that are formulated in a visual language should exploit the metric characteristics of the configuration (i.e., distances between objects), even if only topological constraints are considered for making matches. In the case that topological queries are expressed with a command language [35], the composition-based pre-processing can only be used, as it always ensures that constraints that were not evaluated are satisfied.

In this work, pre-processing strategies were analyzed considering time and results of a similarity-based query process. The findings have implications on future work as they are useful not only for pre-processing queries, but for processing a whole database in order to create an indexing schema that organizes spatial interrelations between objects. Because only physically close interrelations are needed, one could drastically reduce the number of interrelations that need to be stored by a database. An aspect to be considered for future work is the potential of systematically selecting pre-processing strategies depending on the database and/or the query's characteristics. For example, constraints that were eliminated by both pre-processing strategies may indicate that there is a good chance of having a good balance between quality of results and performance of query evaluation by using neighborhood-based preprocessing.

References

[1]   Egenhofer, M.: Query Processing in Spatial-Query-By-Sketch. *Journal of Visual Languages and Computing.* 8:(4) (1997) 403-424.

[2]   Papadias, D., Mantzouroguannis, M., Kalnis, P., Mamoulis, N., and Ahmad, I.: Content-Based Retrieval using Heuristic Search. *ACM-SIGIR Conference on Research and Development in Information Retrieval,* Berkeley, CA, (1999), 168-175.

[3]   Papadias, D., Mamoulis, N., and Delis, V.: Algorithms for Querying Spatial Structure. in Gupta, A., Shmueli, O., and Widom, J. (eds.), *24th VLDB Conference,* New York, NY, (1998), 546-557.

[4]   Rodríguez, A. and Godoy, F.: A Content-Based Approach to Searching Spatial Configurations. in Egenhofer, M. and Mark, D. (eds.), *GIScience 2002, Lecture Notes en Computer Science 2478,* Springer-Verlag, Berlin (2002), 260-275.

[5]   Rigaux, P., Scholl, M., and Voisard, A.: *Spatial Databases: with Application in GIS.* Academic Press, San Diego, CA (2002).

[6]   Egenhofer, M. and Frank, A.: LOBSTER: Combining AI and Database Techniques. *Photogrammetric Engineering & Remote Sensing.* 56:(6) (1990) 919-926.

[7]   Park, H.-H., Lee, C.-G., Lee, Y.-J., and Chung, C.-W.: Early Separation Filter and Refinement Steps in Spatial Query Optimization, *International Conference in Database Systems for Advanced Applications,* (1999), 161-169.

[8]   Clementini, E., Sharma, J., and Egenhofer, M.: Modeling Topological Relations: Strategies for Query Processing. *Computers and Graphics.* 18:(6) (1994).

[9]   Aref, A. and Samet, H.: Optimizing Strategies for Spatial Query Processing. *7th International Conference on Very Large Databases,* Barcelona, Spain, (1991), 81-90.

[10]   Samet, H. and Aref, W.: Spatial Data Models and Query Processing. *Modern Database Systems,* ACM Press (1995), 338-360.

[11]   Kriegel, H., Brinkhoff, T., and Schneider, R.: Efficient Spatial Query Processing. *IEEE Data Engineering Bulletin.* 16:(3) (1993) 10-15.

[12]   Egenhofer, M.: Deriving the Composition of Binary Topological Relations. *Journal of Visual Languages and Computing.* 5:(2) (1994) 133-149.

[13]   Blaser, A., *Sketching Spatial Queries,* Ph.D. Thesis. In Department of Spatial Information Science and Engineering, 2000, University of Maine: Orono, ME.

[14]   Florence, J. and Egenhofer, M.: Distribution of Topological Relations in Geographic Datasets,. *ACSM/ASPRS Conference,* Baltimore, MD (1996).

[15]   Papadias, D., Arkoumanis, D., and Karacapilidis, N.: On the Retrieval of Similar Configurations. in Poiker, T. and Chrisman, N. (eds.), *8th International Symposium on Spatial Data Handling,* International Geographical Union, Vancouver, Canada (1998), 510-521.

[16]   Papadias, D., Kalnis, P., and Mamoulis, N.: Hierarchical Constraint Satisfaction in Spatial Databases. *Proceeding of the Annual Meeting of the AAAI,* Orlando, FL, (1999), 142-147.

[17]   Meseguer, P.: Constraint Satisfaction Problems: an Overview. *AICOM.* 2:(1) (1989) 3-17.

[18] Egenhofer, M. and Sharma, J.: Assessing the Consistency of Complete and Incomplete Topological Information. *Geographical Systems*. 1:(1993) 47-68.

[19] Egenhofer, M. and Franzosa, R.: Point-Set Topological Spatial Relations. *International Journal of Geographical Information Systems*. 5:(2) (1991) 161-174.

[20] Randell, D., Cui, Z., and Cohn, A.: A Spatial Logic Based on Regions and Connection. in Nebel, B., Rich, C., and Swarthout, W. (eds.), *Principles of Knowledge Representation and Reasoning, KR '92*, St. Charles, IL: Morgan Kaufmann, Cambridge, MA (1992), 165-176.

[21] Egenhofer, M. and Al-Taha, K.: Reasoning About Gradual Changes of Topological Relations. in Frank, A., Campari, I., and Formentini, U. (eds.), *Theories and Methods of Spatio-Temporal Reasoning in Geographic Space. Lecture Notes in Computer Science 639*, Springer-Verlag, Pisa, Italy (1992), 196-219.

[22] Gaede, V. and Günther, O.: Multidimensional Access Method. *ACM Computing Surveys*. 30:(2) (1998) 170-231.

[23] Egenhofer, M. and Shariff, A.: Metric Details for Natural-Language Spatial Relations. *ACM Transactions on Information Systems*. 16:(4) (1998) 295-321.

[24] Godoy, F. and Rodríguez, A.: A Quantitative Description of Spatial Configurations. in Richardson, D. and van Oosterom, P. (eds.), *Spatial Data Handling*, Springer-Verlag, Ottawa, Canada (2002), 299-311.

[25] Tarski, A.: On The Calculus of Relations. *Journal of Symbolic Logic*. 6:(3) (1941) 73-89.

[26] Mackworth, A.: Consistency in Networks of Relations. *Artificial Intelligence*. 8:(1977) 99-118.

[27] Maddux, R.: *Some Algebras and Algorithms for Reasoning about Time and Space*. Department of Mathematics, Iowa State University: Ames, IO, (1990)

[28] Smith, T. and Park, K.: Algebraic Approach to Spatial Reasoning. *International Journal of Geographical Information Systems*. 6:(3) (1992) 177-192.

[29] Tobler, W.: Cellular Geography. in Gale, S. and Olsson, G. (eds.), *Philosophy in Geography*, D. Reidel Publishing Company, Dordrecht, Holland (1979)

[30] Toussaint, G.: The Relative Neighborhood Graph of a Finite Planar Set. *Pattern Recognition*. 12:(1980) 261-268.

[31] Jaramcyzk, J. and Toussaint, G.: Relative Graph and their Relatives. *Proceedings of the IEEE*. 80:(9) (1992) 1502-1517.

[32] O'Rourke, J.: *Computational Geometry*. Cambridge University Press, Cambridge, MA (1993).

[33] Preparata, F. and Shamos, M.: *Computational Geometry: An Introduction*. Springer-Verlag, Berlin (1985).

[34] Bacchus, F. and Grove, A.: On the Forward Checking Algorithm. in Montanari, U. and Rossi, F. (eds.), *Principles and Practice of Constraint Programming, Lecture Notes in Computer Science 976*, Springer-Verlag, Berlin (1995), 292-309.

[35] Egenhofer, M.: Spatial SQL: A Query and Presentation Language. *IEEE Transactions on Knowledge and Data Engineering*. 6:(1) (1994) 86-95.

Logical Data Expiration
for Fixpoint Extensions of Temporal Logics

David Toman

School of Computer Science, University of Waterloo
Waterloo, Ontario, Canada N2L 3G1
david@uwaterloo.ca

Abstract. We study the differences between the future and the past fragments of fixpoint extensions of first-order temporal logics in their relationship to expiration of database histories. We show that while the past fragment admits a bounded expiration operator, the future one requires retaining data of size bounded from below by a function linear in the length of the history. We also discuss fragments of future fixpoint temporal logic for which bounded expiration operators can exist.

1 Introduction

Evolution of data is common to most database and information systems. While it is often sufficient to retain only the most current version of a database, many applications of information systems require maintaining information about the past states of the database as well, often in the form of a history of the evolution of the data set. This functionality might be required, among other uses, for archival, analytical, and/or legal reasons.

However, archiving past data indefinitely is costly and in many situations, it is not feasible to retain all past data. In addition, even if collecting an ever growing history of the past states of the database were possible, querying such large data sets might become prohibitively expensive. To address these problems, various techniques have been proposed to identify parts of a history that are no longer needed and subsequently removing such parts. These techniques range from ad-hoc administrative approaches [10, 16] to logical, query-driven expiration algorithms [2, 20]. These algorithms are based, in general, on analyzing queries posed over a history to determine which parts of the current history can be removed without affecting answers of these queries with respect to the current history and all possible extension of the current history. A recent survey chapter [21] discusses many of these approaches and the state of art in the field in detail.

In this paper, we study query-driven approaches to data expiration in the context of *fixpoint extensions of first-order temporal logic*. The main results of the paper are as follows.

1. We present a technique that, for (a fixed set of) queries formulated in the past fragment of fixpoint first-order temporal logic, allows substantial amounts

T. Hadzilacos et al. (Eds.): SSTD 2003, LNCS 2750, pp. 380–393, 2003.

of historical data to expire, while preserving answers to the given queries. In particular, we show that the amount of data that has to be retained is independent of the length of the history and depends only on the size of the active data domain and the query.

2. We show that such a technique cannot be developed for the future fragment. Moreover, we show that there are queries in this fragment for which the size of the retained data is bounded from below by a function linear in the length of the history.

The results demonstrate a large gap between the behavior of the past and future fragments of fixpoint first-order temporal logics with respect to data expiration. The gap can be traced to the interaction between (data) quantifiers and fixpoint operators. In particular, and despite of the popularity of the future fragment of *propositional* temporal logic in many other areas of computer science [22, 23, 24], the future fragment, as a query language over database histories, exhibits a severe deficiency that relates to the ability to expire past data, when compared to the past fragment.

The paper is organized as follows: Section 2 provides the necessary background definitions. Section 3 discusses related approaches. Section 4 defines a bounded expiration operator for past fixpoint temporal logic queries. Section 5 shows that expiration operators for future fixpoint temporal logic queries require linear space (in the length of the database history) to store the residual data. Section 6 concludes with directions for future work.

2   Definitions

In this section we formally introduce database histories, fixpoint extensions of temporal logic as a query language over such histories, and a basic framework in which data expiration can be studied.

2.1   Temporal Databases and Fixpoint Temporal Logics

Temporal databases provide a uniform and systematic way of dealing with historical data [5]. For the purposes of this paper we only consider *transaction-time* temporal databases—temporal databases that collect information about modifications of a standard relational database in a form of a *history*.

Intuitively, a relational database history records the facts that the instance of the database at time i was D_i in a (time-instant indexed) sequence of successive database instances (states of the history). A linear order of the sequence is implied by the natural ordering of the time instants with respect to the flow of time. The discrete and linearly ordered nature of the set of time instants—the temporal domain—also yields the notion of previous and next states in the database history in terms of consecutive time instants. Therefore we assume, without loss of generality, that time is modeled by natural numbers with the usual linear order. In particular natural numbers will be used to index the individual states in histories. From a temporal database point of view, the histories can be viewed as append-only, transaction-time temporal databases [5, 17].

Definition 1 (History) *Let ρ be a relational signature. A history H is a finite integer-indexed sequence of databases*

$$H = \langle D_0, D_1, \ldots, D_n \rangle$$

where D_i is a standard relational database over ρ. We call D_i a state of H at the time instant i.

The data domain $\mathbf{D}_H$ of H is the union of all (data) values that appear in any relation in D_i at any time instant i; the temporal domain $\mathbf{T}_H$ is the set of all time instants that appear as indices in the history H.

Histories allow us to formulate queries that span multiple database states. To facilitate querying, many *temporal query languages* have been developed [5, 17, 18, 19]. Among the more popular choices, temporal logic based query languages play a significant role, mainly due to their ease of use, well-defined semantics, amenability to implementation, and well-studied theoretical properties.

In this paper we focus on μTL, a fixpoint extension of first-order temporal logic (FOTL). The extension is realized by extending the syntax with a *fixpoint operator* of the form $\mu X.Q$ where X is a *relational variable* standing for a (new) predicate symbol over the free variables of Q. The intuitive meaning of such an operator is the (least) solution to the $X \equiv Q$ sentence. The following definition gives the syntax of μTL used in this paper.

Definition 2 (Syntax of μTL) *A μTL formula (or query) is an expression in the grammar*

$$Q ::= r(x_1, \ldots, x_k) \mid x_i = x_j \mid Q \wedge Q \mid \neg Q \mid \exists x.Q \mid \bullet Q \mid \bigcirc Q \mid \mu X.Q.$$

where $x_1, \ldots, x_k$ are (data) variable names and r and X predicate symbols. The $\bullet$ and $\bigcirc$ temporal connectives stand for the "previous time" and "next time" modalities, respectively. We also assume that each occurrence of the $\mu X.Q$ subformula in a μTL formula uses a distinct symbol X.

We say that a μTL formula is guarded *if for every subformula of the form $\mu X.Q$ all occurrences of X in Q are in the scope of one or more occurrences of either the $\bullet$ or the $\bigcirc$ connectives (but not both).*

We say that a μTL formula is well-formed *if for every subformula of the form $\mu X.Q$ all occurrences of X in Q are guarded or positive. We also require data variables in well-formed formulas to be range-restricted [1, 6].*

We define the past fragment of μTL to be the well formed μTL formulas that use only the $\bullet$ connective (we denote this fragment by PastμTL), and the future fragment, that uses only the $\bigcirc$ connective (denoted by FutureμTL).

In the rest of this paper we consider only well-formed μTL formulas in one of the above fragments. The well-formedness requirement guarantees unique answers to μTL queries over *finite histories*[1].

Definition 3 (Semantics of well-formed μTL formulas) *Let H be a finite history $\langle D_0, D_1, \ldots, D_n \rangle$, θ a substitution of values from $\mathbf{D}_H$ for variables, and $t \in \mathbf{T}_H$ a time instant. The semantics of μTL is defined as follows*

$$
\begin{aligned}
&H, \theta, t \models r(x_1, \ldots, x_k) \text{ if } (x_1\theta, \ldots, x_k\theta) \in R^t \\
&H, \theta, t \models x_i = x_j && \text{if } \theta(x_i) = \theta(x_j) \\
&H, \theta, t \models Q_1 \wedge Q_2 && \text{if } H, \theta, t \models Q_1 \text{ and } H, \theta, t \models Q_2 \\
&H, \theta, t \models \neg Q && \text{if not } H, \theta, t \models Q \\
&H, \theta, t \models \exists x_i.Q && \text{if there is } a \in \mathbf{D}_H \text{ such that } H, \theta[a/x_i], t \models Q \\
&H, \theta, t \models \bullet Q && \text{if } t - 1 \in \mathbf{T}_H \text{ and } H, \theta, t - 1 \models Q \\
&H, \theta, t \models \bigcirc Q && \text{if } t + 1 \in \mathbf{T}_H \text{ and } H, \theta, t + 1 \models Q \\
&H, \theta, t \models \mu X.Q && \text{if } H, \theta, t \models Q^\omega[\emptyset/X]
\end{aligned}
$$

where R^t is the instance of r in D_t and Q^ω is the countably infinite unfolding of the fixpoint operator[2].

An answer to a FutureμTL query Q with free variables $x_1, \ldots, x_k$ with respect to a history H is the relation

$$
Q(H) = \{(a_1, \ldots, a_k) \in \mathbf{D}_H^k : H, [a_1/x_1, \ldots, a_k/x_k], 0 \models Q\},
$$

where 0 is the time instant associated with the first state in H. Similarly, an answer to a PastμTL query Q with free variables $x_1, \ldots, x_k$ with respect to the history H is the relation

$$
Q(H) = \{(a_1, \ldots, a_k) \in \mathbf{D}_H^k : H, [a_1/x_1, \ldots, a_k/x_k], n \models Q\},
$$

where n is the time instant associated with the last state in H.

Note that the temporal variables used in the semantic definitions are *restricted to the temporal domain of the history* $\mathbf{T}_H$. Thus, for finite histories, $\bullet Q$ is false in 0-th state of H independently of Q. Similarly, $\bigcirc Q$ is false in the last state of the history[3].

Standard first-order temporal operators can be defined in the appropriate μTL fragment.

---

[1] For infinite histories or when mixed guards are allowed we have to require guarded occurrences of X to be positive as well in order to guarantee uniqueness of least fixpoints and in turn of query answers.

[2] Since the history is finite, there will always be a unique fixpoint that can be reached after finitely many steps of unfolding of Q.

[3] We briefly discuss alternatives to this definition, including the consideration of possibly infinite histories, in Section 3.

Example 4 The classical **since** and **until** connectives can be defined (assuming discrete time domain) by the following guarded (and positive) fixpoint formulas:

$$\varphi \text{ since } \psi = \mu X.\varphi \wedge \bullet(\psi \vee X),$$
$$\varphi \text{ until } \psi = \mu X.\varphi \wedge \bigcirc(\psi \vee X);$$

this definition exactly mirrors the standard *unfolding rule* for these connectives (we are assuming for simplicity that φ and ψ have the same sets of free data variables; otherwise we could simply use standard equivalences to remedy this situation). Additional connectives, e.g., the $\square$ ("always in the future"), $\lozenge$ ("eventually in the future"), $\blacksquare$ ("always in the past"), and $\blacklozenge$ ("sometime in the past") connectives can be defined in terms of **since** and **until** [7].

2.2   Expiration Operators

Since database histories grow over time, a clear approach to controlling the space needed to store the history is an important issue. These approaches range from administrative tools for discarding obsolete parts of the history to formal, query-driven approaches—those that only discard data that can be shown not to be needed subsequently for answering (a fixed set of) queries over the history. The following definitions follow the development in [21], a recent survey of data expiration for historical databases.

Definition 5 (Expiration Operator)
Let $\mathcal{L}$ be a temporal query language over database histories and $Q \in \mathcal{L}$ a query in the language. We define an expiration operator *for Q as a triple*

$$\mathcal{E}(Q) = (0^{\mathcal{E}}, \Delta^{\mathcal{E}}, Q^{\mathcal{E}}).$$

The first two components, $0^{\mathcal{E}}$ and $\Delta^{\mathcal{E}}$, provide an inductive definition of the actual expiration operator as follows:

$$\mathcal{E}(\langle\,\rangle) = 0^{\mathcal{E}} \qquad \text{(initial state),}$$
$$\mathcal{E}(H; D) = \Delta^{\mathcal{E}}(\mathcal{E}(H), D) \qquad \text{(extension maintenance),}$$

where $\langle\,\rangle$ is the empty history and $H; D$ is the extension of a history H by an additional state D. The result of the (inductive) application of these functions define the result of the expiration process with respect to extensions of a history. We call the result $\mathcal{E}(H)$ the residual history.

The third component, $Q^{\mathcal{E}}$, is a query over the residual history that mimics the original query Q. The three components must maintain the following soundness condition:

$$Q(H) = Q^{\mathcal{E}}(\mathcal{E}(H)) \qquad \text{(answer preservation).}$$

In general, there is no restriction on the structure of $\mathcal{E}(H)$, in particular we do not insist that this value has to conform to a particular data model, e.g., the data models of H or D.

This definition allows us to study the properties of various expiration operators, in particular the space needed to represent the residual history $\mathcal{E}(H)$. The space can be measured in terms of the length of the history ($|\mathbf{T}_H|$), the size of the active data domain ($|\mathbf{D}_H|$), and the size of the query, $|Q|$. Of particular interest is the dependence of $|\mathcal{E}(H)|$ on $|\mathbf{T}_H|$, since the length of the history grows over time. We are especially interested in expiration operators that guarantee a *bounded history encoding* [2], an encoding for residual histories whose size does not depend on the length of the history but only on the sizes of the active data domain and the query. This measure is probably the most interesting one, since we assume that the query (and thus also its size) is fixed and we have no control over the size of the active data domain $\mathbf{D}_H$: a user transaction can append arbitrarily large *next* state to the current history.

3 Related Work

There are two main approaches to data expiration. The first approach is based on administrative rules and policies for identifying data to be expired and has been considered by Skyt, Jensen, *et al.* [10, 16].

The focus of this paper, however, is on logical query-driven data expiration and on the limits of such approaches for powerful temporal query languages. The first result in the paper extends Chomicki's approach [2, 4] to enforcing temporal integrity constraints formulated in past first-order temporal logic (PastTL) to queries formulated in *fixpoint extensions* of first-order temporal logic (μTL and, in particular its past fragment PastμTL), a language strictly more expressive than first-order temporal logic. Indeed, PastμTL allows formulation of queries (and properties) that cannot be formulated in PastTL [24], e.g., the "p is true in every even state" property.

The second, negative result on the future fragment of μTL complements the work of Lipeck, Saake, *et al.* [9, 11, 12, 13, 14, 15] on enforcement of temporal integrity constraints formulated using *biquantified* future temporal formulas[4]. The lower bound result in this paper shows that neither this approach, nor any other approach, can be extended to full FutureμTL while maintaining bounded size of the residual histories. In particular, it proves that there cannot be a finite automaton that can accept histories that satisfy a particular FutureμTL sentence[5].

Infinite Histories and Potential Satisfaction. The paper only considers *finite* histories. However, there is an alternative to this approach: finite histories can be considered to be *finite prefixes* of infinite (or complete) histories. Queries

---

[4] A biquantified future TL formula allows quantification over the data domain either only outside the scope of temporal connectives or fully within all temporal connectives.

[5] Such an automaton always exists when μTL is restricted to the propositional setting [22, 23].

are then evaluated with respect to the infinite histories (using essentially the same semantic definitions; the only difference is that an infinite temporal domain is allowed for histories).

However, since only finite portion (a prefix) of the history is available at a particular (finite) point in time, we need to define answers to queries with respect to *possible completions* of the prefix to a complete history. Such approaches, in the first-order setting, run into serious decidability problems; Chomicki and Niwinski have shown that potential satisfaction is not decidable for closed PastTL formulas nor for biquantified formulas FutureTL formulas [3]. Thus considering query evaluation in this setting is not feasible for any sufficiently rich temporal query language (for more in-depth discussion see [21]).

4   An Expiration Operator for Past Fixpoint TL

In this section we develop an expiration operator for the PastμTL fragment and show that this operator guarantees a bounded history encoding for the residual history. The approach is based on an extension of the ideas of Chomicki [2, 4] for the past fragment of first-order temporal logic with the traditional **since** and $\bullet$ connectives.

The proposed operator maintains a sufficient amount of *temporal* information needed to evaluate a given PastμTL query as an instance of an *extended database schema*.

Definition 6 (Extended Database Schema)
Let φ be a PastμTL query over a database schema ρ. We define

$$\rho \cup \{r_\psi(x_1, \ldots, x_k) : \bullet\psi \text{ is a subformula of } \varphi$$
$$\text{with free variables } x_1, \ldots, x_k\}$$

to be the extended database schema *for φ. The predicate symbols r_ψ must not appear in ρ. We call predicates that belong to ρ user-defined and the new predicates r_ψ auxiliary.*

The expiration operator is defined as a set of *materialized view* maintenance rules. The definition of the rules is based on the *unfolding property* of the fixpoint operator, $\mu X.Q \equiv Q(\mu X.Q)$. Before we define the operator itself, we need an auxiliary technical definition.

Definition 7 *Let φ be a PastμTL formula of the form $\mu X.\psi$ such that ϑ is a subformula of ψ containing the fixpoint variable X free. We define the X-closure of ϑ in φ to be the formula $\vartheta[X/\mu X.\psi]$, i.e., in which all occurrences of X have been replaced by their fixpoint definition.*

For ψ a subformula of φ with free fixpoint variables $X_1, \ldots, X_k$ we define the closure (with respect to the fixpoint variables and φ) to be the PastμTL formula $\psi[X_1/\mu X_1.\psi_1, \ldots, X_k/\mu X_k.\psi_k]$.

This definition guarantees, that for every subformula ψ of a given PastμTL query φ, we can find a PastμTL formula ψ' in which all fixpoint variables X_i are in the scope of the appropriate fixpoint operator. Due to the unfolding rule, such a formula always exists and is equivalent to the original formula in the context of φ.

Definition 8 (Expiration Operator)

Let $\rho = (r_1, \ldots, r_k)$ be a database schema and Q a PastμTL query. We define an expiration operator $\mathcal{E}$ for Q as follows:

- We define $\emptyset^{\mathcal{E}}$ to be a constant instance of the extended schema defined as

$$\emptyset^{\mathcal{E}} = (\emptyset, \ldots, \emptyset, \emptyset, \ldots, \emptyset);$$

- Let $D = (R_1, \ldots, R_k)$ be a new state of the history, and $\bullet\psi_1, \ldots, \bullet\psi_l$ be all temporal subformulas of Q. We define the $\Delta^{\mathcal{E}}$ operator as follows

$$\Delta^{\mathcal{E}}(\mathcal{E}(H), D) = (R_1, \ldots, R_k, \emptyset, \ldots, \emptyset) \qquad \text{for } H = \langle \, \rangle$$
$$\Delta^{\mathcal{E}}(\mathcal{E}(H), D) = (R_1, \ldots, R_k, \psi_1^{\mathcal{E}}(\mathcal{E}(H)), \ldots, \psi_l^{\mathcal{E}}(\mathcal{E}(H))) \quad \text{otherwise,}$$

where $\psi_i^{\mathcal{E}}$ is the closure of ψ_i in which all occurrences of temporal subformulas $\bullet\vartheta$ were replaced by r_ϑ.
- We define $Q^{\mathcal{E}}$ to be the query Q in which all occurrences of temporal subformulas $\bullet\vartheta$ were replaced by r_ϑ.

Note that the definition of $\Delta^{\mathcal{E}}$ has to take into account the *special* treatment of the temporal connective $\bullet$ on state 0 (cf. Definition 3) by making explicitly the instances of the auxiliary predicate symbols r_ψ corresponding to $\bullet\psi$ empty.

Theorem 9 $\mathcal{E}$ *is an expiration operator for PastμTL that guarantees bounded encoding of residual histories. Moreover, for guarded PastμTL formulas, $Q^{\mathcal{E}}$ and the components of $\Delta^{\mathcal{E}}$ are first-order queries.*

Proof. Correctness, $Q(H) = Q^{\mathcal{E}}(\mathcal{E}(H))$, follows by induction on the length of H and the observation that the view maintenance rules $\psi_i^{\mathcal{E}}$ maintain the instance of r_ψ to be equivalent to $\bullet\psi$ in every state of H.

Bounded history encoding property follows from observing that both $Q^{\mathcal{E}}$ and all the re-materialization rules $\varphi_i^{\mathcal{E}}$ in the definition of $\Delta^{\mathcal{E}}$ only refer to the last instance of the extended database schema and to the current instance of the user-defined predicates—all of which can be represented by finite instances of the extended relational schema—we can easily show that the residual history size does not depend on the length of H.

For guarded formulas, all occurrences of the fixpoint variables are in the scope of $\bullet$ and thus are replaced by the auxiliary predicates. This guarantees $Q^{\mathcal{E}}$ and the rematerialization rules $\psi_i^{\mathcal{E}}$ that are used to define $\Delta^{\mathcal{E}}$ are first-order.

Example 10 Applying the above construction on the fixpoint definition of the standard **since** temporal operator,

$$\mu X.\varphi \wedge \bullet(\psi \vee X),$$

that contains a single temporal subformula, $\bullet(\psi \vee X)$, proceeds as follows. We use an auxiliary predicate $r_{\psi \vee X}$ in the extended schema to maintain the "past" instance of $\bullet(\psi \vee X)$. The currency of the auxiliary relation after a history extension is achieved using a rule based on the closure of the subformula $\bullet(\psi \vee X)$ with respect to X,

$$\bullet(\psi \vee \mu X.\varphi \wedge \bullet(\psi \vee X)),$$

yielding

$$r_{\psi \vee X} := \psi \vee (\mu X.\varphi \wedge \bullet(\psi \vee X))$$
$$= \quad \psi \vee (\mu X.\varphi \wedge r_{\psi \vee X}) \quad = \psi \vee (\varphi \wedge r_{\psi \vee X}).$$

This is essentially the same materialization rule as the rule designed by Chomicki specifically for the **since** connective [2] and implemented using active ECA rules in IBM Starburst by Chomicki and Toman [4].

PastμTL, however, allows queries that cannot be expressed in PastTL [24].

Example 11 Consider the query

$$\mu X.r(x) \vee \bullet\bullet X$$

that collects values in any instance of r for the even states of the history (counted from the end of the history). Note that to do this, we indeed need to collect the values for odd states too. This is automatically achieved by our construction. The temporal subformulas of this query are $\psi_1 = \bullet\bullet X$, and $\psi_2 = \bullet X$. The inductive definitions for auxiliary relations $r_{\bullet X}$ and r_X,

$$r_{\bullet X}(x) := r_X(x) \quad \text{and} \quad r_X(x) := r(x) \vee r_{\bullet X}(x),$$

capture exactly the required sets of values in even and odd states, respectively.

From an implementation point of view, we could use techniques based on ECA (active) database rules to maintain the instances of the auxiliary predicates up to date, similarly to the approach for enforcing integrity constraints formulated in PastTL proposed by Chomicki and Toman [4]. The only difference is in handling rematerialization rules that mutually depend on each other (cf. Example 11), where temporary storage is needed during (a sequential) execution of the *simultaneous assignment*. However, in the case of PastTL, the technique proposed in this paper does not need any such temporary storage, since all the rematerialization rules can be stratified with respect to the "subformula" relationship [4].

Note also, that the rematerialization rules never refer to the *new* state of the user-defined predicate symbols. Thus, it is sufficient to have only *one instance* of these predicates at any time. To achieve this, and unlike [4], the rematerialization rules must be executed *before* a new state is added to the history. This way, the instances of the auxiliary predicates are *advanced* to the next state before changes are made to the instances of the user-defined predicates. This way, the new instances of the auxiliary predicates can be used to answer the maintained query *during* the execution of an update transaction against the user-defined predicates (which will eventually advance these instances from the current state to the next state).

5   A Lower Bound for Future Fixpoint TL

The situation for FutureμTL is completely different since the *unfolding* rule for fixpoints extends toward the (unknown) future of the history. Indeed we show that this difference implies a *linear lower bound* on the size of the residual history.

Example 12 Consider the following FutureμTL query:

$$\varphi = \exists x, y. \Diamond (q(x,y) \wedge \mu X. r(x,y) \vee \bigcirc \exists z. X(x,z) \wedge X(z,y))$$

and all database histories H over the schema $\langle q(x,y), r(x,y) \rangle$ of the form

State	Database instance
0	{} or {$q(a,b)$}
$\vdots$	$\vdots$
n	{} or {$q(a,b)$}
$n+1$	{$r(a,c_1), \ldots, r(c_i, c_{i+1}), \ldots, r(c_k, b)$},

where the constants a, b, and c_j are distinct values in $\mathbf{D}_H$. In other words, in each of the states $0, \ldots, n$, a single fact $q(a,b)$ is either true or false and the instances of r are empty, and in state $n+1$ the instance of r contains a chain of $k+1$ pairs linking the constants a and b. It is easy to see that the above query φ evaluates to true on a history of this form (i.e., $H, 0 \models \varphi$) if and only if

1. in state i the atomic fact $q(a,b)$ is true (for some $0 \leq i \leq n$),
2. there are distinct elements $c_1, \ldots, c_k$ in the domain $\mathbf{D}_H$ such that the atomic facts $r(a,c_1), r(c_1, c_2), \ldots, r(c_k, b)$ are true in state $n+1$, and
3. $k = 2^{n-i} - 1$.

Now let us consider the prefixes H' of all possible histories H of length n, i.e., missing the $(n+1)$-st (last) state. The size of the active domain of the prefixes H' is

$$|\mathbf{D}_{H'}| \leq |\{a,b\}| = 2,$$

and is independent of the length of this history, n. However, the above example shows that adding H's $(n+1)$-st state to H' allows us to "measure" how far in the history we moved past a state containing $q(a,b)$. Thus, to be able to preserve answers of φ under extensions of H' (in particular, to H), we have to retain at least one bit for each of the states $0, \ldots, n$ to record whether $q(a,b)$ was true or false in that state. Therefore, we need at least $\Omega(n) = \Omega(|\mathbf{T}_{H'}|)$ bits to represent the residual history. This observation yields the following theorem.

Theorem 13 *The worst-case space needed for residual histories produced by an arbitrary expiration operator for FutureμTL is bounded from below by a linear function in the length of the original history.*

An immediate consequence of this theorem is a lower bound for full μTL.

Corollary 14 *The space needed for residual histories produced by an arbitrary expiration operator for μTL is bounded from below by $\Omega(|\mathbf{T}_H|)$.*

Expiration Operators for Fragments of FutureμTL. On the other hand, several fragments of FutureμTL that admit bounded history encoding are already known:

- First order temporal logic (FOTL, with both past and future operators) can be embedded into the two-sorted first order logic, 2-FOL. This way, expiration techniques for 2-FOL [20] can be used to define an expiration operator guaranteeing bounded representation for residual histories.
- Biquantified future TL formulas can be handled using automata inspired approaches [9, 11, 12, 13, 14, 15].

The exact boundary between fragments of FutureμTL for which bounded expiration operators exist and those for which such operators cannot exist is not known at this time.

Note, however, that Theorem 13 precludes extending results on expiration of two sorted first-order logic (2-FOL) [20] to 2-FOL extended with general fixpoints while maintaining the existence of bounded history encoding.

Corollary 15 *The space needed for residual histories produced by an arbitrary expiration operator for a fixpoint extension of 2-FOL is bounded from below by $\Omega(|\mathbf{T}_H|)$.*

6   Conclusion

We have shown a significant difference between the behaviour of the past and the future fragments of μTL, when used as a query language for querying database histories. In particular, we have shown that large parts of a history, in an append-only setting, can be expired while maintaining answers to a finite set of queries formulated in the past fragment. On the other hand, for queries in the future fragment, one essentially needs to retain the whole history.

6.1   Future Work

While the picture for the past fragment is essentially settled, the results for FutureμTL are not quite satisfactory: there is a large gap between the biquantified future TL formulas (for which techniques proposed by Lipeck, Saake, *et al.*

[9, 11, 12, 13, 14, 15] can be applied) and full FutureμTL for which there cannot be a bounded expiration operator.

One way in which we can limit the power of FutureμTL, in particular, is by limiting its ability to introduce (unbounded number of) new data variables. A natural restriction along these lines is to consider a fragment in which fixpoint operators are restricted to the temporal domain only. For example, ETL [24] is is an extension of LTL that allows temporal connectives (over discrete time domain) to be defined in terms of *regular expressions*. This extension allows expressing properties like "*p* is true in every even state", that are known to be inexpressible in LTL. FOETL is a first-order extension of ETL. Because the temporal connectives are defined *without* being able to use quantifiers over the data domain $\mathbf{D}_H$, this logic is essentially equivalent to the fragment of FutureμTL in which free fixpoint variables cannot appear in the scope of data quantifiers. We conjecture the following.

Conjecture 16 *There is an expiration operator for future FOETL that guarantees bounded history encoding of residual histories.*

Another way of limiting the power of μTL is to consider decidable fragments of first order, and possibly fixpoint, temporal logics [8]. These fragments may also allow bounded history encoding with respect to potential satisfaction (and thus potential answers to queries).

On a more practical side, we focus on the possibilities of combining nested fixpoint operators in PastμTL formulas, possibly yielding an expiration operator that does not require temporary storage for the past instance of the auxiliary predicates. It is an open question for how large fragment of PastμTL such an operator exists; it is easy to see that this can be achieved for various simple fragments of PastμTL, e.g., for PastTL.

Acknowledgments

The author gratefully acknowledges the Natural Sciences and Engineering Research Council of Canada, the Communications and Information Technology of Ontario and Nortel Networks Ltd. for their support of this research.

References

[1] Serge Abiteboul, Richard Hull, and Victor Vianu. *Foundations of Databases.* Addison-Wesley, 1995. 382

[2] Jan Chomicki. Efficient Checking of Temporal Integrity Constraints Using Bounded History Encoding. *ACM Transactions on Database Systems*, 20(2):149–186, 1995. 380, 385, 386, 388

[3] Jan Chomicki and Damian Niwinski. On the Feasibility of Checking Temporal Integrity Constraints. *Journal of Computer and System Sciences*, 51(3):523–535, 1995. 386

[4] Jan Chomicki and David Toman. Implementing Temporal Integrity Constraints Using an Active DBMS. *IEEE Transactions on Data and Knowledge Engineering*, 7(4):566–582, 1995. 385, 386, 388

[5] Jan Chomicki and David Toman. Temporal Logic in Information Systems. In Jan Chomicki and Gunter Saake, editors, *Logics for Databases and Information Systems*, pages 31–70. Kluwer, 1998. 381, 382

[6] Jan Chomicki, David Toman, and Michael H. Böhlen. Querying ATSQL databases with temporal logic. *ACM Transactions on Database Systems (TODS)*, 26(2):145–178, 2001. 382

[7] Dov M. Gabbay, Ian M. Hodkinson, and Mark Reynolds. *Temporal Logic: Mathematical Foundations and Computational Aspects*. Oxford University Press, 1994. 384

[8] Ian M. Hodkinson, Frank Wolter, and Michael Zakharyaschev. Decidable fragment of first-order temporal logics. *Annals of Pure and Applied Logic*, 106(1-3):85–134, 2000. 391

[9] Klaus Hülsmann and Gunter Saake. Theoretical Foundations of Handling Large Substitution Sets in Temporal Integrity Monitoring. *Acta Informatica*, 28(4), 1991. 385, 390, 391

[10] Christian S. Jensen. Vacuuming. In Richard T. Snodgrass, editor, *The TSQL2 Temporal Query Language*, pages 447–460. Kluwer Academic Publishers, 1995. 380, 385

[11] Udo W. Lipeck. Transformation of Dynamic Integrity Constraints into Transaction Specifications. *Theoretical Computer Science*, 76(1), 1990. 385, 390, 391

[12] Udo W. Lipeck and Dasu Feng. Construction of Deterministic Transition Graphs from Dynamic Integrity Constraints. In *Graph-Theoretic Concepts in Computer Science*, pages 166–179. Springer-Verlag, LNCS 344, 1989. 385, 390, 391

[13] Udo W. Lipeck, Michael Gertz, and Gunter Saake. Transitional Monitoring of Dynamic Integrity Constraints. *IEEE Data Engineering Bulletin*, June 1994. 385, 390, 391

[14] Udo W. Lipeck and Gunter Saake. Monitoring Dynamic Integrity Constraints Based on Temporal Logic. *Information Systems*, 12(3):255–269, 1987. 385, 390, 391

[15] Udo W. Lipeck and Heren Zhou. Monitoring Dynamic Integrity Constraints on Finite State Sequences and Existence Intervals. In *Workshop on Foundations of Models and Languages for Data and Objects. FMLDO'91*, pages 115–130, 1991. 385, 390, 391

[16] Janne Skyt, Christian S. Jensen, and Leo Mark. A foundation for Vacuuming Temporal Databases . *Data and Knowledge Engineering*, 44(1):1–29, 2003. 380, 385

[17] Richard T. Snodgrass, editor. *The TSQL2 Temporal Query Language*. Kluwer, 1995. 381, 382

[18] David Toman. Point-based Temporal Extensions of SQL. In *International Conference on Deductive and Object-Oriented Databases*, pages 103–121, 1997. 382

[19] David Toman. Point-Based Temporal Extensions of SQL and Their Efficient Implementation. In Opher Etzion, Sushil Jajodia, and Suryanarayana Sripada, editors, *Temporal Databases: Research and Practice*, pages 211–237. Springer LNCS State-of-the-Art Survey, 1998. 382

[20] David Toman. Expiration of Historical Databases. In *International Symposium on Temporal Representation and Reasoning*, pages 128–135. IEEE Press, 2001. 380, 390

[21] David Toman. Logical Data Expiration. In Jan Chomicki, Gunter Saake, and Ron van der Meyden, editors, *Logics for Emerging Applications of Databases*, chapter 7. Springer, 2003. 380, 384, 386

[22] Moshe Y. Vardi. A Temporal Fixpoint Calculus. In *ACM Symposium on Principles of Programming Languages*, pages 250–259, 1988. 381, 385

[23] Moshe Y. Vardi and Pierre Wolper. An Automata-Theoretic Approach to Automatic Program Verification. In *IEEE Symposium on Logic in Computer Science*, 1986. 381, 385

[24] Pierre Wolper. Temporal Logic Can Be More Expressive. *Information and Control*, 56(1/2):72–99, 1983. 381, 385, 388, 391

A Multi-representation Spatial Data Model

Sheng Zhou and Christopher B. Jones

Department of Computer Science, Cardiff University
Cardiff, CF24 3XF, United Kingdom
{S.Zhou,C.B.Jones}@cs.cf.ac.uk

Abstract. Geo-referenced information is characterised by the fact that it may be represented on maps at different levels of detail or generalisation. Ideally a spatial database will provide access to spatial data across a continuous range of resolution and multiple levels of generalisation. Existing work on multi-resolution databases has treated generalisation control as one-dimensional. Here we extend the concept of multi-resolution spatial databases to provide support for multiple representations with variable resolution. Therefore the controls on generalisation become multi-dimensional with spatial resolution as one dimension and various types of generalisation style metrics as the other dimensions. We present a multi-representation spatial data model based on this approach and illustrate the implementation of multi-representation geometry in association with an online web demonstration.

1 Introduction

1.1 Multiple Representations of Geographical Phenomena

Geometric objects in spatial databases and GIS are representations of real world geographical phenomena. A single phenomenon may have multiple representations reflecting different perspectives of the observer. The observer's perspective has an aspect of **scale**, which is linked to **resolution** and introduces a limit on the maximum geometric information that may be represented for a particular phenomenon, as well as an aspect of **generalisation criteria** (**GC**) mainly reflecting the purposes of map compilation. Generalisation criteria may be adapted for example to map specifications for topographical maps or for different types of thematic map. They can be associated with **generalisation metrics** (**GM**) in the respective compilation and generalisation procedures, and may be interpreted as the degree of reduction relating to the maximum information that may be represented. Scale and generalisation criteria together control the form of the geometric objects representing a phenomenon as well as the nature of non-spatial properties associated with the phenomenon. In addition, there is also the issue of temporal multiplicity of representations that reflect change of geographical phenomena over time. While fully acknowledging the importance of this issue, we confine our focus here to the problems associated with space.

T. Hadzilacos et al. (Eds.): SSTD 2003, LNCS 2750, pp. 394–411, 2003.

Fig.1 presents an example of multiple geometric representations of a single geographical phenomenon (Isle of Wight, UK). Representation **A** preserves maximum information, as may be found in a topographical map. The series **A**, **B** and **C** are three representations at the same scale/resolution but under different generalisation criteria. **B** is generalised from **A** assuming criteria for thematic maps in which small details are removed. **C** is further generalised from **B** for use for example in a newspaper illustration, with only large details retained. The other series, of **A**, **D** and **E**, demonstrates the impact of scale/resolution change while the same generalisation criteria (i.e. criteria for a topographical map) remain in effect. As scale decreases, maximum information at a certain scale is preserved in the corresponding representations with only redundant data being removed.

Beyond a single phenomenon, scale/resolution and generalisation criteria will also determine what types of phenomena and which particular phenomena will be represented. This results in another level of representational multiplicity corresponding to object selection. Furthermore, the multiplicity of representations is reflected in differences in a phenomenon's non-spatial attributes and the values of these attributes.

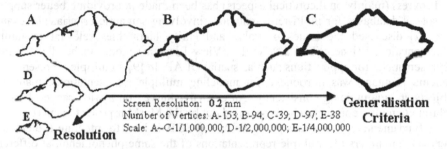

Fig. 1. Multiple geometric representations for a single geographical phenomenon (source dataset derived from original Ordnance Survey map, Crown copyright 2002)

1.2   From MV-SDB and MS-SDB to MRep-SDB

As different representations of geographical phenomena reflect different perspectives and serve different purposes, the efficacy of a spatial database will be increased significantly if multi-representation of geographical phenomena is supported. For example, a web map server could provide "active" maps that are adaptive to users' diverse interests as well as to the varying presentation characteristics of different browsing devices (e.g. printers, desktop CRTs, PDAs and WAP mobile phones).

To an extent, the functionality of multi-representation may be supported in current GIS and spatial databases by simply storing a collection of maps each of which reflects a pre-defined perspective. This approach, which we term **simple multi-version spatial database** or **MV-SDB**, may provide simple and efficient solutions to some applications. However, for many other applications it has severe problems such as potential inconsistency among different maps, high storage/update overhead, and most significantly, lack of flexibility in control over the user's perspective.

In recent years, multi-scale/resolution spatial databases (**MS-SDB**) have attracted increasing interest. On the theoretical side, for example, [1] described a formal model which represents the multi-resolution nature of map features through continuous functions over abstract cell complexes that model the combinational structure of maps. A model for a scale-based space partition hierarchy is described in [2]. "Stratified map spaces" are proposed in [3] as a formal basis for multi-resolution spatial databases. Graphs are used in [4] to describe amalgamation and selection operations caused by resolution change. Examples of experimental implementation include the PR-file [5] for multi-resolution access, and multi-scale geometry [6].

Although MS-SDB support representational multiplicity on the scale/resolution dimension, they do not provide support for variations in generalisation criteria as would be expected of a genuine multi-representation spatial database (**MRep-SDB**). The ideal MRep-SDB will be like every cartographer's dream: given a query scale/resolution value drawn from a **continuous** range and an **arbitrary** set of generalisation criteria reflecting the purpose of the query, a map that exactly meets the requirements is retrieved automatically (and efficiently) with a quality matching (or at least close to) the quality of one generalised by an expert cartographer from a master map. In short, an ideal MRep-SDB should support **on-demand**, **on-the-fly** and **high quality** spatial data retrieval.

Progress (mainly on theoretical aspects) has been made in providing better support in spatial databases for multi-representations involving semantic criteria. For example, [7] discussed the issues of value and entity hierarchies relevant to multi-representation. [8] described a "VUEL" (View Element) model to handle multiple representations for applications such as spatial OLAP. In [9] a multiple representation schema language was introduced for modeling multiple representations, matching objects and maintaining consistency. An extensive survey on a wide range of issues relating to multi-representation was carried out by the MurMur project team[10].

A fundamental issue in designing an MRep-SDB is how to integrate (potentially very large numbers of) multiple representations of the same phenomenon at different levels of detail and under various criteria. The approach currently adopted by most schemes may best be described as a **linked multi-version** approach. Here links are provided between different fixed representations, while intermediate representations, which may be required by services such as intelligent zooming, are interpolated or extrapolated from existing representations [11] by online generalisation procedures.

Because the *status quo* of automatic map generalisation is far from meeting the quality and performance demands to online (or even off-line) generalisation, while acknowledging that map generalisation procedures are the proper tools for generating multi-representations of spatial phenomena, we argue that as much generalisation workload as possible should be moved to a pre-processing stage in order to achieve good performance and maximum flexibility simultaneously. Results of generalisation can then be stored explicitly inside an MRep-SDB to facilitate retrieval and minimize requirements for any post-query generalisation.

In the remainder of this paper, we present a multi-representation spatial data model based on multi-representation geometry. Experimental results of a method to generate multi-representation geometry using a new line generalisation metric are reported and an on-line web demo has been set up. An approach to modelling multiplicity among a set of objects is also presented. Some issues relevant to the design of MRep-SDB design are also addressed briefly.

2   Cartographic Semantics and Multi-representation

Cartographic semantics describe the relation between geographical phenomena and their database representations. In this section, we will discuss those aspects of cartographic semantics relating to our multi-representation spatial data model.

2.1   Scale and Spatial Resolution

Scale (S_{rep}) is the ratio of the physical extent of the presentation medium (*ME*) and the real world extent (*FE*) of the presented contents. Resolution usually refers to the minimum dimension of a feature in a dataset (**database resolution**, R_{db}) or on the presentation medium (**presentation resolution**, R_{rep}). Normally when spatial data are collected for certain purposes, a R_{rep} will be specified. R_{db} is then related to R_{rep} as:

$$S_{rep} = ME \ / \ FE = R_{rep} \ / \ R_{db} \quad \Rightarrow \quad R_{db} = R_{rep} \ / \ S_{rep} = (R_{rep} * FE) \ / \ ME \qquad (1)$$

Unlike paper maps, in a GIS/SDB environment, both *ME* and R_{rep} may have different values on different or the same presentation devices. For a fixed S_{rep}, different R_{rep} corresponds to different R_{db}. This is the reason why (spatial) resolution instead of scale should be used in the context of a spatial database [12]. In discussions below, "resolution" refers to database resolution unless stated otherwise.

2.2   Resolution, Generalisation Criteria and Multiple Representation

Increase in resolution value (i.e. coarsening) will result in simplification of a representation's geometric form. In this context **simplification** refers to processes that normally remove only those elements (e.g. vertices) that are redundant from a resolution point of view while original information is preserved to a maximum. The well-known RDP algorithm [13] when used appropriately may be regarded as an example of such a process. Note that simplification may cause topological change in the original geometric form. In addition, two representations at different resolutions may have different values for a non-spatial attribute (e.g. Landuse). This would typically be due to the level of detail at which a classification hierarchy is applied (for example, *corn* could be generalised to *cereals*) [7].

On the other hand, **generalisation** refers to those processes that remove "details" from the geometric form (which may be the result of previous resolution-driven simplification) or eliminate entire objects in order to highlight the major geometric characteristics of phenomena or maintain a balance of information among different object types according to the criteria imposed.

For a single phenomenon, different GC may be associated with different metrics and/or metric values and will generate different representations at a fixed resolution. Details contained in the geometric form of each representation will vary, as illustrated in Fig. 1. Furthermore, different GC may result in retrieval of representations of different phenomena in the same type hierarchy. For example, at the same resolution, if more details are required, individual buildings could be retrieved; otherwise, the same location may be represented as a built-up area that is the aggregation of a group of buildings.

Two representations of the same phenomenon, such as a land parcel, under different GC may also vary in their attribute values. In this case, attribute values may be drawn from two different value hierarchies. For example, a parcel may be a cornfield under the criterion of current land-use but a residential area under the criterion of planned land-use in urban planning practice.

From a map-wide point of view, coarsening spatial resolution will generally cause a **selection** of geographical phenomena to be presented, as discrete objects fall below the resolution threshold. For a fixed resolution, variation of GC will affect the way phenomena are selected. In addition, change of either resolution or GC may cause **aggregation** of phenomena into new phenomena.

2.3   Incompatibility of Representations

Two representations are said to be incompatible if they should not present simultaneously. **Representation incompatibility** refers to incompatibility among multiple representations of a particular phenomenon or phenomena in the same perception hierarchy (e.g. a group of buildings aggregate to a built-up area). **Topological /proximal incompatibility** may exist between two representations of two different phenomena due to topological or proximal consistency constraints. For example, a generalised representation of a road may leave the initial location of a village on the wrong side of it and, therefore, these two representations are incompatible and a displaced new representation for the village should be retrieved along with this road representation.

3   Multi-representation Geometry and Spatial Object

In this section we introduce the concept of multi-representation geometry (**MRep-Geometry**) which we regard as the basic unit for representing spatial objects in a multi-representation context.

3.1   Generalisation Criteria, Generalisation Metrics and Presentation Space

As previously mentioned, a geometric representation of a spatial phenomenon is defined at a given resolution and under a certain set of GC which describe the purposes of query or map compilation. Generalisation procedures with numerical GM are applied to source data to generate results to meet these purposes. Therefore, a representation may be associated with certain GM values at a given resolution.

Assuming there are $n > 0$ generalisation metrics applied to a dataset (there may be multiple GMs applied to one type of phenomenon and different GMs for different phenomena), we may associate the resolution dimension RES with these n metrics to define an $n+1$-dimensional space $(RES, GM_1, GM_2, ..., GM_n)$ as the **presentation space (PS)** of the dataset. Consequently, any representation of the dataset (or a phenomenon in it) may be mapped to a point in this abstract space.

For the sake of simplicity, in the following discussion we will use a dataset containing one open polyline with one GM applied as an example. Therefore, the PS for this dataset is a 2-D space (RES, GM).

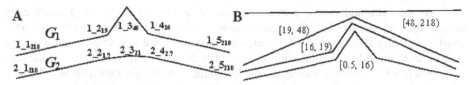

Fig. 2. A-Two Representations of the same phenomenon **B**- Multi-resolution retrieval on G_1

3.2   Multi-representation Geometry

Assuming at resolution *res* and with GM value *gm*, the geometric form of a spatial phenomenon is represented by an instance (G) of one of the well-known geometric types (point, open or closed polyline, chain, polygon, ... or collections of various types), we may denote this representation of the phenomenon as $Rep = (G, PR=\{(res, gm)\})$. We regard such a geometry instance G as a **single-representation geometry** (**SRep-geometry**) and PR as Rep's **presentation range**, which is a point set in the dataset's PS and in this case contains a single point (*res*, *gm*).

As an example an open polyline is denoted as either an *n*-tuple $<p_1, p_2, ..., p_n>$ or a partial ordering $<P, \le >$ on a vertex set $P=\{p_i | i= 1, n\}$ where $\le$ reflects the vertex precedence in the polyline. Fig.2-A illustrates two simple representations of the same phenomenon as $Rep_1 = (G_1, \{(res_1, gm_1)\})$ and $Rep_2 = (G_2, \{(res_2, gm_2)\})$ where $G_1 = <P_1, \le > (P_1 = \{p_{1\_1}, p_{1\_2}, p_{1\_3}, p_{1\_4}, p_{1\_5}\})$ and $G_2 = <P_2, \le > (P_2 = \{p_{2\_1}, p_{2\_2}, p_{2\_3}, p_{2\_4}, p_{2\_5}\})$.

If we follow the multi-version approach, Rep_1 and Rep_2 are two distinct versions of the phenomenon and G_1 and G_2 will be stored separately. Alternatively, we may merge G_1 and G_2 into a single linear structure. Firstly a single graph may be generated from G_1 and G_2 by merging two vertices in G_1 and G_2 into one single vertex if their coordinates are identical and the resulting graph is a DAG. By applying topological sorting on the resulting DAG, we will obtain a linear vertex sequence $MG=<p_1, p_2, p_3, p_6, p_4, p_5>$. Geometrically, $p_i = p_{1\_i} = p_{2\_i}$ except that $p_3 = p_{1\_3}$ and $p_6 = p_{2\_3}$. A vertex p_i in MG has the form of (x_i, y_i, PR_i). PR_i is the vertex's presentation range, which is the union of the presentation ranges of all representations containing this vertex. In our example, $PR_i = \{(res_1, gm_1), (res_2, gm_2)\}$ except that $PR_3 = \{(res_1, gm_1)\}$, as p_3 is in G_1 only, and $PR_6 = \{(res_2, gm_2)\}$ as p_6 is in G_2 only. We regard MG as a **multi-representation geometry** (**MRep-geometry**). Obviously, an SRep-geometry corresponding to a query point (res_q, gm_q) in PS may be easily retrieved from an MRep-geometry by selecting those vertices p_i satisfying $(res_q, gm_q) \in PR_i$.

Specifically, if there exists a query that may retrieve all vertices in an MRep-geometry, we regard such an MRep-geometry as **subsetting** (vertices retrieved by any other queries will be a sub-set of that retrieved by this query); otherwise, it is **non-subsetting** (e.g. p_3 and p_6 in MG will never be retrieved simultaneously).

Several different representations of a spatial phenomenon may be merged into one multiple-representation (**MRep**) containing one MRep-geometry merged from geometries of these representations. Consequently, all representations of the phenomenon may be merged into one or several MReps and a single entity (**Multi-representation spatial object**, or **MRO**) may be used to represent this phenomenon as $MRO=\{MRep_i | i=1, n\}$.

Note that although some representations of a phenomenon are geometrically merge-able, for practical reasons, concerning for example the maintenance of non-spatial attributes that may vary between representations, we may choose not to merge them into a single MRep. In addition, we cannot normally expect to have all the representations of a phenomenon immediately available to merge into MReps. Thus we may need to compute the multiple representations from one or a few detailed representations of a phenomenon.

3.3   Realisation of Simplification and Generalisation Metrics

3.3.1   Geometric Details and Metrics Values

The constituent details in a geometry can be defined in many application-dependent ways, e.g. through their correspondence with inflexion points or skeleton branches [14]. In general we may regard any three or more consecutive vertices in a geometry as a detail. For example, given an open polyline $pl = <p_1, p_2, ..., p_n>$, any sub-tuple $<p_i, ..., p_j, ..., p_k>$ ($i < j < k$; $1 \leq i \leq n\text{-}2$; $2 \leq j \leq n\text{-}1$; $3 \leq k \leq n$) of pl is a **detail** on pl, denoted as $dtl(p_i, p_k)$. In particular, points p_i and p_k are **base points** of the detail and points p_j are **detail points** of the detail. A detail should contain two base points and at least one detail point. A detail is **simplified** if some of its detail points are removed. If new detail points are inserted, the detail is **modified**. Normally we may regard a detail as **removed** if at least one of its base points or all its detail points are removed.

Various relations, such as separate, adjacent, identical, inclusive and nesting, may be defined between two details $dtl(p_a, p_b)$ and $dtl(p_c, p_d)$ on the same polyline. As these relations are not used in the current study, we omit their definitions here.

With the above definition, both simplification and generalisation may be viewed as processes of detail simplification and/or removal (detail modification may also be involved in some algorithms) although the intention of simplification and generalisation are very different. Simplification removes some details while retaining most "critical" points. On the other hand, generalisation normally removes some "critical" points to smooth an object. If we process a detailed representation of a phenomenon with different simplification (normally associated with resolution) and generalisation metric values, different less-detailed representations may be generated, with different vertices/details removed from the original representation (and possibly with some vertices/details added as well). By associating these metric values with the vertices/details removed (or added) and storing these values along with geometric data, different representations of a phenomenon may be retrieved directly without complicated simplification/generalisation processing at query time.

3.3.2   Spatial Resolution, RDP Tolerance and Simplification Metrics

RDP tolerance has been previously adopted in multi-resolution access schemes [5, 6] for representing the spatial resolution dimension. In this study, we will also use the extended RDP tolerance for this purpose, i.e. with tolerance promotion during the process to form a monotonically decreasing tolerance value hierarchy [6].

Several observations may be made on the process of calculating RDP tolerance values (denoted as TOL in the following discussions) of vertices in an open polyline $pl = <p_1, p_2, ..., p_n>$ (see example vertex subscripts in Fig.1-A). For an internal vertex

p_j $(1 < j < n)$ whose TOL value d_j is calculated relative to vertices p_i and p_k (i.e. distance from p_j to line p_i-p_k and $i < j < k$):

- A detail $dtl(p_i, p_k)$ may be defined and measured by d_j which only depends on p_i, p_j and p_k and is irrelevant to other (if any) detail points p_m $(i < m < k$ and $m \neq j)$;
- $d_j \leq d_i$ and $d_j \leq d_k$ (for end-points p_1 and p_n in an open polyline, $ad\ hoc$ TOL definitions are required);
- If there is any other detail point p_m in the detail, $d_m \leq d_j$;
- In a vertex filtering process to select any vertex p_j satisfying $d_j > d_q$ (d_q is a query tolerance value), p_m will never be selected if p_j is not selected; p_j will never be selected if p_i and p_k are not selected; in addition, assuming $d_j > 0$, p_j will be selected for any d_q falling in the range $[0, d_j)$; for the whole polyline, some of its vertices will be selected for $d_q \in [0, d_{max})$ where d_{max} is its vertices' maximum tolerance value;
- Consequently, the above detail $dtl(p_i, p_k)$ may be represented by the internal vertex p_j and its tolerance value d_j;
- Each internal vertex corresponds to one and only one detail that is recognised and hence **effective** in a vertex filtering process.
- If there are m ($\leq n$ if no vertices added) distinct tolerance values $\{d_1, d_2, ..., d_m\}$ generated from the polyline, for any query tolerance value $d_q \subset [d_k, d_{k+1})$ ($k < m$), the same set of vertices (hence the same geometrical representation) will be selected (Fig.2-B).

A mapping mechanism may be defined between tolerance value d and resolution value res (e.g. simply let $res = d$). Therefore, the above tolerance range of a vertex $[0, d_j)$ may be mapped to a **resolution range** $RR = [r_f, r_c)$ ($r_f \leq r_c$) where r_f and r_c are the finest and coarsest resolution bounds of the vertex. If the base resolution of a dataset is r_0 (which conceptually speaking should be greater than 0) and the polyline presents in the initial dataset, we have $r_f = r_0$. Note that for vertices newly added during some other simplification processes or for vertices representing a phenomenon not present in the initial dataset, we have $r_f > r_0$. In addition, under other different simplification algorithms, a resolution range may well possess a more complicated form (such as the union of a few non-overlapping intervals $[r_{f\_1}, r_{c\_1}) \cup [r_{f\_2}, r_{c\_2}) \cup ...$).

Similarly, we may also say that in the above discussion the representation retrieved by $d_q \in [d_k, d_{k+1})$ corresponds to a resolution range $[r_k, r_{k+1})$. This fact implies that a limited (but perhaps large) number of representations (or versions) of a phenomenon are sufficient to support continuous change of query resolution within the resolution range $[r_f, r_{c\_max})$ which is the resolution range of the polyline.

From a multi-representation point of view, the above resolution ranges may be regarded as presentation ranges for vertices and representations on the resolution dimension and the polyline can thus be converted to a polyline which is multi-representational on the resolution dimension.

3.3.3   Generalisation Metrics and Weighted Effective Area

An example of the many available line generalisation metrics is the so-called "effective area" (**EA**) introduced in the Visvalingam-Whyatt (VW) algorithm [15]. The EA of a point p_i $(1 < i < n)$ in an open polyline $pl = <p_1, p_2, ..., p_n>$ is the area of the triangle formed by p_i and the two points p_{i-1}, and p_{i+1} (EA of endpoints p_1 and p_n requires *ad hoc* definition). Unlike the top-down RDP algorithm, the generalisation process of the VW algorithm works bottom-up to iteratively remove the point with smallest EA from the polyline until a predefined EA threshold is reached. When a point is removed, the EA of the two points adjacent to the removed point will be recalculated. Thus if p_i with EA value ea_i is removed, EA of p_{i-1} and p_{i+1} become the areas of triangles $(p_{i-2}, p_{i-1}, p_{i+1})$ and $(p_{i-1}, p_{i+1}, p_{i+2})$ respectively if the new values are **greater** than ea_i. Without setting a fixed EA threshold, we may repeat the process until there are only two (or three for closed polylines) points left.

Like the RDP tolerance, each internal vertex also represents one and only one detail effective in a vertex filtering process based on EA values and this detail may be measured by the *final* EA value of the vertex (i.e. prior to its removal). Consequently, each vertex p_i may be labeled with an EA range [0, ea_i) and the polyline is converted to a polyline which is multi-representational on the EA dimension.

In our current experiment, we have used **weighted effective area** (WEA), a new metric based on EA. Instead of using the area value of the triangle (p_{i-1}, p_i, p_{i+1}) directly, we also take the shape characteristics of the triangle into consideration. A group of weight factors is used to adjust the initial area value to generate a WEA value. These factors are based on measures reflecting flatness, skewness and orientation of the triangle. This new metric (or indeed a family of metrics) provides much more control on detail removal by using different weights and/or weight mapping functions. As it is not directly relevant to the present study, we will not present the details of the WEA metrics here, but the effect of WEA-based generalisation is shown in our experimental results.

3.4   A Method to Compute MRep-Geometry

In the previous sub-section, we have treated resolution and generalisation metric (WEA) dimensions separately. In this sub-section we will demonstrate a method to integrate the two dimensions to compute vertex presentation ranges in the RES-EA space. A single detailed open polyline pl (i.e. G_1 in Fig.2-A) is used as an example. For the sake of simplicity, we use EA as a generalisation metric in the following explanation, while WEA is used in our experiment on a real dataset. In addition, we focus on the states of the three internal points $(p_2, p_3$ and $p_4)$ in pl. We also assume that the base dataset resolution is $r_b = 0.5$ and the maximum resolution and EA values for the polyline (and the two endpoints p_1 and p_5) are *MaxRes* and *MaxEA* whose values may change but are always equal to or greater than those of the internal vertices.

3.4.1   Initial Presentation Ranges

Initial vertex RES and EA values computed from the original polyline are shown in Fig.3-A (labeled on each internal vertex as EA/RES). Therefore the RES value sequence < r_b = 0.5, 16, 19, 48, *MaxRes*> and EA value sequence <0, 593, 940, 2096, *MaxEA*> form two partitions on RES and EA dimensions and the polyline should occupy the region of PR_{pl}={$(res, ea) \mid 0.5 \leq res < MaxRes \wedge 0 \leq ea < MaxEA$ }in the RES-EA space.

For each vertex p_i, it is natural to think its presentation range is PR_i={$(res, ea) \mid 0.5 \leq res < r_i \wedge 0 \leq ea < ea_i$ }. However, because RES and EA dimensions are not independent and different vertices are selected/removed according to RES and EA criteria, it is possible, for example, that a vertex is selected due to the RES criterion while one or both of the base points of the detail represented by this vertex are not selected due to the EA criterion. Consequently, the detail represented by this vertex under RES criterion will not be presented properly from a cartographic point of view.

For the reasons stated above, the initial valid presentation range of the polyline is $PR_{pl\_0} = PR_0 \cup PR_{res} \cup PR_{ea}$, where $PR_0 = \{(res, ea) \mid r_b \leq res < MinRes \wedge 0 \leq ea < MinEA\}$, $PR_{res} = \{(res, ea) \mid MinRes \leq res < MaxRes \wedge 0 \leq ea < MinEA\}$ and $PR_{ea} = \{(res, ea) \mid r_b \leq res < MinRes \wedge MinEA \leq ea < MaxEA\}$. Here $MinRes$ and $MinEA$ are smallest vertex RES and EA values in the polyline (16 and 593 in this example). PR_0 is the region without simplification or generalisation effect, PR_{res} is the region with RDP-simplification effect only and PR_{ea} is the region with EA-generalisation only. The initial valid presentation range of each vertex may be defined similarly by replacing $MaxRes$ and $MaxEA$ with respectively vertex RES and EA bounds r_i and ea_i.

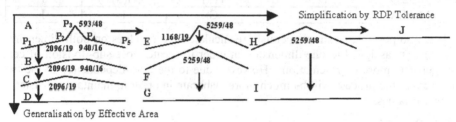

Fig. 3. Computing Mrep-polyline with RDP priority. Vertex labels are AE(final) /RDP values

3.4.2 Expansion of Presentation Ranges

A simple way to expand initial vertex presentation ranges into the region of $\{(res, ea) \mid MinRes \leq res < MaxRes \wedge MinEA \leq ea < MaxEA\}$ is to give priority to one dimension (e.g. RES) and recalculate metric values on the other dimension (e.g. EA) for vertices in representations (Fig.2-B) derived from the initial metric values on this dimension (i.e. RES). In other words, this is a process of "generalisation after simplification" (or "simplification after generalisation" if priority is given to the EA dimension).

Fig.3 illustrates this process while results are shown in Table 1 (which is a **PR-Table**, or presentation-range table, representing the Resolution-Generalisation metric plane). In Table 1, each cell represents a rectangular region (cell-PR) on the RES-EA plane as $\{(res, ea) \mid min\_res \leq res < max\_res \wedge min\_ea \leq ea < max\_ea\}$, e.g. the first (top-left) cell in Table 1 represents $\{(res, ea) \mid 0.5 \leq res < 16 \wedge 0 \leq ea < 593\}$. If a representation (or point, detail, etc.) occupies a cell, its presentation range should contain the cell-PR of this cell. Cells in Table 1 present representations in Fig.3 and   labels of any internal points (p_2, p_3, p_4) in these representations, e.g. the first cell   contains the original polyline (Fig.3-A) which has three internal points indicated in the form of (2/3/4). The PR of a vertex has a more complicated form. In the case of p_2 it is $\{(res, ea) \mid (0.5 \leq res < 16 \wedge 0 \leq ea < 2096) \vee (16 \leq res < 19 \wedge 0 \leq ea < 1168)\}$.

A consequence of this process is that in some vertices the value of the recalculated metric (EA in this case) is increased while the metric value on the other dimension (RES in this case) increases (e.g. p_3 has an EA value of 593 in representation Fig.3-A and the value is increased to 5259 in Fig.3-E). This may generate some odd query results. For example, for a query (r_q, ea_q) ($593 \leq ea_q < 940$), when the value of r_q increases, we will retrieve representations B, E, H or J in Fig.3. Vertex p_3 does not present in B but is present in the simplified representations E and H. To solve this problem, a constraint may be applied to the process to make sure that recalculated metric values should never increase.

Table 1. PR-Table with RDP priority

0 \ 0.5	16	19	48	MaxTol
593	A(2/3/4)	E(2/3)	H(3)	J
940	B(2/4)	E(2/3)	H(3)	J
1168	C(2)	E(2/3)	H(3)	J
2096	C(2)	F(3)	H(3)	J
5259	D	F(3)	H(3)	J
MaxEA	D	G	I	J

It is also possible to simultaneously recalculate metric values on both dimensions with priority assigned to one dimension in order to create more sub-division of cells and generate more representations. However, due to the inter-dependency of the two dimensions, the process will be much more elaborate in order to maintain consistency of metric values.

3.4.3 Discussion

The above method is presented here only for the purpose of demonstrating the general procedure of generating MRep-geometry from detailed single-representation geometric objects. It is simple but the results are not of the highest quality. Some other generalisation metrics associated with other detail definitions may provide better support to handle metric inter-dependency and generate better results. It is also worth noting that results of different metrics may be stored together inside one MRep-geometry to support different generalisation requirements from a single source.

A characteristic of our current method is that there is a one-to-one correspondence between vertices and effective details. Consequently, we attach information relevant to the presentation of a detail to its corresponding vertex and do not need to define details explicitly. For other metrics in which details are defined differently (e.g. [14]), explicit detail definition and storage may be required and references to these details may be stored with vertices affected by these details in the form of constraints. At query time, these constraints can be tested to decide whether a vertex should be retrieved. Such constraints may also be used to resolve incompatibility among multiple representations of different objects.

4   Generalisation Metrics for Multiple Objects

The previous sub-section focuses on a single phenomenon. In this section we use a simple model for point object selection to demonstrate how generalisation metrics for selection can be integrated with spatial resolution to support representational multiplicity among a group of objects.

4.1   A Simple Model for Point Object Selection

Assume in a region with a real world extent of fe_0^2 (constant), there are N_{FLD} point phenomena of a certain type (e.g. residential site) and various other phenomena. The initial task is to construct a spatial dataset at a base dataset resolution of r_0 (derived from the pre-defined initial presentation extent me_0^2 and presentation resolution r_{rep_0} using equation (1) in 2.1).

From a presentation point of view, if we focus on these point phenomena only, r_0 imposes a restriction on the maximum number of phenomena (N_{max_0}) that may be represented in the dataset in order to maintain a reasonable **presentation object density** which may be defined as: $WD(N) = N^k / A_{disp}$. Here N is the number of retrieved objects, k is a weight factor and A_{disp} is the area of the presentation device (me^2 in this case, where me is normalized according to scale to fit fe_0). Therefore we may define $N_{max}(r)$ ($r \geq r_0$) as the **dataset capacity** for this type of phenomena at r and **maximum** WD as (using (1)):

$$WDMax(r) = N_{max}(r)^k / A_{disp} = N_{max}(r)^k / me^2 = (N_{max}(r)^k * r^2) / (fe_0^2 * r_{rep}^2) \qquad (2)$$

Clearly, $N_{max\_0} = N_{max}(r_0)$. Larger r corresponds to decrease of scale or increase of presentation resolution value and will result in smaller N_{max} to maintain the object density at an acceptable level. Therefore, $N_{max}(r)$ represents a resolution-oriented aspect of multiplicity in the process of object selection.

At a given resolution r and assuming that there are sufficient candidates for selection, we may select $N_r \leq N_{max}(r)$ phenomena of this type. This is because, when other types of phenomena are taken into consideration, the space for presenting each type of phenomenon is further restricted and a fine balance among the various types has to be maintained. Consequently, the selection rate (used as a general term here) assigned to a particular type may result in an under-capacity ($N_r < N_{max}(r)$) selection. As the selection rate is affected by the generalisation criteria used to make the dataset, different GC will result in different selection rates for the same resolution r, which represents a semantic aspect of multiplicity of object selection.

Note that the theoretical value of $N_{max}(r_0)$ may exceed the value N_{FLD}. We may either use a universal $N_{max}(r_0)$ for different datasets of the same size under the same GC set, or make $N_{max}(r_0)$ adaptive to the nature of a particular dataset. At present we simply assume that for $N_{max\_0} \leq N_{FLD}$ then $N_0 \leq N_{max\_0}$ phenomena are selected and presented in the initial dataset at r_0.

It is natural to think that objects are selected by their relative importance. When resolution value r increases, at $r = r_i$, the number of objects currently in the dataset will exceed $N_{max}(r_i)$ and the least important object O_i should be removed, leaving N_c objects remaining. Consequently, if the order of selection is fixed, we may say that O_i will present in the dataset within the range of $PR_i = \{(r, N_{sel}) \mid r_0 \leq r < r_i \wedge N_c < N_{sel}\}$, i.e. O_i will be selected only if there are $N_{sel} > N_c$ objects to be selected. PR_i is O_i's **presentation range for selection** in the 2D RES-NUM space (NUM represents object numbers).

To decide the resolution bound r_i at which O_i is removed with N_c objects left, by making a provision that maximum presentation density should remain constant at different resolutions (i.e. $WDMax(r_0) = WDMax(r)$), we have:

$$N_{max}(r) = N_{max\_0} * (r_0 / r)^{2/k} \Leftrightarrow r = r_0 * (N_{max\_0} / N_{max}(r))^{k/2} \qquad (3)$$

$$N_{max}(r_i) = N_c \Rightarrow r_i = r_{0*}(N_{max\_0} / N_c)^{k/2} \qquad (4)$$

For the most important object in the dataset, we have $N_c = 0$ so that *ad hoc* definition is required to decide its coarsest resolution bound. We also assume r_{rep} is not changed in the process. Otherwise, (3) and (4) will possess more complicated forms.

Note that the above derivation has its roots in the so-called "radical law" for feature selection in cartography. From (3) we can also derive $r_0 / r = (N_{max}(r) / N_{max\_0})^{k/2}$. For $k = 4$, we have $r_0 / r = N^2_{max}(r) / N^2_{max\_0}$, which is exactly the basic "radical law" expression for object selection [16].

Number of objects to be selected is certainly not a user-friend query parameter in the process of querying a multi-representation object set described above. Instead we may use **degree of selection** (*DoS*) which is defined as:

$$DoS(r) = N_{sel} / N_{max}(r) \Rightarrow N_{sel} = DoS(r) * N_{max}(r) = DoS(r) * N_{max\_0} * (r_0 / r)^{2/k} \qquad (5)$$

Thus $DoS(r) \in [0, 1]$ as N_{sel} should not exceed $N_{max}(r)$. Under the above provision of a constant maximum presentation object density, it is easy to prove that for the same *DoS* value, the retrieved presentation object density is also approximately constant (since N_{sel} is a discrete integer) at different query resolutions. On the other hand, at the same resolution and for different purposes, a user may use different *DoS* values to control the proportion of objects retrieved relative to the maximum number of objects that may retrieve at the resolution. Note that we have assumed the order of object selection is the same under resolution-driven selection and semantics-driven selection. Otherwise, an additional selection metric will be needed.

A single *DoS* may be of no great interest. However, for a dataset containing more than one type of object, by adjusting *DoS* values for different object types, we may "blend" the source dataset in many different ways to meet users various requirements.

4.2   Selection and Aggregation in Feature Hierarchy

The point object selection model presented above, albeit simplistic, illustrates a general approach for handling representational multiplicity among a group of objects. In normal cartographic practice, selection processing of objects with finite size (length, area, etc.) also obeys some sort of mathematic relations resembling the radical law. Consequently, models similar to the one in 4.1 but with the size and other characteristics of objects taken into consideration may be used to generate multi-representation datasets for these objects.

For an *MRO*={*MRep$_i$*|*i*=1, *n*}, its presentation range for selection is the union of that of its *MRep*s (each of which could contain an MRep-geometry described in section 3). If its *MRep*s are defined according to different semantics, no special treatment will be needed as their retrieval is normally controlled by non-spatial attribute values.

If one *MRep* is derived from the other while resolution decreases, initially the two *MRep*s may be separated on the resolution dimension by the generalisation process. For example an MRO with a *PR* of {(*r*, N_{sel}) | $r_b \leq r < r_{max} \wedge N_c < N_{sel}$} (number of objects is used as selection metric for convenience) contains two *MRep*s as *MRep$_1$*

with $PR_1 = \{(r, N_{sel}) \mid r_b \leq r < r_1 \land N_c < N_{sel}\}$ and $MRep_2$ with $PR_2 = \{(r, N_{sel}) \mid r_1 \leq r < r_{max} \land N_c < N_{sel}\}$. If this is the case, we may choose to move part of PR_1 into PR_2 to provide multiple representations with a certain resolution range $[r_1', r_1)$. Subsequently, we have $PR_1 = \{(r, N_{sel}) \mid (r_b \leq r < r_1' \land N_c < N_{sel}) \lor (r_1' < r < r_1 \land N_c' < N_{sel})\}$ and $PR_2 = \{(r, N_{sel}) \mid (r_1' \leq r < r_1 \land N_c < N_{sel} \leq N_c') \lor (r_1 < r < r_{max} \land N_c < N_{sel})\}$, where $N_c < N_c'$. With this extension, for $r_1' \leq r_q < r_1$, a smaller N_{sel} ($N_c < N_{sel} \leq N_c'$), indicating a low selection rate, will retrieve $MRep_2$; otherwise, $MRep_1$ may be retrieved. Alternatively, a new metric may be used solely for this purpose. This technique also applies to the situation where one MRO is aggregated from a few other MROs residing in the same feature hierarchy (e.g. a built-up area aggregated from a group of buildings).

Finally, due to the flexible nature of an MRep-SDB, potentially there are a great number of incompatible cases among objects, representations of objects or even details in representations caused by topological, proximal or semantic inconsistency. While there is no room to address these issues in detail, we believe most of these cases may be detected and resolved when the multi-representation dataset is generated. Solutions may be stored along with geometric data in the form of persistent constraints and checked at query time to retrieve the correct objects/presentations. For example, in the road-village case presented in 2.3, which representation of the village should be retrieved depends on which road representation is retrieved. Consequently, a constraint recording information on the condition of road retrieval may be attached to the village object and tested at query time.

5   Discussion and Experimental Results

5.1   Experimental Implementation and Results

The method in 4.1 to compute MRep-geometry geometry has been implemented in C++. The RDP tolerance criterion is used as resolution value and WEA is the generalisation metric. Priority is given to RDP and the WEA values are recalculated. As neither of the original RDP and VW algorithms guarantees topological consistency in their output, we also use a fully dynamic 2-D Constrained Delaunay Triangulation package (MGLIB-2) to maintain a triangulation of the dataset during the whole process for detecting topological inconsistency. Currently we do not remove a point causing inconsistency but raise its RES or WEA value and wait until the removal of other points makes this point delete-able. This is the simplest but certainly not the best solution. Without topological consistency checking, the time complexity of this process is roughly $O(n^3)$ for a polyline with n vertices.

Currently the data structure for a vertex in an MRep-geometry is $MRPoint\{x, y, r_{min}, N, R[N], SRWEA[N]\}$. The first three data items are coordinates and the finest resolution bound. $SRWEA[n]$ ($n = 0, N-1$) is the square root of WEA value at resolution range $[R[n-1], R[n])$. In particular, for $n=0$, the resolution range is $[r_{min}, R[0])$. Also, $R[N-1]$ is the coarsest resolution bound for the vertex. Note that if the WEA value is identical at two adjacent resolution intervals, the two intervals are merged. In addition, this is the form for subsetting points with WEA-adjustment only. For other cases, the PR-Table for a point is in the form of a more complicated sparse matrix, for which more sophisticated data structures have to be used.

The test dataset (see Fig.1, 4 and 5) is derived from several Ordnance Survey Land-Form PANORAMA map sheets at a field resolution of 1m. There are five closed objects and 2376 vertices in total while the largest object contains 2336 vertices. We have computed a few statistics on the generated multi-representation dataset. If data items in the above structure *MRPoint* are stored in double precision for coordinates, long integer for N and single precision for others, on average 45.42 bytes (i.e. 29.42 bytes for MRep-data and the average of N is 3.18) are required for a multi-representation vertex. By exhaustive enumeration scanning through all resolution and WEA interval bounds, we also obtain the number of distinguishable representations that we may retrieve from the dataset as 539,066 versions. Note that any geometrically identical representations at separate presentation ranges are **not** counted repeatedly. The total number of vertices in these 539,066 versions is 556,908,339. If the WEA non-increasing constraint is applied (see 3.4.2), the results are 524,212 versions and 540,711,604 vertices.

Although differences between many of these versions are minimal, all these versions are required in order to claim that genuine continuous change of resolution and generalisation metric values is supported under the generalisation procedures we adopt. It is true that due to selection, an object may be deleted at a resolution much smaller than its original coarsest resolution bound. Therefore, many of these versions (i.e. at coarser resolutions and hence containing fewer vertices) would be unnecessary. On the other hand, the size of MRep-geometry would also be reduced as $R[N]$ and $WEA[N]$ are smaller as well.

To demonstrate the representational multiplicity of MRep-geometry, we produced a JAVA applet-based web demo (http://www.cs.cf.ac.uk/user/S.Zhou/MRepDemo/).

In this web demo (Fig.4), we provide an operation mode of "Intelligent Zooming". Under this mode, a screen resolution value and a **"degree of generalisation"** (*DoG*) value is preset.

As subsequent zooming-in/out operations are carried out, the retrieved representations will show a resemblance in generalisation style. Very similar to *DoS*, *DoG* defines a mechanism to map WEA values to a real range of [0, 1]. A *DoG* value of 0 represents "minimum" WEA-based generalisation and 1 the "maximum" generalisation. When the required dataset resolution changes (due to zoom-in/zoom-out), the same *DoG* value will be mapped to a different WEA value accordingly to maintain roughly the same generalisation effect. Therefore, a user may avoid the trouble of having to compute a proper WEA value in order to make an intended query. Fig.5 represents three zooming series under different *DoG* values. From left to right, *DoG* = 0, 0.5, 0.75 and, from top to bottom, scales are $1:10^6$, $1:2.5 \times 10^6$, $1:5 \times 10^6$ and $1:10^7$ respectively. The screen resolution (R_{rep}) is 0.1mm. At each resolution r, *DoG* value is mapped to a WEA value $wea = r^2 {}_* (1 - DoG)^{-2}$ (*DoG* < 1). The number of vertices in each retrieved representation is marked in the figure.

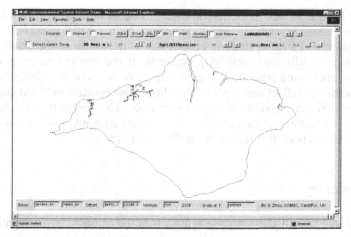

Fig. 4. A Web Demo for MRep-Geometry

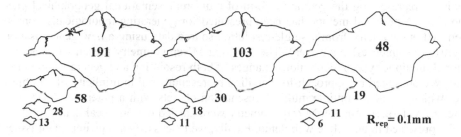

Fig. 5. MRep-Geometry and Intelligent Zooming (drawn at real scale. source dataset derived from original Ordnance Survey map, Crown copyright 2002)

5.2   MRep-SDB Design and Implementation Issues

In this sub-section we will briefly discuss a few key issues relevant to the design and implementation of an MRep-SDB. In an MRep-SDB, a spatial index on a column containing MRO has to support at least four dimensions: the two spatial dimensions, resolution dimension and one or more dimensions representing object selection metrics. As a 3D-Rtree can be used for a multi-resolution SDB [6] with good results, it is natural for us to use N-D-Rtree ($N>3$) to index an MRO column.

Although in this study we have demonstrated that a great deal of generalisation workload may be practically moved to a pre-processing stage, some type of online generalisation may still be required to process results retrieved from a MRep-SDB. One such process is so-called online graphic conflict resolution. Although we might be able to guarantee topological consistency (and proximal consistency to an extent) in the database, proximal inconsistency caused by user actions such as specifying a large symbol size is difficult to handle on the DBMS side and online generalisation procedures are consequently required. Experiments that achieve real-time performance for conflict resolution have been carried out and reported in [17].

Another issue is related to the importance ranking of objects for selection processing. We have assumed such ranking is carried out dataset wide. However, for queries retrieving objects in an area small in comparison to the extent of the dataset, whether such a ranking is still applicable is questionable if the importance of an object depends on whether some other objects are retrieved or not. We may design some more complex metrics to reflect this aspect of locality or use constraints to handle the issue. Alternatively, we may choose to use a query *DoS* value larger than the initially intended value to retrieve some more objects and subsequently apply some online selection procedures upon this relatively small set of objects.

6   Summary

In this paper we have discussed various aspects of the causes of representational multiplicity of geographical phenomena from a map generalisation point of view. We introduced the concept of multi-representation geometry (MRep-geometry) as the basic unit for representing the geometric form of multi-representational geographical phenomena. A practical method has been presented for generating topologically consistent MRep-geometry from a single-resolution source data using a new generalisation metric (weighted effective area). The resulting MRep-geometry presents representational multiplicity with continuous changes of both resolution and generalisation metric. We presented an approach for handling representational multiplicity of an object set which contains multiple multi-representation objects with a potential object type hierarchy. Experiments on MRep-geometry were carried out on a real dataset and results presented in an online web demo. Finally, we discussed various important issues relevant to designing, implementing and using a multi-representation spatial database.

Effective support for representational multiplicity in a spatial database will benefit a wide range of users. We believe the approach presented here holds a clear advantage over previous approaches in storage efficiency, performance and, most significantly, flexibility. Our implementation has (to an extent) demonstrated the practicality of this approach. However, we also acknowledge the huge difficulties in building such an MRep-SDB for even the simplest real-world applications. Predominately, these difficulties concern the automated map generalization required for dataset generation. Issues that will be addressed in more detail in future studies include resolution-dependent proximal consistency, the selection process for linear and areal objects and incompatibility among multiple representations of different objects.

References

[1]   Puppo, E. and G. Dettori. Towards a formal model for multiresolution spatial maps. in Proc. Advances in Spatial Databases (SSD95), LNCS 951. p. 152-169. 1995

[2]   Rigaux, P. and M. Scholl. Multi-scale partitions: Application to spatial and statistical database. in   Advances in Spatial Databases (SSD95), LNCS 951. p. 170-183. 1995. Portland

[3]   Stell, J.G. and M.F. Worboys. Stratified map spaces. in Proc. The 8th International Symposium on Spatial Data Handling. p. 180-189. 1998. British Columbia: Taylor and Francis

[4]   Stell, J.G. and M.F. Worboys. Generalizing Graphs using Amalgamation and Selection. in Proc. Advances in Spatial Databases (SSD'99), LNCS 1651. p. 19-32. 1999: Springer

[5]   Becker, B., H.-W. Six, and P. Widmayer. Spatial priority search: an access technique for scaleless maps. in Proc. ACM SIGMOD. p. 128-137. 1991. Denver, Colorado

[6]   Zhou, S. and C.B. Jones. Design and implementation of multi-scale databases. in Proc. 7th International Symposium on Advances in Spatial and Temporal Databases (SSTD 2001). p. 365-384. 2001. Redondo Beach, CA, USA: Springer

[7]   Rigaux, P. and M. Scholl. Multiple Representation Modelling and Querying. in Proc. IGIS'94, LNCS 884. p. 59-69. 1994. Ascona, Switzerland

[8]   Bedard, Y. and E. Bernier. Supporting multiple representations with spatial databases views management and the concept of <<VUEL>>. in Proc. ISPRS / ICA Workshop Multi-Scale Representations of Spatial Data. 2002. Ottawa

[9]   Friis-Christensen, A., et al. Management of Multiply Represented Geographic Entities. in Proc. International Database Engineering and Applications Symposium (IDEAS'02). p. 150-159. 2002

[10]   The MurMur Consortium. Supporting Multiple Representations in Spatio-Temporal databases. in Proc. 6th EC-GI & GIS Workshop. 2000. Lyon, France

[11]   The MurMur Consortium, MurMur Project Workpackage 3 (Services) Deliverable 9: Other Services. 2001

[12]   Spaccapietra, S., C. Parent, and C. Vangenot. GIS Databases: From Multiscale to MultiRepresentation. in Proc. 4th International Symposium on Abstraction, Reformulation, and Approximation (SARA-2000), LNCS 1864. p. 57-70. 2000. Texas, USA: Springer

[13]   Douglas, D.H. and T.K. Peucker, Algorithms for the reduction of the number of points required to represent a digitised line or its carcature. The Canadian Cartographer, 1973. 10(2): p. 112-122

[14]   van der Poorten, P.M. and C.B. Jones, Characterisation and generalisation of cartographic lines using Delaunay triangulation. International Journal of Geographical Information Science, 2002. 16(8): p. 773-794

[15]   Visvalingam, M. and J.D. Whyatt, Line generalisation by repeated elimination of points. Cartographic Journal, 1993. 30(1): p. 46-51

[16]   Robinson, A.H., et al., Elements of Cartography. 6th ed. 1995: Wiley

[17]   Li, M., S. Zhou, and C.B. Jones. Multi-Agent Systems for Web-Based Map Information Retrieval. in Proc. 2nd International Conference on Advances in Geographical Information Sciences (GIScience 2002), LNCS 2478. p. 161-180. 2002

Learning Similarity with Fuzzy Functions
of Adaptable Complexity

Giorgos Mountrakis and Peggy Agouris

Dept. of Spatial Information Science and Engineering
National Center for Geographic Information & Analysis, University of Maine
348 Boardman Hall, Orono, ME, USA 04469-5711
{giorgos,peggy}@spatial.maine.edu

Abstract. A common approach in database queries involves the multi-dimensional representation of objects by a set of features. These features are compared to the query representation and then combined together to produce a total similarity metric. In this paper we introduce a novel technique for similarity learning within features (attributes) by manipulating fuzzy membership functions (FMFs) of different complexity. Our approach is based on a gradual complexity increase adaptable to problem requirements. The underlying idea is that less adaptable functions will act as approximations for more complex ones. We begin by interpolating a set of planes in the training dataset and due to linearity we get a fast first impression of the underlying complexity. We proceed to interpolate two asymmetrical sigmoidal functions whose initial approximations are calculated from the plane properties. If satisfactory accuracy is not achieved we provide advanced modeling capabilities by investigating FMFs parameters and convolving their output with additional functions.

1   Introduction

In recent years there is a significant increase in geospatial information availability. New sensor technologies together with enhanced data capturing techniques have created extensive data collections. Users that access these collections have diversified needs based on their past experience and/or task at hand. In such complex environments a communication process should be established with the ability to encapsulate user similarity. Similarity parameters should not be predetermined but rather adaptive to different scenarios and requirements even for the same datasets and/or users.

Relational operations like equality or inequality have been used in the past, but in complex database applications with quantitative features a similarity matching approach is applied. Such examples include similarity search within multimedia databases containing images [1], stock extraction based on temporal similarity [15] and retrieval from CAD databases [4]. In order to perform the similarity match efficiently

T. Hadzilacos et al. (Eds.): SSTD 2003, LNCS 2750, pp. 412-429, 2003.
© Springer-Verlag Berlin Heidelberg 2003

an object O is represented by a set of features $O(F^1, F^2, ..., F^m)$ that describe its main characteristics. This way a multidimensional representation of the object's content is created. Each of these features may be represented by feature measures, so for feature i we might have k measures and represent it as $F^i = (f_{i1}, f_{i2}, ..., f_{ik})$. For example a GIS source might be described by two features, qualitative and quantitative attributes ($O_{GISsource}$ (Quantitative, Qualitative)). Each feature can have its own measures, for example Quantitative = (Timestamp, Scale,...).

A database object O is compared to a query description O^q by using matching functions to produce a similarity metric S as follows:

$$S = g\left[h_1\left(t_{11}(f_{11}, f_{11}^q), ..., t_{1k}(f_{1k}, f_{1k}^q) \right), ..., h_i\left(t_{i1}(f_{i1}, f_{i1}^q), ..., t_{ik}(f_{ik}, f_{ik}^q) \right) \right]$$ (1)

In the above equation t_{ik} expresses the similarity between each feature measure, h_i combines similarity results from each feature measure to provide a metric for each feature F^i and g is the overall similarity measure. Value f^q reflects the query value for a feature measure presented to the system. The goal is to define functions t_{ik}, h_i and g so they express user perception of similarity.

Our focus in this paper is function t_{ik}. It is often described by a Euclidean distance (difference). Functions h_i and g receive more attention and are sometimes modeled through complex non-linear functions. However, if function t_{ik} fails to describe the corresponding similarity relationships adequately, its errors propagate in the overall solution and cannot be recovered. This may be the case if function t_{ik} attempts to model asymmetric, non-linear behavior that involves the direct comparison of feature measures. For example, let us consider a geospatial database and a user request for an aerial image of specific ground pixel size for building extraction. User interest decreases gradually (but not necessarily linearly) as pixel size increases to the degree that buildings would not be identifiable. Furthermore the user may have cost considerations (e.g. cost, storage and processing time) associated to a higher resolution acquisition. This translates to a similarity relation that can also be non-linear as resolution improves. So it is easily understood that we need asymmetrical, non-linear relations to model similarity *within each feature measure comparison* (function t_{ik}). Note that this does not necessarily hold true in the combined metric of the feature level (function h_i) or combination of features (function g).

In this paper we present a learning algorithm that attempts to express similarity within dimensions. We concentrate on quantitative attributes that are ordered (e.g. not postal code). We make use of fuzzy membership functions to capture similarity. Fuzzy methods have been used in the past for similarity assessment. For a general review see [14] and for an application in spatial configuration similarity queries [13]. Our contribution is of dual nature, namely:

Support of asymmetrical, non-linear similarity learning within dimensions while the complexity of similarity functions is dynamically adaptable to problem requirements. We do so by gradually increasing the complexity of the underlying function, evaluate results, and if further advanced modeling is required we use the less complex functions as approximations for the next more complex ones. Furthermore, similarity dependence on input parameters is identified, thus accelerating the process. Also, user confidence and prioritization of parts of the input and the output (similarity) space are incorporated by manipulating the weight matrix accordingly.

Establishment of a theoretical framework for function combination through mathematical convolution. This is extremely useful in cases where either internal (by users) constraints are imposed (e.g. periodicity) or external (e.g. by system administrators/designers) restrictions are applied (e.g. real time information availability based on work load).

Our system's similarity results can be incorporated into algorithms that perform multi-dimensional similarity aggregation (e.g. quadratic function).

The rest of the paper is organized as follows. First we present background information on distance functions used previously. Section 3 introduces our approach and the two general similarity functions used, the piecewise linear and the sigmoidal one. The similarity dependence on the input values is also investigated. For cases where sufficient accuracy is not met we developed advanced fuzzy functions as described in section 4. Parameters that were previously constant are now adaptable through the training process. Also the theoretical framework for similarity function convolution is discussed. GIS information retrieval examples showing the functionality of our approach are presented in the next section. Finally we summarize our contributions in the last section (Section 6).

2   Related Work

Our algorithm falls in the general category of lazy learning methods otherwise known as nearest neighbor techniques [6]. Similarity learning is performed by storing examples as points in the feature space and using a distance metric to measure correlation to these points [2]. Usually a Minkowskian p-distance [3] is used to define the similarity measure and is defined as:

$$L_p(\overline{x}, \overline{y}) = \left(\sum_{i=1}^{n} |x_i - y_i|^p \right)^{1/p} \tag{2}$$

In the case that p=2 we have the traditional Euclidean distance metric. If p=1 then the Minkowskian distance expresses the Manhattan distance function. There is also the Quadratic distance that is a weighted form of the multi-dimensional Euclidean. Other functions used are the Mahalanobis [12], Camberra, Chebychen and others. A good overview and corresponding mathematical expressions can be found in [18].

The above functions provide a simple model that allows efficient indexing by dimensionality reduction techniques [7,19]. On the other hand though the simplicity of these functions does not support high adaptability to complex queries. Researchers have come to realize these limitations and have addressed them by a variety of non-linear, complex algorithms. Some of them involve for example neural networks with applications in content-based [9], information [10], and image [5] retrieval. Fuzzy sets have been used in visual retrieval systems [16] and fuzzy integrals approximate similarity in genetic algorithms [8]. Neuro-fuzzy approaches include supervised learning of agent profiles using if-then rules in remote sensing applications [11].

The operation of the above methodologies is concentrated on multi-dimensional similarity aggregation to provide an overall similarity metric. In some cases though the complexity of the problem relies on the similarity calculation within each dimension separately rather than on their combined aggregation. This is frequently the case when querying for GIS datasets. The data mining process might fail because the individual similarity metrics in every dimension were not able to capture user similarity preferences. So the need for more complex similarity functions within dimensions is evident, but what is really the computational cost associated with such an approach? Usually these database collections do not exhibit high dimensionality (e.g. 5-20 dimensions are typically used to index geospatial databases). This leads us to the conclusion that a more computationally intensive algorithm is feasible for improved accuracy. As we will show later, similarity is expressed through continuous functions of not very high complexity order leading to fast computations.

3   Fuzzy Similarity Functions

In this section we present the two function classes we use, the piecewise planar and sigmoidal ones. We discuss how the resulting planes of the piecewise solution can provide approximations for the non-linear sigmoidal functions. We also investigate similarity dependence on inputs by examining plane parameters.

3.1   Approach Overview

In order to adapt similarity to user preferences we developed a relevance feedback algorithm. Users are presented with a variety of pairs of requested and returned values and are asked to provide a similarity metric for each pair. They can also provide a similarity confidence level for the similarity response and prioritize parts of the input and output space. The corresponding training dataset is created and used as input for our similarity learning method.

For our training we make use of several similarity models as expressed through a variety of fuzzy membership functions (FMFs). Our approach is simple yet effective: gradually increase the complexity of the underlying function until an acceptable solution is reached. We begin the process by interpolating a set of planes to the training dataset (fig. 1). We examine the resulting accuracy and if it is within the predefined specifications we end the process. If not, we examine the obtained plane parameters. This analysis leads to a decision whether similarity is dependent on the query value, their difference metric or the actual database and query values. Building on that we interpolate two asymmetrical sigmoidal functions whose initial approximations are calculated from the plane properties. If required accuracy is not achieved we provide further modeling capabilities by parameterizing the FMFs parameters. At the last stage we obtain the best possible set of FMFs expressing user similarity as presented through the training set.

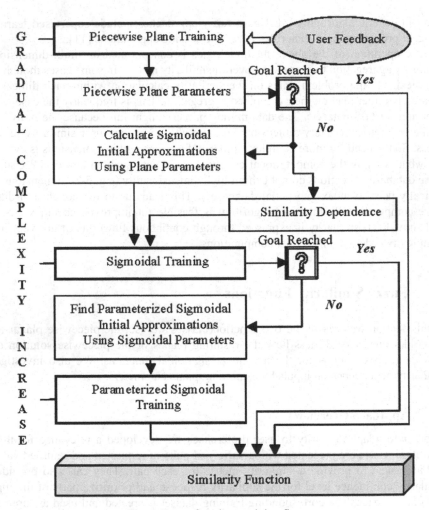

Fig. 1. Fuzzy functions training flow

3.2 Piecewise Planar Similarity Function

Mathematical Formulation. Our simplest set of functions is composed by two piecewise planar solutions to support asymmetrical cases. Let function $\text{Sim}_{\text{Planar}}$ (•) represent an FMF mapping of the two-dimensional input space to the one-dimensional similarity space:

$$\text{Sim}_{\text{Planar}}: \Re^2 \rightarrow \Re^1 \tag{3}$$

The function inputs are query and database values $[X_Q, X_{DB}]$ where $X_Q \in \mathbf{X_Q}$, $X_{DB} \in \mathbf{X_{DB}}$. Depending on which half plane the input parameters rely on ($X_Q > X_{DB}$ or $X_Q \leq X_{DB}$), two separate training datasets are created. Each half plane solution is independent from the other. The similarity function **Sim**$_{\text{Planar}}$ (•) expressing the relation between a database value X_{DB} compared to a query value X_Q is:

$$Sim_{Planar}(X_Q, X_{DB}) = \begin{cases} a_1^R(i)X_Q + a_2^R(i)X_{DB} + a_3^R(i) & if\ X_Q \le X_{DB} \\ a_1^L(i)X_Q + a_2^L(i)X_{DB} + a_3^L(i) & if\ X_Q > X_{DB} \end{cases} \quad (4)$$

Parameters a_1, a_2 and a_3 define the planes used for the corresponding half (left and right). Index i specifies the current plane under examination for each half. Our solution is composed by a collection of planes. Specifically, five planes are used to model similarity in each half plane (i.e. i = [1,2,3,4,5]). Each plane expresses similarity within certain range, for example plane #5 represents similarity for $X_Q > X_{DB}$ where **Sim**$_{\text{Planar}}$ ∈ [1-tb, 1]. An example of the plane configuration for the left half is shown in figure 2. Axes X and Y correspond to the inputs of our process, namely X_Q and X_{DB}. The Z axis represents the similarity output and is calculated based on the plane similarity function. A 2D section of the 3D function is presented in figure 3. This section shows the similarity function for a specific query value X_Q (the white line of figure 2). Such sections of the planes are used after the system is trained to calculate similarity of candidate database values to a specific user query.

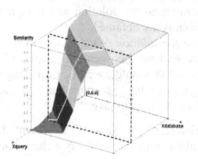
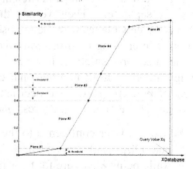

Fig. 2. Piecewise planar similarity function   **Fig. 3.** 2D section for specific query request

Within our process we use exactly five planes in each half for two reasons:

1. *To address ranges where similarity function is almost parallel to the X_QX_{DB} plane.* The *tb* threshold expresses a similarity range of values close to 1 and 0 that will be mapped on planes #5 and #1 respectively. The use of *tb* allows the exclusion of non-active [X_Q, X_{DB}] pairs in terms of similarity gradient. Slight variations that might exist in similarity values close to 0 or 1 could lead the terms a_1 and a_2 to become very small with an unstable solution. In essence we use this threshold as a backup for cases where we might not obtain a solution so we assign a direct value. Furthermore, we want to be able to handle cases where expected similarity might follow a linear behavior but be active only in portion of the [X_Q, X_{DB}] space. The *tb* value defines the starting and ending point of planes #2 and #4 respectively (fig. 3).

2. *To provide approximations for more complex functions that follow.* The *m* threshold defines the range above and below the 0.5 similarity value that is used to define the similarity modeling range of plane #3. The role of this threshold will be explained in the sigmoidal function family, where it is used as a parameter approximation. Planes #2 and #4 are used to model similarity in-between planes #1, #3 and #5, bringing the total number of planes to five.

Mathematical Solution. The solution of this system can be found by using least squares. Our planes have some specific properties that we would like to propagate in the solution. These properties result from enforcing continuity between successive planes so there would be no similarity discontinuities. The continuity requirement provides the following constraints for each half of the solution:

1. The footprints of each plane on the $X_Q X_{DB}$ plane should be parallel to each other. In other words the slope should be the same, which is expressed as a constant ratio between parameters $a_1(i)$, $a_2(i)$.
2. Successive planes should intersect at the specific similarity value as defined by thresholds *tb* and *m*. This is enforced mathematically by having the two successive planes and a third plane with [Sim_{Planar}= constant] intersect at a common line.

In order to make our system efficient first we perform a fast linear interpolation for each plane separately. Then we add the constraints to the solution and after a few iterations the new planes with the imposed continuity are obtained.

Another interesting modification involves the *formulation of the weight matrix* **W** in the least squares solution. If we assume independency between the samples of the training dataset then all non-diagonal elements of **W** would be zero. Each diagonal element of **W** corresponds to a specific training sample that is presented as a [X_Q, X_{DB}, Sim] point. This element can express one or more of the following:

- $W_{confidence}$: User confidence to the specified response [Sim] of the presented inputs [X_Q, X_{DB}]. For example, users might return a similarity value of 40% while being 80% sure for their response.
- W_{input}: Users/database designers desire the capability to prioritize the training set based on how important a part of the input space is. In essence, based on the [X_Q, X_{DB}] value a metric is assigned showing the influence/significance of that section of the input space to the overall solution. For example, if users are requesting satellite imagery they might want the system to adapt more accurately to years close to 2000 than 1985 due to information availability.
- W_{output}: Users/database designers might also want to guide the solution to be more accurate in specific parts of the output (similarity) space. This weight metric is solely dependent on the output value provided. For example a better fitting might be desired to higher similarity values (e.g. >70%) rather than lower ones (e.g. <30%).

The overall effect of the three cases is expressed in the calculation of matrix **W** as:

$$\mathbf{W} = \mathbf{W}_{confidence} * \mathbf{W}_{input} * \mathbf{W}_{output} \tag{5}$$

If any of the three intermediate weight matrices is not a factor then it can be substituted by the identity matrix. If none of them is specified, **W** will be omitted from the least squares solution.

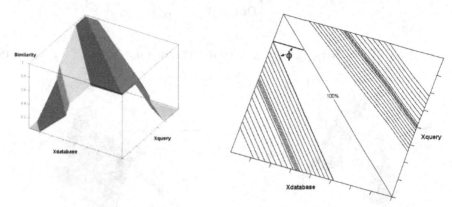

Fig. 5. Asymmetric planar similarity function   **Fig. 6.** Planar function contour plot

3.3   Similarity Dependence on Input Values

After the plane parameters are calculated we compute the average rotation angle (φ_P) over the Z (similarity) axis. For each plane it is given by:

$$\varphi_P = \arctan(\frac{-a_1(i)}{a_2(i)}) \tag{6}$$

Angle φ_P should be the same for all planes in every half because we enforced the condition of having parallel footprints on the $X_Q X_{DB}$ plane. In figure 5 we show a piecewise planar similarity function. A contour plot representing similarity isolines is presented in figure 6. The calculating angle φ_P is the angle between the footprints (or the isolines since they are parallel) and the $X_{database}$ axis.

Our interest in this angle comes from the fact that based on its value similarity dependency on the input values can be extracted. Two special cases are identified and presented hereafter.

Angle $\varphi_P \approx 45^o$

In some cases the calculated angle might be close to the 45 degrees (fig. 7). This translates in the plane equation as $a_1(i) \approx -a_2(i)$. By substituting that to the plane equation we have for each half plane:

$$Sim_{Planar}(X_Q, X_{DB}) = \begin{cases} a_1(i)X_Q + a_2(i)X_{DB} + a_3(i) \\ \\ a_1(i) \approx -a_2(i) \end{cases} \Rightarrow \tag{7}$$

$$Sim_{Planar}(X_Q, X_{DB}) = \begin{cases} a_1(i)X_Q - a_1(i)X_{DB} + a_3(i) \\ \\ Dist = (X_Q - X_{DB}) \end{cases} \Rightarrow \qquad (8)$$

$$Sim_{Planar}(X_Q, X_{DB}) = a_1(i) * Dist + a_3(i) \qquad (9)$$

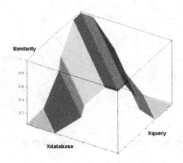

Fig. 7. Rotation angle $\varphi_P \approx 45^o$ **Fig. 8.** Rotation angle $\varphi_P \approx 90^o$

So we come to the conclusion that similarity is not dependent on the actual values of $[X_Q, X_{DB}]$ but only on their Euclidean distance $[Dist = X_Q - X_{DB}]$. Equation 9 shows that the planes can be replaced by lines providing a significant computational gain since a three-dimensional problem is downsized to a two-dimensional one.

Angle $\varphi_P \approx 90^o$

For the case that angle φ_P approaches the 90 degrees mark (fig. 8) the calculation formula of the angle provides $a_1(i) \ll a_2(i)$. With proper substitution in the plane equation we have:

$$Sim_{Planar}(X_Q, X_{DB}) = \begin{cases} a_1(i)X_Q + a_2(i)X_{DB} + a_3(i) \\ \\ a_1(i) \ll a_2(i) \end{cases} \Rightarrow \qquad (10)$$

$$Sim_{Planar}(X_Q, X_{DB}) \approx a_2(i)X_{DB} + a_3(i) \qquad (11)$$

This translates into similarity dependence only on the X_{DB} value. So our system has the ability to recognize that user preference is not dependent on the actual request. But they still have a preference to the returned dataset which is expressed by equation 11.

An example of this nature might involve cases where different users access the same dataset and only their combined knowledge of the problem could express similarity in a comprehensive manner. Each user based on his/her expertise might provide part of the solution without necessarily being able to identify neither the overall similarity trend nor the "ideal" dataset that they might want. This might be the case in a remote-sensing application. Different experts might examine several images of different wavelengths. They would all be looking be a specific temporal instance of the phenomenon under investigation (e.g. iceberg separation). The problem would be that none of them knows the exact time and they all express their preference based on their expertise on the training datasets.

Our system design will overcome this problem based on a combined training dataset from a variety of users. If all users are looking for the same dataset the plane angle has a high possibility of being close to 90°. In this case their similarity behavior should be expressed by a 3D surface similar to the one of figure 8. Since their preference revolves around a specific query value and only that, a 2D line can replace the 3D planes, which is consistent with the formulation of equation 11.

3.4   Sigmoidal Similarity Function

Mathematical Formulation. After the plane interpolation is performed, an accuracy assessment through a fitting error is done. If the results are not as desired a more complex function is necessary. To capture *non-linear* similarity relations between a query and a stored metric attribute we use a modified sigmoidal fuzzy relationship function. Sigmoidal functions are popular in the neural network community and have been used in the GIS field as predefined similarity functions for spatiotemporal trajectory matching [17]. Our similarity function is composed by two separate sigmoidal functions to compensate for asymmetrical cases. The similarity function Sim(•) for a database value X_{DB} compared to a query value X_Q is:

$$Sim_{Sigmoidal}(X_Q, X_{DB}) = \begin{cases} \dfrac{1}{1+e^{-a_R(X_R)}} & \text{if } X_Q \leq X_{DB} \\[4pt] X_R = (X_Q - X_{DB} - c_R)\cos\varphi_R + (X_Q + X_{DB} + c_R)\sin\varphi_R \\[8pt] \dfrac{1}{1+e^{-a_L(X_L)}} & \text{if } X_Q > X_{DB} \\[4pt] X_L = (X_Q - X_{DB} - c_L)\cos\varphi_L + (X_Q + X_{DB} + c_L)\sin\varphi_L \end{cases} \quad (12)$$

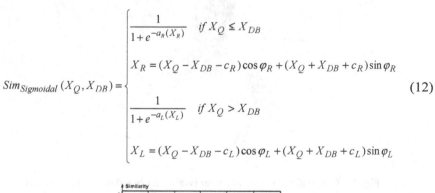

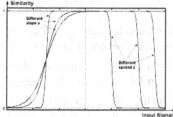

Fig. 9. Slope and spread influence on sigmoidal's shape

The parameters c_R and c_L specify the translation along the database axis. The slope of each sigmoidal function is expressed through a_R and a_L respectively. An important characteristic of the sigmoidal function is the large range of modeling capabilities. Efficient manipulation of the slope can result in representing a variety of cases, ranging from a linear up to a step-like behavior (fig. 9). This diversified capability together with the large operational range on the input space and the mathematical continuity of the function (first derivative exists everywhere) establishes the sigmoidal as appropriate solution from a variety of available fuzzy membership functions.

Initial Approximations and Parameter Calculation. In a non-linear solution such as this there is always the problem of initial approximations. This is where the fast plane interpolation becomes multipurpose. We use the angle φ as calculated before for the initial value of the rotation angle of the sigmoidal (for computational consistency $\varphi = \varphi_P - 45^o$). Also from the mathematical properties of our sigmoidal we know that spread c corresponds to the value where the sigmoidal similarity function will return 0.5 as output (fig. 10).

That is the main reason we introduced plane #3 earlier and the threshold m. We want m to be as small as possible but at the same time include enough samples to have an accurate result. So using the properties of plane #3 we calculate:

$$c = \frac{-(0.5 - a_3)}{a_2} \tag{13}$$

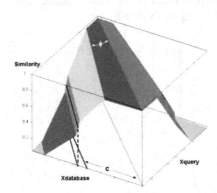

Fig. 10. Calculating sigmoidal initial parameters based on planar solution

The slope parameter cannot be calculated accurately directly from the planes. So in order to get an initial value we use the temporary values for φ and c, and an equal (in number) random subset of the training data for each of the five planes. A least square solution gives an approximation for a with φ and c being fixed.

After all three temporary values are calculated a final refinement takes place with the whole training set. In order to calculate the sigmoidal parameters a least squares solution is implemented through an iterative process. We use the A*δX=L formula where A is the matrix containing the partial derivatives with respect to the unknowns, δX contains the unknowns and L is the observation matrix. The solution is given by $\delta X = (A^T W A)^{-1} A^T W L$. W is the weight matrix as defined previously.

4   Advanced Fuzzy Similarity Functions

When the underlying complexity of the problem is high the already presented similarity functions might not be able to adequately model it. For these cases we present a more adaptable set of functions with higher modeling capabilities. We do so by introducing functions with higher input dependency. Later in this section we also present the theoretical framework for similarity function convolution. Even though this is not part of our training process its significant applicability is noticeable.

4.1   Parameter Substitution by Input-Dependent Functions

In more complex behavior function parameters might not be independent of the query and/or database value. For example spread parameter c of a sigmoidal FMF may depend on the query value X_Q so c will not be constant throughout the input space (e.g. $c = c_0 + t X_Q^2$, c_0 and t are constants). Such a case might exist when users are more tolerant (in a non-linear fashion) towards query deviations as the query value increases. A detailed example is presented in section 5.1.

Mathematically this is expressed as follows: Let function $F(\bullet)$ represent an FMF mapping of the two-dimensional input space to the one-dimensional similarity space:

$$F: \Re^2 \to \Re^1 \tag{14}$$

The function inputs are query and database values $[X_Q, X_{DB}]$ where $X_Q \in \mathbf{X_Q}$, $X_{DB} \in \mathbf{X_{DB}}$. Let $\mathbf{P}$ be the set of the n parameters that formulate this function:

$$\mathbf{P} = [p_1, p_2, ..., p_n] \tag{15}$$

In this case function $F(\bullet)$ can be expressed as:

$$F(X_Q, X_{DB}| \mathbf{P}) \tag{16}$$

Now if we assume that each parameter p_i is not constant but is expressed by function $\mathbf{P_i}(\bullet)$ and is dependent on values $[X_Q, X_{DB}]$. Also function $\mathbf{P_i}(\bullet)$ with i = [1,2,..., n] has its own set of parameters K_i. This leads to the general expression of function $F(\bullet)$ which is :

$$F(X_Q, X_{DB}| [\mathbf{P_1}(X_Q, X_{DB}| K_1), \mathbf{P_2}(X_Q, X_{DB}| K_2), ..., \mathbf{P_n}(X_Q, X_{DB}| K_n)]) \tag{17}$$

For example let's examine the sigmoidal function of equation 12. Similarity function $F(\bullet)$ will be represented as:

$$F(X_Q, X_{DB}| a, c, \varphi) = \frac{1}{1 + e^{-a((X_Q - X_{DB} - c)\cos\varphi + (X_Q + X_{DB} + c)\sin\varphi)}} \tag{18}$$

The number of parameters is three, namely a, c, and φ (n=3). Let $\mathbf{P} = [p_1, p_2, p_3]$ be the corresponding functions of these three parameters. For simplicity let's assume that $[p_1, p_3]$ are constants and only p_2 is substituted by function $\mathbf{P_2} (X_Q, X_{DB}| K_2)$. An example of such function could be:

$$P_2 (X_Q, X_{DB}| c_o, c_1, c_2) = c_o + c_1 X_Q^2 + c_2 X_{DB} \qquad (19)$$

In this case we would have $K_2 = [c_o, c_1, c_2]$. So instead of trying to solve for parameters $[a, c, \varphi]$ our new more complex system would have higher modeling capabilities and would be expressed by a new set of parameters $[a, c_o, c_1, c_2, \varphi]$. The new set of parameters would be approximated initially by the solution obtained in the previous less complex solution, which in this example would happen if we set as initial approximations $[a^{new}, c_o^{new}, c_1^{new}, c_2^{new}, \varphi^{new}] = [a^{old}, c^{old}, 0, 0, \varphi^{old}]$.

4.2   Convoluting Function Output

We further enhance the operational range of our FMFs by introducing another important theorem. This time we do not alternate the properties of a function. Instead we combine more than one function to compose the underlying similarity signal. Such cases facilitate more complex user preferences that a single function could not express. An example would be periodicity combined with gradual decreasing interest (example 5.2). Combination of functions has another potential application that does not necessarily coincide with user perception of similarity. It rather expresses database system requirements and/or constrains that might exist. They can be static or adjust in real time depending on system sources. They can also vary depending on user position in the hierarchy (e.g. restricted access systems).

We allow the combination of functions by convolving their signals in the input space. Let function $\mathbf{F}(\bullet)$ represent an FMF mapping and function $\mathbf{G}(\bullet)$ be for instance an administrative constrain. We have:

$$\mathbf{F}: \Re^2 \rightarrow \Re^1, \; \mathbf{G}: \Re^2 \rightarrow \Re^1 \qquad (20)$$

Inputs for these functions are query and database values $[X_Q, X_{DB}]$ where $X_Q \in \mathbf{X_Q}$, $X_{DB} \in \mathbf{X_{DB}}$. We define the convolution of functions $\mathbf{F}(\bullet)$, $\mathbf{G}(\bullet)$ as their multiplication throughout the input space $\Re^2$. If function $\mathbf{H}(\bullet)$ is the resulting new function it can be represented as:

$$\mathbf{H} (X_Q, X_{DB}) = \mathbf{F} (X_Q, X_{DB}) * \mathbf{G} (X_Q, X_{DB}) \qquad (21)$$

This new mapping function would also project the two-dimensional input space into the one-dimensional similarity space:

$$\mathbf{H}: \Re^2 \rightarrow \Re^1 \qquad (22)$$

Here we should note that we do not support training of function $\mathbf{G}(\bullet)$ and/or retrain function $\mathbf{F}(\bullet)$. Such a task would be extremely difficult due to the higher amount of parameters and the correlations in-between them. At this point we present the theoretical framework behind it and we investigate possible applications of it. Such training is reserved for future work.

5   Functionality Examples of Our Model

In the following sections we introduce a series of examples using our method. Increasingly challenging similarity tasks are presented showing our model adaptability. Our applications are inspired by common but complex user preferences within geospatial environments. We begin with similarity learning in the scale dimension, continue in the temporal one and conclude with a connection speed example.

5.1   Scale Similarity

Let's consider users who are querying a GIS database and specifically request imagery of a particular scale (pixel ground size) that will be used for airport traffic monitoring. Their interest decreases gradually (but not necessarily linearly) as scale decreases to the degree that planes would not be identifiable. This expectation holds true for $X_Q <$ X_{DB}. Such a case is presented in the right half of figures 11 and 12.

After training, the resulting function in the right half is a sigmoidal one with a variable slope a. The variable slope is able to express user alterable tolerance based on their asking pixel size. The larger the requested pixel size the more flexible they are about additional pixel size. That does not happen in a linear fashion so a gradual decrease of a (slope) can model that.

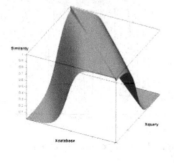
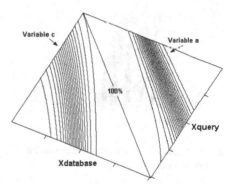

Fig. 11. Sigmoidal fuzzy similarity function   **Fig. 12.** Sigmoidal similarity isolines

Furthermore the user may have a cost function in mind associated with a better than requested resolution (e.g. price, storage, and processing time). This translates to a similarity relation that can also be non-linear as pixel size improves ($X_Q > X_{DB}$). The rate of similarity decrease does not change so slope remains the same (i.e. the isoline distance). But depending on the query pixel size the user expresses the associated cost by allowing a larger range of 100% similarity as query value increases. In other words, if they ask for 50m resolution they will consider that a 40m resolution does not add any additional cost so they assign similarity to be 100%. But if they ask for a much finer resolution this tolerance range will be much smaller due to for example higher price or manipulation cost.

5.2   Temporal Similarity

Another typical request involves the temporal footprint of a GIS source. One task might require the investigation of periodical phenomena. Such scenarios can incorporate dual preference. For example the main focus might be a specific year, but years close by would be acceptable too. This can be expressed by a sigmoidal function for each half (fig. 13 dotted line). Another preference could result from the specifics of the problem which might require information only during specific months (seasons). A sinusoidal function is used to model such preference (fig. 13 solid line).

Users would like though to combine both of these two requirements in the overall similarity computation. In order to do so we convolve the sigmoidals with the sinusoidal function which results in the similarity surface of figure 13. A specific example is shown in figure 14. A user wants to study a disease associated with the leaves of deciduous trees that appeared in 2000. The two asymmetrical sigmoidal functions express his/her preference to datasets before and after 2000, respectively. Note the different similarity gradient that shows datasets of earlier dates would be more suitable than datasets of later dates. Also this query requires datasets only through the summer months since in the winter time the trees lose their leaves. This is expressed through the sinusoidal function with a periodicity of a year. The combined result of the sigmoidal and sinusoidal functions shows user preferences for this task.

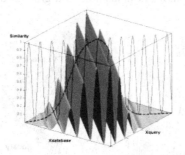

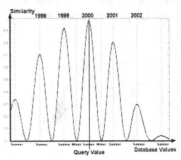

Fig. 13. Sigmoidal with sinusoidal similarity functions convolution

Fig. 14. Time periodicity example

5.3   Server Connection Similarity

In this example we examine the application of constraints to user similarity functions. These constraints can be imposed by the database administrator or by system design, and can be fixed or adaptable to real-time monitoring of the database system.

To accommodate the vast volume of GIS datasets, data warehouses might be created leading to dataset availability through a variety of servers. Depending on their connection speed users might query for servers of analogous speed. Due to high demand all fast servers at some point might be overloaded. Then the system administrator might exclude these servers from the candidate ones being afraid that this might result into denial of service. So he/she creates a function such as the sigmoidal of figure 15 with solid black line. Then the user similarity preference (dotted line) will be convolved with the system constrain and would provide a new similarity surface, the one of figure 15. In figure 16 a contour plot shows the exact effect of the filtering function that was imposed. Servers with connection much faster than 10Mbit would not be accessed even though they would have been under normal circumstances.

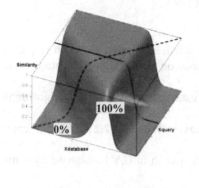

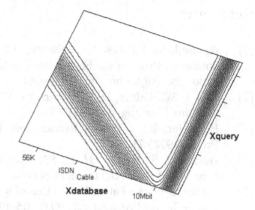

Fig. 15. Sigmoidal with sigmoidal similarity functions convolution

Fig. 16. Connection speed example with similarity isolines

6   Conclusion

In this paper we have proposed a novel method for similarity learning within dimensions. Our approach is based on a gradual complexity increase based on problem requirements. We use a variety of fuzzy membership functions to model the similarity signal. Back-propagation is used to train the fuzzy similarity functions. Initially, planes are interpolated and an analysis of the similarity dependence on the input space is performed. Based on the plane angle the system identifies cases where similarity is independent of the query value or dependent only on the distance metric between query and database values. This way the process is simplified and a significant computational gain is achieved. Also formulation of the weight matrix can enforce more accurate fitting in specific areas of the input space or specific similarity outputs, as well as support incorporation of user confidence in the provided response.

Our gradual complexity increase is expressed through different sets of functions. Their specific design allows the use of properties from less complex functions as approximations for the following more complex ones. By doing so a high convergence rate is achieved in the least squares solution. In the advanced functions we enhance complexity by adding non-constant behavior to the function parameters. We also presented a theoretical framework for similarity function combination through mathematical convolution. Incorporation of the convoluted functions in the gradual training flow is a future challenge. However, overall function adjustability as expressed through GIS query examples is indicative of superior modeling capabilities.

Acknowledgments

This work is supported by the National Science Foundation through grants DG-9983445 and ITR-0121269.

References

[1]   Agrawal, R., Faloutsos, C., Swami, A.: Efficient similarity search in sequence databases. Proc. of the Fourth Intl Conference on Foundations of Data Organization and Algorithms. (1993) 69-84

[2]   Aha, D.W., Kibler, D. F., Albert, M. K.: Instance-Based Learning Algorithms. Machine Learning. 6 (1991) 37-66

[3]   Batchelor, B.G.: Pattern Recognition: Ideas in Practice. New York: Plenum Press. (1978) 71- 72

[4]   Berchtold, S., Kriegel, H.-P.: S3: Similarity Search in CAD Database Systems. Proc. ACM SIGMOD Conf. (1997) 564-567

[5]   Carkacioglu, A., Fatos, Y.-V.: Learning Similarity Space. Proc. of Intl Conference in Image Processing. (2002) 405-408

[6]   Cover, T. M., Hart, P. E.: Nearest neighbor Pattern Classification. Institute of Electrical and Electronics Engineers Trans. on Information Theory. 13 (1) (1967) 21-27

[7]   Gionis, A., Indyk, P., Motwani, R.: Similarity search in high dimensions via hashing. Proc. of the 25th Intl. Conf. on Very Large Data Bases (VLDB). (1999) 518–529

[8]   Ishii, N., Wang, Y.: Learning Feature Weights for Similarity Measures using Genetic Algorithms. Proc. of IEEE Intl Joint Symp. on Intelligence and Systems. (1998) 27-33

[9]   Lim, J.-H., Wu, J.-K., Singh, S., Narasimhalu, A. D.: Learning Similarity Matching in Multimedia Content-Based Retrieval. IEEE Transactions on Knowledge and Data Engineering. 13 (5) (2001) 846-850

[10] Mandl, T.: Tolerant Information Retrieval with Backpropagation Networks. Neural Computing & Applications. 9 (4) (2000) 280-289

[11] Mitaim, S., Kosko, B.: Neural Fuzzy Agents that Learn a User's Preference Map. Proc. of 4th International Forum on Research and Technology Advances in Digital Libraries (1997) 25-35

[12] Nadler, M., Smith, E. P.: Pattern Recognition Engineering. New York: Wiley (1993)

[13] Papadias, D., Karacapilidis, N., Arkoumanis, N.: Processing Fuzzy Spatial Queries: A Configuration Similarity Approach. International Journal of Geographic Information Science (IJGIS). 13 (2) (1999) 93-128

[14] Pappis, C.P., Karacapilidis, N.I.: A comparative assessment of measures of similarity of fuzzy values. Fuzzy Sets and Systems. 56 (21) (1993) 171-174

[15] Rafiei, D., Mendelzon, O.: Similarity-Based Queries for Time Series Data. Proc. ACM SIGMOD Conf. (1997) 13-25

[16] Santini, S., Jain, R.: Similarity Measures. IEEE Transactions on Pattern Analysis and Machine Intelligence. 21 (9) (1999) 871-883

[17] Vlachos, M., Gunopulos, D., Kollios, G.: Robust Similarity Measures for Mobile Object Trajectories. Proc. of DEXA Workshops. (2002) 721-728

[18] Wilson, D. R., Martinez, T. R.: An Integrated Instance-Based Learning Algorithm. Computational Intelligence. 16 (1) (2000) 1-28

[19] Yi, B.-K., Faloutsos, C.: Fast Time Sequence Indexing for Arbitrary Lp Norms. Proc. of the 26th Intl. Conf. on Very Large Data Bases (VLDB). (2000) 385-394

Spatial Similarity Queries with Logical Operators

Konstantinos A. Nedas and Max J. Egenhofer

National Center for Geographic Information and Analysis
Department of Spatial Information Science and Engineering
University of Maine, Orono, ME 04469-5711, USA
{kostas,max}@spatial.maine.edu

Abstract. Traditional spatial querying assumes that a user specifies exactly the constraints of valid results, and that the result set contains only those items that fulfill exactly the query constraints. The nature of spatial data, however, makes it difficult for a user to always guess correctly the values stored, while exhaustive enumerations of acceptable alternatives to the ideal target would become a tedious process. Likewise, values that deviate somewhat from the query constraints should be part of a ranked result set as well. This paper develops methods for the retrieval of similar spatial information, in particular when several similarity constraints with logical combinations must be compared and integrated. The first set of methods is concerned with spatial similarity reasoning over null values by denoting the semantics of different types of null values with explicit identifiers that imply different degrees of uncertainty. The second set of methods contributes to a consistent and comprehensive methodology for spatial similarity retrieval in response to complex queries with combinations of logical operators. We provide an exhaustive list of spatial query scenarios with conjunctions, disjunctions, and negation and present justified solutions for each case. Since these computational methods are founded on fundamental psychological knowledge about similarity reasoning, they are particularly well suited for generating similarity results that match with users' intuitions.

1   Introduction

Today's spatial database systems are built on exact matches for spatial information retrieval. Geographic information systems (GISs) and multimedia databases, however, require a different paradigm for spatial information retrieval, emphasizing similarity over equality, mainly for three reasons:

- The data provider-data user gap is wide due to the differences between the stored spatial data and the user's knowledge of these spatial data while querying. People may know only approximately what they are looking for, so that they need to adopt an exploratory way of accessing spatial data. For

T. Hadzilacos et al. (Eds.): SSTD 2003, LNCS 2750, pp. 430–448, 2003.

instance, when querying an archive of satellite imagery based on such properties as color or texture, an exact match is rarely expected.

- The *spatial-intuition gulf* between people who request spatial information and the models in spatial information systems becomes more apparent as spatial information systems are growing beyond the state of being tools of experts, as a wider and more diversified audience uses them on a daily basis. It is inconceivable that GIS users share a common context and views about reality. The lack of standard, cognitively-plausible formalizations of spatial properties of geographic phenomena makes it even harder to support comprehensive, yet flexible methods for spatial information retrieval.
- The *verbal-visual competition* of requesting spatial information verbally while presenting spatial query results graphically puts an undue cognitive load on users. Thinking spatially is supported only in a very limited way at the query-formulation stage, but alternative visual query modalities, such as sketching, often come closer to a user's mental model of a spatial query than a verbal expression. By their very nature, however, such visual requests for spatial information retrieval are imprecise.

This diversity of background and expertise, combined with ill-defined spatial standards, explains why users' spatial queries often fail to coincide with any stored data.

A successful similarity model for GISs would help eliminate the restrictions imposed by exact matches, thereby providing satisfactory reasoning mechanisms for semantically similar results. Satisfactory results imply a match of methods for spatial similarity retrieval with human perception and cognition. The major obstacle to this goal is the elusiveness and complexity of similarity, which is difficult to describe by formal logical theories or represent with mathematical models; therefore, the focus should be on providing reliable similarity measures that are consistent with people's intuition, rather than conveniently conforming with theories that may have appealing mathematical properties, but contradict human similarity reasoning. This is the main view advocated in this paper. Our approach builds on important findings from psychology, where human similarity has been extensively investigated for decades.

Determining similarity in GISs usually leads to a dichotomy of similarity measures due to the character of spatial entity instances. Objects that represent those instances in a GIS are usually presented as a 3-tuple {thematic attributes, geometric attributes, ID} [1]. Geometric attributes are associated with an object's topology and metric details, whereas thematic attributes capture spatial but non-geometric information. For example, an island as a spatial object may have a name and a population as its thematic attributes, while a shape description provides the value for its geometric attribute. Because of this duality, methods that assess similarity among spatial objects can be divided to separate procedures for geometric similarity assessment and thematic similarity assessment. The overall spatial similarity of two spatial objects is a combination of their geometric and thematic similarity values. Spatial information systems that address objects explicitly have a third dimension of similarity that corresponds to the classes to which the entities belong [2]. Therefore, a formal model for similarity in spatial information systems needs to distinguish three levels of similarity: (1) semantic similarity among entity classes, (2) geometric similarity among entity instances, and (3) thematic similarity among entity instances.

Information systems that record spatial properties explicitly store information about shape and spatial relations as qualitative values. In such a setting, spatial similarity information that is typically derived from the geometric representations is determined much like thematic similarity. For example, rather than storing the geometry of Greek islands and their settlements in the form of a topological data model, spatial relations among islands and between islands and settlements are captured explicitly (e.g., <Crete, disjoint, Thira>, <Thira, disjoint, Karpathos>, <Iraklio, inside Crete>, <Oia, inside, Thira>). Thematic information of such spatial entities is then available within the same framework (e.g., <Crete, populationPerSquareKilometer, 64>, <Thira, populationPerSquareKilometer, 92>) so that a single approach for assessing spatial similarity suffices. The scope of this paper is such an integrated view of spatial similarity.

This paper addresses spatial similarity assessment for queries with multiple constraints. In such scenarios, a query processor must integrate similarity values over Boolean operations, including spatial similarity assessments that involve null values. We develop a set of methods that aim at providing a consistent and comprehensive methodology for spatial similarity retrieval in response to complex queries formed by combinations of logical or relational operators. Logical operators combine separate spatial constraints using such logical connectives as *and*, *or*, and *not*, whereas relational operators refer to such predicates as *greater than* or *less than*. In support of such queries, we also develop a set of methods for spatial similarity reasoning over null values by denoting the semantics of different types of unavailable values with explicit identifiers that imply different degrees of uncertainty. The paper investigates spatial similarity from a conceptual rather than implementation point of view. Issues pertaining to efficiency or optimization of the algorithms as well as to details of lower-level access to the database are beyond the scope of this work.

The remainder of the paper is organized as follows: section 2 provides background information on similarity measures, null values, and complex similarity queries. Section 3 argues for the need of different similarity methods depending on the attributes' types, such as nominal, ordinal, interval, ratio, and cyclic. Problems that arise when null values are part of similarity assessment are addressed in section 4, where we develop a model for null-value similarity. Cognitively plausible methods for similarity assessments with relational and logical operators are addressed in sections 5 and 6, respectively. Conclusions and future work are discussed in section 7.

2   Related Work

2.1   Similarity Measures

Similarity and difference are tightly related concepts [3]. Definitions of *difference* usually coincides with the distance between the representing points of two entity instances in a conceptual space, so that it is equated with a measure of the dissimilarity between the entities. Popular models for similarity assessment distinguish geometric, featural, transformational, and network approaches.

- *Geometric models* [4, 5, 6, 7, 8] view entities as points in an arbitrarily-dimensional space. The distance between the points corresponds to the measure of *dissimilarity*. Similarity is usually derived as some linear, exponential, or Gaussian function of the distance [9, 10]. Geometric models yield a symmetric and transitive similarity relation.

- *Transformation models* are geometric models that rely on a transformational distance that is expressed as the number of operations required to transform one object into the other [11, 12]. Whereas transformational models are especially useful for visual configurations, geometric models apply better to entities that differ along quantitative variables.

- *Featural models* have a qualitative foundation [13]. Rather than estimating similarity as a function of distance, featural models infer directly a similarity measure from common and different features of the entities under comparison. Common features increase similarity, whereas different features decrease it. Since feature-matching is a set-theoretic approach, it is neither dimensional nor metric and, therefore, symmetry and transitivity do not necessarily hold.

- *Network models* provide explicit support for similarity assessments among hierarchically organized concepts. The closer two concepts are in a network, the higher their semantic relation [14]. An intuitive way of evaluating semantic similarity between two concepts in a network is through their semantic distance, which is typically expressed as the shortest path between two nodes in the network and defined as the sum of the number of edges between them [15,16]

2.2   Null Values

Null values refer to attributes that have no value stored. Database theory recommends the elimination of null values through proper database design and normalization; however, even in the most carefully designed systems null values are often unavoidable due to inability to collect all the required information about an entity, schema restructuring, or tradeoffs between performance and normalization. Null values introduce ambiguities related to the meaning of the missing attribute values [17]. Our concern is to address the implications that derive from null values when such values are encountered during a similarity assessment process.

A simple but rudimentary way of dealing with null values is to assign the value *zero* to the similarity measure between two values when one of them is null [18]. This approach, however, misses the different semantics that a null value may carry—for instance, up to 14 different types in ANSI/SPARC [19]. Only a subset of three different interpretations, however, is vital for a formal treatment with respect to their meaning.

Unknown null values were initially investigated by Codd [20]. An unknown value (*unk*) states that a precise value exists, but is currently missing. This model was later extended to include *non-applicable* types of nulls [21]. A non-applicable null (*dne* for does not exist) means that the value is unavailable because the specific attribute is not applicable for an object.

Zaniolo [22] introduced the no-*information* null (*ni*). A no-information value is more generic, subsuming *unk* and *dne* types of nulls. It states that the value is missing either because it exists but is unknown or because it does not apply for that object. The advantage of this approach is that it is conceptually simpler and allows more efficient evaluation of queries. The tradeoff is that it is less informative and hence may result in loss of potentially useful information, since it is inadequate in expressing the full spectrum of semantic interpretations that null values may have.

Vassiliou [23] is concerned with *unk, dne*, and *inconsistent* nulls. The domain of the database is extended to include the values "*missing,*" "*inconsistent,*" and "*non-applicable,*" where *non-applicable* is treated as a regular precise value.

Morrissey [24] provided a comprehensive treatment with the distinction of *unk, dne, p-domains*, and *p-ranges. P-domains* specify that a missing value is one out of a list of values, whereas *p-ranges* state that the missing value is within a particular range. A *p-domain* applies better to attributes with an enumerated domain of finite elements, whereas a *p-range* applies is more suited to attributes whose values vary along a continuum. For instance, a *p-range* of, say, (20-50) means that the precise value is between 20 and 50. In response to a query, one set of objects captures the exact matches, while another set captures objects with one or more null values that could possible be exact matches. While this approach is concerned with the retrieval of possible exact matches, we are interested in finding similar results that, among others, encompass possible exact matches.

The common denominators of these approaches seem to be *unk, dne*, and *ni* nulls and this is the set that we will use in our approach.

2.3   Complex Similarity Queries

Conjunctive queries refer to the combination of constraints using the logical operator *and*, for instance, "Find objects where attribute A has value x *and* attribute B has value y." Similar combinations can be obtained with the use of disjunctions and negation. The evaluation of each constraint yields a separate similarity value, so that the key issue becomes how to combine the similarity values. Two popular approaches are:

- The geometric approach which calculates the *mean* as the average of the similarity values. The use of attribute weights that indicate each attribute's salience within the overall similarity assessment offers a refinement of this process. While appropriate for conjunctions, there are no corresponding operations that would support disjunctions or negations.
- The fuzzy-logic approach which, for conjunctive queries, resorts to selecting the *minimum* of the similarity values. Under a fuzzy set interpretation, the extent to which an object in a database satisfies a query becomes a matter of degree. The core of such a fuzzy set (i.e., elements with a membership value of 1) comprises the set of all exact matches to a query. The fuzzy sets concepts of intersections, unions, and complements correspond to the three fundamental scoring rules for conjunctions (Equation 1a), disjunctions (Equation 1b), and negations (Equation 1c), respectively [25, 26].

$$\mu_{A \wedge B}(x) = \min\{\mu_A(x), \mu_B(x)\} \tag{1a}$$

$$\mu_{A \vee B}(x) = \max\{\mu_A(x), \mu_B(x)\} \tag{1b}$$

$$\mu_{\neg A}(x) = 1 - \mu_A(x) \tag{1c}$$

In this paper we argue, however, that fuzzy logic is inappropriate for expressing similarity measures, especially for conjunctions and negations. We advocate the use of a weighted mean instead, and provide arguments based on widely accepted psychological principles.

3   Modeling Thematic Spatial Similarity

To process spatial similarity queries, we map similarity into the quantitative realm, enabling an ordering of the quality of matches. The mappings result in a normalized value of 1 representing an exact match and a value of 0 denoting a complete difference (i.e., no similarity). While the standardized result of the mapping provides a unified framework for high-level, abstract similarity operations, the ways in which the attribute values are mapped onto the similarity interval differ widely. Since similarity is not a unitary concept [27, 28], favoring the use of one model over another depends on the specifics of each attribute, because each model carries different innate assumptions and emphasizes different properties of similarity.

To account for the diversity of attribute types, each attribute needs to carry its similarity operation (i.e., an algorithm that is tailored to the attribute type to assess similarity). Generic classes of algorithms, however, may be developed for attributes that behave the same way. An important set of categories is based on the four *scales of measurement* [29], referring to cognitive and structural commonalities that are typically found in capturing data. The basic types of attributes are those whose values denote nominal, ordinal, interval, ratio, and cyclic measurements.

- A *nominal* attribute type describes values that can be distinguished by equality, for example, the names of Greek Islands, such as Thira, Crete, and Karpathos
- An *ordinal* attribute type captures the sequence of the values, without any reference to how big the differences are. An example of an ordinal attribute type is the landmass of Greek islands, such as Crete > Karpathos > Thira. The values themselves are not enough to establish this ordering, however, because in differing contexts, other orderings could apply (e.g., Karpathos > Crete > Thira as the popularity among tourists who prefer undeveloped islands).
- An *interval* attribute type adds to the ordinal data type the information about how far apart the ranked individuals are. For example, the data type *highestPointOfIsland*—Crete 2,453 meters; Karpathos 1,140 meters; and Thira 567 meters—is of type *interval*.

- A *ratio* data type adds an absolute zero to an interval type. An example is island population—540,000 for Crete; 7,000 for Thira; and 4,600 for Karpathos.
- A *cyclic* attribute type orders ordinal, interval, and ratio types such that the last element in a sequence becomes also the first element of the next round. For example, if a new ferry service always went from Sitia on Crete over Pigadia on Karpathos to Anthinios on Thira, and then back to Sitia to start the next round in the same sequence, then this ferry route would be of type *cyclic*.

A particular problem with comparing spatial configurations for similarity appears when the two items to be compared are of different cardinality. For example, one traveler's route (an ordinal value) was Thira < Karpathos < Crete. Two others traveled such that Crete < Karpathos < Thira and Thira < Crete. While the two trips with three island stops can be compared based on the differences of the islands in the sequence—each of Thira and Crete are two steps apart in the sequences—the route with just two stops does not fit into this pattern as it is questionable how to account quantitatively for the missing piece.

4   Null Values in Spatial Similarity Assessments

To handle efficiently the different semantics of nulls, DBMSs must extend the domain of attributes in the system with the codes *unk*, *dne*, and *ni*, rather than using only the generic code *null*. Similarity between a null value and any other value of an attribute A may be derived from Equation 2, where a and b are the respective minimum and maximum values that define the range of A, x_q is the query value, and $Sim_A(x_q, a)$ and $Sim_A(x_q, b)$ are measures of similarity between x_q and a and x_q and b, respectively.

$$\forall x_q \big|(x_q \neq dne, unk, ni) \ Sim_A(x_q, null) = \begin{cases} \min(Sim_A(x_q, a), Sim_A(x_q, b)) & \text{if } null = unk \\ 0 & \text{if } null = dne \\ 0 & \text{if } null = ni \end{cases} \quad (2)$$

A comparison between a *dne* and a query value is indeterminate, because *dne* does not exist, whereas the query value exists. We choose to view this existence vs. non-existence of a value as the maximum possible dissimilarity and, therefore, assign a similarity measure of 0 to the pair of *dne* and any query value. Unlike *unk* and *ni*, a *dne* mark should always be treated by the database as a precise value, whether it is encountered in a stored object or specified in a query as the desired value to be retrieved. *Unk* and *ni* nulls, on the other hand, are treated as precise values only when a user queries the system by using them. Such queries are meaningful in the sense that the user may be looking for all missing values in the database in order to update them. In this case a symbolic matching is necessary. In all other cases where *unk* and *ni* values are compared with precise query values, they should be treated as placeholders instead and follow the substitutions (Equation 2); here, the matching is semantic, rather than symbolic [21].

The *unk* code represents knowledge that the actual value, although missing, belongs to the set of values that are allowed in the attribute range [31]. Due to uncertainty we assume minimum similarity and, therefore, substitute *unk* with the domain value that maximizes the distance from the query value x_q. In cases of quantitative attributes, this value is logically either the minimum or the maximum as implied by the domain of the attribute or as specified via an explicit constraint. Hence, we only have to evaluate two results. For qualitative attributes the algorithm may perform only when we are dealing with a finite domain of values. In this case, however, all of the values have to be checked in order to choose the one that minimizes similarity. In the case that the user queries specifically for *unk* values, no substitution takes place and *unk* values are the only exact matches, followed by *ni* values.

The *ni* value is a lower level placeholder for either *unk* or *dne* nulls and is the least informative. For the case of a query specifying any value other than *dne* to be retrieved for a particular attribute, we choose the worst-case scenario and let *ni* values be treated as *dne* values and thus assigned zero similarity. However, during output presentation, tuples with *ni* values must be ranked higher than *dne* in terms of similarity, because they leave open the possibility of existence. If the query, however, asks to retrieve specifically the tuples that have a *dne* value for the attribute, then the order is reversed, since *dne* values are exact matches, and *ni* values the next best results, with everything else excluded. In more realistic scenarios that account for the vast majority of database queries, users will enter precise values, and retrieve similar results, free of nulls.

For example, given the relation in Table 1, for each record, information exists about the type of the accommodation, the category of luxury, the total number of rooms, and the restaurant types that may exist within the establishments. Let the range of possible rooms for accommodations vary from 5 to 70 and explicitly stated so by a constraint. The query for hotels that have 50 rooms and also include a *Greek* restaurant requires similarity assessment with null values. *Dameia Palace* is a good result, because it is a hotel, the value for beds is relatively close to that of the query, and an *Italian* restaurant—also Mediterranean cuisine—exists on its premises. *Caldera Apartments* would be the second best match, followed by *Santorini Palace*. The reason for *Santorini Palace* being ranked so low is because of its *unk* value for rooms. This value will be substituted with number 5, since this is the value in the allowable range for *rooms* that minimizes similarity. If, however, there was a database constraint stating that hotels of category *A* must have between 40 and 70 rooms, then *unk* would be substituted by the number 70, and we would obtain an ordering in which *Santorini Palace* is the most similar result, followed by *Dameia Palace* and then *Caldera Apartments*. *Sun Rocks* is the least similar match, because it is not a hotel and has no restaurants. The similarity between the query value for a *Greek* restaurant and the *dne* value would evaluate to zero.

Table 1. Relation *accomodations* with attributes that include null values

Name	Type	Category	Rooms	RestaurantType
Sun Rocks	Apartments	B	10	dne
Dameia Palace	Hotel	A	70	Italian
Caldera Apartments	Apartments	A	30	Italian
Santorini Palace	Hotel	A	unk	Greek

This approach offers a semantically enhanced and elegant method when dealing with null values, especially when combined with consistency constraints that may be inserted as rules in the database and reduce the uncertainty for certain facts. Specifying the types of null values with different codes allows for more expressive power, both during the modeling of a database, as well as during the retrieval from it. The procedure adopts a pessimistic view when encountering *unk* values, following always a worst-case scenario and substituting *unk* with the most dissimilar value possible. Approaches that are based on probabilities, information content, or entropy [24] do not apply for similarity assessments as they aim at locating probable exact matches. For example, if the values of two tuples in the database are the *p-domains* [Greek, Chinese], [Greek, Italian] and a query asks for a Greek restaurant. Since Italian cuisine is more similar to Greek cuisine than to Chinese, it is logically inferred that the second *p-domain* is always a better similarity match for the query. However, information content or entropy measures would yield equal estimates when assessing the probability of whether these two values are exact matches or not.

5   Similarity Assessments for Queries with Relational Operators

Relational operators extend the concept of an exact match to that of a range match. Besides the equality operator, relational operators determine whether one value is greater or less than another. Specifying queries with relational operators is meaningful only on terms that have a natural order on a scale; therefore, their usage applies to ratio, interval, ordinal, and—in some cases—cyclic attributes.

In a relational query users refer to a range of values, whereas in a query with an equality operator they refer to a single value. Therefore, we are dealing with a query range R_q instead of a query value x_{q_i}. The range may be a closed or an open interval. We denote the endpoints of the range with r_1 and r_2. For instance, in a query of $x \geq 100$, r_1 is the number *100*, and r_2 is plus infinity. Similarity between the range R_q specified by the user and any database value x_i of an attribute A is derived by Equation 3, where $Sim_A(r_1, x_i)$ and $Sim_A(r_2, x_i)$ are measures of similarity between r_1 and x_i and r_2 and x_i respectively. The justification for Equation 3 is that if an attribute value x_i is contained in the range R_q defined by the relational operator, then it is an exact match and, therefore, receives a similarity measure of *1*. If x_i is outside of the range, then its similarity is determined by the algorithm chosen for the attribute. Relational operators are typically pertinent only to quantitative attributes where similarity is derived as a function of distance. In order to estimate the distance, we choose from the range of values that constitute exact matches the one that is closer to x_i. This value will logically be either the minimum or the maximum value of the range R_q (i.e., either r_1 or r_2).

$$Sim_A(R_q, x_i) = \begin{cases} \max(Sim_A(r_1, x_i), Sim_A(r_2, x_i)) & \text{if } x_i \notin R_q \\ 1 & \text{if } x_i \in R_q \end{cases} \quad (3)$$

For example, for a query for all buildings in downtown Iraklion, Crete that occupy an area between 40,000 and 60,000 square feet (i.e., $r_1 = 40,000$ and $r_2 = 60,000$), every building whose area is within the specified interval is an exact match. For buildings with an area value x_i outside of the interval, similarity is a function of the distance from x_i to r_1 if x_i is less than 40,000, or from the distance of x_i to r_2 if x_i is greater than 60,000 (Figure 1).

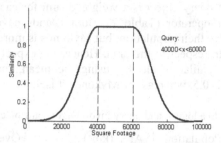

Fig. 1. Similar results to a query involving relational operators

6   Similarity in Spatial Queries Expressed with Logical Operators

Querying a system with logical operators is based on concepts from Boolean algebra. The fundamental logical or Boolean operators include the connectives *and*, *or*, and *not*. This section investigates retrieval of similar results to Boolean queries.

6.1   Queries with *and* on Different Attributes

The use of *and* requires that all the values that it connects be present in the results. Terms joined by the *and*-operator are called conjuncts. In a typical *and*-query the conjuncts are values of two or more different attributes; therefore, the operator *and* is used to allow queries that simultaneously engage multiple attributes of an object. For instance, if A_1 and A_2 are two attributes of a class, the expression $A_1(x)$ *and* $A_2(y)$ means that the user wants to retrieve those objects for which the attribute A_1 has the value x and the attribute A_2 has the value y. For each attribute, similarity between the query value and the stored values is calculated with the algorithm that has been assigned to that attribute. The overall similarity measure between the reference object O_q, characterized by the query values of the user, and any other object (i.e., record) O_i in the database is a weighted sum of the similarity measures obtained for each of the attributes. This measure is captured in Equation 4, where $A_1, ..., A_n$ are the n attributes connected by the *and*-operator, x_q and x_i are the pair of query and database values for an arbitrary attribute A_k, and Sim_A is the similarity measure obtained for that pair. The coefficient ω_k represents the weight assigned to attribute A_k.

$$Sim_{A_1,...,An}(O_q,O_i) = \sum_{k=1}^{n} \omega_k Sim_{A_k}(x_q,x_i) \qquad (4)$$

Consider for instance a user who wants to retrieve islands with a population of 10,000 habitants and an area of 70km^2. The logical expression for this query is Population(10,000) *and* Area(70). Similarity between the value 10,000 and the values of the stored database objects for the attribute Population is derived from an algorithm appropriate for ratio values that has been assigned to the attribute. The same occurs for the other conjunct about the area. The combined similarity for each database record to the reference query object is a weighted sum for each of the attributes that are linked by the *and*-operator (Table 2). Both islands have the same degree of similarity with respect to their population, but Mykonos is more similar than Santorini to the query value with respect to the area. Hence, we expect that Mykonos will be returned as the most similar result. By using the mean, the combined similarity measure for Santorini is 0.5, whereas for Mykonos it is 0.7.

Table 2. Similar results to a logical and query involving two attributes, both equally weighted

Island	Population	Area (km^2)	Overall Similarity
Mykonos	7,000 (0.5)	75 (0.9)	0.7
Santorini	7,000 (0.5)	90 (0.5)	0.5

The validity of this result is verified by an important finding from psychology, [32, 27, 8, 33] according to which the perceived distance between two stimuli varying along a number of separable dimensions is given by their "city-block" distance metric in the space defined by the dimensions (Equation 5). The term *city-block* means that one travels along the dimensions to get from one point (i.e., stimuli) to the other instead of taking the shortest path (i.e., Euclidean distance). Separable dimensions are those that correspond to highly analyzable and non-related attributes such as length and weight, (or population and area in Table 2). Most databases use attributes that correspond to separable dimensions. The coefficient w_i corresponds to the weight assigned to dimension i. The weights must sum up to one.

$$d_C(x, y) = \sum_{i=1}^{n} w_i \cdot |x_i - y_i| \qquad (5)$$

Equation 4 computes perceived similarity, whereas Equation 5 computes perceived dissimilarity. The two measures add up to 1. Hence, the weighted mean implies that the overall similarity is the inverse of the overall perceived distance according to a measure that has proved to yield consistent results with human reasoning. One may argue that non-linear functions such as Shepard's [10] exponential formula or Nosofsky's [9] Gaussian function will give more realistic results. These monotonic functions are indeed preferred during the similarity assessment within individual attributes. At this point of the assessment, however, where similarity measures for each attribute have already been derived and only their integration remains, such functions will just change the similarity scores for each tuple in the set of retrieved similar results, but the ordering from most to less similar object will be preserved. Hence, if the system has a threshold of retrieving 20 similar results, it will retrieve the same set and in the same order, regardless of whether we use the weighted mean or a non-linear monotonic function.

The justification provided clarifies the shortcomings of approaches based on fuzzy logic. The minimum operator that is used in such work [34, 35, 36] is too restrictive, because it only takes into consideration the similarity of one attribute (Equation 1a). For instance, Santorini and Mykonos would both receive an overall similarity value of

0.5 (Table 2). This seems counter-intuitive. Even if one kept adding extra attributes in the database, for all of which the similarity was *0.9* for Mykonos and *0.5* for Santorini, the two islands would still be ranked as equally good results for the query. We do not make the claim here that fuzzy logic is flawed, but rather that the choice of minimum as a fuzzy aggregation operator when reasoning for similarity is erroneous and counter-intuitive. In fact, most of the researchers seem to be somewhat troubled by their results. Santini [37] reports problems between judgments of similarity with his model and others that were experimentally obtained, and admits that the minimum is too restrictive for conjunction. The same is admitted by Ortega *et al.* [26], as well as Fagin [38] who justifies the use of minimum because it has attractive properties that are quite useful in optimizing the algorithms for faster access to the database.

Accuracy and *correctness* of a computer-produced similarity measure and the suitability of an algorithm are only reflected in their fidelity to human behavior, perceptions, and intuition. It makes no sense to succumb to the niceties of a well-defined theory or model when it does not comply with human reasoning, which is the primary objective of all efforts on semantically similar information retrieval.

1.2   Queries with *and* on the Same Attribute

An alternative but rather unorthodox use of *and* occurs when the conjunction is used to connect values of the same attribute. If *A* is an attribute for a class of objects, the expression *A(x) and A(y)* means that the user wants to retrieve those objects for which the attribute *A* simultaneously has the values *x* and *y*. We are not dealing here with fuzzy variables to which an object may belong simultaneously with different degrees of membership, but rather with multi-valued attributes (i.e., attributes that have a set of values for an entity). Comparing a multi-valued property of two objects requires a different logic than comparing a single-valued property. The similarity measure in this case relates two sets of values, rather than two individual values, and describes how similar one set is to the other.

One approach to finding similarity among multi-valued attributes is to arrange the values of the sets in pairs, and then separately compute the similarity for each pair. The overall similarity of the sets is the maximum possible sum of the similarity measures for each pair, divided by the number of formed pairs. This sum may also be weighted, meaning that the user may specify different weights on different values of the set. The first step of this approach consists of constructing a matrix in which the rows represent the values of one set and the columns the values of the other. The coefficient in a cell of the matrix is the similarity measure for the pair represented in that cell. The second step is to examine the different permutations of pairs that may be constructed and choose the one that gives the maximum sum. For a matrix of order *n*, the number of possible permutations is *n!*.

An example is the multi-valued property *Color* for buildings. Assume a semantic similarity matrix (Table 3) that stores the similarity coefficients between various colors and create the instances *Building$_1$_Color(blue, red)* and *Building$_2$_Color (blue, black)*. If a user's query is to find a building that is *blue and red*, then *Building$_1$* is an exact match. In order to find the similarity of *Building$_2$* to *Building$_1$* with respect to their colors, we examine the possible combinations of their values (Figure 2). The columns represent the colors of *Building$_1$* and the rows the colors of *Building$_2$*. Each cell stores a similarity coefficient for a pair of colors, as specified in the similarity matrix of Table 3. There are two possible ways to combine the colors of the two buildings. One is to take the sum of the similarity measures, denoted by *italic* numbers, and the other is to take the sum of the similarity measures, denoted by **bold** numbers. In the first case the overall similarity of the sets is the sum of 0.7 and 0.3 divided by the number of formed pairs, which is 2. The result is 0.5. In the latter case the overall similarity is the sum of 1 and 0.2 divided by 2, which yields 0.6. This is the maximum possible sum, therefore, the measure of similarity between the two sets.

Table 3. Similarity matrix for a color attribute

	yellow	red	blue	black
yellow	1	0.5	0.2	0.1
red	0.5	1	0.3	0.2
blue	0.2	0.3	1	0.7
black	0.1	0.2	0.7	1

Our approach to multi-valued attributes captures indirectly a combination of featural and geometric similarity models. Pairs of values that are common in two sets have a similarity coefficient of 1 assigned to them, and thus are likely to be included in the combination of pairs, which yields the maximum sum; therefore, common values are counted as common features and contribute significantly to the overall similarity of the sets compared. For the rest of the pairs, which comprise of different values in each set, we estimate their similarity, rather than adopting the binary logic of featural models that treats them only as distinctive features.

Building 1

		blue	red
Building 2	blue	1	*0.3*
	black	*0.7*	**0.2**

Fig. 2. Similarity between sets of values for a multi-valued attribute

A problem arises when the sets have different cardinalities. For instance, consider the entity instances *Building₁_Color(yellow, red)* and *Building₂_Color(yellow, red, blue)*. If we follow the same process, then the combination of pairs that yields the maximum sum is given by the two highlighted cells (Figure 3a) and the similarity between two sets is computed from Equation 6.

$$Sim_{color}(B_1,B_2) = \frac{Sim(yellow,yellow)+Sim(red,red)}{2} = 1 \qquad (6)$$

Neglecting the additional color value of *Building₂* leads to an obviously incorrect result, which presents the two buildings as identical with respect to their colors. What is not represented in this similarity measure is the existence of one additional color for one of the buildings. To rectify this problem we may extend the smaller set in the assessment with *dne* nulls up to the cardinality of the larger set (Figure 3b). The addition of the pair *(blue, dne)* in the formula that yields similarity for the sets

(Equation 7) reflects the existence of one additional color in *Building*$_2$, and allows us to obtain a similarity result that corresponds better to the real-world situation.

Building 2 \ Building 1	yellow	red
yellow	1	0.5
red	0.5	1
blue	0.2	0.3

(a)

Building 2 \ Building 1	yellow	red	dne
yellow	1	0.5	0
red	0.5	1	0
blue	0.2	0.3	0

(b)

Fig. 3. (a) Similarity between sets of different cardinalities, **(b)** Extending sets of different cardinalities with *dne* nulls

$$Sim_{color}(B_1,B_2) = \frac{Sim(yellow,yellow) + Sim(red,red) + Sim(blue,dne)}{3} \approx 0.7\,. \quad (7)$$

1.3 Queries with *or* on the Same Attribute

The use of *or* requires that at least one of the values that it connects be present in the results. Terms joined by the *or*-operator are called disjuncts. In a typical database *or* query the disjuncts are values of the same attribute. If A is an attribute of a class of objects, the expression *A(x) or A(y)* means that the user wishes to retrieve objects for which the value for attribute A is either x or y. As in the case with relational operators there is not one query value but a set of query values. The difference, however, to queries expressed through relational operators is that the set of query terms is not represented by a range, but by a finite number of distinct values. Similarity is derived from Equation 8, where $Q=[x_1,x_2,...x_n]$ is the set containing the n values connected by the *or*-operator in the query expression, and x_i is any stored value for attribute A in the database.

$$Sim_A(Q,x_i) = \begin{cases} \max(Sim_A(x_1,x_i), Sim_A(x_2,x_i), ..., Sim_A(x_n,x_i)) & \text{if } x_i \notin Q \\ 1 & \text{if } x_i \in Q \end{cases} \quad (8)$$

Any value x_i contained in Q is an exact match. For values of x_i that do not belong to the set Q, the process consists of examining the similarity between x_i and all the values that belong to Q. The similarity is derived by the algorithm that has been assigned to the attribute A. Since all values in Q are exact matches, we choose the one that gives the largest similarity measure for x_i, when compared with it, that is, the similarity of x_i is determined by its distance from the closest exact match. For example, assume a query on a quantitative attribute A asking to retrieve the records where the value of A is 400 or 600. The expression for this query is *A(400) or A(800)*. Any object with a value of A that is 400 or 800 is an exact match. For objects that have a different value x_i for A, we choose the maximum similarity measure obtained for the pairs *(400, x_i)* and *(800, x_i)* as this is computed from the algorithm that has been assigned to attribute A (Figure 4).

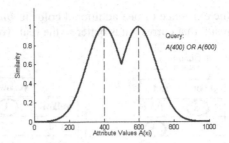

Fig. 4. Similar results to a logical *or*-query involving one attribute

1.4   Queries with *or* on Different Attributes

Specifying queries with *or* where the disjuncts are values of different attributes constitutes uncommon practice, but is still a viable option for the database users. If A_1 and A_2 are two attributes of a class, the expression $A_1(x)$ *or* $A_2(y)$ means that the user wants to retrieve those objects for which the attribute A_1 has the value of x, or those objects for which the attribute A_2 has the value of y. For each attribute, similarity between the query value and the stored database values is calculated with the algorithm that has been assigned to that attribute. If $Q=[A_1(x_q),A_2(x_q),...,A_n(x_q)]$ is the set containing n query values (x_q) of n different attributes connected by the *or*-operator, and $A_k(x_q)$ and $A_k(x_i)$ are the pair of query and database values for an attribute A_k with $k=1,...n$, then the similarity between the reference object O_q, characterized by the query values of the user, and any other object (i.e., record) O_i in the database is derived from Equation 9.

$$Sim_{A_k}(O_q,O_i)=\begin{cases} \max(Sim_{A_k}(x_q,x_i)) & \text{if } A_k(x_i) \notin Q \\ 1 & \text{if } A_k(x_i) \in Q \end{cases} \qquad (9)$$

A database object that matches any or a number of the values contained in Q for some attributes A_k is an exact match. When none of the object's values $A_k(x_i)$ is identical to the query value $A_k(x_q)$ for an attribute A_k, then we separately examine the similarity of the pairs $(A_k(x_i), A_k(x_q))$ for all attributes A_k connected by the *or*-operator. The similarity measure chosen is the maximum found during this process. For example, consider the query *Building_Type(hospital) or Capacity(150)* (Table 4). Regardless of its value for the attribute *Capacity,* object 1 is an exact match because it matches the query value for the attribute *Building_Type.* Similarly, object 2 is also an exact match because it matches the query value for the attribute *Capacity.* For objects 3 and 4 the similarity between their values and the query value for each of the attributes is calculated separately, and the larger of those measures is the overall similarity assigned to the object with respect to the user's query.

Table 4. Similar results to a logical *or*-query involving two attributes

ID	BuildingType		CapacityInBeds		Overall Similarity
1	hospital	100%	100	46%	100%
2	clinic	83%	150	100%	100%
3	health center	75%	50	21%	75%
4	medical center	50%	5	10%	50%

1.5   Queries with *not*

Values that the *not*-operator takes as arguments are not present in the results. If A is an attribute for a class of objects, the expression *not A(x)* means that the user wants to retrieve any object, except those that have a value of x for attribute A. The similarity of an arbitrary database object O_i with respect to a query expressed by the *not*-operator is derived by Equation 10, where x_i represents the stored database value for attribute A of object O_i, and x_q is the value specified by the *not* operator.

$$Sim_A(O_i) = \begin{cases} 0 & \text{if } x_q = x_i \\ 1 & \text{if } x_q \neq x_i \end{cases} \tag{10}$$

Negations are another area where fuzzy based implementations of similarity to complex queries suffer. Equation 1c is used to assess similarity of database objects to the query. Its effect is that it returns as most similar results the objects that are most dissimilar to the value negated in the query. This approach does not scale up well to human reasoning, and might even return paradoxical results. For instance, if a user queries for a hotel but not in the center of a city this does not necessarily mean that she would like to find a hotel in the middle of the desert or on the top of a mountain, while one in the suburbs would be acceptable. Therefore, the role of negations in information retrieval is as a means to avoid undesirable associations, or in general, to eliminate unwanted tuples from the set of retrieved results. Hence, it should be interpreted by a similarity query processor, as it has always been interpreted traditionally in the classic logic paradigm.

The combination of a conjunction and a negation over the same constraint—*A(x) and not A(x)*—can be interpreted as "find the objects that simultaneously have and do not have the value x for attribute A." Although in classic logic this is a contradiction, in a similarity setting it can be interpreted as a request to retrieve all similar results for a query, excluding those that are exact matches.

7   Conclusions

To address the emerging needs for flexible yet powerful spatial information retrieval, we developed a model for spatial similarity assessment with complex constraints. First, we showed that an enhanced treatment of null values is possible if their different semantics are explicitly represented in the system with different identifiers that imply different degrees of uncertainty. Then we provided a comprehensive framework for dealing with similarity assessments under Boolean and relational operators. We followed widely accepted findings about similarity from the field of psychology.

Current implementations of complex similarity assessments that use fuzzy logic have limitations, especially for conjunctions and negations. Although disjunctions perform realistically with a fuzzy logic interpretation of the *or*-operator, negations require a traditional classic logic interpretation. On the other hand, conjunctions need a compensatory use of the *and*-operator, with all of the individual similarity estimates contributing to the final score. An interesting case of conjunction occurs when the aggregated terms refer to values of the same attribute. Such queries are possible in systems that allow storage of multi-valued attributes. We developed a new set of methods to support them.

Future research will address the determination of weights for conjunctive queries based on context, and the design of appropriate user interfaces for similarity queries. We are also interested in finding optimal threshold specifications for the similar results and efficient ways of presenting them to the users.

Acknowledgments

This work was partially supported by the National Science Foundation under grants IIS-9970123 and EPS-9983432 and the National Imagery and Mapping Agency under grant numbers NMA202-97-1-1023 and NMA401-02-1-2009. Max Egenhofer's work is further supported by the National Institute of Environmental Health Sciences, NIH, under grant number 1 R 01 ES09816-01, and the National Imagery and Mapping Agency under grant numbers NMA201-00-1-2009 and NMA201-01-1-2003.

References

[1]   Bishr, Y. (1998) Overcoming the Semantic and Other Barriers to GIS Interoperability. *International Journal of Geographical Information Science* 12(4): 299-314.

[2]   Rodriguez, A., Egenhofer, M., and Rugg, R. (1999) Assessing Semantic Similarities Among Geospatial Feature Class Definitions. in: *The 2nd International Conference on Interoperating Geographic Information Systems*, vol. 1580, pp. 189-202, Vckovski, A., Brassel, K., and Schek, H., (Eds.), Zurich, Switzerland.

[3]   Mill, J. (1829) *Analysis of the Phenomenon of the Human Mind*. vol. 2, Baldwin and Cradock, London.

[4]   Richardson, M. (1938) Multidimensional Psychophysics. *Psychological Bulletin* 35: 659-660.

[5]   Torgerson, W. (1952) Multidimensional Scaling: I. Theory and Method. *Psychometrika* 17(4): 401-419.

[6]   Shepard, R. (1962) The Analysis of Proximities: Multidimensional Scaling with an Unknown Distance Function. I. *Psychometrika* 27(2): 125-140.

[7]   Shepard, R. (1962) The Analysis of Proximities: Multidimensional Scaling with an Unknown Distance Function. II. *Psychometrika* 27(3): 219-246.
[8]   Nosofsky, R. (1991) Stimulus Bias, Asymmetric Similarity, and Classification. *Cognitive Psychology* 23: 94-140.
[9]   Nosofsky, R. (1986) Attention, Similarity, and the Identification-Categorization Relationship. *Journal of Experimental Psychology: General* 115: 39-57.
[10] Shepard, R. (1987) Toward a Universal Law of Generalization for Psychological Science. *Journal of Science* 237: 1317-1323.
[11] Imai, S. (1977) Pattern Similarity and Cognitive Transformations. *Acta Psychologica* 41: 433-447.
[12] Hahn, U. and Chater, N. (1997) Concepts and Similarity. in: *Knowledge, Concepts, and Categories*, Lamberts, L. and Shanks, D., (Eds.), Psychology Press/MIT Press, Hove, U.K.
[13] Tversky, A. (1977) Features of Similarity. *Psychological Review* 84(4): 327-352.
[14] Quillian, M. (1968) Semantic Memory. in: *Semantic Information Processing*, Minsky, M., (Ed.) MIT Press, Cambridge, MA.
[15] Rada, R., Mili, H., Bicknell, E., and Blettner, M. (1989) Development and Application of a Metric on Semantic Nets. *IEEE Transactions on Systems, Man, and Cybernetics* 19(1): 17-30.
[16] Budanitsky, A. (1999) *Lexical Semantic Relatedness and its Application in Natural Language Processing*. Computer Systems Research Group, University of Toronto, Toronto, Technical Report CSRG-390.
[17] Elmasri, R. and Navathe, S. B. (2000) *Fundamentals of Database Systems*. Addison Wesley Longman Inc.
[18] Richter, M. (1992) Classification and Learning of Similarity Measures. in: Studies in Classification, Data Analysis and Knowledge Organization, Springer Verlag.
[19] Bachman, C., Cohn, L., Florance, W., Kirshenbaum, F., Kuneke, H., Mairet, C., Scott, E., Sibley, E., Smith, D., Steel, T., Turner, J., and Yormark B., (1975) Interim Report: ANSI/X3/SPARC Study Group on Data Base Management Systems. *ACM SIGMOD Record* 7(2): 1-140.
[20] Codd, E. (1979) Extending the Database Relational Model to Capture More Meaning. *ACM Transactions on Database Systems* 4(4): 397-434.
[21] Codd, E. (1986) Missing Information (Applicable and Inapplicable) in Relational Databases. *ACM SIGMOD Record* 15(4): 53-78.
[22] Zaniolo, C. (1982) Database Relations with Null Values. in: *Proceedings of the ACM Symposium on Principles of Database Systems*, pp. 27-33, Los Angeles, CA.
[23] Vassiliou, Y. (1979) Null Values in Data Base Management: A Denotational Semantics Approach. in: *Proceedings of the 1979 ACM SIGMOD International Conference on Management of Data*, pp. 162-169, Bernstein, P., (Ed.), Boston, MA.
[24] Morrissey, J. (1990) Imprecise Information and Uncertainty in Information Systems. *ACM Transactions on Information Systems* 8(2): 159-180.

[25] Santini, S. and Ramesh, J. (1996) Similarity Queries in Image Databases. in: Proceedings of CVPR '96, International IEEE Computer Vision and Pattern Recognition Conference.

[26] Ortega, M., Rui, Y., Chakrabarti, K., Porkaew, K., Mehrotra, S., and Huang, T. (1998) Supporting Ranked Boolean Similarity Queries in MARS. *IEEE Transactions on Knowledge and Data Engineering* 10(6): 905-925.

[27] Torgerson, W. (1965) Multidimensional Scaling of Similarity. *Psychometrika* 30(4): 379-393.

[28] Goldstone, R. (1994) The Role of Similarity in Categorization: Providing a Groundwork. *Cognition* 52: 125-157.

[29] Stevens, S. (1946) On the Theory of Scales of Measurement. *Journal of Science* 103(2684): 677-680.

[30] Chrisman, N. (1995) Beyond Stevens: A Revised Approach to Measurement for Geographic Information. in: *Twelfth International Symposium on Computer-Assisted Cartography, Auto-Carto 12*, Charlotte, NC.

[31] Lipski, W. (1979) On Semantic Issues Connected with Incomplete Information Databases. *ACM Transactions on Database Systems*: 262-296.

[32] Attneave, F. (1950) Dimensions of Similarity. *American Journal of Psychology* 63: 516-556.

[33] Nosofsky, R. (1992) Similarity Scaling and Cognitive Process Models. *Annual Review of Psychology* 43.

[34] Santini, S. and Ramesh, J. (1997) The Graphical Specification of Similarity Queries. *Journal of Visual Languages and Computing* 7(4): 403-421.

[35] Fagin, R. (1998) Fuzzy Queries in Multimedia Database Systems. in: Proceedings of the Seventeenth ACM SIGACT-SIGMOD-SIGART Symposium on Principles of Database Systems, Seattle, WA.

[36] Ramakrishna, M., Nepal, S., and Srivastava, D. (2002) A Heuristic for Combining Fuzzy Results in Multimedia Databases. in: *Proceedings of the thirteenth Australasian conference on Database technologies*, Melbourne, Victoria, Australia.

[37] Santini, S. and Ramesh, J. (2000) Integrated Browsing and Querying for Image Databases. *IEEE Multimedia* 7(3): 26-39.

[38] Fagin, R. (1996) Combining Fuzzy Information From Multiple Systems. in: *15th ACM Symposium on Principles of Database Systems*.

Exploiting Spatial Autocorrelation to Efficiently Process Correlation-Based Similarity Queries

Pusheng Zhang*, Yan Huang, Shashi Shekhar**, and Vipin Kumar**

Computer Science & Engineering Department, University of Minnesota
200 Union Street SE, Minneapolis, MN 55455, USA
{pusheng,huangyan,shekhar,kumar}@cs.umn.edu

Abstract. A spatial time series dataset is a collection of time series, each referencing a location in a common spatial framework. Correlation analysis is often used to identify pairs of potentially interacting elements from the cross product of two spatial time series datasets (the two datasets may be the same). However, the computational cost of correlation analysis is very high when the dimension of the time series and the number of locations in the spatial frameworks are large. In this paper, we use a spatial autocorrelation-based search tree structure to propose new processing strategies for correlation-based similarity range queries and similarity joins. We provide a preliminary evaluation of the proposed strategies using algebraic cost models and experimental studies with Earth science datasets.

1 Introduction

Analysis of spatio-temporal datasets [17, 19, 20, 11] collected by satellites, sensor nets, retailers, mobile device servers, and medical instruments on a daily basis is important for many application domains such as epidemiology, ecology, climatology, and census statistics. The development of efficient tools [2, 6, 12] to explore these datasets, the focus of this work, is crucial to organizations which make decisions based on large spatio-temporal datasets.

A spatial framework [22] consists of a collection of locations and a neighbor relationship. A time series is a sequence of observations taken sequentially in time [4]. A spatial time series dataset is a collection of time series, each referencing a location in a common spatial framework. For example, the collection of global daily temperature measurements for the last 10 years is a spatial time series dataset over a degree-by-degree latitude-longitude grid spatial framework on the surface of the Earth.

---

* The contact author. Email: pusheng@cs.umn.edu. Tel: 1-612-626-7515

** This work was partially supported by NASA grant No. NCC 2 1231 and by Army High Performance Computing Research Center contract number DAAD19-01-2-0014. The content of this work does not necessarily reflect the position or policy of the government and no official endorsement should be inferred. AHPCRC and Minnesota Supercomputer Institute provided access to computing facilities.

T. Hadzilacos et al. (Eds.): SSTD 2003, LNCS 2750, pp. 449–468, 2003.

Correlation analysis is important to identify potentially interacting pairs of time series across two spatial time series datasets. A strongly correlated pair of time series indicates potential movement in one series when the other time series moves. However, a correlation analysis across two spatial time series datasets is computationally expensive when the dimension of the time series and number of locations in the spaces are large. The computational cost can be reduced by reducing the time series dimensionality or reducing the number of time series pairs to be tested, or both. Time series dimensionality reduction techniques include discrete Fourier transformation [2], discrete wavelet transformation [6], and singular vector decomposition [9].

Our work focuses on reducing the number of time series pairs to be tested by exploring spatial autocorrelation. Spatial time series datasets comply with Tobler's first law of geography: everything is related to everything else but nearby things are more related than distant things [21]. In other words, the values of attributes of nearby spatial objects tend to systematically affect each other. In spatial statistics, the area devoted to the analysis of this spatial property is called spatial autocorrelation analysis [7]. We have proposed a naive uniform-tile cone-based approach for correlation-based similarity joins in our previous work [23]. This approach groups together time series in spatial proximity within each dataset using a uniform grid with tiles of fixed size. The number of pairs of time series can be reduced by using a uniform-tile cone-level join as a filtering step. All pairs of elements, e.g., the cross product of the two uniform-tile cones, which cannot possibly be highly correlated based on the correlation range of the two tile cones are pruned. However, the uniform tile cone approach is vulnerable because spatial heterogeneity may make it ineffective.

In this paper, we use a spatial autocorrelation-based search tree to solve the problems of correlation-based similarity range queries and similarity joins on spatial time series datasets. The proposed approach divides a collection of time series into hierarchies based on spatial autocorrelation to facilitate similarity queries and joins. We propose processing strategies for correlation-based similarity range queries and similarity joins using the proposed spatial autocorrelation-based search trees. Algebraic cost models are proposed and the evaluation and experiments with Earth science data [15] show that the performance of the similarity range queries and joins processing strategies using the spatial autocorrelation-based search tree structure often saves a large fraction of computational cost.

An Illustrative Application Domain

NASA Earth observation systems currently generate a large sequence of global snapshots of the Earth, including various atmospheric, land, and ocean measurements such as sea surface temperature (SST), pressure, precipitation, and Net Primary Production (NPP) *. These data are spatial time series data in nature.

---

* NPP is the net photosynthetic accumulation of carbon by plants. Keeping track of NPP is important because it includes the food source of humans and all other organisms and thus, sudden changes in the NPP of a region can have a direct impact on the regional ecology.

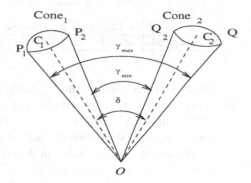

(a) (Reproduced from [10]) World-wide climatic impacts of warm El Nino events during the northern hemisphere winter

(b) Angle of Time Series in Two Cones

Fig. 1. El Nino Effects and Cones

The climate of the Earth's land surface is strongly influenced by the behavior of the oceans. Simultaneous variations in climate and related processes over widely separated points on the Earth are called teleconnections. For example, every three to seven years, an El Nino event [1], i.e., the anomalous warming of the eastern tropical region of the Pacific Ocean, may last for months, having significant economic and atmospheric consequences worldwide. El Nino has been linked to climate phenomena such as droughts in Australia and heavy rainfall along the eastern coast of South America, as shown in Figure 1 (a). D indicates drought, R indicates unusually high rainfall (not necessarily unusually intense rainfall) and W indicates abnormally warm periods. To investigate such land-sea teleconnections, time series correlation analysis across the land and ocean is often used to reveal the relationship of measurements of observations.

For example, the identification of teleconnections between Minneapolis and the eastern tropical region of the Pacific Ocean would help Earth scientists to better understand and predict the influence of El Nino in Minneapolis. In our example, the query time series is the monthly NPP data in Minneapolis from 1982 to 1993, denoted as T_q. The minimal correlation threshold is denoted as θ. This is a correlation-based similarity range query to retrieve all highly correlated SST time series in the eastern tropical region of the Pacific Ocean with the NPP time series in Minneapolis. We carry out the range query to retrieve all time series which correlate with T_q over θ in the spatial time series data S, which contain all the SST time series data in the eastern tropical region of the Pacific Ocean from 1982 to 1993. The table design of S could be represented as shown in Table 1. This query is represented using SQL as follows:

select SST from S where correlation(SST,T_q) $\geq \theta$

Table 1. Tables Schema for Table S and Table N

S: SST of the Eastern Pacific Ocean   N: NPP of Minnesota

Longitude	Latitude	SST (82-93)

Longitude	Latitude	NPP (82-93)

Another interesting example query is to retrieve all the highly correlated SST time series in the eastern tropical region of the Pacific with the time series of NPP in all of Minnesota. This query is a correlation-based similarity join between the NPP of Minnesota land grids and the SST in the eastern tropical region of the Pacific. The table design of Minnesota NPP time series data from 1982 to 1993, N, is shown in Table 1. The query is represented using SQL as follows:

select NPP, SST from N, S where correlation(NPP,SST) $\geq \theta$

Due to large amount of data available, the performance of naive nested loop algorithms is not sufficient to satisfy the increasing demands to efficiently process correlation-based similarity queries in large spatial time series datasets. We propose algorithms that use spatial autocorrelation-based search trees to facilitate the correlation-based similarity query processing in spatial time series data.

Scope and Outline

In this paper we choose a simple quad-tree like structure as the search tree due to its simplicity. R-tree, k-d tree, z-ordering tree and their variations [16, 19, 18] could be other possible candidates of the search tree. However, the comparison of these spatial data structures is beyond the scope of this paper. We focus on the strategies for correlation-based similarity queries in spatial time series data, and the computation saving methods we examine involve reduction of the time series pairs to be tested. Query processing using other similarity measures and computation saving methods based on non-spatial properties (e.g. time series power spectrum [2, 6, 9]) are beyond the scope of the paper and will be addressed in future work.

The rest of the paper is organized as follows. In Section 2, the basic concepts and lemmas related to the cone definition and boundaries are provided. Section 3 describes the formation of the spatial autocorrelation-based search tree and the correlation-based similarity range query and join strategies using the proposed spatial autocorrelation-based search tree. The cost models are discussed in Section 4. Section 5 presents the experimental design and results. We summarize our work and discuss future directions in Section 6.

2   Basic Concepts

Let $x = \langle x_1, x_2, \ldots, x_m \rangle$ and $y = \langle y_1, y_2, \ldots, y_m \rangle$ be two time series of length m. The correlation coefficient [5] of the two time series is defined as: $corr(x, y) = \frac{1}{m-1} \sum_{i=1}^{m} \left(\frac{x_i - \overline{x}}{\sigma_x} \right) \cdot \left(\frac{y_i - \overline{y}}{\sigma_y} \right) = \widehat{x} \cdot \widehat{y}$, where $\overline{x} = \frac{\sum_{i=1}^{m} x_i}{m}$, $\sigma_x = \sqrt{\frac{\sum_{i=1}^{m} (x_i - \overline{x})^2}{m-1}}$, $\overline{y} = $

$$\frac{\sum_{i=1}^{m} y_i}{m}, \ \sigma_y = \sqrt{\frac{\sum_{i=1}^{m} (y_i - \overline{x})^2}{m-1}}, \ \widehat{x}_i = \frac{1}{\sqrt{m-1}} \frac{x_i - \overline{x}}{\sigma_x}, \ \widehat{y}_i = \frac{1}{\sqrt{m-1}} \frac{y_i - \overline{y}}{\sigma_y}, \ \widehat{x} = \langle \widehat{x}_1, \widehat{x}_2,$$

$\ldots, \widehat{x}_m \rangle$, and $\widehat{y} = \langle \widehat{y}_1, \widehat{y}_2, \ldots, \widehat{y}_m \rangle$. Because the sum of the $\widehat{x}_i^2$ is equal to 1:
$\sum_{i=1}^{m} \widehat{x}_i^2 = \sum_{i=1}^{m} (\frac{1}{\sqrt{m-1}} \frac{x_i - \overline{x}}{\sqrt{\frac{\sum_{i=1}^{m} (x_i - \overline{x})^2}{m-1}}})^2 = 1$, $\widehat{x}$ is located in a multi-dimensional

unit sphere. Similarly, $\widehat{y}$ is also located in a multi-dimensional unit sphere. Based
on the definition of $corr(x, y)$, we have $corr(x, y) = \widehat{x} \cdot \widehat{y} = \cos(\angle(\widehat{x}, \widehat{y}))$. The
correlation of two time series is directly related to the angle between the two
time series in the multi-dimensional unit sphere. Finding pairs of time series
with an absolute value of correlation above the user given minimal correlation
threshold θ is equivalent to finding pairs of time series $\widehat{x}$ and $\widehat{y}$ on the unit multi-
dimensional sphere with an angle in the range of $[0, \theta_a]$ or $[180° - \theta_a, 180°]$ [23].

A cone is a set of time series in a multi-dimensional unit sphere and is characterized by two parameters, the center and the span of the cone. The center of
the cone is the mean of all the time series in the cone. The span τ of the cone is
the maximal angle between any time series in the cone and the cone center. The
largest angle($\angle P_1 O Q_1$) between two cones C_1 and C_2 is denoted as γ_{max} and
the smallest angle ($\angle P_2 O Q_2$) is denoted as γ_{min}, as illustrated in Figure 1 (b).
We have proved that if γ_{max} and γ_{min} are in specific ranges, the absolute value
of the correlation of any pair of time series from the two cones are all above θ
(or below θ) [23]. Thus all pairs of time series between the two cones satisfy (or
dissatisfy) the minimal correlation threshold. To be more specific, if we let C_1
and C_2 be two cones from the multi-dimensional unit sphere structure and let
$\widehat{x}$ and $\widehat{y}$ be any two time series from the two cones respectively, we have the
following properties(please refer to [23] for proof details):

1. If $0 \leq \gamma_{max} \leq \theta_a$, then $0 \leq \angle(\widehat{x}, \widehat{y}) \leq \theta_a$.
2. If $180° - \theta_a \leq \gamma_{min} \leq 180°$, then $180° - \theta_a \leq \angle(\widehat{x}, \widehat{y}) \leq 180°$.
3. If $\theta_a \leq \gamma_{min} \leq 180°$ and $\gamma_{min} \leq \gamma_{max} \leq 180° - \theta_a$, then $\theta_a \leq \angle(\widehat{x}, \widehat{y}) \leq 180° - \theta_a$

If either of the first two conditions is satisfied, $\{C_1, C_2\}$ is called an All-True
cone pair (All-True lemma). If the third condition is satisfied, $\{C_1, C_2\}$ is called
an All-False cone pair (All-False lemma).

3   Strategies for Correlation-Based Similarity Queries

In this section, we describe the formation of a spatial autocorrelation-based
search tree and strategies for processing correlation-based similarity range
queries and joins using the proposed search tree.

3.1   Spatial Autocorrelation-Based Search Tree Formation

We explore spatial autocorrelation, i.e., the influence of neighboring regions on
each other, to form a search tree. Search tree structures have been widely used
in traditional DBMS (e.g. B-tree and B+ tree) and spatial DBMS (quad-tree,

R-tree, R^+-tree, R^*-tree, and R-link tree [16, 19]). To fully exploit the spatial autocorrelation property, there are three major criteria for choosing a tree on the spatial time series datasets. First, a spatial tree structure is preferred to incorporate the spatial component of the datasets. Second, during the tree formation the time series calculations such as mean and span should be minimized while still need to maintain a high correlation (high clustering) among time series within a tree node. Third, threaded leaves where leaves are linked are preferred to support sequential scan of files which are useful for high selectivity ratio correlation queries. Other desired properties include depth balances of a tree and incremental updates when the time series component changes.

Algorithm 1 Spatial_Similarity_Search_Tree_Formation

Input: 1) $S = \{s_1, s_2, \ldots, s_n\}$: n spatial referenced time series
         where each instance references a spatial framework SF;
    2) a maximum threshold of cone angle τ_{max}
Output: Similarity Search Tree with Threaded Leaves
Method:
    divide SF into a collection of disjoint cells C
    /* each cell is mapped to a cone. */
    $index$ = 1;
    while ($index$ < $C.size$)
        $C(index).cener$ = Calculate_Center(C, index);
        /* cone center is the average time series within the cone. */
        $C(index).angle$ = Calculate_Span(C, index);
        /* cone span is the max angle between any time series and the
        cone center within the cone. */
        if ($C(index).angle$ > τ_{max})
            split cell $C(index)$ into four quarters C_{11}, C_{12}, C_{13}, C_{14};
            insert four quarters into C at position $index + 1$;
            set C_{11}, C_{12}, C_{13}, C_{14} as $C(index)$'s children;
        else
            $index$ ++ ;
            insert $C(index)$ at the end of the threaded leaf list;
    return C;

We choose a simple quad tree with threaded leaves which satisfies the three criteria. Other tree structures are also possible and will be explored in future work. As shown in Algorithm 1, the space is first divided into a collection of disjoint cells with a coarse starting resolution. Each cell represents a cone in the multi-dimensional unit sphere representation and includes multiple time series. Then the center and span are calculated to characterize each cone. When the cone span exceeds the maximal span threshold, this cone is split into four quarters. Each quarter is checked and split recursively until the cone span is less than the maximal span.

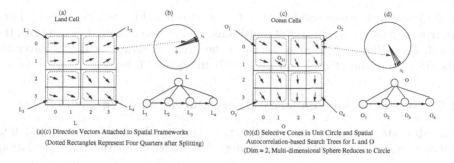

(a)(c) Direction Vectors Attached to Spatial Frameworks
(Dotted Rectangles Represent Four Quarters after Splitting)

(b)(d) Selective Cones in Unit Circle and Spatial
Autocorrelation-based Search Trees for L and O
(Dim = 2, Multi-dimensional Sphere Reduces to Circle

Fig. 2. An Illustrative Example for Spatial Autocorrelation-Based Search Tree Formation

The maximal span threshold can be estimated by using an algebraic formula analyzed as follows. Given a minimal correlation threshold θ $(0 < \theta < 1)$, $\gamma_{max} = \delta + \tau_1 + \tau_2$ and $\gamma_{min} = \delta - \tau_1 - \tau_2$, where δ is the angle between the centers of two cones, and the τ_1 and τ_2 are the spans of the two cones respectively. For simplicity, suppose $\tau_1 \simeq \tau_2 = \tau$. We have the following two properties (Please refer to [23] for proof details):

1. Given a minimal correlation threshold θ, if a pair of cones both with span τ is an All-True cone pair, then $\tau < \frac{\arccos(\theta)}{2}$.
2. Given a minimal correlation threshold θ, if a pair of cones both with span τ is an All-False cone pair, then $\tau < \frac{180°}{4} - \frac{\arccos(\theta)}{2}$.

We use the above two properties to develop a heuristic to bound the maximal span of a cone. The maximal span of a cone is set to be the minimal of the $\frac{\arccos(\theta)}{2}$ and $\frac{180°}{4} - \frac{\arccos(\theta)}{2}$.

The starting resolution can be investigated by using a spatial correlogram [7]. A spatial correlogram plots the average correlation of pairs of spatial time series with the same spatial distance against the spatial distances of those pairs. We choose the starting resolution size whose average correlation is close to the correlation which corresponds to $\min(\frac{\arccos(\theta)}{2}, \frac{180°}{4} - \frac{\arccos(\theta)}{2})$.

Example 1 (Spatial Autocorrelation-Based Search Tree Formation). Figure 2 illustrates the spatial autocorrelation-based search tree formation for two datasets, namely land and ocean. Each land/ocean framework consists of 16 locations on the starting resolution. The time series of length m in a location s is denoted as $F(s) = F_1(s), F_2(s), \ldots, F_i(s), \ldots F_m(s)$. Figure 2 only depicts a time series for $m = 2$. Each arrow in a location s of ocean or land represents the vector $< F_1(s), F_2(s) >$ normalized to the two dimensional unit sphere. Since the dimension of the time series is two, the multi-dimensional unit sphere reduces to a unit circle, as shown in Figure 2 (b) and (d).

Both land and ocean cells are further split into four quarters respectively due to the spatial heterogeneity in the cell. The land is partitioned to $L_1 - L_4$

and the ocean is partitioned to $O_1 - O_4$, as shown in Figure 2 (a) and (c). Each quarter represents a cone in the multi-dimensional unit sphere. For example, the patch L_2 in Figure 2 (a) matches L_2 in the circle in Figure 2 (b). All leaves are threaded, assuming that L_1 to L_4 and O_1 to O_4 are all leaves.

3.2   Strategies for Similarity Range Queries and Similarity Joins

The first step is to pre-process the raw data to the multi-dimensional unit sphere representation. The second step, formation of spatial autocorrelation-based search trees involves grouping similar time series into hierarchical cones using the one described in Algorithm 1. The query processing functions called may be related to similarity range query or similarity join, depending on the query types.

Algorithm 2 Correlation-Based Similarity Query Algorithm

Input: 1) $S^1 = \{s_1^1, s_2^1, \ldots, s_{n_1}^1\}$: n_1 spatial referenced time series
where each instance references a spatial framework SF_1;
2) $S^2 = \{s_1^2, s_2^2, \ldots, s_{n_2}^2\}$: n_2 spatial referenced time series
where each instance references a spatial framework SF_2;
3) a user defined correlation threshold θ;
4) query time series denote T_q ;
5) a maximum threshold of cone angle τ_{max}^1
6) a maximum threshold of cone angle τ_{max}^2

Output: pairs of time series each from S^1 and S^2 or T_q and S^2 with
correlations above θ;

Method:

```
    Pre-processing(S^1); Pre-processing(S^2);                          (1)
    T_1 = Spatial_Similarity_Search_Tree_Formation(S^1, τ^1_max );    (2)
    T_2 = Spatial_Similarity_Search_Tree_Formation(S^2, τ^2_max );    (3)
    if range query                                                     (4)
    /* assume to find highly correlated time series with T_q in S^2.*/ (5)
       Similarity_Range_Query(T_2, T_q,  θ);                          (6)
    else if similarity join                                            (7)
       Similarity_Join(T_1, T_2, θ);                                   (8)
```

Strategies for Range Queries Given a query time series T_q, we want to search all highly correlated time series from the spatial time series dataset S^2 with T_q. In general, strategies to process range queries include scan-based approaches and search tree-based approaches [8]. The scan-based approaches probe each individual nodes one by one. The search tree-based approach starts from the root of the tree and branches to a node's children only when certain conditions are satisfied, e.g., the minimal bounding box of the child contains the querying element.

Algorithm 3 Similarity_Range_Query

Input: 1) T: a spatial autocorrelation-based search tree with
threaded leaves;
    2) T_q: the query time series denote;
    3) a user defined correlation threshold θ;
Output: all time series each from S whose correlations with T_q are
above θ;
Method:
    traverse T; for each cone c on the route do   (1)
        $Filter\_Flag$ = Cone-level_Join(T_q, c, θ);   (2)
       if ($Filter\_Flag$ == ALL_TRUE)   (3)
          output all time series in the cone c (4)
       else if ($Filter\_Flag$!= ALL_FALSE)   (5)
          if c is a leaf node   (6)
              for all pair T_q and s from c do   (7)
                  $High\_Corr\_Flag$ = Instance-level_Join(T_q, s, θ);   (8)
                 if ($High\_Corr\_Flag$) output s;   (9)
          else for each c' of c's children do   (10)
              Similarity_Range_Query(c', T_q, θ)   (11)

We adopt two common strategies to traverse the spatial autocorrelation-based search tree (step 1), namely threaded-leaves-only strategy and tree-based strategy. Note that the query time series T_q can be treated as a cone with a cone span 0. The threaded-leaves-only traversal only visits all the leaf nodes of the tree. The pairs of time series formed by T_1 and each time series in a leaf node which satisfies the All-True lemma will be output. The pairs of time series formed by T_1 and each time series in a leaf node which satisfies the All-False lemma will be ignored. An individual time series in a leave node which fails both All-True and All-False lemmas will be visited. The tree-based traversal starts from the root and checks the All-True and All-False lemmas. The children of non-leaf nodes which fail both All-True and All-False lemmas will be visited until a leaf node is reached. For leaf nodes, the process is the same as that in the threaded-leaves-only traversal.

Example 2 (A Similarity Range Query). The range query with respect to O_{11} and L in Figure 2 (a) and (c) is applied as shown in Table 2. For the threaded-leaves-only traversal, all leaf cones are checked against O_{11} for correlation. The total cost is the sum of 4, which is the filtering cost, and 4, which is the refinement cost. For the tree-based traversal, O_{11} is first checked with L against the All-True and All-False lemmas. If both of them fail, all of L's four children, which are all leaf nodes, are checked. Three of them satisfy the All-False Lemmas and one needs refinement where individual time series are checked against O_{11} for correlation. The total correlation computation is the sum of 5 and 4, which is the refinement cost. For this particular example, the tree-based traversal is more expensive than the threaded-leaves-only traversal.

Table 2. The Range Query with Respect to O_{11} in Example Data

Tree-Based Traversal			Threaded-leaves-only Traversal		
Ocean-Land	Filtering	Refinement	Ocean-Land	Filtering	Refinement
$O_{11} - L$	No	No			
$O_{11} - L_1$	No	4	$O_{11} - L_1$	No	4
$O_{11} - L_2$	All-False		$O_{11} - L_2$	All-False	
$O_{11} - L_3$	All-False		$O_{11} - L_2$	All-False	
$O_{11} - L_4$	All-False		$O_{11} - L_2$	All-False	

Strategies for Similarity Joins Spatial join operations are usually divided into a filter step and a refinement step [19] to efficiently process complex spatial data types such as point collections. In the filter step, the spatial objects are represented by simpler approximations such as the MBR (Minimum Bounding Rectangle). There are several well-known algorithms, such as plane sweep [3], space partition [13] and tree matching [14], which can then be used for computing the spatial join of MBRs using the overlap relationship; the answers from this test form the candidate solution set. In the refinement step, the exact geometry of each element from the candidate set and the exact spatial predicates are examined along with the combinatorial predicate to obtain the final result.

Algorithm 4 Similarity_Join

Input: 1) T^1: a spatial autocorrelation-based search tree with
        threaded leaves ;
    2) T^2: a spatial autocorrelation-based search tree with
        threaded leaves;
    3) a user defined correlation threshold θ;
Output: all pairs of time series each from leaves of C^1 and C^2 with
        correlations above θ;
Method:

traverse T_1 via threaded leaves; for each c_1 from T_1 do	(1)
traverse T_2; for each c_2 T_2 do	(2)
$Filter\_Flag$ = Cone-level_Join(c_1, c_2, θ);	(3)
if ($Filter\_Flag$ == ALL_TRUE)	(4)
output all pairs in the two cones	(5)
else if ($Filter\_Flag$!= ALL_FALSE)	(6)
if c_2 is a leaf node	(7)
for all pair s_1 from c_1 and s from c do	(8)
$High\_Corr\_Flag$ = Instance-level_Join(s_1,s_2, θ);	(9)
if ($High\_Corr\_Flag$) output s_1 and s_2;	(10)
else for each c' of c's children do	(11)
Similarity_Join(c_1,c',θ)	(12)

For a join between two spatial autocorrelation-based search trees, we traverse one tree in a threaded-leaves-only manner and traverse the other tree in either

Table 3. Join in Example Data

Tree-Based Traversal			Threaded-leaves-only Traversal		
Ocean-Land	Filtering	Refinement	Ocean-Land	Filtering	Refinement
$O_1 - L$	No				
$O_1 - L_1$	No	16	$O_1 - L_1$	No	16
$O_1 - L_2$	All-False		$O_1 - L_2$	All-False	
$O_1 - L_3$	All-False		$O_1 - L_3$	All-False	
$O_1 - L_4$	All-False		$O_1 - L_4$	All-False	
$O_2 - L$	All-False				
			$O_2 - L_1$	All-True	
			$O_2 - L_2$	All-True	
			$O_2 - L_3$	All-True	
			$O_2 - L_4$	All-True	
$O_3 - L$	No				
$O_3 - L_1$	All-True		$O_3 - L_1$	All-True	
$O_3 - L_2$	All-True		$O_3 - L_2$	All-True	
$O_3 - L_3$	All-True		$O_3 - L_3$	All-True	
$O_3 - L_4$	No	16	$O_3 - L_4$	No	16
$O_4 - L_4$	All-True				
			$O_4 - L_1$	All-True	
			$O_4 - L_2$	All-True	
			$O_4 - L_3$	All-True	
			$O_4 \quad L_4$	All-True	

a threaded-leaves-only manner (single loop join) or a tree-based manner(nested loop join). Other traversal combinations such as tree matching are also possible but are beyond the scope of this paper; they will be addressed in future work. For each leaf c_1 in the first search tree, a process similar to the range query with respect to c_1 is carried out.

Example 3 (A Similarity Join). The join operation between the cones in Figure 2 (a) and (c) is applied as shown in Table 3. For the nested loop join, each leaf ocean cone is checked with the land cones. The cost of the threaded-leaves-only traversal is the sum of 16, which is the filtering cost, and 2×16, which is the refinement cost. For the single loop join, each ocean cone is checked with the land cones starting with the root L. Its children will be visited only if neither the All-True or All-False lemmas turns out to be true. As can be seen, some All-False cone pairs and All-True cone pairs are detected in the non-leaf nodes and their descendents are not visited at all. The cost of the tree-based traversal is the sum of 12, which is the filtering cost, and 2×16, which is the refinement cost.

Lemma 1 (Completeness and Correctness of the Range Query Algorithm). *The Similarity_Range_Query algorithm is complete and correct.*

Proof Sketch:
Given a query time series T_q, for the threaded-leaves-only traversal, a pair of time

series T_q and T' having a correlation value greater than the user given threshold can only be dismissed when it is in a pair of cones satisfying the All-False lemma or in Instance-level_Join (step 8 in Algorithm 3). The All-False lemma ensures no false-dismissal in the first case and the instance level pairwise checking will not false dismiss either. Any pair of time series found having a correlation value greater than the user given threshold either comes from an All-True cone pair (step 4 in Algorithm 3) or from individual correlation checking (step 9 in Algorithm 3). The All-True lemma ensures no false-admission in the first case and the individual checking will not false admit any pair either.

Given a query time series T_q, for the tree-based traversal, pairs formed by T_q and individual time series in a non-leaf node will be output if they satisfy the All-True lemma; pairs formed by T_q and individual time series in a non-leaf node will be dismissed if they satisfied the All-False lemma. The children will not be visited in both of these cases. This will not result in a false dismissal or false admission for any pair because of the All-True, All-False lemmas and the fact that the union of the time series sets of a non-leaf node's children is the same as the time series set of their parent. The children of a non-leaf node which does not satisfy the two lemma will be visited recursively. As in the threaded-leaves-only traversal, the leaf node will also be checked against the All-True and All-False lemmas. The completeness and correctness can be argued similarly.

Lemma 2 (Completeness and Correctness of the Join Algorithm). *The Similarity_Join algorithm is complete and correct.*

Proof Sketch:
The Similarity_Join algorithm is similar to the Similarity_Range_Query algorithm with a set of query time series organized as threaded leaves. The completeness and correctness proofs are similar to those in Lemma 1.

4   Cost Models

In this section, we provide simple algebraic cost models for correlation-based similarity range queries and joins(all-pair queries) in spatial time series datasets. The correlation analysis of spatial time series is a CPU intensive task, and the CPU cost is at least as important as the I/O cost for datasets with a long sequence of time series. Furthermore, the number of correlation computations could also be used to measure the computational cost of correlation analyses in different system configurations. Therefore, the number of correlation computations is used as the unit of cost in the cost models. We will investigate a cost model that includes the I/O cost of query processing in spatial time series data in future work.

As we discussed in Section 3, the proposed algorithms for correlation-based similarity queries include the construction of a similarity search tree and query processing using the spatial autocorrelation based search tree. Therefore the cost model of a correlation based similarity query, $Cost$, consists of $Cost_{construct\_tree}$, the cost of the formation of the similarity search tree for data, and $Cost_{query}$, the cost of query processing. We denote the fraction of leaf cones satisfying the All-True or All-False lemmas as FAR (the filter ability ratio). The cost models for similarity range queries and similarity joins are introduced respectively in the following subsections.

4.1   Cost Models for Correlation-Based Similarity Range Queries

Let T_q be the query time series and the objective of the correlation-based simi- larity range queries be to retrieve all highly correlated time series with T_q from a spatial time series data S. As discussed in Section 3, there are two query strategies for similarity range queries: matching using a threaded-leaves-only traversal and matching using a tree-based traversal. The costs of the formation of the search tree are the same for the two range query strategies, denoted as $Cost_{construct\_tree}$. Let T denote the search tree for the dataset S and $|T|$ denote the number of nodes in T. Assume the average number of the time series in a leaf cone is n_l. We discuss the cost of query processing for the similarity range queries using the two strategies as follows.

The threaded-leaf-only strategy scans all leaf cones linearly, and prunes all All-True and All-False cones. Let $FAR_{threaded\_leaf}$, which denotes the filtering ability ratio for this strategy, represent the percentage of All-True and All-False cones in all leaf cones. Let L denote the threaded leaf cone set in the search tree and $|L|$ denote the number of leaf cones in L. This strategy scans each leaf cone once, and the refinements occur for the cones which cannot be filtered. The cost of the refinement step is $|L| \times (1 - FAR_{threaded\_leaf}) \times n_l$. Therefore the cost of query processing for this strategy is:

$$Cost_{range\_query}^{threaded\_leaf} = |L| + |L| \times (1 - FAR_{threaded\_leaf}) \times n_l$$

The tree-based strategy traverses all branches in the search tree. It stops traversing when the root cone of this subtree is an All-True or All-False or leaf cone. Let N_t denote all the nodes(cones) visited in the tree-based traversal and $|N_t|$ denote the number of nodes in N_t. Let FAR_{tree_based}, which denotes the leave node filtering ability ratio for this strategy, represent the percentage of All-True and All-False cones in all visited leaf nodes. The cost of the refinement step is $|L| \times (1 - FAR_{tree\_based}) \times n_l$. Therefore the cost of query processing for this strategy is:

$$Cost_{range\_query}^{tree\_based} = |N_t| + |L| \times (1 - FAR_{tree\_based}) \times n_l$$

Since both strategies construct the same search trees, the filtering ability ratios are the same for the range query processing using the two strategies, i.e., $FAR_{threaded\_leaf} = FAR_{tree\_based}$. Hence the costs of the refinement step for the two strategies are the same. When the filtering ability ratio of a range query increases, the number of nodes visited using the tree-based strategy, $|N_t|$ often tends to decrease.

4.2   Cost Models for Correlation-Based Similarity Joins

Let S_1 and S_2 be two spatial time series datasets. The objective of the correlation based similarity join is to retrieve all highly correlated time series pairs between the two datasets. As discussed in Section 3, there are two query strategies for a similarity join: the nested loop approach, which iterates the threaded leaves of both search trees, and the single loop approach, which iterates the threaded leaves of one search tree and traverses the other search tree in a checking and branching manner. The costs of the formation of search trees denoted as $Cost_{construct\_tree}$ are the same for the two join strategies. Let T_1 and T_2 denote the search trees for the dataset S_1 and S_2 respectively. Let $|T_1|$ and $|T_2|$ denote the number of nodes in T_1 and T_2 respectively. Let L_1 and L_2 be the leaf cone sets for T_1 and T_2 respectively, and $|L_1|$ and $|L_2|$ be the number of leaf cones in L_1 and L_2 respectively. Assume the average numbers of the time series in leaf cones are n_{l1} and n_{l2} for L_1 and L_2 respectively. We will discuss the cost of the query processing for the join processing using the two strategies as follows.

The strategy using a nested loop of the threaded leaf cones is a cone-level join between two leaf cone sets of the two search trees. Let FAR_{nested_loop}, which denotes the filtering ability ratio for this strategy, represent the percentage of All-True and All-False cones in the nested loop join. The cost of the nested loop join is $|L_1| \times |L_2|$, and the cost of refinement is $|L_1| \times |L_2| \times (1 - FAR_{nested\_loop})$. The total cost of join processing using the nested loop of leaf cones is:

$$Cost_{join}^{nested\_loop} = |L_1| \times |L_2| + |L_1| \times |L_2| \times (1 - FAR_{nested\_loop}) \times n_{l1} \times n_{l2}$$

The strategy using a single loop of tree-based traversal chooses the search tree with the smaller number of leaf cones as the outer loop, and choose the other as the search tree in the inner loop. Without losing the generality, we assume that the leaf cone set of T_1 is chosen as the outer loop and T_2 is chosen as the search tree in the inner loop. Let N_{t2} denote all the visited nodes in the search tree T_2 and $|N_{t2}|$ denote the number of nodes in N_{t2}. Let FAR_{tree_based}, which denotes the leaf node filtering ability ratio for this strategy, represent the percentage of All-True and All-False cones of the leaf nodes in the nested loop join. We match each leaf cone center in the outer loop with the inner search tree T_2. Therefore each matching is a special range query for each leaf cone with multiple time series inside, and the cost is $|N_{t2}| + |L_2| \times FAR_{single\_loop} \times n_{l1} \times n_{l2}$ The total cost of the joins using the single loop is:

$$Cost_{join}^{single\_loop} = |L_1| \times (|N_{t2}| + |L_2| \times (1 - FAR_{single\_loop}) \times n_{l1} \times n_{l2})$$

5   Performance Evaluation

We wanted to answer two questions: (1) How do the two query strategies improve the performance of correlation-based similarity range query processing? (2) How do the two query strategies improve the performance of correlation based similarity join processing?

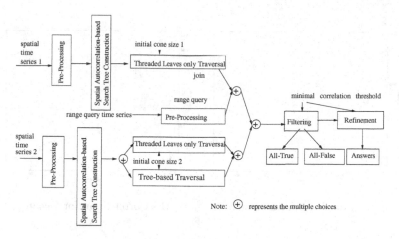

Fig. 3. Experimental Design

We evaluated the performance of the proposed query processing strategies with a dataset from NASA Earth science data [15]. In this experiment, correlation-based similarity queries were carried out between the Sea Surface Temperature (SST) in the eastern tropical region of the Pacific Ocean(80W - 180W, 15N - 15S) and Net Primary Production (NPP) in the United States. The NPP time series from 2901 land cells of the United States and the SST time series from 11556 ocean cells of the eastern tropical region of the Pacific Ocean were obtained under a 0.5 degree by 0.5 degree resolution. The records of NPP and SST were monthly data from 1982 to 1993.

Figure 3 describes the experimental setup to evaluate the different strategies for similarity range query and join processing. As we noted in Section 3, there are two proposed strategies for the query processing: threaded-leaves-only traversal and tree-based traversal. We investigated the two strategies for range similarity queries. For the similarity joins, we chose the threaded-leaves-only traversal for the outer loop, and we evaluated the two query strategies in the search tree of the inner loop.

Here we briefly discuss the selection of parameters for the experiments. As we stated in Section 3, the range of the maximum threshold of cone angles, τ_{max}, is related to the minimal correlation thresholds θ and it is bounded by the minimal of the $\frac{\arccos(\theta)}{2}$ and $\frac{180°}{4} - \frac{\arccos(\theta)}{2}$. In our application domain, one of constrains is the need for fast search tree construction. We begin with the construction of a search tree using a starting cone size. The starting cone sizes depend on the nature of the data and can be roughly estimated using correlograms. The spatial correlogram plots the average correlation of pairs of spatial time series with same spatial distance against the spatial distances of those pairs. A coarse starting cone size is enough to construct the spatial autocorrelation-based search tree. Figure 4 represents the correlograms of samples from the eastern tropical

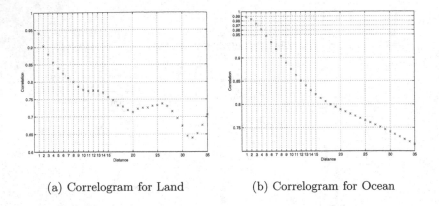

(a) Correlogram for Land   (b) Correlogram for Ocean

Fig. 4. Empirical Correlograms for Land and Ocean Samples

region of the Pacific Ocean and the United States and illustrates the relationships between the pairwise distances and correlations among the samples. The x-axis represents the distances of the ocean-ocean/land-land pairs in the unit of degree, and the y-axis represents the correlations of the time series of the ocean-ocean/land-land pairs. According to this figure, the ocean demonstrates higher spatial autocorrelation than the land. The land does not show as strong spatial autocorrelation as the ocean, and we will vary the starting cone size only for the eastern tropical Pacific Ocean in the experiment for simplicity. The land cone size was fixed at 1×1.

5.1   Correlation-Based Similarity Range Query Processing

This section describes a group of queries carried out to show the savings of the two strategies for a correlation-based range similarity queries. The SST data for the eastern tropical region of the Pacific ocean was chosen as the inner loop to construct a spatial autocorrelation-based search tree. The query time series were from the NPP data in the United States. We carried out the range queries in the spatial autocorrelation-based search tree for SST. All time series in SST, which correlates with the query NPP time series over the given minimal correlation threshold θ, are retrieved. We chose the starting cone size for the eastern tropical region of the Pacific Ocean to be 8×8. (Assume that we have built the spatial autocorrelation-based search tree for the SST time series in the inner loop before we carried out the queries.)

The brute force strategy scans all the time series in SST linearly. The cost of the brute force range queries is equal to $|SST|$, where $|SST|$ denotes the number of time series in the SST data. Here we define the saving ratio as the percentage of cost savings of a range query processing compared to the cost of a range query using the brute force strategy measured in the unit of number of correlation computations. And we define the average saving ratio for multiple

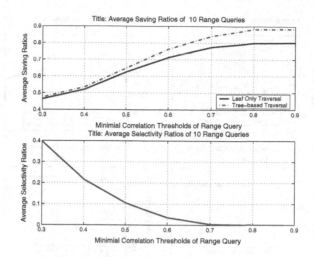

Fig. 5. Savings and Selectivity Ratios for Range Query Processing

range queries as the mean saving ratio for these range queries. We define the selectivity ratio for a range query as the fraction of query results of time series among all the time series in the dataset. And we define the average selectivity ratio for multiple range queries as the mean selectivity ratio for these range queries.

We randomly chose 10 NPP time series from the United States and carried out the correlation-based similarity range queries using the two different strategies respectively with the SST data from the eastern tropical region of the Pacific Ocean. The geographical locations of the 10 query time series were widely spread in the United States. The average selectivity ratios for the 10 queries at the different minimal correlation thresholds are illustrated in the lower plot of Figure 5. As the minimal correlation threshold increased from 0.3 to 0.9, the average selectivity ratio decreased from 0.4 to 0. The average saving ratios using the two query strategies for the 10 queries at the different minimal correlation thresholds (0.3-0.9) are presented in the upper plot of Figure 5. The solid line represents the average saving ratios for the threaded-leaves-only traversal strategy, which range from 0.46 to 0.80. The dash-dot line represents the average saving ratios for the tree-based traversal strategy, and the saving ratios range from 0.48 to 0.89.

As the selectivity ratio decreases, more and more non-leaf nodes(cones) in the search tree are identified as All-True or All-False cones in the query processing using the tree-based strategy. Thus the tree-based strategy often outperformed the threaded-leaves-only strategy as the selectivity ratio decreased.

5.2   Correlation-Based Similarity Join Processing

This section describes a group of experiments carried out to show the net savings of the two strategies for the correlation-based similarity joins. The NPP

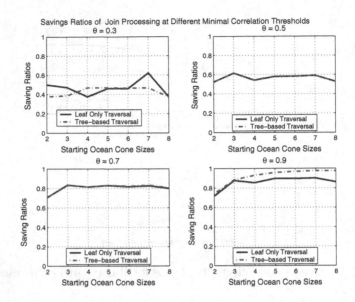

Fig. 6. Savings for Join Processing

time series dataset for the United State was chosen as the outer loop. As we discussed in the selection of parameter, the cone size for the NPP data was fixed at 1×1. The SST time series data for the eastern tropical region of the Pacific Ocean was chosen as the inner loop. A spatial autocorrelation-based search tree was constructed for the SST data. (Assume that we have built the spatial autocorrelation-based search trees before we carried out the similarity join operations.)

The cost of a brute force strategy is $|NPP| \times |SST|$, where $|NPP|$ and $|SST|$ are the number of the time series in NPP and SST respectively. Here we define the saving ratio as the percentage of cost savings of a join processing compared to the cost of a join using a brute force strategy measured in the unit of number of correlation computations. We define the selectivity ratio for a join as the fraction of join results of time series among the cross product of the two spatial time series datasets.

The selectivity ratios for the join processing of the NPP data and SST data are shown in Table. 4. As the minimal correlation threshold of the joins increased from 0.3 to 0.9, the selectivity ratio decreased from 0.39 to 0.

The saving ratios of the join processing using the two strategies are shown in Figure 6. Each subplot represents the saving ratios of the join processing for the two strategies using the search tree beginning with the different starting ocean cone sizes at a fixed minimal correlation threshold. The starting cone sizes for the eastern tropical region of the Pacific Ocean vary from 2×2 to 8×8. The saving ratios were presented at the different minimal correlation thresholds as shown in Figure 6.

Table 4. Selectivity Ratios for the Join between NPP data and SST data

Minimal Correlation Thresholds	0.3	0.4	0.5	0.6	0.7	0.8	0.9
Selectivity Ratios	0.39	0.22	0.11	0.04	0.005	0.0006	0

The saving ratios of the join processing using both strategies increases as the minimal correlation threshold of the joins increases. When the selectivity ratio is high, more leaf nodes(cones) are possibly traversed in the join processing using the tree-based strategy. The threaded-leaves-only strategy often tends to outperform the tree-based strategy at a high selectivity ratio. However, the tree-based strategy often outperformed the threaded-leaves-only strategy as the selectivity ratio was decreased.

In summary, the experimental results show that the query processing using the two query strategies saves a large fraction of the computational cost. The performance of the query processing using the two strategies is robust to the starting cone sizes, and it offers stable savings for the different starting cone sizes.

6   Conclusion and Future Work

We investigated the processing strategies for correlation-based similarity range queries and joins using a spatial autocorrelation search tree. Algebraic cost models were proposed and evaluation and experiments with Earth science data [15] show that the performance of the query and join processing strategies using the spatial autocorrelation-based search tree structure saves a large fraction of computational cost.

In future work, we would like to explore other search tree candidates, such as k-d tree, R-tree, and R-link tree. We plan to incorporate I/O costs into our cost models and carry out the comparison of experimental results with the prediction of algebraic cost models. We will also carry out a comparison study between the proposed query processing strategies with other indexing techniques [2, 6, 9] in spatial time series data.

Acknowledgments

We are particularly grateful to NASA Ames Research Center collaborators C. Potter and S. Klooster for their helpful comments and valuable discussions. We would also like to express our thanks to Kim Koffolt for improving the readability of this paper.

References

[1] NOAA El Nino Page. http://www.elnino.noaa.gov/.   451

[2] R. Agrawal, C. Faloutsos, and A. Swami. Efficient Similarity Search In Sequence Databases. In *Proc. of the 4th Int'l Conference of Foundations of Data Organization and Algorithms*, 1993. 449, 450, 452, 467

[3] L. Arge, O. Procopiuc, S. Ramaswamy, T. Suel, and J. Vitter. Scalable Sweeping-Based Spatial Join. In *Proc. of the 24th Int'l Conf. on VLDB*, 1998. 458

[4] G. Box, G. Jenkins, and G. Reinsel. *Time Series Analysis: Forecasting and Control*. Prentice Hall, 1994. 449

[5] B.W. Lindgren. *Statistical Theory (Fourth Edition)*. Chapman-Hall, 1998. 452

[6] K. Chan and A.W. Fu. Efficient Time Series Matching by Wavelets. In *Proc. of the 15th ICDE*, 1999. 449, 450, 452, 467

[7] N. Cressie. *Statistics for Spatial Data*. John Wiley and Sons, 1991. 450, 455

[8] R. Elmasri and S. Navathe. *Fundamentals of Database Systems*. Addison Wesley Higher Education, 2002. 456

[9] Christos Faloutsos. *Searching Multimedia Databases By Content*. Kluwer Academic Publishers, 1996. 450, 452, 467

[10] Food and Agriculture Organization. Farmers brace for extreme weather conditions as El Nino effect hits Latin America and Australia. http://www.fao.org/NEWS/1997/970904-e.htm. 451

[11] R. Grossman, C. Kamath, P. Kegelmeyer, V. Kumar, and R. Namburu, editors. *Data Mining for Scientific and Engineering Applications*. Kluwer Academic Publishers, ISBN: 1-4020-0033-2, 2001. 449

[12] D. Gunopulos and G. Das. Time Series Similarity Measures and Time Series Indexing. *SIGMOD Record*, 30(2), 2001. 449

[13] D.J. DeWitt J.M. Patel. Partition Based Spatial-Merge Join. In *Proc. of the ACM SIGMOD Conference*, 1996. 458

[14] S.T. Leutenegger and M.A. Lopez. The Effect of Buffering on the Performance of R-Trees. In *Proc. of the ICDE Conf., pp 164-171*, 1998. 458

[15] C. Potter, S. Klooster, and V. Brooks. Inter-annual Variability in Terrestrial Net Primary Production: Exploration of Trends and Controls on Regional to Global Scales. *Ecosystems*, 2(1):36–48, 1999. 450, 463, 467

[16] P. Rigaux, M. Scholl, and A. Voisard. *Spatial Databases: With Application to GIS*. Morgan Kaufmann Publishers, 2001. 452, 454

[17] J. Roddick, K. Hornsby, and M. Spiliopoulou. An Updated Bibliography of Temporal, Spatial, and Spatio-Temporal Data Mining Research. In *First Int'l Workshop TSDM*, 2000. 449

[18] H. Samet. *The Design and Analysis of Spatial Data Structures*. Addison-Wesley Publishing Company, Inc., 1990. 452

[19] S. Shekhar and S. Chawla. *Spatial Databases: A Tour*. Prentice Hall, ISBN:0130174807, 2003. 449, 452, 454, 458

[20] S. Shekhar, S. Chawla, S. Ravada, A. Fetterer, X. Liu, and C.T. Lu. Spatial Databases: Accomplishments and Research Needs. *IEEE TKDE*, 11(1), 1999. 449

[21] W.R. Tobler. *Cellular Geography, Philosophy in Geography*. Gale and Olsson, Eds., Dordrecht, Reidel, 1979. 450

[22] Michael F. Worboys. *GIS - A Computing Perspective*. Taylor and Francis, 1995. 449

[23] Pusheng Zhang, Yan Huang, Shashi Shekhar, and Vipin Kumar. Correlation Analysis of Spatial Time Series Datasets: A Filter-and-Refine Approach. In *the Proc. of the 7th Pacific-Asia Conf. on Knowledge Discovery and Data Mining*, 2003. 450, 453, 455

Automatically Annotating
and Integrating Spatial Datasets

Ching-Chien Chen, Snehal Thakkar, Craig Knoblock, and Cyrus Shahabi

Department of Computer Science & Information Sciences Institute
University of Southern California, Los Angeles CA 90089,
{chingchc,snehalth,knoblock,shahabi}@usc.edu

Abstract. Recent growth of the geo-spatial information on the web has made it possible to easily access a wide variety of spatial data. By integrating these spatial datasets, one can support a rich set of queries that could not have been answered given any of these sets in isolation. However, accurately integrating geo-spatial data from different data sources is a challenging task. This is because spatial data obtained from various data sources may have different projections, different accuracy levels and different formats (e.g. raster or vector format). In this paper, we describe an information integration approach, which utilizes various geo-spatial and textual data available on the Internet to automatically annotate and conflate satellite imagery with vector datasets. We describe two techniques to automatically generate control point pairs from the satellite imagery and vector data to perform the conflation. The first technique generates the control point pairs by integrating information from different online sources. The second technique exploits the information from the vector data to perform localized image-processing on the satellite imagery. Using these techniques, we can automatically integrate vector data with satellite imagery or align multiple satellite images of the same area. Our automatic conflation techniques can automatically identify the roads in satellite imagery with an average error of 8.61 meters compared to the original error of 26.19 meters for the city of El Segundo and 7.48 meters compared to 15.27 meters for the city of Adams Morgan in Washington, DC.

1 Introduction

Automatically and accurately aligning two spatial datasets is a challenging problem. Two spatial datasets obtained from different organizations can have different geographic projections and different type of inaccuracies. If the geographic projections of both datasets are known, then both datasets can be converted to the same geographic projections. However, the geographic projection for a wide variety of geo-spatial data available on the Internet is not known. Furthermore, converting datasets

T. Hadzilacos et al. (Eds.): SSTD 2003, LNCS 2750, pp. 469–488, 2003.
© Springer-Verlag Berlin Heidelberg 2003

into the same projection does not address the issue of different inaccuracies between two spatial datasets. Despite the fact that GIS researchers have worked on this problem for a long time, the resulting conflation [22] algorithms still require the manual identification of control points. Automatic conflation techniques are necessary to automatically integrate large spatial datasets. One application of automated conflation techniques is to accurately identify buildings in the satellite imagery. Computer vision researchers have been working on trying to identify features, such as roads, buildings, and other features in the satellite imagery [19]. While the computer vision research has produced algorithms to identify the features in the satellite imagery, the accuracy and run time of those algorithms are not suited for these applications.

We developed the Building Finder application, which integrates satellite imagery from Microsoft Terraservice with the street information from U.S. Census TIGER/Line files and building information from a white page web source to identify buildings in the satellite imagery. The Building Finder queries the streets from a database containing street network information. The result of the query is a set of tuples consisting of street name, city, state and zip code, which is used to query the Switchboard white pages agent to find the addresses related to those streets. The result of the Switchboard white pages website is then provided to the geocoder agent, which in turn provides the latitudes and longitudes for the addresses. The Building Finder also obtains a satellite image from Terraservice for the given area of interest. Finally, the latitude and longitude points representing different addresses and information representing different streets is superimposed on the satellite imagery.

A key research challenge in developing the Building Finder is to accurately integrate road network vector data with the satellite image. Different information sources utilize different projections for spatial information and there are various inconsistencies in the spatial information. For example, the spatial projection utilized for the satellite imagery is not the same as the spatial projection utilized for the TIGER/Line files, and due to local elevation changes some road locations in the TIGER/Line files are inaccurate. Due to these problems, finding accurate locations of the buildings in the satellite image is a very challenging problem. The Building Finder utilizes techniques described in this paper to find accurate locations of the buildings in the satellite image.

In this paper, our focus is on efficiently and completely automatically reducing spatial inconsistencies between two geo-spatial datasets originating from two different data sources. The spatial inconsistencies are due to the inaccuracy of different data sources as well as different projections used by different data source. Traditionally GIS systems have utilized a technique called conflation [22] to accurately align different geo-spatial datasets. The conflation process can be divided into the following subtasks: (1) find control point pairs in two datasets, (2) detect inaccurate control point pairs from the set of control point pairs for quality control, and (3) use the accurate control points to align the rest of the points and lines in both datasets using triangulation and rubber-sheeting techniques.

Applications, such as the Building Finder, cannot rely on a manual approach to perform conflation, as the area of interest for the Building Finder application may be anywhere in the continental United States. Manually finding and filtering control points for a large region, such as, the continental United States, is very time consuming and error-prone. Moreover, performing conflation offline on two datasets is also not a viable option as both datasets are obtained by querying different web sources at run-time. In fact, satellite imagery and vector data covering the whole world are available from various sources. The vector data and the satellite imagery obtained from different sources do not always align with each other and manually finding control points for the entire world is a very daunting task. Therefore, an automatic approach to find accurate control point pairs in different geo-spatial datasets is required. Our experimental results show that using our algorithm, we can completely automatically align two geo-spatial datasets.

The remainder of this paper is organized as follows. Section 2 describes two different algorithms to automatically identify control point pairs in two geo-spatial datasets. Section 3 describes an algorithm to filter out inaccurate control point pairs from the automatically generated control point pairs. Section 4 describes a modified conflation process to align two geo-spatial data sets. Section 5 provides the results of utilizing our approach to identify road network in the satellite imagery. Section 6 discusses the related work. Section 7 concludes the paper by discussing our future plans.

2   Finding Control Points

A control point pair consists of a point in one dataset and a corresponding point in the other dataset. Finding accurate control point pairs is a very important step in the conflation process as all the other points in both datasets are aligned based on the control point pairs. Section 2.1 describes a technique to find control points by querying information from existing web services. Section 2.2 describes a technique to generate control points using localized image processing.

2.1   Using Online Data

The Internet has a wide variety of geo-spatial and textual datasets available on the web. Intuitively, the idea behind finding control points using the online data sources is to find some feature points on one of the datasets and utilize sources on the Internet to find the corresponding points on the second dataset. In case of the Building Finder, Microsoft Terraservice provides the satellite imagery dataset. Terraservice also provides different types of feature points, such as churches, buildings, schools, etc through the Terraserver Landmark Service. The points provided by Terraserver Landmark Service align perfectly with the satellite imagery, i.e. the points line up with corresponding features in the satellite imagery. Therefore, the feature points provided can be used as control points on the satellite imagery. The feature points extracted from the Terraserver Landmark Service provide name of the point, latitude and longitude for each point. One way to find corresponding point on the TIGER/Line files is to find the address of each feature point and geocode the addresses using the TIGER/Line files. However, the landmark feature points only provide name, type, and coordinates of the important points in various categories, such as churches, hospitals, etc. Table 1 shows some example landmark points queried from Microsoft Ter-raService.

As shown in Figure 1, the corresponding feature control points in the second da-taset are identified by integrating information from several online sources. In case of the Building Finder, the second dataset is the TIGER/Lines vector data. The Building Finder queries the relevant yellow page web sources for the landmark points in vari-ous categories and finds a list of all points in the area for a category. We utilize ma-chine learning techniques described in [17] to query web sources as if they are data-bases. Online yellow page sources are often incomplete or have some inaccuracies, so the Building Finder integrates information from the following yellow page web sources: (1) The Yahoo Yellow Pages, (2) The Verizon Superpages, and (3) The White pages. Next, we find the geographic coordinates for the addresses of the yellow page points using a geocoder that utilizes vector data from TIGER/Line files, i.e., the second dataset, to find geographic coordinates for the given addresses. This geocoded point provides the corresponding point on the TIGER/Line files. Some sample feature points identified by this method are shown in Table 2.

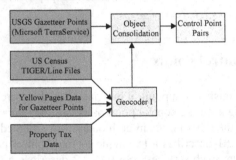

Fig. 1. Finding Control Points Using Online Sources

Table 1. TerraServer Landmark Feature Points

Feature Name	Type	Latitude	Longitude
Church of Christ	Church	33.91971	-118.4079
El Segundo Christian Church	Church	33.91811	-118.4179
El Segundo Public Library	Library	33.92391	-118.4169
El Segundo Foursquare Church	Church	33.92154	-118.4175
First Baptist Church	Church	33.92531	-118.4099

Fig. 2. Resulting Control Points

As shown in Table 1 and Table 2, the landmark names extracted from the yellow page sources do not exactly match with the landmark names from the Terraservice. Furthermore, different yellow page sources refer to different landmarks using different names. The Building Finder application utilizes the record linkage techniques [25] to identify matching point pairs from the landmark points obtained from Microsoft TerraService and the landmark features queried from different yellow page web sources. The record linkage techniques identify textual similarity between the records by utilizing different transformations, such as, acronym, substring, and stemming. The matching point pairs can be used as the control point pairs to conflate two data sources.

The corresponding landmarks on both the imagery and vector data are good candidates for control point pairs. However, we must address the following challenges: First, the landmark points are not uniformly distributed on the imagery. Hence, there may not be enough landmark points in some areas to find sufficient control point pairs. Due to this problem, the available landmark points may not produce enough control point pairs to capture local transformations between the two geo-spatial datasets. We address this issue by utilizing a technique termed region growing, which is described in Section 4.3. Second, some landmarks are big entities that cover a large area. For example, a school may cover a rectangular area of 200 pixels width and 200 pixels height on a 1m/pixel resolution image, and the center of the school building is chosen as the representative for the landmark. The geocoder may geocode the point at the center of the rectangle, which would turn out to be different than the center of the building. We addressed this issue by utilizing small entities, like churches and police stations, as control points.

2.2   Analyzing Imagery Using the Vector Data

We also explored the use of image analysis to identify control point pairs. Various GIS researchers and computer vision researchers have shown that the intersection points on the road networks provide an accurate set of control point pairs [8, 10]. In fact, several image processing algorithms to detect roads in the satellite imagery have been utilized to identify intersection points in the satellite imagery. Unfortunately, automatically extracting road segments directly from the imagery is a difficult task due to the complexity that characterizes natural scenes [11]. Moreover, processing an image of a large area to extract roads requires a lot of time.

Integrating vector data into the road extraction procedures alleviates these problems. We developed a localized image processing technique that takes advantage of the vector data to accurately and efficiently find the intersection points of various roads on the satellite image. Conceptually, the spatial information on the vector data represents the existing knowledge about the approximate location of the roads and intersection points on the satellite imagery. We improve the accuracy and run time of the algorithms to detect intersection points in the satellite image by utilizing the knowledge from the vector data. First, our localized image processing technique finds all the intersection points on the vector data. For each intersection point on the vector data, the localized image processing technique determines the area in the satellite image where the corresponding intersection point should be located. Finally, the image processing techniques are applied to these small areas to identify the intersection points on the satellite imagery. The area size of selected areas is much smaller than the entire image. The area is determined from the intersection points on the vector data and the directions of the road segments intersecting at these points.

The localized image processing technique may not be able to find all intersection points on the satellite image due to the existence of trees or other obstructions. However, the conflation process does not require a large number of control point pairs to perform accurate conflation. Therefore, for a particular intersection point on the vector data, if the corresponding image intersection point cannot be found within the certain area, it will not greatly affect the conflation process. We discuss the more detailed procedure in the following sub-sections.

Table 2. Extracted Feature Points from Online Sources

Feature Name	Address	Latitude	Longitude
Church of Christ El Segundo Hilltop Community	717 East Grand Ave	33.91961	-118.4079
El Segundo Christian Church	223 West Franklin Ave	33.91751	-118.4139
El Segundo Public Library	111 W Mariposa Ave	33.92331	-118.4159
Foursquare Church Of El Se-gundo	429 Richmond Street	33.92124	-118.4145
First Baptist Church of El Se-gundo	591 East Palm Avenue	33.92501	-118.4049

2.2.1   Road Networks Intersection Detection

The process of finding the intersection points on the road network from the vector data is divided into two steps. First, all candidate points are obtained by examining all line segments in the vector data. In this step, the endpoints of each line segment in the vector data are labeled as the candidate points. Second, the connectivity of these candidate points is examined to determine if they are intersection points. In this step, each candidate point is examined to see if there are more than two line segments connected at this point. If so, this point is marked as an intersection point and the directions of the line segments that are connected at the intersection point are calculated.

2.2.2 Imagery Road Intersection Detection (Localized Image Processing)

The intersection points and the road directions from the vector data are utilized to identify the corresponding intersection points on the satellite image. The algorithm to identify intersection points in the imagery takes the following parameters: the satellite image, coordinates of the corner points of the satellite image, set of intersection points detected from the vector data, and the area size parameter. The area size determines the size of the rectangular area around the intersection point examined by our localized image processing algorithm. The area size parameter can be determined based on the accuracy of the two data sets. One option is to utilize the maximum error or offset between two datasets. We utilized the information from the US Census Bureau survey [16] to determine the area size parameter. The area size parameter can also be estimated by the following incremental procedure: First, randomly pick an intersection point on the vector data. Next, mark the location in the image at the same coordinates as the intersection point from the vector data. Start with a very small area size and gradually increase the area size until some clear linear features within the area are recognized. Note the value of the area size parameter. Repeat this procedure for a few intersection points and pick the maximum area size.

For each intersection point detected from the vector data, the localized image processing technique picks a rectangular area in the satellite image centered at the location of the intersection point from the vector data. The existing edge detection techniques from [18] are used to identify linear features in the area. An accumulation array [21] technique is utilized to detect line segments from the linear features. The detected linear features and directions of the lines from the vector data are the key variables used to determine the score for each linear feature (on the imagery) in the accumulation array. The line segment formed by the images' linear features with the highest score in the accumulation array pinpoints the location of the edges of the roads. The intersection point of the detected lines is most likely the corresponding intersection point on the satellite imagery.

The localized image processing avoids exhaustive search of all intersection points on the entire satellite image and often locates the intersection point on the satellite image that is the closest intersection point to the intersection point detected from the vector data. Moreover, this technique does not need to extract road segments for the entire region. Only partial road segments near the intersections on the satellite image need to be extracted. Extracting road segments near the intersection point is easier than extracting all road segments, as the road sides closest to the intersections are often two parallel strong linear features, which are easier to identify. Figure 3 depicts the intersection points on vector data and the corresponding intersection points on imagery. The rectangular points are the intersection points on the vector data, and the circular points are the intersection points on the images.

3   Filtering Control Points

Both techniques discussed in Section 2 may generate some inaccurate control point pairs. As discussed in Section 2.1, the approach to identify control point pairs using

online data sources may produce inaccurate control point pairs due to temporal inconsistencies between data sources and the size of the various features. Meanwhile the
localized image processing may identify linear features, like tree clusters, building
shadings, building edges and some other image noise, as road segments, thus detecting
some inaccurate control point pairs. For example in Figure 3, the control point pairs
1, 2 and 3 are inaccurate control point pairs.

The conflation algorithm utilizes the control point pairs to align the vector data
with the satellite image. The inaccurate control point pairs reduce the accuracy of the
alignment between two datasets. Therefore, it is very important to filter out inaccurate
control point pairs. While there is no global transformation to align imagery and
vector data, in small areas the relationship between the points on the imagery and the
points on the vector data can be described by a transformation and a small uncertainty
measure. The transformation segment can be attributed to different projections used
to obtain the imagery data and the vector data, while the small uncertainty measure is
due to the elevation changes in the area or due to the inconsistencies between the
datasets. Due to the above-mentioned nature of the datasets, in a small region the
control points on the imagery and the counterparts on vector data should be related by
similar transformations. Therefore, the inaccurate control point pairs can be detected
by identifying those pairs with significantly different relationship as compared to the
other nearby control point pairs. We used the vector median filter (VMF) [1] to filter
out inaccurate control points.

Fig. 3. The intersection points (rectangles) on vector data and the corresponding intersection
points (circles) on imagery

3.1   Vector Median Filter (VMF)

Vector Median Filter (VMF) [1] is a mathematical tool for signal processing to at-
tenuate noise, and it is a popular filter to do noise removal in image processing. The
VMF accepts the data points as vectors, e.g., in our case a 2D vector with latitude and
longitude differences between the points in the control point pair, and filters out the
data points with the vectors significantly different from the median vector.

The geographic coordinate displacement between the points of each control point pair in a small area can be viewed as a 2D vector, termed control-point vector. The starting point of the vector is the control point on the vector data and the end point is the control point on the image. Because the spatial inconsistencies between the imagery and vector data in a local area are similar, the control-point vectors whose direction and length are significantly different from the others are characterized as an inaccurate control-point vector. Due to the similarities of these control-point vectors, the directions and lengths of them can be represented by the vector median. We modified the vector median filter to assist us in identifying the control-point vectors that are significantly different. This helped to obtain the best matching set of control points.

Vector median has similar properties as the median operation. Intuitively, the median vector is the vector that has the shortest summed distance (Euclidean distance) to all other vectors.

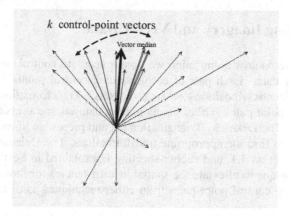

Fig. 4. The distributions of twenty-one control-point vectors in Figure 3(k =11)

The inputs for a vector median filter are N vectors $\vec{x}_i$ (i= 1, 2, 3, ... N) and the output of the filter is the vector median $\vec{x}_{vm}$. We revised the output of vector median filter to accommodate not only $\vec{x}_{vm}$, but also k closest vectors to the vector median. We defined the distance D:

$$D= \|\vec{x}_k - \vec{x}_{vm}\|_2$$

where $\vec{x}_k$ is the k-th closest vector to $\vec{x}_{vm}$.

Then, the output of our vector median filter is

$$\{\vec{x}_i \mid \text{where } \|\vec{x}_i - \vec{x}_{vm}\| \leq D \}$$

As shown in Figure 4, the modified Vector Median Filter selects the k closest vectors to the vector median as the accurate control point pairs. The possible value of k is an integer between 1 and N. Large value of k provides more control-point vectors, but may not filter out all inaccurate control point pairs. If the number of inaccurate control point pairs exceeds the half of the size of control-point pairs, then the vector median would be one of the inaccurate vectors. The Vector Median Filter can only work when the median vector is not inaccurate. Thus, the number of inaccurate control-point vectors should not exceed half the control-point vectors. Therefore, control point pairs with the $\left\lceil \frac{N}{2} \right\rceil$ closest vectors to the vector median should be the most accurate control point pairs. Towards this end, we kept the $k = \left\lceil \frac{N}{2} \right\rceil$ closest vectors to the vector median and filtered out the rest of the control point pairs. As a result, some accurate control-point vectors may be lost. However, the missing control point pairs would not greatly affect the conflation results, as some of the selected control point pairs close to the lost accurate control point pairs have similar directions and displacements.

4   Conflating Imagery and Vector Data

After filtering the control point pairs, we obtain accurate control point pairs on imagery and vector data. Each pair of corresponding control points from the two datasets indicates identical positions on each datasets. Transformations are calculated from the control point pairs. Other points in both datasets are aligned based on these transformations. The Delaunay Triangulation [5] and piecewise linear rubber sheeting [28] are utilized to find the appropriate transformations. The Delaunay Triangulation is discussed in Section 4.1, and rubber-sheeting is explained in Section 4.2. Moreover, a novel technique to alleviate the spatial inconsistencies for those areas where we cannot exploit any control point pairs from either techniques, is discussed in Section 4.3.

4.1   Triangulation

To achieve overall alignment of imagery and vector data, vector data must be adjusted locally to conform to the imagery. It is reasonable to align the two datasets based on local adjustments, because small changes in one area should not affect geometry at longer distances. To accomplish local adjustments, the domain space is partitioned into small pieces. Then, local adjustments are applied on each single piece. Triangulation is an effective strategy to partition domain space to define local adjustments.

There are different triangulations for the control points. One particular triangulation, the Delaunay triangulation, is especially suited for conflation systems [22]. A Delaunay triangulation is a triangulation of the point set with the property that no point falls in the interior of the circumcircle of any triangle (the circle passing through the three triangle vertices). The Delaunay triangulation maximizes the minimum angle of all the angles in the triangulation, thus avoiding triangles with extremely small angles. We perform the Delaunay triangulation with the set of control points on the vector data, and make a set of equivalent triangles with corresponding control points on the imagery. The Delanuay triangulation can be built in O(n*log n) time in worst case, where n is the number of control points.

4.2   Piecewise Linear Rubber-Sheeting

Imagine stretching a vector map as if it was made of rubber. We deform the vector data algorithmically, forcing registration of control points over the vector data with their corresponding points on the imagery. This technique is called "Piecewise linear rubber sheeting" [28]. There are two steps to rubber sheeting. First, the transformation coefficients to map each Delanuay triangular on vector data onto its corresponding triangular on the imagery are calculated. Second, the same transformation coefficients are applied to the road endpoints inside each triangle to transform the road endpoints (on the vector data) within the triangle. The conflated road network is constructed from these transformed endpoints.

Piecewise linear rubber sheeting based on triangles with extremely small angles (i.e., long and thin triangles) results in distorted conflation lines. Since the Delanuay triangulation avoids triangles with extremely small angles, it alleviates the problem. The details of the triangulation techniques and the piecewise linear rubber-sheeting algorithms are described in [15, 22, 28].

4.3   Region Growing

We propose a technique named "region-growing" to alleviate the spatial inconsistencies for those areas where there are no feature points to perform conflation (such as landmarks or intersection points) on the vector data and imagery. New control points are obtained by extrapolating existing control points. Using these new control points, the region with the control points can be expanded. This can also save time by reducing the need to detect intersection points or landmarks. However, if the existing control points are not accurate, the new control points will not be accurate either. In practice, "region-growing", "control points from online data sources" and "control points from intersection detections" could be combined to generate new control points for conflation.

Figure 5 illustrates the vector data for some streets in the city of El Segundo before conflation. Figure 6 shows the road network after applying our conflation technique, using VMF-filtered online data sources as control point pairs. Figure 7 shows the road network after applying conflation technique, using VMF-filtered intersection points as control point pairs.

5   Performance Evaluation

We evaluated our approaches to accurately integrate different geo-spatial datasets by integrating data from two different datasets. The first dataset was the vector data (road networks), and the second dataset was satellite imagery. These datasets are described in detail in section 5.1. The purpose of the integration experiment was to evaluate the utility of these algorithms in integrating real world data. We are interested in evaluating the two approaches to generate the control point pairs and the effect of the filtering techniques. Moreover, we were interested in measuring the improvement in the accuracy of the integration of two datasets using our techniques. To that end, we performed experiments to validate the following:

Hypothesis 1:   Performing automated conflation using the automated control point identification techniques described earlier (with no filters) improves the accuracy of the road identifications.

Hypothesis 2:   The automated filtering techniques improve the accuracy of the road identifications for both automated control point identification techniques.

Hypothesis 3:   The combination of the localized image processing using intersection points and the modified Vector Median Filter provides the best results.

Section 5.1 describes the experimental setup and the datasets used to evaluate our methods. Section 5.2 discusses performance of the two automatic control point identification algorithms without any filters. Section 5.3 describes the improvement due to the Vector Median Filter.

Fig. 5. The road network before conflation

Fig. 6. After applying conflation, utilizing VMF-filtered online data sources

Fig. 7. After applying conflation, utilizing VMF-filtered intersection points

5.1   Experimental Setup

The following are two different datasets used for our experiments: (1) Satellite imagery: The satellite imagery used in the experiments is the geo-referenced USGS DOQ images with 1-meter per pixel resolution. Microsoft TerraService web service [2, 3] was utilized to query the satellite imagery for different areas and (2) Vector data (road networks): The road network from the TIGER/Line files [26] was used as the vector data. The TIGER/Line files dataset was developed by the U.S. Bureau of the Census. In general, the TIGER/Lin files dataset has richer attribution but poor positional accuracy. As shown in Figure 5, the road network is TIGER/Line files and there are certain spatial inconsistencies between the satellite imagery and TIGER/Line files.

The automatic conflation system was developed in C#. The output of our conflation algorithm was a set of conflated roads for the TIGER/Line files. The experiment platform is a Pentium III 700MHz processor with 256MB memory on Windows 2000 Professional (with .NET framework installed). Our experiments were done on the City of El Segundo, California, and a region of the city of Adams Morgan, District of Columbia. We obtained similar conflation performance for these two cities. Therefore, in the following sub-sections, we will take the city of El Segundo as an example to explain our conflation results, and list the conflation result of city of Adams Morgan for reference. The experiments on the city of El Segundo covered the area with latitude from 33.916397 to 33.93095, and longitude from -118.425117 to -118.370173. It is a region of 5.2Km by 1.6Km (a 5200x1600 image with 1m/pixel ground resolution). There are approximately 500 TIGER/Line segments (i.e. about 500 endpoints) on this region. The Adams Morgan data covers a 2.8Km by 2.4Km rectangular area with corner points latitude and longitude (-77.006, 38.899) and (-76.974, 38.879) and contains 300 road segments. Most roads in both the cities are 15 to 30 meters in width. Both automated conflation techniques are order of magnitude faster compared to the other computer vision algorithms to detect features in the satellite imagery.

In order to evaluate our approaches, we compared the conflated roads with the accurate roads. The accurate roads were generated by conflating the TIGER/Line data using the control point pairs provided manually. The road endpoints on the imagery were represented by the endpoints of the high accuracy road networks. The experiments used all the road endpoints in the conflated data and measured the displacement of the road endpoints compared to the corresponding road endpoints in the accurate road network. The mean and the standard deviation of the point displacements are used to evaluate the accuracy of the algorithms.

5.2   First Set of Experiments: Online Data vs. Intersection Points

In the first set of experiments, we compared the mean standard deviation, and displacement range of the manually conflated road network with the road network generated using online data and intersection points as control point pairs respectively.

The experimental results are listed in Table 3, and the displacement distributions of the conflated roads' endpoints are shown in Figure 8. The X-axis of this Figure depicts the displacement between endpoint on the conflated roads and the equivalent endpoint on satellite image. The displacement values are grouped every 5 meters. The Y-axis shows the percentage of conflated points that are within the displacement range represented by the X-axis. For example, as shown in Figure 8, when utilizing unfiltered intersection points to generate conflated roads, 48% of the conflated roads' endpoints have less than 10 meters displacement from the corresponding satellite imagery points. While utilizing unfiltered online data, we obtained 13% of the points within 10 meters displacement. Considering the original TIGER/Lines, there are no points within 10 meters displacement from the imagery.

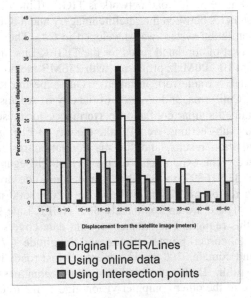

Fig. 8. The displacement distributions of road endpoints (online data vs. intersection points) for city of El Segundo

As shown in Table 3, the method utilizing unfiltered intersection points resulted in a smaller mean displacement than the TIGER/Lines and the conflated roads generated by the unfiltered online data. Therefore, the automated conflation approach using the control pairs obtained by using the localized image processing technique with no filter improves the accuracy of the integration process. However, the automated conflation using the unfiltered online control point pairs, resulted in lower accuracy as compared to the original TIGER/Lines. The key reasons for the inaccurate results are that the landmark points obtained from the online sources are not uniformly distributed and the control point pairs are often inaccurate (because of the spatial inconsistencies between the online data sources). The inaccuracy of the control point pairs is accumulated when applying region growing to generate new conflated roads, resulting in almost half (44%) of the conflated points having greater than 25m displacement as shown in Figure 8. However, the performance of both approaches is significantly improved by filtering out the inaccurate control point pairs.

5.3   Second Set of Experiments:
Filtered Control Points vs. Unfiltered Control Points

In the second set of experiments, we utilized the Vector Median Filter to filter out inaccurate control point pairs from the control point pairs generated using online data sources or localized image processing. We identified the road network in the satellite imagery using the filtered control point pairs. Finally, the conflated roads were compared with the manually conflated road network to evaluate their performance.

The experimental results are listed in Table 4, and the displacement distributions of the conflated road endpoints are shown in Figure 9. The meanings of X-axis and Y-axis of Figure 9 are the same as Figure 8. As shown in Table 4, conflated lines using VMF-filtered online control point pairs increase the accuracy of the original data by about 40%. Moreover, the intersection control points with the Vector Median Filter leads to a displacement error that is less than 50% of the displacement error for the original vector data.

From Figure 9, we can see that when using VMF-filtered intersection points as control points, more than 60% of the conflated road endpoints are within 10 meters displacements from the image. Only 2.8% of the endpoints have displacements greater than 25 meters. After visual checking, we found most of these points are close to the margins of our experiment region. It is reasonable to have low accuracy points around the margins, since long and thin Delanuay triangles were constructed around the margins. The small value of standard deviation (6 meters) of conflated roads generated using VMF-filtered intersection points indicates that most points' displacements are close to the mean displacement of 8.6m. Although the standard deviation is one meter greater than the standard deviation of the TIGER/Lines (5 meters) data, the range of displacement from the image is much smaller than the TIGER/Lines' range of displacement. This means that majority of endpoints of conflated roads using the VMF-filtered intersection control points are more accurate than TIGER/Lines' endpoints.

484   Ching-Chien Chen et al.

Table 3. Comparison of original road network with conflated roads

Dataset	Mean point displacement	Standard Deviation	Mean +- std. deviation
Original TIGER/Lines El Segundo	26.19	5	(21.19, 31.19)
Online control points El Segundo	27.41	16.25	(11.16,43.66)
Intersection control points El Segundo	15.48	13.41	(2.07, 28.89)
Original TIGER/Lines Adams Morgan	15.27	3.31	(11.96, 18.58)
Intersection control points Ad-ams Morgan	11.74	9.71	(2.03, 21.45)

Table 4. Results after filtering

Dataset	Mean displacement	Standard deviation	Mean +- std. deviation (meters)
Original TIGER/Lines for El Segundo	26.19	5	(21.19, 31.19)
Intersection cps + VMF-filter for El Segundo	8.61	6	(2.61,14.61)
Online cps + VMF-filter for El Segundo	15.92	8.38	(7.54, 24.3)
Original TIGER/Lines for Adams Morgan	15.27	3.31	(11.96, 18.58)
Intersection cps + VMF-filter for Adams Morgan	7.48	4.81	(2.67, 12.29)

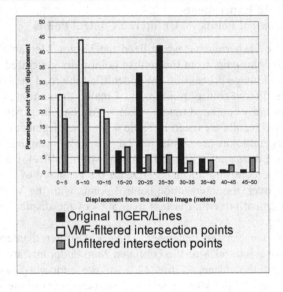

Fig. 9. The displacement distributions of road endpoints (VMF-filtered vs. unfiltered intersection points) for city of El Segundo

From Table 3 and 4, we conclude that all methods to perform automated conflation, except the method utilizing unfiltered online data, result in more accurate alignment of the vector data with the satellite imagery and more accurate road identifications compared to the original road network. Therefore, using any combination of the automatic control point identification techniques and the automatic filters results in better alignment. This validates hypothesis 2.

From Table 4, we also see that the mean displacement of conflated roads utilizing VMF-filtered intersection points is three times better than the original TIGER/Lines and almost two times better than the result without using the filter. Finally, conflation using intersection control point pairs and the VMF filter provides the most accurate result. This validates hypothesis 3.

6   Related Work

Currently, there are commercial products that utilize conflation techniques to provide integrated geospatial data. For example, NEXUS [20] was proposed by Nicklas to serve as an open platform for spatially aware applications. Since all kinds of spatial data can be integrated into the NEXUS system, it is a vital prerequisite that identical spatial objects from different datasets be matched in advance. Toward this end, the conflation technique discussed in [27] was applied to accomplish vector to vector dataset integration in the NEXUS system. Yuan and Tao proposed a componentware technology to develop conflation components and they demonstrated their approach for vector-to-vector conflation [29]. A commercial conflation product, MapMerger [6], also performs vector-to-vector conflation with limited human intervention to consolidate multiple vector datasets.

Advances in satellite imaging technology are making it possible to capture geospatial imagery with ever increasing precision. Remotely sensed images from space can offer a resolution of one meter or better. Utilizing imagery to vector conflation, this accurate imagery can assist in updating the relatively poor positional accuracy but rich attribution vector datasets, such as TIGER/Lines. To perform imagery to vector conflation, some spatial objects must be extracted from imagery to serve as control points. However, autonomous extraction of spatial objects from satellite imagery is a difficult task due to the complexity that characterizes natural scenes. Various approaches were developed over the past few years to automatically or semi-automatically conflate imagery and vector data covering the overlapping regions. Most of these approaches detect the counterpart elements on the datasets, then apply traditional conflation algorithm (i.e. establishing the correspondence between the matched entities and transforming other objects accordingly) [9, 21, 23, 24]. These approaches are different, because of the different methods utilized for locating the counterpart elements.

Some approaches directly extract the features from imagery and convert them to vector format, then apply the typical map-to-map [12, 22] or linear conflation algorithm [7]. Extracting features directly from imagery and converting to vector format is a tough task. Taking the road extraction as an example, there exist many algorithms for extracting roads utilizing the characteristics of roads as prior knowledge [9, 21, 23, 24], while none of them give good results in all circumstances [11, 13] and most of them are time-intensive.

Other alternative approaches utilize existing vector databases as part of the prior knowledge. Integrating existing vector data as part of the spatial object recognition scheme is an effective approach. Vector data represents the existing prior knowledge about the data, thus reducing the uncertainty in identifying the spatial objects in imagery. Hild and Fritsch [14] processed vector data to extract vector polygons and performed image segmentation on imagery to find image polygons. Then, a polygon matching (or shape matching) algorithm is applied on both images and vector to find a set of 2D conjugate points. In order to obtain a successful matching between an image and vector data, the datasets must contain polygonal features like forest, villages, grassland or lakes. This approach will fail when polygonal features can not be found, like in the high resolution urban areas. Flavie and Fortier [10] tried to find the junction points of all detected lines, than matched the extremities of the road segments with the image junctions. Their method suffers from the high computation cost of finding all possible junctions of detected lines on images. Another approach, which utilizes the road axes detected from vector data to verify the extracted line segments to determine where the roads are, was proposed in [4]. This approach uses the vector data knowledge only for checking the extracted lines, thus it also takes a long time to detect road segments.

Our proposed conflation approach takes the knowledge, such as online data sources or road segment direction and road intersections provided by vector data to alleviate the problems of finding control points from aerial images. Therefore, we can efficiently acquire control points on imagery. VMF filter is utilized to remove inaccurate control point pairs to obtain better alignments. The VMF filter uses the fact that the control points on the vector data and the counterparts on the imagery are related by similar transformations in a small region.

7   Conclusion and Future Work

The main contribution of this paper is the design and implementation of a novel information integration approach to automatically annotate and integrate spatial datasets. Our approach utilizes the online data sources and intersection points detected by localized image processing as control points. Moreover, the inaccurate control points are removed by our proposed filter. Experimental results on the city of El Segundo and the city of Adams Morgan demonstrate that our approach can accurately align and annotate satellite images with vector data.

We plan to further improve the integration result by an iterative conflation process. The process could work as follows: the vector-image conflation operations, automatic control point pairs generation and vector to imagery alignment, are alternately applied until no further control point pairs are identifiable. We also intend to extend our approach in several ways. Extending our approach to integrate multiple satellite images of the same area is one possible topic. Our approaches can be utilized to align both spatial image datasets with some other spatial vector dataset. Another possible topic is extending the localized image processing technique to improve the performance of the Building Finder application. Although the Building Finder application has successfully integrated information from various geo-spatial data sources to locate the buildings in the imagery, the boundaries of the buildings are represented by rectangles instead of the exact building edges. Utilizing the localized image processing within each rectangle to further refine the building boundaries is a promising future research direction.

Acknowledgements

We would like to thank Dr. Jose-Luis Ambite for his comments on various aspects of this project. We would also like to thank Bo Han for his help with online control point identification. This material is based upon work supported in part by the Defense Advanced Research Projects Agency (DARPA) and Air Force Research Laboratory under contract/agreement numbers F30602-01-C-0197 and F30602-00-1-0504, in part by the Air Force Office of Scientific Research under grant numbers F49620-01-1-0053 and F49620-02-1-0270, in part by the United States Air Force under contract number F49620-01-C-0042, in part by the Integrated Media Systems Center, a National Science Foundation Engineering Research Center, under cooperative agreement number EEC-9529152, and in part by a gift from the Microsoft Corporation.

References

[1]   J. Astola, P. Haavisto, and Y. Neuvo. *Vector Median Filter. In Proceedings of IEEE*. 1990.

[2]   T. Barclay, J. Gray, E. Strand, S. Ekblad, and J. Richter, *TerraService.NET: An Introduction to Web Services*, Microsoft Corporation.

[3]   T. Barclay, J. Gray, and D. Stuz, *Microsoft TerraServer: A Spatial Data Warehouse*. 1999, Microsoft Corporation.

[4]   A. Baumgartner, C. Steger, C.Wiedemann, H. Mayer, W. Eckstein, and H. Ebner., *Update of Roads in GIS from Aerial Imagery: Verification and Multi-Resolution Extraction*. IAPRS, 1996. **XXXI**.

[5]   M.d. Berg, M.v. Kreveld, M. Overmars, and O. Schwarzkopf, *Computational Geometry: Algorithms and Applications*. Springer-Verlag, 1997.

[6]   ESEA, Inc., Map Merger: Automated conflation tool for ArcGIS, http://www.conflation.com/map_merge/ 2002

[7]   S. Filin and Y. Doytsher. A Linear Conflation Approach for the Integration of Photogrammetric Information and GIS Data. IAPRS. 2000. Amsterdam.

[8]   M.A. Fischler and R.C. Bolles, Random Sample Consensus: A Paradigm for Model Fitting with Applications to Image Analysis and Automated Cartography. Communications of the ACM, 1981. **24**.

[9]   M.A. Fischler, J.M. Tenenbaum, and H.C. Wolf, Detection of Roads and Linear Structures in Low Resolution Aerial Images Using Multi-Source Knowledge Integration Techniques. ComputerGraphics and Image Processing, 1981. **15**(3): p. 201-223.

[10]   M. Flavie, A. Fortier, D. Ziou, C. Armenakis, and S. Wang. Automated Updating of Road Information from Aerial Images. American Society Photogrammetry and Remote Sensing Conference. 2000.

[11]   A. Fortier, D. Ziou, C. Armenakis, and S. Wang, Survey of Work on Road Extraction in Aerial and Satellite Images, Technical Report. 1999.

[12] F. Harvey and F. Vauglin. Geometric Match Processing: Applying Multiple Tolerances. Proceedings of International Symposium on Spatial Data Handling (SDH). 1996.

[13] C. Heipke, H. Mayer, and C. Wiedemann, *Evaluation of Automatic Road Extraction.* IAPRS, International Society for Photogrammetry and Remote Sensing, 1997. **32**(3-2(W3)).

[14] H. Hild and D. Fritsch, Integration of vector data and satellite imagery for geocoding. IAPRS, 1998. **32**.

[15] J.-R. Hwang, J.-H. Oh, and K.-J. Li. Query Transformation Method by Delaunary Triangulation for Multi-Source Distributed Spatial Database Systems. ACMGIS. 2001.

[16] J.S. Liadis, GPS TIGER Accuracy Analysis Tools (GTAAT) Evaluation and Test Results. 2000, TIGER Operation Branch, Geography Division.

[17] I. Muslea, S. Minton, and C.A. Knoblock, *Hierarchical Wrapper Induction for Semistructured Information Sources.* Autonomous Agents and Multi-Agent Systems, 2001. **4**(1/2).

[18] R. Nevatia and K.R. Babu, *Linear Feature Extraction and Description.* Computer Graphics and Image Processing, 1980. **13**: p. 257-269.

[19] R. Nevatia and K. Price, Automatic and Interactive Modeling of Buildings in Urban Environments from Aerial Images . IEEE ICIP 2002, 2002. **III**: p. 525-528.

[20] D. Nicklas, M. Grobmann, S. Thomas, S. Volz, and B. Mitschang. A Model-Based, Open Architecture for Mobile, Spatially Aware Applications. International Symposium on Spatial and Temporal Databases. 2001. Redondo Beach, CA.

[21] K. Price, *Road Grid Extraction and Verification.* IAPRS, 1999. **32 Part 3-2W5**: p. 101-106.

[22] A. Saalfeld, Conflation: Automated Map Compilation, in Computer Vision Laboratory, Center for Automation Research. 1993, University of Maryland.

[23] W. Shi and C. Zhu, The line segment match method for extracting road network from high-resolution satellite images. GeoRS, 2002. **40**(2).

[24] C. Steger, H. Mayer, and B. Radig. The Role of Grouping for Road Extraction. Automatic Extraction of Man-Made Objects from Aerial and Space Images (II). 1997. Basel, Switzerland.

[25] S. Tejada, C.A. Knoblock, and S. Minton, *Learning Object Identification Rules for Information Integration.* Information Systems, 2001. **26**(8).

[26] U.S.Census Bureau - TIGER/Lines, http://www.census.gov/geo/www/tiger/ 2002

[27] V. Walter and D. Fritsch, *Matching Spatial Data Sets: a Statistical Approach.* International Journal of Geographic Information Sciences, 1999. **5**.

[28] M.S. White and P. Griffin, *Piecewise Linear Rubber-Sheet Map Transformation.* The American Cartographer, 1985. **12**(2): p. 123-131.

[29] S. Yuan and C. Tao. Development of Conflation Components. Proceedings of Geoinformatics. 1999.

Location- and Time-Based Information Delivery in Tourism

Annika Hinze[1] and Agnès Voisard[1,2]

[1] Computer Science Institute, Freie Universität Berlin, Germany
{hinze,voisard}@inf.fu-berlin.de
[2] Fraunhofer ISST, Berlin, Germany

Abstract. Today's mobile devices allow end users to get information related to a particular domain based on their current location, such as the fastest route to the nearest drugstore. However, in such Location-Based Services (LBS), richer and more targeted information is desirable. In many applications, end users would like to be notified about relevant events or places to visit in the near future according to their profile. They also do not wish to get the same information many times unless they explicitly ask for it. In this paper, we describe our system, TIP (Tourism Information Provider), which delivers various types of information to mobile devices based on location, time, profile of end users, and their "history", i.e., their accumulated knowledge. The system hinges on a hierarchical semantic geospatial model as well as on an Event Notification System (ENS).

Keywords: Location-based services, event notification system, user-defined profile, context-awareness

1 Introduction

Today's mobile devices allow end users to get information that belong to a particular domain based on their current location. Examples include the address of the nearest drugstore or even the fastest route to it. However, in such *Location-Based Services (LBS)*, more complex and targeted information is desirable, such as information based on the present time or on the near-future. Moreover, in most applications, end users would like to be notified about relevant events or places to visit in their domain of interest, i.e., according to their profile. Last but not least, end users do not wish to get the same information many times unless they explicitly asked for it.

Delivering different types of information based on location, time, profile of end users, and their "history" - which leads to accumulated knowledge - is concerned with many issues that range from high level profile definition languages to wireless transmission of information. A whole range of applications concerns scheduling assistance, i.e., the best way(s) to combine time and location. Take for example a set of "mobile" events such as a tennis tournament, a film festival, a trade fair, or a conference. An end user would like to optimize his or her

T. Hadzilacos et al. (Eds.): SSTD 2003, LNCS 2750, pp. 489–507, 2003.

path through events/places (i.e., company booths or tennis courts or conference rooms) he or she is interested in. An intelligent system would deliver a list of options in terms of paths that combine the time and the location of the visitors as well as their interest and their possible priorities (some events, e.g., an invited talk, should not be missed). Such applications fall under the general topic of combinatorial optimization which is not the focus of the present paper.

Instead we are concerned here with applications involving mobile end users who already acquired knowledge on a particular area and who would like to get more information at a certain location, at a certain time, on particular topics and to relate pieces of information (current and past) with each other. A typical application is that of a tourist walking around in a region. If this person already visited a place he or she does not want to be reminded of basic historical facts related to that place. He or she would rather like to get further information related to the place in question. This is similar to Internet usage, where successive clicks provide more and more specialized information. However, to our knowledge, there is no available systems making connection with pages visited before (history) and offering the notion of personal profile. Besides, a mobile device used in tourism, such as a cellular phone or a *Personal Digital Assistant (PDA)*, has particular requirements. First, the amount of information that can be presented is limited. This means that the information should be conveyed in a simple form. Web page like layout is unacceptable. In addition, the computing power of such a device is restricted and many operations as well as rendering need to be performed elsewhere.

The information delivered to the users is extracted, and then combined, from various databases, such as a spatial database storing maps and an event database (e.g., concert or film time table), referred to as *scheduled event database* in the following. However, we are concerned with applications that go beyond pure database querying. In the applications considered here, end users get information they did not explicitly asked for. This push behavior comes from one of the following two situations: (1) Based on a certain profile, time, or location, targeted information is automatically extracted from the various databases, combined, and delivered to the user; or (2) external events not stored in a database (e.g., cancellation of a concert) but of relevance for the user are sent.

A solution that comes to mind is to extend an *Event Notification System (ENS)* or an active database. Event notification services, or alerting services, are increasingly used in various applications such as digital libraries, stock tickers, traffic control, or facility management. The idea is to react to a particular event by taking a certain action. Combining ENS and LBS in this context means considering the following features:

- Personal profiles.
- History-dependent information delivery.
- Spatial/spatio-temporal information organized hierarchically.
- Spatial/spatio-temporal[1] information organized in a semantic network such that facts can be related to each other.

---

[1] Note that considering pure temporal information does not make sense here.

In this paper, we offer an environment that combines the structured information, the various profiles, and all possible events. We use operators as means to navigate though the semantic network of information. A typical example of operators is proximity in several dimensions, as in "*near*" this position, "*near*" in time, or "*near*" in a semantical context. This is referred to as *proximity search* (in various dimensions) in the following.

A few remarks are noteworthy. First, in this paper we are not concerned with technical details such as the transmission of information from the mobile device to the server and vice versa. The fact, for example, that the *Global Positioning System (GPS)* is not operational inside a building and that the system may need to be coupled with a wireless *Local Area Network (LAN)* - as it was done for instance recently in a Tokyo museum - is not our concern here. Second, we are not concerned with privacy issues either even though these issues are definitely crucial. We assume, however, that end users send both their location to the server and selected information from their history. This means that users' history is stored on the portable device. Finally, the way the information is eventually conveyed to the user - through drawings, voice, texts, using the *Short Messaging System (SMS)*, in general unified messages - is not our focus here.

This paper is organized as follows. Section 2 presents related work. Section 3 introduces our reference application, which is a description of the information delivered to a tourist in the city of Berlin. Section 4 is concerned with the combination of LBS and ENS. It presents the major concepts as well as the architecture of our system, TIP, and a description of the information organization. Section 5 concerns the matching of profiles and events. Finally, Section 6 presents our conclusion and our ongoing and future work.

2 Related Work

Several system exist that process context-aware and location-based information. Two major approaches can be distinguished: services for outdoor experiences and services focussing on indoor activities. Examples of outdoor services include tourist guides, such as Nexus [32], Guide [6], Crumpet [25], and the Oldenburg guide [3]. Examples of indoor systems include museum guides, e.g., Hippie [23], Electronic Guidebook [15], and Rememberer [9]. Substantial consideration has been given to database modeling and querying of moving objects (e.g., in [28, 31, 30, 10, 12], to cite only a few). [28] distinguishes three query types: instantaneous (evaluated once at definition), continue (evaluated regularly after definition), and persistent (sequence of instantaneous queries evaluated at every database update). However, special mechanisms for profile definition and event filtering are not discussed in this approach. In the context of location based services, continuous queries are of particular interest. Most systems only consider only queries regarding the changes in user location (e.g., in the Oldenburg guide). Extensive research on location-based services focuses on the technical challenges of interaction with the moving users or the spatiotemporal observation of moving objects in general.

In most systems, the context is merely the user location measured either at certain access points (e.g., in Electronic Guidebook) or at a given location (e.g., in Nexus). That is, continuous queries, or profiles, only consider the user location. Additional contexts to consider would be, e.g., user interest, local time, and technical communication parameters. However, only few systems encompass the notion of events or profiles. In the Guide system, tourists are actively informed about general events, such as the opening hours of a museum. This information is broadcasted to all user of the system, whether they are interested or not. Similarly, users are informed about each available sight. In the Nexus predecessor, VIT, keyword profiles are used to select the information sources by topic (similar to advertising). In Crumpet, the information delivered on request is sorted according to user interests. Additionally, pro-active tips are delivered to interested users. The user's interest is defined in terms of profiles that are gradually adapted to the user based on specific user feedback. The Oldenburg guide uses continuous queries regarding the the spatiotemporal location of the users as profiles. Information about (moving) objects is delivered depending on its importance to the user, where importance depends on the spatial distance between object and user.

A large variety of event notification systems has been implemented, as for example SIFT [35], Salamander [21], Siena [4], OpenCQ [20], Elvin [26], Gryphon [29], NiagaraCQ [5], LeSubscribe [24], Hermes [8], and A-TOPSS [18]. The few ENS used in the context of tourist information have been focussing on traveller support in travel planning and route guidance, e.g., in the Genesis system [27]. For event notification systems, we distinguish document-centered approaches from event centered approaches. In document centered systems, the events are the publication of a new document. These systems are called publish/subscribe systems or systems for *Selective Dissemination of Information (SDI)*. Examples are SIFT, NiagaraCQ, Hermes and A-TOPSS (see above). In most event centered systems, the message reporting an event is formatted as attribute-value pairs.

As far as profile definition languages are concerned, it is common to distinguish subject-based from content-based filtering. In the former, the profiles are subjects or topics in which the events are ordered. Content-based filtering allows for a more fine-grained filtering, better adapted to the system users. The profile definition languages used in content-based ENS mirror the characteristics of the systems: document-centered systems use concepts from Information Retrieval, such as keyword-based search (e.g., SIFT and Hermes) or XML query languages (e.g., NiagaraCQ and A-TOPSS). Event-centered systems use Boolean combinations of predicates on attribute values. Additionally, several of these systems carry the notion of composite events that are temporal combinations of events, such as a sequence. Composite events have been extensively studied in active databases [11, 16, 36]. Only few sophisticated profile definition languages using composite events have been implemented [19, 14]. A combination of concepts from active databases and event notification systems are Event Action Systems (EAS). In such systems (e.g., in Yeast [17]) the user profile defines an action that is triggered by a certain event. In several aspects our work is very close to EAS, for example, in the detailed action definition.

Active Badges [33], the ultrasonic-based Bat system [34], or Radar based on wireless LAN [1]. Location systems for outdoor activities may use a wireless phone location system such as the US E911 [7] or GPS [22]; for an overview of location systems see [13]. [2] studied the impact of technical parameters such as computing power of the client, speed and throughput of the network connection on the on the client interaction.

3   Example Application

This section describes a typical application in the tourism domain, which will serve as a reference in this paper. We first briefly describe our application scenario and then detail the information that the mobile user gets on the mobile device.

3.1   Application: A Tourist in Berlin Downtown

Let us consider a tourist in Berlin on Saturday, February 22, 2003, with the following profile. This person has been visiting major European cities for over a week. She is for the first time in Berlin and is interested in (i) basic architectural facts in the city; (ii) wall-related facts; and (iii) Jewish history. This person has a few items to visit on her agenda but would like to be notified whenever something of interest with respect to both her location and profile occurs. Besides, she gets hungry after a while and has quite particular requirements in terms of restaurants.

Following is the planned trajectory of the tourist (see map in Figure 1) described in terms of major points of interest and addresses.

1. Starting point: **Synagogue** (Oranienburger Strasse 38)
2. **Reichstag** (Platz der Republik)
3. **Brandenburg Gate** (Strasse des 17. Juni)
4. **Potsdamer Platz**
5. End point: **Jewish Museum** (Lindenstrasse 9)

Note that due to unexpected events and slight changes of plans, the trajectory will eventually not be the shortest path through all these locations, even though they will all be included, as illustrated further.

3.2   Delivered Information and Interaction with the User

We suppose that the tourist walks around with a PDA. The information that she gets on the device as well as the actions taken by the system are represented through the successive PDA screens displayed in Figure 2.

This simple figure illustrates many aspects of the system and in particular many kinds of events. The five rows of PDA screens represented on the figure

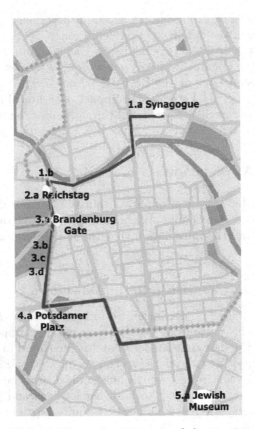

Fig. 1. Planned trajectory of the tourist

correspond to the five major locations (addresses) of the tourist's trajectory, as given in Section 3.1. The tourist starts at the Synagogue (1), walks, gets the notification that she is crossing the former wall, goes to the Reichstag (2), faces the Brandenburg Gate (3), walks, gets the notification that she is walking along the wall, goes to Potsdamer Platz (4), walks, poses a LBS query, and finally ends up at the Jewish Museum (5) where she gets more information.

In the figure, basic information from the system is displayed in normal font on the screen while recommendations and further information are displayed in italics. The fact that the user is walking is materialized by arrows linking screens. The various events considered by the system are indicated between star symbols. The fact that the location of the tourist is sent to the system is indicated by **Send location**. When there is a new location, two menu fields are displayed: *Information* and *Architecture Information*, as indicated in italics on the screens. The former is equivalent to asking more general information at a particular location (i.e., major monuments at this location) while the latter takes the profile of the end user (i.e., interested in architecture) into account. The option chosen

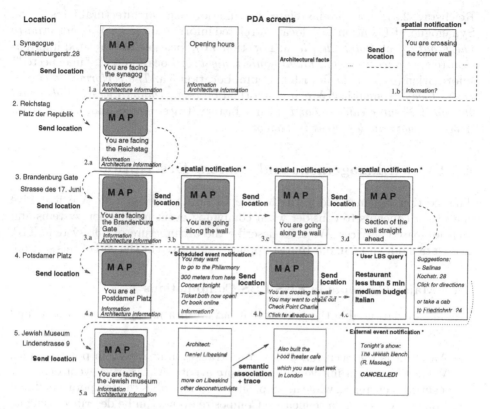

Fig. 2. Successive PDA screens

by the user is highlighted on the screen. As for the numbering of the PDA screens , each time a "Send location" event occurs the number of the major location is followed by a letter (in order to reference a new location).

Tourist Side/Mobile Device Actions. As we can see from Figure 2, the end user "sends" her location to the system. This is done automatically, periodically. She also sends queries to the system. These are of two kinds:

- Place-related query, such as in Location 3.a, when facing the Brandenburg Gate and pressing the "Information" button , which is equivalent to asking *What is this monument?*
- Service, such as *Find an Italian restaurant, medium budget, less than 5 minutes walk* (Location 4.c).

System Actions. As far as the system is concerned, it uses the current location and time of the tourist to either answer LBS queries or to provide her with more information. Further information includes: more basic information (e.g., at the

Reichstag, 2.a), more profile-related information (e.g., architectural facts at the Synagogue, at Location 1.a), location-related information (e.g., *You may want to check out Check Point Charlie*, at Location 4.b), location/time related information (e.g., *Concert at the Philharmonie tonight*, at Location 4.a), "unexpected" information (e.g., at the Jewish museum, Location 5.a, *The performance is cancelled today*), semantically-related information (e.g., *Daniel Libeskind also built the Food Theater café in London*) and history/trace-related information (e.g., *You saw that café last week in London*).

4   Event Management and System Description

This section is concerned with the overall notification system. We first give the major concepts to consider when combining event notification systems and location-based services. We then describe the architecture of our system, TIP. The data model used in our tourist application is given at the end of this section.

4.1   Major Concepts in ENS-LBS Combinations

The main terms used in the context of event notification systems are *events* and *profiles*.

- An *event* is the occurrence of a state transition at a certain point in time. We distinguish primitive and composite events: A primitive event describes a single occurrence, while a composite event describes the temporal combination of events (e.g., a sequence). Composite events can be described using an event algebra [14]. Composite event operators are, e.g., sequence $(E_1; E_2)_t$, conjunction $(E_1, E_2)_t$, disjunction $(E_1|E_2)$, and negation $(\overline{E_1})_t$. For example, a *sequence* $(E_1; E_2)_t$ occurs when first $e_1 \in E_1$ and then $e_2 \in E_2$ occurs. The parameter t defines in the profile the maximal temporal distance between the events. The occurrence time $t(e_3)$ of the sequence event instance $e_3 := (e_1; e_2)$ is equal to the time of e_2, i.e., $t(e_3) := t(e_2)$.
  We distinguish *events instances* from *event classes*. An event class is defined by a query. The event class is the set of all events that are selected by the query. Concrete event instances are denoted by lower Latin e with indices, i.e., $e_1, e_2, \ldots$, while event classes are denoted by upper Latin E with indices, i.e., $E_1, E_2, \ldots$. The fact that an event e_i is an instance of an event class E_j is denoted *membership*, i.e., $e_i \in E_j$.
- A *profile* is a (standing) query executed on the incoming events. In ENS, the result of an event successfully evaluated against a certain profile is a notification about the event. Unmatched events are rejected.

In the LBS context, we need to specify the terms events, actions (notification), and profiles that define the actions to be carried out after certain events occur.

Events in LBS. We distinguish location events that are user-related from external events that are independent of the users:

- **Location Events** are events that are connected to a specific user, time, and location. A location event occurs when the user presses the *Information*-button.
- **External Events** are caused by external sources that send event messages to the system. External events are also connected to a certain time, location, and profile and are pushed to the concerned users. An example of external event is *The play "The Jewish Bench" is cancelled this evening.*

Location events trigger a system reaction that results in the dissemination of information to the respective users. External events are, depending on the users' profile and location, forwarded to selected users.

Actions/Information Dissemination. In an ENS, the action that is triggered by an event is the possible forwarding of the event information. Similarly, SDI services forward filtered documents or parts of documents. In our system, the following three forms of actions are distinguished:

- **Information Delivery.** In this case, the action defined in the profile specifies the information data to be selected from the database and to be sent to the user. The selected information data depends on the location event, its time and location, on the event history, on the user/generic profiles, and on the semantic network of the information data. Depending on personal profiles, only selected information about a certain sight - or attraction - is delivered. Depending on generic profiles, additional information may be delivered about the interconnection of sights already seen, such as at Location 5.a in the reference example. The scenario also illustrates two examples of *spatial notification*. The first one concerns the fact that the tourist crosses the former wall (at locations 1.b and 4.b), the second one that the tourist is walking along the wall (locations 3.b and 3.c). The first notification requires an intersection query between a trajectory and the geometry of an object of interest (here, the wall), the second one a proximity query between the trajectory and an object of interest.
- **Recommendations.** Here, additional information about semantically-related items is given. The selected information depends on the information event, its time and location, the history of events, the user profile, and the semantical network of information data. A representative example is the one occurring at Location 4.b (*You may want to check out Check Point Charlie*).
- **Scheduled/External Message Delivery.** In this form of action, the delivery depends on the external/scheduled event, the time and location it refers to, and the user profile. An example of scheduled event occurs at Location 4.a, while an example of external event is given at Location 5.a.

Profiles/Conditions. In our system, the profiles are similar to triggers in active databases or profiles in an event action system. In contrast to profiles in ENS, the profile structure is not defined as event-condition(-notification) but as event-condition-action. The action is defined as the selection of information from the various databases. This information is not extracted from the event message as in typical SDI systems but from the system databases described further (more precisely, it is a semi join). We distinguish the following three kinds of profile:

- **Personal Profiles** are associated with end users. They are either defined explicitly by the end user or inferred from user actions applying user profiling techniques. The personal profile influences the information selected for the user. An example of a personal profile is "Send only information about architectural facts". Simple personal profiles consist of keywords selecting topics of information. More advanced personal profiles may consist of attribute-value pairs or database queries that specify certain information. For example, the recommendation of restaurants may be based on user profiles defining the food style (e.g., Italian), the price level (e.g., moderate), and additional restrictions (e.g., vegetarian).
- **Generic Profiles** are defined in the service. They are based on a general structural relation between the information data. An example of a generic profile is "Advise the visit of sights that are in the same semantical group and have not been visited yet". Simple generic profiles may use only the most recent location event, while sophisticated generic profiles are based on users event histories.
- **Application Profiles** are application-specific profiles defined by an application expert, e.g., the provider of the tourist information. Application profiles mirror semantical relationships between objects of interest. For example, a tourist information guide provides specific information to be delivered if the tourist visits in Berlin the German Dome at Gendamenmarkt *after* the French Dome. This action cannot be described in generic profiles, because it requires application knowledge.

4.2   Architecture of TIP (Tourism Information Provider)

Figure 3 depicts the architecture of the whole system. The TIP notification system is composed of mobile devices and the TIP server. The server disseminates information based on: time, location, and profiles. We now describe the components in more detail.

Mobile Devices. The application scenario described in the previous section illustrates the need to send a location at any time and to ask basic queries. A critical issue is the visibility of the history. For privacy reasons, the history should be stored on the device. This means that each time end users pose a query their history should be shipped to the system. It is up to the user to make parts of the history visible. In other words, location/time events can be removed from the history (e.g., the end user did not want to mention that she was in that café in London last week).

TIP Server. The system hinges on three thematic databases, which are:

- **Profile Database.** This database contains generic profiles as well as personal profiles.

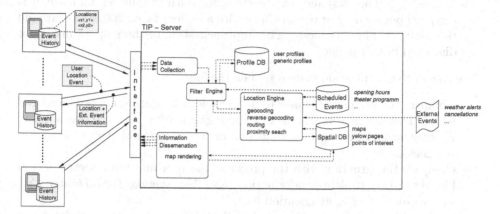

Fig. 3. Architecture of TIP

- **Scheduled Event Database**. This database contains any unexpected event (e.g, weather-related alert) as well as events that have a limited validity in time such as concert schedules and various programs.
- **Spatial Database**. This databases encompasses more than (vector) maps of the area. It contains *Points Of Interests (POI)* such as museums, restaurants - all classified through categories - or teller machines. They are organized in a semantical network. POIs are gathered in semantic clusters.

Note that external events are not stored in a database but are coming from an external source.

In addition, the location engine maps locations to maps themselves and assists users in geospatial-related operations. The basic operations are:

- **Geocoding**. Through this operation, the end user gives an address and the system returns a (longitude, latitude) pair, which may be used to find places of interest in a certain area.
- **Reverse Geocoding**. Through this operation, which is mostly used here, the user sends a (longitude, latitude) pair and the system returns an address.
- **Routing**. As seen from the typical LBS query in the example (i.e., *Where can I find an Italian restaurant nearby*, at Location 4.c) we need navigation tools. The algorithms usually use a two-sided[2] (memory-bounded) A* algorithm to route someone from one coordinate to another (note that geocoding/reverse geocoding are often coupled with this algorithm).
- **Proximity Search**. This is a broad issue as it concerns many dimensions: time, location, and semantics. The buffer allowed in each dimension can be set by default depending on the profile of the user (e.g., when walking,

---

[2] Unless the arrival time is an issue in which case we need a 2-pass algorithm.

"nearby" means about 2 minutes for this particular tourist, when considering distances, 200 meters) and may be changed. With the spatial database, it is a typical point query or region query with a buffer of e.g., 200 meters around the location (plus fuzziness). The implementation of these operators is not discussed in this paper.

The role of the notification system is then the following:

- Compare the profile of the user to deliver relevant information (architectural facts). This information can be of various granularity (e.g., at Location 5.a., *Further information on Libeskind, i.e., more architectural work by him* after the click).
- Compare the situation with the profile of the user and the relevant part of his/her history to deliver information (e.g., *You saw the Food Theater Café in London last week,* at Location 5.a).
- Look for relevant information in the scheduled event and spatial databases by applying spatio-temporal operators (e.g., *You may want to go to the Philharmonie where there is a concert tonight,* at Location 4.a, or *You are crossing the former wall* at locations 1.b and 4.b).
- Look for external events (e.g., *Performance cancelled,* at Location 5.a).
- Process typical LBS queries (e.g., *Italian restaurant nearby* at Location 4.c).

4.3   Data Model

The data model used in our application is depicted in Figure 4 as an entity relationship diagram. The main entities we consider are the following. On the information delivery side: Location, Object of interest (which belongs to a Semantic Class), Item of interest, Information (e.g., information delivered to a user *at a certain level in the hierarchy of information.* On the user side: User/user profile. Finally, on the event side: History and Event (e.g., location event, scheduled event, or external event).

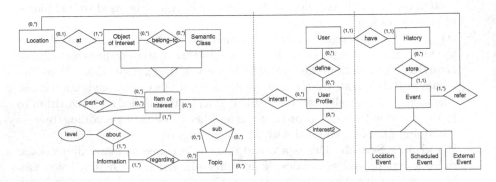

Fig. 4. Data model used in TIP

The object of interest is a sight or attraction. A semantic class is a generalization of sights, e.g., churches in Berlin. The item of interest encompasses objects and classes – it is an artificial component to support the uniform access to objects and classes. For each item of interest, the service stores a hierarchy of information (indicated by a level). End users define profiles regarding certain items and topics, e.g., architecture. In the event history, for each end user, the events are stored together with their location and occurrence time. We do not get into detail here regarding the location concept as we focus on the various events and profiles. We assume that an end user has a location at a certain time, which is a 0-dimensional entity in a 2-dimensional space. The location associated with an object of interest is a (two-dimensional) area.

5 Matching Profiles and Events

This section describes the various profiles handled in TIP as well as the way to deliver relevant information to the user based on a traversal of the hierarchical semantic structures according to the data model given in Figure 4.

5.1 Defining User Profiles

A user profile specifies information of interest for an end user. We assume here the simple form of subject-based user profiles. In the TIP system there exists a hierarchy of subjects that a user can subscribe to. Subscribing to a subject in the hierarchy implies considering subjects in the partial tree having the selected subject as root-node. A user profile is used within generic profiles and application profiles. It has no specific actions defined.

5.2 Defining Generic Profiles

For the formal definition of profiles, we use a notation inspired by *Event-Condition-Action (ECA)* rules in active databases enhanced by logical operators: ON event IF condition DO action.

We use the notation given in Table 1 to refer to the various data sources. The methods used for the profile descriptions are shown in Table 2. Let E_1 be a given set of location profiles.

One remark is necessary regarding the *covers* predicate between an object and a location. The expression $covers(object, location)$ means that the area of the object of interest (e.g., a square) includes the considered location.

1. **General Information, without User Profile.** A simple location event le_1 occurs ($le_1 \in E_1$) when a user u_1 is at location l_1 at a certain point in time. If it is the kth occurrence of this event in the user history ($le_1^{[k]} \in E_1^{[k]}$), and if general information exists at the kth level for an object that is near this location, this information is sent.

Table 1. Notations used in this paper

Variable	Description
L	set of all locations in the database
I	set of all information data in the database
O	set of all objects of interest in the database
T	hierarchy of topics
G	set of semantic groups in the database
$H(u)$	visible history of user u
$P(u)$	user profile of user u containing a set of topics and items

Table 2. Methods used for profile definition

Method	Description
$covers(object, location)$	true if the object covers the location, false otherwise
$member(object, group)$	true if the object is referred to in that semantic group, false otherwise
$near(location1, location2)$	true if the two locations are near each other (see further, e.g., based on a user preference), false otherwise
$soon(time)$	true if $time$ is near the current time
$above(t)$	set of all topics between t and the root topic $general$ of T plus t (transitive closure required)
$below(t)$	set of all child topics of topic t in T plus t (transitive closure required)
$send(information)$	send $information$ to the user
$recommend(object)$	recommend $object$ to the user

> **ON** location event $u1.le1$
>
> **IF** $u1.le1.location \in L \wedge \exists o \in O : covers(o.location, u1.le1.location) \wedge$
> $\exists k \in \mathbb{N} : \forall j \in \mathbb{N} : 0 \leq j < k \rightarrow \exists l(j) \in L \wedge near(l(j), u1.le1.location) \wedge$
> $l(j) \in H(u1) \wedge \exists i(o, k, general) \in I$
>
> **DO** $\forall o$ (as above) $: send(i(o, k, general))$

2. **Information that Matches the User Profile.** A simple location event le_1 occurs ($le_1 \in E_1$) when a user u_1 is at location l_1 at a certain point in time. The information is sent if: If it is the kth occurrence of this event in the user history ($le_1^{[k]} \in E_1^{[k]}$) and some information exists for a topic that is a subtopic of a user profile and an object exists near this location. The

default profile is *general* (see 1.). The information sent depends on the level (k^{th}) and on the history of topics.

ON location event $u1.le1$

IF $u1.le1.location \in L \land \exists o \in O : covers(o.location, u1.le1.location) \land$

$\exists k \in \mathbb{N} : \forall j \in \mathbb{N} : 0 \leq j < k \rightarrow l(j) \in L \land near(l(j), u1.le1.location) \land$

$l(j) \in H(u1) \land \exists t \in P(u1) : \exists i(k, below(t)) \in I$

DO $\forall o$ (as above), $\forall t$ (as above) : $send(i(o, k, t))$

3. **Recommendation of Objects that Are Near by (Semantically, Spatially).** All objects that are near object o are recommended, if they have not been visited yet.

ON location event $u1.le1$

IF $u1.le1.location \in L \land \exists o \in O : covers(o.location, u1.le1.location) \land$

$\exists g \in G : member(o, g) \land \exists q \in O \land member(q, g) \land q \neq o \land q \notin H(u1)$

DO $\forall o$ (as above), $\forall q$ (as above) : $recommend(q)$

4. **Information Related to a Semantic Group.** Information about a group this object o belongs to, if the user has already visited two objects in the group.

ON location event $u1.le1$

IF $u1.le1.location \in L \land \exists o \in O : covers(o.location, u1.le1.location) \land$

$\exists g \in G : member(o, g) \land \exists q \in O \land member(q, g) \land q \neq o \land q \in H(u1) \land$

$\exists k \in \mathbb{N} : \forall j \in \mathbb{N} : 0 \leq j < k \rightarrow \exists l(j) \in L \land$

$(near(l(j), u1.le1.location) \lor near(l(j), q.location)) \land l(j) \in H(u1)$

$\land \exists i(g, k, general) \in I$

DO $\forall o$ (as above), $\forall g$ (as above) : $send(i(g, k, general))$

5. **External Events that Are Near by (Temporally, Spatially) and Do Match the User Profile.**

ON external event $ex1 \land$ location event $u1.le1$

IF $ex1.location \in L \land (near(ex1.location, u1.le1.location))$

$\lor soon(ex1.timeref)) \land (ex1.topic \in P(u1) \lor ex1.item \in P(u1))$

DO $send(ex1.info)$

5.3   Defining Application Profiles

A number of combinations of events are conceivable for application profiles. In general, they are formed by a number of events that happened in the user history combined with a current event. We can define this composite event using our algebra as briefly introduced in Section 4.1. We now show two examples.

- Several events $E_1, E_2, \ldots E_{n-1}$ without a specified order happened before the current event E_n: The profile is defined as a sequence of a composite and a primitive event, where the composite event is a conjunction of the previous events $(E_1, E_2, \ldots E_{n-1}); E_n$.
- Several events $E_1, E_2, \ldots E_{n-1}$ happened at a certain order before the current event E_n: The profile is defined as a sequence of events $E_1; E_2; \ldots; E_{n-1}; E_n$.

Combinations of the two forms for composite events can also be considered. Additionally, time intervals may be defined to ensure that the history events occurred within a certain time span, e.g., $((E_1, E_2, \ldots, E_{n-1})_\infty; E_n)_t$ Here, the history events are in no special order, and the last history event occurred no longer than time span t before the current event E_n.

6   Conclusion

In this paper, we presented our TIP (Tourism Information Provider) environment to allow end users to get relevant information based on four criteria: (i) their current location, (ii) the current time, (iii) their profile, and (iv) their accumulated knowledge. At present, relevant information based on location is offered by many phone companies as location-based services (LBS). Time-related information is provided by event notification systems (ENS). However, to the best of our knowledge, no system at this point allows one to obtain information based simultaneously on the four criteria cited above. Our approach gathers all these concepts in a single framework based on mobile devices, various databases, and event notification services.

Delivering information based on profiles means matching a profile definition with various predefined profiles stored in a database. Delivering the right information according to the four criteria cited above is an innovative aspects which presents many challenges, from a high level of abstraction down to a technical level. At a high level, the information of possible relevance needs to be organized in an efficient semantic way, such as topic maps. At a more technical level, because of privacy issues, some information - the history - needs to be periodically sent from the mobile device to the system. This encompasses the physical means of sending information. Because sending the whole history of the user each time would not be sensible, we also have to find the most appropriate amount of information to be sent. At present, we send the whole visible history, which is the history that the user is willing to make public (private information is hidden by simply removing it from the history). We are currently working on a heuristic approach to make the best usage of the history with respect to the information stored in the various databases. We also record the trajectory of the tourists in order to send them appropriate location-related information (referred to a spatial notification earlier).

At a first sight, many aspects of TIP may seem similar to successive mouse clicks from a static user in an Internet browsing session. However, we are not aware of any system, even on the World Wide Web, that would deliver customized information based on a user profile and on his or her history. In addition, in our approach, we also had to consider the small amount of information that can be delivered on mobile devices, hence to convey the information in a simple manner.

TIP is currently under implementation at the Freie Universität Berlin. The implementation is done in Java^{TM} using Oracle 9i^{TM}. The spatial database is stored in Oracle Spatial ^{TM}. We are also in the process of specifying memorization levels for end users. The application described in this paper assumes a perfect user memory. This prevents the system from repeating information which was already delivered. For instance, a tourist who is in Berlin for the second time and who is interested in wall-related history may not want to be reminded many times that the wall was built in August 1961. However, a tourist who does not have a good memory would like to be reminded of certain facts, even basic ones. Hence, an end user with this profile should be able to specify his or her memorization level.

Eventually, our goal is to implement a platform that will be able to combine location, time, profile, and history in scheduling tasks, for instance in trade fairs where people want to visit booths within a certain time interval, based on their profile but also on the information they accumulated and their priorities (e.g., visited booths in the past may have a low priority during a further visit, or a high one if the person wants to see it again or to show it to someone). One of the major issues here concerns the definition of various profiles. Profiles may be pre-defined. They may also be inferred using data mining techniques. As far as the platform is concerned, it hinges on combinatorial optimization algorithms, which we plan to introduce in our system by modifying the location engine.

We also investigate many of the issues presented in the paper in the context of a large joint project between Fraunhofer ISST and the Institute of Computing Technology (ICT) of the Chinese Academy of Sciences, focusing on Personalized Web Services for the Olympic Games 2008 which will take place in Beijing.

Acknowledgements

We wish to thank the anonymous referees for their constructive comments.

References

[1] P. Bahl and V. N. Padmanabhan. RADAR: An in-building RF-based user location and tracking system. In *INFOCOM (2)*, pages 775–784, 2000. 493

[2] T. Brinkhoff. The impact of filtering on spatial continuous queries. In *10th Intl. Symposium on Spatial Data Handling (SDH 2002)*, 2002. 493

[3] T. Brinkhoff and J. Weitkämper. Continuous queries within an architecture for querying XML-represented moving objects. In *Proceedings of the 7th Intl. Symposium on Spatial and Temporal Databases (SSTD)*, volume 2121 of *Lecture Notes in Computer Science*, pages 136–154, Heidelberg/Berlin/New York, 2001. Springer Verlag. 491

[4] A. Carzaniga. *Architectures for an Event Notification Service Scalable to Wide-area Networks*. PhD thesis, Politecnico di Milano, Milano, Italy, 1998. 492

[5] J. Chen, D. DeWitt, F. Tian, and Y. Wang. NiagaraCQ: A scalable continuous query system for internet databases. In *Proc. of the ACM SIGMOD Conf. on Management of Data*, 2000. 492

[6] K. Cheverst, K. Mitchell, and N. Davies. The role of adaptive hypermedia in a context-aware tourist GUIDE. *Communications of the ACM*, 45(5):47–51, 2002. 491

[7] Federal Communications Commission. FCC wireless 911 requirements fact sheet, 2001. available at http://www.fcc.gov/e911/. 493

[8] D. Faensen, L. Faulstich, H. Schweppe, A. Hinze, and A. Steidinger. Hermes – a notification service for digital libraries. In *ACM/IEEE Joint Conference on Digital Libaries*, 2001. 492

[9] M. Fleck, M. Frid, T. Kindberg, E. O'Brien-Strain, R. Rajani, and M. Spasojevic. From informing to remembering: Ubiquitous systems in interactive museums. *Pervasive Computing*, 1(2):13–21, 2002. 491

[10] L. Forlizzi, R. H. Güting, E. Nardelli, and M. Schneider. A data model and data structures for moving objects databases. In *Proc. of the ACM SIGMOD Conf. on Management of Data*, 2000. 491

[11] N. H. Gehani, H. V. Jagadish, and O. Shmueli. Composite event specification in active databases: Model & implementation. In *Proceedings of the Intl. Conference on Very Large Data Bases (VLDB)*, 1992. 492

[12] R. H. Güting, M. H. Böhlen, M. Erwig, C. S. Jensen, N. A. Lorentzos, M. Schneider, and M. Vazirgiannis. A foundation for representing and quering moving objects. *Transations of Database Systems (ACM TODS)*, 25(1):1–42, 2000. 491

[13] J. Hightower and G. Borriello. Location systems for ubiquitous computing. *Computer*, 34(8):57–66, 2001. 493

[14] A. Hinze and A. Voisard. A parameterized algebra for event notification services. In *Proceedings of the 9th International Symposium on Temporal Representation and Reasoning (TIME 2002), IEEE Computer Society*, 2002. 492, 496

[15] S. Hsi. The electronic guidebook: A study of user experiences using mobile web content in a museum setting. In *Proceedings of the IEEE Intl. Workshop on Wireless and Mobile Technologies in Education (WMTE)*, 2002. 491

[16] H. V. Jagadish and O. Shmueli. Composite events in a distributed object-oriented database. In *Proceedings of the International Workshop on Distributed Object Management*, 1992. 492

[17] B. Krishnamurthy and D. S. Rosenblum. Yeast: A general purpose event-action system. *ACM Transactions on Software Engineering*, 21(10), 1995. 492

[18] H. Liu and H.-A. Jacobsen. A-topss - a publish/subscribe system supporting approximate matching. In *Proceedings of the Intl. Conference on Very Large Data Bases (VLDB)*, pages 1107–1110, 2002. 492

[19] L. Liu and C. Pu. Complex event specification and event detection for continual queries. Technical report, OGI/CSE, Portland, 1998. available at ftp://cse.ogi.edu/pub/tech-reports/. 492

[20] L. Liu, C. Pu, and W. Tang. Continual queries for internet scale event-driven information delivery. *IEEE Transactions on Knowledge and Data Engineering*, Special issue on Web Technologies, 1999. 492

[21] G. R. Malan, F. Jahanian, and S. Subramanian. Salamander: A push-based distribution substrate for internet applications. In *USENIX Symposium on Internet Technologies and Systems, Monterey, California, December 8-11, 1997*, volume 32, 1997. available at http://www.eecs.umich.edu/~rmalan/publications/mjsUsits97.ps.gz. 492

[22] J. C. Navas and T. Imielinski. Geocast - geographic addressing and routing. In *Mobile Computing and Networking*, pages 66–76, 1997. 493

[23] R. Oppermann, M. Specht, and I. Jaceniak. Hippie: A nomadic information system. In *Proceedings of the First International Symposium Handheld and Ubiquitous Computing (HUC)*, 1999. 491

[24] J. Pereira, F. Fabret, H. Jacobsen, F. Llirbat, R. Preotiuc-Prieto, K. Ross, and D. Shasha. LeSubscribe: Publish and subscribe on the web at extreme speed. In *Proc. of the ACM SIGMOD Conf. on Management of Data*, 2001. 492

[25] S. Poslad, H. Laamanen, R. Malaka, A. Nick, P. Buckle, and A. Zipf. Crumpet: Creation of user- friendly mobile services personalised for tourism. In *Proceedings of 3G 2001 - Second International Conference on 3G Mobile Communication Technologies*, 2001. 491

[26] B. Segall, D. Arnold, J. Boot, M. Henderson, and T. Phelps. Content Based Routing with Elvin4. In *Proceedings of the AUUG2K Conference*, 2000. 492

[27] S. Shekhar and A. Fetterer. Genesis: An approach to data dissemination in advanced traveler information systems. *IEEE Bulletin of the Technical Committee on Data Engineering*, 19(3):40–47, 1996. 492

[28] A. P. Sistla, O. Wolfson, S. Chamberlain, and S. Dao. Modeling and querying moving objects. In *ICDE*, pages 422–432, 1997. 491

[29] R. Strom, G. Banavar, T. Chandra, M. Kaplan, K. Miller, B. Mukherjee, D. Sturman, and M. Ward. Gryphon: An information flow based approach to message brokering. In *Proceedings of the International Symposium on Software Reliability Engineering*, 1998. 492

[30] J. Su, H. Xu, and O. H. Ibarra. Moving objects: Logical relationships and queries. In *Proceedings of the 7th Intl. Symposium on Spatial and Temporal Databases (SSTD)*, volume 2121 of *LNCS*, Heidelberg/Berlin/New York, 2001. Springer Verlag. 491

[31] M. Vazirgiannis and O. Wolfson. A spatiotemporal model and language for moving objects on road networks. In *Proceedings of the 7th Intl. Symposium on Spatial and Temporal Databases (SSTD)*, Heidelberg/Berlin/New York, 2001. Springer Verlag. 491

[32] S. Volz and D. Klinec. Nexus: The development of a platform for location aware application. In *Proceedings of the Third Turkish-German Joint Geodetic Days – Towards A Digital Age, Istanbul, Turkey*, 1999. 491

[33] R. Want, A. Hopper, V. Falcao, and J. Gibbons. The active badge location system. *ACM Transactions on Information Systems*, 10(1):91–102, 1992. 493

[34] A. Ward, A. Jones, and A. Hopper. A new location technique for the active office. *IEEE Personal Communications*, 4(5):42–47, 1997. 493

[35] T. W. Yan and H. Garcia-Molina. The SIFT information dissemination system. *ACM Transactions on Database Systems*, 24(4):529–565, 1999. 492

[36] S. Yang and S. Chakravarthy. Formal semantics of composite events for distributed environments. In *Proceedings of the International Conference on Data Engineering (ICDE)*, pages 400–407, 1999. 492

Building a Robust Relational Implementation
of Topology

Erik Hoel, Sudhakar Menon, and Scott Morehouse

Environmental Systems Research Institute
380 New York Street, Redlands, CA 92373
{ehoel,smenon,smorehouse}@esri.com

Abstract. Topologically structured data models often form the core of many users' spatial databases. Topological structuring is primarily used to ensure data integrity; it describes how spatial objects share geometry. Supporting topology within the context of a relational database imposes additional requirements – the complex topological model must retain integrity across transactional boundaries. This can be a problematic requirement given the complexities associated with implementing safe referential integrity structures in relational databases (e.g., bulk data loading into a topologically structured model) [19, 5]. Common implementation techniques such as allowing dangling pointers (i.e., null foreign keys) complicates the issues for client applications that consume these models. In this paper, we revisit the problem of building a robust and scalable relational implementation of a topologically structured data model. We propose a different approach to representing such models that avoids many of the traditional relational database problems associated with maintaining complex semantic models.

1 Introduction

Topological data structures have been used to represent geographic information for over thirty years [7, 24]. The topological model has been the basis of a number of operational systems (see, for example TIGER/db [4], ARC/INFO [22], or TIGRIS [14]). These systems have been based on binary file and in-memory data structures and support a single-writer editing model on geographic libraries organized as a set of individual map sheets or tiles.

Recent developments in geographic information systems have moved to database-centered information models. One aspect of this work has been to replace the file system with a relational database engine as the persistence mechanism for geographic information. However, replacement of the physical I/O layer is only one aspect to consider when designing a "database GIS". Other aspects of the database concept must also be considered.

- What is the generic spatial information model and what are the associated spatial operators?
- How does the design support multiple, simultaneous writers?

T. Hadzilacos et al. (Eds.): SSTD 2003, LNCS 2750, pp. 508-524, 2003.

- How is the semantic integrity of the data model declared, maintained, and enforced?
- How to design a system which performs well and can scale to support hundreds of simultaneous users?
- How to design a system which can support very large continuous spatial databases, containing millions of geographically interrelated objects (e.g., the road network of the United States or the land ownership fabric of Austria)?

Database GIS involves more than simply exporting classic GIS data structures to a normalized relational schema. Database GIS must also address the functional aspects of being a database as well: the integrity model, the transaction model, and performance/scalability issues. Otherwise database GIS implementations run the risk of becoming "off-line data repositories" (at best) or "write-only databases" (at worst).

The representation of topological data models using relational database concepts and engines should be of interest to the database research community as well as to geographic information scientists. The data model serves as an excellent case study for considering problems of information modeling and, especially, for evaluating architectures for the management of semantic integrity.

In this paper, we describe a design for modeling GIS topology using relational concepts and database engines. This design is the basis for our implementation of topology in the ArcGIS geographic information system.

In the first section, we introduce the logical model of GIS topology. We then consider a physical database implementation using the conventional notions for mapping entities and relationships to tables and the conventional primary key / foreign key referential integrity model. Problems in this approach are discussed. We then present an alternative implementation of the topology model which uses an unconventional approach to the problem of database integrity and transaction management.

2   What is GIS Topology?

Topological data structures for representing geographic information are a standard topic in geographic information science (see [Güti95], for example, for an excellent definition of the mathematical theory underlying this information model). In general, the topological data model represents spatial objects (point, line, and area features) using an underlying set of topological primitives. These primitives, together with their relationships to one another and to the features, are defined by embedding the feature geometries in a single planar graph. Such datasets are said to be "topologically integrated".

The model associates one or more topological primitives (i.e., nodes, edges, and faces [16]; or 0-cells, 1-cells, and 2-cell in the TIGER parlance [3, 8]) with spatial objects of varying geometry type (i.e., points, lines, and polygons respectively). More specifically, a feature with point geometry is associated with a single node element, a feature with line geometry is associated with one or more edge elements, and a feature with polygon geometry is associated with one or more face elements. This is depicted in Fig. 1 as the generic topology model.

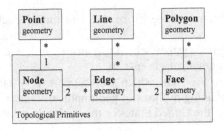

Fig. 1. Generic topology model

There are additional relationships between the topological elements themselves as is also shown in Fig. 1. A node element may or may not be associated with a collection of edge elements. A face element may be associated with one or more edge elements. Finally, an edge element is associated with two node elements and two face elements. The relationships between nodes and faces may either be implicit or explicit. We have represented these relationships between nodes and faces as implicit within Fig. 1.

A concrete example, showing a specific instance of this model is shown in Fig. 2. The database consists of three classes which represent real geographic entities: Parcels, Walls, and Buildings. In the example, there is one instance of each class. In practice, these classes could contain millions of instances. The wall and the building are coincident with the western boundary of the parcel as shown.

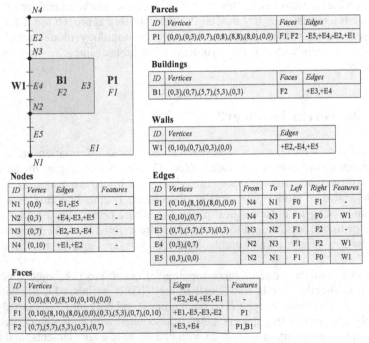

Parcels

ID	Vertices	Faces	Edges
P1	(0,0),(0,3),(0,7),(0,8),(8,8),(8,0),(0,0)	F1, F2	-E5,+E4,-E2,+E1

Buildings

ID	Vertices	Faces	Edges
B1	(0,3),(0,7),(5,7),(5,3),(0,3)	F2	+E3,+E4

Walls

ID	Vertices	Edges
W1	(0,10),(0,7),(0,3),(0,0)	+E2,-E4,+E5

Nodes

ID	Vertex	Edges	Features
N1	(0,0)	-E1,-E5	-
N2	(0,3)	+E4,-E3,+E5	-
N3	(0,7)	-E2,-E3,-E4	-
N4	(0,10)	+E1,+E2	-

Edges

ID	Vertices	From	To	Left	Right	Features
E1	(0,10),(8,10),(8,0),(0,0)	N4	N1	F0	F1	-
E2	(0,10),(0,7)	N4	N3	F1	F0	W1
E3	(0,7),(5,7),(5,3),(0,3)	N3	N2	F1	F2	-
E4	(0,3),(0,7)	N2	N3	F1	F2	W1
E5	(0,3),(0,0)	N2	N1	F1	F0	W1

Faces

ID	Vertices	Edges	Features
F0	(0,0),(8,0),(8,10),(0,10),(0,0)	+E2,-E4,+E5,-E1	-
F1	(0,10),(8,10),(8,0),(0,0),(0,3),(5,3),(0,7),(0,10)	+E1,-E5,-E3,-E2	P1
F2	(0,7),(5,7),(5,3),(0,3),(0,7)	+E3,+E4	P1,B1

Fig. 2. An instance of the generic topology model

It is interesting to note that the objects have both set and list-based properties. For example, the geometry of an edge is defined by a list of coordinates and the object references to the edges participating in a line feature (e.g., W1) are ordered and oriented to properly represent the orientation of the linear feature. Edges and vertices of polygons are oriented clockwise (with the interior of the polygon on the right). For clarity, we have showed attributes, such as object geometries, redundantly in multiple object classes. In some physical implementations of the model, these geometries would only be stored once, on edge primitives for example, and instantiated via queries for other features.

After examining this example, it is clear that the logical topology model is a complex graph model, containing ordered object associations based on the geometric embedding of the objects in two-dimensional space. It should also be clear that common queries, such as "draw a map of all buildings" or "find features contained within a given parcel" require ordered navigations of relationships, not simply set operations.

Given the inherent complexity of this representation, it is important to reflect upon why people want topology in their spatial datasets in the first place – i.e., what are the fundamental requirements. At a high level, topology is employed in order to:

- Manage shared geometry (i.e., constrain how features share geometry).
- Define and enforce data integrity rules (e.g., no gaps between features, no overlapping features, and so on).
- Support topological relationship queries and navigation (e.g., feature adjacency or connectivity).
- Support sophisticated editing tools (tools that enforce the topological constraints of the data model).
- Construct features from unstructured geometry (i.e., polygons from lines).

The logical topology model provides a theoretical basis for this functionality. For example, the constraint "buildings must not overlap one another" can be expressed by the topology constraint "faces may only be associated with a single feature of type building". Similarly, the problem of creating polygons from unstructured lines can be stated as: "calculate edges, faces, and nodes from lines; create a feature on top of each resulting face".

In GIS, topology has historically been viewed as a physical spatial data structure that directly implements the objects of the logical topology model. However, it is important to realize that this physical data structure is only useful because it is a tool for data integrity management, spatial queries / navigation and other operators. It is possible to consider alternate implementations of the logical topology model which also support this functionality. In effect, topology must be considered as a complete data model (objects, integrity rules, and operators), not simply as storage format or set of record types.

3   Conventional Physical Implementation

The logical topology model can be implemented for relational database engines in a straight forward fashion as a normalized relational model with explicit representation of topological primitives using keys (primary and foreign) to model the topological relationships (see Fig. 3). We can call this the conventional relational topology model.

This implementation uses referential integrity constraints [13, 20] to declare integrity rules for the topology. Join tables are employed to support many-to-many relationships between the features and their associated topological primitives (in databases which support array types, the join tables may be replaced by lists of foreign keys embedded in the feature and primitive tables). In addition, the geometry of the features is normalized - that is, it is assembled from their associated topological primitives. Fig. 4 illustrates our sample dataset example in this model.

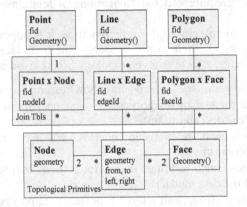

Fig. 3. Conventional relational topology model with join tables (e.g., Line x Edge)

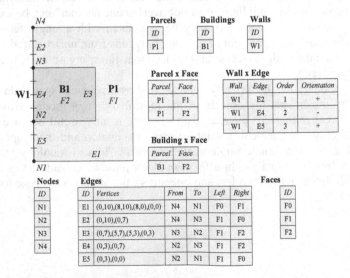

Parcels

ID
P1

Buildings

ID
B1

Walls

ID
W1

Parcel x Face

Parcel	Face
P1	F1
P1	F2

Wall x Edge

Wall	Edge	Order	Orientation
W1	E2	1	+
W1	E4	2	-
W1	E5	3	+

Building x Face

Parcel	Face
B1	F2

Nodes

ID
N1
N2
N3
N4

Edges

ID	Vertices	From	To	Left	Right
E1	(0,10),(8,10),(8,0),(0,0)	N4	N1	F0	F1
E2	(0,10),(0,7)	N4	N3	F1	F0
E3	(0,7),(5,7),(5,3),(0,3)	N3	N2	F1	F2
E4	(0,3),(0,7)	N2	N3	F1	F2
E5	(0,3),(0,0)	N2	N1	F1	F0

Faces

ID
F0
F1
F2

Fig. 4. An example instance of the conventional relational implementation

There are a number of advantages to this physical implementation. First, there is a direct and rather trivial mapping to the logical topology model. There is conceptual comfort for many users because all of the topological primitives are explicitly persisted, as are many of the primitive topological relationships. The geometry itself is only represented once within the database. Finally, there is a degree of client independence given that the topological primitives and relationships can be edited using standard SQL updates.

However, there are a number of serious problems with this implementation, these relate to:

- the performance of typical queries,
- the maintenance of semantic integrity in the model, and
- the performance and complexity of typical updates.

3.1   Query Performance

Although this implementation eliminates redundant storage of geometric information for features, complex queries are required to instantiating the features' geometry (the most common query for most GIS software) [28]. For example, to fetch the geometry of the parcel P1, a query must combine information in four tables (Parcels, Parcel x Face, Faces, and Edges) and use external geometric/topological logic to correctly assemble the geometry of the Parcel. When this query must be performed iteratively – to draw all parcels, for example – we end up nesting complex queries or executing nested cursors in the application code. In general, navigational access to relationships (dereferencing pointers) is significantly slower with relational technology that with other technologies (e.g., object databases [17]).

3.2   The Integrity Mechanism

A more fundamental problem relates to the integrity of the database. Despite the use of (and paying the performance cost for) referential integrity constraints, the integrity and consistency of the topology data model cannot actually be defined using the conventional referential integrity model!   Referential integrity constraints simply declare that "if a foreign key is not null, then the referenced primary key exists". This is a very weak (one might almost say meaningless) basis for managing the integrity of the topological data model. For a consistent state of the data model, there must be no null references and the geometry of the primitives must be consistent with the objects and references. The conventional referential integrity model has no means for declaring such "semantic" constraints, much less enforcing them.

The integrity of a topology is a global property of the set of entities comprising the topology, rather than constraints or behavior attached to individual entities. Topology integrity must be validated by considering a complete set of updates as a whole. This validation logic must analyze the geometric configuration of features in the changed area to ensure that the topology primitives and relationships are correct. This validation logic executes externally to the core relational integrity model.

It is possible to execute arbitrary business logic in response to data updates using triggers. Such a mechanism could be used to accumulate change information, and then execute global validation logic. However, active relational databases (i.e., those supporting constraint and trigger mechanisms) continue to have lingering implementation and performance drawbacks [5, 26]. Database extensions that are implemented as trigger-based services (that may or may not be automatically generated) where the complexity of the domain is non-trivial (e.g., business rules, supply chain management, rule-based inference systems, and topology) suffer from several fundamental problems:

- difficulty of implementation (subtlety of behavior, primitive debugging tools),
- performance problems and scalability with complex trigger collections (lack of sophistication of trigger processors), and
- lack of uniformity (portability between RDBMSs, though this will be helped by the SQL-99 standard [11]).

For these reasons, complex semantic behavior (also known as the business objects) is more commonly implemented in shared code running in an application server tier.

3.3   Complexity of Updates

Simple edits to a topological data model can result in a complex sequence of changes to the associated topology primitives and relationships. Consider a simple edit to the sample dataset of Fig. 4: let's move the building one unit to the right. The changes necessary in the data model are shown in Fig. 5.

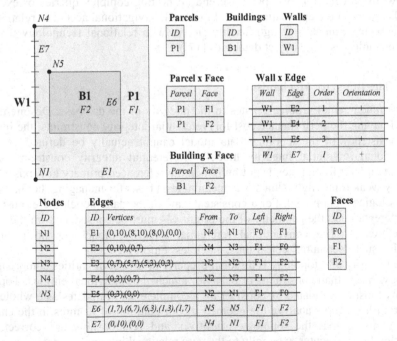

Fig. 5. An example instance of the conventional relational implementation. In this example, deleted rows are indicated with the horizontal strike through; new rows are in italics

This edit to the geometry of a single feature requires that we validate the geometry and topology of the effected area. The edit requires updates and inserts to multiple tables: Edges, Nodes, and Edges x Walls. These updates must either be made correctly by the application prior to executing the validation logic.

The example also raises an interesting point related to the "lifecycle semantics" of topological primitives. These spatial objects do not correspond to any feature in either the real or legal-boundary worlds [25]. They exist solely as constructs of the topology for a given configuration of features. How is "identity" defined for such objects? In the example, did we replace edges E2, E4, and E5 with E7 or should we have updated one of the existing edges? These lead to additional complexity when we deal with identifier generation, historical data management, and other factors. By making topological primitives explicit entities in the model, we have another set of business objects to manage.

Update operations on the explicit topology implementation are complex (irrespective of whether stored procedures/triggers or client-side code is employed). This complexity is closely related to performance concerns when persisting topological primitives in relational databases. The performance difference can be quite significant when compared with existing file-based topology solutions (e.g., orders of magnitude). It is important to note that the increased server side processing required with the complex trigger mechanisms will impact server scalability [5].

These considerations, reinforced by practical experience implementing the normalized model using prototype software led to the development of an alternative approach, described in the following section.

4   Alternative Physical Implementation

In order to address some of the problems inherent in the conventional topology physical implementation, we describe a new model that is currently hosted within the ArcGIS Geodatabase [10, 32]. With this model, we make three fundamental departures. First, we relax the conventional transactional model and allow the incremental validation of the topology (i.e., validation is performed as a bulk process at certain user-defined intervals or events). Thus, features with geometry that has not been topologically validated can be maintained within the model. This has a significant impact upon the user's editing experience where each individual edit operation does not need to topologically restructure the area being edited. Second, we cache geometry in the features rather than only in the topological primitives in order to eliminate relationship navigation for common queries (e.g., drawing the features). Third and finally, we use logic external to the relational database for geometric and topological validation.

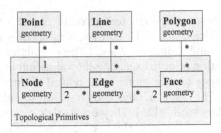

Fig. 6. Geodatabase topology model

It is possible in the generic model (r.e., Fig. 1) to obtain topological primitives from feature geometry; similarly, it is possible to obtain feature geometry from topological primitives [28]. Effectively, the geometry found in features is a dual representation of the geometry that would be found on the topological primitives. We have chosen to simplify and streamline the generic explicit topology model and to not persist both representations.

The topological primitives are not persisted as a special type of feature; instead, feature geometry is persisted and topological primitives (along with their geometry) are inferred. The process of topological integration (validation) results in vertex equality where features share underlying topological primitives. Given vertex equality, reconstruction of topological primitives is straight forward. Vertices on feature geometries in this scheme play the same role as that assigned to embedded foreign keys in data structures that explicitly model topological primitives.

Topological primitives and relationships are only instantiated during the process of topological validation or when required by the client application (note that this aspect is similar to MGE where topology is selectively built but the topological primitives are not persisted in the RDBMS [15]). The primary reason for this alternative approach is that it is easier (faster, more scalable) to recreate an index (e.g., the topological primitives) than to do all the bookkeeping necessary to persist and retrieve it from the database while preserving the database transaction model (note that we have also found the same to be true when modeling networks as well as surfaces – i.e., TINs). Additionally, it is frequently the case that the portion of the topological primitives necessary for an operation is small relative to the entire topology (e.g., editing a few block groups in a localized area within TIGER).

It is important to note that for this approach to be viable from a performance standpoint, it is critical that there exist a high performance topology engine that validates the portion of the topology in question (see the description below) as well as instantiate the topological primitives for the given collection of features within the topology [29, 30].

At a high level, topology within the Geodatabase consists of a collection of feature classes (homogeneous collections of features), topology rules, and other metadata used to support the validation model. This metadata includes dirty areas, topology errors, and the cluster tolerance. An example instance of the topology implementation is shown in Fig. 7.

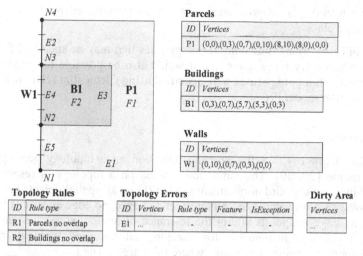

Fig. 7. An example instance of the Geodatabase topology implementation

4.1 Topology Rules

Topological integrity is defined with respect to a collection of topology rules. *Topology rules* are used to define constraints on the permissible topological relationships between features in one or more feature classes that participate in the topology. Topology rules are considered part of the topology metadata; they are not considered metadata associated with the feature classes that participate in the topology. The collection of topology rules that are associated with the topology are selected on the basis of which topological relationships are important for the user's model. There is no fixed set of topology rules that are associated with all topologies; instead, topologies may be specified with zero or more rules (note that one significant utility of a topology without any topology rules is that Milenkovic's third normalization rule – see Section 3.2 - are enforced on the features as a byproduct of validation).

Topology rules are checked when the topology is validated. When a topology rule is violated, a topology error object is generated. This topology error may be represented as a special type of feature that may itself be persisted. At a later point following the validation, the user may then review the topology error objects and the error conditions may be corrected. Topology rule violations do not prevent the validation operation from successfully completing.

Examples of topological rules that may be applied to polygon features include:

- The interiors of polygons in a feature class must not overlap (they may however share edges or vertices).
- Polygons must not have voids within themselves or between adjacent polygons (they may share edges, vertices, or interior areas).
- Polygons of one feature class must share all their area with polygons in another feature class (i.e., they must cover each other).

- The boundaries of polygon features must be covered by lines in another feature class.

There are of course numerous other topology rules that may be specified for each of the different geometry types. Note that it would also be possible for a system to be designed where all topology rules were specified using Clementini relationships [6] or the 9-Intersection model [9].

4.2   Validation

The validation process is a fundamental operation on a topology performed by a topology engine [29, 30]. The validation process on a topology is responsible for ensuring Milenkovic's third normalization rule [21] on all spatial objects participating in the topology are respected (i.e., no intersecting edges, no edge endpoints within the tolerance, no edge endpoints within the tolerance of another edge). In addition, the validation process is responsible for checking all specified topology rules and generating topology errors at locations where rules are violated.

The basic processing flow for the validation process within the topology engine is as follows:

- Load all the feature geometries and associated topology metadata (topology rules, feature class weights, and cluster tolerance).
- Crack, cluster, classify, and topologically structure the nodes and edges.
- Create new topology error instances when topology rules are found to be in violation. Delete pre-existing error instances if the rules are no longer in violation.
- Update the feature geometries as necessary (i.e., if their geometries were modified during the establishment of the Milenkovic conditions).
- Update the dirty areas associated with the topology.

It is important to note that the validation process does not need to span all features within the topology dataset. A validation can be performed on a subset of the space spanned by the dataset. This is a complex task given that it will require the validation of topology rules using partial information (e.g., certain error instances may only be partially contained within the region being validated).

4.3   Dirty Areas

A topology can have an associated *dirty area* – a dirty area corresponds to the regions within the topology extent where features participating in the topology have been modified (added, deleted, or updated) but have yet to be validated. When the geometry of a feature that participates in a topology is modified, the extent of the dirty area is enlarged to encompass the extent of the bounding rectangle of the modified geometry (note that other simplified geometry representations may also be employed - e.g., convex hulls). This is depicted in Fig. 8. The dirty area is persisted with the topology. In order to ensure that the topology is correct, the topology in the dirty areas will need to be validated.

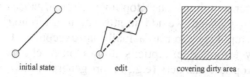

initial state   edit   covering dirty area

Fig. 8. Example of dirty area creation following a feature edit. The dirty area is depicted by the hatched square

It is not necessary to validate the entire space spanned by the dirty area at one time; instead, a subset of the dirty area can be validated. If the dirty area is partially validated, the original dirty area will be clipped by the extent of the region that is validated.

Allowing users the ability to validate a portion of the dirty area is a pragmatic requirement of supporting extremely large seamless topologies – for example, when a topology is first created, or when the topology metadata (e.g., topology rules, etc.) is modified, the entire extent of the topology is dirty. If users were not provided with the capability to validate a portion of the dirty area, the user would be required to validate the entire topology which could prove to be a very lengthy process (e.g., up to a week of processing time for large topological datasets derived from TIGER/Line Files [27]). This would be impractical for large enterprise datasets.

4.4   Topology Errors and Exceptions

A *topology error* is generated for each instance of a topology rule that is determined to be invalid during the validation process (an example is shown in Fig. 9). Topology rules are commonly specified as a required topological relationship that must hold between collections of features in one or more feature classes. Topology errors are associated with the topology; inspection of the error will enable a user to determine why the error was generated. Topology errors have an associated geometry that is used to position the error in the topology dataset. Topology errors are persisted with the topology.

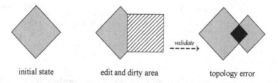

initial state   edit and dirty area   topology error

Fig. 9. Example of an edit (polygon creation) followed by a validation where the topology rule is "polygons must not overlap". The generated topology error is depicted by the black diamond

We have observed with large enterprise topologies that it is sometimes the case that certain topology error instances are acceptable. For example, within the Census Bureau's TIGER/db [4] DB system, there is a general rule that American Indian Reservations may not overlap. There are however two instances where this general rule is purposefully violated (e.g., the Lualualei and Mashantucket Pequot reservations in Hawaii, and the Spokane and Schaghticoke reservations in

Washington). In order to support such topology error instances where the topology rules are purposefully violated, we add an attribute to a topology error that indicates whether or not the topology error is actually an exception (to the rule). Marking purposeful topology errors as exceptions allows other clients of the topology to handle them in appropriate manners (e.g., report generators that indicate the number of errors in the topology – this is often used as a quantitative measure of quality within the topological dataset). Note that it should also be possible to demote an exception to error status.

4.5   Complexity of Updates

Simple edits to the Geodatabase topological data model can result in rather simple changes to the associated topology metadata (e.g., dirty areas). Consider a simple edit to the sample dataset of Fig. 7 where the building is moved one unit to the right. The changes necessary in the data model are shown in Fig. 10. More specifically, the geometry of the building feature is updates and the dirty area extent of the topology is unioned with the initial and final geometry of the building that was updated (i.e., the polygon (0,3),(0,7),(6,7),(6,3),(0,3)). No other modifications to the persisted representation are necessary.

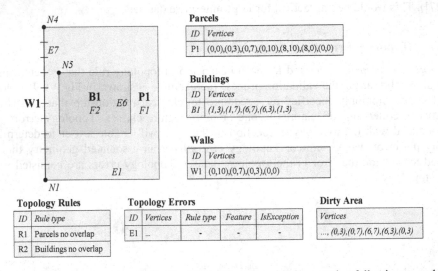

Parcels

ID	Vertices
P1	(0,0),(0,3),(0,7),(0,10),(8,10),(8,0),(0,0)

Buildings

ID	Vertices
B1	*(1,3),(1,7),(6,7),(6,3),(1,3)*

Walls

ID	Vertices
W1	(0,10),(0,7),(0,3),(0,0)

Topology Rules

ID	Rule type
R1	Parcels no overlap
R2	Buildings no overlap

Topology Errors

ID	Vertices	Rule type	Feature	IsException
E1	...	-	-	-

Dirty Area

Vertices
..., (0,3),(0,7),(6,7),(6,3),(0,3)

Fig. 10. An example instance of the Geodatabase topology implementation following an update to the building geometry (r.e., Fig. 7). In this example, updated rows are in italics (i.e., the geometry of the building and the vertices of the dirty area)

5   Implementation Experience

This new topology model has been implemented and is currently shipping with ESRI's ArcGIS 8.3 product. It is fully supported within a multi-user versioned database environment. It has been used to validate very large topologies, including a dataset derived from the features contained within the entire collection of the Census Bureau's TIGER/Line files (53.5 million features; 30 million lines, 23.5 million polygons [18]). A small portion of this dataset in the vicinity of the U.S. Capitol in Washington, DC is shown in Fig. 11. Other large datasets that have been validated are summarized in Table 1.

Table 1. Summary statistics of large topologies validated

Dataset	feature count	topology rule count
TIGER (U.S. National)	53.5 million	83
LPI, New South Wales, Australia	22.6 million	41
Cook County Assessor (Illinois)	4.3 million	16
Calgary Legal Cadastre (Canada)	2.1 million	5

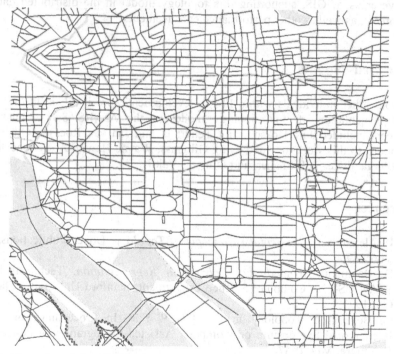

Fig. 11. Example of the TIGER dataset taken from the vicinity of the U. S. Capitol in Washington, DC

6   Conclusion

In this paper we described the logical model of GIS topology. We considered a common physical database implementation using the conventional notions for mapping entities and relationships to tables and the conventional primary key / foreign key referential integrity model. Problems in this approach were discussed. We then presented an alternative implementation of the topology model which used an unconventional approach to the problem of database integrity and transaction management.

The presented design serves as the basis for our implementation of topology in the ArcGIS geographic information system. This new models offers increased flexibility in terms of defining which rules constitute a valid topology. This topology model is supported in a multi-user long transaction (i.e., versioned) environment where multiple users may simultaneously edit the same geographic area within the topology extent. This new model has been implemented and is currently shipping with the ArcGIS 8.3 product.

Our future work will focus on experimentation with dirty area management policies that are more useful for the client (i.e., require less revalidation) without incurring considerable computational expense during version reconcile, applying the dirty area model to effectively support partial processing in other computationally intensive areas of GIS, supporting this topology model in the distributed database environment, as well as other performance enhancements.

Acknowledgements

Numerous other individuals within ESRI Development were involved in the design and implementation of this topology model in the ArcGIS 8.3 product. Key developers included Jeff Jackson, Jim Tenbrink, and Jan van Roessel. Other large contributors to this work included Craig Gillgrass, Wayne Hewitt, Andy MacDonald, Doug Morganthaler, Jeff Shaner, and François Valois.

References

[1]   P. Alexandroff. *Elementary Concepts of Topology*. Dover Publications, New York, 1961.

[2]   B. Baumgart. *Winged-edge Polyhedron Representation*. Technical Report STAN-CS-320, Computer Science Department, Stanford University, Stanford, CA, 1972.

[3]   G. Boudriault. Topology in the TIGER File. In Proceedings of the 8th International Symposium on Computer Assisted Cartography (Auto-Carto 8), Baltimore, MD, 1987.

[4]   F. Broome and D. Meixler. The TIGER Data Base Structure. *Cartography and Geographic Information Systems*, 17 (1), January 1990.

[5]   S. Ceri, R. Cochrane, and J. Widom. Practical Applications of Triggers and Constraints: Successes and Lingering Issues. In *Proceedings of the 26th International Conference on Very Large Data Bases (VLDB'00)*, Cairo, Egypt, 2000.

[6]   E. Clementini, P. Di Felice, and P. van Oosterom. A Small Set of Formal Topological Relationships Suitable for End-User Interaction. In *Proceedings of the Third International Symposium on Large Spatial Databases (SSD'93)*, Singapore, June, 1993.

[7]   D. Cooke, and W. Maxfield. The Development of a Geographic Base File and its Uses for Mapping. In Urban and Regional Information Systems for Social Programs: Papers from the Fifth Annual Conference of the Urban and Regional Information Systems Association. Kent, OH: Center for Urban Regionalism, Kent State University, 1967.

[8]   J. Corbett. *Topological Principles in Cartography*. Technical Paper 48. Bureau of the Census, Washington, DC, 1979.

[9]   M. Egenhofer and J. Herring. *Categorizing Binary Topological Relations Between Regions, Lines, and Points in Geographic Databases*. Technical Report, Department of Surveying Engineering, University of Maine, 1990.

[10] ESRI. *Building a Geodatabase*. Prepared by Environmental Systems Research Institute, ESRI Press, Redlands, CA, 2002.

[11] P. Gulutzan and T. Pelzer. *SQL-99 Complete, Really*. Miller Freeman, Lawrence, Kansas, 1999.

[12] R. Güting. Realm-Based Spatial Data Types: The ROSE Algebra. *VLDB Journal*, 4 (2), 1995.

[13] M. Hammer and D. McLeod. Semantic Integrity in a Relational Database System. In *Proceedings of the 1st International Conference on Very Large Data Bases (VLDB'75)*, Framingham, Massachusetts, September 1975.

[14] J. Herring. TIGRIS: Topologically Integrated Geographic Information System. In *Proceedings of the 8th International Symposium on Computer Assisted Cartography (Auto-Carto 8)*, Baltimore, MD, 1987.

[15] Intergraph Corp. *GIS: The MGE Way*. Intergraph Technical Paper, October 1995.

[16] ISO TC 211/WG 2. Geographic Information – Spatial Schema. Technical Report, Second Draft of ISO 19107, International Organization for Standardization, 1999.

[17] W. Kim, editor. Modern Database Systems: The Object Model, Interoperability, and Beyond. ACM Press, New York, 1995.

[18] C. Kinnear. The TIGER Structure. In Proceedings of the 8th International Symposium on Computer Assisted Cartography (Auto-Carto 8), Baltimore, MD, 1987.

[19] V. Markowitz. Safe Referential Integrity Structures in Relational Databases. In *Proceedings of the 17th International Conference on Very Large Data Bases (VLDB'91)*, Barcelona, September 1991.

[20] W. May and B. Ludäscher. Understanding the Global Semantics of Referential Actions using Logic Rules. *ACM Transactions on Database Systems*, 27 (4), December 2002.

[21] V. Milenkovic. Verifiable Implementations of Geometric Algorithms Using Finite Precision Arithmetic. In *Geometric Reasoning*, The MIT Press, Cambridge, Massachusetts, 1989.

[22] S. Morehouse. ARC/INFO: A Geo-Relational Model for Spatial Information. In *Proceedings of the 7th International Symposium on Computer Assisted Cartography (Auto-Carto 7)*, Washington, DC, March 1985.

[23] J. Munkres. *Topology*. Second Edition, Prentice-Hall, Englewood Cliffs, New Jersey, 2000.

[24] T. Peucker and N. Chrisman. Cartographic Data Structures. In *The American Cartographer*, 2 (2), April 1975.

[25] P. Rigaux, M. Scholl, and A. Voisard. *Spatial Databases with Application to GIS*. Morgan Kaufmann, San Francisco, 2002.

[26] E. Simon and A. Kotz-Dittrich. Promises and Realities of Active Database Systems. In *Proceedings of the 21ˢᵗ International Conference on Very Large Data Bases (VLDB'95)*, Zürich, Switzerland, 1995.

[27] U. S. Census Bureau. *2002 TIGER/Line Technical Documentation*. Prepared by the U. S. Census Bureau, Washington, DC, 2002.

[28] P. van Oosterom, J. Stoter, W. Quak, and S. Zlantanova. The Balance Between Geometry and Topology. In *Proceedings of the 2002 Symposium on Spatial Data Handling (SDH'02)*, Ottawa, Canada, July 2002.

[29] J. van Roessel. A New Approach to Plane-Sweep Overlay: Topological Structuring and Line-Segment Classification. *Cartography and Geographic Information Systems*, 18 (1), 1991.

[30] J. van Roessel. Supporting Multi-Layer Map Overlay and Shared Geometry Management in a GIS. In *Computational Cartography – Cartography Meets Computational Geometry, Dagstuhl Seminar Report 252*, M. Molenaar, M. van Krefeld, and R. Weibel, editors, September 1999.

[31] P. Watson. *Topology and ORDBMS Technology*. Laser-Scan White Paper, Laser-Scan Ltd., January 2002.

[32] M. Zeiler. Modeling Our World: The ESRI Guide to Geodatabase Design. ESRI Press, Redlands, CA, 1999.

Author Index

Lecture Notes in Computer Science

For information about Vols. 1–2646
please contact your bookseller or Springer-Verlag

Vol. 2687: J. Mira, J.R. Álvarez (Eds.), Artificial Neural Nets Problem Solving Methods. Proceedings, Part II. 2003. XXVII, 820 pages. 2003.

Vol. 2688: J. Kittler, M.S. Nixon (Eds.), Audio- and Video-Based Biometric Person Authentication. Proceedings, 2003. XVII, 978 pages. 2003.

Vol. 2689: K.D. Ashley, D.G. Bridge (Eds.), Case-Based Reasoning Research and Development. Proceedings, 2003. XV, 734 pages. 2003. (Subseries LNAI).

Vol. 2691: V. Mařík, J. Müller, M. Pěchouček (Eds.), Multi-Agent Systems and Applications III. Proceedings, 2003. XIV, 660 pages. 2003. (Subseries LNAI).

Vol. 2692: P. Nixon, S. Terzis (Eds.), Trust Management. Proceedings, 2003. X, 349 pages. 2003.

Vol. 2693: A. Cechich, M. Piattini, A. Vallecillo (Eds.), Component-Based Software Quality. X, 403 pages. 2003.

Vol. 2694: R. Cousot (Ed.), Static Analysis. Proceedings, 2003. XIV, 505 pages. 2003.

Vol. 2695: L.D. Griffin, M. Lillholm (Eds.), Scale Space Methods in Computer Vision. Proceedings, 2003. XII, 816 pages. 2003.

Vol. 2697: T. Warnow, B. Zhu (Eds.), Computing and Combinatorics. Proceedings, 2003. XIII, 560 pages. 2003.

Vol. 2698: W. Burakowski, B. Koch, A. Bęben (Eds.), Architectures for Quality of Service in the Internet. Proceedings, 2003. XI, 305 pages. 2003.

Vol. 2701: M. Hofmann (Ed.), Typed Lambda Calculi and Applications. Proceedings, 2003. VIII, 317 pages. 2003.

Vol. 2702: P. Brusilovsky, A. Corbett, F. de Rosis (Eds.), User Modeling 2003. Proceedings, 2003. XIV, 436 pages. 2003. (Subseries LNAI).

Vol. 2704: S.-T. Huang, T. Herman (Eds.), Self-Stabilizing Systems. Proceedings, 2003. X, 215 pages. 2003.

Vol. 2706: R. Nieuwenhuis (Ed.), Rewriting Techniques and Applications. Proceedings, 2003. XI, 515 pages. 2003.

Vol. 2707: K. Jeffay, I. Stoica, K. Wehrle (Eds.), Quality of Service – IWQoS 2003. Proceedings, 2003. XI, 517 pages. 2003.

Vol. 2709: T. Windeatt, F. Roli (Eds.), Multiple Classifier Systems. Proceedings, 2003. X, 406 pages. 2003.

Vol. 2710: Z. Ésik, Z. Fülöp (Eds.), Developments in Language Theory. Proceedings, 2003. XI, 437 pages. 2003.

Vol. 2711: T.D. Nielsen, N.L. Zhang (Eds.), Symbolic and Quantitative Approaches to Reasoning with Uncertainty. Proceedings, 2003. XII, 608 pages. 2003. (Subseries LNAI).

Vol. 2712: A. James, B. Lings, M. Younas (Eds.), New Horizons in Information Management. Proceedings, 2003. XII, 281 pages. 2003.

Vol. 2713: C.-W. Chung, C.-K. Kim, W. Kim, T.-W. Ling, K.-H. Song (Eds.), Web and Communication Technologies and Internet-Related Social Issues – HSI 2003. Proceedings, 2003. XXII, 773 pages. 2003.

Vol. 2714: O. Kaynak, E. Alpaydin, E. Oja, L. Xu (Eds.), Artificial Neural Networks and Neural Information Processing – ICANN/ICONIP 2003. Proceedings, 2003. XXII, 1188 pages. 2003.

Vol. 2715: T. Bilgiç, B. De Baets, O. Kaynak (Eds.), Fuzzy Sets and Systems – IFSA 2003. Proceedings, 2003. XV, 735 pages. 2003. (Subseries LNAI).

Vol. 2716: M.J. Voss (Ed.), OpenMP Shared Memory Parallel Programming. Proceedings, 2003. VIII, 271 pages. 2003.

Vol. 2718: P. W. H. Chung, C. Hinde, M. Ali (Eds.), Developments in Applied Artificial Intelligence. Proceedings, 2003. XIV, 817 pages. 2003. (Subseries LNAI).

Vol. 2719: J.C.M. Baeten, J.K. Lenstra, J. Parrow, G.J. Woeginger (Eds.), Automata, Languages and Programming. Proceedings, 2003. XVIII, 1199 pages. 2003.

Vol. 2720: M. Marques Freire, P. Lorenz, M.M.-O. Lee (Eds.), High-Speed Networks and Multimedia Communications. Proceedings, 2003. XIII, 582 pages. 2003.

Vol. 2721: N.J. Mamede, J. Baptista, I. Trancoso, M. das Graças Volpe Nunes (Eds.), Computational Processing of the Portuguese Language. Proceedings, 2003. XIV, 268 pages. 2003. (Subseries LNAI).

Vol. 2722: J.M. Cueva Lovelle, B.M. González Rodríguez, L. Joyanes Aguilar, J.E. Labra Gayo, M. del Puerto Paule Ruiz (Eds.), Web Engineering. Proceedings, 2003. XIX, 554 pages. 2003.

Vol. 2723: E. Cantú-Paz, J.A. Foster, K. Deb, L.D. Davis, R. Roy, U.-M. O'Reilly, H.-G. Beyer, R. Standish, G. Kendall, S. Wilson, M. Harman, J. Wegener, D. Dasgupta, M.A. Potter, A.C. Schultz, K.A. Dowsland, N. Jonoska, J. Miller (Eds.), Genetic and Evolutionary Computation – GECCO 2003. Proceedings, Part I. 2003. XLVII, 1252 pages. 2003.

Vol. 2724: E. Cantú-Paz, J.A. Foster, K. Deb, L.D. Davis, R. Roy, U.-M. O'Reilly, H.-G. Beyer, R. Standish, G. Kendall, S. Wilson, M. Harman, J. Wegener, D. Dasgupta, M.A. Potter, A.C. Schultz, K.A. Dowsland, N. Jonoska, J. Miller (Eds.), Genetic and Evolutionary Computation – GECCO 2003. Proceedings, Part II. 2003. XLVII, 1274 pages. 2003.

Vol. 2725: W.A. Hunt, Jr., F. Somenzi (Eds.), Computer Aided Verification. Proceedings, 2003. XII, 462 pages. 2003.

Vol. 2726: E. Hancock, M. Vento (Eds.), Graph Based Representations in Pattern Recognition. Proceedings, 2003. VIII, 271 pages. 2003.

Vol. 2727: R. Safavi-Naini, J. Seberry (Eds.), Information Security and Privacy. Proceedings, 2003. XII, 534 pages. 2003.

Vol. 2731: C.S. Calude, M.J. Dinneen, V. Vajnovszki (Eds.), Discrete Mathematics and Theoretical Computer Science. Proceedings, 2003. VIII, 301 pages. 2003.

Vol. 2733: A. Butz, A. Krüger, P. Olivier (Eds.), Smart Graphics. Proceedings, 2003. XI, 261 pages. 2003.

Vol. 2734: P. Perner, A. Rosenfeld (Eds.), Machine Learning and Data Mining in Pattern Recognition. Proceedings, 2003. XII, 440 pages. 2003. (Subseries LNAI).

Vol. 2743: L. Cardelli (Ed.), ECOOP 2003 – Object-Oriented Programming. Proceedings, 2003. X, 501 pages. 2003.

Vol. 2745: M. Guo, L.T. Yang (Eds.), Parallel and Distributed Processing and Applications. Proceedings, 2003. XII, 450 pages. 2003.

Vol. 2749: J. Bigun, T. Gustavsson (Eds.), Image Analysis. Proceedings, 2003. XXII, 1174 pages. 2003.

Vol. 2750: T. Hadzilacos, Y. Manolopoulos, J.F. Roddick, Y. Theodoridis (Eds.), Advances in Spatial and Temporal Databases. Proceedings, 2003. XIII, 525 pages. 2003.